MW01273053

The ABC's of FOOD

A Study of Food As History, Story, Tradition and Nutrition

A Food Encyclopedia
Compiled, Edited and Written by

Louise Ulmer and Richard S. Calhoun
with
Contributing Food Experts

Front Cover by T. Marie Smith

Back Cover Art by EbooksOnThe.net

Food Guide Pyramid Illustrations by
Anne Catharine Blake

It's all about Food

Peach Blossom Publications
Williamsport, Pennsylvania

ISBN 0-941367-20-7

THE ABC's OF FOOD

Articles
Activities
Attractions
Cooking Schools
Encyclopedia
Festivals
Glossaries
History
Recipes
Stories
Terms
Web Addresses

Especially arranged for use in
Young People's Cooking Classes
and
Schools with Vegetable Gardens

Library of Congress Control Number 2001 130760

The ABC's of Food
First Edition

With Special Thanks to

our fellow researchers and writers:

Joyce Ackermann, Erville Allen, Regina Anthonypillai, Walter V. Barnett Jr.,

Barbara Belknap, Karon Booth, Kelly Brown, John Calhoun,

Anna V. Damiani-Becker, Eric Diesel, Bernice Erickson, Elizabeth Giles,

Roberta Greenwald, Kathleen Grinley, Julia B. Hans, Billie Jean Hepp,

Susan Holloran, Eva Holmes, Cheryl Hoyer, Gretchen Huesmann,

Linda Huntington, Carol Iocco, Donna Joyal, Echo Lewis, Diana Lowry,

Kelly McHugh, Joan MacDonald, Virginia McNear, Holly Martin

JoAn W. Martin, Chef Laurel Miller, Lad Moore, Evelyn Neuhaus,

Marie Prato, Alice Reeve, Pamela Schmidt,   Jean B. Seymour,

Renee Shepherd, T. Marie Smith, Pat Smithdorff, Livia Sparangna,

Irene Squire, Mary Eddy Stewart, J. Wendy Thomas, Sandra Trainor,

Fay O. Valley, Carol Wilson.

NOTE:

All telephone numbers and internet addresses are subject to change.

NUTRITION FACTS

were computed using

MasterCook II by Arion Software, Inc.

All Nutrition Facts are subject to change by USDA and FDA.

The ABC'S of FOOD is unillustrated but you can find many photographs and additional information by clicking on the internet addresses within the text.

Aa

ABALONE: (ab-a-low-nee) These ear-shaped shellfish are found on rocks in the warm waters of the Pacific Ocean from California to Alaska. The molluscs are generally red or pink in warmer southern waters, orange colored in the northern waters. They are also found in other oceans, except the western Atlantic.

 In southern California waters, abalone average six inches, but have been found growing up to a foot in length. Red is the favorite species. In Alaskan waters, the shell is much smaller, with an average of about three inches. Some shells are used to make mother-of-pearl buttons.

The abalone has a large, oval "foot" muscle it uses to adhere firmly to rock, especially when disturbed. It takes a crow bar to remove the larger abalones and strong hunting-type knife to dislodge the smaller ones. It is the foot that is the edible part.

Commercial abalone fishing is forbidden in United States waters. Except for man, its main enemy is the sea urchin.

Before it is cooked, the tough muscle needs to be tenderized, which is done by pounding with a mallet. Larger muscles should be cut into thin strips before pounding. The delicious clam-like muscle adds flavor to chowder and can be found canned in specialty food markets. If sliced thin and tenderized, the muscle can be sautéd in butter and eaten like a steak. **Nutrition facts:** A 3-ounce serving has 89 calories, 6 calories from fat, .7g total fat (1%), .1g saturated fat (1%), 72.3mg cholesterol (24%), 256mg sodium (11%), 5.1g carbohydrates (2%), zero fiber, 14.6g protein (29%), zero vitamin A, 3mg vitamin C (3%), 26mg calcium (3%), 2.7mg iron (3%), and 213mg potassium.

HUNTING THE ELUSIVE ALASKAN ABALONE
by Richard S. Calhoun

Living on the water in southeastern Alaska has advantages, especially if you like fishing, and that's my favorite pastime.   I was just waking up when Pete walked into my bedroom and asked, "Richard, do you want to pick some abalone?
     "What time is it?" I asked.
     "It's four-thirty," Pete answered. "There's a minus tide, so picking should be easy."
     "Okay!" I reached for my hip boots.
     "You're not going to wear hip boots are you?" Pete asked. "It's not wise to wear hip boots in a skiff," Pete commented.
     "But, it's all I have. I only have one pair of shoes and I can't get them wet or Mom will kill me."

I looked in to see if Dad was awake. Both he and Mom were still asleep. Pete was already down on the dock and in the skiff. He was waving for me to hurry up. "We'll row over to that island," Pete said as he pointed to an island about a mile away. "There should be lots of abalone over there."

"But that's nothing but a rock pile. We can't even get ashore."

"We're not going ashore," Pete replied. "We will pick them from the skiff."

"How are we going to do that?" I asked. "When I lived in California, divers in wet suits swam down and pried them off the rocks with tire irons."

"California abalone are bigger than ours. See this pole? I tied a fish hook on the end of it. We will pick the abalone with this pole."

We crossed the channel to the island. The water was kicking up with about a foot chop. Every once in awhile a wave splashed over the sides. With a bucket, I bailed out the water. Once at the island the water was calmer, but with some surges up on the rocks. Pete looked over the edge of the skiff into the water. "See any abalone?" I asked.

"No, not yet, just a bunch of gum boots."

"What's a gum boot?"

Pete put the pole in the water, hooked a gum boot and pulled it up. "Here's one just for you," Pete laughed.

The gum boot was black on top, about four inches long and an inch wide. I turned it over and saw it had one big yellowish sucker muscle. The black side was arched, but there wasn't a hard shell.

"Are they good to eat?" I asked.

"I don't know," Pete answered. "I have never heard of anyone eating one. I suppose if you were real hungry, you could."

We pushed the boat along the rocks. Pete continued to peer in the clear water off the bow of the stiff. The water wasn't very deep and the bottom was sandy.

"See any yet?" I asked.

"No, there's too much sand. Sand clogs up the abalone gills. Also there are many starfish and sea urchins and not enough seaweed."

"What does starfish have to do with abalone?" I asked.

"Starfish eat abalone, as do the sea urchins."

"Oh, I get it. Does the abalone eat seaweed?"

"Yes," answered Pete.

Just then a surge of water pushed the bow of the skiff up on the rocks and the stern went under water. Pete grabbed for the rocks and was out of the skiff. I stood up trying to grab a rock, but couldn't get to one. Cold water started to fill up my hip boots and I couldn't swim or even dog paddle because of the water weight in my boots. I felt like I was in one of those gangster movies where someone had their feet cemented in a wash tub and being dumped in the ocean. Pete saw I was in trouble and threw me the bow rope.

"Here, catch the rope!" he commanded, as he held on to the other end of the rope. He pulled me over to a rock and I grabbed hold for dear life. The water was still surging and banging me up against the rocks. With all my strength I slowly pulled myself out of the water.

"Wow!" I exclaimed. "I thought I was a goner in that ice cold water."

Pete and I managed to pull the skiff up on the rocks and dump out most of the water. It was hard work, because we were not on level ground and a skiff full of water is really heavy. We climbed back into the skiff. I managed to remove my hip boots and dumped out the water.

"Now you see why you don't wear hip boots in a skiff!" Pete exclaimed.

"I see what you mean," I replied.

Pete rowed around to the calmer side of the island where the water wasn't surging so much. Even though we were both wet and cold, we continued to look for abalone.

"I found some!" Pete yelled. "Hand me the pole."

Pete hooked one after another and before long we had a couple dozen abalone. They were small, about three inches in diameter and the shell was black. The muscle foot was a yellow-orange in color.

"What do we do with them now?" I asked.

Pete grabbed an abalone and with his knife cut the muscle out of the shell. With the butt handle of the knife he hit the middle of the cut muscle with one sharp blow. "That tenderizes them," he said. He threw the shell in the water.

"Hey, don't throw the shells away, I want to save them," I requested.

Pete handed me his knife and said, "They're all yours. You clean them as I row back to shore."

I picked up one and cut it out of the shell and hit the muscle with the handled of the knife. "That's not hard enough," Pete ordered, "Hit 'em hard or they will be tough like shoe leather."

We tied up to the dock and Dad was there to greet us. "Richard, where have you been?" he shouted.

"Pete and I went abalone picking." I answered.

Dad looked at the abalone muscles in my hand and said, "They are too small. That's against the law."

Pete interrupted and said, "They don't get much bigger in Alaska."

"Richard, why are you all wet?" Dad asked angrily. "Did you have to dive down to get them?"

"No," I answered. "The skiff filled with water when we ran up on the rocks and I fell in."

Mom met me about halfway down the boardwalk and asked, "Where were you? Why are you all wet?"

I repeated what happened as we walked to the house. "I'm going to change my clothes. You can cook the abalone for breakfast."

"I don't know how to cook abalone," Mom replied.

"I will show you how," said Pete.

I changed my clothes and returned to the kitchen. Pete fried the abalone for a couple of minutes, while Mom made some buttermilk biscuits. The abalones had sort of a sweet clam taste and were surprising good, much better than clams.

"The next time you plan to go out in the skiff, you tell us where you are going," ordered Dad. "You would have drowned if Pete wasn't there to save you."

"Okay." I didn't argue.– From *Cheechako, by* Richard S. Calhoun,

ACEROLA: Native shrub of topical America with a red, juicy, sweet, sometimes tart fruit. Eaten fresh, made into juice, or ice cream. Low in calories, it has a fair source of vitamin A and is one of the best sources of vitamin C in the world with 100 times more than oranges, ounce for ounce. .

ACORN: Acorns are the nuts borne by oak trees. Most types are not edible by humans but certain kinds that grow around the Mediterranean are similar to chestnuts. Other types have been eaten in times of famine. In North America a few species are edible and helped keep the Native Americans and Colonists alive during the long bleak winters. Acorn meal or acorn flour was used much like cornmeal. The best of the group is from the California black oak.

ACORN SQUASH: This fall and winter vegetable belongs to the gourd family and is native to America. Like other members of the squash family, it may have originated in Peru. When the first European settlers arrived in America, the acorn squash was introduced to them by the Native Americans. The name comes from the word "*asquash*" which means "eaten green." The acorn squash has a hard green shell and can grow up to eight inches long. The sweet inside has a yellow-orange flesh with many seeds. Generally, the acorn squash is baked. It is cut in half, seeds and fiber scraped out. It is placed, cut-side down, on a cookie sheet and baked in a hot oven for up to an hour. The squash can also be cut into rings and steamed. **Nutrition facts:** A ½-cup serving has 28 calories zero fat and sodium, 7.3g carbohydrates (2%), zero fiber, 6g protein (1%), 239 IU vitamin A (5%), 8mg vitamin C (13%), 23mg calcium (2%), .5mg iron (3%), and 244mg potassium.

ADDITIVES:

OH NO! I JUST ATE TETRAHYDROFURAN!

That's right. You just finished a refreshing cold beverage, a scoop of ice cream and downed a little cream filled cake, and now you're reading the ingredients on the labels. What are all those names that few of us can pronounce and why are they in foods?

Real home-made ice cream contains milk, cream, sugar and fruit. So what are monoglycerides, cellulose gum, and carrageenan found in some ice creams? And why didn't my cookbook call for them? Food additives are in almost everything. Are they safe? The answer: Yes and no.

One thing consumers have going for them: The Food and Drug Administration (FDA) must approve all food additives before they can be used. However, some people are sensitive to some natural foods, such as soy products and dairy products. Being exposed to just one ingredient might cause you no harm, but by combining with other ingredients, a chemical reaction could take place and could make you very ill.

The good news is many additives are added to protect you. Some **fight bacteria**, others retard spoilage, another adds nutrients, and some just add flavor. Back in the late 1930s, a slogan was introduced, "Better Living Through Chemistry," and many thought that to be true. Yes, it was true in many ways, but not for everyone. It was found that some of those chemicals caused cancer, infections and other health problems.

Take **nitrites** for an example. Nitrites prevent botulism, yet when added to your natural stomach chemicals, they can cause cancer in some people. The problem, no one really knows just how much of a good thing (chemicals) will cause a bad thing (illness) to happen. When food is cooked, it loses color, so **dyes** are added to make food look more appetizing. The Romans used saffron to color rice dishes yellow and at the same time it added flavor. Annatto, seed of the tropical lipstick tree, is a vegetable dye that has been used in butter for more than 700 years. Now annatto is used to color margerine and cheese. Green coloring is added to mint products, because when mint extracts are used there is no green color. People just expect mint products to be green.

Again, coloring just makes food more appetizing. **Red Dye Number Two** was supposed to cause cancer in some lab animals, but how much red dye must be consumed for the same reaction in people - a pint, a quart, or a gallon a day? It's unknown and few of us would even consider drinking a glass of red dye. Nevertheless, Red Dye Number Two was removed.

Additives are not just added to packaged foods. Additives are added to fruits and vegetables growing in the fields, and additives are added to live animals as well. Additives have been around for thousands of years. **Salt and sugar** were used as preservatives. As you know, too much salt and sugar is not good for you. When you see the word "sodium" you know that salt is involved in that additive. When you see the words **"calcium"** or "casein," it probably came from milk. And the word "gum" came from plants that you might eat anyway.

Oh yes, **tetrahydrofuran** is a synthetic flavoring for beverages, ice cream and other sweets. It is not known to be toxic. Hope that makes you feel better, or does it? If you are concerned about food additives or would just like to know more about them, plan a visit to your library and check out the book *Consumers Dictionary of Food Additives* by Ruth Winter. This book is written in everyday language that you will understand. You can find what is safe for you, and what might cause you harm. Some people think if you can't pronounce it, you shouldn't eat it.

THOSE LITTLE CREAM-FILLED CAKES

That little cream-filled cake you ate has all kinds of additives. Some of the chemical names you may recognize, but others you will not, unless your are a food chemist. Here are a few types. **Mono and diglycerides**, a vegetable emulsifier derived from soybeans and used to keep the cream filling from separating into water and fat. **Calcium casinate** is a protein derived from milk that adds body and flavor to the cream filling. **Sodium stearyl lactylate** conditions the dough to make it tender and extends the life of the cake, some think up to a dozen years or more. **Cellulose gum** is made from the interlining of plants and is used to prevent sugar from crystallizing in the icing, and also is a thickening agent.

ADOBO: Native of Madagascar. A 2-inch green fig. Low in calories, high in fiber.

ADZUKI BEANS: Originating in China, these small, reddish-brown beans with a white ridge along one edge, have a sweet, nutty flavor. Adzuki are also called *aduki* and *azuki* beans. They are grown in the Midwestern United States, as well as Asia. In China, adzuki beans are often served on New Year's Eve to bring courage and good fortune in the coming year. Also ancient Chinese folk wisdom says that the kidneys govern the emotion of fear. The adzuki bean is considered a source of courage that helps people meet challenges bravely.

They are lower in fat, have more iron, are easier to digest, and produce less gas in the stomach than most beans. Adzuki beans combine well with other foods. For example, add some cubes of peeled winter squash during the last 30 minutes of cooking. Also rice, onions, and celery can be added to make patties and fried. Adzuki beans are available in most health food stores. In China and Japan, adzuki beans are processed into a sweet red paste and are added to vegetable recipe mixtures. **Nutrition facts:** A ½ cup serving has 147 calories, zero fat and sodium, 28.5g carbohydrates, zero fiber, 8.7g protein (17%), zero vitamins A and C, 32mg calcium (3%), 2.3mg iron (13%), and 612mg potassium. One cup of cooked adzuki beans has as much iron as four ounces of lean steak, more folate than a cup of cooked spinach, and about as much protein as four tablespoons of peanut butter.

AFRICAN OIL PALM: Native of Africa. The branches are loaded with reddish to blackish fruits in clusters of 200 fruits. Source for palm oil. Sap is made into wine. Very high in calories and fats, especially in saturated fat.

AGARICUS MUSHROOMS: They are commonly known as White Mushrooms. Agaricus account for about 90% of all mushrooms cultivated in the United States. They vary in color from creamy white to light brown and range in sizes from small (button) to jumbo (stuffers). They have a mild and woodsy flavor when eaten raw, and the flavor intensifies when cooked. Freshly picked have closed veils (caps that fit closely to the stem) and a delicate flavor. When mature, with open veils and darkened caps, they develop a richer, deeper taste.

 Use fresh in salads and for dips. Can be sautéd, braised, stir-fried, and grilled on shish kebabs. Use in casseroles. Great on pizzas! Can be marinated with garlic and thyme. --*Mushroom Council*

AGRICULTURAL LIBRARY

NATIONAL AGRICULTURAL LIBRARY

Imagine a library with a bookshelf 48-miles long. Yes, 48- miles! On this shelf are more than three million volumes of books that covers all aspects of agriculture. Along with the books are related journals, computer software, audio visuals and other materials in many formats. The collection is in 75 different languages.

All this describes the American National Agricultural Library (NAL). Of course the bookshelf is not all one length, but if all the shelves are added up in this building, they would measure 48-miles in length.

Formed in 1862, the NAL is the largest agricultural library in the world. The library serves everyone who needs agricultural information. This includes students along with farmers, scientists, policy makers, and school teachers.

Suppose a farmer would like to convert a chemically-intensive corp production to alternative modes of insect and weed control. The farmer would find this information at NAL. At the same time a chicken rancher is looking for suppliers of hatchery equipment. The rancher only needs to consult with the NAL. Also eager school teachers who want to develop a nutrition education program for students will find the NAL has the answers. One way to obtain this information is on the Internet.

In addition to the Internet, NAL provides traditional library services, which include programs that teach how to identify, locate and obtain needed information.

Scientific research supported by NAL information is a potent weapon in food safety. such as elimination of pests and diseases. The information and database services of the NAL are vital to sustain a viable agricultural economy, in a healthy environment. NAL users ensure safe, abundant, affordable and high-quality agricultural products for American consumers. Additional information on the NAL is available by writing: **United States Department of Agriculture**, Agricultural Research Service (ARS), National Agricultural Library, 10301 Baltimore Avenue, Beltsville, MD 20705-2351 or call (301) 504-57555. www.nal.usda.gov

AKEE is the fruit of a North African tree in the same family as the lychee. It looks peachy on the outside but has segments similar to an orange. It is eaten raw or cooked.

ALA: See BULGUR WHEAT

À LA CARTE (a-la-kart) is used to describe a restaurant menu where each dish is ordered and paid for separately.

À LA KING is a white sauce with a combination of chopped vegetables and poultry, seafood, or eggs. Useful as a food stretcher, it is usually served over toast, pasta, rice, or potatoes.

À LA MODE, in America, means to top a dessert with a scoop of ice cream.

ALBACORE: Albacore is the queen of the tuna family (see TUNA). Its pure white meat is the best for canning, and is usually in cans marked, "solid pack." Fresh albacore is available in some seafood markets. Albacore can be used for all recipes calling for tuna or other canned fish. **Nutrition facts:** A 3-ounce serving (tuna) has 122 calories, 39 calories from fat, 4.2g total fat

(6%), 1.1g saturated fat (5%), 32.3mg cholesterol (11%), 33.2mg sodium (1%), zero carbohydrates and fiber, 19.8g protein (40%), 1,857 IU vitamin A (37%), zero vitamin C, 7mg calcium (1%), .9mg iron (5%), and 214mg potassium.

ALFALFA SPROUTS: A member of the legume family, alfalfa originated in southwestern Asia. Alfalfa is one of the most nutritious crops, because it is rich in protein, minerals, and vitamins. The main use for alfalfa is farm animal feed. It's also an excellent source for the honeybees. Alfalfa is used to increase the vitamin content in prepared foods, and serves as a base for many multivitamins. Alfalfa seeds produce quick sprouts. Sprouts taste good mixed in salads and in sandwiches. Sprouts can be added to soups and omelets. They can even be marinated, steamed, and sautéd. Never cook sprouts more than five minutes. (See BEAN SPROUTS and SPROUTS) **Nutrition facts** per ½ cup 5 calories, zero fats and sodium, zero carbohydrates, .4g fiber (2%), .7g protein (1%), 26 IU vitamin A (1%), 1mg vitamin C (2%), 5mg calcium (1%), and .2mg iron (1%).

ALLIGATOR: Unlike the crocodile, which is found in several parts of our world, the alligator is only found in the freshwater swamps, lakes, and bayous of the southeastern United States, and in the basin of the Yangtze River in China. They are hunted for both their meat and their hides.

The best meat is about a foot-long section just behind the back legs. This white meat is tender and juicy, and has a taste like a combination of chicken, pork, and fish. The tail is cut like pork chops, then salted, peppered, floured and fried until golden brown.

Alligator can be substituted in many veal recipes, and is especially good in scallopini. The meat is available in many meat markets in Louisiana and nearby states. **Nutrition facts:** Alligator is a food, low in both calories and fat; high in vitamin B-12 and iron and good for the heart. .

ALLIGATOR AT WILDLIFE GARDENS
by Betty Provost

Would you like to feed an alligator? You can at Wildlife Gardens. In our park you can relax on the porch and feed alligators as they swim by without fear of an attack. You can explore nature trails and see native plants, deer, owls, otters, turtles and other wild animals, or take day or night boat tours into the back water of the swamp. My husband will also fix you a Cajun breakfast with a crayfish omelet, 7-UP biscuits, and his specialty, "Alligator A La James."

Here's how he makes it:
1. He makes a marinate of 7-UP, mustard, lemon juice,
Tony Chachere's Creole seasoning (a mixture of salt, cayenne
pepper and garlic powder), and hot sauce.
2. Slices 1 pound of alligator meat into 1 inch cubes.
3. Marinates the meat for 3 days in the refrigerator.
4. Drains the marinate and reserves it.

5. Dices 4 onions and sautés in butter until brown.
6. Piles the alligator meat in the middle of an iron
skillet and tops with the cooked onions. Pours the marinate
on top and cooks over medium-high heat until all the sauce
is gone. His recipe makes 4 servings.

If you would like to visit with us, write: Wildlife Gardens,
5306 North Bayou Black Drive, Gibson, LA 70356.

ALLSPICE: The allspice berry grows in the West Indies and is related to the myrtle family. It is picked green and dried in the sun, which intensifies the flavor and the aroma. Don't let the name fool you. Allspice is not a combination of spices, but just one spice. It received its name because it resembles a combination of cinnamon, nutmeg and cloves in taste. Allspice is also known as Jamaica pepper, and Jamaica seems to have a monopoly on the spice, but it is available throughout the American tropics.

Allspice is available both whole and ground. It is used in countless recipes for meats, vegetables, breads, and other baked goods. Also used in pickling and preserving meats, fruits, and vegetables.

When Columbus sailed across the Atlantic, he became the first European to find allspice, and he took it back to Spain on his return trip.

Activity

Do a taste and smell test to see how allspice is alike or different from cinnamon, nutmeg and cloves, or combined. Can you tell allspice from apple pie spice? Pumpkin pie spice? How do the tastes compare?

ALMOND: The almond is related to the peach tree and is believed to have originated in the Mediterranean region. The almond tree is a robust, long-lived tree with gorgeous pink and white blossoms. All it requires, it has been said, is hard, dry ground. The famous Spanish almonds of Valencia, Spain grow in such ground, kept alive by their long roots that grow deep into the ground. Spain harvests over 33,000 tons of almonds every year.

There are two kinds of almonds, sweet and bitter, with many varieties of each. The bitter variety contains prussic acid, a poison, which must be processed-out first before almond flavoring is made.

Almonds were brought to the United States by early Spanish missionaries and are now commercially grown in California.

Almonds are mentioned in the Bible, first in Genesis (43:11-12): *"Their father Israel said to them, '... then do this: take in your baggage, as a gift for the man, some of the produce for which our country is famous: a little balsam, a little honey ... and almonds.'"*

Because almond flowers appeared before any other, the ancient Phrygians believed the blossoms to be the father of all life. The ancient Greeks honored the almond as a symbol of fertility. And, the almond is the mark of heavenly hope to the Moslems.

Almonds are used in countless recipes. Almost any recipe can be given added texture and interest with the crunch of almonds. Almonds are main ingredients in baking by the Scandinavians, Spanish, Greek, and Near Eastern countries. Oriental artists and poets grow almonds as much for beauty as for food.

Marzipan can be made with tinted almond paste, molded into confectionery fruits, animals and other fun shapes. Germany and Denmark are famous for their marzipan. The famous Spanish candy called turron is almond nougat. See TURRON. **Nutrition facts** per 1/4 cup: 209 calories, 156 calories from fat, 18.5g total fat (29%), 1.8g saturated fat (9%), zero cholesterol and sodium, 7.2g carbohydrates (2%), 3.9g fiber (15%), 7.1g protein (14%), zero vitamins A and C, 94mg calcium (9%) and 1.3mg iron (7%). www.almond.org; www.almondsarein.com; www.bluediamondgrowers.com.

ALMOND OIL. Almond oil is popular in many European countries and available here in health food stores. For thousands of years, almond oils have been used in cosmetic creams to soften the skin.

ALOE VERA: A member of the lily family and originally a native of the Mediterranean. Grows well in pots and on window sills. When commercially grown, powder or juice can be sold as a digestive aid or laxative. Keep a plant at home for quick burn relief. Low in calories, and a good source for vitamin C. Aloe Vera drinks are available in health food stores.

ALTOIDS®, "The Original Celebrated Curiously Strong Mints"® were first produced in England at the turn of the 19th century during the reign of King George III. Smith and Company (established 1789) the small London firm which later developed the original "curiously strong" recipe, later became a part of Callard & Bowser, a prestigious English confectionery founded in 1837. Today Altoids are made to the same exacting standards as the original recipe developed nearly 200 years ago. In its familiar red tin, the candy has recently become popular in the United States among lovers of peppermint because of its truly bold flavor. Altoids also come in equally bold cinnamon and spearmint.

AMERICAN DAIRY ASSOCIATION: An organization for the promotion of dairy products. www.diarycenter.com

AMERICAN DAIRY FARMERS: For milk product information see www.ilovecheese.com.

AMERICAN DIETETIC ASSOCIATION: Organized "to serve the public through the promotion of optimal nutrition, health, and well-being." Nearly 70,.000 members, the ADA sets standards of quality for professional practice in all areas of dietetic practice. It was founded in 1917 under the leadership of Lulu C. Graves, first president and Lenna F. Cooper, co-founder, in Cleveland, Ohio. The ADA Foundation funds new and existing programs with scholarships and awards, education and research projects that promote public health and well-being. www.eatright.org.

AMADINE: There are several kinds of almond-based pastries under this name. It may be a tart, pie or fancy cake, large or small.

AMARANTH: This grain was a staple of the Aztecs of Mexico and has recently been rediscovered. It can be found in some health food stores. The tiny grain has a nutty, spicy flavor and is high in protein. Amaranth can be popped like corn, made into flour for making pasta, and is found in some breakfast cereals. **Nutrition facts** per ½ cup cooked cereal: 365 calories, 56 calories from fat, 6.4g total fat (10%), 1.6g saturated fat (8%), zero cholesterol, 20.5mg sodium (1%), 64.5g carbohydrates (22%), 14.8g fiber (59%), 14.1g protein (28%), zero vitamin A, 4mg vitamin C (7%), 149mg calcium (15%), and 7.4mg iron (41%).

AMARANTH LEAVES: Also known as mirah and redroot and mistakenly called pigweed. Green amaranth, when steamed, tastes just like spinach with a nutty flavor. Spinach grows best during the cooler spring months, whereas, amaranth likes the hot weather. Amaranth is harvested from late spring to early fall. Look for soft, fuzzy, light green leaves that sprout from a beet red root in early summer. The crinkled heart-shaped green leaves have deep purple veins. Amaranth is native to the Americas. However, most of the Amaranth is imported from southeast Asia. **Nutrition facts:** A ½ cup serving has 31 calories, 3 calories from fat, .4g total fat, zero saturated fat, 23.7mg sodium (1%), 4.7g carbohydrates (2%), zero fiber, 2.5g protein (6%), 3,451 IU vitamin A (69%), 51mg vitamin C (85%), 254mg calcium (25%), 2.7mg iron (15%), and 723mg potassium.

AMARANTH SEEDS: Once green amaranth begins to flower, the leaves turn tough and bitter, the seeds start to mature. By the end of summer, the flower spikes may hold hundreds of dark seeds. The seeds are used for making cereal and flour.

Spanish conquistadors first learned of amaranth seed cakes when they saw the Aztecs devote pastry cakes to worshiping their gods. Later the Spanish forbade the growing of amaranth to help stamp out pagan worship. The same mealy pasta Aztecs thought good enough only for gods is used today in tamales.

 As a cereal, amaranth becomes very sticky when cooked. Best to mix with corn, onions and beans as a side dish at any meal. When made into flour, it has a strong, sweet, spicy, nutty flavor. Adventurous cooks use it to accent wheat flours for making cookies, muffins, pancakes, waffles, and other baked goods. Substitute 1 part of amaranth flour for 3 parts of whole wheat flour.

Whole amaranth seeds can be sprinkled on dinner roles like poppy seeds before baking. Because it requires little water to grow, amaranth are among the seeds being tested to flourish drought stricken parts of the Third World. **Nutrition facts:** Amaranth seeds are high in calories, fat, fiber, protein, calcium, iron, and are a fair source for vitamin C and potassium. Since Amaranth seeds are used in small amounts, exact daily values percentages are not available.

AMAZON TREE GRAPE: Native of Brazil. Small fruit with a single seed, thin skin, and sweet flesh.

AMBARELLA: Native of the South Pacific. Large, yellow, oval, sweet fruit, with a spiny stone seed. Eaten fresh, made into preserves or jelly.

AMBROSIA: Said to be the food and drink of the Greek gods, who would give immortality to those who partook of it. Today it's a dessert made by combining fruits, juices, and coconut.

AMERICAN BEAUTYBERRY: Native of Florida. A small 1/8-inch fruit, eaten fresh.

AMERICAN CHEESE: A processed pasteurized cheese product made from one or more different kinds of natural cheeses. The cheese(s) are ground and heated, then stirred with an emulsifier and water to make a smooth cheese. American cheese is easy to slice and to melt. American cheese is a good choice when making sauces for vegetables and pasta. American cheese also comes as a spreadable cheese in jars, tins, and squirt bottles. Kraft American Processed Cheese was introduced in 1916 by J.L. Kraft and Brothers of Chicago. Sales proved Americans loved American cheese. **Nutrition facts:** A 2-ounce serving has 213 calories, 159 calories from fat, 17.7g total fat (27%), 11.2g saturated fat (56%), 53.5mg cholesterol (18%), 368.6mg sodium (15%), zero carbohydrates and fiber, 12.6g protein (25%), 686 IU vitamin A (14%), zero vitamin C, 349mg calcium (35%), .2mg iron (1%), and 92mg potassium.

ANCHOVIES: These finger-sized fish are found mostly in the Mediterranean Sea, with some schools in the warm currents from Peru to California. Unfortunately, El Nino and pollution have taken their toll on the anchovy. Because they deteriorate quickly when exposed to air, fresh anchovies are not found in seafood markets. The small fish are caught in nets and immediately salted to preserve them. Anchovies are available in most supermarkets canned with salt and oil. You may find them canned flat or rolled around a caper, or as anchovy paste. Anchovies are generally served as appetizers, or used as a topping on pizzas. If the anchovies are too salty for your taste, soak them for about 15 minutes in cold water or milk, drain, and pat dry. Anchovies are also the key ingredient in some sauces, such as Worcestershire and Caesar dressings, and is the basic ingredient in Southeast Asian fish sauces. **Nutrition facts** per tablespoon: 19 calories, 7 calories from fat, .7g total fat (1%), .2g saturated fat (1%), 8.9mg cholesterol (3%), 15.4mg sodium (1%), zero carbohydrates and fiber, 3g protein (6%), zero vitamins A and C, 22mg calcium (2%) and .5mg iron (3%).

ANGEL FOOD is a high, delicate cake using egg whites as the leavening agent and containing no fat in the recipe.

ANGELICA: An herb grown commercially in northern Europe (Germany and France), which, except for a few private gardens, is not grown in the United States. All parts of the plant--seeds, leaves, stems and roots--are used in cooking from soup to desserts. The stem is imported, but not the leaves. The taste is similar to juniper berries. In Europe the stems are eaten as a vegetable, like cooked celery. The leaves are added to salads and candied for cake decorations. The plant was called "angel's plant," because herbalists believed it to have heavenly powers against disease. The distilled oil of angelica seeds is treasured by perfume makers. Check your vegetable department. It can be found in some American markets. Also, candied stalks have been sold in the US, called "French rhubarb." Candied angelica is a specialty of Niort, France.

ANISE: (Pronounced either *an-is* or *an-ees*) Also called Aniseed. While anise is used as a spice, it is really an herb, because it belongs to the parsley family. The plant grows about two feet tall, has feather-type leaves, and the tiny fruit is gray-brown in color. The taste is similar to licorice and is often used to flavor licorice candy.

Anise originated in the Mediterranean, where it is still grown commercially (especially in Turkey) and has been used by the Greeks, Hebrews, and Romans for centuries. Emperor Charlemagne in the 8th century grew it in his German gardens and it has been popular ever since. Scandinavian cooks flavor their breads with crushed aniseeds. In Italy it is a flavoring used in liqueurs. The Chinese add it to meat and vegetable combinations, and Europeans use it to flavor stews, seafood, and vegetables such as carrots, cauliflower and beets.

Aniseeds are sold whole, so to release the flavor, crush them between two sheets of wax paper with a rolling pin.

Anise is also used in medicines, as a flavor and as a stimulant. Both the smell and the taste come from an oil which contains anethole. It's the anethole that is used to make perfumes and flavorings. The Chinese anise comes from a plant related to the magnolia and is known as "star anise." This oil is used the same as aniseed oil.

ANNATTO (also called the Lipstick Tree): From tropical America. Red, spiny pods, 1 ½-inches long in clusters. Used to color margarine.

ANNONA FAMILY: The atemoya, pond apple, soursop, guanabana, sugar apple, custard apple, and sweetsop are one family–the annona.

ANTELOPE: There are no true American antelope. They are native to Africa and Asia. The antelope found in America are descendants of zoo animals that were introduced in the wild in the 1940s. Antelope resemble deer in both body and eating habits. In the U.S., there are more than 150 ranches which have herds for domestic use. The meat is much leaner than beef. The male is

.8% fat, the female is 5.2% fat. This makes it an important meat for those on low fat and low cholesterol diets. The meat is sometimes available in supermarkets; often sold as venison. The meat can be roasted, broiled, or braised, and is usually coated with lard or wrapped in strips of salt pork before cooking. **Nutrition facts:** A 3-ounce serving has 97 calories, 16 calories from fat, 1.7g total fat (3%), .6g saturated fat (3%), 80.8mg cholesterol (27%), 43.4mg sodium (2%), zero carbohydrates and fiber, 19g protein (38%), zero vitamins A and C, zero calcium, .27mg iron (1%), and 300mg potassium. www.brokenarrowranch.com.

ANTIPASTO is an Italian term for a first course which contains no pasta. It means "the food before the pasta." It is usually served as the salad course, an attractive arrangement of vegetables, cold meats, and cheeses with Italian dressing. You may also see it spelled "antepasto."

APPETIZER is a small portion given prior to a meal to help create an appetite. Various appetizers include canape, dips, hors d'oeuvre, nibbles, and relishes.

APPLE: Ever since Eve picked that first "apple" off the tree in the Garden of Eden, apples have played a part in mythology, science, art, and history. Archaeologists argue about the Garden of Eden story, because they believe Eve ate a peach, a quince or an apricot, since apples were unknown in the Middle East during the time of Genesis. When the Christians told the story about the Tree of Knowledge, it was the Northern Europeans who assumed it was the apple.

Newton discovered the law of gravity when an apple fell on his head, and in recent history, John Chapman, better known as **Johnny Appleseed,** scattered seeds across Ohio.

The apple is a member of the rose family. Today there are more than 7,000 different kinds, however, only about 50 are grown commercially in the United States.

Apples come in red, green, yellow, and combinations. The flesh is white, yellow, or pinkish. The taste can be anything from tart to sweet. Apples are eaten raw, can be cooked, frozen, canned, or dried. Prior to refrigeration, apples stored in a cool place were about the only fruit that could make it through the winter months without spoiling.

There's a saying, **"An apple a day will keep the doctor away."** Here's why. **Nutrition facts:** An apple has 81 calories, 4 calories from fat, .5g total fat (1%), zero saturated fat and sodium, 2 .1g carbohydrates (7%), 3.7g fiber (15%), .3g fiber (15%), .3g protein (1%), 73 IU vitamin A (1%), 8mg vitamin C (13%), 10mg calcium (1%), .3mg iron (1%), and 159mg potassium. www.usapple.org; www.apples.ne.com; www.bestapples.com;

NORTH CAROLINA APPLE FESTIVAL

This annual apple festival is held over the Labor Day weekend during harvest time in Hendersonville, North Carolina. The event begins Friday morning with an apple pancake breakfast followed with an apple recipe contest and auction. Also included: an open house at the historic Johnson Farm, orchard tours, bake sales, and the Big Apple Breakfast on Sunday. Additional events: antique cars, tennis tournament, doll show, gem and mineral spectacular, model railroad displays, antique aircraft, and a street dance. Festival ends on Monday with Joe's Super Smiling Kids Parade and the King Apple Parade. For complete information write: **North Carolina Apple Festival Headquarters,** P.O. Box 886, Hendersonville, NC 28793 or phone (828) 697-4557.

APPLE BUTTER is only similar to butter in that both are a spread for bread. Apple butter is a thick apple sauce, made sweeter and spiced with cinnamon for eating on bread and cakes. Apple butter gets its unique taste from the addition of apple cider. Apple butter has been around a long time, since it has always been one of the best ways to preserve ripe apples. There are also peach, plum and other fruit butters. **Nutrition facts** per tablespoon: 36 calories, zero fats and sodium, 9.3g carbohydrates (3%), .6g fiber (2%), zero protein and vitamin A, 1mg vitamin C (2%), zero calcium and iron, and 38mg potassium.

THE NATIONAL APPLE MUSEUM

Scotch-Irish settlers established apple orchards in Biglerville, Pennsylvania prior to the arrival of the Germans. With shipping by the railroads and new fruit processing methods, today this area is one of the most intensive fruit culture regions in the country. The Biglerville Historical and Preservation Society has done much research on pioneer families, land settlements and genealogy.

In 1990 the Society opened The National Apple Museum to honor the founders of the apple industry. This one-of-a-kind museum displays exciting exhibits in the 1857 restored bank barn. Some of the exhibits include early deeds and warrants written on sheepskins with plot plans of the early settlers identified; window-maker ladders, sprayers, portable forge and other machinery; quality control display of peelers, cider presses and a vinegar generator; an 1800s kitchen with dough tray, dry sink, woodstove, and table and chairs; early orchard photos; a honey bee display; and an historic country store with authentic fixtures, advertising and original merchandise.

Guided tours are available weekends April through October. The museum is located just seven miles north of Gettysburg on route 394. For more information write: **The National Apple Museum,** 154 West Hanover Street, Biglerville, PA 17307 or phone (717) 677-4556.

WASHINGTON APPLE COMMISSION VISITORS CENTER

Washington state, with its 3,500 apple growers, produces ten-billion apples annually, which is more than half of all fresh apples grown in the United States. To honor the apple industry, the Washington Apple Commission has opened a Visitor Center north of Wenatchee, along the Columbia River, in central Washington. Visitors have the opportunity to sample a variety of apples and apple juices from the crunchy red delicious to the tart Granny Smith. The center answers an assortment of questions: Why do apples turn red? (It takes cool nights to turn apples from green to red.) Why do some apples crunch? (It's tiny water cells that explode when you bite into them.) Why does "An Apple A Day Keep the Doctor Away"? (It's the fiber.) These and other questions are answered in their apple industry movie. The gift shop offers apple souvenirs from apple t-shirts to apple telephones. For more information call (509) 663-9600 or write to the Washington Apple Commission, P.O. Box 18, Wenatchee, WA 98807. There is also a visitor center in Yakima, Washington

.

THE APPLE BLOSSOM FESTIVAL

In the spring, fragrant apple blossoms, as well as peach and cherry blossoms, adorn the mountain air in Pennsylvania's Adams County. During the first full weekend of May, the Apple Blossom Festival is held in Arendsville. Along with homemade arts and crafts, watch apple bobbing and apple pie eating contests, antique cars, antique tractors and rides, antique gas hit-and-miss engines, an antique cornmeal engine, orchard tours, and lots of live entertainment. Food is foremost with all kinds of apple treats, cider, fritters, pies and lots more. If you don't receive your fill of apples during this spring event, plan to return in early October for the National Apple Harvest Festival. While in Adams County, plan to visit the National Apple Museum in nearby Biglerville. For more information write: **Adams County Fruit Growers Association,** P.O. Box 515, Biglerville, PA 17307 or phone (717) 677-7444. —*Kathy Kleiner*

APPLE MOLASSES: Whoa! Isn't molasses made from sugar cane? True! But it can be made from other foods containing sugar. Benjamin Franklin in March 1741 in his *The General Magazine and Historical Chronicle* published an article on a new way to make molasses from apples. In part it read:

 "The Manner of Making it is thus; you must grind and press the Apples, and then take the Juice and boil it in a Copper till three Quarters of it is wasted, which will be done in about 6 Hours gentle boiling and by that Time comes to be of the Sweetness and Consistency of Molasses."

Apples in Early America

Unfortunately, it is not possible to duplicate Franklin's recipe. For the most part, early apples were hard, small, and sour, sometimes referred to as "pig apples" and often were fed to pigs. Grafting a branch onto an existing tree is the only way to guarantee the variety of apple to be produced. One of the more interesting varieties produced was the Wolf River apple. It had a circumference in many instances of fourteen inches, large enough to make an apple pie from just one apple!

The apple used to make apple molasses was called the "Summer Sweeting." This and other apples faded away, especially in the 1930's when the WPA destroyed all abandoned apple orchards. Even though the Summer Sweeting is no longer available, apple molasses can be made from any quality cider. However, the sweetness and quality will not compare to the original apple molasses as describe by Franklin in his magazine.

20

You Can Make Apple Molasses

You can make apple molasses by boiling down one gallon of cider for about three hours, until it is about one-sixth the original volume. Be **very very careful** with any boiling liquid. Care must be taken not to overcook, because the liquid thickens considerably while cooling. In fact, it could cool down to a jelly. If this happens, mix in a little cider to bring it to the desired consistency. In Vermont, apple molasses is known as boiled cider where it is still made by the Willis Wood family of Springfield and sold. – October 1985 *Early American Life*

APPLE PIE: One of American's favorite pies, made with spiced apples baked in a crust.

OH MY! THAT'S SOME APPLE PIE!
by Gretchen Huesmann

Ever dive into a pie as long as a swimming pool? Ever sink your teeth into a dessert a foot deep? That's just what the city of Wenatchee, Washington did when they created (and ate!) the World's Largest Apple Pie!

Why?

While doing some research, Pauline Sweeny, secretary to the North Central Washington Museum, ran across photographs of a 2,200 pound apple pie made by Wenatchee residents in 1938. With further research, she found a clipping from England in 1982 that an English chef baked a 30,000 pound pie. When Keith Williams, director for the museum heard, he thought it was un-American to have England hold this record, after all, "Mom and apple pie" seems to be an American motto. Wenatchee decided to beat that record and so they baked a 38,000 pound apple pie.

What did it take to make the Titanic-size tart? The recipe included the usual ingredients: flour, sugar, and apples. However, this mammoth pie required mammoth amounts:

3,927 pounds of sugar and brown sugar,
3,175 pounds of flour,
100 pounds of cinnamon
1,227 pounds of shortening, and
16 pounds of salt!

Oh yes, and 36,333 pounds of Red and Golden Delicious, Fuji, and Granny Smith apples! That's enough ingredients for **70,000 servings of apple pie**, or enough to feed all the fans at a major league baseball stadium.

While several local businesses donated the pre-mixed crust, filling, and topping ingredients, the main ingredient needed was volunteers. Hundreds of people gathered on the morning of August 16, 1997 to assemble and bake the pie in one day. Before dawn the volunteers began washing, coring, and slicing truckloads of apples. Others worked on the giant pie crust, rolling gobs of dough onto table-size aluminum foil and hoisting it into the rectangular pan. As the crust took shape, the prepared apples were dumped into the pan. **Football players in surgical clothing** used **cement spreaders** to level the fruit and to stir in brown sugar and cinnamon. A crumb topping provided the finishing touch.

Just How Do You Bake the World's Largest Apple Pie?

That question proved to be the biggest challenge. A committee of architects and engineers had to create a one-of- a-kind oven, big enough to cover the enormous pie pan (set on concrete highway barriers) and provide the heat as well. They designed a dome-like structure made of steel tubing covered in chicken wire, aluminum foil, and insulation, a material which holds in heat. Propane gas heated the oven. In all, 600 gallons of propane gas were used, that's about 133 barbecue's worth! Computerized sensors inside the oven and pan controlled the temperature.

A towering crane carefully lifted the oven and set it over the pie. An average pie bakes about an hour. This spectacular sweet slowly baked the rest of the afternoon. As the sun tipped toward the western mountains, a crowd of spectators, tired volunteers, and the media gathered for the official ceremonies. The people hushed when the crane slowly lifted the oven. A warm spicy scent drifted overhead. Someone whispered, "Oh my! That's some apple pie."

The official judges measured the colossal creation: 44 feet long, 24 feet wide, and 11 ½ inches deep! "We have the world's largest apple pie!" the announcer declared.

The crowd cheered. It had been a long exhausting day, but there was just one more task to complete. With plates, bowls, and buckets, the hungry crowd massed around the pool-size pan for their all-you-can-eat portion of the World's Largest Apple Pie.

When Pauline Sweeny was questioned, "Will Wenatchee compete if a larger apple pie is baked somewhere else?" She replied, "Not in my lifetime, if I have any say about it!"

NORTH CENTRAL WASHINGTON MUSEUM

Wenatchee, Washington calls itself **"The Apple Capital of the World."** More than half of all the apples grown in the United States come from the state of Washington, and the town of **Wenatchee** is in the center of this industry. The North Central Washington Museum has an excellent apple exhibit. Of special interest is a working antique apple sorting and packing line containing an apple wiper and a catapult sorter. There's also an audio visual presentation. The apple exhibit is connected by a skybridge from the main museum, which houses pioneer and Native American exhibits, and provides demonstrations and cultural programs of this agricultural region. For more information, write: **North Central Washington Museum,** 127 South Mission Street, Wenatchee, WA 98801-3039, or phone (509) 664-3340. --*Pauline Sweeny*

WHEN IS AN APPLE NOT AN APPLE?

At a church picnic, everyone enjoyed an apple pie. Afterwards they were amazed to learn the pie had no apple at all but was made from zucchini squash. The "green squash" in that apple pie recipe bakes up exactly like apples. The zucchini has no flavor of its own so the taste comes from the apple pie spices. See PIE HISTORY and ZUCCHINI.

Activity

SLICE AN APPLE, EXPLORE THE SIZE OF THE WORLD

Pretend you are on a giant spaceship, speeding through space. Like being lost in the wilderness, you are going around in circles. Do you know where you are? You're on the Spaceship Earth, traveling around and around a big ball of fire, year after year, going in the same direction. Are you giving much thought to this excursion and the spaceship you are on?

Let's take an apple and examine the spaceship Earth. Cut an apple into four equal pieces, from top to bottom. Set three of the segments aside for a moment. The one remaining segment is the land on your Earth spaceship. Cut this segment in half. One piece represents uninhabited land. Land that is too dry, too wet, too hot, or too cold for you. This includes deserts, swamps, river basins, mountain tops, and land covered with ice. The other piece, or one-eighth (1/8) of the spaceship Earth is part of the land where you live.

Take this usable land piece and cut it into four equal pieces and set aside three of these segments. One segment, or one-thirty-second (1/32) of the habitable spaceship is where humans can grow food. Pretty small, isn't it? Take this small piece and cut a tiny slice. This represents three-one-hundredth (1/300) of the spaceship surface. All of your drinkable water comes from this area and is the reason you must help to protect this water for your survival.

Now go back to the three large segments first cut, each represents a quarter (1/4) of the spaceship Earth. All of these segments represent the spaceship's oceans. Take one segment and cut it in half. This one-eighth of the spaceship surface represent the productive zones of the oceans. The rest supports very little life. Now cut this one-eighth segment into four equal pieces. One piece (one-thirty-second) represents the productive ocean area along the Pacific coast of North America, one of the richest regions of the ocean. Take this one-thirty-second segment and cut off a very thin slice. This tiny segment represents the top three hundred feet of the ocean through which light can penetrate and support photosynthesis. Without light there would be no life. *Almost all of the ocean's life is concentrated in this narrow surface region.*

Now examine the leftover pieces of your spaceship Earth. It's all garbage, little used, and of no value. Now look at the few pieces that are of value. Pretty small isn't it? Now you understand the spaceship Earth and why you and your friends need to protect it for food and water and everyone's survival. –RSC in *Cobblestone*

23

APPLESEED, JOHNNY:
THE LIFE AND LEGEND OF JOHNNY APPLESEED

Yes, Johnny Appleseed was a real live person. His correct name was John Chapman. He was born in Leominster, Massachusetts, September 26, 1774. He spent his boyhood years in East Longmeadow. In his late teens, Johnny migrated to western Pennsylvania and settled for a time in Warren, near Pittsburgh. From there he traveled west by horseback, canoe (usually two canoes tied together, one of which carried apple seeds he had gathered from western Pennsylvania cider presses), and by foot into the Ohio valley. He lived the life that many folks today relegate more to legend than history.

According to legend, Chapman was a strange looking man of medium height, raggedly dressed, barefoot (even in the winter). To cover his long, brown hair, he used a tin pan, which served the dual purpose of hat and a stew pot in which he cooked his food -- often just cornmeal mush. He wore little clothing, mostly cast-off garments from the settlers, or a garment made from a coffee sack with holes cut in it for his head and arms. He said clothes should not be worn for adornment, only for comfort. He was a vegetarian, eating no meat or fish, since he believed it was wrong to take the life of another just to procure food. This belief contributed to his zeal for urging people to plant vegetables and grow fruit trees. Except for later in life when he lived with a relative in Mansfield, Ohio, he had no home, and as he traveled he preferred to sleep in the forest. At times he would sleep indoors during foul weather, on the floor in front of the fireplace, with his kit as a pillow.

LEGEND MIXED WITH FACTS

As he traveled he would inform the settlers that his name was John Chapman, that he was a Swedenborgian Christian preacher, and he came to plant apple seeds. As he traveled the streams and rivers he would stop and plant apple seeds wherever he found suitable ground. He not only kept ahead of the settlements, but returned each year to care for the trees he had planted. His favorite apple was the Rambo. His visits were looked forward to with delight and no cabin door was ever closed to him. To the men and women he was a news carrier. To the children he was a friend and a playmate. He taught the boys to make sleds and wagons, and to the girls he gave ribbons for their hair. He became first known as the "apple seed man," later known as John Chapman, and finally given the nickname of Johnny Appleseed.

For fifty years John traveled Ohio, Indiana, and other states, planting and caring for his apple trees, teaching farmers apple culture, and assisting them in planting and caring for orchards, and preaching good news. Today, it is rare thing to find a farm in the country he traversed that does not have at least a couple of his apple trees. He had several apple tree nurseries and it was at one of those he was tending that the weather became cold and soon snow fell. That night he spent in the home of a friend, and by morning he had developed pneumonia. He died soon thereafter. He was buried just north of Fort Wayne, Indiana. He had become a living legend during his seventy one years, fifty of which were planting apple seeds. Johnny was survived by a half-sister, who related stories about him. She told of his love for the sight of flowers on the open prairie, the undisturbed forests, and how he looked upon nature as his friend. He was never known to injure or kill any living thing except one rattlesnake, and he always regretted killing that snake.

THE REAL JOHNNY APPLESEED

Part poet, part philosopher, part mystic, perhaps out of touch with the goals and aspirations of his contemporaries, but infinitively attuned to the larger harmony of the universe, John Chapman, better known as Johnny Appleseed, occupies a special place in the long line of dreamers, innovators, and statesmen who have contributed to America's greatness. --*International Apple Institute*

JOHNNY APPLESEED'S PRAYER
O, the Lord is good to Me,
And so I thank the Lord, For giving
me the things I need, the sun,
the rain and
the apple seed.
The Lord is good to me.
Amen

APRICOT: The apricot tree originated in Asia, where it still grows wild, and is related to the peach. The Chinese have cultivated apricots for more than 4,000 years. The tree doesn't do well in a cold climate, because a late frost will kill the blossoms. Apricots do well in the Middle East and the Mediterranean countries.

The first apricots in the United States were brought by the Spanish to California in the 1770s, where they are still grown commercially in the Santa Clara valley. Most apricots are picked green, because a ripe apricot must be eaten almost immediately. Let the green apricot ripen at room temperature. They can be refrigerated for up to five days. Apricots are also available canned, dried, and made into preserves.

It is believed only about five percent of the population in the United States has tasted a tree ripened apricot, because they don't ship well. In fact, the tree ripened apricot is so delicate, it can almost spoil being hand-carried from the tree to the house. But anyone who has tasted a tree ripened apricot will never forget the honey- sweet, tangy taste. Pure ambrosia! **Nutrition facts:** An apricot has 17 calories, zero fat and sodium, 3.9g carbohydrates (1%), .9g fiber (3%), .5g protein (1%), 923 IU vitamin A (18%), 4mg vitamin C (6%), zero calcium, .2mg iron (1%), and 105mg potassium. www.apricotproducers.com

AQUACULTURE: The farming of fish and shellfish is playing an important role in meeting the global demand for fishery products as the population continues to expand and fishery stocks approach their biological limits. Some of the United States fresh and salt water fishery farms raise: Catfish (see CATFISH FARMING), crayfish, lobsters, mussels, oysters, salmon, shrimp, tilapia, and trout. Aquaculture is more than the taking of eggs and producing fish for table food.

Balanced feed for fish and shellfish must be produced; female sex control with hormones must be studied; care must be taken for recirculating water systems and water temperatures. There are diseases that can wipe out whole ponds in a short time. Waste management from the ponds is another problem. Students who would like to enter the Aquaculture profession, write to: **World Aquaculture Society,** 143 J.M. Parker Coliseum, Louisiana State University, Baton Rouge, LA 70803.

ARACA: Native of South America. Small, yellow, subacid fruit, used to make jam and jellies.

AROMA, in cooking, means an agreeable fragrance from food and cooking.

ARROWROOT: Arrowroot is a starch obtained from tropical plant tubers. Arrowroot is used as a thickening agent in place of flour or cornstarch in puddings, sauces, and soups. Easy to digest, arrowroot is often used in baby food, and for those with digestion problems. Arrowroot is not as popular in American cooking as it is in Great Britain, where cookbooks are full of arrowroot recipes. Arrowroot is best used in low temperature cooking, such as making puddings with eggs. Arrowroot can be substituted for flour or cornstarch in recipes, but use only half as much. Cook the recipe only until thick, without excessive stirring. The name comes from its use by Native Americans in the treatment of arrow wounds.

ARTICHOKE: The artichoke, a member of the thistle family, is one of the most misunderstood vegetable foods. It has been cultivated in Europe for centuries before arriving in America. The French settlers brought artichokes to Louisiana, and the Spanish missionaries brought them to California. Today, they are also grown in Florida. The plant likes to grow in a cool, foggy, and frost-free climate. **Nutrition facts:** An artichoke has 60 calories, zero fat, 120.3mg sodium (5%), 13.5g carbohydrates (4%), 6.9g fiber (28%), 4.2g protein (8%), 237 IU vitamin A (5%), 15mg vitamin C (25%), 56mg calcium (6%), 1.6mg iron (9%), and 474mg potassium.

HAVE YOU EVER EATEN AN ARTICHOKE? Here's How!

First time eaters might question the artichoke for a couple of reasons. First, it's a thistle, and aren't thistles prickly plants? Who wants to eat something that has stickers?

Second, the name has the word "choke" in it, and the question is, "Will I choke when I eat it?" Don't worry, there are no stickers to eat, and by following these simple directions, you won't choke. It's actually a flower bud and the name comes from an Italian word having nothing to do with choking.

Cooking an Artichoke

Cut off stem at base; remove small bottom leaves. If desired, trim tips of leaves and cut off top 2 inches of the artichoke. Stand the desired amount artichokes upright in a deep saucepan in a single layer. Add boiling water 2-inches deep in the pan. Cover; simmer gently 35 to 45 minutes. Test for doneness when base pierces easily with a fork. Be careful to avoid steam. Drain; serve or chill for later. Artichokes are good hot or chilled.

Eating Is Fun and Easy!

Pull off one leaf at a time, holding it by the pointed end and dip the base of the leaf, if desired.
Pull the base of the leaf through your teeth to remove the soft, pulpy portion. Discard the remaining leaf. When the leaves have been eaten, spoon out the fuzzy center at the base; discard. The bottom, or heart of the artichoke is entirely edible. Cut into small pieces. Dip if desired, and enjoy.

Artichoke Dips

Artichokes are tasty plain, but dips do add flavor, bringing out more of the artichoke taste. Some like to dip it in melted butter; others prefer mayonnaise, salad dressing, or sour cream. Try making your own dip:

Creamy Ranch Dip: Combine 1/4 cup nonfat plain yogurt and 1/4 cup lowfat Ranch salad dressing. Mix well.

Honey Mustard Dip: Combine 1/4 cup prepared mustard with 2 tablespoons each of cider vinegar and honey. Mix well. -- *California Artichoke Advisory Board*

ARTIFICIAL SWEETENERS: First there was **saccharine**, an artificial sweeter that was discovered about 100 years ago. It has been used in soft drinks and chewing gum for years. However, even though it has a sweet flavor, it leaves a bitter aftertaste.

In 1981 along came **aspartame**, which was an improvement, however, when heated, it broke down and lost its sweetness. Recently two new sweeteners have been introduced, **acesulfarme K** and **sucralose.** Both have been added to diet beverages.

Laboratory scientists are still looking at saccharin, because in massive doses it was found to develop cancer in the urinary tract of rats. However, vitamin C given to rats also produced problems with the rats' urinary system, so the final result on saccharin is inconclusive.

Even with these artificial sweeteners, Americans overall have gained weight. There's still fat in most foods and even replacing sugar with an artificial sweetener in a doughnut will not turn that delight into a health food. It was also found that by cutting the calories in half on many products, many thought it was okay then to eat twice as much.

A plus for artificial sweeteners is that they are helpful for diabetics and they don't cause tooth decay.

While the food industry is celebrating, consumers still should use caution, since some health experts say artificial sweeteners are nothing to cheer about. Some nutritionists think if artificial sweeteners were only a minor food additive, it wouldn't matter very much, but they are being used in enormous quantities, and experts are still not sure they are safe. Weigh the choices. The best solution is to learn to enjoy the natural taste of as many foods as possible so that you won't want added sugar or artificial sweeteners.

ARUGULA: The leaves have a peppery, sweet-tangy flavor, adding pizzaz to even the blandest lettuces. It adds the same punch as green onions, but without the aftertaste. Arugula can also be added to other greens, nuts, and even fruit, such as apples and pears. In France it is known as *roquette*, and in England they call it "rocket salad." In Italy it grows wild and they call it *rucola*. It has the taste of regular arugula, but is a little more tangy and spicy. In Italy the leaves are added to almost everything including most hardy dishes, pasta, and pizza. Even the spicy, yellow flowers are edible and are added to garnishes. **Nutrition facts** per ½ cup: 3 calories, zero fats and sodium, zero carbohydrates and fiber, .3g protein (1%), 237 IU vitamin A (5%), 2mg vitamin C (3%), 16mg calcium (2%), and .2mg iron (1%).

ASAFETIDA: An aromatic gum, a member of the parsley family. Asafetida is mainly grown in Iran and India. It smells like strong garlic. It is dried, crushed, and sold as powder. In the distant past, people wore it in small bags like a necklace around their necks, as protection from disease. The smell was so bad it was believed to keep away anything, even diseases. It is still used, in very small amounts, to break down the indigestible enzymes in beans and cruciferous vegetable, such as cabbage. It is available in powdered and lump form in Indian and Mid-East markets. Medically, it has been use to prevent spasms and flatulence.

ASIAGO CHEESE: A creamy Italian cheese with a hard shell made from whole milk. Asiago is used for eating and cooking. It has a piquant flavor. Asiago is also aged and grated.

ASPARAGUS: The fifth most popular vegetable in America is the asparagus. It is a member of the lily-of-the-valley family. Asparagus is native to Asia Minor where it still grows wild. It was first brought to Europe about 200 BC. Our pioneers brought it to America and it quickly spread across the United States. Green asparagus is available fresh from early February to late June.

A white variety is also available, which is milder in flavor, and generally more tender than the green variety. Some think the smaller the stalk, the more tender they are. This is not true. It's the greener ones that are the most tender, whether the stalks are thin or thick.

Both green and white asparagus is available canned. Asparagus can be eaten raw or steamed, hot or chilled. Asparagus is not just a dinner food; it is enjoyable at any meal. Try steamed or canned asparagus topped with poached eggs for breakfast, or an asparagus sandwich for lunch made with deviled ham and pimiento cheese. If you tried canned asparagus and thought it was too mushy and didn't enjoy it, don't be prejudiced. Give fresh asparagus a chance, either steamed or raw with a dip. **Nutrition facts:** A ½ cup serving has 15 calories, zero fat and sodium, 3g carbohydrates (1%), 1.4g fiber (6%), 1.5g protein (3%), 391 IU vitamin A (8%), 9mg vitamin C (15%), 14mg calcium (1%), .6mg iron (3%), and 183mg potassium. www.calasparagus.com; www.washingtonasparagus.com.

STOCKTON ASPARAGUS FESTIVAL

It's the celebration of the Rolls Royce of vegetables. The Stockton Asparagus Festival features mouth-watering flavors and aromas that fill the air with such delights as asparagus pasta, beef-n-asparagus sandwiches, asparagus stir fry, and the all time favorite deep fried asparagus. These dishes and more are all prepared fresh on site in the 8,000 square feet Asparagus Alley Kitchen. For the "I don't eat asparagus crowd," there's asparagus pickles, asparagus jelly, asparagus salsa, and even an asparagus cake. Give it a try, you will like it. This event is held the fourth weekend in April during the height of the asparagus harvest in Stockton's (California) Oak Grove Park. Events include a 5k fun run, an arts and crafts show, lots of entertainment for all ages, and the *Concours d'Elegane* with more than 200 makes and vintages of cars. There are also cooking demonstrations by celebrity chefs where you will learn the ins and outs of preparing asparagus. Between events, take a stroll along the lake, where you are followed by geese and ducks looking for a handout, or take a nap in the shade of a giant oak tree. For information write: **Stockton Asparagus Festival,** 306 East Main Street, Suite 310, Stockton, CA 95202, or phone (209) 467-8001.

ASTRONAUT FOOD: Special provisions have to be made for eating when traveling in outer space. Food not only has to be preserved but has to take up as little space and weight as possible. Weightlessness is a special condition that affects the way astronauts eat in space. Space travelers can eat standing up, sitting down, or floating throughout the cabin upside down. Astronauts eat with a baby-size spoon, and they must eat slowly and carefully so that food doesn't fall off the spoon and float around the cabin.

Activity

Try eating like an astronaut. Place a mat on the floor next the wall. Stand on your head and rest your feet against the wall (might need a friend to hold up your feet). Take a bite of a piece of fruit, chew and swallow. What happens? Try eating a cookie. Do all the crumbs go in your mouth or do you drop some on the floor? Try eating something messy, like spaghetti with sauce. What happens? Try eating chocolate pudding. What happens? Try the same experiment by sitting in a chair with the back lying down on the floor. If you do this experiment with friends, see who does the best job of consuming the food with the least mess.

Activity
BE A NASA ASTRONAUT AT HOME

You can experience many of the astronaut foods at home, only under different conditions.

DISCOVER YOUR RDA WITH THE FOOD GUIDE PYRAMID All astronauts must receive Recommended Dietary Allowances (RDA) of vitamins and minerals necessary to perform in the environment of space (see the Food Guide Pyramid to plan your balanced daily meals).

FIND YOUR BEE DAILY REQUIRED CALORIE INTAKE

Caloric requirements are determined by the National Research Council formula for Basal Energy Expenditure (BEE). To figure your BEE, use the following formula:
For females: 655 + (9.6 x your weight in kilograms) + (1.7 x your height in centimeters) - (4.7 x your age) = BEE.
For males: 66 + (13.7 x your weight in kilograms) + (5 x your height in centimeters) - (6.8 x your age) = BEE.
With the answers you will need to know the amount of daily calories needed for space travel.

CALORIE COUNTDOWN

Today's space lunch menu has the following foods and calories:
Macaroni and cheese, 309 calories
Asparagus with sauce, 85 calories
Green beans with sauce, 63 calories
One slice of bread, 75 calories
One shortbread cookie, 45 calories
Chocolate pudding, 175 calories

1. For lunch, one astronaut ate an extra slice of bread and two extra cookies. What was the total calorie count of the meal?
2. One astronaut had one extra portion of green beans with sauce, but no asparagus. What was the total calorie count of the meal?
3. How many more calories did the first astronaut eat than the second?

MAKE A SPACE SHUTTLE BREAKFAST
You will need:
Powdered eggs (available as camping stores)
Tang
Freeze-dried banana
A breakfast roll

Step 1. Add water to Tang.
Step 2. In a non-stick pan, add powdered eggs and water
per instructions, stir, beat, and scramble on medium heat.
Step 3. Rehydrated the freeze-dried bananas per instructions.

Step 4. Eat.

Compare this space breakfast to your Earth breakfast.

GO SHOPPING

Visit your supermarket and see how many packaged foods can you find. Make a list. Choose foods packaged in paper, foil, or plastic. No metal cans or glass jars, and no large packages, only individual servings. Visit the food section of a camping store and make a list of available dehydrated and freeze-dried foods. With your list, plan a six-day menu for the Space Shuttle. For the fun of it, make a meal with some of the foods from your list for you and your friends. Be sure to sample some freeze-dried ice cream for dessert. Make notes who likes what and why, and what foods are disliked and why. Plan a day long hike and take only space foods from your list. Report on how each one worked in the wild. --*National Aeronautics and Space Administration* (NASA) See SPACE.

ASPIC: a nonsweet "jelly" made from vegetable juice or meat stock, such as cold chicken broth. Aspic salads are made by adding bits of vegetables, meats, or eggs, and molding it with gelatin into various shapes.

ATALANTIA: Native of India. A 3/4-inch yellow bitter fruit, eaten fresh.

ATLANTIC SALMON: Unlike the Pacific Ocean, the Atlantic Ocean only has one species of salmon. Atlantic salmon are found in the northern waters from North America to Europe Atlantic salmon. Unlike the Pacific salmon, Atlantic salmon swim upstream to spawn two or more times. **Nutrition Facts** per 3 ounces: 121 calories, 50 calories from fat, 5.4g total fat (9%), .9g saturated fat (4%), 46.8mg cholesterol (16%), 37.4 mg sodium (2%), 0 carbohydrates and fiber, 16.8g protein (34%), 0 vitamin A and C, 10mg calcium (1%) and .7mg iron (4%).

ATEMOYA: Native of tropical America. A member the annona family, and considered the best of the family. Atemoya is a large, smooth, sweet fruit, eaten fresh, made into a drink or ice cream.

AU GRATIN (awe-grah-tin) is a cooking process done in a hot oven or under a broiler, which produces food with a crisp golden crust.

AU JUS (awe-zhoo) is a natural meat juice which is served with the meat. It is not a gravy.

AU NATUREL means food plainly done without special sauces and seasonings. A food in a natural state.

AVOCADO: Although it's a fruit, the avocado is usually eaten as a vegetable. In Nicaragua they cook the avocado. In Ecuador it is made into a soup. Brazilians make avocado ice cream. Well, it is a fruit!

Spanish explorers found the avocado in the early 1500s. Central American natives called it *ahucati* and the Spanish modified into *aguacate*. It is also known as an **"alligator pear."**

Avocados are grown in southern California, along the Rio Grande in Texas, and in Florida. Peak period is from early winter into mid spring. Available in supermarkets almost year 'round.

Avocados grown in the United States are about the same size and shape as a pear. Central American varieties can weigh as much as a small watermelon. The avocado has a nutty flavor with a buttery texture. Coarse dark green skin makes them easy to peel. Avocados are usually eaten raw, often made into a dip such as guacamole. Sliced avocados make a neat sandwich with mayonnaise (and a thin slice of onion). **Nutrition facts:** Unlike most fruits, the avocado is high in both fat and calories. A ½-cup serving has 186 calories, 146 calories from fat, 17.7g total fat (27%), 2.8g saturated fat (14%), zero sodium, 8.5g carbohydrates (3%), 6.8g fiber (27%), 2.3g protein (5%), 707 IU vitamin A (14%), 9mg vitamin C (15%), 13mg calcium (1%), 1.2mg iron (7%), and 692mg potassium. www.avocago.org; www.calavo.com.

Bb

BABA: A leavened cake usually made with raisins, steeped in syrup or rum, and baked in tall molds. The name possibly comes from the resemblance of the plump round loaf to a stocky peasant woman. The word means "old woman" or "grandmother." The recipe probably came from Italy, since it resembles the *panetonne*.

BABKA: A coffee cake flavored with orange rind, rum, almonds and raisins.

BACON: The word "bacon" comes from the French. It originally referred to "the meat on a pig's back." Later, in England, it meant, "a side of pig's meat." It used to mean pork of any kind but today it means certain cuts cured and smoked. Being a British production, there are various British cuts and cures. It was originally sold by the cheesemongers instead of the butchers. Bacon was a staple in all but the poorest households since cured cuts kept well and provided cooking fat and seasoning for vegetable cookery. Even today many people think nothing flavors vegetables like a touch of bacon grease.

British bacon slices are called **rashers**. **Canadian bacon** is the center muscle of a pig's back.

Curing means to preserve the meat from deadly bacteria. Preserving by drying and smoking is done with salt, brown sugar, and saltpeter.

Depending upon the feed given to the pigs, the types of wood, and the blend of spices used in smoking, bacon tastes may have slight variations. Bacon is usually found packaged sliced, thick or thin. Short and irregular slices are boxed and sold as bacon "ends." These are useful in cooking when slices are not needed.

Most bacon is pan fried. The slices are turned often over low heat and not allowed to smoke, because the bacon will obtain a burnt flavor. Drain the fat from the pan often to keep the bacon crisp. Bacon can also be baked, broiled, or microwaved. After cooking, drain on paper towels. **Nutrition facts** per 3 slices of regular sliced bacon: 109 calories, 85 calories from fat, 9.4g total fat (14%), 3.3g saturated fat (17%), 16.2 cholesterol (5%), 303.2mg sodium (13%), zero carbohydrates & fiber, 5.8g protein (12%), zero vitamin A & calcium, 6mg vitamin C (11%), and .3mg iron (2%).

ARKANSAS BACON

Have you heard the expression, "Eating high on the hog?" It means eating the best part. This refers to Arkansas bacon from the Ozarks. This bacon comes from the upper part of the pork shoulder, where's there's more lean meat and less fat, and other choice lean cuts. Arkansas bacon is dry-rubbed with sugar and deep hickory smoked with no added water.

Arkansas bacon is cooked like any other bacon, either fried or broiled. It is important that Arkansas bacon be fried very slowly over low heat and turned frequently to prevent burning. Save the drippings to make red-eye gravy. Arkansas bacon makes an excellent Eggs Benedict, but better known as "eggs Ozark" in Arkansas. Arkansas bacon and ham can be order from **Ozark Mountain Family**, P.O. Box 77, Farmington, AR 72730-0037 or phone (800) 643-3437. They also have other smoked meats, such as chickens and turkey.

BACTERIA: Some food bacteria is toxic and can be life threatening. The most common is botulinum. Others include salmonella, *clostridium perfringens,* and *staphylococci.* Raw poultry is the main source of salmonella bacteria. Sauces and gravies which are kept warm, not hot, will cause staphylococci to grow. **Reheating** will kill the organism **but not the toxin.** Reheating can be more dangerous than eating it as it is. **Toss out if not 100% sure.** See FOOD SAFETY

To avoid problems, follow these rules: #1. **Wash your hands** with antiseptic soap after washing poultry and other meats. #2. **Disinfect** cutting board (2 teaspoons of bleach in a gallon of water) after cutting poultry. #3. **Keep hot foods hot** (above 140°F), and **cold foods cold** (below 45°F), #4. **Wash all** cutting boards, knives and other utensils between uses. #5. Do not use a cloth towel for drying; either **air dry** or dry with a clean paper towel you will discard. .

BAEL FRUIT: Native to India, has a 4-inch round, hard shell. The pulp is eaten fresh, made into a beverage, or makes a great sherbet. The root and bark are said to be good to reduce fever.

BAGELS: Bagels, which originated in south Germany, were part of the Jewish cuisine in northeast America, and generally served with cream cheese and lox (smoked salmon). The name comes from a Yiddish word meaning bracelet.

Today bagels have become popular throughout the United States. Basic bagel dough is made with yeast, allowed to rise like all yeast bread products, then shaped like a doughnut and allowed to rise once more. The bagel is first simmered in water, then baked until a golden brown. The finished product is bland in taste, with a hard crust, and a chewy interior. Some bagels are also made with eggs presenting a yellow interior.

Bagels come in varieties fortified with dried fruits (raisins, apples, cranberries, cherries, blueberries, etc.); spiced with cinnamon; covered with seeds (poppy, sesame, caraway, etc.); coated with dried onions and garlic, filled with sun-dried tomatoes, cheddar cheese, jalapeño peppers, chocolate chips, nuts; sweetened with honey. The basic dough sometimes varies as with pumpernickel and sourdough.

As a popular breakfast treat, bagels are sliced (carefully) and toasted, then topped with jam, peanut butter, or any favorite topping. In the southern United States the southerners call them, "northern biscuits." For lunch they make great sandwiches with meat, cheese, lettuce, etc. Try using a bagel in place of a hamburger bun for your next hamburger. A plain white bagel has about the same nutrition values as a slice of white bread.

BAIN-MARIE: This term means to keep foods hot by placing one cooking vessel into another vessel of hot water. The set of pans made especially for this is called a double-boiler. As a method of melting things like chocolate, the microwave has mostly replaced the double-boiler today.

BAKE: To cook with dry heat, especially in an oven.

BAKED ALASKA: The dessert has been around a long time, at least since 1866 when a Paris chef served it to impress a Chinese delegation visiting that city. According to one source, an American, Dr. Rumford, is given credit for the invention of the dessert. Rumford knew egg white is a poor conductor of heat. Based on the knowledge, the chef prepared hard vanilla ice cream over sponge cake and topped the whole thing with meringue. Sealed with the frothy egg white, the heat of toasting the meringue for a few moments in a oven could not reach the ice cream. The meringue can also be flamed.

Another story says the recipe was created in New York's Delmonico Restaurant in 1867 to celebrate the purchase of Alaska Territory from Russia.

"When I lived in Alaska, I made it once with Neapolitan ice cream. While everyone enjoyed it, they had never heard of it. Most thought I was a bit strange." –RSC

BAKING MIXES: Premixed dry ingredients can be made ahead to speed preparation time. Commercial mixes are available in the supermarkets.

MAKE YOUR OWN BAKING MIXES

When the recipe calls for a prepared mix and the prepared mix is not available, make your own. Since your mix will not contain preservatives, store them in a tightly closed container in the refrigerator. When your recipe calls for a baking mix, measure per recipe and follow recipe instructions.

BISCUIT MIX

4 cups flour
2 tablespoons baking powder
1 tablespoon sugar (optional)
2 teaspoons salt
1 cup shortening (for flakier biscuits, use 2 cups)

1. Combine the dry ingredients thoroughly.
2. Cut in the shortening with a pastry blender only until mixture looks like course crumbs. Do not over mix.

BUTTERMILK BISCUIT MIX

1. To the Biscuit Mix add 1/3 cup of dry cultured buttermilk powder.
2. Reduce baking powder to 4 teaspoons.
3. Add 1 teaspoon of baking soda.

PANCAKE MIX

2/3 cup flour
1/3 cup whole wheat flour
(Whole wheat flour can be replaced with all-purpose flour)
1 teaspoon baking powder
½ teaspoon baking soda
2 tablespoons sugar

Mix above ingredients thoroughly.
Recipe can be doubled, tripled, etc.

BUTTERMILK PANCAKE MIX

1. Add 3 tablespoons dry culture buttermilk powder to
the Pancake Mix recipe.

HOT ROLL MIX

2 cups flour
1 package dry yeast

35

1/4 teaspoon salt
1/4 cup powdered dry milk

SWEET ROLL MIX

1. Add 1/3 cup sugar to Hot Roll Mix.

MUFFIN MIX

4 cups flour
½ cup sugar
2 tablespoons baking powder
1 teaspoon salt
1/3 cup dry powdered milk

BUTTERMILK MUFFIN MIX

1. Replace 1/3 cup of dry powdered milk with 8 tablespoons of dry cultured buttermilk powder.
2. Reduce the baking powder to 4 teaspoons.
3. Add 1 teaspoon of baking soda to the Muffin Mix recipe.

CORNMEAL MUFFIN MIX

1. Add 1 cup of cornmeal to the Muffin Mix recipe.
2. Decrease flour to 3 ½ cups.

BAKING POWDER RECIPE

You have run out of baking powder and you need some in a hurry. Make it yourself with this simple recipe.

2 teaspoons cream of tartar
1 teaspoon baking soda
1 teaspoon cornstarch

Combine all ingredients well. Makes 4 teaspoons.

SELF-RISING FLOUR RECIPE

If the recipe calls for self-rising flour, and you don't have any, you can make your own.

If the recipe calls for:

½ cup flour	add 3/4 teaspoon baking powder, and 1/4 teaspoon salt.
3/4 cup flour	add 1 teaspoon baking powder, and 1/4 teaspoon salt.
1 cup flour	add 1 ½ teaspoons baking powder, and ½ teaspoon salt.
1 1/4 cups flour	add 1 3/4 teaspoons baking powder, and ½ teaspoon salt.
1 ½ cups flour	add 2 1/4 teaspoons baking powder, and ½ teaspoon salt.
1 3/4 cups flour	add 2 3/4 teaspoons baking powder, and 3/4 teaspoon salt.
2 cups flour	add 1 tablespoon baking powder, and 3/4 teaspoon salt.
2 ½ cups flour	add 3 ½ teaspoons baking powder, and 1 teaspoon salt.
3 cups flour	add 4 ½ teaspoons baking powder, and 1 1/4 teaspoons salt.

BAKING POWDER: Packaged baking powders have been on the market since the early 1850s. However, it wasn't until 1889 when William M. Wright of Chicago, developed a product with a mixture of saleratus (baking soda) and cream of tartar that commercial baking powders were reluctantly accepted by the cook. Wright felt a need for a better version. With experimentation, he worked out a formula for a new baking powder; a double-acting one that began its leavening action when mixed into dough, then produced a second leavening in the heat of the oven. Two of the main ingredients in double-acting baking powder are sodium aluminum sulfate (for leavening) and calcium sulfate (maintains leavening). Baking powder also contains corn starch as stabilizer (to keep the powder from reacting in the can) and bicarbonate of soda. See BAKING SODA

Prior to the invention of baking powder, pear lash (or pearl ash) was used as a leavening agent. It was made from leaching wood ashes and was called, "potash." Potash was made by adding lye water to wood ashes and letting the water evaporate to a powder. Pear lash was purified potash. It only had some leavening action and did not produce a finished product like today's commercially made baking powder. www.hulman.com

BAKING SODA: The original name was "saleratus" and was developed in England. It came to America in 1839, packaged in a bright-red wrapper, and with a free recipe card. In those early days, soda salesman rode into town in decorated wagons pulled by a team of horses. With the sound of bells and a blast of a trumpet, everyone knew the soda man had arrived. In this day and age, it's hard to imagine that joyous event, since today baking soda comes in a small box easy to overlook on the market shelf.

The chemical formula is $NaHCO_3$ and is mostly used in baking as a leavening, but also makes a good cleaning agent. Plus it will soothe the itch from bug bites and sunburn. Baking soda is required in baking recipes where acid ingredients, such as buttermilk, vinegar, and fruit juices are also used. It is even used in recipes also containing baking powder and cream of tartar, where acids from chocolate, sour cream, brown sugar, apples, etc. are mixed together. A dough made with baking soda needs to be baked immediately because at room temperature most of the leavening gas will escape. However, if refrigerated, dough can be baked at a later time. This is what makes refrigerated biscuits possible in the supermarkets. You can do the same at home.

BAKLAVA is a pastry made famous in Greece and Middle Eastern cookery. It is made of filo (phyllo) pastry layered with honey, butter, and nuts. www.dessertsonus.com.

BAMBOO SHOOTS: Native to Asia, bamboo shoots are a basic ingredient in oriental recipes. The shoots come from the inner white part of young bamboo grass. Shoots are obtained by stripping off the tough bamboo outer layer. The shoots are then cut into strips, ready for cooking. Not all bamboo grass produces edible shoots. In fact, depending upon the season, the shoots will have different flavors, especially in the summer when the shoots are bitter. Bamboo shoots are available canned in either brine or water and imported from the Orient, mostly from Japan and Taiwan. The shoots are added to stews, soups, and stir fry dishes. Shoots have a mild taste similar to an artichoke. Shoots are low in calories, about 25 calories per 3 ounces. **Nutrition facts** per 1/4 cup: 10 calories, zero fat and sodium, 2g carbohydrates (1%), .8g fiber (3%), 1g protein (2%), zero vitamin A, 2mg vitamin C (3%), zero calcium, and .2mg iron (1%).

BANANA: Bananas originated in the Malaysian jungles of southeast Asia. It is believed the first Europeans to eat bananas were members of Alexander the Great's expedition to India in 327 BC. In some lands bananas were considered the principal food, so much that during the ivory and slave trade, travelers carried roots of the plant to the Middle East and Africa. The Portuguese traders carried the roots from Africa to the Canary Islands, where today bananas are still grown commercially. www.dole.com; www.chicquita.com.

When the Spanish explorers came to the New World, so did bananas. According to Spanish history, Franciscan Friar Tomas de Berlanga in 1516 brought roots to the fertile soil in the Caribbean. From there they went into Mexico and south through Central America all the way to Brazil.

There are some 30 species of bananas, which look and taste different from each other. Some bananas cannot be eaten raw and must be cooked. Those are usually enjoyed as a vegetable. The most popular of this variety is the "plantain." Bananas also find their way into many desserts. Green tipped bananas are best for frying.

To ripen bananas, place in a brown paper bag with an apple or tomato overnight. Yellow bananas are prime for eating as is or for slicing on top of cold cereals. Placing the banana in the refrigerator at this stage will keep them fresh for up to two weeks. The skin will darken, but not the insides. Once brown freckles form on the skin, this indicates the maximum sweetness. If you prefer to eat yours less ripe, use the riper ones for baking breads and muffins. **Nutrition facts:** Bananas are rich in potassium, which revitalizes muscle power and maintains body fluid balance. One banana contains 105 calories, 4 calories from fat, .6g total fat (1%), .2g saturated fat (1%), zero sodium, 26.7g carbohydrates (9%), 2.7g fiber (11%), 1.2g protein (2%), 92 IU vitamin A (2%), 10mg vitamin C (17%), 7mg calcium (1%), .4mg iron (2%), and 451mg potassium.

APRIL FOOL'S DAY BANANA
by Sandra Trainor

Activity:

My mother was a practical joker. In fact several generations of her family were jokers. I guess you could say my family tree grows nuts. So when it came to April Fools Day, jokes abounded, and this is my favorite joke. Image peeling a banana and finding it already sliced. How could this be? Did it grow this way? Or maybe someone took the banana out, sliced it, then placed it back inside its peel? No, that couldn't be - what glue could stick well enough to reseal a banana peel? So how did a sliced banana get inside an unpeeled banana peel? Here's how:

You'll need:
1 banana
1 threaded needle

1. Notice that along the banana peel there are several lines from the top near the stem down to the bottom. Along one of these lines and about an inch up from the bottom, push a threaded needle in. Have the needle come out of the next line to its right.
2. Continue "sewing" around the banana in the same circular direction until you have both ends of the thread coming out the same hole where you started.
3. Gently pull both ends of the string toward you. As you pull, the banana inside the peel will slice.
4. Do this about every inch all the way up to the top of the banana. Remove threads.
5. Give the banana to a friend, and watch their amazement as a sliced banana emerges out of a never before peeled banana peel.

THE WHOLLY USEFUL BANANA PLANT
by Regina Anthonypillai

The tall banana plant looks like a tree, but it is not a tree because it has no woody trunks or boughs. It looks so much like a tree that an animal can be tied to the "trunk" of the banana plant and enjoy the roof-like shade of its large leaves. The banana is a giant herb plant and in the same family as the lily. The stalk of the banana is composed of soft, overlapping leaves and can grow 25 feet high, making the banana plant the largest on earth without a woody stem. Only three or four weeks after the banana root has been planted in the ground, suckers appear and leaves begin to unfold from the suckers. Fully expanded leaves on mature plants look like enormous, drooping feathers. Tough feathers! Even in tropical storms, banana leaves will shred rather than break off and leave the tender fruit unprotected.

When the leaf formation is complete, a flowering stem emerges from the top and large bud develops. As each purple leaf of the bud unfolds, a double roll of small flowers develop into tiny green bananas. Each flower becomes an individual banana and is known as a "finger." Each cluster consists of 10 to 20 bananas. Most plants have five to nine clusters, called "hands," so one plant can easily yield 100 bananas. **Banana flowers** that haven't turned into fruit are cut off and cooked as a side dish to eat with rice.

It can take four to twelve months for the hands to develop. Farmers put the stems in large plastic bags to protect the bananas from wind and insects. Bananas are picked green and shipped in

39

refrigerated ships to markets around the world. Thanks to the wonders of shipping, people in the **United States eat about 11-billion ripe bananas** annually. Fried bananas and dried banana chips are popular as snacks. Banana fruit has a smooth but bitter yellow skin, which cannot be eaten by humans but serves as a delicious meal for cows.

In tropical lands the large **banana leaves** are used as an umbrella in an emergency. In India, the leaves are also used to wrap food like rice and curry. Food wrapped in banana leaves and cooked has a rich smell. People wrap rice and curry first in a banana leaf, and then cover this with paper to take it with them when going on a picnic. Indian cooks use the dry leaves like nonstick spray on a frying pan to cook roti (a kind of bread). In parts of Latin America, tamales are wrapped in banana leaves, rather than corn husks. Meat is sometimes wrapped and roasted, or cooked with banana leaves for added flavor, just as you would cook with herbs. As a symbol of fruitfulness, in some countries the whole banana plant, with its fruit and purple flowers, is cut and used as decoration for weddings. Two trees form a little niche for the bride and groom to sit under, a symbol of their happy home.

The banana plant dies soon after bearing fruit. The **dead plant**, not wasting any part of itself, is cut down and buried to make the soil rich. The old plant becomes food for the young plants, called "daughters," that spring forth from its roots. Daughters produce a flowering stem and the process continues year after year producing more daughters and more bananas. Where only a small growing space is available, bananas will feed more people than wheat would.

BANANA SPLIT: The person who invented this soda fountain extravaganza is an unnamed hero. It is made by cutting a banana lengthwise in a long dish and adding three scoops of ice cream. These are topped with three different toppings, swirled with whipped cream, and crowned with a maraschino cherry and nuts.

BANGAR NUT: This seed-filled fruit originated in east Africa. The seeds are roasted or fried. Eating too many seeds will have a laxative effect. The flowers smell offensive, and the Latin name for this flower, *stercus*, means manure.

BANNOCK: A round Scottish oatmeal cake which was baked in the embers of the fireplace, then toasted on a griddle. The name comes from "hearth bread."

BANQUET: A lavish meal, usually accompanied by speeches, music and dancing, given to a large number of people. Today a banquet is given for holidays, state occasions, weddings, and any kind of formal celebration.

BAOBAG: This large tree is native to Africa and has 8-inch long brown fuzzy fruit. When dried the pulp tastes like cream of tartar. The leaves are cooked and eaten.

BARBADOS CHERRY: This large, red, juicy berry, native to the American tropics, is also known as acerola. Sweet or sour, the berries are eaten fresh, made into juice and tea. Barbados cherries are high in vitamin C.

BARBADOS GOOSEBERRY: A Madagascar tree fruit used for pies and preserves. The sour green fruit is high in vitamin C.

BARBECUE: A method of cooking meat, and some vegetables and fruits, over an open fire, usually charcoal. Some barbecue units today use propane gas as the open fire. "To barbecue" is the verb form, meaning to cook by barbecuing.

BARBEDWIRE CACTUS: If you are in Florida, look for this red, spiny 2-inch fruit, and eat some fresh.

BARD: A process where meat is wrapped with bacon or salt pork, which lubricates meat while cooking, especially extra lean meats like filet mignon, chicken breast, and some game meats. The bard fat is usually discarded after cooking.

BAR-LE-DUC: A jam originally made in Bar-le-duc, France, from currants and honey. The seeds were pushed out with a needle. In America the seeds are left in.

BARLEY is the oldest of the cultivated cereals in Europe and the Near East. It may even be older than rice. In ancient times it was the most important food grain, but it was replaced by other cereal grains. Today it is still used as food, but more often as animal fodder and for making malt for beer. The oldest known remains of barley were discovered in Syria, dating from about 8000 BC. Gradually, over the centuries, barley fell out of favor as wheat was found to make better, lighter breads. Today you can find barley in the hot cereal section. It is still used in soups and meat dishes too. The grains, or pearls, add texture, thickening and interest to a dish.

BASIL: Basil is a member of the mint family. It was native to southern Asia and the Middle East, and long grown in Europe for cooking and medical purposes. Basil is an annual herb and will grow in almost any warm climate. Basil comes in a half dozen varieties, ranging from light green to purple leaves. The word, "basil," is Greek and means "king." The royalty at that time preferred the purple color, perhaps because the pungent fragrance was fit for a king's house, according to herbalist John Parkinson. Sweet basil is most commonly used in flavoring seafoods, salad dressings, soups, and tomato dishes. Basil may be used dried or fresh. Basil oils are also used in perfumery and incense. www.mellissa.com

BLISSFUL BASIL

If you were marooned on a desert island, and had the choice to grow just one herb, what would you chose? Consider basil, since it is the most versatile of all herbs. There are three groups: scented, Italian, and Oriental.

Scented Basils

These exotic fragrances and pretty forms will add texture and perfume to your garden and kitchen. **Cinnamon Basil** has a spicy scent, especially when the leaves are brushed up against, and the fragrance of cinnamon fills the air. Cinnamon basil makes a wonderful tea, added to jellies, chutneys, curries, sweet and sour dishes, and for meat and chicken marinades. **Lettuce Leaf Basil** is one of the oldest known basils. The four inch long leaves have a mild spicy, sweet flavor. Use lettuce leaf basil mixed in salads, replace lettuce with it in sandwiches, or shred the leaves to make a delicious sauce for vegetables and pasta. **Red Rubin Purple Leaf Basil** is highly fragrant and makes a nice addition to salads and pastas. Add red rubin to make a scented vinegar. **Purple Ruffled Basil** is one of the most ornamental basils with three to four inch skinny dark purple leaves with deeply fringed and ruffled edges, and contrasting light rosy-lavender flowers. **Broadleaf Sweet Basil** is one of the most popular commercial varieties. This is one of the best for making pesto, great for salad garnishes.

Italian Basils

From the Mediterranean comes a distinctly different strain of sweet green basils. **Napoletano Basil** comes from Southern Italy, has light green leaves, a very sweet fragrance and mellow, rich flavor that adds a buttery flavor to almost any dish. Chop some with parsley and sprinkle over sliced tomatoes. **Fino Verde Compatto Basil** is one of the smallest varieties growing about a foot tall and is preferred by many Italian chefs because they can easily measure the small one inch green leaves. The sweet pungent leaves can be added with a bit of oregano, crushed garlic and olive oil then spread on toasted sourdough bread.. **Genova Basil** has an intense perfumed flavor, with a haunting taste. Italian chefs make a quick paste with a little olive oil and add it to soups and casseroles just before serving. **Greek Basil** is the smallest, growing only up to nine inches tall. Great for growing in window boxes and indoors on a kitchen windowsill. The leaves are extremely fragrant and can be used is almost any recipe calling for basil.

Oriental Basils

Basils from the Pacific Rim countries bring on new and exciting flavors. **Thai Lemon Basil** has a concentrated fragrance and Flavor of sweet lemon. Crush the leaves when adding to rice dishes, fish and poultry recipes, or salads and marinades. **Siam Queen Basil** has a combination sweet clove-mint scent and is wonderful mixed in chutneys, marinades and jellies. Fragrant basil makes almost every dish a feast for your senses. One word of warning. Some of the deep purple leaves will tend to add color to food, hence, best not to use with chicken and white cream soups and sauces, as the result may not be very appetizing.

Drying and Storing

Basil is basically a summer plant, so the question comes up how to preserve the leaves for winter use? One of the easiest is to **oven-dry** them. Place leaves on a cookie sheet and place in a 180°F oven for several hours. If your oven doesn't go down that low, leave the door ajar. The microwave in another way to dry them. Place leaves on a paper towel, set the microwave to run for thirty seconds, turn and mix, repeat, for up to about total of three minutes. Dried basil needs to be stored in airtight containers in a cool, dark pantry. It is best to keep the leaves whole, crush them when used to release the flavor oils. Basil can also be frozen in water or olive oil. Put a handful in a blender with just a little water or olive oil and blend into a paste, then fill the chopped leaves in ice cube trays.

Grow Year Round

In warm regions, basil can be grown year round. In cooler climates, grow basil indoors so that it receives several hours of sunlight each day. Indoor plants are not as hardy as those growing outdoors, so it is best to plant a few seeds every couple of weeks. For an excellent source for basil seeds contact **Shepherd's Garden Seeds,** 30 Irene Street, Torrington, CT 06790-6658 or phone (860) 482-3638 for a catalog.

BASMATI RICE: A long-grain, aromatic, hulled rice imported from the Himalayan mountains of India. It is aged one year to develop its full flavor. A must for Indian and Middle Eastern cuisine. Available in white and brown. **Nutrition facts:** A ½ cup serving has 341 calories, 4 calories from fat, .5g total fat (1%), zero saturated fat and sodium, 75.8g carbohydrates (25%), zero fiber, 7g protein (14%), zero vitamins A and C, 18mg calcium (2%), and 1.2mg iron (7%).

BASS: There are many varieties of bass fish found in both fresh and saltwater. The most common fresh water bass are found in the upper Mississippi River system and the Great Lakes. These seldom exceed 5 pounds. The most common are white and yellow bass. Saltwater bass are found in both the Atlantic and Pacific Oceans. Atlantic bass weight up to 4 pounds, while in the Pacific the striped bass weigh up to 20 pounds.

Baked and stuffed are popular methods for cooking, but bass can also be poached, fried or broiled. Bass is a favorite of gourmets, because the meat is delicate, tender, and moist. **Nutrition facts:** A 3-ounce serving of bass has 97 calories, 30 calories from fat, 3.1g total fat (5%), .7g saturated fat (3%), 57.8mg cholesterol (19%), 59.5mg sodium (2%), zero carbohydrates and fiber, 16g protein (32%), 85 IU vitamin A (2%), 2mg vitamin C (3%), 68mg calcium (7%), 1.3mg iron (7%), 303mg potassium, and a good source for phosphorous.

BASTE: To moisten food while cooking, usually by brushing or pouring on fat.

BATCH: An amount produced at one baking.

BATTER: A mixture of liquid and flour, usually with other ingredients, thin enough to pour. A pourable dough.

BATS: No, bats are not a gourmet food. Bats do have an important role in the food chain by consuming insects which eat plants, vegetables and fruit. Bats protect crops. A single bat can eat up to 3,000 bugs a night at the rate of more than 500 insects an hour. There are some colonies of bats which can eat up to 250-tons of insects in a single night. Some farmers house bats to use in organic farming, thus reducing a dozen pesticide sprayings to one or two a year.

Bats (like nighthawks) help control the insects at night, other birds help control insects during the day. Bats, like bees, help in pollination and dispersing of seeds. Bats play an important role in saving tropical fruits, especially mangoes, dates, figs, and avocados. If you would like to control insects around your home, install both bird and bat houses on your property. If you would like to know more about bats or would like to build a bat house, write to the **Bat Conservation International, Inc.**, P.O. Box 162603, Austin, TX 78716-2603 or phone (512) 327-9721 or (800) 538-BATS. – - *Mark Kiser*

BAVARIAN CREAM: A chilled egg custard dessert made with gelatin and enriched with whipped cream, then chilled.

BAY LEAF: The bay leaf is from a small laurel shrub and is native to the Near East and the Mediterranean regions. Bay leaves are generally dried and just one leaf can do wonders for the flavor of a simple dish. Bay leaves are used in most Mediterranean recipes, as well as in French cooking. The leaves are used in chowders, soups, marinades, stews, casseroles, and in water containing meats such as corn beef and ham. Add a bay leaf or two to the water when cooking potatoes, onions, or tomatoes, and other fresh or frozen vegetables. It will add a distinctive flavor. It's best to leave the bay leaf whole (an eaten crushed bay leaf can be lodged in the throat, causing a person to choke). However, if the recipe calls for it to be crushed, wrap the crushed leaves and other herbs in cheese cloth which can be discarded at the end of the cooking process. www.melissa.com

BEACH PLUM: Beach plums grow wild along the Atlantic seacoast from Virginia to Canada. The fruit, a member of the plum family, has the combined taste of grape, plum, and cherry. However, the fruit is quite bitter and sour, and seldom eaten raw. Even the birds won't eat them. Beach plums make an excellent jelly or jam.

BEANS: Beans are one of the world's oldest cultivated plants. They are known to have grown more than 5,000 years ago in Europe. Beans are a member of the legume family with peas, lentils and peanuts. Except for a few varieties, only the seeds are eaten. Bean seeds are eaten fresh or dried for later use. **Don't eat beans from the castor-oil plant or catalpa tree; they are toxic** and can cause death. See DRIED BEANS.

The **kidney bean and the lima bean** are native to the Americas. It is believed these beans originated in Peru, since they were first cultivated by the Incas.

Beans are feeding the world, especially in countries where meat is not generally available. Beans can grow in almost any soil, even poor soil, and with their high protein content, they make an excellent meat substitute. Fresh and frozen green beans are available year round, as are packaged dried beans. Beans are higher in protein than most vegetables and have fair amounts of A and C vitamins

BEAN FACTS & FOLKLORE

The secret of Jack's magic beanstalk beans remains a mystery. The history of mankind is full of such folklore, demonstrating the part these tiny legumes have played in the course of civilization. The true history of beans is no less interesting than folklore.

Most varieties originated in Africa, Asia, and the Middle East. It is thought that beans were brought into the Americas by the first nomadic tribes who crossed the Bering Strait into Alaska. There is evidence the **Aztecs** in Mexico used beans as staple food as early as the 10th century. **Large lima beans** were born high in South America's Andes by the **Incas**, and brought to California by ship from Peru.

In the 1600s on the **East Coast, Native Americans** grew such good bean crops they were able to teach the European settlers to plant corn and beans together. That way bean vines could climb the cornstalks for support. Beans and corn just naturally combine well. The colonists also learned to cook corn and beans together in a dish the Native Americans called *musicickquatash*, now popular as **succotash**. The beans fixed nitrogen in the soil to nourish the corn, and the corn supported the bean vine. From the Native Americans, America's early settlers learned how to make Boston baked beans, and bean soup. From our friends south of the border came refried beans and chili with beans. .

Harvesting

Most bean varieties are planted from late spring to midsummer. The exception are garbanzo beans. **Garbanzos** do not like intense heat.

When the pods are plump with beans, the vines are cut and laid in wind rows to air dry. After the pods dry, the plants are picked up and the pods are shelled. The dried beans are cleaned and packaged for your supermarket shelves. All this was once done by hand. Today there are machines to do much of it commercially, but it is still done by hand at home.

Nutrition

Beans are best know for protein. Eaten with small supplements of meat, dairy products, or grains, they supply all essential amino acids. Beans are prized as an energy food. Their carbohydrates supply "working" calories. They digest slowly, satisfy hunger longer, and the calorie count is low. Beans supply B vitamins that help turn food into energy and keep digestive and nervous systems healthy. Beans supply iron for building red blood, calcium and phosphorous for strong bones and teeth, and fiber for regularity. **Nutrition facts** per 1 cup **string beans**: 74 calories, zero fat and cholesterol, 14.3mg sodium (1%), 17g carbohydrates (6%), 4.3g fiber (17%), 4.3g protein (9%), 1590 IU vitamin A (32%), 39mg vitamin C (65%), 88mg calcium (9%), and 2.5mg iron (14%). **Nutrition facts** per 1 cup cooked **dried white beans**: 249 calories, 6 calories from fat, .6g total fat (1%), .2g saturated fat (1%), zero cholesterol and sodium, 44.9g carbohydrates (15%), 11.3g fiber (45%), 17.4g protein (35%), zero vitamins A and C, 161mg calcium (16%) and 6.6mg iron (37%).

Beans for the World

About half the **baby lima** beans grown in California are sent to Japan and made into a confectionery paste called *anko*.

The "Belle of Dixieland" is the **black-eyed** bean, or black-eyed peas, as they are known down there. Peas are Soul Food down South and are becoming popular from border to border as Yankees and Westerners teach it tasty new tricks. Garbanzo beans, so named by the Spaniards, are known as **chick peas** in many other lands. The small **white bean** is a Boston aristocrat. The bluebloods of old Boston made this compact bean famous the world over as "New England Baked Beans." **Edamame** is the Asian soybean you can snack on like nuts or eat in the pod.

Make beans your way. They can be a main meal dish or a side dish. You can make with meat or serve them vegetarian, maybe with a little cheese. You can make them hot and spicy with chili powder and jalapeño peppers or sweet with brown sugar and molasses. Serve them sour with vinegar or lemon juice or combine seasonings for a sweet-sour taste. –**California Dry Bean Advisory Board**

BEANS IN THE NEWS -THEN AND NOW
A Light Look at Bean History

Beans have been making history long before the Knights of the Round Table. As a matter of fact, they have been mentioned in very ancient history books. Here are some headlines stories you might have seen down through history:

525 BC news bulletin: "Pythagores (pi thag or us), noted Greek philosopher, sage, and mathematician found dead! Was it by his political enemies, or his allergy to fava beans?"

325 BC: It is reported that the poor in Athens, Greece existed on greens, beechnuts, turnips, wild pears, dried figs, barley paste, grasshoppers (yes!) and fava beans.

1526 AD: Money by the pound! In a history of the West Indies, Spanish explorer Pedro de Alvarado says "in Nicaragua everything is bought with **cacao beans** (source of chocolate); however cheap or expensive." Forget dollars, fill your wallet with cocoa beans!

1528: Pope Clement VII wishes for gold, but gets beans! Spanish explorer, Hernando **Cortéz introduced haricot beans** to Spain from Aztecs or Incas in the New World. On his return,

Cortez presented them to Pope. The kidney shaped beans were called *fagioli,* in association with fava beans, the only bean known in Europe at that time.

1621: Suffering Succotash! The welcoming Native Americans showed Massachusetts colonists how to plant beans in their corn hills. Both rich and poor colonists baked beans for their Saturday night supper, just before their weekly bath.

1640: In France, a new word appears in *Oudin's Dictionary.* The word is **haricot** for **fagioli** beans brought to France by Catherine de Medici in 1533. Imagine it taking five years for beans to get from Spain to France! Did they walk by themselves? Actually, all transportation of new ideas being slow in those days, that was fairly fast.

1875: **Navy Beans** at Sea! Burnham and Morill Company of Portland Maine, produced the first canned baked beans. They were the white bean variety known as "pea," but later became known as "navy" beans because they went to sea with the ocean fishermen. Today, you can have the same beans from supermarkets, sold as "B&M Baked Beans."

1800s: A study shows: Preference for beans you eat depend a great deal on your heritage, availability, and to some extent on the government. Yes, the government. Free government surplus foods usually include beans. In the 1800s the American government allotment of food for the Ojibway natives in Minnesota introduced them to salt pork, bacon, and pinto beans. Today, Minnesotans, especially the Native Americans, still prefer pinto beans.

1930s: Beans for Depression! During the Great Depression, the Slovakians in Minnesota survived on bean and noodle soup. And a great many others too. In the South, it was beans and greens.

More About Beans

There are **bush beans**, also called snap beans, and vine beans or pole beans. The names describe the way they grow. Pole beans, whether growing on corn stalks, poles, or trellises all produce more beans in less space, than the bush varieties. Snap or bush beans from your supermarket are usually eaten fresh or cooked. If you have your own garden and use no chemicals, you can pick and eat the beans straight from the plant. Just stay away from the bean plants if they are at all damp. You'll spread plant disease. The United States grows about 30- million hundredweight (hundred pound bags) beans just for **dry bean use** every year. These bean include: pinto, pea, garbanzo, and navy. Some of them are bush and some pole varieties.

Annuals grow and die in one year with the exception of lima beans. They are a pretty perennial vine in their native tropics. In North America they act like an annual, because they can't take the cold. Most beans are planted after the soil temperature reaches sixty degrees. The exception is the garbanzo bean. They produce better in cool temperatures. If you use canned beans in a recipe, discard the liquid, and rinse them before use.

The more beans you eat, the better you'll feel.
We should eat beans at every meal.
--Virginia G. McNear

Activity
Bean Bonanza

Buy some beans (they are cheap) and make the following projects:

1) Make a bean poster by gluing a few samples of each kind to poster board and labeling each according to name. 2) Pour a sampling of each variety into a gallon jar, counting each bean as you go, and allow your friends to guess the total for a prize. Also see if they can guess and name how many varieties are in the jar? Show them the names on your bean poster.

3) For a gift or just for a nice kitchen display, layer different color and kinds of beans in a large glass jar. Store with the lid on. If special cooking instructions are needed, write out the instructions and store them folded inside the jar on top of the beans.

TRADITIONS AND HOLIDAY BEANS

Greeks eat a great many bean dishes, especially in the week before Easter. They have a traditional fish and bean dish which is eaten after a funeral. Jewish traditions include a special party when a baby cuts its first tooth. The grandmother makes a special soup with beans, rice, bulgur, barley, and meat. Italians use beans as a main ingredient in minestrone soup and *pasta fagioli*. At Christmas, southern Italians use lupine beans. These beans must be boiled, then soaked for a week, with frequent changes of water. Scandinavians make a *bruna bonor* or brown bean dish for Christmas. It is sweet and sour, and may use both nutmeg and molasses. New Year's Day wouldn't be New Year in the American south without black-eyed peas. July 4th, the national picnic favorite is hot baked beans. – *Virginia G. McNear*

BEAN HOLE BEANS

Maine's early settlers, especially those in the logging camps, cooked beans in large pots, buried in the ground surrounded by hot coals. Now for a quarter of a century, the Broad Cove Church of Cushing, Maine bakes their beans as a fund raiser almost like the early pioneers once did, except with some modern appliances, such as a gas stove.

The **"Bean Hole Bean" project** begins at nine on Friday morning. The men dig holes in the ground, line the holes with rocks, build fires with oak and other hardwoods and fill the holes with the red hot coals. The men take two hour shifts, adding more wood. Also very early Friday morning, the women start preparing the beans. Ten pounds of soldier and pea beans are soaked with cold water in each large blue enamel canner pot. About two in the afternoon, the water is poured out, fresh hot water is added, then cooked by boiling until you can blow on the beans and the skin flakes up from the beans. The cooking water is then poured off and the mixing begins by laying salt pork cubes in the beans with brown sugar, molasses, dry mustard, salt and pepper. The pots are then filled with boiling water, and the lids tied down with clothes hanger wire. Very carefully, to avoid spilling, men carry the pots to the fire holes. The hot coals are shoveled out and the bean pots put down into the hot rocks. The coals are then put back around the pots to fill up the space. A steel plate is placed on the pot which is then topped with sand and dirt to hold in the heat. Heavy canvas is placed on top to keep out any rain that might happen. The beans are cooked for 24 hours.

During the history of this event there has never been a failure. On July 13, 1996, hurricane Bertha blew in while the weather was cool, breezy and foggy, there was no rain as the men worked hard on Friday building the red hot coals. Once the bean pots were placed in the holes, the rain started. It poured, the wind blew, but the event went on as scheduled with a great crowd that Saturday night.

When the "Bean Hole Bean" project started, just two holes were dug. Today four holes are used, but as people hear about the event, the church members plan on additional holes. Along with two kinds of bean hole baked beans, hot dogs, cole slaw, home-baked breads, and various pies are served. --*Jeannette Chapman*

BEAN SPROUTS: Various kinds of sprouts have been a favorite in Oriental recipes, and now people have found other ways to enjoy them. The most popular are bean sprouts, available fresh in many supermarkets and health food stores. Sprouts are also available canned. Sprouts can be eaten raw in a salad or a sandwich. They can also be sautéd with an onion and/or green peppers. Of course, chop suey or chow mein is not complete without the sprouts. Try adding them to a stew or soup just before serving. **Nutrition facts:** A ½ cup serving has 16 calories, zero fat and sodium, 3.1g carbohydrates (1%), .9g fiber (4%), 1.6g protein (3%), zero vitamin A, 7mg vitamin C (11%), 7mg calcium (1%), .5mg iron (3%), and 77mg potassium. Strange as it may seem, the vitamin C value is greater in a sprout, than in the whole dried bean (5%).

BEAR: Bear meat is not as common in wild game eating households as deer or elk. However, if the bear is young and tender, and hasn't yet learned to fish, it should be tasty enough for anyone. Just in case the bear is a little tough, it's best to grind into hamburger. Young bear chops are quite good, especially with lots of added onion and lemon juice. For a juicy and tender rump roast, season the meat with onion soup mix, a can of mushroom soup, wrap tightly in aluminum foil, and roast very slowly at 300° F for 4 hours. Can also be done in a crockpot.

Since game can have a so-called "gamey" taste, extra ingredients are sometimes added to mask that flavor. Sometimes bear meat soaked overnight in salt, vinegar, and water will have the fishy taste removed, but not always. Or a good marinade made with spices, herbs, and juniper berries might do the trick.

Braise small chucks of bear meat with vinegar, soy sauce, onion, and green pepper for about an hour until tender. During the last 20 minutes, add some pineapple jam.

An old bear, especially one that has learned to fish, can be dry and tough. As one old timer once said, "The bear was so tough, you couldn't put a fork in the gravy."

Bear meat must be thoroughly cooked to avoid trichinosis disease. Meat should be falling off the bone as a test for doneness, or as we say, "fork tender."

BEARNAISE: (ber-nayz) A French sauce made with egg yolks, butter, wine, vinegar, shallots, pepper, parsley and tarragon; used on baked, broiled or cooked meats.

BEATEN BISCUIT: The dough is beaten with a mallet (or rolling pin, some say) for 30 to 60 minutes, rolled out, cut, and baked slowly. There are better, faster, and easier ways to get biscuits. Beating is supposed to serve the same purpose as kneading. "Kneading puts in air and mixes the dough. Beating doesn't do either. I made them once. Never again!" –RSC

BÉCHAMEL: (bay-sha-mel**)** A French white sauce made with flour, butter and milk; delicious with eggs, meats, and vegetables.

BEECHNUT: An edible nut from the beech tree. The tree grows in temperate regions of Europe and North America, also found in the Andes, New Zealand and Australia. It has smooth, ash-grey bark and is related to the oak and chestnut trees. The nut is 50% oil, used mostly for pig food, especially in Europe. The Southern Beech grows an edible fungus, sometimes used as cattle feed. Beech-Nut is a brand name food producer. Beech-Nut gum has no beechnut that we know of.

BEEF: Beef comes from cattle. Most of the beef we eat comes from steers (males are castrated when very young) and heifers (females which have never borne a calf). Depending upon the cut, beef can be fried, broiled, roasted, stewed braised and boiled. Beef can be cured to make beef bacon, corned beef (from the brisket). Beef can be dried (chipped beef and jerky), and freeze-dried (mostly used for camping). Variety meats include the brains, hearts, kidneys, liver, and tongue. As with all meat, **refrigeration is important** to control harmful bacteria. This bacteria is mostly on the outside of the meat, so it is okay to cook the inside rare. Ground beef must be cooked well done to kill all of the bacteria. Beef comes in a variety of grades with prime the most expensive. Choice grade is the most popular, followed by the good grade. Meat is graded depending upon the fat content and if the meat is well marbled, which makes the meat more tender. **Nutrition facts:** Beef can be high in saturated fat, cholesterol, and calories. A 3-ounce steak can contain up to 37% fat and 375 calories. Beef is an excellent source of protein, iron, vitamins B2 (riboflavin) and niacin. www.sdbeef.org; www.beef.org; www.nybic.org

OPERATION T-BONE

Audubon, Iowa, is famed for its livestock and annually holds the Operation T-Bone celebration in mid-September. The celebration began in 1951 when the cattle shippers invited banker Albert Kruse to ride with them to Chicago. Mr. Kruse declined after hearing others tell how drafty and uncomfortable the caboose ride could be in the late, cold fall. However, he said they would make the trip if a Pullman car was provided. A Pullman car was arranged, and Mr. Kruse, along with the cattle shippers and businessmen made the trip in grand style. Operation T-Bone caused quite a stir when the train pulled into Chicago's stockyards. This event was covered by news reporters as far away as England. To honor this event, the Audubon Jaycees' constructed the world's largest Hereford bull. It is made of steel and concrete, stands thirty feet high, and named Albert. There is a parade, a horse show, a tracker pull, Junior High Jump Basket Bounce, kids roping contest, crafts, and entertainment. There's also an array of food: fresh baked cinnamon rolls and pies, barbecued beef, funnel cakes, and all kinds of beverages. At noon on Saturday is the T-Bone Hamburger Feed, and in the evening is the T-Bone Banquet. For more information write: **Audubon Chamber of Commerce**, P.O. Box 66, Audubon, IA 50025-0066.

BEER: The making of beer is one of the oldest occupations known, since it was enjoyed more than 5,000 years ago by ancient civilizations. Beer can be made from a variety of cereal grains, wheat, millet, barley, rice, and corn. Today it is mostly made from barley that has been germinated in water and dried, and with hops and cultured yeast. Beer was the most common drink in England before tea was brought from Asia. In early America, beer was a chosen drink, even at breakfast, because it was more pure than water. Old cookbooks generally had a recipe to make beer, since most households made their own. Because they were so much easier to make, coffee and tea replaced beer at breakfast, when they became readily available. Coffee and tea required only boiling water. Beer varieties include ale, lager, porter, and stout. Lager is the most popular in America. Beer is lower in alcohol than wine and other spirits. Some meat, seafood, and cheese recipes call for beer or ale. When cooked, the alcohol completely evaporates, leaving only a slight taste and usually an enjoyable sauce.

BEETS: Beets probably originated in the Mediterranean area. They were enjoyed by early Romans and still enjoyed in Italy. The Dutch also like beets, and cultivated several varieties. Russians created a wonderful beet soup called borstch. See BORSTCH.

Most beets have a large red root. However, there are yellow beets, and beets striped with red and white. Red beet juice is used for natural fabric dye. Summer is the peak growing season. Planting should be done either before or after the real hot weather. Beets require more water than most vegetables. If the ground dries out too much beets become woody. When purchasing fresh beets look for smooth and firm texture. Smaller beets are the most tender.

Unwilted tops of beets can also be cooked much like spinach. Young leaves can be used fresh in salads. Beets can be boiled or baked, should be cooked whole, then peeled. The beets can be served whole, sliced, diced, or shredded. Reheat beets in a little of the beet water, add butter or margarine, and maybe a little lemon juice or vinegar. Beets are available year round canned or pickled. **Nutrition facts:** The saying that beets are "good for your blood" is true. They are also good for all of your body! A ½ cup serving of beets has 29 calories, zero fat, 53g sodium (2%), 6.5g carbohydrates (2%), 1.9g fiber (8%), 1.1g protein (2%), 26 IU vitamin A (1%), 3mg vitamin C (6%), 11mg calcium (1%), .5mg iron (3%), and 221mg potassium. The tops are more nutritious, with 1,162 IU vitamin A (23%) 6mg vitamin C (10%), and only 4 calories. www.members.aol.com/asga/cal/htm

BELCH: It is the custom in some cultures to burp or belch, as it is also called, after eating to show appreciation for the food. In this country is considered rude, except for babies. See also INDIGESTION and FLATULENCE.

JOHNNY BELCHES WHEN HE EATS

Early settlers once thought Native Americans lacked humor. This is not so, writes Matthew W. Stirling, author of *Indians of our Western Plains*. The tribesmen of a Blackfoot village bestowed the name on one of theirs, "Johnny Belches When He Eats." Johnny was embarrassed when people laughed at him. He requested a name change to the tribal council. For such a name change, it is the custom to furnish a feast for the council's powwow. Johnny furnished a small steer for the occasion. The council met and give him the new name, "Johnny Does Not Belch When He Eats." It is unknown whether Johnny liked his new name or not. --RSC

BELL PEPPERS: One of the more popular sweet peppers; originated in the Americas. They are eaten raw in salads and dips, or cooked as part of a sauce or stuffed with meat and other ingredients. Bell peppers, also called bull-nosed peppers, come in green, yellow, red, orange, and brown colors. Since the colored ones are expensive, cook with the greens and use the colored ones for salads and garnishes. **Nutrition facts** per ½ cup serving: 26 calories, zero fats and sodium, 6.2g carbohydrates (2%), 1.8g fiber (7%), .9g protein (2%), 613 IU vitamin A (12%), 87mg vitamin C (144%), 9mg calcium (1%), .4mg iron (2%), and 172mg potassium.

BERMUDA ONIONS: A mild flavored onion, the Bermuda is a large, flat onion, and white or yellow in color. Bermudas are available during the spring months. Once the only sweet onion, and available only in season, it has been largely replaced as other sweet onions are now available all year round. **Nutrition facts** per ½ cup serving: 22 calories, zero fats and sodium, 5g carbohydrates (2%), 1g fiber (4%), .7g protein (1%), zero vitamin A, 4mg vitamin C (6%), 11mg calcium (1%), .1mg iron (1%), and 90mg potassium.

BEURRE MANIÉ: (burr-mahnee)A thickening agent made with flour and butter and added at the end of the cooking process.

BEURRE NOIR: (burr-nwah) Browned butter.

BEVERAGE is a loose term for any liquid that can be drunk. It could be a glass or milk or orange juice, a cup of coffee or tea, or a carbonated soft drink or a bottle of beer. This would include colas, shakes, frappes, smoothies, soft drinks, alcoholic drinks, and all kinds of milk. Hence, drinks can be natural or man-made. The root word, *bibere*, comes from the Latin to the French to the Middle English, meaning "to drink."

BIGARADE: A French cooking term wherein a recipe is flavored with rind and/or juice of an orange, especially a bitter orange.

BIGNAY: This small tree is native to Malaysia and has long currant-like clusters. These make an excellent juice, jelly and wine.

BILBERRY: See BLUEBERRY

BILIMBI: This small tree growing in the Malayan region, has green, sour, cucumber shaped fruit, suitable for pickles and preserves.

BIND: A French cooking term which means to hold separate ingredients together, such as the way eggs combine in mayonnaise and flour combines in sauces.

BIOTECHNOLOGY FOR FOOD: What is food biotechnology? It's a process of modifying plants, animals, and microorganisms to produce an abundant supply of better tasting, more nutritious foods. For thousands of centuries, farmers have been selecting, sowing, and harvesting seeds that produce food products. Though they didn't understand the underlying scientific principles involved --namely, that they were **moving and modifying genes** by the thousands -- early farmers have been harnessing biology for centuries to make and modify their plants. Therefore, farmers unknowingly moved and changed genes to improve food. Modern biotechnology allows food producers to do the same thing -- knowingly and with deliberate purpose. With agricultural biotechnology, humans can now move or change one gene at a time.

There are many food biotechnology choices. Let's look at two, squash and tomatoes: Do you know how yellow crookneck squash has been improved in recent years? Not likely. Most just take for granted that it will be in the supermarket's fresh produce sections every summer and fall. Thanks to biotechnology, squash farmers can grow higher quality food at the same or lower price, and use chemicals more judiciously in the growing process. This news is welcomed by health, cost, and environmentally conscious consumers.

Among other farming problems are **insects** called aphids. **Viruses** can claim as much as 80% of a squash crop each year. Before, farmers could do nothing to stop the viruses directly; instead, they sprayed chemicals to kill the aphids. Through biotechnology, modern plant specialists use precision enzymes to cut out the protein coats that surround all viruses. In short, the **plants are vaccinated.** In turn, the plants develop their own protection to the virus. This protective immunity becomes a part of the plant's genetic make-up and is passed along to future generations of plants. This same biotechnology is being developed for potatoes, tomatoes, cantaloupes, watermelons, and cucumbers.

Would you rather buy tomatoes that were picked while still hard and green and then treated with ethylene gas to turn them red? Or would you prefer tomatoes left on the vine until redness appears, then picked and shipped directly to market with more homegrown flavor? Soon you will have that choice to make, thanks to plant breeders and genetic tools that enable them to understand tomatoes better.

The genes responsible for ripening have been known to tomato breeders since the 1950s. But until recently, no one had been able to turn down the expression of these genes because no one understood how these genes functioned in the tomato itself. More than anything else, the new tools of biotechnology have given modern plant breeders the ability to understand how specific genes actually work in tomatoes. With this increased understanding, breeders now can work with specific genes and get specific results. Researchers discovered that by putting a copy of a gene that causes softening into the tomato plant backwards, they could slow down the softening process. This has resulted in better tasting tomatoes.

These new methods are being applied to melons, peaches, bananas, and papayas. Before long, biotechnology will produce better tasting tomatoes, because they will be able to stay on the vine longer; friendlier squash that will no longer need to be sprayed; healthier cooking oils with less saturated fat; less food related allergies; fruits and vegetables that will contain higher levels of vitamins and minerals; and at the same time a reduction in the overall chemical use in the farming environment, and the scaling back of other agricultural inputs that will not be used because so many fewer acres will be necessary to plant.-- ***International Food Information Council***

BIRD: A way to make meats go further by rolling thin meat around a bread or vegetable stuffing, which is then simmered in stock or gravy. They are also called "rolls" and "*roulades*."

BIRD GRAPES: Native to south Florida, the ½-inch round, black grapes grow in clusters, to eat fresh or as jelly.

BIRIBA: A large yellow Amazon fruit, the sweet white pulp of which is eaten fresh.

BISCUIT: (bis-kit) A French term meaning "cooked twice." The word is applied to various kinds of small, thin baked goods. In England it's a cookie or cracker. In Italy it's a frozen dessert. In America it's a quick bread, leavened with baking powder or soda and cut into cookie size before baking. The small size speeds the baking time. Biscuit varieties are too numerous to list. In America, the most common form is baking powder biscuits served hot.

BISCUIT MIX: Toward the end of the 1800s, food mixes were starting to be prepared. Some of these mixes could make several recipes: hot biscuits, coffee cakes, pancakes and waffles. Generally the only difference was the amount of liquid added to the mix. You can make your own hot biscuit mix at home. See BAKING MIXES.

BISON: (by-sun) Also known in America as buffalo, a wild animal that once ran in herds across the American West. Native Americans hunted and used every part of the animal for food and clothing. Over-hunted by the white settlers, their number reduced to almost extinction. Today the bison is making a comeback and plentiful enough to be offered in restaurants around America. Buffalo burger tastes like beef, perhaps moister and more flavorful. Watch for it on the menu as you travel around the country and try it. "Buffalo" also applies to other kinds of oxen in Asia and Africa. www.bisonranch.com

BISQUE: (bisk) A rich soup made with seafood. Bisque, a French word, also refers to some frozen desserts made with fruit and nuts.

BITTER MELON: Also known as bitter gourd, this vine is native to the Old World tropics, with 2 to 8-inch orange, bitter fruit. Eaten cooked. The leaves are made into a medicinal tea. Also available in health food stores as an herbal remedy. www.gardenofdelights.com

BITTERS: A liquid made from bitter roots, barks, herbs, and plants such as the orange. Bitters help stimulate the appetite, as well as aiding in digestion. Health food specialists say American's have an aversion to anything bitter and so will avoid bitter foods. They recommend eating more horseradish and bitter herbs.

BLACK BEANS: Also known as turtle beans, these beans are much smaller than a kidney bean. The black to grey skin hides a white interior. However, after cooking, the whole bean turns black. Slightly sweet, they go well with many other vegetables as well as by themselves. Black beans are grown mostly in **Mexico, Central and South America**, and are available dried in many supermarkets and Latin American food stores. They make an excellent soup, and when mushed are great refried. The cooked whole beans can also be mixed half and half with rice and topped with a little sour cream and served as a side dish. In **Nicaragua** and **Costa Rica**, they are called *gallo pinto*. In **Brazil** they are often baked with pork products. **Nutrition facts:** A ½ cup serving of cooked dried black beans contain 114 calories, 4 calories from fat, .5g total fat (1%), .1g saturated fat (1%), zero sodium, 20.4 carbohydrates (7%), 7.5g fiber (30%), 7.6g protein (15%), zero vitamins A and C, 23mg calcium (2%), 1.8mg iron (10%), and 305mg potassium.

BLACKBERRIES: In the British Isles they are called brambles. The blackberry is one of the most abundant wild shrubs in Europe and America. There are over 2000 varieties. When unripe they are red; when ripe they are a purple-black. Blackberries can be eaten fresh with cream and sugar or topped on a breakfast cereal. They can also be cooked in a pie or made into jam. When picking blackberries, if the cap stays on the berry, it isn't ripe enough to pick. The season runs from June through September. Fresh blackberries should be eaten almost immediately, or they can be refrigerated unwashed for up to 2 days. Wash just prior to eating. Blackberries are also available canned and frozen. Beginning with the early Greeks, blackberries have long been used for medicinal purposes and in herbal remedies. **Nutrition facts:** A ½ cup serving has 37 calories, zero fat and sodium, 9.2g carbohydrates (3%), 3.6g fiber (14%), .5g protein (1%), 119 IU vitamin A (2%), 15mg vitamin C (25%), 23mg calcium (2%), .4mg iron (2%), and 141mg potassium. www.moodyfarms.com

BLACK COD: See SABLEFISH.

BLACK-EYED PEAS: A favorite bean in the Southern United States is the black-eyed pea. The white bean has a black or yellow spot in the oval. Hopping John, a Southern dish, is made with black-eyed peas, bacon, onions, and rice. **Nutrition facts:** A ½ cup serving has 99 calories, 4 calories from fat, .5g total fat (1%), .1g saturated fat (1%), zero sodium, 17.8g carbohydrates

(6%), 5.6g fiber (22%), 6.6g protein (13%), zero vitamins A and C, 21mg calcium (2%), 2.2mg iron (12%), and 238mg potassium.

BLACKENED: a Cajun recipe wherein fish, chicken, beef, shrimp, etc. are coated with butter and hot spices and fried over very high heat quickly. The process produces intense smoke so it is best to cook this way outdoors. The spices and the smoke blacken the meat with a thin, dark outer crust. www.chefpaul.com

BLACK PEPPER: (Piper nigrum). Attila the Hun, when holding all of Rome hostage, demanded 3,000 pounds of peppercorns as tribute. In medieval Europe, pepper was traded for gold, ounce for ounce. Piper nigrum is a broad-leaved, woody vine; grown in the tropics on trees and poles. They grow densely packed flower spikes. The fruits are harvested, usually, while still green. The fruits are dried until the single hard seed is wrinkled and dark gray/black. It is then packaged as peppercorns, or ground into the familiar black pepper. The milder white pepper is from the same plant; but the seeds are ripe when picked, and the flesh is removed before grinding. Red or pink peppercorns are the lowest fruits on the spike, and their appearance signals "time to pick the green ones." In addition to table use, pepper is used in liniments, gargles, and insecticides. These seeds should **not be confused with the Brazilian pepper tree**, which is not pepper, and the seeds of this tree only resemble black pepper.

BLACK SAPOTE: Native to Mexico, this tropical persimmon also grows well in south Florida. The dark green-to-black fruit, is eaten fresh and made into desserts. Known as the "chocolate pudding fruit." www.gardenofdelights.com

BLACK SUGAR PALM: In the Philippines we find a brown fruit that takes two years to ripen, but which is not eaten, because it burns the mouth. The male flower produces sap which is made into sugar. Sago starch is made from the trunk.

BLACK WALNUTS: North American Native Americans relied heavily on black walnuts for their food. The oil was used to season their food. Nut meats when ground were used to thicken vegetable and meat dishes. Black walnuts are not generally eaten plain, but are better when combined with other ingredients, especially cookies, and muffins, and for making candy and ice cream. **Nutrition facts** per 1/4 cup used in cooking: 190 calories, 147 calories from fat, 17.7g total fat (27%), 1.1g saturated fat (6%), zero cholesterol and sodium, 3.8g carbohydrates (1%), 1.6g fiber (6%), 7.6g protein (15%), 93 IU vitamin A (2%), 1mg vitamin C (2%), 18mg calcium (2%), 1mg iron (5%), and 164mg potassium.

WALNUT TIME IN THE OZARKS

One of the most walnut producing areas today is the Ozark Mountain region of Arkansas and Missouri. Every fall, when ripe black walnuts drop from the plentiful walnut trees there, the walnuts are gathered in the wild, often by families for fun or income, and taken to shelling machines. Many commercial shelling machines are mobile and owners take them to stations along the roadsides to wait for walnut pickers to bring their bulging gunny sacks of nuts for shelling. Nuts are shelled, then weighed and sold for commercial use or taken home for personal use.

Walnuts require considerable effort before they can be enjoyed because of the green outer shell and the hard inner shell. Once the outer shell is removed, there is still the inner shell to crack. The time honored way is to whack them with a hammer on a brick. Special nut pickers are needed to remove the nutmeat. Not long ago, everyone had a walnut tree on their property. Kids gathered the nuts and stored them until holiday time or it was too cold to play outside. Then the task of cracking and picking out the nuts fell to older children and granddads. Grandma's job was to make the cakes and pies to go with the nuts. Perhaps it's still that way where families have time and nut trees of their own. It's still not uncommon for Ozarkians to buy 100 pounds of black walnuts to shell during the winter when there's nothing else to do. *–LU*

BLANCH: To briefly cook foods in boiling water of freezing and canning. Also helps to slide skins from fruit and vegetables.

BLANCMANGE: (blah-manzh)A French name for a cold snow white pudding. The name (blanc manger) in French meant "white food" and since there are so many such dishes, the origin is hard to trace.

BLANQUETTE: (blahnk-ett) A French term used to keep meat, such as veal and chicken, white while cooking it in a sauce.

BLEND: (Noun) A mixture of ingredients.   (Verb) To thoroughly mix two or more ingredients.

BLINI: (blee-nee) A Russian and Polish term for pancakes made with buckwheat flour and leavened with yeast. They are served as an appetizer with cream and caviar. Traditional blini are baked in specially designed cast iron pans, just the right size for one blini and sold in sets of six. Their association with Russian holy days goes back to the Middle Ages.

BLINTZ: A Jewish term for pancakes that are stuffed with fruit and/or cheese, and served with sour cream.

BLUEBERRY: Today the name is fairly standard for the small, round, bluish fruits of the *Vaccinium* bush. Wild blueberries once grew all over North America. Today, blueberries are grown commercially in many states where there is sufficient acid soil and rain.   Western Europe and New Zealand also produce fine blueberries. Blueberries, like their cousins, the cranberries, will grow in acid, boggy places where other things will not grow well. New England colonists called the blueberries "huttleberries", "whortleberries", "huckleberries" and also "bilberries" (like their European cousins). Like all the other native berries, these supplied food for Native Americans. See Also HUCKLEBERRIES. Huckleberries are quite different from blueberries. Huckleberries are rounder and nearly tasteless.

■ Blueberries, a staple of our early ancestors, they are as much a part of our heritage as country quilts.

■ Blueberries were loved by the Native Americans. When the Colonists arrived, the natives shared their blueberry secrets. The natives dried the wild berries in the sun, then beat them to a powder. The powder was added to cornmeal, water and honey to make a pudding called *sautauthig*.

■ The Native Americans beat dried blueberries into venison, which was then smoked and dried. They also made a tea from the roots, which was used as a relaxant for women during childbirth.

■ Blueberries originated wild in North America. Cultivated, they thrive from Newfoundland south to Florida, plus Arkansas, Michigan, Oregon, Washington and British Columbia.

■ Fresh blueberries are available from early May into September. Frozen and canned blueberries are available year-round. Fresh blueberries should be stored in the refrigerator and used as soon as possible.

■ Blueberries contain more vitamin A, more than any other berry. One cup of blueberries supplies one-third of daily requirements of vitamin C, at only 82 calories per cup.

■ Blueberries are fuel to combat diabetes and cancer. – ***North American Blueberry Council.***
Nutrition facts per ½ cup: 41 calories, zero fats and sodium, 10.3g carbohydrates (3%), 2g fiber (8%), .5g protein (1%), 73 IU vitamin A (1%), 9mg vitamin C (16%), zero calcium and .1mg iron (1%). www.wildblueberries.com; www.blueberries.com; www.state.nj.us/agriculture www.blueberry.org

BLUEBERRY ARTS FESTIVAL

During the height of the blueberry harvest in August, the three day Blueberry Arts Festival is held in Ketchikan, Alaska. The main event is a juried art show held in the Alaska State Office Building. ne of the Festival highlights is the Kids Slimy Slug Races. Each contestant places his or her slug in the middle of a large table, the first slug to reach the edge is the winner. All the slugs are named, such as Banana Beauty and Streaked Lightning. This event is held outside, rain or shine (usually rains), in the Methodist Church parking lot. A Blueberry Pie Eating Contest is open to all kids, as is the Fun Run and the Spelling Bee. There are lots of games of chance and entertainment. Many of the entertainers are Alaskan Natives and includes the Gigglefeet Dance Festival by the Saxman Tribal House, and a street dance (again rain or shine) by the Potlatch Band. Other entertainers with colorful names include Red Hoochie and The Tomcods, Blind Dog Salmon, Daflunkillation, and the Blueberry Pie Band. There's lots of food: salmon barbecue, crab legs, blueberry crepes, blueberry baked goods, and of course pizza and corndogs For more information write: **Ketchikan Area Arts & Humanities Council**, 338 Main Street, Ketchikan, AK 99901 or phone (907) 225-2211.

BLUE CHEESE: A crumbly semi-soft cheese with blue veins of mold in a white interior. Used for eating and cooking. Tastes similar to Roquefort cheese.

BLUEFISH: Bluefish are found along the Atlantic coast and range from 3 to 5 pounds. The are bluish on the top with a silver belly. They can be baked, broiled or pan fried.   "Blues" are found all over the world by other names. **Nutrition facts:** A 3-ounce serving has 105 calories, 34 calories from fat, 3.6g total fat (6%), .8g saturated fat (4%), 50.2mg cholesterol (17%), 51mg sodium (2%), zero carbohydrates and fiber, 17g protein (34%), 338 IU vitamin A (7%), zero vitamin C, 6mg calcium (1%), .4mg iron (2%), and 316mg potassium.

BOCKWURST: This stuffed sausage originated in Germany and is made from pork and veal, seasoned with cloves, sage, mace and other spices. It is a fresh sausage and must be cooked well done like any fresh sausage prior to eating. One difference between bockwurst and bratworst is the seasoning. **Nutrition facts:** A 3-ounce serving has 261 calories, 214 calories from fat, 23.5g total fat (36%), 8.6g saturated fat (43%), 50.2mg cholesterol (17%), 939.8mg sodium (39%), zero carbohydrates and fiber, 11.3g protein (23%), zero vitamins A and C, 14mg calcium (1%), .6mg iron (3%), and 230mg potassium.

BOIL: A liquid heat method of cooking. A term used when a liquid reaches the vaporizing stage and bubbles break on the surface. Water boils at 212 degrees at sea level, but the temperature decreases as elevations increase. Foods are boiled to make them tender and to kill bacteria.

BOK CHOY: A member of the cabbage family that has long white stalks and green, crinkled leaves. An important ingredient in many Chinese recipes. **Nutrition facts** per ½ cup serving: 5 calories, zero fats, 22.8mg sodium (1%), zero carbohydrates, .4g fiber (1%), .5g protein (1%), 1050 IU vitamin A (21%), 16mg vitamin C (26%), 38mg calcium (4%), and .3mg iron (2%).

BOLOGNA: America bologna, also called baloney, is made with pork, beef, veal, ham, chicken, and turkey, or a combination of these. Bologna can't be considered a true bologna as originally made in Bologna, Italy during the Middle ages. The original bologna was made with pork and beef, and smoked. In Italy, bologna is known as *mortadella*.

In Lebanon, Pennsylvania, a special bologna is made with ground beef, spiced, and then smoked slowly for a long period. It is called Lebanon bologna, also "summer bologna." Smoking prevents quick spoilage, therefore it could be carried in lunch pails during hot weather. Bologna must be refrigerated and should be eaten within 5 days after it is once cut. Bologna is good in sandwiches, can be cubed for salads, cooked into casseroles and added to cooked vegetables. For a special treat, try roasting a large chuck on the barbecue. **Nutrition facts:** Bologna is high in both fat and calories. A 3 ounce serving has 210 calories, 155 calories are from fat, 16.9g total fat (26%), 5.9g saturated fat (29%), 50.2mg cholesterol (17%), 1007mg sodium (42%), zero carbohydrates and fiber, 13g protein (26%), zero vitamin A, 30mg vitamin C (50%), 9mg calcium (1%), and .7mg iron (4%).

BOMBE: (bomb) A fancy round or melon-shaped frozen dessert, combining two or more layered frozen mixtures, such as ice cream and sherbet.

BONBON: The French word for any small candy or "goodie." Today it is most often applied to chocolates but the meaning is much broader.

BONIATO: (bon-yato) Better know as the sweet potato, this vine originated in tropical America. Only the tubers are eaten.

BONITO: A saltwater fish which belongs to the mackerel family and is found in both the Pacific and Atlantic oceans. Most of the commercially caught bonito is canned in flakes and chunks and sold as tuna. It's rare to find fresh bonito in the market. However, when available it can be fried, baked or poached. **Nutrition facts:** A 3-ounce canned in water has 99 calories, 7 calories from fat, .7g total fat (1%), .2g saturated fat (1%), 25.5mg cholesterol (9%), 287.5mg sodium (12%), zero carbohydrates and fiber, 21.7g protein (43%),

BORDEAUX: (bor-doe) A term referring to gourmet food cooked on the delicate side, often seasoned with mushrooms. Also a wine originating in Bordeaux, France.

BORDELAISE: (bor-da-laze) a seasoned brown sauce made with red wine and served with steak. It originated in Bordeaux. France.

BOROJO: This small tropical tree has medium size fruit with seedy brown pulp to be eaten fresh.

BORSCH: (also spelled Bortsch) (borsh) A Russian beet soup.

BOUILLABAISSE: (bwee-ya-baiz) French chowder or different kinds of fish, shellfish, and other ingredients.

BOUILLON: (bwee-yo) This is a French word and means, "to boil." Bouillon is broth, a by-product of simmering meat, poultry, fish or vegetables in water. In Paris there was once a chain of restaurants called "bullions" because the main dish they served was cheap, boiled beef soup. Americans pronounce it "boolyun."

If beef broth is clarified, it is usually called, "consommé." Many chefs save all liquids after cooking one of the above foods, then simmer it down to concentrate it and use this liquid in cooking other foods. At one point the liquid is cooled and the fat removed. Bouillon has almost no calories. Bouillon is used to add taste and liquid to dry cuts of meat, casseroles, or soups.

Commercially made bouillon cubes are mostly salt and sugar with added fat, cornstarch and some flavorings and spices. Generally one cube added to a cup of water has about 5 calories, no fat or protein, but does have 35% or more of sodium depending upon the brand. Don't be fooled, these cubes are not true bouillon. Beef bouillon is also called "beef tea" and a favorite nourishment for the ill. **Nutrition facts:** 48 IU vitamin A (1%), zero vitamin C, 9mg calcium (1%), 1.3mg iron (7%), and 202mg potassium.

BOUQUET GARNI: (boo- key gar- nee) A bouquet of herbs and spices tied together and added to slow-cooking dishes such as soups. The bouquet is discarded after cooking. The herbs and spices can also be tied into cheesecloth and easily discarded.

BOURBON WHISKEY: An alcoholic beverage made with at least 51% corn, plus rye or barley. Bourbon usually has an amber color. The name came from where it originated, Bourbon, Kentucky. Bourbon whiskey is sometimes used in flavoring meats and baked goods. When used in cooking, all the alcohol is cooked out, leaving only the flavor. When used to soak a cake, most of the alcohol will remain. **Nutrition facts:** Bourbon has no nutritional values, with 1 ½ ounces ranging from 100 to 125 calories, depending upon the proof.

BOYSENBERRIES: The cultivated hybrid of the North American Blackberry. This edible berry was obtained by crossing the blackberry, raspberry, and loganberry. It is large like a loganberry, has the flavor of a raspberry, and the color of the blackberry. It is sweeter than the wild blackberry or raspberry. The berry is named after American horticulturist Rudolph Boysen. Boysenberries are eaten and used the same as blackberries. **Nutrition facts** per ½ cup: 33 calories, zero fats and sodium, 8.1g carbohydrates (3%), 2.6g fiber (10%), .7protein (1%), 44 IU vitamin A (1%), 2mg vitamin C (3%), 18mg calcium (2%) and 5mg iron (3%).

BRAISE: To fry by browning in fat before adding a minimum of liquid and allowing to cook slowly. Braising is done to seal juices inside for tenderness.

BRAINS: Edible brains are available from beef, veal, pork and lamb. When cooked, they are easy to digest, and they are often given to young children and invalids. Mild flavored, they are usually served with scrambled eggs. However, they can also be breaded and fried. Brains are extremely perishable and must be used immediately. Even if refrigerated, they should be consumed within 24 hours. Brains are no longer recommended by the public health services.

BRAN: The outer layer of cereal grains is bran. Bran, as well as the germ, is separated during the flour-making process.. All-purposed white flour contains no bran. Whole-wheat flour contains bran. Separated bran, such as oat bran, is added when baking some breads and muffins, and as an ingredient in some breakfast cereals. The packages will generally say "with oat bran" or "added bran) for customer convenience. **Nutrition facts:** Bran is a good source of B vitamins, dietary fiber, and fair amounts of iron. Bran is low in calories, and about 105 calories in 1 cup of 40% nonsweetened bran flakes.

BRANDY: An alcoholic beverage made from grapes. After the liquid is distilled, it can be 50% or more in alcohol content. Brandy is judged by aroma and the smoothness in the taste. Brandy is made in all wine-making countries, with France receiving the credit for the best brandy, especially that made in the town of Cognac. Brandy can also be made from fruit and is labeled as such. Peaches, apples, pears, plums, cherries, and some berries are fermented into brandy. When brandy is used in cooking, the alcohol evaporates during the process so only the taste remains. Some dishes add brandy just prior to serving and set the brandy aflame, which is called, "flambé."

BRATWURST: A highly seasoned German sausage. See BOCKWURST.

BRAZIL NUTS: Did you know you could be killed by a falling Brazil nut? Read on. This is just one of the many amazing facts about Brazil nuts.

Not all nuts are nuts, and this is true with Brazil nuts. The Brazil nut is the seed from a giant tree grown wild in the Amazon of South America. Attempts have been made to grow them in the southern United States, but the climate is not warm enough, so the experiment failed.

The tree is enormous, up to 150 feet tall, growing up in the dense jungles of the Amazon River basin, and almost nowhere else. It does not flourish in captivity, as it were. The tree is unclimbable, so harvesters have to wait until the tree is ready to drop its precious fruit. The fruit is about coconut size and wooden like a coconut shell. If you haven't seen a coconut, that's about the size of a medium cantaloupe. Harvesting is dangerous. Inside, the 12 or more nuts are arranged like orange segments. In Brazil they have several names but the most common is "cream nuts" because of the flavor. The shells are used as ornaments or burned as fuel. –LU **Nutrition facts** per 1/4 cup: 230 calories, 194 calories from fat, 23.2g total fat (36%), 5.7g saturated fat (28%), zero cholesterol and sodium, 4.5g carbohydrates (1%), 2g fiber (8%), 5g protein (10%), zero vitamins A and C, 62mg calcium (6%), and 1.2mg iron (7%)

BREAD: Bread has been made in various forms for thousands of years, long before modern methods have restyled what we eat today. No one knows who made bread first, but it may have been the ancient Egyptians (who kneaded dough with their feet) or maybe the ancient Chinese found a way to make it out of rice. Over the eons, bread has been made from all kinds of ingredients besides wheat. In most countries, wheat could only be afforded by the wealthy. Bakers made their bread out of processed white flour, since white flour was considered more elegant. The peasants, on the other hand, made their bread out of various coarse grains. The irony is that the poor were healthier than the rich from eating healthier varieties and more fiber, among other reasons. The poor also made bread from beans and peas, called "horse bread."

The Greeks, the Romans and, finally, the English set many of today's standards for the amounts of water and flour used, and how to handle the dough/bread before, during and after baking. **Basic bread is made from four essential ingredients**: Flour, yeast, salt and liquid. Oils, sugar and eggs are optional. Bread is one part of the food pyramid and one of the few foods eaten at all three meals. Bread provides nutritional values, such as carbohydrates and niacin for energy, protein for growth, iron for red blood cells, thiamine for digestion, and riboflavin for healthy skin. www.rhodesbread.com

FROM TORTILLAS TO TOAST
A Brief History of Bread
by Wendy Thomas

Chomp! You take a big bite into your peanut butter and jelly sandwich. The jelly oozes between your teeth and peanut butter sticks to the roof of your mouth as you suddenly wonder where bread came from. No, not the supermarket. Who was the first person to make bread?

Bread is a baked food made from ground grain, beans or nuts. There is no proof that primitive men and women baked bread. Archaeologists, people who study the lives and cultures of ancient man, have found pieces of fossilized bread 4,500 years old by a lake in Switzerland. This early bread was made from a porridge of ground nuts or grain and cooked over hot rocks. The result was a hard, flat cake that looked very much like the tortillas that you find in Mexican restaurants. So, how did the soft, fluffy kind of bread arrive?

Many people think that it was the **ancient Egyptians** who discovered the secret of leavening bread. Leaven is a word meaning "fermenting dough" or "yeast." Yeast cells occur in the air all around us. Perhaps one day, long ago, an Egyptian baker left some uncooked dough out longer than intended, yeast cells landed on the dough, fed on the sugar in the dough, which then produced carbon dioxide gas that causes bread to rise. When the bread was baked, the people who ate it must have been very excited with this new soft texture. So bakers began to keep back some of the uncooked dough to add to later batches. They didn't know why it worked, they just knew it did.

With the discovery of leavened bread, people no longer cooked bread on stones and ovens were invented. Those **early ovens were chambers** made of stones or bricks with horizontal ledges or grates. A fire was built between the bottom ledges and the bread was baked in the middle. Egyptians made so much bread, because they had so many slaves to feed, they used kids to knead large batches with their feet.

It was in **ancient Greece and Rome** that bread was first baked in commercial bakeries as well as in people's homes. In Rome, a school for bakers was formed in the first century A.D. by the Emperor Trajan.

During the Middle Ages, as European towns and cities grew, baking became more of a commercial enterprise. Technology and ovens improved. Beaters were developed for kneading the dough, which had formerly been done by hands or feet. This meant larger batches of bread could be produced with less work so more people could be fed in a day.

In the Americas, **Native Americans** made bread from corn. When the European settlers arrived, they learned to make cornbread from them. Later, the Native Americans used the wheat that settlers brought with them. America's population grew and more bakeries sprang up everywhere. White bread, made from bleached flour, became popular as people grew more wheat.

Some strange methods of bleaching the flour were used. In the nineteenth century, some bakers used chalk dust as a bleaching agent, but fortunately these practices were banned as the baking industry became more government regulated. In the year 1910 nearly all bread baked in this country was baked at home, but by the 1960's most was produced in commercial bakeries. Today's bread is often sliced and wrapped in plastic, something earlier people could never have imagined! Well, now you know something of how bread came to be. Have you every wondered when buttering your morning toast, who was the first person to toast the bread? See UNLEAVENED BREAD.

WONDER BREAD

You have taken a bite into a slice of soft textured white bread and liked the delicious taste. Chances are it was a slice of Wonder Bread. Wonder Bread began in **1921 in Indianapolis**, Indiana as an unsliced pound-and-a-half loaf. This new bread was named by Elmer Cline, a vice president of the Taggart Baking Company. He came up with the name at a balloon Race. When he saw the sky filled with hundreds of colorful balloons, to him that pattern signified "wonder." "That's it," Cline said, "I'll call it Wonder bread." Cline designed the bread wrapper with colorful balloons. He had the company trucks painted with more balloons. To debut his new bread, thousands of helium-filled balloons were handed out to kids in Indianapolis neighborhoods with messages attached, urging their mothers to try the new Wonder bread.

This new "light" bread caught on quickly and soon bakeries across the United States were making a similar bread. Other bakers even used the name "Wonder," and all claimed they used the name before Taggart Baking Company used it.

In **1925**, Continental Baking Company bought Taggart and soon sold Wonder Bread coast to coast. In **1930**, **they sliced it** for the first time. The public became very suspicious at first, but once they tried it, became enthusiastic. In **1941** Continental supported the new government enrichment program and added vitamins and minerals to Wonder bread. In 1970, Wonder bread became the first national baking company to list nutrition information on the wrapper, along with the dates for freshness. This move was in response to the whole grain bread revolution that threatened to make white breads extinct. Americans loved the bread they grew up with and today it is still a family favorite. Wonder bread was endorsed by television heroes Howdy Doody and Buffalo Bob. The bread that **"helps to build strong bodies 12 ways**," was praised in song by the "Happy Wonder Bakers" cartoon quartet. In 1995 Interstate Brand Corporation bought out Continental and continues to make the original white bread.

BREAD CRUMBS can be made from either fresh or dried bread. Fresh crumbs are made from 2 to 3 day-old bread. They can be made by pulling apart with your fingers or in a food processor. Generally fresh bread crumbs are used for thickening in gravies and meat loaves. You can made your own dried bread crumbs by laying bread slices on a cookie sheet and baking in a 250ºF slow oven until dry. Cool the dried bread, break up in a food processor, than place back on the cookie sheet in the slow oven and bake until the desired color. Generally light-colored are used for breading fried foods and topping for casseroles. Brown dried crumbs are best used as a topping for foods that require little or no more cooking. Dark brown crumbs are made by adding 1 cup of dried brown crumbs with 1/3 cup of butter or margarine in a skillet and cooked over medium heat until the desired color is obtained. They crumbs should be used immediately and are used the same are brown dried crumbs. www.contadina.com

BREAD, TO: (verb) To apply a coating of flour, bread, or cracker crumbs to the outside of meat before frying or baking. The meat is dipped into an egg mixture first to cause the breading to cling to the meat while it cooks. Some vegetables, such as fried green tomatoes, can be breaded and fried.

BREADFRUIT: Children reading *Mutiny on the Bounty* always wonder, "What on earth is breadfruit?" We could say it belongs to the jakfruit family but that doesn't help American kids much. The fruit is round, about the size of a soccerball. The inside is like a melon. The outside has a hexagonal pattern like a pineapple skin. You will remember that Captain Bligh was obsessed with bringing 1000 plants of the breadfruit from the south sea islands to the East Indies for cultivation. The mutiny on the *Bounty* ruined that trip but he later made a return voyage and did manage to get his plants to Jamaica in 1793. The seedless variety did grow so well there that Jamaica is still the main producer of seedless breadfruit. The seeded kind grows well in other Caribbean islands.

Breadfruit, like its relative, jakfruit, has a flavor you either love or hate. Most people outside of Asia have never acquired a taste for it. Perhaps they just don't know how to fix it. The seedless form is picked green and roasted, fried or boiled. Roasted or fried in fat, it can be compared to roasted potatoes. Boiled it is gluey and unappetizing to Western tastes. Fans of the fruit describe it in various ways. Some say it's like Yorkshire pudding. Some say they have had it cooked like mashed potatoes with meat dishes. It can even be sliced, dried, and ground to make a flour for bread, which is where it gets its name. In Hawaii, they sometimes use it like taro for making poi. Versatile as it is, the fruit has provided nourishment for thousands of years. The seeded kind is mostly grown for the seeds themselves, which are said to taste like chestnuts if roasted. *–LU* www.gardenofdelights.com

BREAKFAST: The most important meal of the day is breakfast. Yet in many households it is a rare treat when everyone can sit down to breakfast together. One of today's problems is time, especially when both parents are working. Thus many kids go to school or out to play without breakfast. Breakfast provides the needed energy to start the day. Kids who eat breakfast perform better in school and have more energy to play sports. The same goes for adults; those who eat breakfast perform better at work. There are ways to make breakfast easier.

The simple answer is to arise earlier. However, to a non-morning person this is not an easy solution. Many breakfast recipes can be made the night before, refrigerated, and baked while dressing. Also, the supermarket has many breakfast items on the shelves and in the freezer which can be served in minutes. Anyone who can use a toaster, oven and/or microwave can have a healthy breakfast. Start with a glass of juice and a bowl of cereal topped with fruit, or pop a frozen waffle in a toaster and top with syrup or honey, and end breakfast with a glass of milk. In the refrigerator there might be leftovers from last night you can reheat. Almost anyone can fix a simple breakfast for the needed energy to start the day right. Many schools offer free breakfast programs.

THE MEN WHO CHANGED BREAKFAST
by Carol A. Wilson

What did you have for breakfast this morning? You probably had a bowl of cereal. Ever wonder what people ate for breakfast before there was cereal?

Oriental people usually have rice or fruit for a light breakfast. Western people had to cook their breakfasts - big, hearty breakfasts. Eggs, biscuits and gravy, fried potatoes, ham, steak, sausage, bacon, pancakes, cornmeal mush, lots of coffee, and would you believe it, a pie for dessert?

DR. JACKSON'S GRANULA

The first so called "instant" breakfast cereal originated at a water cure clinic in Danville, New York. In 1858, Dr. James C. Jackson had experimented with wheat to make a healthy breakfast food and produced what he called, **Granula**, the first cold, ready-to-eat breakfast cereal. The ingredients for Jackson's cereal were baked in an oven and looked like one huge graham cracker, although much harder. This cracker was ground into large crumbs, placed in a large glass, then the glass was filled with milk. Soaking began the night before so that by morning the Granula had absorbed the milk, expanded, and softened. The contents were poured into a bowl, cream and sugar added. By today's standard, "ready to eat," means instant, just pour from box into a bowl and enjoy. Today, Granula would not merit the title of a "ready-to-eat cereal." However, at that time it was popular, healthful, easy to prepare and tasty. Competition forced Granula out of business in 1921.

KELLOGG'S FLAKES

Flaked cereal, as we know it today, was invented by accident by brothers Dr. John Harvey Kellogg and Will K. Kellogg in 1895 at their Battle Creek Sanitarium, in Battle Creek, Michigan. Dissatisfied patients rebelled against the vegetarian menu with meat substitutes made from dry nuts and tasteless grains. Some patients would even sneak out and enjoy a steak at a local restaurant. The brothers conducted a series of experiments to develop a good tasting substitute for the hard and tasteless bread on the menu. They cooked wheat, forced it through granola rollers, then rolled it into long sheets of dough. One day after cooking the wheat, the Kelloggs were called away. Although the wheat was stale when they returned, the brothers decided to see what would happen when the tempered grain was forced through the rollers. Instead of the usual long sheets of dough, each wheat berry was flattened into a small thin flake. When baked, the flakes tasted crisp and light. At the time they were unaware they had invented flaked cereal. These flakes were an instant hit with the patients. In fact they were so good that when the patients returned home, they wrote back requesting the flakes be sent to them by mail. The flakes were called **Granose**, packaged in ten ounce boxes and sold for fifteen cents each. At that time no one thought of eating a cold breakfast. Even the Kellogg brothers meant their cereal to be a health snack, not breakfast food. The Kellogg's continued to experiment and in 1898 developed the process of flaking corn.

POST'S TASTY TOASTIES

One of Kellogg's patients was Charles William Post. Post wasn't pleased with the Kellogg Sanitarium, so formed his own, the La Vita Inn. For two years he experimented with wheat, bran and molasses combinations. Finally, on New Year's Day, 1895, Post made a cereal beverage he called **Postum** for sale to the public. Post continued to experiment with various grains. He made a cereal of wheat, malted barley, salt and yeast which was baked in the form of bread sticks. The sticks, after being baked, were shredded and broken into small chunks, then rebaked, ground and sifted to a uniform size. This became **Grape-Nuts**. In 1904, Post introduced corn flakes and called it Elijah's Manna. The public rejected the name, so he renamed it **Post Toasties** in 1907.

PERKY'S SHREDDED WHEAT

In 1892, Henry D. Perky stopped at a hotel in Nebraska and noticed a man eating an unfamiliar breakfast food. It was boiled wheat. The man explained he suffered from indigestion and boiled wheat was one of the few foods that he could enjoy. Perky, who also suffered from indigestion, tried the boiled wheat and found that it helped him considerably. He conceived a machine to make a whole wheat product, a machine with a pair of steel rollers, one smooth and the other grooved. Water-softened whole wheat berries were put into the machine and from it were extruded stringy filaments which could be folded up into little biscuits. These wheat biscuits were moist and spoiled in a few days. Perky solved this problem by baking the biscuits the day after they were manufactured, hence **Shredded Wheat Biscuits** were invented and his bakery was opened in 1901 in Niagara Falls, New York. In 1928 Nabisco acquired Perky's bakery, which was called Nabisco until 1993 when sold to Kraft/Post.

DANFORTH OF PURINA

Purina Mills in Saint Louis, Missouri had created animal foods. Seeing the success of cereal companies, they decided to enter the cereal market. William H. Danforth cooked grains until they were mushy. The grains were poured into shallow vats where men in rubber boots tore the lumps apart with rakes. After drying, the smaller lumps were further reduced, flaked, and baked. This was called **Purina Wheat**.

RALSTON'S CHEX

Danforth asked health guru, Dr. Ralston with his million followers to endorse his new cereal. Ralston agreed and his name was added to the cereal. In 1902, ads boasting Ralston Purina Cereals found a welcome home on the breakfast table. Further ads claimed that Ralston Barley Food Builds Brain and Muscle, Purina Health Flour is much better for the family than white bread, and Ralston Hominy Grits - "My! but it's good!" Shortly thereafter, the famed red and white checkerboard boxes were designed. It wasn't until 1933 that the company began marketing a bite-sized, shredded biscuits called Shredded Ralston. The name was later changed to **Chex**, and a new line of cereals products were made with rice, corn and other grains. Today Purina makes only animal food.

ALEXANDER'S "SHOT FROM GUNS" PUFFS

Like other cereal companies, **Quaker Oats** bakers were experimenting with grains. In 1902, Dr. Alexander P. Anderson invented a method to puff rice and wheat. Steamed under pressure, the grain expanded eight times. In 1904, **Quaker Puffed Rice** was shot from guns at the Saint Louis World's Fair. It was coated with caramel and sold as candy. It took several years before these puffed grains were sold as breakfast cereals.

BATTLE CREEK'S CEREAL WARS

Shortly after the turn of the century, more than forty companies were making cereals, a dozen of them in Battle Creek alone. In those few years, the cereal industry was born and today supermarkets carry an assortment of colorful boxes full of flaky, raisiny, nutty, marshmallowy breakfast treats in all shapes, sizes and colors. It took men like Jackson, the Kellogg brothers, Post, Perky, Danforth, and Anderson to change breakfast forever.

WORLD'S LONGEST BREAKFAST TABLE

During the cereal boom in Battle Creek, Michigan around the turn of the century, more than 300 cereal and coffee substitute companies were formed, but only a few survived. One of the largest to survive is the Kellogg Company. In celebration of Kellogg's 50th anniversary, the Kellogg Golden Jubilee was held in downtown Battle Creek on June 28, 1956. More than 200 picnic tables were set up to feed an estimated 7,000 people. Almost 15,000 showed up. People ate the cereal topped with cream and left with the bowls, spoons, napkins and Golden Jubilee hats.
The event was so successful that since 1976 it has been an annual event. Kellogg's, Post and General Mills companies all take part. Cereal, juice, milk and donuts are served to more than 40,000 people. Now called the Battle Creek Cereal Festival, the event includes the Miss Cereal City Pageant, parades, arts and craft show, races, strawberry festival, farmers' market and amusement rides. For information on this June event, contact: **Battle Creek Visitor Bureau**, 34 West Jackson Street., Suite 4, Battle Creek, MI 49017 or phone (616) 962-2240

BRIE CHEESE: A mild to pungent creamy cheese made from whole milk. Similar to Camembert. It originated in Ile-de-France. Emperor Charlemagne was fond of it. One poet called it "the cheese worth its weight in gold."

BRINE: A salt solution for preserving meats and vegetables and for pickling.

BRITTLE: An easy and ancient form of candy made by pouring caramelized syrup over nuts. When cooled, the syrup will be hard enough to crack. Favorite in America are peanut brittle and pecan patties. Similar confections are popular all over the world where nuts are grown or available.

BRIOCHE: (bree-ohsh) A rich, cake-like yeast bread made with butter and eggs, and generally baked with a round top head.

BROCHETTE: (bro-shet) French word for skewer, the long thin rod for broiling chunks over an open fire or barbecue pit. A tiny medallion of beef or pork. Smaller than a fillet mignon.

BROIL: To cook under a heat source in a kitchen range. Broiling can also be done over a heat source such as a barbecue.

BRISKET: The breast portion of beef. The brisket is cooked fresh, or cured into corn beef, or made into pastrami. Brisket can be boiled, braised or roasted slowly. **Nutrition facts** per 4 ounce serving, fresh: 354 calories, 276 calories from fat, 30.1g total fat (46%), 12.1g saturated fat (61%), 12.1g saturated fat (61%), 82.8mg cholesterol (28%), 72.6mg sodium (3%), zero carbohydrates and fiber, 19.2g protein (38%), zero vitamins A and C, 8mg calcium (1%), 1.8mg iron (10%), and 283mg potassium.

BROCCOFLOWER® : A hybrid of broccoli and cauliflower. It looks like green cauliflower. It's milder in taste than either. Broccoflower seed was discovered in Holland and was bought to the United States by Tanimura & Antle of Salinas, California in 1988. Many who dislike broccoli or cauliflower like this new combination of tastes. When purchasing Broccoflower, look for light green heads that feel firm, heavy and compact. It is generally more expensive than broccoli and cauliflower, and because it has not grown in popularity, it is sometimes hard to find. Use and cook as you would cauliflower. *Broccoflower is a registered trademark of Tanimura & Antle.* **Nutrition facts**, ½ cup serving: 13 calories, zero fat, 15mg sodium (1%), 2.6g carbohydrates (1%), 1.3g fiber (5%), 1g protein (2%), zero vitamin A, 23mg vitamin C (39%), 11mg calcium (1%), .2mg iron (1%), 151mg potassium, and a good source for vitamin B6.

WHAT WOULD POPEYE SING TODAY?

In its cartoon heyday, in both the comics and cartoon movies, "Popeye the Sailor Man" demonstrated that the world's great vegetable was spinach. A squinting and muscular Popeye would, in one gulp, directly from the can, down spinach to make him strong enough to rescue his love, Olive Oyl, from his arch-rival Bluto. It's still a mystery why Popeye didn't swallow his pipe at the same time. Olive was forever being chased and abducted by Bluto. She'd holler to Popeye for help, but he always lacked stamina to respond until he gulped down that can of spinach. Popeye never was interested in the flavor of spinach and it is questionable if he ever did taste it. If Popeye had started his day with an iron-rich bowl of Wheaties®, he might of had time to savor the goodness of spinach before rescuing Olive. After he gulped down the spinach, he would sing, "I'm strong to the finish, cause I eats me spinach."

Some say Popeye was created to encourage kids to eat foods that were good for them, usually healthful vegetables that many kids didn't like. In early times, people didn't understand vitamins and minerals, but they knew they were good for better health. In Popeye's heyday, folic acid had just been discovered in green leafy vegetables. While everyone thought it was the iron that created Popeye's strength, it might have really been folic acid, along with vitamin C and a combination of B vitamins that did the job. Popeye was a sailor, and it was known that seamen with a prolonged shortage of vitamin C would develop scurvy. Similarly, tiredness was caused by an iron-deficiency. We'll never know what was really making Popeye so tired, but spinach always came to his rescue. There's a new vegetable, Broccoflower®, that could have been Popeye's hero and, perhaps, done a better job. With as much folic acid, five times the vitamin C, and about the same amount of iron per serving of spinach, Broccoflower® would be a better choice to regain his strength. However, Popeye's song wouldn't have worked, "I'm strong to the finish, cause I eats me Broccoflower," it just doesn't rhyme, and rhyming is very important because it usually helps preserve wisdom from one generation to the next. How about, I'm strong by the hour, cause I eats me Broccoflower®! Broccoflower® is a vegetable of our time. It's so naturally sweet and buttery tasting, that most kids like it from the first bite. Of course history cannot be rewritten, since Broccoflower® didn't exist in the 1930's when Popeye was defending Olive Oyl's virtue. So let's let Popeye rest in peace, but maybe his grandchildren will try Broccoflower.® How about you? What rhyme can you make with Broccoflower? James Scala, Ph.D. Broccoflower® is a registered trademark of Tanimura & Anlte, Inc. Wheaties® is registered trademark of General Mills, Inc.

BROCCOLI: Broccoli has been a favorite vegetable for more than 2,000 years in the eastern Mediterranean area. The Italians first brought it to the New World. Broccoli is related to cauliflower and cabbage. Broccoli is available the year round, with the peak crop during the fall months. When purchasing broccoli, look for dark green heads; buds should be tightly closed. If yellow buds appear, broccoli is over matured and will be bitter.

Broccoli is best when streamed tender crisp for about 10 minutes. Broccoli can be eaten hot with a little salt, pepper and butter, or is good cold in a salad, either cooked or raw. For a special treat make broccoli soup topped with Parmesan cheese. Broccoli is great in stir fried dishes, such as Chinese stir fry. About 90% of American's broccoli comes from California. **Nutrition facts:** A ½ cup serving has 12 calories, zero fat and sodium, 2.3g carbohydrates (1%), 1.3g fiber (5%), 1.3g protein (3%), 678 IU vitamin A (14%), 41mg vitamin C (68%), 21mg calcium (2%), .4mg iron (2%), 143 potassium, and an excellent source of riboflavin.

BROTH: The thin soup which results from boiling meat and water. Also called bouillon.

BROWN: The process of scorching food surfaces, especially meat, to seal in the juices before baking or slow cooking. Browning is done by frying the meat's top and bottom until it forms a brown or cooked crust but is still raw inside.

BROWN RICE: Brown rice is the whole rice grain. There are several varieties of brown rice. The long grain tends to remain separated and fluffy when cooked. Best used in pilafs, stir-fries, rice salads and curried vegetables. The taste is distinctly different from white rice but delicious. The organic brown rice is similar to long grain, but stickier. A favorite source of potassium and fiber. **Nutrition facts:** A ½ cup serving of long grain has 342 calories, 24 calories from fat, 2.7g total fat (4%), .5g saturated fat (3%), zero cholesterol and sodium, 71.5g carbohydrates

(24%), 3.2mg fiber (13%), 7.4g protein (15%), zero vitamins A and C, 21mg calcium (2%), 1.4mg iron (8%), and 206mg potassium.

BROWNIE: The origin is not known, but they go back at least to 1897 when they were listed for sale in the Sears-Roebuck catalog. Thick, chewy, moist, rich chocolate describes a bar cookie called a brownie. Some brownies are thick like fudge, while some are light like a cake. And there are even light colored brownies made without chocolate with a butterscotch flavor. Some are almost pure chocolate, while some are mixed with nuts. Some are plain, maybe with a little powdered sugar, or frosted. Most brownie lovers prefer a dense, chewy brownie and if that is your choice, try this recipe.

½ cup butter
½ cup sugar
2 tablespoons water
6 ounces semisweet chocolate morsels
1 teaspoon vanilla
2 eggs
3/4 cup flour
1/4 teaspoon baking soda
1/4 teaspoon salt
½ cup walnuts or pecans, chopped

1. In a sauce pan, mix the butter, sugar and water. Slowly bring to a boil, stirring constantly.
2. Add chocolate and vanilla, continue to cook until the chocolate is melted and the mixture is smooth.
3. Remove from the heat, beat in the eggs, one at a time.
4. In a small bowl, blend the dry ingredients.
5. Slowly mix in the dry ingredients into the chocolate mixture.
6. Fold in the nuts.
7. Pour into an 8x8-inch cake pan. Bake in a preheated 325° oven for 25 to 30 minutes.
8. Cool completely in the pan, then cut into 2-inch squares.
Makes 16 brownies.

Nutrition facts per brownie: 180 calories, 100 calories from fat, 11.7g total fat (18%), 5.7g saturated fat (29%), 41.9mg cholesterol (14%), 120.1mg sodium (5%), 18g carbohydrates (6%), .8g fiber (3%), 2.9g protein (6%), 268 IU vitamin A (5%), zero vitamin C, 11mg calcium (1%), .8mg iron (5%) and 75mg potassium.

BRUNCH: A combination of breakfast and lunch served in mid-morning, usually on holidays and Sundays.

BRUSH CHERRY: A small, purple Australia fruit used to make jelly.

BRUSSELS SPROUTS: Brussels sprouts appeared on European tables more than 400 years ago. Until recently, they were considered a luxury vegetable. It is thought that they originated in Brussels, Belgium, since that was the main export center. If you think they look like little cabbages, you are right. The plant is a tall stalk with a leafy top, and along the stalk are a series of miniature cabbages. When purchasing Brussels sprouts, look for very small heads. The larger heads can produce a strong bitter taste, and they take longer to cook. Cook in a small amount of boiling water for about 5 minutes, but never longer than 10 minutes. Adding a dash or two of nutmeg helps to bring out the flavor. The sprout tops are sold as greens. **Nutrition facts:** A ½-cup serving has 19 calories, zero fat and sodium, 3.9g carbohydrates (1%), 1.9g fiber (7%), 1.5g protein (3%), 389 IU vitamin A (8%), 37mg vitamin C (62%), 18mg calcium (2%), .6mg iron (3%), and 171mg potassium.

BUCKWHEAT: Buckwheat grows wild in Central Asia and Siberia where it originated. It is also cultivated worldwide. It is not a member of the wheat cereal grasses, but is a member of the same family as rhubarb, sorrel and dock. The plant likes a cool climate and will grow in the poorest soils. Today it is a staple grain served as a vegetable in Russia and other parts of Europe where it is known as, "kasha." Kasha can be purchased in the hot cereal aisle or health food section of most supermarkets. In the United States, buckwheat helped to feed the early settlers. Buckwheat flour is often added to pancake flour. In can be cooked as a cereal, boiled like rice, and eaten with cream and sugar, or butter and maple syrup. See BLINI. **Nutrition facts:** A ½-cup of buckwheat has 292 calories, 24 calories from fat, 2.9g total fat (4%), .6g saturated fat (3%), zero sodium, 60.8g carbohydrates (20%), 8.5g fiber (34%), 11.3g protein (23%), zero vitamins A and C, 15mg calcium (2%), 1.9mg iron (10%), and 391mg potassium.

BUDDHA'S HAND: This citrus originated in India. Its thick rind makes citron candy and preserves. www.frieda.com.

BUFFALO: A member of the ox family which is wild in Africa and domesticated in Asia. The American Bison is related. See BISON.

BUFFET: (bu-fay) The word comes from the French and applies to any table arrangement where foods are laid out for the guests to help themselves.

BULGUR WHEAT: Also known as "ala," bulgur is cracked wheat that has been partially cooked. It is good at breakfast with milk and sugar, makes a wonderful chilled salad, or a side dish cooked with vegetables. It's easy to cook. Use one part of bulgur with two parts water or chicken stock; simmer for 5 minutes; fluff, cover and let it sit for 10 minutes. Or, pour boiling liquid over bulgur, cover and let it sit for 1 hour. **Nutrition facts:** A ½ cup serving has 76 calories, zero fat and sodium, 16.9g carbohydrates (6%), 4.1g fiber (16%), 2.8g protein (6%), zero vitamins A and C, 9mg calcium (1%), .9mg iron (5%), and 62mg potassium.

BUISSON: (bwee-son) You know those gorgeous and clever arrangements of food (usually fruits) stacked into pyramids shapes you see around the holidays. Remember? They look like little Christmas trees? The arrangements have a name–buisson. Next time you see one, knock your friends out when you explain, "Wow, what a spectacular buisson!" It means "bush."

BULLOCK'S HEART: Also known as custard apple. The fruit is of poor quality, but it is eaten fresh in tropical America.

BUNS: The name is applied to any individual sized loaves or bread or rolls. Such miniature loaves comes in a multitude of shapes and sizes, mostly round. They are called "Brötchen" (little bread" in Germany.

BUÑUELOS:

History

In 1973, San Antonio, Texas celebrated with the HemisFair. Texas and Mexico folk wanted to get involved in the World's Fair in some important way. Tony Specia remembered his wife's grandmother making a Spanish-Mexican pastry, buñuelos (pronounced, boo-nyoo-ay'-los). He told his friend, David Carter, and the two went into business. They knew fair goers like snacks, especially snacks they can enjoy while walking, and buñuelos was just that. Tony's wife's grandmother, Señora Trinidad Bustillos Guterrez, use to make the buñuelos the old-fashioned way by rolling out the dough and stretching it on her knees. The two partners, knowing this was a slow process, made the six inch round disks with a machine that stretched the dough paper thin and cut it into six-inch round disks. The buñuelo looks like a flour tortilla. The dough is made with flour and eggs, deep fried in peanut oil, and sprinkled with a mix of cinnamon and sugar. Tony says, "The recipe is a secret, but what makes our buñuelos different from others is that we add a sweet syrup to the dough."

Holiday Fare

Buñuelo comes from the phase, *¿Es buñuelo?* meaning: "It is nothing?" The phrase is said to a person who doesn't take time to do things right, a failure. Needless to say, the buñuelos were not a failure at the fair, as the crackly little discs sold like, well, hotcakes! Today, the original recipe is still being made as three workers make 5,000 of the light, crispy, cinnamon-and- sugar dusted delicacies a day. Everyone in San Antonio wants them for Christmas and New Year's parties because not only do they taste good, they're considered to bring good fortune. Popular the year around, buñuelos are eaten at all occasions or no occasion at all! --RSC

BURBANK, LUTHER: GARDENER TO THE WORLD

The next time you bite into a French fry, savor a plum, or crack open a walnut, you should thank Luther Burbank. He created more than **800 new plants** that permanently changed America's farms. His plants included apples, berries, cherries, figs, grapes, nectarines, peaches, plumcots, quinces, chestnuts, walnuts, plums and prunes, plus vegetables, herbs and flowers. The most famous of his creations was the Burbank Russet potato, which is now known as the Idaho potato.

Burbank was born in Lancaster, Massachusetts in 1849. He devoted ten or more hours daily to create new plants. First he worked with strawberries in Massachusetts, but his strawberries never attained the popularity of his other fruits. His favorite was the "robusta" strawberry. Burbank's first horticultural discovery was the Burbank potato.

The Plant Wizard

From a rare "Early Rose" potato seedball, he developed a blight-resistant, fine-grained, long potato. He offered a reward for a second potato seedball, but he never saw another one.

At the age of 26, with $150 in his pocket, he set out to find a botanical paradise. When he arrived in Santa Rosa, California in 1875 he wrote home: "This is the chosen spot of all the earth as far as Nature is concerned." Burbank started a small nursery with the help of his mother and sister. In 1881 he received an order for 20,000 prune trees, which other nurserymen said was impossible. He used a new technique called "June-budding," the grafting of prune buds onto early-budding almond trees. He delivered 19,500 prune trees and the influential grower spread the news proclaiming Burbank **a "Plant Wizard."**

His work on the plum, formed a basis for the plum and prune industries of the world. Burbank imported plum varieties from Europe and Japan. He hybridized them with American plums and created more than 100 other varieties. Unfortunately, many of his plants no longer exist or are only found in private gardens. One of his more unusual developments was the "iceberg white blackberry." The berry was actually transparent, the seeds being visible inside. The public didn't accept it, since they preferred more colorful pies.

Even Wizards Make Mistakes

At the turn of the century, Southern California had a shortage of vegetables and fruit. Burbank developed a variety of rhubarb used as a spring vegetable and a substitute for fruit. Once the availability of fresh fruit increased, the market for rhubarb slackened. When he created the "sunberry" in 1905, it was thought to be poisonous and inedible. This news caused controversy throughout the horticultural world. His credibility was further damaged after he sold the sunberry, changed the name to **"wonderberry,"** and made exaggerated claims for it in his advertising.

Burbank was also criticized for crossing plums with apricots, a new species he called **"plumcots."** It wasn't until other plant breeders duplicated this breed that he was given credit. While plumcots are available in many supermarkets, they are still not a popular fruit. Burbank developed a Chinese climbing plum, he called *"Mao-li-dzi."* The name didn't catch on, but the fruit did in New Zealand. Today it's called "kiwi." Kiwi's are now grown in California and are very popular.

Burbank also improved many food plants, including tomatoes, often lengthening their growing season. When he received an order for peas to grow to uniform size and maturity, he developed five new strains in graduating sizes. One of his most difficult hybrids was the elephant garlic. He experimented with various wild garlic species, especially those from Chile.

A Green Legacy

In 1919 he introduced the garlic "elephant," about three times larger than regular garlic. After Burbank's death in 1926, friends found many new plants in his gardens in both Santa Rosa and nearby Sebastopol and named them after him. Because of Burbank's Elberta peach, he was inducted into the **National Inventors Hall of Fame in 1986**.

Burbank was labeled a plant wizard and praised as a mystic. But others branded him as a charlatan and damned him as an infidel for interfering with God's creation. During his life, scientists visited his nursery to try to provoke doubts in his discoveries and inventions. All came away convinced that they had met a genius. Burbank had countless visitors to his gardens, including Helen Keller, Jack London, Thomas Edison, Henry Ford and Harvey Firestone.

As with many popular heroes, Burbank weathered many storms. Some included the misuse of his name in phony financial schemes. The fact was, Burbank was too busy with what he loved best, working with plants, to pay attention to such details. Fortunately, his popularity withstood the occasional failed schemes.

Today you can visit his home, green house, and gardens on the corner of Santa Rosa and Sonomas Avenues in downtown Santa Rosa. To find out more about his life and the many plants he developed, request a list of available books from: **Luther Burbank Home and Gardens**, P.O. Box 1678, Santa Rosa, CA 95402. Of special interest is the humorously illustrated book for elementary students: *Here a Plant, There a Plant, Everywhere a Plant, Plant!* For middle grade students and young adults request information on *Yesterday and Today,* and for older readers there is *A Gardener Touched With Genius.*

BURDEKIN PLUM: Another small purple fruit used to make jelly in Australia.

BUTTER: This basic food is animal fat derived from whole milk. Churning cream turns the butterfat into a solid. Butter is available both salted and unsalted. Supermarket butter is made from cow's milk. In other parts of the world, butter is made from the milk of sheep, goats, horses, camels, water buffaloes, and yaks. It is believed butter was first made by herdsmen who carried milk in a container made from an animal stomach. As the milk was carried over long distances, the sloshing divided the fat into butter and the remaining liquid into buttermilk (or yogurt).

Butter is best when used as a bread spread or a topping for cooked vegetables. It can be used for sautéing, but must use low heat because it browns easily. See GHEE. It is also used as shortening in baking recipes, either melted or mixed with sugar or flour. U.S. federal law states that butter must contain at least 80% milk fat. In Europe, especially France, butter has a higher fat content. Butter compared with margarine contains the same amount of fat. But the fats are different kinds. Butter has cholesterol. Margarines are butter substitutes made of vegetable or grain oils. See TRANS FATTY ACIDS. Because of the fat content, many fat free butter substitutes have been developed. Fat free substitutes do not contain fat, have no cholesterol, no calories and no real butter taste.

Butter substitutes do not work the same as butter in cooking and baking so be take care what you substitute. Often the package will carry the message "not for baking" or something similar. **Nutrition facts:** Butter has 100 calories per tablespoon, of which all of the calories come from fat, 11 grams total fat (17%). There are 7 grams saturated fat (36%), 30mg cholesterol (10%), and 90mg sodium (4%) in salted butter. www.landolakes.com.

MAKE FRESH BUTTER AT HOME

No one knows for sure who first made butter or how it was discovered. Some believe it was a herdsmen carrying milk in a bag. The milk sloshed in the bag, separating the contents into butter and whey. You can make it at home, it only takes cream, salt (if desired), and an electric mixer.

2 cups whipping cream
½ teaspoon salt (optional)

1. Place cream in small mixing bowl.
2. Whip on high speed with electric mixer for about 10 minutes. After cream begins to curdle, add salt, and place a towel over top of mixing bowl to prevent liquid from splattering.
3. Whip until solid pieces form.
4. Drain off liquid (refrigerate this liquid and enjoy the real taste of buttermilk when chilled); rinse butter with water and drain again. Squeeze off excess water.
5. Wrap in plastic wrap and refrigerate.

Unsalted butter keeps for up to two weeks. Salted butter keeps for up to one month. Salt is both used as an added taste and as a preservative. Makes about ½ pound of butter. You can also churn your own butter by shaking half and half in a gallon jar until butter forms. The jar allows you to observe the whole process. *--American Dairy Assocation*

BUTTER BEANS: Found in the southern U.S., "butter beans" are extra large, dried lima beans. In some areas, speckled purple beans are called, "butter beans" or "calico beans."

BUTTERED EGGS: Our ancestors have been wonderfully creative in finding ways to preserve food for the winter long before they had refrigeration. No one knows who thought this one up, but the idea is still used in Cork County, Ireland where it has a long history. Irish farmers spread their hands with butter and then rolled warm fresh eggs in their hands to coat the eggshell. When the egg cools, the buttered shell acts like a waxy barrier to keep air and germs out of the egg. This helps to keep the egg for up to six months. When cooked, the butter adds a touch of flavor since some of it has seeped into the egg from the shell. "Buttered eggs" might also mean scrambled eggs in older cookbooks.

BUTTERHEAD LETTUCE: A small, soft, succulent lettuce. The inner leaves are light yellow and have a buttery feel, hence the name. The outer leaves are light green. The taste is sweeter than most lettuce. Two of the most common varieties are Bibb and Boston. **Nutrition facts** per ½ cup: 4 calories, zero fats and sodium, zero carbohydrates, .3g fiber (1%), .4g protein (1%), 275 IU vitamin A (6%), 2mg vitamin C (4%), 9mg calcium (1%), and .1mg iron (1%).

BUTTERMILK: This is the milk left over after churning butter. True buttermilk is a thin liquid with little butter globules. Commercial buttermilk is made from non-fat milk with a culture and is thick and smooth. Cultured buttermilk is more appetizing in appearance than real buttermilk. Salt is usually added to buttermilk No one knows who took that first sip of buttermilk. It is known that butter has been made for more than 5,000 years. Ancient Hindus based the market value of their cows on the amount of butter churned from their milk. Early colonists brought butter-making to America. These homemakers found many ways to utilize the butter-flecked fluid left over from home buttermaking.

Churning butter was an arm-aching job. It started with cool cream, which was jostled about in a deep wooden tub for quite awhile. When the milkfat particles (butter) separated from the cream, the remaining fluid was drained off for use as a nourishing beverage and as a cooking ingredient. Factory production of butter began about 1860, but most butter was still being churned on the farms until the 1920's. Creameries began to use the churned buttermilk in dried form in the 1940s for more efficient use in baked goods, as well as in pre-packaged mixes.

Today, buttermilk is made by fermentation, a bacterial action. The bacteria is grown or cultured under laboratory conditions. Once added to skim milk, the bacteria multiply and convert some of the milk sugar lactose to lactic acid. The acid gives the milk that tart flavor. The thickness is the result of bacterial action on the milk protein. It is then pasteurized to destroy remaining bacteria. Pasteurising forms butter granules that gives the appearance of churned buttermilk. In some dairies the containers are labeled "churned," but probably it is not real churned buttermilk. Unfortunately, with the new modern production methods, little, if any, buttermilk is left over from butter making.

Buttermilk, like all fluid milk, should be refrigerated. It will keep for up to two weeks, but should be used during the first week after the container has been opened. Freezing buttermilk is not advised, since it causes separation of the water and solids. If frozen, thaw in the refrigerator. Stir gently and use for cooking.

You can churn your own butter by shaking half-and-half cream in a gallon jar until butter forms (see MAKE FRESH BUTTER AT HOME). The jar allows you to observe the whole process. From the liquid left over after the butter comes out, you can taste real buttermilk.

Buttermilk is used in recipes, especially baked goods. When buttermilk is used in baking, baking soda must be added in place of or part of the baking powder. Liquid buttermilk can be replaced with cultured dry buttermilk powder. Mix the dry powder with other dry ingredients and add water to equal the amount of fluid buttermilk called for in the recipe. Use one tablespoon of buttermilk powder for each 1/4 cup of liquid buttermilk.

In Scandinavia they make a buttermilk soup with is enjoyed as a luncheon meal or as a dessert with cookies. In the southern U.S., buttermilk is made into a pie and is used in cornbread recipes. **Nutrition facts:** Buttermilk has the same nutrition as non-fat milk, with about 90 calories per 8 ounces. It is high in protein, calcium, and riboflavin. – RSC. www.sacofoods.com

BUTTERMILK SUBSTITUTE: Add one teaspoon lemon juice or vinegar to enough milk to make one cup. Stir and let set for 5 minutes. This makes 1 cup of buttermilk.

BUTTERNUT: A native nut from North America, sometimes called a "white walnut." Once common, they are rare today. The nutshell provided a wonderful natural dye for fabrics. During the American Civil War, the uniforms of the South were so often dyed with butternut that the soldiers were sometimes referred to as "the Butternut Brigade." The nut grows in clusters inside a husk, making it difficult to shell. Butternuts are grown in the eastern U.S. from Maine to Georgia and west to the Dakotas and south as far as Arkansas. The nut is used in cooking, mainly in cookies and cakes. **Nutrition facts** per 1/4 cup serving: 214 calories, 166 calories from fat, 19.9g total fat (31%), .5g saturated fat (2%), zero cholesterol and sodium, 4.2g carbohydrates (1%), 1.7g fiber (7%), 43 IU vitamin A (1%), 1mg vitamin C (2%), 19mg calcium (2%), and 1.4mg iron (8%),

BUTTERNUT SQUASH: This one is a winter squash with a hard light brown shell. Many are somewhat pear shaped, having seeds in a small hollow in the base. The flesh is orange and the flavor is sweet. They can be pealed, cubed and steamed, or cooked in a small amount of water. Or, they can be left with the peeling on, cut in half lengthways, seeded, and baked. Baking provides the best flavor. Peak season is late fall, but some are available from August to March. They can be stored in a cool place for several months. **Nutrition facts:** A ½-cup serving has 32 calories, zero fat and sodium, 8.2g carbohydrates (3%), zero fiber, .7g protein (1%), 5,460 IU vitamin A (109%), 15mg vitamin C (25%), calcium (3%), .5mg iron (3%), and 246mg potassium.

BUTTERS: A fruit spread, such as apple butter, which is cooked longer (to thicken) than apple sauce. Butters are like jam made from apples, apricots, pears, and yes–from peanuts.

BUTTERSCOTCH: A flavor combining butter and brown sugar used in candies and deserts.

Cc

CABBAGE: Of all the vegetables, cabbage is eaten by the most people around the world. It has been enjoyed for more than 4,000 years in Europe, Africa, and Asia. The original wild cabbage, called sea cabbage, grew along the coasts of European countries. It was spindly, more like kale, and had no head. Cabbage heads didn't appear until about 100 BC and were still rather small. By the Middle Ages, gardeners had learned to cultivate the wide heads we know today.

Cabbage came to the Americas in 1541 with Jacques Cartier, who planted it in Canada. But the first immigrants to plant cabbage successfully were probably the Germans after 1669. In Alaska, cabbage heads of 100 pounds are not uncommon.

Cabbage can be eaten in hundreds of recipes, raw or cooked. It is available with white, green or red leaves. Cabbage come in many shapes, from firm tight head, to loose curly heads, and can grow in almost any climate. Cabbage can be made into soup, braised with butter, boiled with meats, and fried with apples. Shredded cabbage can substitute for lettuce in green salads. Leaves are used to wrap up rice and meat for Greek and Arab recipes. Two of the most popular cabbage dishes are coleslaw and sauerkraut. **Nutrition facts:** A ½ cup serving has 8 calories, zero fat and sodium, 1.9g carbohydrates (1%), zero fiber, .4g protein (1%), 44 IU vitamin A (1%), 18mg vitamin C (30%), 16mg calcium (2%), .2mg iron (1%), and 86mg potassium.

CABBAGE PALM: Better known as "hearts of palm," they are the tender hearts of several kinds of palm trees. Fresh cabbage palm is only available in the tropics. It is available canned at most supermarkets. The taste is bland, but cooked with butter and lemon juice, or mixed into a salad and topped with dressing, it has a delicate taste.

CACAO: Sometimes called the chocolate tree, properly, it's *Theobroma cacao*. The tree is native to the Amazon but is now found in most tropical climates. The tree is a widely branching evergreen that may grow to 40 feet. It is kept at 20 feet on plantations. Woody, football shaped fruit, up to a foot long, develop from white-pink, fragrant flowers which appear on the trunk and main branches. About 50 bitter seeds are found in the gelatinous pulp. When the pulp is fermented, the beans become less bitter. Then they are dried, roasted, shelled, and processed. More than 50% of the bean is fat. Cocoa butter, which has endless uses by the cosmetic and food industries. . The fat-free, powdered residue is cocoa. Chocolate is made by combining the cocoa with cocoa butter, milk or cream, vanilla, and sweeteners. Cocoa contains caffeine and theobromine, both stimulants. See CHOCOLATE.

CACTI: Yes, some of the desert plants are edible. See CACTUS PEAR.

CACTUS PEAR: Also known as "cactus apple" and "prickly pear," it's the red seed fruit picked from the flat cactus stems found in northern Mexico and southwestern United States. The pears have a high content of water and often serve thirsty people and animals crossing the dessert. Care must be taken to remove the sharp spines before eating. The stems are also eaten, especially in Mexico, and both the stems and pears are made into preserves and candy. Cactus pears are low in calories and have a sweet, mild flavor. Best eaten raw, chilled with a little sugar and lemon juice. Their beautiful magenta color makes them prized as a food garnish.

CAFÉ AU LAIT: Double strength coffee and an equal amount of very hot milk, both poured into the cup at the same time. The fashion began in Vienna in the 17th century. It was the favorite dish of Marie Antoinette.

CAIMITO: Also called star-apple, produces 2-3-inch long green or purple fruit, which is eaten raw.

CAJUN COOKING:

In 1976 Clyde LeBlanc wrote *The Good Earth* cookbook and it was published by the *Houma-Terrebonne Bicentennial Commission*. This is his introduction to his book.

THOUGHTS OF A CAJUN BREAKFAST

(Original spelling retained)

"All cooking, eating, and even cook books got to start somewhere, so I guess we start with breakfast - *le petit déjeuner* (the little un-fasting, literally) or just plain *déjeuner* (day-zhun-ay) in Terrebonne, Louisiana. First, we got to have the coffee, black, strong, pure, very little at a time; *la goutte* (the sip). Dripped slowly, it is more of a licquer than a beverage, and even the *café-au-lait* (coffee with milk) for the children is pretty strong stuff. The 'cadien breakfast is got to be a solid meal. He get up early, work up a appetite for a couple of hours, and is ready for grits, eggs, biscuits, boudin, grillades, smother potato, fig preserve, butter, cream cheeze, and fruit - whatever he have, or all of it. These is mostly the food he raise himself, or he can get close by. If he is a farmer, he have plenty of meat, eggs, vegetable; if he is a fisherman, he have plenty of seafood, some meat, and rice and potatoes, syrup, can milk and coffee, so he make out. Have you ever see a child eat a breakfast of fried shrimps, or onions? If that is what you got, you eat it; and some kind of way, it seems to work out good, even if it is not a balance meal, like they say nowadays.

And nowadays, too, you can get plenty of fresh foods, because they is plenty of rice, and tomatoes, oranges, and lemons, and even plenty of vitamin pill if you make some mistakes in eating, so everything is take care of in this *new trishon* they tell us all about. When the weather is nice, and I get up early, sometime I just sit in my yard and watch the "good earth" come to life. The chickens and the birds is up first, but they don't beat the farmers and the fishermans by much, and the shrimp peelers is gone to the factory long before the birds is even think of wake up. So by the time the sun get up enough to see what you is eating, you is usual hungry enough to enjoy a good breakfast, no matter what it is. Even at the oil rigs, where breakfast can be day or night, they work hard enough to eat good.

Even the childs, who got to go to school on the bus, get up early enough to do they work and eat breakfast before they leave, which is kind of early, especial with the 'daylight save time', which the sun don't pay no mind to, and which just make it harder to go to bed early enough to get up in the morning sooner. Sometime I think we is more international than Acadian, down here. We got all the good foods of the American Indian, the African, the Asian, the European, and the Acadian. Sometime I go to sit and rock on the poach at Mr. Pellegrin store, and read his phone book for recreation. I try to figure out all them name in Terrebonne, which sound like German, French, English, Chinese, Scotch, Spanish, Indian, African, Italian, and so many other, it seem to me that our cooking must have come from all over the world, and the reason we make it so good is that we take the time and trouble to cook and eat all the good thing we got here like they deserve. Anyway, we got a start on our story of the cooking and the people of Terreboone. Enjoy it in good humor and *appetit!*"– *Reprinted with permission by Linda LeBlanc Thibodaux*

CAKE: A sweetened dough that is leavened with baking powder or with egg whites (like angel food cakes). After baking, the cake is usually frosted, sometimes filled between the layers. Before making a cake, lay out all ingredients, cooking utensils, prepared pans, read the recipe twice, and preheat the oven for at least 10 minutes. Follow directions precisely. It's important that you don't make any substitutions and always level off each dry measurement with a knife. To test for when the cake is done, use a toothpick and insert in the center. If is comes out dry, the cake is done. www.bettycrocker.com www.tastykake.com

LITTLE SHORT CAKE FINGERS

A History of Hostess Baking Company

Those little handheld, packaged snack cakes have been around since 1919 when D.R. "Doc" Rice originated the first chocolate cupcake for the Taggart Baking Company. The same year that William B. Ward, founder of Continental Baking Company, began making Hostess cakes. Continental purchased Taggart in 1925. In 1930, Jimmy Dewar, Continental's manager in Chicago saw the need for a new, low-priced product that could be sold during the Depression period. Continental made shortcakes during the strawberry season, but the rest of the year, those little cake pans sat idle. Dewar's idea was to make the same little cakes and inject a banana cream filling to be sold year round. Times were tough, money was tight during those depression years, so the "Little Short Cake Fingers," as they were first called, sold two to a pack for a nickel.

Dewar was not totally pleased with the Little Shortcake name. On a trip to Saint Louis, he saw a billboard advertising "Twinkle Toe Shoes." Dewar picked up on that name, and renamed his little cakes, "Twinkies." Sales took off, and the item became the top Hostess-line seller. Twinkies haven't changed much since their introduction, although technology and packaging have improved texture, softness and color. During the 1940s, vanilla-flavored creme filling replaced the original banana creme.

The first Twinkies were hand-filled one at a time, with a piston-type filler. Today they can make 52,000 hourly. While the cooled cakes are still upside-down in the pans, the creme filling is injected in them through three small injection tubes using air injection. Immediately after being filled, the Twinkies pans are turned over, and the cakes ride a short conveyor belt to be fresh wrapped.

Hostess "Sno Balls" snack cakes were the next big hit and were created by Ellis Baum in 1947. Sno Balls get the name from their outer marshmallow frosting rolled in coconut. Inside is a chocolate cupcake. It was Doc Rice who taught employees how to properly dip, then roll Sno Balls. First one employee would dip the cakes in marshmallow and quickly pass it on to the next employee who would roll the ball in coconut. Today machines have taken over this job of dipping and rolling, but the Sno Balls still have the same great taste. At first all were white. Next pink was introduced, and now during different times of the year you have green Sno Balls for Saint Patrick's Day; yellow and lavender for Easter; red, white, and blue for the Fourth of July; and orange for Halloween. Other colors are sometimes added for a special event, such as orange and blue when the Denver Broncos were in the National Football League playoffs.

Everyone has afavorite way of eating a Sno Ball. Some prefer to eat it bite by bite out of hand. Some like to peel off the marshmallow and eat it first or last. And, there are some that like to shove the whole Sno Ball into the mouth all in one bite. With a fork? Yes, that's possible too.

Hostess Continue to Create New Snacks

Today Hostess makes a whole array of snacks and breakfast cakes. What will come next, is anyone's guess. Hostess has plans, so be on the lookout for their next sweet sensation! Hostess, Twinkies, Suzy Q's, Ding Dongs, O's, and Choco-Bliss are registered trademarks of *Interstate Brands Corporation*.

CAKE FLOUR: When flour is being refined, it's a process of separating the endosperm from the bran and germ. When this process is totally complete, and only the heart of the endosperm remains, you have cake flour. Cake flour is also known as "fancy" and "short patent" flour. **Tips**: When a recipe calls for cake flour and it isn't available, measure carefully one cup of flour without tapping the cup (this packs the flour), then remove 2 tablespoons. Also note that when using cake flour, the batter requires more beating than all-purpose flour. However, too much beating will make the cake tough. Beat after each addition only until smooth with no lumps.

CAKE YEAST: Also known as compressed yeast. A 2/3 ounce package of cake yeast is equal to 1 ¼ ounce package of dry yeast or 2 teaspoons of active bulk yeast. Dry yeast will keep longer than cake yeast. Cake yeast must be refrigerated and used within two weeks. Generally, you will obtain equal results with either cake or dry yeast. Look for yeast cakes in the dairy case.

CALABASH is one of the edible gourds. It grows a hard shelled fruit 3 to 6-inches. The seeds are cooked prior to eating, and the young fruits are pickled. The sweet calabash grows in South America and Africa.

CALABURA are also known as Panama berries and Jamaica cherries. The small red or yellow berry is sweet and aromatic enough to eat fresh. Also made into jam and tarts.

CALAMARI: See SQUID.

CALAMANSI is a cross between Mandarin orange and the kumquat which is prized in Filipino cooking. The juice is used in all the ways one uses lemon.

CALAMONDIN is a member of the citrus family, originating in the Philippines. The small round sour fruit can be found in juice, preserves, and marmalade.

CALICO BEANS: See BUTTER BEANS

CALIFORNIA FOODS See CUISINE.

CALOOSA GRAPE a south Florida fruit. Eaten fresh, and made into jelly.

CALORIE: The unit of measurement for food energy from fats, proteins, and carbohydrates. Calories give us a way to measure fuel (calories) needs and fuel (energy) consumption. If the body ingests more calories than it needs for fuel, the surplus calories are stored in the body as fat to be used at a later time. The exact wording in the *American Heritage Dictionary* is "a unit of energy-producing potential equal to the amount of heat that is contained in food and released upon oxidation by the body."

CAMEMBERT (kam-em-bear): Camembert is one of the most famous soft cheeses. The French village of Camembert gave it its name and still produces the true Camembert cheese. The town was famous for good cheeses as early as 1708. True Camembert is made from untreated cow's milk, and not less than 45% fat. A natural, local blue mold gives the Camembert cheese its individual taste and appearance.

CAMERANO CHEESE: A mountain goat milk cottage cheese made in Spain.

CAMEL MILK: In arid Africa and other Arab lands, camel milk is the preferred beverage choice of nomadic people, since it takes less to feed a camel than a cow. Camel milk is a valuable source of protein, and is nutritionally complete. A camel can provide up to 10 gallons of milk a day. Camels can be a source of meat, but are generally too valuable for other purposes to be eaten.

CANAPE´ (can-a-pay): The French word is applied to appetizers or *hor d'evers,* especially crackers or cut bread with cheese or meat topping.

CANDLE TREE from Central America produces 18-inch yellow, candle shaped fruits. Although edible, "candles" are tough with poor flavor. Mostly used for livestock feed.

CANDY: A sweet confection made with sugar, honey, corn syrup, fruit juices or other sweeteners. Candy has only calories, sometimes fat, but usually no nutritional values.

Candy in History

During **ancient times** the Egyptians, Arabs and Chinese prepared confections of fruit and nuts candied in honey.

In Europe during the **Middle Ages**, the high cost of sugar made sugar candy a delicacy available only to the wealthy.

Boiled sugar candies were known in the **17th century** England and in the American colonies.

Homemade hard candies, such as peppermints and lemon drops became popular **in early 1800s** America. In the same time period, candy developed rapidly with the discovery of sugar beet juice and the advancement of mechanical appliances.

The **penny candies** were the most popular in the **19th century**. Some candy was as high as a penny each, while some were as low as five for a penny. Hard to believe! Penny candies are still available today. Of course they are now more than a penny, and are generally sold by the pound. Some of the "penny" candies you can find without much trouble are jelly beans, Boston baked beans, lemon drops, buttermints, malted milk balls, and root beer barrels. But have you ever tasted anise or clove drops? How about Mary Janes or licorice pastels?

By the **mid-1800s**, more than 380 American factories were producing "penny candy," which was sold loose from glass cases in general stores.

When Étienne **Guittard** arrived in San Francisco, his intent was like so many other Forty-Niners, to strike it rich in the gold fields. Instead, his fortune came by way of fine chocolate making, a skill he learned in his uncle's shop in France. His most famous candy were **nonpareils**, a smooth, creamy-rich, one-inch chocolate wafers covered with tiny sugar sprinkles that melted in your mouth.

Famous Names in Candy History

Pastel wafers of sugar, corn syrup and dextrose were developed in 1847. It wasn't until **1901** that they were marketed by the acronym name **NECCO** (New England Confectionery Company). www.necco.com

Tootsie Roll, created in 1896, was the first wrapped penny candy. It was following by a number of penny products, one of the most popular was the "Guess What?" that contained two pieces of taffy and a small toy.

In 1900, the Dutch made the first **chocolate apple-shaped candy**. Today, there are other versions made with orange and other flavorings. When banged on the table, the ball will explode into 18 perfect slices. In some areas, you'll only find these at Christmas time.

The chewy, fruit-flavored morsels **Jujubes** and **Jujyfruits**, were developed by Henry Heide of New Brunswick, New York and were popular in the late **1910s.** Now part of Hershey.

In 1912, **LifeSavers** were first produced. The round white peppermints had holes in the middle that made them look like a life preserver on a ship. First produced by Clarence A. Crane of Cleveland, Ohio.

In **1912**, **Goo Goo Supremes** were made. Goo Goos are two and one-half-inch round clusters of chocolate covered by caramel and marshmallow, topped with pecans. There are many imitations, but few are equal to the original.

In **1918**, the **Cherry Mash** was created. The creamy center is made of mashed maraschino cherries, rolled in ground peanuts and then covered in milk chocolate.

Walnettos, a chewy caramel with walnuts, was a favorite in the **1920s**. Once you taste a Walnetto, you will never forget the flavor. **NECCO** Wafers were another favorite early in the 20th century. A roll of Neccos were reputed to last through two movies and a cartoon.

Originally, **salt water taffy** was considered penny candy, usually two or three for a penny in the **1930's**. Today the best taffy is made along our ocean coastlines. Whether the salt air has anything to do with it, is anyone's guess. The original salt water taffy was made by **Fralinger's** Candy Store in Atlantic City, New Jersey. Fralinger's claims all others were only imitations, because theirs were the best - just soft enough so they didn't pull out your teeth, yet chewy enough that the full flavor lingered.

Chuckles, the jellied candy coated with sugar crystals, was produced by Fred W. Amend of Chicago, Illinois in **1921.**

In **1924**, the honey-favored taffy bar with bits of almond, **Bit-O-Honey**, was produced by the Schutter-Johnson Company of Chicago, Illinois.

In **1931**, a candy maker added a bit too much vanilla to a batch of marshmallow. Instead of hardening with it cooled, the marshmallow remained smooth and flowing. The candy maker poured it into milk chocolate two inch cups, and **Valomilks** were born. If you find a Valomilk, be careful when you bite into this creamy, sweet sensation, because the marshmallow will run down your chin. –*National Confectioners Association*

OLD-FASHIONED CANDY

What has happened to all the old-timed candies you ask? Many companies were purchased by other candy companies, such as Hershey's and Nestle. However, everything listed in this article are still made, some by the original company, and are available. Look for companies that feature items from yesteryear, not just candy, but cookware and kitchen appliances. One such company is **The Vermont Country Store of Weston, Vermont**. Not only does the store have all in stock, along with other candies, they also offer mail order service. For a catalog, write: The Vermont Country Store, P.O. Box 3000, Manchester Center, VT 05255-3000 or call them (802) 362-2400.

Activity

You might be too young to experience the taste of some of the candies of yesteryear. It's even possible your parents have never enjoyed sucking a piece of horehound or sassafras drops. Have some family fun and check with your grandparents to see what they remember of old-fashioned candy. You might awaken some sweet memories they would love to share! Write down such memories for the family history.

A Game for All

Here's a game for your next long, boring car trip. See how long the people in the car can keep up taking turns naming kinds (including brand names) of candy. You'll be surprised just how many there are and how many you can remember. It makes the trip a lot sweeter.

CANDY, CLEAR:

CLEAR TOY CANDIES

In 1894, Philadelphia children discovered something new in the confectionery window on North Tenth Street. Candy maker Fred Regannes had filled the window with a rainbow of candies that looked like glass gleaming in the sunshine. "Are they real?" the children asked. "Taste," said Mr. Regannes.

Today, over one hundred years later, descendants of the Regannes family still delight candy lovers with the time-honored tradition of jewel colored sweets. Sold all year round, the toys really come into their own at Christmas season for gift-giving and as ornaments. Another reason for making the candies in the winter time is purely practical. Heat and humidity are the natural enemies of the candy trade. Boiling candy is difficult and dangerous work so conditions need to be ideal. Patience pays off in a crystalline candy beloved by all. Today there are only a handful of professionals who still make clear molded candies by hand. One of the busiest is Kay Helm, who carries on the tradition of her Regannes relatives.

Candy Molds

Clear candy molds were once made almost exclusively by Thomas Mills and Brothers, a Philadelphia foundry established in 1864. Mold making is demanding art in itself. Since the Mills stopped make molds back in the 1960s, antique molds are highly prized and sought after by candy makers. Automated candy makers used reproductions of the early molds. The first molds were pewter or cast iron. Modern reproductions are usually cast of aluminum. Candy supply houses offer some in very heavy plastic. Anything less cannot take the heat.

A FUNNY STORY

*From the family history of Mary Dodd of Pennsylvania comes this interesting note. "Two fakers went from street to street and charged admission to see a 'glass eating' exhibition. The showmen's trade secret was a clear toy bottle mold in which they made candy bottles that looked like glass. Before the eyes of the audience, they would smash the bottles and eat the pieces, leaving the viewers convinced they had devoured brown glass." For candy making supplies on the internet, contact: www.kitchenkrafts.com For a complete line of clear candies call or write **Kay Helm,** 153 Welliver Road, Danville, PA 17821, phone (570) 275-1227. – LU*

CANISTEL from Central America is also known as egg fruit and yellow sapote. Variable in size and shape, the fruits are yellow or orange, eaten both fresh and cooked.

CANOLA OIL: A neutral-flavored, all-purpose cooking oil, made from rapeseed (a wild mustard), is widely grown in Japan and Canada, and popular there long before coming to the U.S. It is known as rapeseed oil in other parts of the world. Use to sauté vegetables, bake, and to make salad dressings. It works well in high temperature application like deep and stir-frying. Canola oil is lower in saturated fat than corn oil. **Nutrition facts:** One tablespoon has 120 calories, 120 calories from fat, 13.6g total fat (21%), 1g saturated fat (5%), 8g monounsalturated fat, 4g polyunsaturated fat, and zero cholesterol.

CANTALOUPE: (can-ta-lope)A variety of the muskmelon. Melons originated in Asia and were enjoyed by Mediterranean people during ancient times. The cantaloupe receives its name from Cantalupo, Italy, where the melon was first cultivated in Europe for the Pope's table in the early 1700's. California's Imperial Valley is the main producer, growing special plants resistant to mildew. Other varieties are grown commercially in warm southern climates from California to Texas. Modern strains can be grown in summer gardens all over the United States. Cantaloupes are available year round; however, the main season is during the summer months. Ripe cantaloupes are fragrant, with the stem end soft and slightly sunken. Cantaloupes are best fresh, but can be frozen and made into sorbet. Cantaloupes can carry a toxic bacteria on the skin and should be washed well before cutting. **Nutrition facts:** A ¼ wedge has 47 calories, 3 calories from fat, .4g total fat (1%), zero saturated fat and cholesterol, 12mg sodium (1%), 11.2g carbohydrates (4%),1.1g fiber (4%), 1.2g protein (2%), 4,304 IU vitamin A (86%), 56mg vitamin C (94%), 15mg calcium (1%), .3mg iron (2%), and 413mg potassium. www.duda.com

CAPERS: A native of the Mediterranean, they are the unopened flowers of the caper bush. The flower buds are preserved in salt and vinegar. Capers are added to sauces and served on eggs, rice, seafood, vegetables, and salads. Smaller buds, called "nonpareil," are the tenderest and the most expensive. Capers are cultivated in France. Roguevaire, France is the caper capital of the world, but capers are also big in Spain and Italy.

CAPON: Capons are male chickens butchered while still immature (4-8 pounds) to keep them small and tender for roasting or braising whole. **Nutrition facts** per 4 ounces: 192 calories, 129 calories from fat, 14g total fat (22%), 4.1g saturated fat (21%), 72.1mg cholesterol (24%), 38.9mg sodium (2%), zero carbohydrates and fiber, 14.4g protein (31%), 750 IU vitamin A (15%), 2mg vitamin C (4%), 9mg calcium (1%), and 1.2mg iron (7%).

CAPSICUM: A pod-bearing plant native to tropical America as early as 7000 years ago. This plant is not related to the black pepper vine of Asia. The pods come in a variety of sizes, and colors. The taste ranges from mild, like paprika, to red hot chilies. The hot capsicum peppers (chilies) must be used with discretion. The pepper is made from both the pod and the seeds, with the seeds having the most heat. The mild, rounded green and red peppers are also capsicums but are called "green" or "bell" peppers in English. Columbus, so an not to confuse his newly discovered chili peppers with the black peppers of the East Indies, call the South American peppers "pimientos." Capsicum is the botanical name for both kinds–chilies and bell peppers.
See PEPPERS.

CAPULIN from Central America produces a fruit that is made into preserves.

CARAMBOLA, from Malaya, is also known as star fruit in this country. The yellow fruit makes jelly, preserves, and juice. Great sliced fresh and added to green salads with a fruit dressing. Sliced crosswise, the fruit resembles a five-point star. Available in many supermarkets.

CARAMEL CANDY: Caramel and toffee are hard to tell apart. Both begin with sugar, milk and butter. Toffee can have other flavors but caramel has its own flavor. Caramel has the same texture but caramel has a more chocolatey look and taste. Caramel and chocolate are often used together as in caramel filled chocolate bonbons or caramel coated nut rolls dipped in chocolate.

CARAMELIZE: A culinary term referring to burnt sugar that adds color and flavor to foods. To make, heat a heavy skillet over medium heat, add 1 cup of sugar, stirring constantly until sugar just forms golden-brown syrup. Remove from the heat and use immediately.

CARAWAY SEEDS: One of the oldest herbs known to man. From the Arabic (*karaweiia*), it is mentioned in earliest Egyptian medical books. Caraway seeds, which originated in Asia Minor, were used by the people of Europe 1500 years B.C. The Germans brought the seeds to Maine in the 18th century, where they still grow and harvested for sale. Not only the seeds are used for seasoning, but the young leaves as well. Even the roots can be steamed and eaten as a vegetable. Caraway seeds are added to soups, cheeses, vegetables, meat, and baked goods, such as rye bread. For the maximum amount of flavor, the seeds should be crushed to release their oils.

CARBONATED: A beverage made with the addition of carbon dioxide, creating fizzing action. Most bottled soft drinks are carbonated.

CARDAMOM: Also Cardamon. As early as 500 BC, the dried spice called cardamom, a member of the ginger family, was carried by spice traders on the Spice Road out of India to the North. It still grows in India, especially the Malabar region. It also is cultivated in Guatemala, Mexico, Sri Lanka, Tasmania and Papua New Guinea. It is the third most expensive spice after saffron and vanilla.

CARDOON: Related and tastes like artichoke, but looks more like celery. To the Greeks and Romans, it was a great delicacy and remained so as its fame spread all over Europe in the following centuries. Even today it is cultivated in Southern Europe and North Africa. In this country it is considered a weed. When prepared correctly, is quite tender, with the inner stalks best. Cardoon can be boiled, sautéd, or breaded and deep fat fried, and served with a white or tomato sauce. **Nutrition facts:** A ½ cup serving has 18 calories, zero fat, 151.3mg sodium (6%), 4.4g carbohydrates (1%), 1.4g fiber (6%), .6g protein (1%), 107 IU vitamin A (2%), 2mg vitamin C (3%), 62mg calcium (6%), .6mg iron (4%), and 356mg potassium.

NONNA'S WONDERFUL WEED FEED
by Marie Prato

Both of my grandmothers were born in Italy. When they were young, living off the land was a necessity and my grandmothers learned to make a meal out of whatever was available - including flowers and weeds. After they moved to the United States and had families, my grandmothers taught their children and grandchildren, including me, how to find and eat delicacies that most Americans consider nuisance plants.

Whenever my father's mother came to visit our home on Long Island, we would go hunting together. Armed with pails, plastic bags, and scissors we would start searching for dandelions. Working our way up and down the road, we would snip each delicate stem near the ground and drop the stalks in one of the pails.

When both our pails were full, Grandma and I would head back to the house. But before going inside, we would stop at my father's garden. Heading right to the squash section, we looked over each flower on the squash plants as if we were examining a rare diamond. After running our hands under and over each thin, orange blossom to make sure they were free of rot and holes, we cut off the best flowers for our meal and put them in our plastic bag.

Now the real work began. After placing the dandelions in a strainer, I ran warm water over them until they were clean. Snipping each yellow flower off of the steams, I placed the tops in a separate plastic bag. The dandelion flowers would be used later by my grandmother to make dandelion wine. The stems, however, were for eating. After placing the dandelion stems in a large bowl, my grandmother poured a mixture of olive oil, vinegar, salt and pepper on top of them. This was going to be our salad. Then we started on the squash flowers. Grandma divided the flowers into two piles - one pile was for shredding and the other pile of flowers for cooking whole. I took the pile of squash flowers to be shredded and tore them into one inch sections. After mixing the shredded flowers into a bowl filled with pancake batter, they were ready to be cooked. Grandma poured the thick batter into a greased frying pan about six inches wide. When the pancake was golden brown on both sides, she flipped it onto a large tray and started the next pancake.

After the pancakes were done, we started on the pile of squash flowers that hadn't been shredded. Each large blossom was dipped in egg, rolled in flour, then fried in olive oil. After a few minutes, the ends of the squash flower would curl and the flour coating would turn crisp and brown. I could hardly wait until my father came home. Dinner started with the dandelion salad. Tender and juicy, each stem that had been marinating in its olive oil mixture was savored as we worked our way through the bowl. Then we were ready for the main course.

Each squash-flowered pancake filled our entire dinner plate as we tried to make room for the fried squash flowers. Due to my diligent shredding, each and every bite of the pancake has at least one piece of the juicy orange flower in it. And on the inside of each thin, crispy flour shell was a whole moist and tender squash flower. But my Grandma on my mother's side had her own specialty when it came to weeds. Once or twice a year, she and I would go to my aunt's place in upstate New York near the Pennsylvania border and hunt. Armed with buckets and a hooked knife, Grandma and I would walk into the woods hunting for cardoons. Using her hooked knife, Grandma would cut the tough fiber plant just below the dirt. After shaking the loose dirt off the celery- like stalk, she would put the weeds in the pail.

Cleaning the cardoons was much more difficult. After cutting off the leaves and some of the tough outer stems, we would place the cardoons in a strainer. Dirt and insects seemed to cling to every crevice of the stringy, tough stems as we laboriously washed them again and again. When they finally passed my grandmother's inspection, she peeled off the stringy outer layer from each of the stalks and cut them into four or five inch sections.

After the stalks were peeled and cut, grandma would put them in a pot of water with a little bit of lemon juice and boil them. When the cardoons were tender, grandmother would take them out of the pot, put three of them together and braid them. Each braid was then dipped in a beaten egg and then rolled in bread crumbs. When all the stalks were ready to be cooked, she took out her heavy frying pan. Putting in a few drops of olive oil, grandmother fried the cardoon braids until they were a rich golden brown. Although the cardoons looked like celery, they tasted more like artichoke. And sweet! The crisp cardoons were so sweet on the inside it was almost like having dessert. We never had to worry about what to do with the leftovers. No matter how many weeds my grandmothers and I picked, there never was anything left!

CARMINE: A natural red food coloring, also called cochineal. It comes from the cochineal insects, a family of red scale insects that feed on cacti from the American Southwest to Central America.

CAROB: Also called the locust bean in its native Mediterranean area. It also has the nickname of "Saint John's bean" because the Biblical prophet John the Baptizer lived on locust beans and honey while he lived in the Judean desert. A member of the legume family, the bean pods grow up to eight inches long, about as long as a new pencil.

The ancient Greeks and Arabs used the seeds to weigh their gold and jewels because, by some miracle of nature, each bean can be counted on to weigh 0.18 grams or six thousandths of an ounce. This became the standard unit of weight we know as the carat, or 0.2 grams. The word carat came from the tree's Latin name, *Ceratonia siliqua*. As other foods became more abundant, the carob lost favor though the beans were fed to pigs or ground up for a coffee substitute in hard times. Only recently the carob was found to be useful as a substitute for chocolate. It is sweet, low in fat, and similar to the cocoa bean, but with more nutrients than the cocoa bean. Carob bean gum is used as a thickening agent and as a replacement for chocolate. Most often found in health food stores.

CARP: Is native to Asia, a relative of the goldfish. The large black fish has been introduced to many rivers and lakes around the world. While prized in Europe, it's not a favorite fish in America, because it muddies up the waters, making the water uninhabitable for other fish. Best eaten during the late fall to early spring months, when they taste less "muddy." Carp can be skinned and soaked in salt water to remove some of the muddy taste. Carp can be fried, poached, or baked. **Nutrition facts:** A 3-ounce serving has 108 calories, 45 calories from fat, 4.8g total fat (7%), .9g saturated fat (5%), 56.1mg cholesterol (19%), 41.7mg sodium (2%), zero carbohydrates and fiber, 15.2g protein (30%), zero vitamin A, 1mg vitamin C (2%), 35mg calcium (3%), 1.1mg iron (6%), and 283mg potassium.

CARP DELIGHT: A Story
by Kelly Ann Brown

Carp are not eaten by many Americans, because of it's muddy taste. Although you might not enjoy carp, most Europeans are fond of them. Try this recipe and *bon appetit*!

1 garlic clove
2 teaspoons lemon juice
¼ cup pineapple juice
1 red pepper
2 tomatoes, quartered
1 red onion, sliced
½ teaspoon salt
½ teaspoon pepper
1 cedar board

1. Massage the carp with fruit juices.
2. Cover the carp with the vegetables.
3. Season with salt and pepper.
4. Add the garlic last.
5. Place the prepared carp on a fragrant cedar board, and cover with aluminum foil.
6. In a preheated 350° oven, cook for about 2 hours
7. Carefully remove from the oven, open the foil, being careful as not to let the steam burn you. Check to see if the fish is white and flaky. If it is, carefully wrap up the fish in the foil and drop into a garbage can.
8. Eat the board. It should be tasty and tender. Be careful of splinters.

Nutrition facts are not available, as I can't compute the nutriments of the cedar board. Cedar doesn't have many calories, no fat or cholesterol, minimum amount of sodium, no vitamins, but a fair source of minerals. –RSC

CARROTS: An age old vegetable, carrots have been cultivated for more than 2,000 years in Europe. Carrots were brought to America in the early 1600s. Some say carrots are best when young and slender, while others say carrots must be fully mature for the best taste. When purchasing carrots, buy those with fresh looking green tops, but once home remove the tops, wash the carrots, place in a plastic bag, and refrigerate. If the tops are left on, the tops will draw moisture from the carrot. If buying carrots without tops, do not purchase cracked ones. Some super carrots have been developed with five times the beta carotene which is converted to vitamin A in the body. They are being introduced in countries where the diet is lacking in vitamin A. In preparing carrots, young carrots do not need to be peeled, just scrub with a stiff brush. Mature carrots should be peeled to remove the dirt. Carrot can be eaten raw, boiled in water, or baked whole in the oven. Strange at it might seem, cooked carrots are better for you than raw carrots, as cooking partially dissolves the cellulose, making more nutrients available. **Nutrition facts:** A one-half cup serving has 24 calories, zero fat, 19.2mg sodium (1%), 5.6g carbohydrates (2%), 1.7g fiber (7%), .6g protein (1%), 15,460 IU vitamin A (309%), 5mg vitamin C (9%), 15mg calcium (1%), .3mg iron (2%), and 178mg potassium. www.styorganics.com. www.valleyfruit.com.

CARUSSA is native to South Africa. It produces a red fruit that is eaten fresh, added to salads, mashed into a sauce, or squeezed into milky colored juice.

CAS from Central America, produces a yellow, soft acid pulp that is eaten fresh, jellied or juiced.

CASABA: This, like many melons, originated in Persia (Iran). Most of the casabas are grown in California and best when harvested in the early to mid fall. The flesh is white when ripe and has almost a mild cucumber taste. When purchasing, look for a yellow rind, with no green on the skin, and a softening at the blossom end. **Nutrition facts:** A ¼ wedge has 107 calories, 3 calories from fat, .4g total fat (1%), zero saturated fat and cholesterol, 49.2mg sodium (2%), 25.4g carbohydrates (8%), 3.3g fiber (13%), 3.7g protein (7%), 123 IU vitamin A (2%), 66mg vitamin C (109%), 20mg calcium (2%), 1.6mg iron (9%), and 861mg potassium.

CASABANANA comes from tropical America. Fruit resembles an orange or purple cucumber. Mature fruit is made into a beverage.

CASHEW: This rich, kidney-shaped nut is native to tropical America and is the seed of the marañon fruit. Today most of the cashews are imported from India and are popular cooked in many India dishes, especially in curry recipes. Cashews are available roasted, unroasted, dry-roasted, salted, and unsalted. Cashews are eaten fresh, added to salads and stir-fries, used in stuffings, ground into cashew butter, and make great cashew brittle. Cashews are high in fat, but contain some protein and iron, with some B vitamins. Three ounces of cashews have more than **500 calories. Nutrition facts** per ¼ cup: 187 calories, 133 calories from fat, 15.7g total fat (24%), 3.1g saturated fat (15%), zero cholesterol and sodium, 9.3g carbohydrates (3%), 1.2g fiber (5%), 5.3g protein (10%), zero vitamins A and C, 13mg calcium (1%), and 1.3mg iron (7%)

CASSAVA, also called yuca in its native Latin America and the Caribbean, the roots are cooked and eaten like potatoes. The starch is a source for making tapioca..

CASSEROLE: There are two meanings: 1) A heat proof vessel for baking or 2) a combination of foods either simmered on top of the stove or baked in an oven, called, "one-dish meals." Casseroles are easy to make, require little watching, and usually use inexpensive meats, vegetables, or leftover foods.

CASSIA: (cash-ya) A spice also called "false cinnamon." It goes by various names and comes from different parts of the Orient but it's still a poor relative of cinnamon. It was said in the

Middle Ages that cinnamon was for lords but cassia was for common people. Cassia is a good spice in itself. Cassia is reddish brown whereas true cinnamon is tan.

CASSOULET: (cas-soo-lay) A bean, vegetable, and meat (generally a combination of sausage, pork, lamb, and duck) stew from France, simmered on top of the stove. The name comes from the earthenware vessel in which it is cooked.

CATFISH: This fish has feelers, which resemble whiskers on a cat, hence the name. There are both fresh and salt water catfish. The most important for eating is the channel catfish that can weight up to 10 pounds. Usually feeding near the surface of the water and are less muddy-tasting than bottom feeders. Catfish can be cooked in many ways, but frying is the preferred method, especially breaded and deep fat fried. **Nutrition facts:** A 3-ounce serving has 81 calories, 23calories from fat, 2.4g total fat (4%), .6g saturated fat (3%), 49.3mg cholesterol (16%), 36.6mg sodium (2%), zero carbohydrates and fiber, 13.9g protein (28%), 43mg vitamin A (1%), 1mg vitamin C (1%), 12mg calcium (1%), .3mg iron (1%), and 304mg potassium.

CATFISH FARMS: Most commercial catfish are raised in ponds which were once cotton fields that have been diked. The ponds are aerated and monitored for oxygen levels to keep water fresh and the catfish alive. Farmers who once grew cotton can now raise a cash crop of catfish instead.

How did the catfish ever become a farm animal? It happened when word got out catfish were delicious fried and cuddled up with hush puppies. Channel catfish was chosen to farm, because they are the fastest growing and best tasting. Also channel catfish will rise to the top for feeding, unlike other catfish that prefer to feed off yucky bottom stuff.

Producing farm-raised channel catfish begins with mating mature catfish. Each female can lay more than 4,000 eggs annually. Once the eggs are laid and fertilized, they are collected and taken to hatcheries. The eggs hatch after seven days. The young catfish are called "sac fry" because of the attached yolk sacs that supply their food. Once the sacs are depleted, the baby catfish begin to swim in ponds where they grow into fingerlings about six inches long. They are then placed in catfish ponds.

The catfish are fed a puffed, high-protein, floating food pellet made up of soybeans, corn, wheat, vitamins, and minerals. Because of this special formula, the catfish has a subtle taste and has no "fishy" odor. The clay-lined ponds, plus top feeding, helps to eliminate the "muddy" taste common in non-farmed catfish. After 18 months, the fish weigh about 1 ½ pounds and are ready to be harvested. They are taken alive to the processing plants. In takes less than 30-minutes to clean and process a catfish. Some are shipped iced-fresh immediately, while others are fast-frozen to 40° below zero. This freezing method preserves the taste and quality. Catfish are available in most supermarkets nationwide as whole fish, steaks, fillets, strips, and nuggets. Some are marinated, breaded, or pre-cooked in frozen dinners.

Catfish must pass stringent taste tests at the ponds where they are raised and undergo inspections by the United States Department of Commerce at the processing plants. Catfish have gone from a traditional Southern delicacy to the fifth most popular fish in America. Catfish are served in restaurants throughout the country. *--The Catfish Institute*

CATTLEY GUAVA is from Brazil, also known as strawberry guava. It produces a small red or yellow fruit that is eaten fresh or made in jelly.

CAULIFLOWER: Mark Twain said cauliflower was "just cabbage with a college education." This advanced form of cabbage has been enjoyed in the Mediterranean regions for more than 2,500 years and came to America about 200 years ago. It looks like one single flower, but it is actually made up of a bunch of little flowers, called "florets." Some growers have experimented with new varieties, one was a shade of purple. Recently Broccoflower was developed by combining cauliflower with broccoli, presenting a green color. Cauliflower can be eaten raw or cooked. Raw florets are great tossed in a salad or can be served as an appetizer. **Tips**: When cooking cauliflower, steam in a small amount of water. Do not overcook, it should be tender crisp and white. **Nutrition facts"** A ½ cup serving has 13 calories, zero fat, 15mg sodium (1%), 2.6g carbohydrates (1%), 1.3g fiber (5%), 1g protein (2%), zero vitamin A, 23mg vitamin C (39%), 11mg calcium (1%), .2mg iron (1%), 151mg potassium, and a good source for vitamin B6.

CAVIAR is black or red salted roe (fish eggs). The most prized roe comes from beluga, a member of the sturgeon family. Caviar also comes from herring, carp, salmon, cod and whitefish. The eggs are sieved, washed, pressed lightly, and salted. Caviar is generally served as an appetizer on a piece of toast, but is also mixed in dressings for salads, and added to wine sauces for fish.

CAYENNE PEPPER: Also known as red pepper. See CAPSICUM

CECROPIA, a plant from tropical America, produces a 3-inch, hollow, edible fruit with soft, sweet flesh and many small seeds. The sap, latex, is used like rubber.

CELERIAC: A variety of celery, also know as "celery root," because it grows at the base of the stem and looks like a turnip. It was developed in the 17th century by Italian and Swiss botanists. Celeriac is seldom eaten raw, but when cooked can be served hot or chilled. Tips: When buying, select smaller roots, because larger roots tend to be woody and hollow. After roots and tops are cut off, celeriac is best peeled, sliced or diced, and cooked with just enough water to cover. It will take 20 to 30 minutes. Serve plain with a little butter or cream. To serve as a salad, cook and chill in a marinate of French dressing. **Nutrition facts:** A ½ cup serving has 30 calories, zero fat, 78mg sodium (3%), 7.2g carbohydrates (2%), 1.4g fiber (6%), 1.2g protein (2%), zero vitamin A, 6mg vitamin C (10%), 34mg calcium (3%), .6mg iron (3%), and 234mg potassium.

CELERY: This herb has grown wild in Europe and Asia since ancient times and was bought to the U.S. in the early 19th century. The first mention of garden cultivated celery comes from France in 1623. After that it soon began to be a favorite in family plots. The two main varieties are "golden

heart" and "pascal." Golden heart celery is wrapped in paper to prevent the celery from turning green. Pascal is a tall, green variety, and the variety most likely found in the supermarket. Celery can be eaten raw, fried, boiled, or braised. Use the inner stalks for eating, the outer stalks for cooking. **Nutrition facts:** A ½ cup serving has 10 calories, zero fat, 52.3mg sodium (2%), 2.2g carbohydrates (1%), 1g fiber (4%), .5g protein (1%), 80 IU vitamin A (2%), 4mg vitamin C (7%), 24mg calcium (2%), .2mg iron (1%), and 172mg potassium.
www.styorganics.com

CELERY ROOT: See CELERIAC

CELERY SEED: Seed of the celery dried and used as seasoning for it's bitter zip to salads and stews.

CEREAL: The seeds or grains from grass. The most common are barley, corn, oats, rice, rye, and wheat. These grains are used in making flour (bread, cakes and other baked goods), pasta, and breakfast cereals. Cereal grains have been used for more than 10,000 years. Buckwheat, millet and sorghum, while made into flour and breakfast cereals, are not true grass cereals. Each grain has three elements: the thin outer layer called "bran," the embryo (also called the "germ"), and the endosperm, which is the largest part of the seed. Whole grain flours contain all three, while all-purpose white flour contains mostly the endosperm. www.generalmills.com
www.kelloggs.com; www.kraftfoods.com

CEREAL CITY USA:
KELLOGG'S CEREAL CITY USA
by Jennifer Kingen

Battle Creek, Michigan, the Cereal Bowl of America, presents Kellogg's Cereal City USA. The fun starts before you enter the doors as an authentic glockenspiel (bell tower clock) uniquely shaped as a grain silo announces the time. Many of Kellogg characters, Snap! Crackle! Pop! Toucan Sam, and Tony the Tiger greet and entertain guests. The cereal story begins with an actual cereal production line with the making of corn flakes. At the end of the line you will be able to taste the newly created flakes, warm out of the oven. On the **Historical Timeline tour** you will meet Dr. John Harvey Kellogg, Will Keith Kellogg, and Charles William Post, who tell their cereal stories.

In Cereal City, you can see *The Best to You Revue, Cereal Bowl of America,* and *A Bowl Full of Dreams.* Walk on the cobblestone streets between the theaters are cartoon-like buildings with interacting exhibits relating to health, nutrition, and the cultural impact cereals have made on the world.

In the *Red Onion Grill* you can enjoy dinner specialties, as well as novelty foods made from cereal products. If you would like to take Tony the Tiger home, visit *The Factory Store* for stuffed animals and collectibles. Would you like your own personalized cereal box with your own face on it? You can purchase one. For visitor information, write: **Kellogg's Cereal City USA,** 171 W. Michigan, Battle Creek, MI 49017 or phone 1-616-962-6230. Kellogg's Cereal City USA, Snap!, Crackle!, Pop!, Toucan Sam, and Tony the Tiger are registered trademarks of the Kellogg Company.

CERIMAN is from Mexico and Central America, the vine produces green cucumber-shaped fruit, eaten fresh and made into preserves. The fruit tastes like a combination of banana and pineapple.

CEVISHE (SEVICHE) (se-vee-shay) is a special dish in South and Central America. These are raw fish fillets marinated in lime and lemon juice with olive oil and spices and served as an appetizer. The names seems to come from the Spanish, *cebiche,* for fish stew. The acid of the limes produces an effect on the fish almost the same as cooking it. Thus the fish is not really raw.

CEYLONESE TREE, a forbidden fruit as the seeds are narcotic.

CEYLON GOOSEBERRIES are small, dark purple, sour berries for jelly, preserves, and juice.

CEYLON SPINACH is so called because the vine's leaves are eaten as a vegetable.

CHAFING: A method of cooking or warming at the table. A chafing dish has a small candle underneath for cooking or keeping hot.

CHALLAH (Pronounced and sometimes spelled "hallah.") is a Jewish Sabbath bread made with eggs and white flour. The loaf is twisted or braided and topped with sesame seeds. Two loaves are served at each meal of the Sabbath day to remind Jews of the manna that fell from heaven during their years of wildness wandering. For Jewish New Year it is round, symbolizing the completion of the old year and hopes for a perfect new year. The name comes from the bit of dough that is traditionally torn off and baked symbolically for the priests. "Challah" means "the priest's share." Today it is a popular bread in Jewish bakeries. Challah makes wonderful French toast when cut 3/4-inch thick and soaked overnight in the refrigerator, then baked or fried.

CHANTILLY: A whipped cream that has generally been sweetened and/or flavored to be used with foods such as whipped into potatoes or made into a sauce.

CHARD: Also know as Swiss chard, is a member of the beet family, but only the top leaves are eaten. Chard is best cooked like spinach, in a small amount of water, but can be sautéd in butter. **Nutrition facts:** A ½ cup serving has 3 calories, zero fat, 38.3mg sodium (2%), zero carbohydrates, .3g fiber (1%), .3g protein (1%), 594 IU vitamin A (12%), 5mg vitamin C (9%), 9mg calcium (1%), .3mg iron (2%), and 68mg potassium.

CHARICHUELA is a South American fruit with yellow rind whose soft, white, low acid pulp is eaten fresh.

CHARLOTTE: A gelatin dessert containing flavored whipped cream, molded into a form lined with sponge cake or lady fingers. The name most likely comes in honor of England's Queen Charlotte (1744-1818) wife of King George III. Most famous of all is Apple Charlotte. France and Russia have somewhat different versions. There are two types. One is baked and served warm with cream. The other is a cold, gelatin mold type. The cold one looks spectacular and is easier to make than it looks.

A Charlotte Anyone Can Make

Line a circular baking pan or deep dish with lady fingers standing side by side. Fill the inside with vanilla ice cream. Refreeze. When ready to serve, turn the charlotte upside down on a serving dish. Garnish with fruit or ice cream toppings.

CHAUD-FROID: (show-fwah) A French term meaning "hot-cold." A sauce made hot, stiffened with gelatin and served cold with meat and vegetables. Aspic is an example.

CHAYA. In the Yucatan, the leaves are cooked twice (to remove the poison) in two waters, and eaten as a vegetable. The fresh leaves will irritate the skin.

CHAYOTE: It's a fruit of the gourd family from tropical America. At one time it was the principle food of the Mayans and Aztecs. The taste is bland, hence needs to be combined with other vegetables and meats or well seasoned. Chayote can be boiled, fried, and baked. Two popular recipes are 1) au gratin with cheddar cheese; and 2) stuffed with ground beef, rice, tomatoes and baked. **Nutrition facts:** A ½ cup serving has 16 calories, zero fat and sodium, 3.6g carbohydrates (1%), 2g fiber (8%), .6g protein (1%), 37 IU vitamin A (1%), 7mg vitamin C (12%), 13mg calcium (1%), .3mg iron (1%), and 99mg potassium.

CHEESE: A product made from milk after the curd has been separated from the whey. At this point the curd is treated in a number of ways to make a variety of cheeses. Nonprocessed natural cheese is made directly from the curds, while process cheese (also called American) is made from natural cheese that has been ground, heated and emulsified into a smooth product. Some of the more popular natural cheeses out of about 350 different kinds are: Asiago, Blue, Brie, Camembert, Cheddar, Colby, Cottage, Cream, Edam, Feta, Gouda, Jack (or Monterey), Limbuger, Mozzarella, Muenster, Neuchatel, Parmesan, Provolone, Ricotta, Romano, Roquefort, and Swiss.

Cheese is a good source for protein and calcium. Most cheese is high in calories, fat, and sodium. Cottage and cream cheese are the lowest in calories. Many of the low-fat and nonfat cheeses lack taste, but are gaining in popularity as the flavors are improved. These low-fat and nonfat cheeses are not used in cooking, as cooking reduces the flavor and turns the consistency into a rubbery mass. www.kraftfoods.com; www.castro-cheese.com; www.ilovecheese.com www.cabotcheese.com.

Activity: Buy a variety of cheeses and crackers and have a cheese tasting party.

CHEESECAKE: A rich cake made basically with cream cheese, blended with cottage cheese, ricotta, pot cheese, or farmer's cheese. Most cheesecakes have a pastry shell or graham cracker crust. The combined acid of the cheese and sugar give it a mild, lemony taste. www.elicheesecake.com.

CHEDDAR CHEESE: Made from whole milk, colored a deep orange, eaten fresh or used for cooking. Cheddar is mild when fresh, but grows more sharp with aging.

CHEF: A French term meaning, "chief." The chef is a professionally trained cook and the head of the kitchen.

SO YOU WANT TO BE A CHEF?

The first question that comes to your mind is "How do I prepare to become a chef?" First, you must have an interest in food, enjoy working in the kitchen, and currently you should be preparing some of your favorite dishes.

How Do I Begin?

In school, take available cooking courses. Most culinary schools do not have a prerequisite for food study in the middle grades or even high school, but it all helps. Some culinary schools will require you to have at least six months of food service, which includes working in a professional kitchen where at least fifty percent of the food is prepared on the premises. You could be a volunteer in a soup kitchen, hospital, or the like. You might have to start as a dish washer, or in another non-cooking position and work your way up to a cooking position. Most fast food restaurant employment doesn't count, since most of the food is not prepared on the premises.

How Much Does it Cost?

Your second question might be, "How much does it cost to attend a culinary school?" Tuition can be as high as $8,000 per semester or about $30,000 for a two-year course. To this you must add the cost of living which can be $1,500 to $2,000 per semester. Financial aid is generally available, along with grants, and federal and state loans. During the course, most schools have an arrangement where you will work in a restaurant, hospital kitchen, or a bakery between your first and second year. This could be at a summer resort, in a test kitchen for a cooking magazine, a helper on a TV food program, on a cruise ship, or in a famous gourmet restaurant.

Employment and Salaries?

And the third and most important question, "Where will I be employed and how much will the starting wage be?" From a good culinary school you should receive three job offers paying $23,000 or more annually. Like your externship, you will have many choices where you will start your employment. Prior to attending a culinary school you should visit your library and study cookbooks, food manuals, and food videos, and watch chefs prepare recipes on TV shows.

Can I Specialize?

While most schools will offer an overall food course, you might want to specialize, such as in baking breakfast breads or making table-side desserts, and this should be considered when picking a culinary school. Ask your vocation advisor at your school for a list of culinary schools and write to them for their catalogues. Most schools will offer you a list of their famous graduates. If one is located near you, request an interview with this chef for additional advise. If at all possible, plan to visit several culinary schools before you make your final choice. Most offer tours, and some offer week long courses during school vacation-time for middle grade and high school students. It's important to be happy and satisfied with your first choice, so ask lots of questions and be sure your have made the right choice. – RSC

CHERIMOYA grows in the tropical highlands of Peru and Ecuador Inside the rough green skin is a sweet, juicy, creamy flesh and flavored with hints of banana, pineapple, papaya, and mango. Eaten fresh (best chilled), served as a dessert, or diced and added to fruit salads and yogurt.

CHERRIES JUBILEE was created to honor Queen Victoria at her Golden Jubilee celebration in 1887. That first version did not contain ice cream. Since cherries were her favorite, it was a simple dish of cherries poached in thickened syrup to which warmed brandy was added and set aflame at the last minute. Ice cream got added later by the famous Chef Escoffier.

CHERRY: This fruit originated in Asia Minor, probably in the Black Sea region. Settlers brought the tree to Massachusetts in the early 1600s. Most colonial homes had cherry trees, as did George Washington's home. Cherries grow abundantly and are much loved in Russia.

There are two types of cherries, sweet and tart. The sweet are the larger heart-shaped. **Bings** and **Royal Anns** are two of most popular sweet cherries found in the supermarkets. Tart cherries are used in cooking pies, jellies, jams. The most popular is the tart **Montmorency** cherry. **Maraschino** cherries are made from sweet cherries which are bleached, then cooked in a sugar syrup with a little bitter almond flavoring, and added color. Maraschino cherries were developed in Italy 300 years ago. The French improved on them. Fresh cherries are available from May through August, depending on the location and the variety. **Nutrition facts:** A ½ cup serving has 36 calories, 3 calories from fat, .3g total fat (1%), zero saturated fat and sodium, 8.5g carbohydrates (3%), .9g fiber (4%), .7g protein (1%), 674 IU vitamin A (13%), 1mg vitamin C (2%), 10mg calcium (1%), .4mg iron (2%), and 96mg potassium. www.califcherry.com www.nwcherries.com

CHERRY-OF-THE-RIO GRANDE is from Brazil. The small, dark purple, sweet fruit is eaten fresh.

CHERVIL: This "fine" herb plant, resembling parsley, is an annual that grows up to 2-feet tall. It's easy to grow in gardens and in pots. Chervil is used for flavoring omelets, potatoes, soups, salads and stews. Fresh leaves and boiled roots can be eaten as a vegetable. **Nutrition facts:**. A ½ cup serving has 36 calories, 4 calories from fat, .6g total fat (1%), zero saturated fat and cholesterol, 12.6mg sodium (1%), 7.4g carbohydrates (2%), 1.7g fiber, 3.5g protein (7%), zero vitamins A and C, 205mg calcium (20%), 4.9mg iron (27%), and 720mg potassium.

CHESTNUT: The tree originated in Asia Minor. Today the chestnut tree is found throughout the northern hemisphere from Europe to Asia and still in some parts of Canada. Chestnuts once flourished in the New England states and south through the Appalachia's to Alabama. Few of the trees remain, after fungus from Asia in the early 20th century killed off most of the trees. Most chestnuts today are imported from Spain and Italy. However, we are happy to report at least one place is growing chestnut trees successfully in the U.S. Shady Grove Farms in Washington are growing enough trees to sell chestnuts commercially. www.chestnutsource.com.

In America's eastern cities, roasted chestnuts may still be sold by street venders from fall to early spring. In Europe chestnuts are ground into flour for making bread and other baked goods, as well as a thick soup. In Italy they are used in a chocolate dessert. Clifford Wright tells us in *A Mediterranean Feast* that chestnuts were one of the staple foods of the poor in Europe. In the Provence region of France, there is a mountainous area known as the "Chestnut Zone." Workers were paid in pounds of fatback and white chestnuts. Chestnuts can be boiled, braised or roasted, eaten as a vegetable, combine with other vegetables, and used for stuffing poultry. Chestnuts are low in fat and calories, high in fiber, and contain some protein, iron, and B vitamins.

CHICKEN: The birds originated in the jungles of southeastern Asia and have been domesticated for more than 4,000 years. European explorers found them tasty and brought them to Europe in the 3rd century B.C. Chickens came to U.S. with the colonists in the early 1600s. At that time they were raised mainly for their eggs and feathers. Feathers were, and still are, prized as pillow stuffing. Chickens are divided into groups: Fryers weigh from 1 to 3 ½ pounds, roasting Capons 4 to 8 pounds, Cornish up to 2 pounds for roasting and broiling, and stewing hens with less tender meat weigh up to 5 pounds and are boiled or braised. Egg laying hens are not eaten until they no longer produce eggs. Mass-produced chickens are raised crowded together and under supervised conditions to be brought to market in exact sizes and weights.

Free-range chickens, which are allowed to forage for food on their own, are often called "love" chickens because they live happier lives. These chickens taste much better than mass-produced birds, since they are allowed to eat a variety of foods. Chickens that exercise have more dark meat, such as in the legs. Since chickens seldom fly and don't exercise their wings, wing meat is lighter in color. Chicken needs to be cooked well done without any pink color in the meat. Whether roasting or frying, the internal temperature should be 200°F when done. **Nutrition facts 3 ounce white meat:** 117 calories, 59 calories from fat, 6.3g total fat (10%), 1.8g saturated fat (9%), 43.5mg cholesterol (15%), 42.9mg sodium (2%), zero carbohydrates and fiber, 14.2g protein (28%), 56 IU vitamin A (1%), 1mg vitamin C (1%), 7mg calcium (1%), and .5mg iron (3%). **Nutrition facts: 3**

ounces dark meat: 142 calories, 94 calories from fat, 10.3g total fat (16%), 2.9g saturated fat (15%), 56.4mg cholesterol (19%), 51.1mg sodium (2%), zero carbohydrates and fiber, 11.6g protein (23%), 97 IU vitamin A (2%), 2mg vitamin C (3%), 7mg calcium (1%), and .7mg iron (4%).

CHICKPEAS: Also known as garbanzo beans and native to southern Europe. Chick-peas are an important food in Asia, Africa, and Central America. Chickpeas come in red, white, and black, with the white the most popular. The nutty flavored peas are served by themselves, cooked in soups and stews, or in salads and sauces. **Nutrition facts:** A ½ cup serving has 134 calories, 19 calories from fat, 2.1g total fat (3%), .2g saturated fat (1%), zero cholesterol and sodium, 22.5g carbohydrates (7%), zero fiber, 7.3g protein (15%), zero vitamin A, 1mg vitamin C (2%), 40mg calcium (4%), 2.4mg iron (13%), and 239mg potassium.

CHICORY: A wildflower herb, member of the endive family, looks like a small blue daisy. It originated in Europe, where it still grows wild, it has been a salad green farm crop in America since the turn of the century. A dash of chicory, with its slightly bitter taste, is added to green salads. In Louisiana it is prized for its long roots. The roots are roasted, ground, and added to coffee, and sold as "New Orleans Creole coffee." Chicory is widely used in herbal remedies.

CHICOZAPOTE from Mexico and Central America has large, brown-skinned fruit, with sweet tan pulp, eaten fresh, and made into sherbet.

CHIFFON: (shi-fahn) A light-textured cake or pie made with whipped egg whites.

CHIFFON CAKE: (shi-fahn) Chiffon cake is a true Hollywood original. The name comes from the shiny, light-as-air, silken fabrics popularly used for Hollywood ball gowns. The "light as chiffon" cake was invented by 64-year-old insurance salesman Henry Baker, who added salad oil to the basic sponge cake recipe. His chiffon cakes became the darling of his celebrity neighbors. So that he could keep his career as baker and not have to go back selling insurance, Baker kept his closely guarded recipe a secret. For twenty years, he only made his cake for the public on special occasions. In 1948 he finally decided to divulge his secret recipe to a radio food show personality in Minneapolis and then sold his recipe to General Mills. The flour milling company introduced the chiffon cake as the first new cake in 100 years. Tips: When making a chiffon cake, it is necessary to follow the directions exactly as written and to add ingredients in the order given. It is important that the oil be added before the egg yolks, if not, the cake will have eggy streaks. The egg yolks must be beaten until they're thick and lemon-colored, or your cake could have an eggy bottom layer. As with any sponge cake recipe, the egg whites must not be overbeaten or underbeaten. The beaten egg white must be folded in gently, not stirred hard.

CHIFFONADE: (shi-fon-aid) Sorrel, endive or lettuce cut into strips, softened in butter or cream and used as a garnish for soups. Also refers to a French salad dressing with shredded vegetables and chopped hard-cooked eggs.

CHILI: A tropical American plant which produces pods that are mild to hot. Red or cayenne pepper is just one of the products from the hotter varieties. Green bell pepper is one of the mildest and is quite popular stuffed and baked. When the red bell pepper is dried, it is ground and made into paprika. Bell peppers can be eaten fresh or cooked. Jalapeños are one of the most popular peppers and can be mild to very hot, depending upon the variety. They are used to make hot sauces, and added to stews, salsa and chili dishes. Jalapeños are eaten raw, roasted, and stuffed. Habañeros are one of the hottest, some 50 times hotter than jalapeños. They are used fresh or made into salsas. It is said they taste like apricots, but since they kill all taste buds, it's not known for sure if this is true. See CAPSICUM.

CHILI FARMING IN NEW MEXICO
by Louise Ulmer

In New Mexico, the unofficial state symbol has become the chili pepper. Hot peppers spice up everything from T-shirts and ball hats to dishes and Christmas trees. Hatch Valley is the largest chili-producing area in the nation. The state's hot sunlight and cool nights are ideal for that special New Mexican taste. The state has been breeding chili plants for over 100 years. Today's university researchers are developing plants that can withstand diseases, viruses, and bacteria better than the older varieties.

Chili peppers are the Number 1 cash crop in 1998, bringing in more than $58 million. Nearly 400 farmers in New Mexico grow hot peppers. Researches keep trying to breed the perfect chili pepper. They try to arrive at the right "hotness" by crossing the jalapeño with be bell pepper. They also get some nice ornamental colors like purple, but pepper lovers don't like their peppers "cuted up." They want green or red. With all those peppers it might look like Christmas all year long in the lower Rio Grande Valley. And that's how they like it in New Mexico.

CHILI CON CARNE: A Mexican import made with meat, beans, onions and chili powder. Red kidney beans can be added. Today it is said there are as many chili recipes as there are Texans.

CHILI SAUCE: A sweet sauce made with tomatoes, vinegar, onions, sweet peppers and seasonings. Available mild or hot.

CHILL: To remove heat from food by placing on ice or in the refrigerated for a short time. Do not over chill, as it deprives flavor in food, especially salads, fruits, and seafood.

CHINESE BROCCOLI: While Chinese broccoli has a slightly delicate broccoli flavor, the taste to many is between bok choy and mustard greens. Unlike broccoli, Chinese broccoli is grown for its fleshy stems, which must be peeled prior to cooking. Chinese broccoli can be used in most broccoli recipes.

CHINESE GOOSEBERRY, better known as kiwi, grown in New Zealand and California, is available in supermarkets and health food stores. The fuzzy brown skin covers a sweet green pulp, eaten fresh, and made into preserves.

CHINESE OKRA is better known as loofah. Loofah grows on a vine. The green, 18-inch, cucumber-shaped fruit can be eaten as a vegetable when very young. Older fruits are dried and the insides used for scrubbing, cleaning, and bathing.

CHINESE PARSLEY: See CILANTRO

CHINESE RAISIN comes from Japan and China, produces a small fruit, eaten fresh, or dried.

CHINOOK SALMON: See KING SALMON

CHINQUAPIN: (chinky-pin) A tree once growing wild and plentiful in the southern United States with a fruit similar to the chestnut in appearance and taste. Like the chestnut, the tree has been dying off. **Activity**: If you know of any such rare or unusual trees, not just this one, contact your nearest university department of agriculture, tree specialists, or naturalist to let them know so the trees can possibly be saved from extinction.

CHIPOTLE are smoked jalapeños, often canned in a mixture of tomato sauce, vinegar and spices called *adobo*.

CHITTERLINGS (chit-luns): The intestines of young pigs. They are cleaned and soaked in brine for 24 hours, then washed a half dozen times more. Chitterlings can be boiled with onions, herbs and spices. Boiled chitterlings can be breaded and deep fat fried. **Nutrition facts** per 3 ounces: 214 calories, 170 calories from fat, 19.7g total fat (30%), 6.7g saturated fat (34%), 135.2mg cholesterol (45%), 29.8mg sodium (1%), zero carbohydrates and fiber, 8.6g protein (17%), zero vitamin A, 3mg vitamin C (6%), 17mg calcium (2%), and 1.6mg iron (9%).

CHIVES: A smaller member of the onion family, gown for their tubular leaves. Chives add a mild onion flavor to almost any food. Popular in salads, dressings, toppings. www.melissa.com

CHOCOLATE: A product made from the cacao tree, sometimes called the chocolate tree, that is native to the Amazon basin.

Chocolate is full of caffeine and theobromine, both stimulants. This is why soldiers have carried it with them since the Civil War. Strangely enough, it is also soothing to the mind.

Chocolate comes in many grades from unsweetened to sweet. Unsweetened, it is used for cooking and is ideal for a deep-bodied flavor in baking. Semisweet is used for making candy, frostings, sauces, and baking, especially in chocolate chip cookies. Sweet chocolate is mostly used for making chocolate beverages. Milk chocolate is sweet chocolate with the addition of dried milk.

One tablespoon of chocolate chips contain 51 calories, of which half the calories come from fat. Except for a little iron, potassium, and antioxidant, there are few health benefits, just good taste. www.nestle.com

CHOCOLATE - "FOOD OF THE GODS"

Chocolate begins with a bean, a cacao bean. This bean has been mashed and eaten for centuries. "Food of the Gods," was the name given by Swedish botanist Carolus Linnaeus, founder of the modern system of classifying life forms, by giving each life form a genus and species name.

The scientific name of this bean is *Theobroma cacao* which means "food of the gods" and has been worshiped as an idol by the Mayans of Mexico and Central America for more than 2,000 years. Prior to 1492, the Old World knew nothing of the cocoa bean. **Christopher Columbus** returned with some beans and presented them to the Court of King Ferdinand and Queen Isabella. It was thought they were almonds and the court was not impressed.

In 1519, Hernando Cortez tasted a bitter drink called *cacahuatt* prepared for him by Montezuma II, the last Aztec emperor. While Cortez was looking for gold, it was the cacao beans the Aztecs treasured the most. Cortez took some cacao beans back to Spain where the chocolate drink was made heated with cane sugar (and possibly with vanilla and cinnamon). This formula was kept a secret for nearly 100 years, since it was only to be enjoyed by nobility. Eventually, the secret was revealed and the chocolate drink's fame spread to other lands.

By the mid-1600s, the chocolate drink had gained widespread popularity in France. One enterprising Frenchman opened the **first hot chocolate shop in London**. By the 1700s, chocolate houses were as prominent as coffee houses in England.

The **New World's first chocolate factory** opened in 1765 the Massachusetts Bay Colony by the Walter Baker Company. Sixty years later, Conrad Van Houten, a Dutch chemist, invented a press that made cocoa powder and enabled confectioners to make chocolate candy by mixing the powder, cocoa butter with finely ground sugar.

Domingo **Ghiradelli** of Italy began making chocolate in San Francisco during the California Gold Rush of 1849. His original factory still stands and you can visit it at Ghiradelli Square on the famed Fishermen's Wharf. Also during the Gold Rush, Étienne Guittard arrived in California from Paris, bringing with him the knowledge obtained from his uncle's Paris chocolate factory. Guittard Chocolate Company is still family owned.

First Milk Chocolate

In 1876, **Daniel Peter,** a Swiss candymaker, experimented for eight years and developed milk chocolate by adding condensed milk to chocolate liquor (a nonalcoholic by- product of the cocoa bean's inner meat). He sold his creation to his neighbor, **Henri Nestle.** In 1879, Rudolphe Lindt, also of Switzerland, gave chocolate a smoother texture through a process called "conching. Conching is a "kneading" action, where rollers plow back and forth through the chocolate mass, some for hours, others for days. The conching name was derived from a Greek term meaning "sea shell" and referred to the shape of old mixing vats where particles in the chocolate mixture were reduced to a fine texture. This process is still used today to further refine chocolate. Nestle developed the **Nestle's Crunch Bar** in 1938, and chocolate chips in 1939.

Milton Hershey set up his first confectionery shop in Philadelphia at the age of 19 in 1879. It wasn't until 1907 that he first made **Hershey's Kisses**. Today more than 20- million Kisses are made per day. In 1913, another Swiss confectioner, Jules Suchard, introduced a process to produce filled chocolates.

The **Milky Way** (1923) put the **Mars** Candy company on the map. The original Three Musketeers bar of the 1930s originally had three parts: chocolate, vanilla and strawberry. It became all chocolate in the 1940s.

Surveys have revealed that 48% of Americans like chocolate candy best. It was also revealed that kids in the middle grades like chocolate candy more than they did in elementary school. Today the average American eats almost twelve pounds of chocolate (candy, hot chocolate, etc.) per year. That's not a record, Denmark citizens enjoy almost thirty pounds per person a year.

Today, some **chocolate factories offer tours**. An important note, all chocolate manufacturers **must meet standards** as set forth in the rules and regulations of The Food and Drug Administration. Even with these laws, there are still secrets. It's the chocolate chef who must guard his formula for blending beans, time intervals, temperatures, and proportions of ingredients. Hence, a visit to a chocolate factory will reveal no secrets to you, but you will be impressed by the cleanliness and the gleaming appearance of all the machinery used to make chocolate. – *The Chocolate Manufacturer's Association*

EASTER RABBIT WIZARDRY

The owners of a tiny candy store in Lancaster, Pennsylvania had no idea they were about to make candy history when they made molded Easter treats. Joseph Royer and Joe Huber carved models out of paraffin wax. Then they set the wax chickies and bunnies into liquid plaster. After the plaster hardened, they melted the wax, which left a hollow mold, perfect for shaping candy. Children bought the candy bunnies and eggs as fast as they could be made. Before long the candy makers from all over were coming around, trying to learn the secrets of molded candies. Mr. Royer trained a few apprentices, one of them a teenager named Milton Hershey. Young Hershey later grew up to form his own candy business. His first business didn't make magic, but he became a real wizard in milk chocolate. The apprentice Easter rabbit molder became so famous that a whole town was named after his chocolate business. Remember this next you have a Hershey's chocolate Easter bunny from Hershey, Pennsylvania.

FIREHOUSE ART CENTER CHOCOLATE FESTIVAL

At the Firehouse Art Center Chocolate Festival in Norman, Oklahoma, every February, on the first Saturday preceding Valentine's Day, chocolate takes new forms in the minds and at the hands of artists. While the artists are at work, so are professional chefs and home-kitchen bakers creating the most delicious chocolate desserts to compete for cash prizes. . In recent years artists have created a garden pool of sculpted chocolate, complete with flowers and a fish-fountain spouting chocolate milk; whimsical forest animals; one hundred and one Dalmatian puppies emerging from cocoons; "Rub-a-dub-dub, Two Pigs in a Tub;" and lots more. Artists melt it, mold it, shave it, sculpt it, carve it, and even throw chocolate on a potter's wheel. Prizes are awarded for most humorous, most creative, and most elegant. Chocolate never is boring. Chocolate Festival in Norman, every year. For more information write: **The Firehouse Art Center,** 444 South Flood, Norman, OK 73069 or phone (405) 329-4523. *--Linda Sexton*

GRANDMA'S HOT CHOCOLATE
by Kelly McHugh

Megan ran down the stairs. She slid across the hall floor into the kitchen. "Hey, Jennifer, Grandma isn't feeling well. What can we do?" Megan asked her older sister.

"We could make her favorite, hot chocolate," Jennifer replied.

"Yeah," said Megan, "when we get sick Grandma always makes us her special hot chocolate. Do you have her recipe?"

"Yes, but it's a secret, so don't tell anyone. Here it is, I wrote it down once while Grandma was making it."

½ cup dark chocolate chips
2 cups milk
¼ teaspoon vanilla
Marshmallows

Jennifer put the chocolate chips in a saucepan and put it on a low burner. Once the chocolate chips began to melt, she slowly poured in the milk and stirred until the milk was hot. Megan poured in the vanilla and a handful of miniature marshmallows. Carefully the hot chocolate was poured in Grandma's favorite yellow mug. The girls took it to Grandma, who was resting in her bedroom.

Grandma took a sip and a smile came on her face as she said, "Thank you girls."

"Do you know the story of chocolate?" asked Grandma.

"Yes, it was the Aztecs," replied Megan. We studied that in the third grade."

"Did you know the Aztecs once flavored their chocolate with red pepper?" asked Grandma.

"Yuck," replied Jennifer.

"It was the Spanish who first used sugar, and kept it a secret for more than a hundred years," Grandma said. "And, it was the French who discovered a way to make chocolate candy bars."

"We sure have come a long ways since those Spanish explorers bought home chocolate to Europe, haven't we?" Megan said.

"That's right!" replied Grandma, "and I feel better already."

CHOKECHERRY: A native of North America, it's a small wild cherry that grows on a very large bush. Eaten raw, the chokecherry has a puckery taste. Best when made into jelly or jam.
Like other American berries, it went into *pemmican* made by the Native Americans.

THE MONTANA CHOKECHERRY FESTIVAL

The lowly, small, maroon-colored, and puckery tasting chokecherry that grows wild in Montana reigns supreme on the first Saturday after Labor Day in Lewistown, Montana, with their annual Chokecherry Festival. Family fun starts with a pancake breakfast served, with (what-else) chokecherry syrup. One of the highlights of the day is the Chokecherry Pit-Spitting contest. The Chokecherry Culinary Contest boasts delights all using chokecherries as an ingredient, and the public can taste the entries. For more details, write: **Lewistown Area Chamber of Commerce**, P.O. Box 818, Lewistown, MT 59457; or phone (406) 538-5436. *--Gloria A. Keller*

CHOP: (verb) Means to cut vegetables and meats into small pieces. (noun) It also refers to a tender cut of meat, such as a pork or lamb chop, with the bone attached.

CHOP SUEY is a Chinese specialty invented by Chinese immigrants at the end of the 19th century to please American customers. It's a mixture of chicken or pork strips simmered with chopped vegetables and bean sprouts.

CHORIZO SAUSAGE: Highly seasoned, smoked pork containing red pepper, pimiento, garlic and paprika. Some chorizo are in firm links. Some chorizo when removed from the casing is soft and fluid. Chorizo is found in most supermarkets and Latin American food stores.

CHOWDER: A hearty cream soup which usually, but not always, contains seafood and vegetables.

CHUM SALMON: Also known as "ketas" (in Alaska they are also called dog, fall, chub, or calico), average 8 pounds, and available as fillets, steaks, or whole in fish markets. Chum is the meatiest and firmest of all salmon, having mild flavor, with pink flesh, and lower in fat than most other salmon varieties. Chum can be sautéd, baked, steamed, or poached.

CHUTNEY: "Chutney" is the general name for a relish made of some combination of herbs, spices, fruits and vegetables. The English word came from the Hindustani word *chatni*. When India was part of the British Empire, many British people came to work there in government offices and trading companies or as members of police forces and army units. Some brought their families and settled in India and in what is now Pakistan. Among the Indian foods popular with the British was *chatni*, which they pronounced "chutney." They brought recipes for it back to England. British bottled chutneys now have their own personalities. In India, the chutney is prepared fresh with each meal.

Now, with the proliferation of Indian restaurants, chutney has become well-known in most parts of the world. Chutney can be made and served fresh or it can be preserved in glass jars. Herb chutneys are made with such ingredients as mint leaves, green chilies, ginger, coriander leaves, mangoes and coconut. Onions and yogurt are also sometimes used. Because herb chutneys do not keep well, they are eaten fresh.

Preserved chutneys are made with fruits (pears, apples, apricots and mangoes) or with vegetables, such as carrots, tomatoes and tamarind. These are chopped and cooked with sugar, vinegar and spices. Raisins, dates, almonds or walnuts may be added. Mango and tomato chutneys are among the most popular kinds. Chutneys are served as an accompaniment with curries, stews, poultry, meat, and most vegetables. Some are sweet, some are sour, some are cooked, some are not, and most are spicy. –*Joyce Ackermann*

CIDER: Apples are ground into pulp and the juice is pressed from the pulp. The pulp and juice can be strained to make clear cider. Cider can be sweet or fermented (hard) . Sweet cider is considered the same as apple juice when made at home. When made commercially, sweet cider is pasteurized so it won't spoil. Modern American cider contains preservatives to keep it from fermenting beyond the legal limit.

By English standards, American cider isn't cider at all, but merely apple juice. The alcoholic content of hard cider varies from 2% to a potent distilled spirit called, "applejack," or cider brandy. **In Colonial times**, cider was the national beverage, made so by the abundance of apples, pears, and peaches. In a good year, a single village of forty families might put up 3,000 barrels of cider in the 1720s. As it aged, it became more intoxicating, but at least it was preserved to help people through the long winters. **Nutrition facts:** One cup serving has 117 calories, zero fat and sodium, 29g carbohydrates (10%), .3g fiber (1%), zero protein and vitamin A, 2mg vitamin C (4%), 17mg calcium (2%), .9mg iron (5%), and 295mg potassium. Applejack has 628 calories, zero everything else, and 90g alcohol.

CIDER VINEGAR: A sour liquid made by fermentation of apple cider. See VINEGAR.

CILANTRO: (sil-ant-row) Also known as "Chinese parsley," it is used in Mexican and Asian cookery. It adds a citrusy-spicy flavor to salsas, poultry and fish dishes, dried beans, stir fry recipes. The seed of the cilantro plant is coriander.

CINNAMON: Cinnamon trees belong to the laurel family. Cinnamon is the bark of the tree, dried and rolled up to make a tube. The most prized kinds come from Sri Lanka and China. Most of the cinnamon used in the United States is cassia (imported from Indonesia). Cassia is not considered true cinnamon but most people don't know the difference. Today your cinnamon may be a mixture of both, though you won't see that on the box. The people of Mexico prefer Ceylon's milder flavor. Cinnamon is available in sticks and ground. Cinnamon is not only used in baking, but in some countries it is added to meat, fish, beans, and vegetables. Oil of cinnamon comes from the ripe fruit of the shrub along with some of the bark.

CIOPPINO: A complicated fish stew conceived in California.

CITRON: Originating in northern India, the fruit resembles a grapefruit sized lemon, growing on a small thorny tree. Only the tough, greenish-yellow skin is used, because the pulp is too acid. The fragrant peel is treated in brine to remove the bitter oil and to bring out the flavor. It is then candied and is available in halves or diced for fruitcake, Italian desserts, and other recipes.

CITRONELLA makes lemon grass candles to ward off bugs. See LEMON GRASS.

CITRUS: A native of tropical Asia, this family of fruit trees include oranges, lemons, limes, limetts, kumquats, tangerines, and grapefruit (pomelo). Except lemons and limes, all are eaten raw, and all are made into juice. There are many citrus varieties and hybrids. Some of the more popular are: **Kumquats** are the smallest of the citrus family. Try one. Pop the whole thing in your mouth and chew. Most people only eat the raw skin. **Kings** are a cross between the orange and the mandarin. **Mandarins** are native of China, now grown and imported from Japan. **Temples**, a hybrid of tangerine and orange. **Shaddock** is the original grapefruit and can grow to the size of a watermelon and weight up to 20 pounds. **Tangelos**, a combination of grapefruit and tangerines. According to tradition, the first oranges arrived in the eastern Mediterranean area with Alexander the Great's caravan of 356-323 B.C.   After that, the Arabs cultivated **bitter oranges** as an ornamental plant and as Islam spread to Spain with the Moors it became the famous **Seville** orange of Spain. The modern orange began when at the end of the 18th century a Spanish Catholic priest in Carcagente, near **Valencia,** laid out the first commercial groves. After his success, plantations sprang up on land thought to be worthless. Irrigation made possible a fruit industry which increased tenfold in the next hundred years.   Spain grows the most orange varieties in the world. The Valencias are less popular today because of their seeds when so many seedless varieties are available. See MANDARIN   Watch your supermarket, especially around December, to see newer varieties such as the sweet **Clementines**. **Nutrition facts:** Citrus fruit is a good source of vitamin C, are low in calories, and a good source for potassium and fiber.
www.caltreefruit.com; www.cffa.org; www.florida.com/floridacitrus;

CITRUS PARADISI, also known as "forbidden fruit," was discovered in 1750 on the island of Barbados. We know it as grapefruit. It is thought to be a mutation or hybrid of *citrus grandis,* which had been introduced there in the 1600s.

CLABBER: Clabbered milk is milk that has soured naturally with curds that have not been separated from the whey. Clabber is another word for curdled. It can be used for drinking and baking like buttermilk. Old timers used to let milk sour naturally to make their own buttermilk. Or if milk has become too old and sour, it need not be thrown out but can be used in recipes as buttermilk.

CLAM: There are many kinds of clams found around the world. Soft-shell clams are found from North Carolina to Greenland. **Hard-shell** clams are found along the Atlantic seaboard and the Gulf of Mexico to Texas. In Pacific and Alaskan waters, are a variety of clams, some of which have been transplanted from the Atlantic. One of the most famous Pacific clams is the **Pismo** clam, where the shell can be six or more inches across. The largest Pacific clam, **geoducks**, can weigh up to eight pounds with a three foot neck. Clams, such as the **Little Neck** clams found along the New England coast, are eaten raw. Larger clams are steamed, fried, broiled, baked or made into chowder. Fresh clams are found in coastal stores. Canned clams are available whole or minced, and bottled clam juice. Tips: Clams should be alive just prior to preparing. Soak clams in salt water, sprinkle cornmeal over the clams, the clams will eat the cornmeal, cleaning out their stomachs. For frying and chowder, pry open the clams with a knife; cut out the mussel on each side of the shell; cut off the neck. Discard the neck. If there is any poison in the clam, it will be in the neck. **Nutrition facts:** A 3-ounce serving has 63 calories, 8 calories from fat, .9g total fat (1%), zero saturated fat, 28.9mg cholesterol (10%), 47.6mg sodium (2%), 2.2g carbohydrates (1%), zero fiber, 10.9g protein (22%), 255 IU vitamin A (5%), 11mg vitamin C (18%), 39mg calcium (4%), 11.9mg iron (66%), and 267mg potassium.

THE PISMO BEACH CLAM FESTIVAL

Every mid-October for over 50 years, California's Pismo Beach hosts a Clam Festival. Along with a parade, carnival, games, art show, and entertainment, there are many contests from kayak surfing to sand castle sculpturing. And of course, lots of food. The favorite event is the Pismo Clam Dig, open to kids of all ages. Yes, the clams have been planted with numbers on the shells for prizes of cash and gifts. There's also the Clam Chowder Cook-Off, open to both professionals and amateurs. Prizes are awarded for the best flavor, most creative, and the wildest names. All chowder must be prepared before the contest and brought in crock pots. You can sample and vote on your favorite. One unusual event is the **World's Worst Poetry Contest**, with bad puns, and terrible rhymes. The only rule of the contest is the poem must contain the word "Pismo" and it should be horrible. For details, write: **Pismo Beach Visitors Bureau,** 581 Dolliver, Pismo Beach, CA 93449, or phone (805) 773-4382.

CLARIFY: A means of making liquids and fats pure and clear, by separating the solids from the liquids. Examples are clarified butter and consommé soups.

CLEMENTINE: A small, sweet, seedless tangerine of the Mandarin orange family.

CLOVES: An unopened flower bud belonging to a tree in the myrtle family, originating in the Spice Islands. Prized since Medieval times for taste, scent, and medical properties. Now the main supply comes from islands off the east coast of Africa, Madagascar and Zanzibar. The tree has been transplanted in other tropical countries, such as Brazil and the West Indies. The clove tree is a pyramidal evergreen. The broad shiny leaves are fragrant, as are the tiny yellow flowers, which are seldom allowed to bloom. When the pink buds turn bright red at the base, they're picked and sun-dried to the reddish brown that we know.

During the Han dynasty (207 BC to 220 AD), Chinese court visitors were required to hold cloves in their mouths, while addressing the Emperor. By the fourth century the English had heard about the aromatic flower buds, and traded with the Arabs for them. In the 17th and 18th centuries there were fierce trade wars between the Dutch and Portugese over cloves. The Dutch, owners of the island Ambon, destroyed all the trees on the other islands. Finally, the French managed to cultivate some on their islands.

Cloves are available whole or ground, and used in baking (fruitcake, gingerbread), vegetables (onions, pickled beets) fruits (peaches, pears), and fruit juices (cider). While most of the cloves are used in cooking, a large number are distilled for clove oil. Oil of cloves is used in the home for toothaches, and dentist use it in fillings. Cloves are also used to scent soaps and pot-pourris. In many countries clove tea, made by steeping the cloves in boiling water, is used to cure nausea, and get rid of gas. Chinese use oil of clove to treat diarrhea and hernia. Tincture of clove oil is said to be an effective treatment for athlete's foot.

CLUB SODA: Club soda is carbonated water. It makes whatever it is combined with fizzy. It also has other uses far removed from food. It works to remove certain stains because the bubbling action floats the stain particles to the surface where they can be wiped up.

PRESERVE THE PAST FOR THE FUTURE
by Echo Ann Lewis

Wait - don't drink that club soda! Remember the yellowing, tattered treasure map handed down to you from your grandfather? Or the letters from you grandmother, who, when she was ten, wrote to her big brother in the United States and told him all about their daily home life back in Ireland? If you want to keep those pieces of paper for long enough to give to your children some day, you can help keep them from yellowing any further or crumbling with age by washing them in a solution made up of club soda and a few other essential ingredients. Here are the instructions and the materials you'll need in order to preserve the past for the present and the future.

Materials needed

1. One quart of club soda, available in grocery stores.
2. Milk of magnesia liquid or tablets, available in grocery and drug store.
3. A plastic, aluminum, enamel, glass or stainless steel pan about ten inches by fifteen inches, and two and a half inches deep.
4. White blotting paper, found in stationery stores.
5. Paper towels.

Preparing the solution

1. Remove the cap from a quart bottle of cold club soda.

2. Drop in two teaspoonsful of milk of magnesia liquid or two crushed milk of magnesia tablets.
3. Replace the bottle cap and shake the closed bottle gently to mix the ingredients evenly.
4. Put the bottle back in the refrigerator. The solution will be stronger if kept cold.
5. After ten minutes, take the bottle out and shake it gently again.
6. Put bottle back in the refrigerator.
7. After ten more minutes, take the bottle out and shake it gently again.
8. Put bottle back in the refrigerator.
9. After ten more minutes, shake gently again for the third and last time. This should dissolve any white powder left in the bottom of the bottle.
10. Allow the bottle to sit undisturbed in the refrigerator for at least thirty minutes or until any undissolved powder settles to the bottom of the bottle.

Treatment Procedure

1. Pour the clear solution carefully into the pan.
2. Place the papers to be treated in the solution one-by-one. Gently press each sheet of paper fully into the solution before adding the next sheet.
3. Let the papers soak for at least twenty to thirty minutes. Do not soak for more than an hour or two. That would be harmful to the papers.
4. Raise and lower the papers three or four times to make sure they all get soaked with fresh solution.
5. Remove the sheets from the pan and allow the excess solution to drain away. The solution left in the pan can now be thrown away.
6. Let the sheets dry in the air (you could put them on a clean screen) until they are just damp.
7. Now place the sheets of paper one-by-one between sheets of blotting paper.
8. On top of the blotting paper, place one or two heavy books, so the sheets dry flat. Change the sheets of blotting paper now and then, if necessary.

When the papers are completely dry, your job is done, and your treasure map or those special letters of your grandmother, are ready to be enjoyed and treasured by another generation to come. How does this work? It's in the chemistry. Papers become yellow and aged when they contain acid or are stored with other papers containing acid. The University of Chicago developed the magnesium carbonate formulae to de-acidify (de-acid-i-fye) papers. The formula contains alkaline to neutralize acid. The paper soaks in alkaline which remains behind after drying to help prevent the development of more acid and more aging.

CLUSTER FIG is native to India and produces an edible fig.

COAT: (verb) "To coat" means to cover food with flour or crumbs prior to sautéing or baking, Coating preserves the inner moisture. The best way to coat is to first dip the vegetable or meat into milk, then into flour, then into a beaten egg, and finally into the crumbs.

COBBLER: A deep dish fruit pie, sometimes without a bottom crust, topped with either a pie or biscuit crust. Also, a cobbler refers to a cold fruit drink with the addition of wine or liquor, and garnished with fruit and mint. "To cobble" meant to patch or put together, which makes sense for the way pies are made.

COCKTAIL: Generally a combination of two or more ingredients, either made with vegetables or fruits or alcoholic beverages. Also an appetizer made with cut up vegetables, fruit, and/or seafood served chilled. The origin of the word is not known, but first appeared in America in the early 19th century. It may have been a reference to the several bright colors in the tails of many species of male birds.

COCOA: Fruit of the cacao tree are cocoa beans. Cocoa comes from Brazil and Ecuador, but trees are found throughout the tropics, including Africa. The main use for the cocoa bean is cocoa powder for chocolate. The beans are roasted, ground, and the cocoa butter removed. The beans are ground again into cocoa powder. Cocoa butter is mainly used in making candy and pharmaceutical products. See CHOCOLATE. www.sacofoods.com www.nestleusa.com

COCONA is from South America, an orange colored fruit, sour pulp with many seeds, used to make preserves and jelly.

COCONUT: Tree is native to Malaya, but transplanted to all tropical and many subtropical parts of the world. Coconut seems to have been in the Mediterranean area early, brought by Arab sailors who found it on the island of the Indian Ocean, where it had traveled from Southeast Asia. Coconut is **not a nut, but a fruit**. The outer green husk fruit can grow to 18-inches in length and 8-inches in diameter. After the husk is removed, the inner brown shell contains white meat and a milky liquid. Ripe coconut meat is removed in chucks to be eaten raw or shredded for cooking. Unripened coconut meat has about the same consistency of set gelatin, and is used for making coconut milk. The liquid can be enjoyed as a fresh, cool beverage, or used in recipes.
Coconut meat is also dried to make copra. Pressing copra removes the oil for making soap, margarines, and as a cooking oil. Fresh coconut is available the year around. Shredded coconut is available canned or packaged in bags. **The spelling is coconut, not cocoanut.** Don't be confused. **Nutrition facts:** A ½ cup of shredded coconut meat has 142 calories, 114 calories from fat. 13.4g total fat (21%), 11.9g saturated fat (59%), zero cholesterol and sodium, 6.1g carbohydrates (2%), 3.6g fiber (14%), 1.3g protein (3%), zero vitamin A, 1mg vitamin C (2%), 6mg calcium (1%), 1mg iron (5%), and 142mg potassium. A ½ cup of coconut oil has 940 calories of which 471% is saturated (corn oil has about the same calories, but only 69% is saturated).

COCO PALM, native to South Florida, produces a smooth, white or purple cotton-like pulp eaten fresh.

CODDLE: To cook food in a covered pan by bringing water to a boil and then removing from the heat to let it stand until the desired consistency. This is a common way of cooking eggs.

To cook coddled eggs, cover eggs in water. Bring to a rolling boil. Turn off heat and let eggs stand for 20 minutes. It takes the guesswork out of boiling eggs. You'll have perfect hard cooked eggs every time.

COD FISH: There are many varieties of cod (Pacific cod, gray cod, true cod, treska) in both the North Atlantic and North Pacific waters. Cod was once so plentiful off Cape Cod as far back as 1640, Massachusetts sent 300,000 dried codfish to market. Scrod, a young filleted cod, was one of the first original New England dishes. Cods come in all sizes from less than two pounds to forty pounds. Cod is available fresh, salted, frozen, canned. The meat is white, mild tasting, and easy to digest. It can be prepared by frying, poaching, baking, steaming and broiling. Cod cooks quickly, timing is important not to overcook. In stews and chowders, add cod during the last 10 minutes of simmering. Cod is low in calories and fat, a good source for protein, and has some iron, calcium and B vitamins. From the liver we obtain cod-liver oil. A teaspoon of this oil provides 92% of vitamin A and 112% of vitamin D. It is suggested if you take a multivitamin, not to take cod- liver oil, because it might raise levels of both vitamins above safe limits. **Nutrition facts:** A 3-ounce serving has 70 calories, 5 calories from fat, .6g total fat (1%), .1g saturated fat (1%), 36.6mg cholesterol (12%), 45.9mg sodium (2%), zero carbohydrates and fiber, 15.2g protein (30%), 34 IU vitamin A (1%), 1mg vitamin C (1%), 14mg calcium (1%), .3mg iron (2%), and 351mg potassium.

COFFEE: Originating in Abyssinia (now Ethiopia), these tropical plants are now grown throughout the tropic regions of the world. According to legend, a goat herder noticed his goats acting frisky after eating some berries of a certain bush and tried them himself. Once the man got a taste for them, there weren't many left for the goats. Coffee bushes were first cultivated in Arabia. Brazil is the largest grower of coffee, but other Central and South American countries depend upon coffee as a major part of their economy.

The plants do best in a hot moist climate at about 4,000-foot elevation. When the bean turns red, it is time to pick. All picking must be done by hand to make sure that none of the green beans are mixed in. The red skins are removed, and the beans are allowed to dry in the sun for three weeks. Two more layers of skin are removed before the beans are roasted. There are two types of coffee: **"arabica,"** which is grown in high altitudes and the most expensive, and **"robusta,"** which is cheaper and has more caffeine than arabica beans. A cup of brewed coffee has no calories, about 100 milligrams of caffeine, is a diuretic, may cause calories to burn faster, and can cause heartburn. Contrary to rumor, strong coffee will not sober up a drunk person. And in Great Britain, they drink as much coffee as tea.

ROASTING COFFEE FOR FLAVOR

Gourmet coffees tend to be roasted darker than commercial, brand name coffees. The more common descriptions are:

Cinnamon Roast is a light cinnamon-brown color and has a nut-like flavor.
American Roast has an even, chestnut brown color.

Full City Roast is a dark brown in color and contains no traces of oil on the bean's surface.
Vienna Roast is also a dark brown but with a small amount of oil on the surface of the beans.
French Roast is very dark brown and has large amounts of oil on the surface of the beans.
Italian Roast beans are almost black, with a large amount of oil on the surface and can have a
   strong burnt or bitter taste.

If your parents are adventurous and like the smell of freshly roasted coffee, home roasting
equipment is available at some specialty coffee stores. *--Coffee Development Group*

COFFEE CREAMER: 1) a small jug holding cream. 2) A nondairy product in powder or liquid
form that substitutes for cream in coffee. It's usually made from corn-syrup solids but has the taste
of cream.

COHO SALMON: Also known as "**silvers**" (in Alaska they are also called **red, Jack, hoopid,**
and **blush**), average ten pounds, and are available as fillets, steaks, whole, and smoked in fish
markets. Although a bit higher in calories than most other salmon, coho has low oil content. When
cooked it is necessary not to overcook. The flesh is mild-tasting, and it maintains its orange-red
color throughout cooking. There is a white flesh variety. Cohos can be broiled, baked, poached, or
grilled.

COLA: The evergreen cola tree originated in tropical Africa. It has small, petal-less, yellow
flowers, and produces a seed pod that contains 4 to 15 reddish brown seeds (cola nut). The seeds
smell like roses, but the taste is extremely bitter. A bitter syrup is made by boiling the seeds in
water. The syrup is used in both the beverage and drug industries.

There are 125 cola species, all growing in the rain forests of tropical West Africa. Only two species
are used commercially. Both are now cultivated in the West Indies, Brazil, India, and Sudan.

According to an early Coca-Cola ad, Henry Stanley may never have found Dr. Livingstone, if his
native bearers had not chewed the cola nuts. When first chewing on the nuts, the flavor is bitter,
but it deepens with chewing, and the aftertaste is sweet. The nuts have three times as much
caffeine as coffee. They act not only as a stimulant, but also as a breath freshener. They are widely
used during religious fasts.

Cola beverages contain some caffeine, but not as much as coffee or tea. The main ingredient in a
bottled soft drink is water. Along with the cola syrup are added herbs, spices, natural and fruit
extracts, oils, color or caramel, preservatives, sugar (in diet drinks, a noncaloric sweetener is
substituted), and carbon dioxide gas, which is forced into the liquid just prior to sealing. Sodium
and potassium are also found in colas and come naturally from the water supply. Caffeine from
these nuts is used for respiratory and cardiac stimulation. It is used in nonprescription pain
remedies and energizers. Carbonation in soft drinks, heightens the caffeine effect, thus it is used for
headaches, hangover, and to settle queasy stomachs.

COLA DRINKS: LIQUID CANDY

In 1997, carbonated soft drinks accounted for more than 27% of Americans beverage consumption. This means on an average every man, woman, and child drank more than 18 ounces of soft drinks a day. Kids start drinking soda pop at a remarkably young age, and consumption increases through young adulthood. By the time the average kid is 12, boys drink 28 ½ ounces and girls average 24 ounces a day.

Regular soft drinks provide youths with hefty amounts of sugar and calories. Both regular and diet sodas affect the intake of various minerals and vitamins. Diet drinks which provide no calories or sugar, constitute only 4% that is consumed by boys and 11% by girls. Carbonated drinks account for the single biggest source of refined sugar intake for kids. The U.S. Department of Agriculture (USDA) recommends that active kids eating a daily diet of 2,200 calories should not eat more than 12 teaspoons of sugar a day. Yet, boys consumes 34 teaspoons a day from soda pop and girls average 24 teaspoons. Lots of soft drinks means lots of sugar which means lots of calories. While many nutritionists state that soft drinks and other calorie-rich, nutrient-poor foods can fit into a good diet, this isn't true for young teens.

In 1996 a survey found only 34% of boys and 33% of girls consumed the correct number of daily servings of vegetables as recommended by the USDA Food Guide Pyramid, 11% of fruit for boys and 16% for girls, 29% of dairy for boys and 10% for girls, and few kids met the recommended amounts of grain and protein foods. As teens grow older they double and triple their consumption of soda pop and cut their consumption of milk, fruit juice and other healthy beverages. In 1976 kids drank twice as much milk as soda pop, in 1996 this figure has reversed, now kids drink twice as much soft drink as milk. All this means while kids' calories and sugar go up, important vitamins and minerals go down.

The problem is not so much what happens in the teen years, as what it will mean later in life. Obesity, osteoporosis (especially in women), tooth decay, heart disease, kidney stones are just some of the problems that could occur from the high calorie-sugar teenage diet. It's not necessary to totally eliminate soft drinks and other high calorie foods, but it is necessary to limit your intake and increase your intake of more healthful foods of beverages. Condensed from an article by Michael F. Jacobson, Ph.D. "How Soft Drinks are Harming Americans' Health" Executive Director, *Center for Science in the Public Interest*

COCA-COLA and COKE

Coca-Cola was born on May 8, 1886 in Atlanta, Georgia by pharmacist Dr. John Styth Pemberton, in a brass pot in his backyard. Dr. Pemberton took his new product down the street to Jacobs' Pharmacy where it was sampled and placed on sale for a nickel a glass. It is unknown whether carbonated water was added by choice or by accident.

The name was coined by Dr. Pemberton's bookkeeper, Frank M. Robinson, and he wrote it out in his own unique script, which is still used today. The new soft drink was advertised in the newspaper and soon was available all around Atlanta. Dr. Pemberton didn't realize the potential he had created and just prior to his death he sold his business to Asa G. Candler.

Mr. Candler's flair for merchandising boosted sales to a point where he liquidated his pharmaceutical business. With his brother, John, Frank Robinson, and two other associates they formed their corporation named "The Coca-Cola Company" with $100,000. As the business grew, the first plant outside of Atlanta opened in Dallas, Texas in 1894. The following year, two more plants were opened, one in Chicago, the other in Los Angeles. By 1895, Coca-Cola was available in every state and territory of the United States.

At this time the focus of sales were soda fountains in drug stores and variety stores. In 1894, in Vicksburg, Mississippi, Joseph A. Biedenharn started to bottle Coca-Cola in the rear of his store and sold cases to plantations and lumber camps up and down the Mississippi River.

It was Benjamin F. Thomas and Joseph B. Whitehead of Chattanooga, Tennessee who secured exclusive bottling rights from Mr. Candler to the entire United States. The familiar bottle was designed by Alexander Samuelson in 1915, an employee of the Root Glass Company of Terre Haute, Indiana. It was thought he designed it after the popular hobble skirt of that time. In 1919, an Atlanta banker, Ernest Woodruff and an investment group purchased the company from Mr. Candler for $25-million. Under Mr. Woodruff direction, he created many new merchandising concepts such as the easy-to-carry-home six-bottle pack. Probably the most major objective he achieved was to place Coca-Cola in the hands of thirsty sports fans by venders.

Coca-Cola is now bottled in countries around the world. It actually started in 1900 by Mr. Candler's eldest son, Charles, when he took a jug of syrup with him on a vacation to England. But it wasn't until 1920 before the first European bottler began operating in France. By the outbreak of World War II, Coca-Cola was bottled in 44 countries.

Now bottled in nearly 200 countries, producing millions and millions of servings per day, the Coca-Cola system has successfully provided a moment of refreshment for a small amount of money.

Yes, the history of Coca-Cola is quite a story from the very early beginnings of Dr. Pemberton backyard brew to today's creation of the pleasure to hundreds of millions of people every day. If you have the opportunity to visit Atlanta, you will want to visit the **World of Coca-Cola Museum** with interactive displays and 1,200 Coca-Cola artifacts dating from 1886. At the end of the tour you can visit a 1930's soda fountain and sample Coca-Cola products of the future. The museum is located at 55 Martin Luther King Jr. Drive on the corner of Central Avenue next to Underground Atlanta. *–Coca-Cola Company* www.coca-cola.com

COLANDER: A large, holey, footed utensil used for straining coarse food or pureeing vegetables. Can also be used as a drainer for pasta and such.

COLBY CHEESE: Made from whole milk, deep yellow, a mild, softer variation of cheddar. Begun by Alfred Crowley's dairy in Healdville, Vermont in 1824. Delicious sliced or in cooking.

COLD CUTS are another name for sandwich meats. Meats which have been cured, spiced, smoked, baked, boiled, and/or corned. Examples: bologna, salami, corned beef, liverwurst, and pepperoni.

COLESLAW: At its simplest, it is uncooked, shredded cabbage mixed with a mayonnaise or salad dressing. Recipes vary. Other ingredients could include carrots, onions, celery, pickles, and/or bacon. It was first mentioned in American Dutch cooking and later imported to England. The name comes from the Dutch "*koolsla*," meaning cabbage salad.

COLLARDS: Also called, greens and similar to kale, collards are a member of the cabbage family. Unlike cabbage, collards can grow in hot climates, hence, are found mostly in the southern United States. Boiled with ham or bacon, collard become "soul food." The rich juice, called "pot likker" needs only to be soaked up by cornbread and served piping hot. **Nutrition facts:** A ½ cup serving has 29 calories, zero fat, 18.6 sodium (1%), 6.6g carbohydrates (2%), 3.4g fiber (14%), 1.5g protein (3%), 3,097 IU vitamin A (62%), 22mg vitamin C (36%), 27mg calcium (3%), .2mg iron (1%), and 157mg potassium. www.littlebeanproduce.com

COLONIAL COOKING:

WHAT EVERY COLONIAL COOK HAD TO KNOW

Those early colonial cookbooks were filled with terms and measures that are probably unfamiliar to you. If you are fortunate to find one of these old recipes, see if you can figure it out.

The cook's life wasn't easy. Things that you take for granted, such as butter, had to be washed before it was used because there was no refrigeration. Butter was preserved with salt, so the washing rinsed out the salt and also made it palatable. Also, sugar came in lumps and had to be pounded before it could be measured and used. Today, suppose your mother said,

"Johnny, hurry up and eat your cree, because I need your help with the searce. Also you need to remove some potash from the stove to make a pearl ash for tomorrow's cake and clean the hoop. For dinner you have to help me with the forcemeat. If you help me, I will make your favorite flummery for dessert."

Would you eat your cree? How about putting ashes from the stove into a cake? What the heck is flummery? All sounds "yucky," doesn't it?

GLOSSARY OF TERMS

Cree: Grains, boiled to become a porridge.

Flummery: A jellied dessert, flavored with either orange-flower water or rose water.

Forcemeat: Finely chopped meat seasoned with herbs, used for stuffings or made into meat balls.

Hoop: Cake batter was poured into a deep ring (hoop) made of wood (later of iron) to be baked in an open hearth. Hoop was also know as "garth."

Isinglass: The air bladder of sturgeon fish was dried into sheets and made into a gelatin. Isinglass was used as a clarifying agent.

Lively Emptings: In the bottom of a beer barrel was a yeast sediment used in place of beaten eggs.

Pearl Ash: A leavening made from potash that was combined with sour milk. Some cookbooks spelled it "pear lash" or as one word, "pearlash."

Sack: Imported white wine from Southern Europe.

Saleratus: Refined potash. Today equal amounts of baking soda can replace saleratus in recipes.

Searce: A sieve used to remove sugar lumps and impurities from flour.

Even more confusing were measurements. Every kitchen had a scale, hence items like eggs and flour were weighed. Eggs were small and ranged from eight to twelve eggs per pound. The same goes for flour. It could be anywhere from 3 to 4 ½ cups per pound. Today, some bakers still use weights to measure certain ingredients. George Washington enjoyed a cake made by his wife, Martha. Here is the recipe just as written. Can you make it?

WASHINGTON CAKE

One Pd of Sugar, five Eggs beat light - and separate - Three quarters of a Pd of butter, one pint of milk - a tea spoonful of Pearlash and one and a half Pd of flour, one nutmeg - one Pd of currants. That's it! No mixing or baking instructions. Either you knew how to do it, or you didn't. And what about that one nutmeg? Throw it in whole or grate it? Was it to be large, medium or small?

GLOSSARY OF MEASUREMENTS

Butter the size of an egg = ¼ cup
Butter the size of a walnut = 2 tablespoons
Coffee cup = 1 cup
Dash = 1/8 teaspoon
Dessert spoon = 1 ½ teaspoons
Dram = 3/4 teaspoon
Drops, 20 = ¼ teaspoon liquid
Gill = ½ cup
Lump = 2 tablespoons (butter)

Pinch = 1/8 teaspoon
Pint = 2 cups
Pound of eggs = 8 to 12 eggs
Pound of flour = 3 to 4 ½ cups
Pound of sugar = 2 to 2 ½ cups
Quart = 2 pints
Salt spoon = ¼ teaspoon
Scruple = about ¼ teaspoon
Teacup = 3/4 cup
Tin cup = 1 cup
Tumblerful = 2 cups
Wineglass = ½ gill or ¼ cup

Activity

Open up a cookbook. Find your favorite cake and write the recipe in colonial terms. Make copies for your friends.

COOKBOOKS IN HISTORY

AN 18th CENTURY COOKBOOK

Today's cookbook is easy to read, with ingredients you know and with concise instructions. This was not the case in early day America. In **1772**, a cookbook titled, *the Frugal Housewife, or Complete Woman Cook*, was published and sold by Edes and Gill of Boston. Paul Revere, silversmith, made the printing plates. The book was first published in London and written by **Susannah Carter** of Clerkenwell. The advertising stated: "Any person by attending to the instructions given in this book, may soon attain a complete knowledge in the art of cookery." Read the following biscuit recipe from Carter's book and see if you can understand it:

COMMON BIFCUITS.

"Beat up fix eggs, with a fpoonful of rofewater and a fpoonful of fack, then add a pound of fine powdered fugar, and a pound of flour ; mix them into the eggs by degrees, with an ounce of coriander feeds ; mix all well together, fhape them on white thin paper or tin moulds, in any form you pleafe. Beat the white of an egg, and with a feather rub them over, and duft fine fugar over them. Set them in a an oven moderately heated, till they rife and come to a good colour ; and if you have no ftove to dry them in, put them into the oven at night, and let them ftand till morning."

No, there are no misspelled words. In the 18th century spelling a "f" is used in place of a "s." Earlier a "long s" was used in initial and medial positions in words. This long "s" was shaped like an italic "f", which later became a "f."

There's one ingredient you probably do not recognize, the ingredient "fack." In Carter's book there are many words not found in today's cookbooks. Look over the following words and see how many you can match with the statements:

1. Collaring	a. Diluted condensed milk
2. Fack	b. A food coagulation of wheat flour
3. Flummery	c. To preserve, such as with salt
4. Giam	d. Roll meat up and tie with string
5. Potting	e. A highly season stew
6. Ragouts	f. Milk curdled with wine or cider
7. Sillabubs	g. Jam

ANSWERS: 1 d, 2 a, 3 b, 4 g, 5 c, 6 e, 7 f.

COMBINE: (verb) to mix unlike ingredients.

COMPOTE: A combination of fresh, canned and/or dried fruits, gently cooked in their own juices; served hot or cold as a dessert. A compote dish is a fruit bowl on a stem.

CONCH: The tough meat of this spiral-shelled shellfish which is found in southern waters. It's a prized food of Floridians and Italians. In Florida it's called "conk" and in Italy it's "*scungilli*." The meat must be tenderized by pounding, by use of a tenderizing liquid or powder, or by parboiling. Conch can be sautéd, stewed and made in chowders. Like all shellfish, fresh conch must be alive prior to cooking, and after cooking must be refrigerated and consumed within two days, or frozen.

CONCH APPLE is from the West Indies, also known as sweetcup, produces small yellow-green grape flavored fruit that is made into a beverage.

CONDENSED MILK: Whole milk concentrated by evaporating part of the water. Sweetened. condensed milk has sweetener added. Read the labels carefully. See EVAPORATED MILK.

CONDIMENT: The addition of seasonings to enhance the flavor of food, such as salt, pepper, herbs, and spices. Also the term for sauces such as mustard, ketchup, and steak sauce.

CONFECTION: Candy or any sweet dessert.

CONFECTIONARY: Candy maker or store selling sweets of all kinds.

CONSERVE: A preserve made with a combination of fruits and nuts.

CONSOMMÉ: (con-soo-may) A clear soup made from meat and/or vegetable broth.

COOKBOOKS: See COLONIAL COOKING and Author's names

COOKBOOKS:

OLD AND NEW, FUNNY AND FAR OUT

Something about a well-worn cookbook speaks to us of everyday history and lifetimes of work, sometime ending in joy - sometime in tears. Not every recipe turns out a success. Cooking is hard work. Even if your dinner came in a package that you heated up, someone somewhere spent hours preparing it before you got it. Before that, someone planted the ingredients and harvested them and preserved them. The growing and processing, cooking and packaging of any food takes time and toil. We should all remember that and appreciate how our good food comes to us.

In the beginning there were no cookbooks. There were no recipes - except in the cook's memory. One cook taught another, the way silversmiths taught the working of silver or printers taught printing to an apprentice.

In 1998, an early cookbook published in the United States - *Amelia Simmons' American Cookery 1796*, sold at auction for $22,000. Today people love cookbooks, cherish them, collect them and use more of them than ever before. The average household in 1950 might have five cookbooks but today we don't even stop to count them we have so many. Rick Ellis, food stylist for movies such as *The Age of Innocence* has a collection of nearly 5000.

In 1896 Fanny Farmer published *The Boston Cooking-School Cookbook,* the first one with precise directions. Thus level measurements became standard. No more pinch of this and pat of that. Cooks could expect the same results each time by relying on exact measures every time.

Maria Parloa, at the Boston School of Cooking was considered the first authority on culinary matters in America with her *1884 New Cook Book*. It was Miss Parloa who taught Miss Farmer. Marion Cunningham did a complete revision of The Fannie Farmer Cookbook and is also the author of *The Fannie Farmer Baking Book.*

When automated canning and bottling changed the scene of American cooking, new methods inspired new cookbooks. Brand name foods such as Jell-O came with their own cookbooks, some of which sell for over $100 today.

The first cookbook for children was Mary Frances' *First Cook Book*, the illustrated adventures of kitchen appliances that teach a young girl how to cook. Later (1946) came *A Cookbook for Girls and Boys* by Irma S. Rombauer.

This is the age of abundant food. There are cookbooks for everything and more being printed every day. Some recipes have changed very little over the years, but the constant change of new foods and new technologies for cooking them keep things always in a state of newness. Some people claim "new is better." That depends. It's all a matter of taste. But there is a cookbook somewhere for every taste.

Activity

Maybe you should take an inventory of your family's cookbooks to see if you have something valuable. Remember "valuable" doesn't always means money. Grandma's floury cookbook may not sell at auction but it may be precious to your family. Listed below is just a sampling of the kind of cookbooks you can expect to find at the library or in a personal collection.

EARLY COOKBOOKS:

1727 *The Compleat Housewife* (reprinted in Williamsburg, Virginia 1742)

1746 *The Art of Cookery Made Plain and Easy* by Hannah Glass, London, England

1772 *The Frugal Housewife, or Complete Woman Cook* by Susannah Carter, printing plates by Paul Revere, published by Edes and Gill, Boston (See article: An 18th Century Cookbook with recipe and quiz.)

1796 *American Cookery* by Amelia Simmons, Hartford, Connecticut (First in America)
Books of Cookery by Martha Washington (First First Lady)

1824 *The Virginia Housewife* by Mary Randolph. Most popular early cookbook in the South)

1828, *Seventy-five Receipts, for Pastries, Cakes and Sweetmeats* by A Lady of Philadelphia, Munroe and Francis, Boston

1896 *Ye Gentlewoman's Housewifery* by Margaret H. Hooker, Dodd Mead and Co., New York. Newly released in 1981 by American Review, Lake Scotia, New York under the title: *Early American Cookery*

1972 *The Attic Cookbook*, A Treasury of Old Recipes by Gertrude Wilkerson, Penguin Books, 1972

For information on where you might view these early cookbooks, contact the **American Antiquarian Society,** Salisbury Street and Park Avenue, Worcester, Massachusetts, phone (508) 755-5221. They published the *Bibliography of American Cookery Books* 1742-1860. It might be available at your library. Also the Library of Congress (Washington, DC), historical societies and university libraries have early cookbooks in their collections.

ETHIC COOKBOOKS:

The African Cookbook, Tastes of a Continent, Jessica Harris, Simon and Schuster, New York 1998

Elephant Walk Cookbook, Longteine De Monteiro and Katherine Muestadt (CAMBODIAN CUISINE from the nationally acclaimed restaurant) Houghton-Miffin, Boston, 1998

The Frugal Gourmet on Our Immigrant Ancestors, by Jeff Smith, William Morrow and Co., New York 1990. Jeff Smith has compiled recipes from almost every region around the world, except Italy and China, as he has separate cookbooks for tho se countries.

The Melting Pot (Ethnic Cuisine in Texas), The University of Texas, San Antonio, Texas 1977. A collection of 27 ethic or cultural groups. Available from the Institute of Texan Cultures. Phone (210) 458-2300

SPECIALTY COOKBOOKS:

Complete Book of Spices, Dorling-Kindersley, Ldt. London 1991
Rare Bits, Unusual Origins and Popular Recipes, Ohio University Press, Athens, Ohio 1998
The Bordello Cookbook by Jo Foxworth A cookbook loaded with colorful tales of yesterday's "men's clubs," along with 157 delicious recipes.
The Foraging Gourmet, Katie Letcher Lyle, Lyons and Burford, New York 1997
More Recipes from a Kitchen Garden, by Renee Shepherd and Fran Raboff, Ten Speed Press, Berkerly, California 1995. More than 300 recipes you can make from your own vegetable and herb garden. Phone (888) 880-7228.
The Breakfast Book, by Marion Cunningham, Alfred A. Knopf, New York 1988
Corn Recipes from the Indians by Frances Gwaltney, Cherokee Publications, Cherokee, North Carolina 1988
One Bite Won't Kill You by Ann Hodgman, Houghton Miller, Recipes for picky kids with refrigerated biscuits, blocks of Velveeta and cans of onions rings.
The World's Worst Cookbook, by Mike Nelson, Cool Hand Communications, Boca Raton, Florida 1993. Author Mike Nelson gathered recipes for the worst dishes anyone ever ate. Recipes had to be actual dishes someone prepared and ate, not made up for a joke. A sampling of recipes include: Weiner Water Soup, Liver Meatballs, Sugar Cooked Liver, Ultimate Fish Loaf, Tuna Marshmallow Supreme, Creamed Kraut Macaroni and Spam Hawaiian, Hamburger Jell-O, Chocolate Chili, Castor Oil Cookies

CRAWLING CUISINE COOKBOOKS

Bugs may sound yucky to you, but many people around the world eat insects. It may not be such a bad idea to eat these crawling creatures before they eat you. Find out by reading a bug book or two at your library. Most have recipes.

Bugs for Lunch, by Margery Facklam, Charlesbridge Publishers, Inc., Watertown, MA 1999
Entertaining with Insects, by Ronald L. Taylor and Barbara S. Carter., Order from Salutek Publishing Company, P.O. Box 696, Yorba Linda, CA 92885
The Eat a Bug Cookbook, by David George Gordon, Ten Speed Press, Berkeley, CA 1999 This book offers 33 ways to cook grasshoppers, ants, water bugs, spiders, centipedes, and their kin. Some of the chapters include: The Benefits of Eating Bugs, Beware of Bad Bugs, Cooking with Crickets

REGIONAL COOKBOOKS:

Good Earth by Clyde LeBlanc, Houma, Louisiana,

Cajun-creole Cooking, by Terry Thompson, HP Books, Los Angeles, California 1986
Chef Paul Prudhomme's Louisiana Kitchen, 1-800-457-2857.
The Central Market Cookbook, by Phyllis Pellman Good and Louise Stoltzfus, Good Books, Intercourse, Pennsylvania 1989
The Sharpsteen Museum Cookbook (Napa Valley Specialties) Calistoga, California 1985
Fredericksburg Home Kitchen Cook Book, Fredericksburg Texas 1982
Aunt Bee's Mayberry Cookbook by Ken Beck and Jim Clark, Rutledge Hill Press, Nashville, Tennessee 1960
Log Cabin Cooking (Pioneer Recipes and Food Lore) by Barbara Swell. Available, phone (309) 827-0428.
Cooking the Wright Way by Melba Hunt, Kettering-Moraine Museum, Dayton, Ohio. Phone (937) 299-2722 for information. Author Melba Hunt gathered recipes from the world famous Wright Brothers starting with their cooking experiences at Kitty Hawk, North Carolina. Orville was usually the cook, Wilbur the dishwasher. Both were deeply interested in cooking and even quite fussy about how it was done.
Jane Austin Cookbook, by Maggie Black and Diedre L. Faye, Chicago Reporter, 1995
Authors Maggie Black and Diedre L. Faye have gathered recipes from 1750 to 1820 and have modernized them for present day kitchens. It is believed to be a collection of recipes Jane and her characters might have eaten, compiled in manuscript form, as cookbooks were then unknown.

POPULAR KITCHEN COOKBOOKS:

Better Homes and Gardens New Cookbook, Meredith Press
Woman's Day Encyclopedia of Cookery, Funk and Wagnalls
The Redbook Cookbook, McCall Publishing Co.

For a catalog of old and new cookbooks write to: **Jessica's Biscuit**, 1-800-878-4264

COOKIE: A small cake or sweeten biscuit made with a variety of ingredients and formed into different shapes. Cookies are shaped by several methods: 1) baked like cake and cut into squares; 2) rolled and cut out in shapes; 3) molded by hand; 4) pressed through a hollow tube or cookie press; 5) dropped onto cookie sheets in small mounds called "drop" cookies.

MONSTER COOKIE

In 1996, a cookie company in New Zealand made a giant chocolate chip cooked that measured more than 81 feet across. That's bigger than the width of a basketball court!

Activity: Make your own monster cookie by making a recipe of chip cookies and using a pizza pan, pat it out into one large cookie instead of many small ones. Then it can be cut into small pieces, after baking, which saves time. Or you can decorate it like a cake and present someone with the whole cookie as a gift.

THE PHANTOM BAKERS OF BARNABY STREET

by Echo Ann Lewis

Nine-year-old Becky Petroski plopped onto steps outside their brick apartment building on Barnaby Street. "I'm bored," she complained, flipping her copper pigtails over her shoulders.

Becky's sister Deborah looked up from her crossword puzzle. "What'll we do?"

"Well, I'm going in for a cookie," Becky decided. "That'll help me think."

In the kitchen Becky flung a cupboard door open. No cookies in sight. Becky fetched a stool, and climbed up. She fumbled in the dust on top of the cupboard, reaching behind the waffle iron. No luck. "There's only one thing to do," she muttered. "I'm going to make my own."

"What is going on in here?" Deborah cried, wandering into the kitchen several minutes later. "You're covered with flour!"

Blinking away the flour-dust on her eyelashes, Becky said, "There isn't a single cookie in this whole apartment, so I'm making some."

"You don't even know how to cook!" Deborah yelped.

"I'm going to learn right now," Becky declared. She nearly dropped the egg bowl as she tired to pick the end of one blue hair ribbon out of it.

Deborah sighed, pushing back her perpetually-sliding glasses. "Come on, I'll show you a really easy recipe for raisin cookies.

"Hooray!" Becky cheered. "And I've got an idea!"

"Where's Mom's other apron?" Deborah asked. "Here, tie it for me, will you?"

"Let's wrap up some of the cookies and take them down the street to Anthony. He's sick again."

"Hey," Deborah said, pulling the raisins out of the cupboard. "And what about Miss Taylor? I'm sure she could use some cheering up."

"And Mr. Walker," Becky added. "He hardly ever gets treats. Let's pool our allowances, get a bunch of raisins and stuff, and do a whole secret project!"

"All right!" Deborah cried, scrounging through drawers for wrapping paper and scissors. "This will keep us busy the whole summer. Hello, secret project and goodbye, boredom!"

Buried in mountains of flour and raisins, Becky hardly noticed the next day fly by. At the end of the week, she burst into the apartment and raced to the kitchen.

"Look, Deborah, look!" she cried, waving the current copy of The Barnaby Street Blurb. Our secret project has made the news!" She slapped the neighborhood newspaper onto the table.

Deborah pushed her glasses back and read the headlines. "'Will We Ever Discover the Identity of Those Phenomenal Phantom Bakers of Barnaby Street?'"

COOKING SCHOOLS: Cooking schools are available in every major city. Some only accept adults, but will let kids attend by special invitation. At the same time, many cooking schools are open to all ages. Finding a cooking school might take a little work on your part, since not all advertise. Check with your chamber of commerce, and school and college home economics departments. Also some supermarkets and cookware stores offer cooking demonstrations.

For excellent demonstrations turn on your television to a Public Broadcast Station (PBS). Many PBS stations have cooking shows. One of the best is the *Cooking Secrets of the CIA*. The show is produced by the Culinary Institute of America (CIA) at their New York School, usually with students attending. For a bit of fun, view the Dessert Circus and Yan Can Cook. There are also cooking shows on cable TV, the Food Network and some on Home and Garden Television.

If you plan to grow your own garden, there are two shows, one on PBS, the Victory Garden and the syndicated show, Rebecca's Garden. Both usually have some food tips or a cooking demonstration. See also Martha Stewart Living. A sampling of cooking schools follows: See SO YOU WANT TO BE A CHEF.

THE CULINARY INSTITUTE OF AMERICA

The oldest culinary college in the United State, the Culinary Institute of America, was founded with 50 students in 1946. Today, more than 2,000 full time students, representing every state and several foreign countries, are enrolled in their various programs. The Institute offers two programs culminating in an associate's degree, one in culinary arts and one in baking and pastry arts. Each program is 21 months and stresses hands-on instruction. Students study a number of subjects, including skills development, American and international cuisines, nutrition, seafood cookery, hospitality (appetizers, buffets and reception foods), sanitation, culinary French, meat cutting and fabrication, wines and spirits, purchasing and table service.

Baking and pastry arts students will study topics such as baking math and science, baking, pastries, breads, desserts, ice carving, and *pâtisseries* (advanced desserts). Each 21 month program requires students to complete an 18 week paid externship at an Institute approved food service establishment. Prior to graduation, students will also work in the college's four award-winning, student- staffed public restaurants. The Institute also offers two programs with a bachelor's degree, one in culinary arts management and one in baking and pastry arts management. Each program requires an additional 17 months of study. The Institute has a continuing education program with a number of hands-on courses that run from one to 30 weeks and are offered to professional cooks, bakers, and others experienced in the industry. More than 120 chefs and instructors from 20 countries make up the college's faculty, of which, one-third are certified as Master Chefs.

The main facility is located in New York's Hyde Park in the Hudson Valley. The 150-acre campus includes Roth Hall that houses three restaurants, 36 kitchens and bakeshops, a computer lab, a language lab, and administrative offices. The Conrad N. Hilton Library holds one of the largest collections of culinary publications in the United States with more than 50,000 valumes for student use. There's also a video viewing center, and a 150-seat Danny Kaye Theater where cooking and baking demonstrations are held. The General Food Nutrition Center houses another restaurant, a state-of-the-art kitchen, classrooms, and a nutrition resource center. The J. Willard Marriott Continuing Education Center has cake and pastry shops, lecture halls, and is the home of the Shunsuke Takaki School of Baking and Pastry.

In California's Napa Valley, the Institute's second campus is located at Greystone in Saint Helena. This facility has a Mediterranean restaurant, kitchens, bakeshops, auditorium for cooking demonstrations, and continuing education in food, wine, and hospitality fields. On the campus is a two acre organic garden for students to study the link between the farm and the kitchen. Tours of the Institute are available. Call for days and times. The Hyde Park campus offers a one week **introduction course for high school students.**

For **middle grade** students, Chef Wayne Almquist offers classes in Hyde Park during the summer and on fall weekends. The Institute also produces a television series, Cooking Secrets of the CIA and is aired on many PBS stations. For more information write to **The Culinary Institute of America,** Admissions Department, 433 Albany Post Road, Hyde Park, NY 12538-1499. Or you can phone (800) CULINARY (285-4627) or (914) 452-9430. -- *Mary K. Cowell*

GALLERY 37 CENTER FOR THE ARTS - CULINARY ARTS

This course offers students an opportunity to work in a commercial-style kitchen and learn skills to prepare for job opportunities in restaurants. Emphasis is on traditional language and basic skills. This training program is for Chicago Public School students ages 14 to 21. **Gallery 37 Center of the Arts**, 78 East Washington Street, Chicago, IL 60602 (312) 744-8925; www.gallery37.org

HOMECHEF COOKING SCHOOLS

This school offers demonstrations and workshops. HomeChef offers all courses to both kids and adults. One of the highlights is their "assistant program" where students arrive 90 minutes prior to class and help the teacher prepare for the class, thus offering more hands-on skills.

CORTE MADERA: Town Center (415) 927-3191
NEWPORT BEACH: Fashion Island (949) 718-0114
PALO ALTO: 451 University Ave. (650) 326-3191
PASADENA: 538 South Lake Ave. (626) 744-3399
SACRAMENTO: Loehman's Plaza (916) 487-3191
SAN FRANCISCO: Laurel Village (415) 668-3191
SAN JOSE: Westgate Mall (408) 374-3191
WALNUT CREEK: 1604 Mount Diablo Blvd. (925) 943-3191

Contact their main office for a brochure: Judith Ets-Hokin, **HomeChef Cooking Schools**, 5725 Paradis Drive, Suite 360, Corte Madera, CA 94925 (415) 927-3290 www.homechef.com

KENDALL COLLEGE

Students complete an intensive culinary program, given by chef instructors, leading to bachelor of arts and science degrees, as well as entry positions in baking, health care, and catering. Degrees are also offered in culinary and hotel/restaurant management. A two week summer camp is available to students 16 years and over. Christian DeVoe, **Kendall College School of Culinary Arts**, 2408 Orrington, Evanston, IL 60201, (847) 866-1300, www.kendall.edu

KROGER SCHOOL OF COOKING

Invites guest chefs for classes. Besides regular classes, there are Culinary Kids Camps, Father's and Sons Tailgate Partys, and Mother- Daughters teams for both cooking. "Cooking with Bernard" airs weekends on Channel 33 in the Atlanta area. Bernard T. Kinsella, **Kroger School of Cooking,** 12460 Crabapple Road, Alpharetta, GA 30004, (770) 740-2069.

THE SUSTAINABLE KITCHEN

Two-hour classes are held in various locations in the San Francisco Bay area. Small classes offer lots of hands-on instruction. Most classes held in restaurants and supermarkets. Some begin at the grocery store, purchasing the ingredients for that class. Field trips are also given to farms and dairies. **Chef Laurel K. Miller**, 2030 Felton Street, Berkeley, CA 94705, Phone (510) 665-1446.

SUR LA TABLE

This kitchenware store not only has hard-to-find cookware and tools, but most of the stores also have hands-on demonstration classes for both adults and children. The stores offer a variety of themes including Asian, Italian, Indian, Mexican, South American, Southwestern, canning, BBQ, desserts, holiday and much more. Classes are taught by visiting and local chefs, cookbook authors, and Sur La Table staff. There are free and fee classes that range from $40 to $250.

Scottsdale (AZ), Kierland Commons (480) 998-0118
Berkeley (CA), 1806 4th St. (510) 849-2252
Los Gatos (CA), Old Town Center (408) 395-6946
Newport Beach (CA), Corona del Mar Plaza (949) 640-0200
San Francisco (CA), 77 Maiden Lane (415) 732-7900
Santa Monica (CA), 301 Wilshire Blvd. (310) 395-0390
Chicago (IL) 52-54 East Walton St.
Manhasset (NY), 1468 Northern Blvd. (516) 365-3297
Dallas (TX), 4527 Travis St. (214) 219-4404
Houston (TX), River Oaks Shopping Center (713) 533-0400
Salt Lake City (UT) 10 North Rio Grande St.
Arlington (VA) 1101 South Joyce St. (703) 414-3580
Kirkland (WA), 90 Central Way (425) 827-1311

Some of the stores offer Cooking Camps for the Junior Chef, run two to five days, ages eight to eighteen. Some stores also have shopping and/or cooking tours, such as San Francisco's Chinatown or a Farmers' Market.

Stores are also in Chandler (AZ), Pasadena (CA), Thousand Oaks (CA), Denver (CO), Washington (DC), Cincinnati (OH), Las Vegas (NV). Plano (TX), McLean (VA), and Seattle (WA). For more information write: **Sur La Table**, 1765 6th Avenue, South, Seattle, WA 98134-1608, phone (800) 243-0852 or www.surlatable.com

WESTLAKE CULINARY INSTITUTE

Two hour classes are limited to fifteen kids, providing lots of active participation. Additional classes are offered to both parents and kids. Sylvia Rieman, 4643 Lakeview Canyon Road, Westlake Village, CA 91361, (818) 991-3940.

COQUILLE: (cock-eel) A shell or a shell shaped dish, with food served in it, with or without a sauce, covered with bread crumbs and/or cheese, and placed under a broiler to brown.

CORIANDER: Also known as cilantro, it's a member of the parsley family. Both leaves and seeds are used in recipes. The seeds are sold as coriander, and the leaves are sold as cilantro. Coriander is native to India and the Mediterranean region. The seeds have a taste like a mixture of aniseed, cumin seed, and orange. Unlike some spices, the longer the seed is kept, the more fragrant it becomes. The leaves are mixed into salads, made into salsas, and cooked with beans. The crushed seeds are used in baking, puddings, candies, soups, coffee, and cheese. The ground seeds are mixed with other spices to make curry. The seeds can be sugar-coated and are sometimes found in the center of jawbreakers. It's a wonder anyone bothered with coriander because all parts of the green plant are said to smell like bed bugs. But when ripe the fruits are pleasantly aromatic.

CORKWOOD: A member of the nightshade (potato and tomato) family, is a major source of a seasickness remedy. *Scopolamine* comes from the leaves of the Australian tree. The tree in the wild grows to 40 feet; in cultivation it is kept to shrub size. *Atropine*, also from the leaves, is used in dozens of present day medical treatments.: .

CORN: Also called maize, corn first grew wild as a Mexican grass. Under Aztec cultivation, corn made possible the great civilization from the Aztec to the Zuni. The United States has been called "cornhusker to the world" because nearly half the world's corn is grown here. Columbus and his men were the first Europeans to eat corn. As a curiosity, the explorers took some seeds back to Old world. Within a hundred years, it was grown in almost every European country.

If not for corn, American settlers could not have survived. Today, without corn millions of people and animals would starve. There are thousands of varieties of corn. Kernels come in all colors, including black and mixed. The world's **foremost corn specialist, Walter C. Galinat**, botanist at the University of Massachusetts, actually bred a red, white, and blue corn for America's 1976 Bicentennial. Galinat says that over centuries of cultivation, Native Americans created the plant as we know it now.

Corn is never better than when eaten fresh off the cob, but kernels can be removed for eating the same way as any vegetables. Dried kernels are ground into cornmeal and corn flour for making cornmeal mush, breads, pancakes, hush puppies, and tortillas. Dried kernels can also be soaked and cooked like dried beans.

Available fresh only during warm growing season, corn is on market shelves canned, dried, or frozen. Oil, sugar, syrup, liqueur, wine, and beer can be made from corn and/or corn stalks. Almost everything an American touches, including cloth, paper, cleaning products, and fuel, has been influenced by corn or corn products. **Nutrition facts:** One corn-on-the-cob has 43 calories, 5 calories from fat, .6g total fat (1%), zero saturated fat. cholesterol, and sodium, 9.6g carbohydrates (3%), 1.4g fiber (5%), 1.6g protein (3%), 142 IU vitamin A (3%), 3mg vitamin C (6%), zero calcium, .3mg iron (1%), and 136mg potassium. See also, "Corn the Golden Grain" by Robert Rhoades, *–National Geographic*, June 1993. www.state.nj.us/agriculture www.coloradocorn.com

NATIVE AMERICAN CORN

From the arid valleys of the Southwest to the woodland clearings along the Atlantic seaboard, Native Americans lovingly tended fields of corn, a crop that had no rival as a food source. Their names for it were reverential, often meaning "Our Mother" or "Our Life" and in truth this remarkable member of the grass family supported their world. Legend termed the plant a divine gift to humans, but the story of corn is more complex than that.

In Middle America, around 5500 BC, Native Americans found the way across a great economic divide, leaving behind their total dependence on wild foods and penetrating the mysteries of seed, water, and soil. Corn eluded domestication for perhaps another thousand years, and for a long time it hardly advanced beyond the version that grew in the wild.

Wild corn was an unprepossessing plant with a single bare, inch-long ear holding about fifty small, loosely attached kernels. But around 1500 BC, the novice farmers learned how to create vastly superior hybrids, endowed with multiple ears, protective husks, and cobs that secured row upon row of big, energy-rich kernels.

So superb was corn as a food source that although the Native Americans developed many varieties of the tamed grass over the millennia, they never domesticated another cereal plant. Today this Native American grain is often called "Indian Corn" and generally refers only to varieties of corn that produce ears with multicolored kernels, and people often decorate their homes with the colorful ears in the fall. *--Bernice Erickson*

CORNDOGS: Frankfurters placed lengthwise on a long stick, coated with cornmeal batter and deep fat fried until golden brown.

CORN, DRIED: Americans have been drying corn since the Native Americans taught them how long ago. To be cooked later, it has to be soaked in water overnight before boiling. In Pennsylvania it is still done among farming people.

"When I was a child, I remember my Aunt Agnes making her own dried corn. On the back of her wood-burning cast-iron stove she had large flat pans similar to cookie sheets where she spread out the corn kernels. The low heat from the stove dried the corn slowly. As Aunt Agnes went about her business, she would give the corn a stir now and then so it would dry evenly. When the kernels had dried, she stored them in a special white linen bag she made herself. The full bag would be about the size of a pillow case. This she tied with a rope and hung in the summer kitchen out of the reach of mice. When she needed corn to cook, she would untie the bag and scoop out enough. The corn would stay dry and never mold all winter long." *–Luella Bassett Ulmer*

CORNED MEAT: A process where meat is preserved in brine made up of salt, sugar, and saltpeter. Salt is the preservative. Sugar stops the salt from hardening and the saltpeter preserves and in some cases intensifies the color.

CORNISH HENS: Also known as Rock Cornish Game Hens. They are small chickens, under 2 pounds, used for roasting and broiling.

CORNMEAL: Dried corn kernels ground into coarse meal. Packaged cornmeal comes in white, yellow, and blue. Use white and yellow for cornmeal mush, polenta, cornbread, and muffins. Do you like purple pancakes? If so, try making them with blue cornmeal. Blue cornmeal is higher in protein than yellow, and when cooked, turns lavender in color. **Nutrition facts:** A ½ cup serving has 253 calories, 10 calories from fat, 1.1g total fat (2%), .2g saturated fat (1%), zero cholesterol and sodium, 53.6g carbohydrates (18%), 5.1g fiber (20%), 5.9g protein (12%), 285 IU vitamin A (6%), zero vitamin C and calcium, 2.9mg iron (16%), and 112mg potassium.

STONE GRIND YOUR OWN CORNMEAL

You will need:
Dried corn kernels
Large flat stone (as large as a dinner plate)
Smaller rounded stone (as big as you can hold)
Bowl for holding ground cornmeal

1. Place a handful of corn on the large stone.
2. With the smaller stone, crush, and grind the kernels into powder.
3. Place the fine powdered cornmeal in the bowl, leaving the larger pieces on the flat stone as you add more kernels.
4. Use this ground powder in your cornmeal recipes.
The finer the grind, the nicer the cornmeal will be for baking and cooking.

CORN OIL: A vegetable oil obtained from corn. It has no taste or odor, is used it frying, salad dressings, and baking. Corn oil has no cholesterol; however, it has about the same calories and fat as animal fats. One tablespoon has about 120 calories.

CORN PALACE:

THE WORLD'S ONLY CORN PALACE
by Pam Morgan

You're traveling along Interstate Highway 90 in South Dakota and a billboard reads:

From Ear to Eternity
We're All Ears!
Ear-chitecture
American I-corn

You try to figure out what that means, and ahead another billboard, reads:

To Ear is Human, To Visit, Divine
Corn-ceptural Art
Prepare to be A-maize-d!
Be A-maize-d!

A light goes on in your head, corn! They are talking about corn. Maybe there's something on the radio, you think. You find a radio station and the announcer says, "*You're listening to radio station K O R N from Mitchell, South Dakota, home of the World's only Corn Palace, home of the Kernels high school football team, and the Kernels mascot, a giant ear of corn called Cornelius.*"

Sounds like a strange place, but your curiosity has got the best of you, so you turn off the freeway to downtown Mitchell. On north Main Street a giant Moorish-designed building with minarets, turrets, and kiosks appears. It's the Mitchell Corn Palace.

The building is decorated from top to bottom with native grasses, grains, and a variety of colored corn. It's beautiful! A brochure tells the story. The first Corn Palace was built in 1892 and was home of the first "Corn Belt Exposition" with a display of products from the rich Dakota soil. By 1905 the building was too small for the event, a larger building was built. Again in 1921, the building was judged too small, and a new building was constructed. Every year new decorations are added.

The decorating starts in midsummer with thousands of bushels of colored grains and corn, and is completed for the Corn Palace Festival in September. This 10 day festival features top- name entertainment leaning toward western-country entertainers within the Corn Palace building. On Main street is a carnival with a midway, games, and food concessions. For more information on **The Corn Palace**, telephone: 1-800-257-CORN (2676), or write: Mitchell Area Chamber of Commerce, P.O. Box 776, Mitchell, SD 57301.

CORNSTARCH: A starch obtained from corn and used in powder form to thicken gravies, sauces, and puddings. Cornstarch substitute: 2 Tablespoons all purpose flour equals I Tablespoon of cornstarch. www.cornstarch.com

CORN SYRUP: A clear syrup obtained from cornstarch, available both light and dark. Corn syrup is used as a sweetener in desserts, preserves, soft drinks, and pancake syrups. Corn syrup substitute: 3/4 cup sugar plus ¼ cup water equals one cup corn syrup. For dark corn syrup, use 3/4 white corn syrup plus ½ cup molasses to equal 1 cup dark corn syrup. www.karosyrup.com

CORNUCOPIA: Originally a goat's horn filled with drink or food in an endless supply. Also called a horn of plenty. Today a horn-shaped basket is the centerpiece on many Thanksgiving tables, overflowing with fruit, vegetables, and grains as a symbol of prosperity.

CORTLAND APPLES are a large, mostly dark red apple with distinctive red stripes showing on lighter skin areas. Cortlands are an all-purpose apple with fine white flesh, mild, and tender taste.

COTTAGE CHEESE: It's the fresh curd from either whole or nonfat milk, with cream added, and is available salted and unsalted. It is eaten cold by itself, in salads, in gelatin salads and used for cooking.. Some cooks prefer it over ricotta in lasagna. Some brands are sweeter and creamier than others so try more than one kind to fine one you like. .

COSTMARY: An herb, also known as "sweet Mary" and "Bible leaf," it has a sweet, lemon minty fragrance and is used in teas, cakes, meat and poultry. Use only a little; the flavor is very strong. The name Bible leaf originated from people who use the long leaf as a bookmark in their Bible.

COW: Better know as beef. Also an ice cream drink.

HAVE A COW

Some kids use the phase "Having a cow" as someone having a fit or being extremely upset. In some parts of the country the same phase refers to an ice cream soda. A brown cow is root beer and vanilla ice cream. A purple cow features grape-flavored carbonated beverage. And, of course, there's also the orange cow (with either vanilla or orange sherbet) and the strawberry cow (best with strawberry ice cream).

To make the original vanilla cow, place a scoop of vanilla ice cream in a tall glass. Fill the glass about 3/4 cup of club soda and stir to blend the ice cream and the soda. Add another scoop of vanilla ice cream and enough soda to fill the glass. Serve immediately with a long spoon and a straw.

What other kinds of cows are there? Have you invented a special cow? You do not need to restrict the flavor of ice cream to vanilla. How about a chocolate cow made with chocolate ice cream? Have a cow!

COWPEAS: See BLACKEYE PEAS

COUSCOUS (koos-koos): A Moroccan and North African staple, couscous is processed wheat similar to bulgur wheat but finer. Not a grain, but a pasta made from several grains, it is light in flavor and texture, and absorbs the flavor of foods. In Morocco it is eaten with the fingers. It is made in a special pot called "couscousier." The pot which is very expensive, steams the couscous on a rack. Couscous can be made without this special pot, but care must be observed, as it will burn easily. When the African slaves came to Louisiana, they brought with them couscous and ate it for breakfast. Soon cornmeal replaced couscous and today the cornmeal version is still enjoyed by the Cajuns and they call it, "*couche couche*" (pronounced koosh-koosh).In supermarkets, semolina is often sold as couscous. Couscous is added to stews as a thickening agent, made into a pudding with raisins and spices, made into pasta, baked in bread, and fed to young children as farina. **Nutrition facts:** A ½ cup serving has 100 calories, no fat or sodium, 20.8g carbohydrates (7%), 1.3g fiber (5%), 3.4g protein (7%), zero vitamins A and C, 7mg calcium (1%), .3mg iron (2%), and 52mg potassium.

COYORE PALM produces small, red sweet fruits edible from Puerto Rico.

CRAB: The crab is a crustacean with a shell and ten legs. There are more than 4,500 species of crabs, some as small as one inch, while others can grow up to 12 feet wide from claw to claw. An Alaskan king crab might reach across and touch both walls of a small room. Most common in Atlantic waters are blue crabs, and stone crabs in Florida. The Pacific yields Dungeness and snow crabs. A soft shell crab is a blue crab which has shed its shell. Fresh crabs are found in coastal regions the year around. Cooked and frozen crabs are available in most supermarkets. Fresh crabs must be cooked and refrigerated as soon as possible, and eaten within two days, or frozen. Crab meat is also available canned. Most of the meat is found in the legs and claws, but the sweeter meat is found in the head. Cooked crab meat is used in salads, chowders, casseroles, and crab cakes. **Nutrition facts:** A 3-ounce serving of crab meat has 84 calories, 10 calories from fat. 1.1g total fat (2%), .2g saturated fat (1%), 75.7mg cholesterol (25%), 283.2mg sodium (12%), zero carbohydrates and fiber, 17.5g protein (35%), zero vitamin A, 2mg vitamin C (4%), 86mg calcium (9%), .7mg iron (4%), and 318mg potassium.

CRAB APPLE: A small, very sour apple, wild or cultivated. Too sour to eat, the hard yellow apple is used in jellies and made into canned apple rings, mainly for garnishing other foods. The trees produce breathtakingly beautiful white and pink blossoms. More often today the trees are planted for their beauty than for their apples.

CRAB CAKES: These little fried cakes are made by adding onions, eggs, bread crumbs and seasonings to crab meat.

CRACKER: It is the name for crisp, thin bread, unleavened or leavened. The name comes from the cracking sound when the crunchy bread breaks.

CRACKER CRUMBS: Crackers crumbled to a coarse powder are used for coating meats and vegetables before frying. Graham cracker crumbs are made into pie crust. Cracker crumbs can also be used for topping casseroles and other dishes.

CRACKER JACK is the brand name of a packaged caramel popcorn.

"The More You Eat, The More You Want"

Possibly the best thing that happened to popcorn was the invention of Cracker Jacks in 1871. It happened in Chicago at a humble popcorn street stand. A German immigrant, Frederick William Rueckheim first combined molasses, peanuts and fresh popcorn. From 1871 to 1899, he and his brother Louis sold Cracker Jack in bags at his street stands. The caramel corn sold so fast that Rueckheim had to build a factory to keep up.

Sales increased after the 1908 song *Take Me Out to the Ball Game* gave them a nice bit of free advertising. In the early 1900s the free prize was tucked inside the bottom of the red, white and blue boxes. Today those prizes have become collector's items and the caramel corn tastes just as good. Cracker Jack and his dog Bingo have appeared on the box since 1918, though the company now belongs to Borden since 1964. For more information, read Alex Jarammillo's book *Cracker Jack Prizes* published in 1989 by Abbeville Press.

CRACKLINGS: Our pioneer forefathers and mothers used every bit of the butchered animal that could be used. Cracklings are an example of their creativity and necessity. When fat is rendered from a butchered hog by melting it off in an oven, the skin is left over. That skin is melted until the last drop is gone and the result is a crisp brown chip, somewhat like thick potato chips. They are called cracklings because of the snap when they are broken.

CRAISINS: Dried cranberries, which resemble raisins, thus the name.

CRANBERRY: First known as "crane berries," these red berries were found wild in boggy parts of the northern United States. Most of the cranberry crop comes from Massachusetts, the rest are cultivated in Rhode Island, New Jersey, Wisconsin, Oregon, and Washington. In Sweden, their cranberries are called "lingonberries" and are much spicier than ours.

There are more than a hundred different known varieties of cranberries, many with interesting names such as **Potter's Favorite, Budd's Blues, Centennial** and **Aviator**, which conjure up fascinating pictures of earlier days. Four varieties account for most of the cranberries produced commercially:

Early Black is the standard variety in Massachusetts and New Jersey. A small berry which is blackish red when ripe, usually during the first two weeks of September.
Howes - A standard late variety named for their discoverer, Eli Howes, in 1843 and found in Massachusetts and New Jersey. Howes are oblong in shape, larger than early blacks and ripen later. The fruit turns medium red when ripe.
Searles - Predominant variety in Wisconsin and the most productive of all cultivated cranberries. Berries are deep red when ripe, usually in late September.
McFarlin - Named for Charles Dexter McFarlin of South Carver, Massachusetts, who was the first commercial West Coast cranberry grower in the late 1800's. Now the principal variety in Washington and Oregon,. A nearly oblong berry which ripens late and produces a deep red color.

Cranberry bogs are naturally wildlife friendly with bluegills, herons, turtles, and frogs. Some growers make them even more so by building nesting boxes for bluebirds and kestrels, and erect osprey towers. Cranberries are cooked into a sauce, added to meats and salads, baked into breads and cakes, as well as cookies and pies.

Look for fresh cranberries in the store around mid-October. To freeze fresh berries, just pop a package in the freezer. Canned and frozen cranberries are available year round in supermarkets.
Nutrition facts: A ½ cup of cranberry sauce has 209 calories, zero fat, 40.2g sodium (2%), 53.9g carbohydrates (18%), 1.4g fiber (5%), .3g protein (1%), 28 IU vitamin A (1%), 3mg vitamin C (5%), 6mg calcium (1%), .3mg iron (2%), and 36mg potassium.

PUCKER BERRY
by Bernice Erickson

Ever tasted a red berry that makes your mouth pucker? Long before the Pilgrims came to America, a wild red fruit speckled the marshy areas along the north Atlantic coast each fall. The native Wampanog people who lived there called this berry *ibimi* (ih-bih-mee) or "bitter berry." When the

Pilgrims came to America, the natives shared the *ibimi* with them. The berries helped the newcomers survive the long hard winters, because of their rich vitamins A, C, and B, which are necessary to prevent illnesses.

The Native American had many uses for these berries. One dish they relished was *pemmican*. It was a mixture of dried venison, fat, and *ibimi* pounded into a pulp, patted into cakes and placed on rocks in the hot sun to bake.

The blossoms of the *ibimi*, that bloom in early summer, reminded the Pilgrims of the neck, head, and beak of a European bird, the crane. The settlers started calling *ibimi*, "crane berry," later cranberry. When the cranberries blossom, the small flowers are a pale delicate pink, but so numerous they give the appearance of dusting powder on the green vines. The Pilgrims started bogs near their settlements. Laws in 1773 were written to prevent anyone picking them. Anyone caught picking more than a quart of cranberries before September 20th were fined a dollar and the loss of their cranberries. The settlers had to pick on private land. This was to protect the wild berries so they would grow back each year.

Native Americans used the precious fruit for cooking, dyeing, and healing. Cranberries were boiled with venison, wild onions, and fat to make their favorite dish. They dyed their blankets, and utensils with the red juices. Mashed unripe berries were used to heal scrapes and sores. The Pilgrim women applied their own culinary know-how in developing sweetened preserves, tarts, and cranberry sauce. As early as 1683, a recipe for cranberry juice was published in the *Compleat Cook's Guide*.

"Put a teacupful of cranberries into a cup of water and mash them. In the meantime, boil two quarts and a pint of water with one large spoonful of oatmeal and a very large bit of lemon peel. Then add the cranberries and as much fine Lisbon sugar as shall leave a smart."

Early settlers enjoyed cranberries so much they thought King Charles II would like them, so they sent him ten barrels of cranberries, two hogshead of samp (cornmeal), and 3,000 codfish to appease his wrath against the coining of the Pine Tree Shillings (America's first money).

Cultivation

Within the next three hundred years, Americans learned to tame the wild berries. The first cranberry farm was started in 1816 along the Massachusetts coast. Through hard work, we have "cranberry farms" all over the nation, and throughout the world. Cranberry farms are made from wild bogs, or marshes. Over hundreds of years, dead plants fall to the bottom of the bogs, pressing down on each other making a spongy layer called peat. Cranberries grow well in this layer because it holds moisture.

Cultivation requires clearing bogs of trees, brush, and the top layer of peat, then adding sand to protect the plants from freezing in the winter. Cranberry farmers dig ditches around the bed for irrigation, spraying the plants when there is a danger of frost, and flooding the plants for harvest. As the farmers became educated, they modernized their equipment. Their work became easier, and they were able to grow more cranberries.

Harvesting

When the cranberries are ripe, about mid-October, crews work in shifts to flood the beds. Water reels, called "eggbeaters," are driven through each cranberry bed. Their spinning reels churn the water, and knock the berries off the vines. The berries float on top of the water, and are ready to be collected. Cranberries are collected by miles of yellow rubberized floating tube, or connected wooden slats, called boom. Workers surround the berries with the boom to coral them in a small space. They use long handled screens, or scrapers, to guide them into a conveyor belt that slants up to an open-bed trailer. As the berries move up the belt, streams of shooting water, and puffs of air remove leaves and sticks, called trash. Tractors pull the trailers to a loading area where the cleaned berries roll up another belt into a truck. The truck is then driven to a cooperative or factory, where they are air dried, and sorted by size. The quality berries are packaged, and shipped to stores.

A CAPE COD CRANBERRY LEGEND

Cranberries came to grow on Cape Cod through the intervention of a white dove. During an argument over whose "medicine" was the most powerful, a Wampanaog medicine man cast a spell and mired the Reverend Richard Bourne in quicksand. In order to settle their differences, the two men then agreed to a 15 day marathon battle of wits. Unable to move, the Reverend was kept alive by a white dove which fed him a succulent berry from time to time. The medicine man could not cast a spell on the dove, and he finally fell to the ground exhausted from his own lack of food and water. The spell on the Reverend was then released. In the course of these events, one of those berries fell to the ground and took root - and thus began Cape Cod's cranberry bogs. -- *Ocean Spray Cranberries, Inc.*

THE WARRENS CRANBERRY FESTIVAL

In late September, the world's largest cranberry festival is held in Warrens, Wisconsin. This three day event includes a pancake breakfast topped with cranberry syrup, a farm market, a cranberry marsh and harvest tour, a tour of the Ocean Spray receiving plant, a guided tour of the Cranberry Expo Museum, art and crafts show, a parade, and lots of cranberry foods.

The farm market offers painted pumpkins, corn husk dolls, cranberry honey, chocolate covered cranberries, craisins (sweet dried cranberries), and cranberries in every way possible.
At the Cranberry Expo Museum (the nation's largest museum dedicated solely to preserving the heritage, methods, and equipment of the cranberry industry) you will view unique machinery designed, built, and used by cranberry growers. One of the highlights in the gift shop is cranberry

glassware. No, cranberries are not added to the glass to give it that rich ruby color - gold is. The festival has a number of contests, some of the highlights include a scarecrow contest, the biggest cranberry contest and a cranberry recipe contest. For more information, write: **Cranberry Expo Ltd.**, 28388 Cty EW, Warrens, WI 54666-9501, or phone (608) 378-4878. *--Peggy Anderson*

CRANBERRY BEANS: In Ohio they are called "shellouts," and are similar to pinto beans, except they are white with red speckles.

CRAPPIE: A small freshwater fish originally found in Middle America, but now in lakes across the country. They grow more than a foot long and weight about a pound. They are best breaded with cornmeal and fried in butter.

CRAWFISH: Also known as crayfish, crawdads, and mudbugs, are found in the fresh water around the world. There are also salt water varieties called "sea crawfish." They look like tiny lobsters and have a similar taste. They are boiled, made into soup, and fried. Eating a crawfish takes on an art form. First twist the tail off the body and suck out the fat and juices of the body. Next remove the shell from the tail and with your teeth pull the meat out of the bottom of the tail. It takes about three pounds of crawfish to feed one person. **Nutrition facts:** One pound, with heads, has 350 calories, 39 calories from fat, 4g total fat (6%), 1.3g saturated fat (7%), 518.1mg cholesterol (173%), 263.1mg sodium (11%), zero carbohydrates and fiber, 72.1g protein (114%), 236 IU vitamin A (5%), 5mg vitamin C (9%), 123mg calcium (12%), 4mg iron (22%), 1,371mg potassium.

MUDBUGS

When the French Acadians lived in Nova Scotia, they became very fond of the delicious lobsters found in the region. When the Acadians were forced from the region, it is said they tied strings on the lobsters and carried them on the long walk to Louisiana. It was a long trip and those poor lobsters lost a lot of weight. When they arrived, the lobsters were sorrowful little things, only a fraction of their original size, about the size of a large bug. The lobsters were released in their new home and given the new name, "crawfish." They made their home in the muddy bayous, but never gained back to their original size. They are affectionately known as "mudbugs" by the Cajuns.
−RSC

CREAM: The fatty part of whole milk. It is obtainable in several fat contents from whipping cream (40% fat) to half-and-half (15% fat). Available both sweet and sour.

DEVONSHIRE CREAM

Before milk was required to be homogenized, milk came with cream floating on top. England's Devonshire cream is thick cream. It's like a cross between butter and whipped cream. Also called "clottted cream."

CREAM CHEESE: If you have eaten cream cheese, you probably noticed it isn't like any other cheese. Strictly speaking, it isn't cheese at all. It is cream dried until it's easy to cut, about like butter. Today's cream cheese is a mixture of sur cream and milk, inoculated with lactic-acid (rennet) producing bacteria to give it the right acidity. Most brands are pasteurized to kill the bacteria as soon as their work is completed. In America, Philadelphia Brand Cream Cheese is the gold standard. French cream cheese can have double or triple the cream content. It is available in various fat contents, including a nonfat version. www.creamcheese.com

CREAM GRAVY: Gravy made primarily with milk instead of water. A typical recipe:

2 tablespoons bacon fat or chicken fat
2 tablespoons flour
1 to 2 cups milk
Salt and pepper to taste

1. After the bacon or chicken has been fried, pour off all but 2 tablespoons of fat.
2. Add flour. Cook and stir until flour is browned.
3. Add 1 to 2 cups of milk gradually, stirring constantly to prevent lumps.
4. Add salt and pepper to taste.

CREAM OF TARTAR: A powder made from grapes. Once mixed with baking soda as a leavening agent. Adding cream of tartar to egg whites makes the whipped whites firmer, and when baked, the meringue tolerates the heat better.

CREAM PUFF: A pastry made with flour, boiling water, butter and eggs; usually filled with a variety of cream fillings; sometimes called "eclairs." Puffs are also used for appetizers and filled with cheese, meat and seafood.

CRÉME BRÛLEÉ: (krehm broo-lay) A French dessert meaning "burnt cream." Called the "world's most perfect dessert" by some, it is made with only five ingredients: egg yolks, whipping cream, sugar, brown sugar and vanilla. It's just custard with a brown sugar cap. In English the same dish is called Burnt Cream. The burning part comes from toasting or caramelizing (not really burning) the top crust after the custard is done. Professionals use a welding torch to do the burning but it can be done in the broiler. Toppings and garnishes can be anything from chocolate to raspberries. Savory types omit the brown sugar topping and use things like roasted garlic, onion, and blue cheese.

CRENSHAW: A large melon, sometimes called cranshaw, with a cream-colored rind, salmon-colored flesh. Available in the late summer to early fall. Ripe crenshaws are juicy and full of flavor with a spicy-sweet taste. They are ripe when the rind is a light yellow to golden yellow color, and a minimum of green.

CRIMINI MUSHROOMS (crim-een'-ee): Most commonly called Italian Brown mushrooms. They are closely related and similar in shape to the agaricus mushroom, but with a darker color that ranges from tan to rich brown, and their flavor is deeper, denser, and earthier. Used the same as agaricus mushrooms. Great sautéd in garlic butter, season with oregano, salt and pepper, and served over pasta with Parmesan cheese.

CRISPS: In England and France, crisps are the same as potato chips here.

CRÊPE: (Pronounced krep or crayp) Delicate rolled hot cakes made with a thin egg pancake batter. Can be served with a sauce, fruit, or filled with cheese. Two popular versions are the Jewish blintzes which are filled with cottage or cream cheese and with fruit. The French version is called Crêpes Suzette and are flamed at the table in a chafing dish.

CROAKER: A small Atlantic Ocean fish that makes a croaking noise from the air bladder. Some fresh water varieties are also available. Croakers can be either fried or broiled.

CROCKERY: earthenware cooking items. **Activity:** Make a study of American made crockery to find out what is still available and collectible. You can start in your own home and the homes of your grandparents and work outward to antique stores and flea markets. For a report, you don't have to buy the pieces, just take pictures of them.

CROCKPOT:

CROCKPOT COOKING

There are two basic styles of crockpots:
     1. A **"slow cooker"** has the heating element on the bottom and no removable crock.
2. **"Crockpots"** have the heating coils around the sides and may have a removable ceramic liner (crock part). Both models have low and high settings. Low is about 200°F and high is about 300°F. Two hours on low is about the same as one hour on the high setting.

Crockpot Tips:
■ When the ceramic liner is hot, add only warm or hot liquids, never ice cold foods, or the ceramic could break.
■ Always unplug the crockpot before cleaning it.
■ Never submerge the electrical pot into water. Yes, the removable ceramic liner may be washed with your other dishes.
■ Never remove the cover just to have a peek. The pot will lose too much heat. Because it cooks at such a low temperature, it takes a very long time to build heat back up. This many affect the cooking time. *--Virginia G. McNear*

CROOKNECK SQUASH: See YELLOW SQUASH

CROISSANT: (kraw-sahn) A French flaky, buttery crescent-shaped roll, leavened with yeast .

CROQUETTE:(kroe-ket) A French word meaning "to crunch." Croquettes are usually made with leftovers, such as poultry, fish and rice. Other versions use fresh ingredients such as eggs, potatoes, and nuts. Croquettes are deep fried and usually served with a sauce.

CROUTON: Bread cut into small cubes, fried in oil and browned in the oven. Seasoned croutons are served with soups and salads, and also used in meat and poultry stuffings. Unseasoned croutons can go into bread puddings.

CROUPION: (kroo-peeon) Well, now you have heard everything! It's the tail end of a fowl–where the tail feathers grow. In Britain it's called "the parson's nose." It is said to be tasty but mostly it is ignored. In American we don't have a name for it, but now you can impress everyone and call it by its proper name or its informal British name, should it come up in conversation. Of course, at Thanksgiving when the turkey is carved, you can always start a conversation yourself by asking, "Would anyone care for the croupion?" –LU

CROW:

EAT CROW!

by Charlotte Shidler

If someone said to you, "Eat crow!" you would probably would have answered, "You eat crow!" No, you probably don't hear that expression much anymore, but if you don't know what it means, you can translate it to mean anything from disgrace to dishonor to shame. On the other hand, you could say,"I'll eat crow if . . ." It's that "if" that could mean anything, such as the day my Cousin Suzie said, "I will catch the biggest fish or I will eat crow."

I can remember that day when Cousin Suzie looked forward to a big fish fry on the banks of the Colorado River. As she prepared for the trip, she dashed in and out of the house talking to herself about cornmeal, lemon, butter, all with a gleam of anticipation in her eye. As it turned out, it was one of those days that Cousin Suzie not only didn't catch the biggest fish, she didn't even catch a small one. So here is her receipe for . . .

SMOTHERED CROW

1 crow
Water
Vinegar
Salt
Pepper
Flour
Garlic
Bacon fat
Worcestershire

1. Young birds are best; the older ones may be tough and strong. Sort as to age, dress the crow and cut in half. Allow one crow per person.
2. Soak old crows about 4 hours in water containing a little vinegar and salt.
3. In a heavy skillet, brown a clove of garlic in 1/4-inch of bacon fat. When brown remove the garlic.
4. Salt, pepper and dust the crow with flour.
5. Brown on both sides, move the skillet to the side of the fire and cover skillet. Cook slowly until tender, adding a little hot water from time to time.
6. Season with Worcestershire sauce and serve.

By the time Cousin Suzie finished eating crow, I asked, "How do you tell an old crow from a young crow." Suzie didn't answer as she slung her creel over her shoulder and departed.

CRUET: (krew-et) A fancy glass bottle for oils and vinegars small enough for use at the table.

CRUDITE': (krewd-itay) The French have a word for everything. This one means the vegetables we slice, dice and cut into strips to go with dips.

CRULLER: (kruh-ler) Made from doughnut dough, cut into strips, twisted and fried. The word comes from the Dutch. The crullers seem to be a Pennsylvania Dutch creation.

CRUMPET: They are similar looking to an English-muffin, but are softer and have many surface holes. First baked on a griddle, split, and toasted.

CRYSTALIZE: In cooking, it means to coat or glaze with sugar. It can also mean to bring sugar to a stage of boiling where it begins to form crystals around the sides of the pan.

CRYSTALLIZED BLOSSOMS

Here's a recipe you can make. All you need are edible flowers, such as violets, roses, auriculas, primrose, or pear or cherry blossoms. Since some flowers can be harmful, be sure and let an adult help you select the blooms.

You will need:
Edible blossoms
Paper towels
Egg white
Small paintbrush
Superfine sugar
Waxed paper

1. Rinse well and gently shake off excess water.

2. Pluck blossom from stems and drain the blossoms on
paper towels.
3. Beat an egg white until it is frothy.
4. With a small clean paintbrush, gently paint egg
white on upper and under sides of the blossoms.
5. Immediately sprinkle superfine sugar evenly on each
painted surface and shake off excess sugar.
6. Place on waxed paper to dry for at least two hours.

Crystallized blossoms make delightful cake decorations.
--T. Marie Smith

CUBE: To cut solids into six equal sides of usually ¼ to ½ inches.

CUCUMBER: (Q-cum-ber) A member of the gourd family, they are native to southern Asia. There are many varieties from finger-long stubby cucumbers to greenhouse varieties two feet long. Cucumbers make a glorious array of pickles and salads, but can be made into soup, braised, or baked. The people of India and the eastern Mediterranean have enjoyed them for 4,000 years. A favorite of Roman emperors, the conqueror Charlemagne brought them to France in the 8th century. The Crusaders carried them home to England in the 13th century. Columbus planted them in Haiti in 1494, and thereafter English colonists planted them as a staple, because they were easy to grow and keep by pickling. Once someone thought to marry vinegar with the cucumber, pickling made cucumbers available to everyone. **Nutrition facts:** Cucumbers are 96% water. A ½ cup serving has 3 calories, zero fat, sodium, and carbohydrates, .2g fiber (1%), zero protein, 56 IU vitamin A (1%), 1mg vitamin C (2%), zero calcium and iron, and 37mg potassium.

CUISINE: (kwiz-een) There are two meanings: French style of cooking, and a name for the kitchen.

CALIFORNIA CUISINE

by Chef Laurel Miller

When you think of California, what comes to mind? Probably beaches, Hollywood and Disneyland, right? But what about artichokes, garlic and dairy products? You might not be aware of it, but California is the nation's leading producer of the above foods. The indigenous Native American tribes of what is now California have always eaten game, seafood and shellfish, in addition to planting corn and beans. These staples found their way to California with migrating tribes from Mexico and South America.

Spanish Specialties

Then came the Spanish missionaries who settled California in the 1700s. When the Spaniards arrived, they brought with them such New World ingredients as squash, peanuts, tomatoes, turkey, peppers, chiles, avocados, chocolate, pineapples and vanilla. They planted the seeds of oranges, olives and grapes, the descendants of which today account for California's flourishing citrus, olive oil and wine industries. The missionaries established ranchos, or cattle ranches, throughout California. Beef became, and still is, one of the top industries in the state. Outdoor cooking methods, such as grilling and barbecuing, were the most common means of cooking meat, and it was a way for relatives and neighbors to socialize and celebrate.

Basque Bounty

Much later in the state's history, Basque (a region in the Pyrenees Mountains of France and Spain) immigrants came to California and became cheesemakers and sheepherders, thus establishing a consumer market for the lamb that California is famous for.

Italian Immigrants

Italian immigrants planted California's first artichoke and fennel plants. Armenian farmers settling in the San Joaquin Valley, grew melons, figs, raisins, and pistachios.

Asian Appetites

During the Gold Rush of the mid-1800's, thousands of Chinese laborers came to California to help build the railroad. Their arrival has an enormous impact upon the food and culture of the state, as they introduced such ingredients as ginger, dried mushrooms, and other vegetables, fruit, herbs and spices. Today, San Francisco's Chinatown has the largest community of Chinese outside of China! Because California is situated on the West Coast of the United States, it has also received a great deal of influence from the rest of Asia. People emigrating from Japan, Southeast Asia and the Pacific Rim all contributed their cultures, cooking methods, and foods, which eventually found their way into California kitchens. Think of sushi; *nuoc nam* (a Vietnamese fish sauce); *udon* (a thick Japanese wheat noodle); stir fry; *pad thai* (a Thai noodle dish); dim sum (Chinese dumplings); woks and bamboo steamers. These words may sound foreign, but to the Californian they mean good eating!

Many Climates for Many Foods

In addition to the "melting pot" of different races and cultures that comprise California's population, there is another reason why this state is famous for it's food. California is unique in that it possesses a variety of microclimates. There are arid deserts, lush valleys, foggy coastal regions, snowy mountains, ancient redwood forests, fertile plains, and a vast coastline. The climate is similar to that of the Mediterranean in that is has a high percentage of sunny days year-round, a cooler coastal climate, dry summers, and rainy winters. All of these factors combine to make California the top-ranking agricultural state in the nation.

Thirty million acres of farmland produce 55 percent of the fruits, nuts and vegetables consumed by the United States. California is also responsible for supplying the U.S. and other countries with beef cattle, wheat, lettuce, strawberries, citrus fruit, and dairy products. The state is also home to many small, independent farmers, many of whom grow organic produce and raise livestock, poultry, fish, and shellfish, and handcraft cheese, bread, olive oil, and other food products.

Organic Farms

Organic farmers grow crops without using chemical pesticides, fertilizer and preservatives. Organic farming emphasizes protection and preservation of the soil, water, flora, and fauna by not using chemicals. Organic farmers are helping to ensure that our food supply remains wholesome and safe to eat. California also boast the nation's toughest standards for growing organic food, which has served as a model for other states and countries, and helps to protect the future of our planet.

So What Is California Cuisine?

With all of these different ingredients from around the world mixed up together in one state, how do we know what "California Cuisine" really is? Quality defines what California cuisine is all about. The freshest produce, meat, fish and shellfish are usually cooked simply in order to highlight the natural flavors of the food. Seasonal ingredients are used, which results in truer flavors and supports local farmers. Simple, outdoor methods of cooking such as grilling, or stir frying and searing meat are preferred. California cuisine emphasizes health. Californians are generally health-conscious and active, and the region's cooking reflects that. Monounsaturated olive oil is preferred over butter and lard, and spicy chiles, garlic, herbs and spices are used in place of rich, heavy sauces. Salsas are also an integral part of California cuisine. Originally used as condiments on the ranchos of the 1800s, today's salsas incorporate fresh fruits and Asian flavors, such as a mango, red onion and cilantro salsa, or a salsa with chiles, avocado, sesame oil and watercress.

CALIFORNIA ON THE MENU

It's not so much about creating a crazy mishmash of flavors, but finding flavors that work together and compliment each other, even if the ingredients used comes from different sides of the world.

APPETIZERS
Kalamata Olives and Fresh Basil

Sushi with Avocado, Cream Cheese and Crab

ENTREES
Fresh Salmon with Soy-Wasabi (Japanese horseradish)
Marinade, with Asian Guacamole

Pasta with Local Goat Cheese,

with Over-Roasted Tomatoes

Quesadillas with Shitake Mushrooms
with Fontina Cheese

Roasted Chicken with Hoisin-Sauce Glaze

Lamb with Cabernet Sauce and Braised Fennel

DESSERTS
Chocolate Torte with Passion Fruit Sauce

CULINARY: (kyoo-lyn-air-y) Similar in meaning to "cuisine," pertaining to cooking and the kitchen. From the Latin, meaning kitchen.

CUMIN: Native to the Mediterranean, a cousin of the parsley family, cumin is a highly prized spice, distinctive in Asian curry powders. In Mexico, it is a key spice for preparing chili dishes and tamales. The small herb rarely grows more than six-inches high. The seed is tiny, with a strong slightly bitter taste. Cumin is used worldwide to spice fish, meats, cheese, eggs, poultry, fruit, vegetables, and breads. Cumin is available as whole seeds or ground; use sparingly. The Romans can be thanked for spreading the popularity of cumin all over Europe. By 1250 Crusaders have brought cumin home for medicine and table use. Medieval cooks bragged about roasted peacock flavored with cumin seeds. Ancient scholar Pliny said that eating cumin seed would make a student look pale and scholarly whether he had been studying or not. Most children are not fond enough of the flavor to bother with such a deception. You will hear it pronounced like "kum-in" or "koom-in" or "kyoo-min." Either way is all right.

CUPCAKE: A cake batter baked in muffin tins and frosted. www.tastycake.com.

CURDS: Aged milk separates into whey and curds. The curds are the coagulated, acidic lumps which become the basis of various cheeses.

PLEASE PASS THE CURDS
by Linda Huntington

Hold it! Before you dig into that macaroni and cheese with a fork, think about what you're doing. Do you really want to put that cheese into your mouth? Cheese, you say? Why, that's the basis for half the good things in life -- pizza and cheeseburgers and . . . Maybe. But do you know what it is?

Everyone knows cheese is made from milk, right? Right. But did you know the milk is clotted? Before that sticks in your throat, you should realize "clotted" is a less tasty-sounding way of saying coagulated -- or curdled. You might prefer to think of it as merely "separated."

Coagulation is actually the first step in cheese making. Special bacteria (yes, there are good bacteria) is added to milk, along with a chemical taken from the lining of a calf's stomach. That chemical is called rennin extract. When this strange brew is heated and stirred, a chemical reaction takes place -- the milk is broken down into solid chucks (curds) floating in a liquid (whey, pronounced way).

Do you suppose Little Miss Muffet was taking a break at the cheese factory when she was "eating her curds and whey?" After the milk has coagulated, the whey is poured off and the curds are cut into smaller pieces. The curds are then salted and pressed into molds. The molds are stored to allow the cheese to age or ripen. During the aging process, bacteria along with yeasts and molds from the milk react chemically with each other to produce special flavors and aromas. It can take from several weeks to several years for cheese to ripen. The longer the time, the more zing its flavor has. That is the way cheese is usually made. Sometimes the process is changed to produce different qualities in the cheese. For example, instead of pouring whey off the coagulated milk, the curds may be dipped out. Perhaps the salting is delayed until later in the aging. Cheese makers may add more mold or bacteria during ripening to change the flavor or smell or looks. Sometimes there might be no aging at all. These differences in the cheese making process are the reason there are so many kinds of cheese.

There are about twenty varieties of cheese today, although they are known by more than 400 labels.

Many are named after the town in which there were first made. For example, Limburger cheese was produced in **Lemberg, Belgium** – and Cheddar (you guessed it) in **Cheddar, England**. The kinds most popular here in the United States are Cheddar, creamed cottage or cream cheese, Swiss, and processed. Cheddar is a hard, dyed yellow cheese. It can be either mild or sharp tasting, depending on how long it ages. Unlike other cheeses, Cheddar is baked before it is molded and pressed. Cottage and cream cheese are white. They are not pressed into molds, but simply drained in cloths -- so they are very moist. There is no aging for them. As the names suggest, creamed cottage cheese and cream cheese both contain cream.

Swiss cheese is known for its holes. While the cheese is being made, gas bubbles are formed by the clotted milk bacteria. The cheese is so thick and sticky that the bubbles can't escape. So they are captured in the form of holes. The same bacteria that makes the bubbles give the cheese its unusual nutty taste. **Processed cheese is an American idea**, first produced in 1904. It is made by grinding and melting together several different kinds of cheese. The blends are then run into glass, plastic containers, or foil-lined cartons.

Cheese has been around a long time. One legend says it was discovered by an Arabian trader who started out on a long journey across the desert. He put his milk supply into a bag made from a sheep's stomach. The heat of the sun and the rennin in the sheep's stomach caused the milk to break down into curds and whey. At the end of the day, he drank the liquid whey to quench his thirst -- then he ate the curds. The first cheese! Whether the legend is true or not, cheese has been made and enjoyed for thousands of years. **The Bible records cheese as food 1000 years B.C.** Cheese was included in the supplies aboard the Mayflower when it sailed for America. And cheese is still popular today.

Why? Kids eat cheese because it tastes good. Mothers and other adults like it because it's loaded with good things -- milk protein, important minerals including calcium, vitamin A, niacin, and B vitamins riboflavin and thiamin. All those things grow big, strong bodies full of energy. In spite of the strange path it follows from the cow to the finished product, cheese is as healthful as a glass of milk. See CHEESE and individual names of cheeses.

CURE: To preserve (meat) by salting, smoking or aging.

CURRANTS: Currants come fresh and dried., but don't confuse the two. Fresh currants are a berry. Dried currants are from little grapes. Fresh currants are a member of the gooseberry family, native to northern Europe. They come in red, white, and black colors. Red currants are made into jam and jelly, and are also eaten fresh. White currants are eaten fresh, usually in salads or mix fruit cups. Black currants are made into jam, jelly, and beverages. Fresh currants are available during the summer months with peak season in July. Dried currants are actually a member of the grape family, and look like a tiny raisin. They are a bit tarter than raisins. Dried currants are mainly used for cooking in cakes and cookies. Fresh currants are low in calories and have some vitamin A and C. Dried currants are lower in calories than fresh currants, and are a good source of iron, calcium, and phosphorus. **Nutrition facts** per ¼ cup: 102 calories, zero fats, 26.7g carbohydrates (9%), 2.5g fiber (10%), 1.5g protein (3%),26 IU vitamin A (1%), 2mg vitamin C (3%), 31mg calcium (3%), 1.2mg iron (7%).

CURRY: The traditional curry dish gets its name from *kari* in India. The mame is given to the spice mixture and to the recipe prepared with it. *Kari* is not one standard recipe but a typical blend contains curry leaf, coriander, cumin, mustard seeds, red and black peppers, fenugreek, turmeric, and sometimes cinnamon, cloves, and cardamom. Indian cooks blend their spices right before cooking.

CURRY LEAF comes from Ceylon, the leaves from this small tree are dried and valued as a spice. Names for the leaf vary. The shiny green leaf comes from the *mirraua keonigii* trees that grow wild in Southeast Asia and are cultivated in other tropical countries. Like the bay leaf, the curry leaf is used fresh and put in whole in the recipe until the dish is done and then the leaf if removed. One leaf provides just the right touch of spice.

CURRY POWDER of the kind on our grocery shelves is a pale attempt to imitate the fresh blend of spices used in Indian cooking. It contains some of the dried and powdered ingredients of the mixture used by Indian cooks but what they do with fresh spices cannot be duplicated and canned. See CURRY.

CUSK: A large salt-water fish from the cod family which is found in the North Atlantic Ocean. The lean meat can be prepared in any cod recipe.

CUSTARD: A dessert made with eggs and milk and usually baked. A Spanish version is called *flan* or caramel custard. Pie was long ago called, among other things, *crustards*, from which we get "custard." Fruit and milk pies were *crustards*, because of the crust. Today, recipes for custard are about the same as the earliest pies except the old recipes used more eggs per milk than we do today.

CUSTARD APPLE: A heart shaped fruit of the tropics in several varieties, with sweetsop or cherimoya the most popular. The outside rind looks like it has scales, and the delicate inside flesh is creamy like custard with a bland taste (it has no apple taste). The bland taste can be improved by chilling the pulp and adding a little lime juice. Too perishable for export, the custard apple is available in south Florida, south Texas and southern California during the winter to mid spring. **Nutrition facts:** A ½ cup serving has 78 calories, 4 calories from fat, .5g total fat (1%), zero saturated fat and sodium, 19.5g carbohydrates (7%), zero fiber, 1.3g protein (3%), 26 IU vitamin A (1%), 15mg vitamin C (25%, 3mg calcium (2%), .6mg iron (3%), and 296mg potassium.

CUT IN: To combine fat, such as shortening, with dry ingredients, using a pastry blender, two knives, or a fork.

CZECH FOOD:

NEBRASKA CZECH FESTIVAL

In 1873, C.D. Wilber gave a plot of land to a group of Czech immigrants to build a city. Today it is considered the Czech capital of the United States. Throughout the years, the community of Wilber has retained its Czechoslovakian heritage. Many Old World traditions, as well as the language, are still practiced and observed. Every year in mid summer, Wilber hosts the Nebraska Czech Festival with *Hudba a Tanec Jido a veselost Máme nêco pro kazdého,* meaning "Music and Dance, Food and Fun, We have something for everyone." It's an experience to visit Wilber for a bit of Eastern Europe with small town friendliness and partake in the fun. Festival events include a kids' parade, Czech dancers, Czech Historical Pageant, and an Accordian Jamboree, all in Czech costumes, and if you wish, you can join in Polka dancing. There are Czech foods for every taste bud. Try liver soup, roast duck, roast pork, *Jelitka* (black sausage), *Jitrnice* (white sausage), bread dumplings, kraut, rye bread, apple rings, applesauce, *koláce*, rosettes, and *houska* (a nut and raisin filled strudel). For the kids there are lots of hot dogs, hamburgers, pies, ice cream, and soft drinks. No one will leave Wilber hungry. Two of the Czech specialties are bread dumplings and koláce. Bread Dumplings, better known as *housekove knedliky* to the Czechs, are 1 1/2 inch round dumplings, boiled in water, sliced, and served with meat or poultry. *Koláce* are sweet rolls filled with dried fruit or poppy seeds You can enter one of many events: The Duck and Dumpling Run, *Koláce* Eating Contest, and the Hot Dog Eating Contest. For dates and other information write to: **Wilber Chamber of Commerce**, P.O. Box 1164, Wilber, NE 68465, or phone toll free (888) 494-5237. -- *Brad Kalkwarf*

Dd

DAGWOOD SANDWICH: This sandwich was made famous by Dagwood Bumstead of Chic Young's comic strip, *Blondie*. Dagwood would pile one of everything between two pieces of bread. This sandwich is known by several names: club, hero, pyramid, and skyscraper. There's no set recipe. Just pile your favorite meats, cheeses, vegetables, and spreads between two pieces of bread and enjoy it.

DAIKON: Also known as the Oriental radish, "*omny*," it is a member of the radish family. This white, carrot-shaped vegetable has a similar taste to a red radish, but is milder and sweeter. Daikons add a zesty taste and crisp texture to salads, stir-fry dishes and stews. When daikons are cooked, they have a turnip-like taste. **Nutrition facts:** A 3-ounce serving has about 15 calories, no fat or sodium, good source of fiber, an excellent source for vitamin C (31%), and with some calcium and iron.

DAIRY: A farm or processing plant for milk and milk products. www.dairycenter.com

DAIRY PRODUCTS: Includes all milk and milk products, including cheese, butter, ice cream, and yogurt. www.ilovecheese.com; www.dairycenter.com

HOPKINS COUNTY DAIRY FESTIVAL

Sulphur Springs, the dairy capital of Texas, kicks off the summer with a celebration of their dairy industry. Held in the third week of June, the Dairy Festival has a parade, carnival, and a variety of dairy events. The highlight is the "Homemade Ice Cream Freeze Off." Here you can sample a variety of ice creams and see if you agree with the judges who is the winner. While in Sulphur Springs plan a visit to the Southwest Dairy Museum and Learning Center where you will learn how they used to do it as you view exhibits depicting all facets of milk production and processing from an early farm kitchen to the modern transport and production of dairy products. Of special interest is the museum's old fashion soda fountain that still serves ice cream.

Sulphur Springs has a number of annual festivals. The **Folk Festival** begins the second weekend in May, featuring pioneer experiences from soap making to corn grinding. In September is the Hopkins County Fall Festival and is highlighted by the **Stew Contest** with more than one hundred cooking teams make stew in huge iron pots over open wood fires. The stew meat ranges from chicken to beef to squirrel. For more information on these festivals contact: **Hopkins County Chamber of Commerce,** P.O. Box 347, Sulphur Springs, TX 75483 or phone (903) 885-6515.

PUTNAM COUNTY DAIRY FESTIVAL
WITH UNCLE REMUS

In the beautiful dairylands of central Georgia, the folks of Putnam County celebrate a one day festival in early June to honor their dairy industry. The day begins with road races and a parade, followed with arts and crafts and dairy exhibits. At noon is the big barbeque, and the afternoon is filled with entertainment. During your visit, stop by the museum honoring **Joel Chandler Harris**, the creator of Uncle Remus, Br'er Fox, Be'er Bear, and Be'er Rabbit and hear the stories you once heard as a child. The museum has a collection of first editions of many of his books. For more information on the Putnam County Dairy Festival, write: **Pilot Club of Eatonton**, P.O. Box 3031, Eatonton, GA 31024 or phone the chamber of commerce: (706) 485-7701.

DAMSON: A member of the rose family and a variety of the plum tree. This sour fruit is generally not eaten raw. It is used for cooking in jams, compotes and pies. Damsons are purple, oval in shape, and are available during the summer months in specialty fruit stores. There is also a variety with yellow flesh. Yellow damsons contain more acid than purple plums and taste spicier. The name comes from Damascus, the capitol city of Syria, where they have been growing for thousands of years. Traveling Greeks and Romans took the plums home with them and tried to grow them. When the Crusaders came in the early 1200s, damson plums were among the treasure they brought back to Europe. American plums all began as European imports.

DANCY: See TANGERINE.

DANDELION: Also known as "piss-a-bed," "priest's crown" and "telltime," it's a weed that homeowners love to hate. It grows wild throughout North America, Asia, and Europe. For centuries a dandelion salad heralded the arrival of spring. The leaves have a bitter taste. The roots can also be eaten as a vegetable, or made into a hot beverage and served as a tonic. The diuretic effect accounts for the common French name *pissenlit* or piss-a-bed. It was a diet staple until after World War II, possibly because people were just so tired of depending on the common green and were only too happy to eat other things. It was the lawn care people, not cooks, who labeled the dandelion as a weed. But then, a lot of "weeds" are good food. See WILD FOODS.

Some Native Americans used the root tea for heartburn. Dried leaves make a mild laxative. The most important medical use is in the treatment of liver problems. Dandelion wine is made from dried dandelion flowers. The name comes to us from the French term, which means "tooth of the lion."

To cook the leaves, wash then boil them in ½-inch of water until tender, about 15 minutes. To cook the roots: wash, peel, slice crosswise, bring to a boil in water, drain, butter, and season with salt and pepper. To make a beverage, also known as dandelion-root coffee, roast the roots in a slow oven for about 4 hours. Then grind and use them as in making coffee.

Botanist Peter Gail founded Defenders of the Dandelion in Cleveland, Ohio. He is the author of *The Dandelion Celebration.* **Nutrition facts** per ½ cup: 12 calories, zero fats, 20.9mg sodium (1%), 2.5g carbohydrates (1%), 1g fiber (4%), .8g protein (2%), 3850 IU vitamin A (77%), 10mg vitamin C (16%), 51mg calcium (5%), and .9mg iron (5%).

DANISH: A rich, sweetened yeast dough, made with egg is the basic pastry. To this dough is added all kinds of filling, especially cream cheese, fruit or nuts. The Danish word for "Danish" is "Vienna bread." The pastries the Danish eat in Denmark are nothing like the sweet pastries sold by their name in the United States and Europe. In Denmark, Danish pastries are light and crisp, fresh from the oven and eaten any time of day. www.ohdanishbakery.com.

DASH: Generally means just a little shake from a container, such as a dash of salt and pepper. Always less than 1/8 teaspoon.

DASHEEN: A member of the tropical taro root family, and prized for its starchiness. It is grown commercially in the southern U.S. since 1913 and in most tropical countries. The root grows from egg size to up to six pounds. The brown skins are peeled, the flesh cooked and eaten like potatoes. They have a nutty flavor and more protein than the potato. Best served with salt, pepper and lots of butter or margarine. In the Pacific Islands, dasheen is cooked into a pasty mass of starch called *poi*. **Nutrition facts:** Dasheen has about the same nutrition as taro. One cup of dasheen has about 110 calories, no fat or sodium, high in fiber, with some carbohydrates and protein, a fair source for vitamin C, with some calcium and iron.

DATE: It's the fruit of the date palm tree which originated in Arabia. People of the Indus Valley cultivated date palms as early as 4000 B.C. Date palms need less water than any other food plant and require a hot, low humidity climate to thrive. It is often called the **Tree of Life**. In the Middle East it is said to have 800 uses. Desert people can live for long periods on nothing but dates and milk.

The fruit has a single seed and the flesh is thick and very sweet, so sweet that sugar can be made. Totally useful, the flesh is eaten raw or cooked. The seeds can be roasted, ground, and made into a coffee type beverage. The leaves can be woven and used in building roofs and walls for houses. **Date palm fiber** is made into rope.

In the United States, date palms are grown in Arizona and California deserts. Near Palm Springs, California are many canyons with wild date palms. No one knows if they were planted or native to the area. It is not known if anyone harvests these wild dates.

Packaged dates are available pitted, unpitted, chopped, and dried year round. The rich flavor of dates adds a special dimension to baked bread, cakes, cookies, and muffins. Dates also help keep the baked goods moist longer. Middle Eastern cooks add dates to recipes such as rice and other grains, meat, and vegetables. Combined with butter, dates makes a great spread for pancakes, waffles and nut breads. For a low fat dessert, mix some chopped dates with yogurt and top with some nuts. For quick snacks, stuff dates with almonds and other nuts and roll into powder sugar. Dates can also be stuffed with candied fruit, cheese, and crystallized ginger. **Nutrition facts:** Ten dates have about 240 calories, no fat or sodium. They are a good source for fiber, potassium, and magnesium, and a fair source for some B vitamins. With 57 grams of carbohydrates, dates are a perfect energy-boosting snack. www.home.earthlink.net/-bardmedjool/ www.californiadates.org

NATIONAL DATE FESTIVAL

When the early Spaniards came to California, they brought date palms with them. The first were planted in **San Diego by Father Junipero Serra**. It is believed a date palm must "have its feet in the water and its head in the fires of heaven." California's Coachella Valley fit that description with both the climate and the soil. The date palms were bought to the Valley from Algeria in the 1890s. Today, 95% of the total United States crop comes from the Coachella Valley. To celebrate the date harvest, the National Date Festival is held in mid-February in Indio, California. This event is held in connection with the Riverside County Fair. It is one of the oldest and the most unique events in the West. There are more than 6,000 exhibits and demonstrations, which include: date tasting, date recipes, animals, arts, agricultural, gems and minerals, and floriculture. As with most fairs, carnival rides and games are also provided. The theme, "A Thousand and One Sights," is a magical experience. Two Festival highlights are the spectacular outdoor musical Arabian Nights Pageant, and the hilarious ostrich and camel races. Lots of famous stars provide entertainment for every member of the family. On the closing day is a fiesta, which commemorates the early Mexican influence in California. For information telephone 1-800-811-FAIR. Or write: **Riverside County Fair & National Date Festival**, 3525 14th Street, Riverside, CA 92501. www.datefest.org.

DAUBE: A slow way of cooking meat, similar to braising. In France it is both the method of cooking and a type of dish, the *daubiere*. Now prized as an antique, the *daubiere* is similar to a terrine dish.

DECORATE: Ways of enhancing the appearance of food, such as frosting cakes and cookies with the addition of sprinkles, nuts, candied fruits, raisins, etc.

DECORTICATE: To remove the outer layer of a spice.

DEEP FRY: When frying, the fat must cover the food being cooked. The result should be a crisp exterior and a moist interior. Unlike pan frying, deep frying cooks all sides at once.

DEER: The hunting and eating of deer is more prominent than urban people realize since it is not sold commercially. In many states, families depend on killing a deer during deer season to supplement their meat provision for the coming winter. In the year 2000, Pennsylvania reported a deer population of over 1.4 million. More than 80,000 deer were killed along the highways. If the deer kill is reported and retrieved immediately, it is taken to be used as food for prisoners. Deer hunting is necessary to keep the animal's population down. Pennsylvania farmers reported losses of $76 million from grain crops eaten by wild deer. Pennsylvania deer records are probably typical of other heavily forested states. See VENISON

DEHYDRATE: A drying process that removes water from food without destroying the nutrition values.

DEMITASSE: A small cup of black coffee. Also refers to ½ cup measurement.

DESSERT: A final course of the meal, which may include sweet baked goods, frozen creams, custards, fruit, cheese, and combinations of all these. .

FUNNY NAMES FOR HOMELY DESSERTS

Some names like **"cobbler"** and **"betty"** you have not only heard of, but probably have eaten. A cobbler is a deep dish fruit pie, sometimes with a bottom crust, more likely a top thick biscuit-like crust. A betty on the other hand, is also like a fruit pie, but without a bottom crust and topping made of bread crumbs. How about other desserts with names like: "buckles," "duffs," "flummeries," "fools," "fungies," "grunts," "pandowdies," and "slumps?"

Some of these names are regional and later were applied incorrectly to other deserts, maybe because they were similar or maybe because no one knew what else to call them. A good example is a **flummery** (a Welsh word). Originally it was a jellied pudding made with water and thickened with cereal. Later the name applied to other puddings, some thickened with cornstarch, others with gelatin. If you're Welsh, you still might call all puddings flummery.

A **buckle** is a coffee cake with fruit mixed in the dough and usually having a crumb topping. A **duff** is a pudding boiled in a bag, much like a steamed plum pudding. The English dessert, **"fool"** is fruit whipped with cream. Some call a fool a "flummery." However fool is not cooked, whereas a flummery is. The name **"fungy"** is often interchanged with **"grunts"** and **"slumps."** When a berry grunt is cooked, the berries make a noise while being stewed. Grunts are generally topped with dumplings of biscuit or pie dough. Some grunts are served as a main course, not as a dessert. If the grunt is made with fruits, other than berries, it is a slump, not a grunt. A **"pandowdy"** is a cross between a pudding and a deep dish pie. Once the pandowdy is half cooked, the crust is chopped and mixed into the fruit, then continue to bake. If this dowdying is not done, then it's not a pandowdy, but a cobbler. And a **"slump"** is similar to a grunt, except pie dough is used to top the fruit, and when the dessert cools, it slumps down in the middle. Slumps are often inverted, like an upside down cake, and eaten with cream. –RSC

THE FROZEN DESSERT DILEMMA

Almost everyone likes ice cream and sherbet. Which is best for you? Are you concerned with too much sugar in your diet? Stay away from sherbet. If it's fat you worry about, then it's premium ice cream you should avoid. Both sugar and fat should be eaten in moderation, since there are no nutrients in either, only calories. This chart will help you make the right decision for your next frozen dessert.

Sugar Fat Content:

Ice Cream: ½ cup Premium: 3 teaspoons sugar 12g fat; Regular: 3 teaspoons 7g fat.
Ice Milk: ½ cup, Premium: 3 teaspoons sugar 4g fat; Regular: 3 teaspoons sugar, 3g fat.

Lowfat Frozen Dessert: ½ cup 2 teaspoons sugar, 1g fat.
Frozen Yogurt: ½ cup Regular: 3 teaspoons sugar, 2g fat; Lowfat: 3 teaspoons sugar,1g fat; Nonfat: 3 teaspoons sugar, trace fat.
Sherbet: ½ cup 5 teaspoons sugar, 2g fat.
Sorbet: ½ cup 3 teaspoons sugar, zero fat. *– Human Nutrition Information Service*

DO YOU LOVE DESSERT?

Is your sweet tooth asking for dessert? Are you concerned about calories, sugars and fat?

Tropical Shake

It's nutrient-dense fruit with no added sugars. This shake is an excellent source for vitamin C.

8 ounce canned pineapple, juice pack
1 banana
1 cup skim milk
1 cup orange juice
Ice (optional)

Chill all ingredients. In a blender, blend the undrained pineapple for about 2 minutes. Add the banana, and blend until smooth. Blend in milk, then the orange juice. Serve over crush ice, if desired. Makes 4 servings. **Nutrition facts** per serving: 110 calories, 4 calories from fat, .4g total fat (1%), .1g saturated fat (1%), zero cholesterol, 33mg sodium (1%), 25g carbohydrates (8%), 1.2g fiber (5%), 3.1g protein (6%), 294 IU vitamin A (6%), 40mg vitamin C (66%), 92mg calcium (9%), .4mg iron (2%), and 407mg potassium.

SHAHI TUKRA, A ROYAL DESSERT
by Shazia Hasan

Shahi Tukra was a dessert for the kings and queens who ruled over the Indian Subcontinent several centuries ago. In those days there were no refrigerates or toasters, nor did they have any different flavor extracts. The royal cooks used rose water for flavoring. Instead of toasting the bread, they would fry it in butter. *Shahi Tukra* was left to cool overnight in dishes made of clay and was served to the royal family the next day with red rose petals sprinkled over it. Now is the time to up date this delicious dessert. Enjoy!

1 cup sweetened condensed milk
1 ½ cups water
8 bread slices, white or brown
½ teaspoon flavor extract of your choice (banana, strawberry, orange, etc.)
½ teaspoon food color (optional).
Match the color with the chosen extract (red with strawberry, etc.)

1. Toast the slices of bread to a golden brown. This will harden them a little and prevent them from breaking when cooked in the milk.

2. In a sauce pan, mix the water and milk and put it on low heat. Place the toasted bread slice in the milk. If the sauce pan is too small then dip in each slice for about five seconds. Take the slices out and spread them on a jelly roll pan. (cookie sheet)

3. Continue to heat the milk until it thickens. Add the flavor extract and food coloring. Pour it over the bread slices.

4. Refrigerate for at least an hour and serve cold. For best results, prepare *Shahi Tukra* and refrigerate it overnight.

5. Arrange slices on pretty plates and sprinkle with rose petals, if you have any.

Shahi Tukra can be enjoyed not only as a dessert, but makes a wonderful breakfast as well.

Nutrition facts per slice: 189 calories, 38 calories from fat. 4.2g total fat (7% DV), 2.3g saturated fat (11%), 13.2mg cholesterol (4%), 183.1mg sodium (8%), 33.2g carbohydrates (11%), .6g fiber (2%), 5.1g protein (10%), vitamin A (3%), vitamin C 92%), calcium (14%), and iron (5%).

DEVILED: A highly seasoned food. Deviled ham is spiced ham spread. Deviled eggs are hard boiled eggs cut in half with the yolks scooped out, mayonnaise, mustard, salt, pepper, and sometimes pickle relish added, stirred and then spooned back into the whites, which form a kind of shell for the deviled yolks.

DEVIL'S FOOD: A chocolate cake, deep in color, with rich texture. The name comes as play on words in contrast to Angel Food Cake, which is light and snow white.

DEVONSHIRE CREAM: Prior to the homogenizing of milk, fresh whole milk came with inches of cream floating on top. Sometimes this cream was so heavy you could eat it with a spoon. Devonshire cream is even thicker, and can be produced at home, but only with nonhomogenized, farm fresh milk. It's like a cross between butter and whipped cream. In England, it is always served with tea and scones, and also as a topping on toast, pie and fruit.

DEWBERRIES: Related to the blackberry, and available during the summer months. Dewberries can be interchanged with any blackberry recipe. Only the vines are different. **Nutrition facts:** Dewberries are low in calories, have no fat, contain a fair source of vitamin C and iron.

DICE: To cut food into small cubes, approximately ½ inch or less.

DIET: A selection of food, to gain weight, lose weight, or maintain weight in good health.

SHOULD KIDS GO ON A DIET?

What do the hula hoop, high protein diets, and wearing your clothes backwards have in common? They are all fads. Fads come and go, but when it comes to fad diets, the health effects can be permanent, especially for middle grade and high school students.

Not all students who go on diets need to lose weight. Pressure from friends, and sometimes parents, to be very slim may create a distorted body image. Having a distorted body image is like looking into a funhouse mirror; You see yourself as fatter than you are. Your growing years are a **period of rapid growth and development**. Fad diets can keep you from getting the calories and nutrients that you need to grow properly and that dieting can retard your growth. Stringent dieting may cause girls to stop menstruating and will prevent boys from developing muscles. If the diet doesn't provide enough calcium, phosphorus and vitamin D, bones may not lay down enough calcium. This may increase the risk of osteoporosis later in life.

Instead of dieting because "everyone" is doing it, or because you are not as thin as you want to be, first find out from a doctor or nutritionist whether you are carrying too much body fat for your age and height. The flip side to feeling pressured to be thin is having legitimate concerns about being overweight that adults dismiss by saying, "It's just baby fat" or "You'll grow into your weight." Most girls reach almost their full height once they start to menstruate. Boys usually don't stop growing until age 18.

As with most everything else, **there's a right way and a wrong way to lose weight**. The wrong way is to skip meals, resolve to eat nothing but diet bread and water, take diet pills, or make yourself vomit. You may make it through the end of the week and maybe even lose a pound or two, but you're unlikely to keep the weight off for more than a few months. And inducing vomiting can lead to an eating disorder called **bulimia,** which can result in serious health problems. The more you deprive yourself of the foods you love, the more you will crave those foods. Inevitably, you'll break down and binge. Then you'll not only gain those pounds back, you'll add a more.

Low-calorie diets that allow only a few types of foods can be bad for your health because they don't allow you to get enough vitamins and minerals. Rapid weight loss from very-low-calorie "starvation diets" can cause serious effects for students, such as gallstones, hair loss, weakness, and diarrhea. If going to extremes won't do the trick, what will? Believe it or not, it's as simple as making a few changes in your eating habits to emphasize healthy foods and exercise (good advice even if you don't need to lose weight). A good diet is one that has balance, variety and moderation in food choices.

The best guideline is the **Food Guide Pyramid**. The most important dietary change you can make is to limit the amount of high-fat foods that you eat. Balancing your favorite foods which are usually high in fat with fruits and vegetable which are almost always low in fat; eat a variety of foods to keep from getting bored and make sure your diet is nutritionally sound; and keep portion sizes reasonable so that you can have your "thin" slice of cake. To keep fat intake down, make some simple lower **fat substitutes**:
Drink skim milk instead of whole milk;
Enjoy low-fat frozen yogurt instead of ice cream;
Eat pretzels instead of corn chips;
High-fat foods such as french fries, candy bars, and milkshakes that have no low-fat substitutes should only be eaten once in a while or in very small amounts.

Whether you are overweight or not, **regular exercise** of at least three times a week is important to your look and your feel. If you do lose weight, stepping up your activity level will cause you to burn calories more quickly and help make weight loss easier.

At best, fad or starvation diets and diet pills offer temporary solutions. At worst, they may jeopardize your health. The safest way for you to control your weight is to eat healthy, low-fat diet, and get enough exercise. --*Ruth Papazian* , an article condensed from **FDA Consumer Magazine**, May 1997

HEALTHY EATING

Most families are too busy these days and have less time for planning what to eat. It's a known fact that today's families are not eating a high fiber and low fat diet, nor are they getting enough exercise. What to do about the diet? The answers are simple. You can help by suggesting to your parents these **25 rules**:

1. Eat lots of fruits and vegetables, grains, and beans. Almost all are low in calories and fat.
2. When shopping, and if in a hurry, use bagged cut-up or frozen vegetables.
3. Steam or microwave veggies to retain more vitamins and minerals than in boiling in water.
4. Include lean meat and low fat dairy products five times a week. .
5. Go easy on fats.
6. Switch to reduced or nonfat salad dressings.
7. Eat whole wheat, multigrain, or oatmeal bread, muffins, bagels, and rolls. Whole grains are a good source of fiber, vitamins, and minerals.
8. Spread toast with jelly, jam, or preserves instead of butter or margarine.
9. Top potatoes and vegetables with lower fat content sour cream, yogurt, cottage cheese,
10. Use lemon juice, herbs, or salsa as a topping for vegetables and salads instead of fat products such as butter, mayonnaise, etc.
11. If you prefer butter, mayonnaise, etc., either cut the portion in half or use a lower fat product.
12. Switch to nonfat or 1% dairy products (milk, sour cream, yogurt). There is no loss of calcium in these low fat products.
13. Cut back on cheese or switch to low fat cheeses, but don't eat twice as much!
14. Save french fries and other fried foods for special occasions.
15. Save ice cream and pastries for special occasions.
16. Eat smaller portions of meat, fish, and poultry and use low fat cooking methods (baking broiling) and trim off all fat and remove skin from poultry.
17. Use lower fat luncheon meats, such as sliced turkey or chicken breast, lean ham or lean sliced beef.
18. For snacking, keep a bowl of raisins and other dried fruits available on the kitchen counter. Keep a bowl of cut up vegetables on the top shelf of the refrigerator.
19. Add fruit to your breakfast as a topping to cereals or drink 100% fruit juice.
20. Choose whole grain hot and cold cereals.
21. As you decrease fatty foods, increase lower fat foods.
22. Choose fruit for dessert. For a special dessert, try a fruit parfait with low fat yogurt or sherbet.
23. Add vegetables to sauces. An example, grate carrots and zucchini into spaghetti sauce.
24. Once a week, replace meat with a recipe featuring beans (tacos, burritos, mixed with rice, soup or salad. Use canned beans to save cooking time.
25. Once a week, replace meat with whole grain pasta, brown rice, or bulgur (cracked wheat).

As you see it's a matter of just switching some foods and changing some eating habits. Don't do it all at once, do in a little at a time, especially when it comes to adding fiber to the diet. Do not go on a nonfat diet, unless instructed by a doctor. Every body needs some fat.
--National Institute of Health

DIETARY GUIDELINES FOR KIDS

Many kids eat too many calories and too much fat, and at the same time too little complex carbohydrates and fiber. While diseases caused by vitamin and mineral deficiencies are relatively rare in the U.S., it is still important to take a look at your nutritional intake. Some kids need vitamin and mineral supplements, especially calcium and iron. Food alone cannot make you healthy. Good health depends on your environment and the health care you receive. You must exercise regularly, eat a variety of foods for needed nutrients, consume enough calories for the energy you require, and at the same time maintain a healthy weight. Choose a diet with plenty of vegetables, fruits, and grains; and use sugar, salt, and fats in moderation. For more information see: FOOD GUIDE PYRAMID, LABELING, MINERALS, and VITAMINS. *--U.S. Department of Health and Human Services*

MEDITERRANEAN DIET:

THE MEDITERRANEAN DIET PYRAMID

In 1992, the U.S. Department of Agriculture (USDA) revised the current food guide pyramid as a practical and flexible guide to help Americans create a healthy diet. In 1993, another valuable food pyramid was developed based on the Mediterranean Diet. This diet focuses on an overall eating pattern and groups of foods according to frequency of use . . . a few times per month, a few times per week or daily, unlike the USDA pyramid, which groups foods based on daily recommendations.

The Mediterranean Diet emphasizes plant-based foods (nuts, seeds, and beans, as primary protein sources because they are cholesterol-free and low in saturated fat. The USDA recommends two or three servings of meat, poultry and seafood weekly whereas the Mediterranean Diet recommends people eat lean red meat a few times per month, and poultry, eggs and fish only a few times per week. Thus, the Mediterranean Diet emphasizes food sources high in monounsaturated fat (such as olive oil and nuts) and more fruits and vegetables. Most consumers believe that buts are high in fat. But what most don't know is that fat in nuts is primarily monounsaturated. In addition, nuts and beans are high in protein and a good source of fiber.

Monounsaturated fat is believed to reduce LDL cholesterol levels in the body. LDL cholesterol is considered "bad" cholesterol. There is also an HDL cholesterol, and it is considered "good" cholesterol. HDL cholesterol carries the "bad" cholesterol to the liver whre it is passed from the body.

The Mediterranean Diet recommends daily: olive oil, olives, cheese, yogurt, dairy products, beans, legumes, nuts, fruits, vegetables, bread, grains, pasta, rice, couscous, polenta and bulgur.
– International Conference on the Diets of the Mediterranean

The Mediterranean Diet Pyramid

DILDOE BARBED-WIRE CACTUS: Native to south Florida and the American tropics, the tangled, creeping stems produce spiny red 2-inch fruit that is eaten fresh.

DILL: Native to Asia Minor, this hardy herb grows in temperate climates. The feathery leaves are dill weed, while the fruit is the seed. Both are used fresh and dried. Both are used in salads and salad dressings, cooked with vegetables (cabbage, carrots, and turnips), made into a sauce for fish and shrimp, and added to bread recipes. www.melissas.com.

DILL PICKLES: Also known as a "genuine" pickle, are cured in three different ways.
1. Fresh cucumbers are stored in salt brine tanks for up to three years. Next they are heated to remove the salt, then packed in jars. These pickles remain crisp in the jars.
2. Fresh pack dills are not aged for a long time in the brine. They are pasteurized (heated to kill microorganisms). These dills are less salty, light green when packed, turn dark with age and usually turn soft in the jars.
3. Cold pack dills must be kept under refrigeration at all times and must be consumed within three months. They are never cooked or pasteurized and retain the cucumber texture. These are called "deli dills."

There is also a **cold pack process** where the dills are cured in a high vinegar content in two or three days and are called "overnight dills." All three methods produce the three basic flavors: dill, sour and sweet.

Dill weed can be added at any stage. Kosher dills are made the same way, only with the addition of garlic in the brine. Dill pickles have little or no sugar added. Sour pickles are finished in a solution of vinegar and spices. Sweet pickles are sour pickles that are drained of the brine, then packed in vinegar, sugar and spices.

Activity

Have a pickle tasting party with cheese and crackers. What do you think? What do the three methods have in common? Why is one better than another in your opinion?

DINNER: The main meal of the day, eaten at any time from noon on. City people eat dinner in the evening, while country people are known to eat it at noon. In some countries dinner is followed with relaxation and/or a nap. Supper is a smaller, less formal evening meal.

DIP: (verb) "To dip" means to dunk a food product into a liquid or a soft substance. (Noun) As a noun, it is the name of the liquid or the soft substance. Examples: We dip a cracker into a creamy cheese dip, or tortilla chips into refried bean dip.

DIRTY RICE: Of course, the rice isn't dirty. It's just colored by the seasonings. Cajuns and dirty rice are like bread and butter; they belong together. This one pot meal is usually made with chicken livers and gizzards. Those who dislike innards (giblets) can make this recipe with pork..

DIRTY RICE CAJUN SEASONING MIXTURE

Almost all Cajun recipes are highly spiced. Make up this seasoning and use for other recipes where you want a little heat. Use enough of the mixture to flavor cooked rice to your own taste.

> 2 teaspoons paprika
> 1 ½ teaspoons black pepper, freshly ground
> 1 ½ teaspoons salt
> 1 ½ teaspoons cayenne red pepper
> 1 teaspoon dry mustard
> 1 teaspoon garlic powder
> ½ teaspoon dried thyme
> ½ teaspoon dried oregano

In a small bowl, combine the seasonings, and crush well all ingredients; set aside. Best if made several days in advance to allow the mixture to marry. –*Pamela Schmidt*

DISSOLVE: Adding a solid, such as sugar or salt, to a liquid, so that the solid becomes one with the liquid.

DIVINITY: A creamy, marshmallow candy created by beating hot syrup with beaten egg whites. Most divinity is made with white sugar. When made with brown sugar it's called "seafoam."

DOCK: See SORREL

DOG SALMON: See SALMON.

DOLMA: In Near Eastern cooking it means stuffing vegetables, grains, and/or meat into grape leaves.

DOLPHIN: There are two different kinds of dolphin. One is a mammal which you might have seen in aquariums, as Flipper on TV, or in the movies. The other is a fish found in tropical waters which can reach 5-feet in length. They look nothing alike. It's the fish that's in fish markets, not the mammal. Fillets can be fried, baked, or broiled. **Nutrition facts** per 3 ounces: 72 calories, 6 calories from fat, .6g total fat (1%), .2g saturated fat (1%), 62.1mg cholesterol (21%), 74.8mg sodium (3%), zero carbohydrates and fiber, 15.7g protein (31%), 153 IU vitamin A (3%), zero vitamin C, 13mg calcium (1%), and 1mg iron (5%).

DORMOUSE: As late as the 1600s one could still buy a dormouse pie in France. Yes, it's just what you think. The dormouse is a small rodent who lives in trees and feeds off seeds and berries. The Romans were so fond of dormice that they bred them in captivity in special mud cages. The fattened little mice went into stews, or were coated in honey and poppyseeds and roasted. Alas, today such a delicacy is no longer generally available. –LU See MICE.

DOT: To dot food means to place a small amount of something on top, such as a "dot of butter" on potatoes.

DOUGH: A mixture of flour, liquid, and other ingredients for making bread and other baked goods. Dough is a very stiff batter. We think of cake "batter" and bread "dough."

DOUGHNUT: A small cake with a hole in the middle which has been deep fried or baked.

DOUGHNUTS

Doughnuts with a hole in the middle are probably an American invention. No, not by colonial housewives. Guess again. Archaeologists found petrified rounds of dough in the American southwest. **Native Americans may have had doughnuts first**, but apparently didn't write down their recipe. True, fried cakes in hog fat were popular in Europe and the colonists brought the recipe with them to America.

Why the Hole?

Some people complained that the center sometimes didn't get cooked, so some smart mama cut the middle out. **Dutch cooks filled the hole** with a nut or fruit. Sailors liked the idea because the doughnuts could be slipped onto the spokes of the ship's wheel and kept handy while they steered.

.

Many Names

The name "doughnut" came from the Dutch. They were also called *olykoeks* meaning "oil cakes." The Dutch also twisted two pieces of dough together to become "love knots." Today we call them **crullers**. The Dutch also make a holeless, fried caked, filled with raisins called *oliebollens*. The Pennsylvania Germans called them **fastnachts** (fahs-nocks) and served them for breakfast on Shrove Tuesday or Fastnacht Day. By custom, the last person to arrive at the tables was called a "lazy fastnacht." In New Orleans, the French made them without the hole and called them *beignets*. Whatever you call them, including the modern misspelling,"donuts," it all comes down to the same meaning.

Hole or No Hole

Doughnuts are small cakes, usually with a hole in the center. They can be leavened with either baking powder or yeast. Yeast doughnuts are fried in deep oil while cake (baking powder) types can be baked. Doughnut dough should be soft with just enough flour to roll out. Yeast doughnuts need to rise until double in bulk before frying. Doughnuts are fried in deep oil at 350°F to 375°F. The dough will sink, but will rise in a moment. Immediately turn over and fry until golden brown on the bottom and turn over again and fry until both sides are golden brown. After cutting, baking powder doughnuts should rest about 15 minutes before frying. Doughnuts can be baked in a hot oven (about 400°F), but will spread out and will not have a true doughnut shape. Adding a little more flour will help to hold their shape.

MOTHER ADA DREW URIE

by Fay U. Valley

My mother, being of Scottish decent, always started out breakfast with oatmeal steamed overnight. We worked a small farm in Vermont's Green Mountains, and in the hot afternoons Mom fixed us a refreshing oatmeal drink after pitching hay. Mom baked many items for visitors who vacationed at our lakes. Here are a couple of her favorite doughnut recipes.

RAISED DONUTS

The batter is easy to make. However, if this is the first time you have fried doughnuts, you will **require adult help** because **boiling and deep frying are VERY dangerous processes.**

You will need heavy bottomed fry pans to hole 2-3 inches of oil. Wesson oil is good to fry with because it takes more heat than other oils before it begins to smoke. **Be very careful with hot oil.**

1 cup milk
1/3 cup + 1 teaspoon sugar
1 teaspoon salt
Sprinkle of nutmeg
2 to 3 tablespoons butter
2 1/2 cups flour, sifted
1/3 cup warm water
1 package yeast
1 egg, beaten

1. Scald the milk.
2. Add 1/3 cup sugar, salt, butter and nutmeg.
3. Cool mixture to lukewarm in a large bowl.
4. In a small bowl, soften yeast in water with 1 teaspoon of sugar.
5. Add yeast to cooled milk mixture, with egg and 1 ½ cups flour; beat well.
6. Add more flour to make a soft dough.
7. Knead 3 to 4 minutes, cover and let rise about 1 hour.
8. Knead again for a minute or two.
9. Roll dough, cut into strips and form a figure 8 or cut with a doughnut cutter.
10. Let rise again and fry in a oil that is already heated to 350˚. Doughnuts will sink and then rise again when they are done. Take them out with a slotted spoon when they turn light golden brown.

Drain in a wire rack or waxed paper.
Dip cooked doughnut in hot maple syrup or honey (slightly diluted in water), or sugar syrup, if desired. Makes 1 dozen.

DOVYALIS: Better known at the African gooseberry, it first came from Ethiopia, produces a small orange berry, with a good tart flavor. Best cooked in pies and jellies. A second variety grows in Ceylon with a small, dark purple berry, with a sour, poor flavor. Best cooked into jelly, preserves, or made into juice.

DOWNY MYRTLE: Native to tropical Asia, this shrub produces small, greenish-purple, sweet berries, preferably for jam and pies.

DRAGEES: (drah-gays) Those tiny silver balls for cake decorating.

DREDGE: To coat food with flour, sugar, cornmeal, etc., usually prior to frying or baking.

DRESSING: There are two meanings. 1. A cold sauce added to salads, meats, and fruit. 2. A solid mixture for stuffing meat and poultry. www.dressings-sauces.org; www.mayo.com

DRIED BEANS: Most varieties of legumes can be preserved by drying and later cooked by boiling. See BEANS.

DRY BEAN TIPS
by Virginia G. McNear

If your garden produces too many beans, consider drying them for later use. Leave the plants in the ground until the stalks are nearly dry. Then pull them up, shake the dirt off the roots, tie them in bunches of three or four plants, hang them root side up in a dry place. As soon as they are totally dry, rub the pods off, store the beans in tightly covered jars so they don't spoil. The varieties grown specifically for drying should not be picked until they are thoroughly mature, 90 to 100 days. To determine if they are mature, bite one. You will barely be able to dent it, if it is hard, it is mature.

Beans are sensitive to light. Light lowers the level of vitamin B6. When buying dried beans, avoid beans in bulk bins, they may be cheaper, but you don't get as much nutrition for your money. Store your beans in light, airtight, and moisture proof containers.

To prepare beans: pick them over, remove stones, dirt and wrinkled ones. Wash in cold water, discard any beans that float. Cover with fresh water and soak at least eight hours or overnight. Disregard any recipe that advises you to cook the beans in the soaking water.

Soak dried lima beans for eight hours. The soaked limas will cook in about 30 minutes. White beans are the toughest, they need the longest soaking time.

Never add salt or salted meats (bacon, salt pork or ham) while cooking if you want tender beans. The salt will harden them. Add the salt and meats when the beans are done.

Beans, beans the musical fruit,
the more you eat, the more you toot.
The more you toot, the better you feel.
We should eat beans at every meal.
–Anonymous

Yes, beans can cause the "tooting" gas in your digestion system. Beans contain glycoside (a type of sugar) that your body can not digest. That glycoside is the cause of gas. To cut the gas problem, cover the beans with water, boil for about five minutes, remove from the heat and let them soak for about six hours. Also, adding a dozen or more cloves of garlic helps to cut gas. Discard the water, rinse the beans, add fresh water, and continue to cook them. To test if the beans are done, put a few on a spoon and blow gently on them If the skins peel back if they're done.

DRIED FRUIT: Fruit that has had most of the water removed, a form of preservation.

When purchasing dried fruits, look at the label for those that have been processed unsulphured and dried naturally. (Sulphured fruit tends to retain natural colors.) Natural drying permits the dried fruit to retain the concentrated essence of fresh fruit. Store dried fruit in a cool, dark place, in airtight containers. Dried fruits can be eaten dried or they can be reconstituted with liquid. **To reconstitute** dried fruits, place in a glass bowl. Pour boiling water or fruit juice in a two-for-one ratio and allow to sit for 15 minutes to an hour. Or, cover fruit with room temperature water or juice, cover, and let them sit, refrigerated, overnight. Drain extra liquid, save, and use as liquid for baked goods, hot cereals, or dried fruit compotes. Reconstituted fruit should be refrigerated if not eaten immediately. Fruits cured with fruit juice, such as papaya, do not reconstitute well. www.dfaofca.com

Apples: Add chopped apples and soaking liquid to baked goods such as muffins and quick breads. Add dried apples prior to cooking to hot cereal and granola.
Apricots: Dried apricots can be added to meat and poultry stuffing, fruit compotes, trail mixes, muffins, and cookies. Apricots that are not sulphured are darker in color than those processed with sulphur dioxide.
Bananas: Add to fruit salads and trail mixes.
Currants: Zante currants lend a delicate sweetness to scones, muffins, cookies, and pilafs, and can be substituted for raisins in recipes.
Dates: Use in quick breads, cookies, and breakfast bars. Dates can be stuffed with nuts and rolled in coconut. Add dates to fruit salads.
Figs: Use in cookies, breakfast bars, fruit compotes, chutneys, puddings, and for stuffing poultry. Also great served with cheese as a dessert.
Mangoes: Great in fruit salads, chicken salad, and stir-fries.
Peaches: Use in baked goods and fruit compotes. To make fruit compote, simmer with fruit juice, lemon peel, and a cinnamon stick.
Pears: Simmer pears in water or fruit juice with other fruits, orange or lemon rind, cinnamon and nutmeg, and serve hot as a topping for waffles or pancakes, or with yogurt as a dessert.

Pineapple: Most fresh pineapple is simmered in pineapple juice before drying. Best eaten as a snack, but can be added to cereal, and granola. For a softer texture, soak for a short time in water or pineapple juice.

Prunes: (**Dried Plums**) Use in fruit compotes, roasted chicken dishes, or serve with cheese for dessert. Prunes are a good laxative, but eat them in the morning, not at night before bed.

Raisins: Raisins can be used in cookies, cereals, cooked with grains, granola, and in trail mixes.

Tomatoes: Sun-dried tomatoes provide a tremendous flavor boast to many foods. Marinate tomatoes in olive oil and season with garlic, rosemary, and basil. Marinated tomatoes are great on pizzas and can be added to chicken dishes. *--Whole Foods Market*

DRIP: A process where a flow of liquid is added drop by drop. This is how oil is added to in making mayonnaise to prevent curdling.

DRIPPINGS: Fat or liquid that comes from food when cooking.

DROP: (noun) A small amount of liquid, similar to a dash. (verb) The word also refers to dough or batter being dropped from a spoon for making biscuits, cookies, etc. The word can also mean a small candy with the shape of a teardrop. Think of hard lemon drops or soft chocolate drops or gumdrops.

DR PEPPER: Dr Pepper a breakfast drink! For some, maybe. During the 1930s era, research proved that sugar provided energy and the average person experiences a let- down during the normal day at 10:30 a.m., 2:30 p.m. and 4:30 p.m. This led to the famous Dr Pepper advertising slogan, "Drink a bite to eat at 10, 2 and 4."

Most Misunderstood

Did you wonder why the Dr Pepper commercial calls it the "Most misunderstood soft drink"? While not true, many mothers believed Dr Pepper contained prune juice. Hence, the beverage was given to their children to keep them regular and became a popular breakfast drink.

Waco, Anyone

Dr Pepper is a native Texas soft drink. It originated at Morrison's Old Corner Drug in Waco, Texas, patented in **1885. Dr. Charles Curtis Alderton**, a young pharmacist and medical doctor, working at Morrison's, formulated a blend of fruit-based flavors and tested it on the patrons in the drug store. It was originally advertised as a "**Tonic, Brain Food, Exhilarant**" drink. At first the beverage was known as "WACO," as it was only available in Waco, Texas.

It is assumed that Wade B. Morrison, owner of the drug store, named the new beverage after his first employer, **Dr. Charles Pepper,** a physician and owner of a drug store in Virginia.

Dr Pepper gained such a demand that Alderton and Morrison could no longer produce enough syrup from their soda fountain. Alderton was primarily interested in pharmacy and had no designs on the drink. Morrison asked Robert Lazenby, a beverage chemist, to make and bottle Dr Pepper. He agreed and Morrison and Lazenby continued to develop the beverage further. Dr. Pepper was sampled by 20 million people at the 1904 World's Fair Exposition in St. Louis. This same Exposition also introduced hamburger and hot dog buns, as well as the ice cream cone.

DR PEPPER MUSEUM

In the early 1920s Dr Pepper Company moved to Dallas and the Waco building was closed in 1965. Later Dr Pepper Company donated the building to be used as a museum. Today visitors can enjoy a visit to this historic building and can savor real soda fountain soft drinks. The museum exhibits the history, inventions, production and advertising of soft drinks. The museum is a non-profit organization and not part of Dr Pepper Company. For information on the museum, contact: **Dr Pepper Museum and Free Enterprise Institute** 300 South 5th Street Waco, Texas 76701 Phone (817) 757-1024

DRY: To remove the moisture from the exterior of food.

DRY WATER: Can water be dehydrated into a solid or powdered form to be reconstituted later into a liquid? If so, in what form and what would this liquid be? It's like asking, "What came first, the chicken or the egg?" No, so far, it's not possible to dehydrate water, although many inventors have tried. Today, a new process has been developed and is called "DRiWATER."

DRiWATER

In 1988, inventor G. Lee Avera developed a way to convert water into a thick gelatin form. Harold Jensen joined Mr. Avera, who did the necessary research and developed a marketable product. DriWater is made with three non-toxic ingredients: 98% pure water, and 2% food grade cellulose vegetable gum and aluminum sulfate (ingredients found in many manufactured food products, such as mayonnaise and ice cream). While the ingredients are known, the process to form the thick gel is a secret. This gel is safe around children and pets, however, with any food product, best to avoid contact with the eyes

DriWater has gone under an extensive product testing with government agencies, university research programs and by the private-sector end-users. Field tests have been done in arid desert conditions in Africa, the Middle East, Asia and the United States. In Egypt, two-million trees were planted in the rolling sand dunes and each tree was given three quarts of DriWater. Only seven percent of the trees died, the remaining developed a root system that could be maintained without supplemental moisture. The test was so successful, seventeen-million trees have been planted. These trees will not only produce food, but wood will be used for building the "Sixth of October City" near Cairo.

Every year, two to five percent of commercial grape vines and fruit trees die. While there might be enough moisture for the mature plants, there's not enough for the newly planted young seedlings. One quart packages of DriWater in biodegradable cartons are buried next to the roots of the new plants. This not only supplies the needed moisture, it also speeds up growth. In one cherry orchard, normally it takes five years for the tree to bare fruit. With DriWater, many trees produced fruit in just three years.

The time release of moisture from DriWater happens when bacteria in the soil breaks down the gel. One quart will provide necessary moisture for up to 90 days. Smaller packages of DriWater are available from nurseries and garden centers for home use and provide moisture for 30 days, perfect for watering that small plant while on vacation. If you would like to know more on how DriWater is turning deserts into forests, log on to their web site: www.driwater.com.

DUCK: Domestic ducks were derived from either the **mallard** or the **Muscovy** duck. The mallard is native to the northern hemisphere, the Muscovy is native to Central and South America. The domestic duck is referred to as a duckling and weight 3 to 5 pounds. Ducks can be fried, roasted whole, quartered and broiled or grilled over a barbecue. **Nutrition facts:** Four ounces of duck meat without the skin will have about 150 calories, of which 63 calories come from fat. Ducks are higher in fat than any other poultry of which 13% of it is saturated and 29% cholesterol. Duck is an excellent source of protein, vitamin C, and iron. Duck meat eaten with the skin will raise the calorie content up to almost 460, of which 405 calories come from fat, and 75% is saturated fat.

NICARAGUAN BIRD DOGS
A True Story
by Richard S. Calhoun

When ducks from the United States and Canada fly south for the winter, many fly to Nicaragua. One of the favorite duck habitats is in the marsh lands on the east shore of Lake Managua, in Nicaragua. Tall grasses provides both camouflage and food for the birds.

Shortly after the ducks arrive in Central America from the north, so do hunters from the United States. The hunters are taken to this remote game area by professional guides. It's about an hour's drive east of Managua, half of it on bumpy unpaved roads.

When the vans arrive at the hunting grounds, boys of all ages line up like tin soldiers waiting for the hunters. The kids are clean and neat, and their clothes are freshly pressed. Each hunter must pick out one boy as his or her retriever. The hunters look over the boys to see who might be the fastest. Boys will act as bird dogs because hunters are not permitted to bring their retrievers into Nicaragua.

Alice is the first hunter to pick a boy. She walks up and down the line and stops at one boy who is about 12 years old. She asks, "What is your name?"

The boy looks puzzled, because he doesn't understand English.

Adan, the guide, walks over to the young boy and says, "¿*Cómo te llamas*?"

The boy answers, "Jorge."

"My name is Alice," she replies.

Jorge seems to understand. Jorge is a bit short for his age. He wears a white shirt and blue jeans with patches on his knees. He also has a slingshot around his neck. Some of the boys are barefooted, but Jorge is wearing shoes that look a bit too big for him.

The rest of the hunters pick out their own personal boy retriever. There are always more boys than hunters. Some hunters take two boys with them into the tall grass. Each boy is given a white cotton sack for the "bagged" ducks.

Adan has brought out a wooden rocking chair. He sits down, leans back and shouts in English, "Begin the hunt!"

The morning quiet is broken as kids run into the tall grass to scare out the ducks. The sky is soon filled with birds. The sound of shotguns end the silence. One by one, ducks fall to the ground. Kids run in all directions, picking up downed ducks. So many ducks! No one knows for sure who hits which duck. A contest develops to see which boy brings in the most ducks.

Within an hour the hunt is over. Kids are now covered with mud from head to toe. Jorge is still fairly clean, but his shirt is now wrinkled. All the kids are happy and smiling after the hunt. They seem to have more fun gathering the downed ducks than the hunters who have been shooting.

Jorge came in with ten ducks and Alice gives him five dollars. Each boy is rewarded about a dollar per duck.

The boys drop to the ground with their ducks and clean and remove all the feathers from the ducks. Soon the ground is covered with duck feathers. The ducks are tagged and put in an ice chest. Later they will be frozen to be taken back to the United States. The hunt for this day is over. The boys head down the dusty road toward home with their money firmly grasped in their hands.

Tomorrow there will be another group of hunters. And the same group of boys will be there to greet them. All neat and clean, with freshly pressed clothes.

DUMPLING: A small amount of dough, filled or unfilled, cooked by boiling or steaming. Most popular in America are probably dumplings with chicken or boiled ham. Squirrel and dumplings were a pioneer favorite. Other cultures have other kinds.

FLAT DUMPLINGS, FIRESIDE, AND FAMILY REUNION
by T. Marie Smith

"Mother," asked Kanona, "may I help with the flat dumplings?"

"Pat the corn meal dough very thin and we'll boil them in water until they're done," answered Mother.

They finished cooking and Mother laid the dumplings out on the table to cool while Kanona and her little brother ran to gather firewood. The freezing air hit their noses as they entered the silent forest. The naked trees looked grotesque and their long-since-dried leaves scrunched under the children's moccasins.

"Kanona," whispered Watie, "are there Skillies in here?"

"No, silly," she answered, trying to be brave, "Skillies only come around after sundown, and besides, they will all be driven away when Daddy and Grandfather smoke the dumplings."

They hurried to finish their chores and rushed back to the yard where Father was making the fire. After laying their huge armloads of wood down, the children rushed to the warmth of the house.

"Kanona," said her mother, "you and Watie can split the dumplings and put them into the flat basket."

They were almost finished when Watie excitedly laid the knife on the table and said, "Here's Grandmother and Grandfather." He ran out to be with them.

Grandmother came in. "It looks like these are about ready for the flames," she said as she hugged Kanona.

Outside the fire was burning high and night was beginning to creep in as the men took the basket and everyone gathered around for the ceremony. They slowly passed the basket of flat dumplings through the flames four times, once to the North, East, South, then West, while quietly mumbling the secret words.

"Now, children," Grandfather spoke with confidence, "no Skillies here for another year."

"Right," added their father, "but we must go inside. The night wind brings a freeze."

"Leave the basket outside," said Mother. "It will be ready for our gathering tomorrow." "That smoke was perfect to flavor the dumplings," said Grandmother. "We'll have a wonderful reunion."

The next morning aunts, uncles, and cousins arrived shortly after sun-up and gathered around the huge bonfire that the men had going. While the older men told hair-raising stories about the past, everyone munched on smoked bits of frozen flat bread.

"Is that true, Grandfather?" Kanona tried to sound brave.

"Oh, yes," he answered. "The Skillies were taking me away but your Great-Great -Grandfather threw them a smoked dumpling and they disappeared into the night sky."

Scooting closer to the bright fire the children begged for another story. "And this time tell a true one," said Watie. Everyone laughed.

The smoky flat bread was deliciously cold, the fire was delightfully warm, but the family love was indescribably wonderful.

DUNGENESS CRABS: These crabs are native to the northern Pacific waters. The largest, about 2 ½ pounds, come from the icy, pure Alaskan waters. This succulent crab has a distinctive, almost sweet flavor, and very tender, flaky white meat. Dungeness crabs are available, already cooked and frozen, the year round in most supermarkets and specialty seafood stores. The meat can be enjoyed cold in a leafy green salad or hot in seafood stews and soups. One of the best ways is to steam the crab until hot (can also be microwaved), crack the legs, and dip into melted butter, mayonnaise or your favorite dipping sauce. The meat in the body shell is best used in creamed dishes, bisques, and casseroles. www.alaskaseafood.org

DURIAN: A tree native to southeast Asia, produces sweet, very odorous fruit with sharp protuberances, and is the costliest fruit in the world. The smell is a combination of rotten onions and stale cheese. The smell is so obnoxious that some hotel owners refuse to allow guests to eat them in their rooms or anywhere they might offend the tourists. The fruit is pineapple size, with a thick yellow-green rind, and half inch long thorns. They look hard to eat and they are, because the spiky shells are tough to crack. The central egg-sized, creamy colored seed is sometimes roasted and eaten like chestnuts. The pulp is yellowish with the texture of blancmange (a wonderful vanilla pudding). Durians are eaten fresh, made into preserves, ice cream and candy. Because of their value, the Thai orchards are protected by electric fences and guard dogs. The bad smell obviously does not discourage everyone from enjoying the good taste.

DURUM WHEAT: Also called hard or macaroni wheat, it is mostly made into an unrefined flour and used to make pasta. Pasta made from durum wheat does not disintegrate when cooked and while tender will remain firm. If it hasn't been bleached or stripped of its nutrients, it is very high in protein. Also a good source of gluten for making bread.

DUST: To sprinkle or coat lightly with flour or sugar.

DUTCH OVEN: A cast iron pot for cooking meat, vegetables, and some baked goods. The food is placed in the pot, covered, and placed on the stove top, in a fireplace, or in a 300° oven. The food is cooked slowly, resulting in tender, juicy meat; and flavorful vegetables. The dutch oven can bake biscuits, corn bread, yeast bread, and cakes. Dutch oven can be spelled either as Dutch or dutch oven.

DUXELLES: A process of removing liquid from fresh mushrooms. The mushrooms are then sautéd. The liquid can be used in sauces.

Ee

ÉCLAIR: (ee-kair) A puff pastry filled with creme and glazed with icing. French name for elegant cream puff.

EDAM CHEESE: A reduced fat, semisoft to hard Dutch cheese with a mild flavor, for eating and cooking.

EDAMAME: The Chinese have been cultivating these Asian soybeans for thousands of years, but the name "edamame" is from the Japanese, where they have been eaten almost as long. In Japan they eat the little beans right from the pod as snack food. Americans are discovering the beans as they become available frozen in their pods, frozen shelled, and fresh cooked in their pods. Current research shows that 25 grams of soy protein a day helps reduce the risk of heart disease, which means that ½ a cup of these tasty little green gems supplies 16 grams of complete protein.
The beans also provide vitamin A, fiber, calcium, and a mix of phytochemicals, including isoflavins that act as antioxidants. Those are the things that fight disease in our bodies. These soybeans look like snow peas, except that the beans look more like limas, not peas.

EDDOE: Better known as taro or dasheen, an edible tuber eaten cooked like potatoes. The tender leaves can also be cooked and eaten.

EEL: There are several varieties of this fish that looks like a snake, found in both fresh and salt water. The flesh is tender, rich, and delicate. **Elvers** are immature eels. They are transparent but have reached the shape of eels. At this stage, they are caught and cooked like tiny fish.

The **English** are fond of eel pies and jellied eel. Jellied eel is small pieces of eel in pale green aspic, served in cups, and sprinkled with chili vinegar. The **Japanese** don't just like eels, they love them. They claim it cures the doldrums and revives good health. In Tokyo they have **eeleries** where they slice and grill up to 10,000 eels a day! You can order eel sushi, eel roll or eel fillet served over rice. What does it taste like? One food critic says it tastes like fishy chicken–fatty but light–and better with soy sauce. Roasted eel in tins is about like sardines. In Spain, you can order eel omelettes. But here's the all time best eel story. Baseball's Babe Ruth–it is said– liked eels pickled and smothered with chocolate ice cream. You may feel like Ogden Nash when he wrote,

"I don't mind eels
except at meals
and the way they feels."

Eels must be alive when purchased. Have the fish dealer skin and clean them. The meat is very perishable and should be cooked as soon as possible. Eels can be fried, poached, broiled, baked, or stewed, and can be served hot or cold. Eels are also available smoked and canned. **Nutrition facts** per 3 ounces: 156 calories, 92 calories from fat, 9.9g total fat (15%), 2g saturated fat (10%), 107.2mg cholesterol (36%), 43.4mg sodium (2%), zero carbohydrates and fiber, 15.7g protein (31%), 2955 IU vitamin A (59%), 2mg vitamin C (3%), 17mg calcium (2%), and .4mg iron (2%)

EGG:

CACKLEBERRIES
by Cheryl L. Hoyer

Have you ever eaten a cackleberry? I bet you have. Cackleberries are chicken eggs! A chicken egg is **an amazing creation!**

It takes 24 to 25 hours for an egg to form in the reproductive tract of a hen. The process begins with a **cell** called an "ovum" contained in a thin envelope (**follicle**). **Yolk granules** develop in the ovum until the yolk is large as one in a freshly laid egg. The yolk is freed from the ovary and grasped by the **oviduct**, a long winding tube that leads to an opening under the chicken's tail. As the yolk moves along the oviduct, the rest of the egg is formed in layers. The **shell** is made last in the lower part of the oviduct. The egg usually moves through the oviduct small-end first, but, surprisingly, comes out large end first. When egg-laying time comes, the hen squats and forces the egg from her body through the opening under her tail. Then she cackles! Why? No one knows for sure. Maybe she is very proud and wants everyone to notice what she has done! Or, she may be saying, "What a relief!"

Fertile Eggs

Did you know that not all eggs make baby chickens? The egg must be fertilized, and after being laid, it has to be kept warm (99 to 100 degrees) for 21 days. Warming is done by a hen or by machines called "incubators." Eggs also must be turned every few hours. Turning prevents the chick from sticking to the inside of the shell. Imagine that you are a mother hen. Not only do you have to keep your eggs warm 24 hours a day, but you also have to turn each one of them every few hours, and keep it up for 21 days! Now that's a job!

An egg has four main parts: the **shell, white, yolk**, and the **germ.** The germ is an area the size of a pin-head on the yolk. It develops into a chick in a fertilized egg. You wouldn't notice it, but the white has four layers, two thin and two thick. The thick layer around the yolk is twisted into a rope-like structure called the **"chalaza."** It acts like ropes for a swinging cradle. The chalaza is attached at each end of the egg to the outer thick white layer, anchoring the yolk, but allowing it to move easily. A growing baby chick has a built-in rocking chair

Preparing Eggs

How many ways of preparing eggs can you think of? You can fry, scramble, poach, boil, and make omelets, casseroles, pies, cakes, and candy. Another good thing about eggs is that they will stay fresh for a long time if stored properly. Freshly laid eggs have an air space at the large end. If they are stored with the large end up (just like they are placed in cartons at the store), and kept at temperature just above freezing, they will keep for many months. That's right, months! Are eggs just good food? No way! They are made into soap, paint, ink, shampoo, medicine, and vaccines. Yes, eggs are used to make all of these things and many more. What part of the egg do you think is used to make fertilizer and animal feed? If you said, "the shell" you would be right. Why, eggshells are even used for art. They are broken in pieces, dyed, and used to create mosaic pictures.

Green Eggs or Blue?

Last, but not least, is the fun of dyeing eggs at Easter. If you don't want to go to all the trouble of dyeing eggs, just go to a local farm and ask for eggs from an Aracuana hen. They pop out of the chicken already colored green or blue. Oh, yes they really do!

WITCHES & EGGS
by Eva Holmes

What do witches and eggs have in common? They both play an important part in the Swedish Easter celebration. As is often the case with major holy days, certain superstitions were attached to Easter. Swedish people once believed that there were women who practiced black magic (Easter hags). Hags were thought to gather in a nearby church tower on Maundy Thursday, where they might fly off on brooms to some place called *Bla kulla*.

175

It's told that there once was a brave young man who went to a church late one Easter night. When the witches started to gather, he saw his fiance among them. Astonished, he made a sudden move and the witches discovered him. His fiance looked at him and said, "God bless your beautiful hair!" But the poor man went instantly bald.

People were hesitant to start a fire in the fireplace on Easter morning. The one who first got smoke up the chimney was assumed to be one of the "Easter hags." It was not uncommon that witches got caught in the chimneys on their way home from *Bla kulla*. To be really sure that the chimney was free from magical beings you had to burn nine different types of non-evergreen trees. People did everything they could to protect themselves from ill powers at play during those days. They lit bonfires and shot firearms into the sky in hope to scare off any airborne evildoer. Crosses, stars and other holy symbols were painted on doors. Axes and scythes were hung crisscross over live stock.

Fear of the supernatural has triggered hysterical witch hunts from time to time over the centuries in Sweden, sending unknown numbers of innocent women to their fate. Such grim superstitions have a more cheerful legacy in modern times. Now, on Easter eve Swedish boys and girls dress up as hags and pay visits to their neighbors. Some give a small hand-decorated "Easter letter," hoping for a sweet or a coin in return.

What would Swedish Easter be without a grand bonfire? Weeks ahead, children gather fallen tree branches, old Christmas trees, and anything else that will kindle. Villages vie to see who can build the biggest one. The custom of shooting also lives on, but today firecrackers replace firearms. Hard-boiled eggs are traditionally eaten the evening before Easter Sunday. Elaborate egg-shaped "boxes" filled with sweets are given to the children the next morning. Branches of birch or willow are brought into homes and schools, commemorating Christ's entry into Jerusalem. The tree branches symbolizing the palm fronds laid in front of Jesus. So the next time you celebrate Easter, why not eat a couple of hard-boiled eggs and wish someone you know "*Glad Pask*" (Happy Easter).

Activities

TOSS A CACKLEBERRY

Eggs can be lots of fun, too! Have you ever played Egg Toss? When you play this game, eventually someone will end up with egg on their face, clothes, or shoes, and it might be you! Two players stand about two feet apart facing each other. They take turns tossing a RAW EGG back and forth. Each time a player tosses, that player takes one step back. Continue tossing until the egg breaks. The player with the broken egg is the loser. This game can also be played using teams of two or more groups, with two players on each team. The team who has the most distance between them before breaking the egg is the winner. –*Cheryl L. Hoyer*

ROLLING EGGS AT EASTER

In some villages in Dorset, England, the children have a fun custom during the Easter celebration. Eggs are hand painted, then rolled down the grassy banks of a steep slope. The idea is to see how far the egg will roll without being damaged. The egg that rolls the farthest is the winner. The egg is symbolic of the stone being rolled away from the tomb of Jesus. --*Jean B. Seymour*

EGG IN THE BOTTLE TRICK

If you like to amaze your friends, tell them you can put an egg in a bottle. What you will need:

Hard cooked egg, shelled
Bottle
Boiling water

The chosen bottle must have a slightly smaller neck. Many juice bottles will work perfectly. Show your friends that the egg won't fit into the bottle. Now carefully pour in some boiling water, swirl the water, and pour the water out. Quickly place the egg on the mouth of the bottle. The egg will be sucked into the bottle. The scientific explanation is simple. Heating the bottle causes the air molecules inside to become more active. Some molecules will escape out of the bottle. The egg has sealed the molecules inside. Once these molecules begin to cool, the air pressure inside the bottle will lower as compared to the air outside of the bottle. The outside higher air pressure will push the egg into the bottle, thus equalizing the inside and outside air pressure. Now how do you get the egg out of the bottle?

THE EGG: IS IT RAW OR COOKED?

Suppose you have hard cooked some eggs and by mistake placed them in the carton with raw eggs. How can you tell which is which? No, you don't need to crack the shell to tell. It's easy! **Just spin the eggs, and they will tell you.** On a dinner plate spin each egg. The eggs that spin the longest are hard cooked. Now spin a hard cooked egg with a raw egg, and you will see the raw egg will stop first, while the cooked egg will continue spinning. Another trick is to spin a raw egg, stop it, release it, and it will continue to spin. Try the same with a cooked egg. What happens? Yes, it stops spinning. The scientific explanation involves inertia, the tendency of something to keep moving or remain still. A raw egg has more inertia because the contents are liquid. While you stopped the shell from spinning, the inside of the raw egg was still moving, and this moving liquid started the egg spinning again. --*RSC*

A FEW EGG TIPS YOU NEED TO KNOW

Separating Eggs: It's best to separate eggs when they are cold, since the yolks are less likely to break. Carefully crack the egg in the center, pull apart over a bowl and let the whites pour into the bowl. Pour the remaining yolk into the other half of the shell to remove the remaining whites. If the yolk breaks, even a little yolk in the whites will prevent the whites from beating to full volume. Best to separate the egg in a small bowl, then add the separated whites to a larger bowl with the other whites, thus preventing any yolk to contaminating a whole bowl of whites. If a small bit of yolk falls into the whites, it generally can be removed with the corner of a paper towel.

Beating Eggs: Eggs beat best to full volume at room temperature, whether it is the whole egg, the yolks or the whites. If a recipe requires the egg to be slightly beaten, beat only until frothy or foamy with large air bubbles. When beating only the yolk, use a narrow diameter bowl and beat until thick and lemon-yellow in color.

Beating Egg Whites: Use a bowl with a small rounded bottom when beating egg whites. Egg whites will generally double in volume, so make sure the bowl is large enough. The bowl must be thoroughly clean without even a small trace of fat. When using an electric beater, beat at high speed for best results. Never use a blender to beat egg whites. Most recipes will call for stiffly beaten egg whites, but not dry. Stiffly beaten whites will be foamy with small air cells and the peaks will lean over when the beater is removed. When a recipe requests stiffly beaten whites to the dry stage, the peaks will stand straight up and generally the whites will slip easily out of the bowl. Some recipes require cream of tartar. If not available use ½ teaspoon of vinegar or lemon juice per three egg whites. When beating for meringues, once at the stiff stage, add sugar, one tablespoon at a time, and beat until glossy.

Adding Eggs to a Hot Mixture: Slightly beat the eggs just until blended. Add a small quantity of the hot mixture to the beaten eggs, mixing well. Continue to add more hot mixture until the outside of the bowl feels warm. Then gradually add remaining hot mixture, stirring constantly. If the beaten eggs are added to the hot mixture all at once, the eggs will lump in the hot mixture. Eggs are generally added to a hot mixture to thicken it.

Eggs and Cholesterol

There's a great deal of confusion about eggs. Some nutritionists present serious health claims about cholesterol and fat. Whole eggs contain cholesterol and saturated fat. However, considering that eggs offer an inexpensive way to obtain the highest quality of protein in nature, it makes sense to take a close look at the egg. Egg protein is superior to all other animal and vegetable protein. It's the complete protein with a well balanced combination of amino acids. The egg yolk contains 212.5mg of cholesterol (71%) and 5.1g of fat (1.6g of the egg's fat is saturated or 8%). There's nothing wrong with some cholesterol. It is a type of fat that plays many important roles in the human body, including being part of every cell. Cholesterol is necessary for vitamin D synthesis in the skin and for the production of hormones, and it is a major constituent of brain and nervous tissue.

For those with high blood cholesterol concentrations, it is important to limit cholesterol. Hence, egg yolks would not be nutritionally wise. Most people consume about 450mg of cholesterol per day from animal products (eggs, meat, milk, cheese, etc.). The recommendation is to limit cholesterol intake to no more than 300mg per day to avoid potential health problems. In terms of eggs, this would be about one extra large egg. The egg white has no fat, and has more protein than the yolk (whites have 3.5g or 7%, the yolk at 2.8g protein or 6%). There's no limit to the number of egg whites you can consume, as the egg white has only 17 calories per egg. Do you want scramble eggs with less fat? Scramble one whole egg with four egg whites (makes 2 servings). You will received the quantity, protein and the taste of a complete egg. Also two egg whites can replace one whole egg in most recipes. www.eggland.com

Moderation is the key when it comes to fat. Looking at the **Food Guide Pyramid**, an egg is about a ½ serving (a serving of meat is 2 to 3 ounces). Just limit your daily content on meat to enjoy an egg. Like all protein foods, bacteria is a problem. However, with proper handling and cooking, there should not be a problem. Keep eggs refrigerated in the original carton.

Discard eggs that are broken in the carton. Cooking eggs at 160° will kill almost any bacteria. Whites should be completely set and the yolks begin to set, but not hard. If you like lightly cooked fried eggs, covering the pan will help increase the temperature and kill the bacteria.
Nutrition facts per egg: 74 calories, 46 calories from fat, 5g total fat (8% daily value), 1.6g saturated fat (8%), 212.5mg cholesterol (71%), 63mg sodium (3%), zero carbohydrates and fiber, 6.3g protein (13%), 317 IU vitamin A (6%), zero vitamin C, 25mg calcium (2%) and .7mg iron (4%). -- *American Egg Board*

EGG FRUIT: Native to Central America, this yellow-orange fruit is also known as yellow sapote, popular fresh or cooked.

EGGNOG: A cold beverage made with eggs, sugar, milk and a dash of nutmeg, especially popular at holidays with rum or brandy added.

EGGPLANT: The eggplant, which contains no eggs, is a fruit (a berry), that is eaten as a vegetable. It looks like the squash family but is related to the potato and tomato. It is believed the eggplant originated in the East Indies. The name may come from the small white variety which does look like a hen's egg. Eggplants come in various sizes and shapes. They also come in white, yellow, and red, but purple is most common. Eggplants can be boiled, pan-fried, deep fried, baked, or broiled. They make excellent appetizers, stuffed and baked, or stewed with vegetables and/or meat. Eggplants are found in many classic recipes from the Mediterranean to Asia. When purchasing an eggplant, look for a firm, glossy, smooth skin without soft or brown spots. If the skin is dull, it's overripe. **Nutrition facts** per ½ cup: 11 calories, zero fats and sodium, 2.5g carbohydrates (1%), 1g fiber (4%), .4g protein (1%), 34 IU vitamin A (1%), 1mg vitamin C (1%), zero calcium, and .1mg iron (1%). www.littlebeanproduce.com.

EIGHT-BALL ZUCCHINI: Another summer squash has hit the market. This tennis ball size squash is dark green and tastes like its skinny counterpart. Eight-ball has fewer seeds, hence makes it perfect for stuffing. When stuffed, best to bake it, and it will keep its shape. Eight-ball can also be sliced, then boiled, broiled, or grilled. Another favorite is to coat with an egg and flour mixture and deep fry.

ELDERBERRY: The elderberry tree grows wild all over Europe, West Asia and North America. The flowers, as well as the berries, have been eaten for thousands of years. The flowers are boiled to make a medicinal tea, both in Europe and by Native Americans. Elderberries are still said to be very effective against colds and flu. Since Medieval times, cooks have delighted diners with elderberry flower fritters and elder flowers still go into muffins and pancakes. Perhaps the most popular use for elderberries has long been in wine. A nonalcoholic elderberry cordial is one of the delights of summer when elderberries are common. You may even find elderberries in British chutney, Scandinavian fruit soups, and Swiss candy drops, as well as American jellies. **Neither** flowers nor berries are edible raw since they taste awful and contain a poisonous alkaloid. Cooking destroys the alkaloid. **Nutrition facts** per ½ cup: 53 calories, 3 calories from fat, .4g total fat (1%), zero saturated fat and sodium, 13.3g carbohydrates (4%), 5.1g fiber (20%), .5g protein (1%), 435 IU vitamin A (9%), 26mg vitamin C (43%), 28mg calcium (3%) and 1.2mg iron (6%),

ELEPHANT APPLE: Native to the Philippines, produces a yellow or green 5-inch fruit used in jellies. In India it is cooked as a vegetable.

ELEPHANT GARLIC: A very large, slightly milder form of garlic. Bulbs have been known to weight as much as a pound.

ELEPHANT STEW:

In some regions of the world, only wild game is available. And when it comes to a party for several thousand people, this recipe is often served.

1 elephant, cut up into bite-size pieces
Gravy, either brown or white, your choice
2 rabbits
Salt and pepper to taste

Start this recipe early because it can take one person up to two months to cut up the elephant.

1. Put meat in an extra large pot and cover with gravy.
2. Best cooked outside, over an open fire. Wood offers the best flavor, but some use kerosene since it doesn't take as much time to watch the fire.
3. It will take up to a month to cook, so be patient.
The recipe serves about 4,000, however, if more are expected add the 2 rabbits. Add the rabbits only in an emergency, since many of your guests won't like hare in their stew.
4. Season the stew at serving time.

ELIXIR: An aromatic liquid containing alcohol used for flavoring, also known as "extract."

ELK: A member of the deer family, larger than deer, smaller than moose. The Shawnee natives called them *wapiti*, meaning "white" or "pale." Elk are found in North America, Siberia, Sweden,

Norway, and the Baltics. The meat can be used in any venison recipe. **Nutrition facts** per 3 ounces: 94 calories, 12 calories from fat, 1.2g total fat (2%), .5g saturated fat (2%), 46.8mg cholesterol (16%),49.3mg sodium (2%), zero carbohydrates and fiber, 19.5g protein (39%),zero vitamins A and C, zero calcium and 2.4mg iron (13%)

EMBLIC: Native to tropical Asia, produces a green, sour, round 3/4-inch fruit that is eaten fresh and made into preserves.

EMPIRE APPLES: A medium-size red apple with distinctive striped appearance. Empires are good raw or cooked in pies and sauces. The white flesh is creamy white and semi-firm.

EMU: (emoo) A smaller Australian cousin to the ostrich, emu meat tastes great when barbecued. Like lean beef, it has very little fat and cholesterol. Emu flesh is available in some supermarkets and restaurants that serve game. Emu farming has been tried in the USA with varying degrees of success.

EN PAPILLOTE refers to food that is baked in parchment. As the food bakes, the steam makes parchment puff up like a dome. This French specialty is served on the plate in the parchment and the diner slits open the paper to let the wonderful fragrance escape. The food contents is usually a mild fish, such as pollock, with spinach, tomatoes and mushrooms.

ENDIVE: A salad green native to the East Indies and in the chicory family. Endive has a mildly bitter flavor. In America, its curly leaves add charm to salads. Pennsylvania Dutch cooks toss endive with a hot bacon and vinegar dressing. In Europe it is cooked as a vegetable or in a broth. The main crop is available during the late fall to early spring. Endive likes cool climate, hence, when grown in warmer areas, the very young green leaves need to be picked early for the best flavor. Escarole, another salad green, is related to endive. **Nutrition facts:** Endive is low in calories, is rich in vitamin A, and a fair source for vitamin C and iron.

ENGLISH MUFFIN: A yeast dough cut about 3-inches in diameter and 1-inch thick, and baked on a griddle. To split the muffin open, use a fork all around the muffin and tear apart. Some packaged muffins come precut.

ENGLISH WALNUTS: Also known as Persian walnuts, and cultivated for centuries in the Mediterranean. This wrinkled hard-shell contains two irregular shaped nuts covered with a thin brown skin. In Old England the nut was called *wealhhnutu*, meaning "foreign nut," since it was an import. When brought to America, English walnuts were grafted onto the hardy native black walnut trees to be grown commercially. They soon passed the black walnuts in popularity because the black walnuts are so much harder to harvest and crack. English walnuts are eaten fresh, and added to cakes, cookies, candy, and ice cream. www.walnut.org; www.diamondwalnut.org.

ENOKI MUSHROOMS (Ee-no'-kee): This fragile, flower-like mushroom grows in small clusters with long slender stems and tiny button caps. They are creamy in color, with a mild, light flavor, and a slight crunch. Before use, trim roots at cluster base, and separate stems before serving, and handle with care. Enoki mushrooms are best enjoyed eaten raw in salads and on sandwiches. Also used as a garnish for appetizers, soups, and entrees. Great with Asian dishes.

ENRICHMENT: A process of replacing nutrients to grains.

ENTERCÔTE: It's the meat cut between the 9th and 11th ribs of beef and called "Delmonico" steak.

ENTRÉ: (ahn-tray) French term meaning the main course dish of a meal.

ENZYMES: The dictionary defines, "A complex protein molecule, originating from living cells and capable of producing certain chemical changes in organic substances by catalytic action, as in digestion."

Enzymes are considered the "fountain of life," since without them the body would die. The body is one big chemical factory, and enzymes are needed for every chemical action and reaction. The immune system's function is to fight off all foreign invaders in the body, such as bacteria, viruses, carcinogens, and other chemicals. It relies almost totally on enzymes to do its job. A weakened immune system has less enzymes and it is necessary to replace them. Also enzymes have a limited life and must be replaced regularly.

Enzymes come from food, which converts to more than 3,000 varieties of enzymes needed for various purposes. Unfortunately, food cooked at high temperatures kills all enzymes, so it is imported to eat raw foods or take enzyme supplements. Some important enzymes are in meat, but people don't eat raw meat anymore. Also, lots of food consumed is processed, and that kills enzymes as well. The good news, with a young body, even a small amount of enzymes from food will manufacture in large numbers for the young body's needs. As you grow older, this ability diminishes, and your immune system weakens, allowing disease easy access. So you see why it's important to eat raw vegetables and fruits to keep your enzymes active. Enzymes are a complex subject, worthy of a separate study. On a practical side, eat lots of pineapple and raw cabbage. When you're peeling potatoes, take a bite of the raw potato to aid your digestive enzymes.

ESCALOPE: A dish prepared with thin slices of meat, generally veal, and fried in butter. In Italy it is called *"scaloppine."*

ESCAROLE: A curly member of the lettuce family, similar to endive but with broader leaves.

ESCARGOT: (es-cahr-go) A land mollusk, better known in America as snails. The French and Italians consider them as a delicacy. The best come from the vineyards, so the experts say. In the United States, snails are just another garden pest, and only a few gourmets love them. Snails have little taste; if it weren't for the butter or garlic sauces, they would be bland. Snails are prepared by boiling in water and should be served in their shells. Purists have special snail forks and pincers to

hold them. Oyster forks or a nutpick works just as well. Snails are also available canned.
Nutrition facts per 3 ounces: 68 calories, 14 calories from fat, 1.7g total fat, zero saturated fat and cholesterol, zero sodium, 1.7g carbohydrates (1%), zero fiber, 13.6g protein (21%), zero vitamins A and C, zero calcium, and 3.4mg iron (19%) See SNAILS.

ESPAGNOLE: A French sauce similar to brown sauce.

ESPRESSO: An Italian strong, dark coffee brewed with a special espresso maker that heats the water to boiling so that resulting steam is forced under pressure up through the very fine coffee grounds. The resulting coffee is so rich it has to br drunk in small sips. The coffee requires a special dark roasted coffee bean ground almost to powder. Cappuccino is espresso with hot frothy milk added. The are electric machines and also traditional stove top coffee makers for both espresso and cappuccino. Notice it is not ex-presso. There is no "x" in espresso.

ESSENCE: A concentrated liquid from meat or vegetable stock used for flavoring other foods. Also the distillation of mint, oranges, etc. for flavoring.

EVAPORATE: To remove moisture from a liquid or a solid by boiling.

EVAPORATED MILK: A canned milk from which 60% of the water has been removed. The invention of evaporated milk in cans was a great boon to mankind since milk could the be preserved and transported without spoiling quickly.

ELSIE THE COW AND BEEF BISCUITS
Borden, the Crazy Inventor

Inventor, Gail Borden had many strange ideas during his lifetime. One invention began in 1844, in Galveston, Texas. His wife and son had earlier died from yellow fever. It was known that yellow fever was carried by mosquitoes, and that yellow fever started shortly after the winter months. Borden thought if he could have kept his wife and son chilled for a long period of time, they wouldn't have died.

Borden made a giant refrigerator, which was chilled with ether. He invited the citizens of Galveston to live in his refrigerator for a week. He claimed the white frost would put an end to this disease. The citizens knew Borden was weird, so fortunately no one took him up on his offer. Even though Borden had no formal education, he continued with many inventions. Most of them either didn't work, or were not accepted. One invention, the "beef biscuit," almost succeeded. He boiled down 120 pounds of beef to ten pounds, dehydrated it, mixed it with flour, and kneaded it into biscuits, which he baked. The taste was something between melted glue and molasses, so most people found them disgusting.

However, **Borden's beef biscuits** were described in the *Scientific American* as one of the most valuable inventions at that time. Both the Navy and the Army took an interest and tried them out.

They found the biscuits were yucky and still left you hungry. The biscuits caused headaches, nausea and muscular depression. His beef biscuits did find their way into the California gold fields with the gold seekers and they were taken on an Arctic expedition. Nevertheless, Borden's beef biscuits failed and he went bankrupt in 1852. Failures didn't seem to bother Borden. He knew there was a need for condensing foods. Since potatoes were mostly water, he thought he could reduce the potato to the size of a pill. Why couldn't a pumpkin fit into a tablespoon? Could a watermelon fit on a saucer? While he didn't accomplish those dreams, he did reduce six and half gallons of apple cider down to one gallon, but no one was interested in condensed apple cider.

During the American Civil War, Borden shipped some pure condensed blackberry juice to General Sherman. Sherman gave the juice to some of his sick soldiers and this juice helped cure an epidemic of dysentery that the Army surgeons couldn't control. In the early 1850s, Borden had returned to America on a ship from England. He witnessed many children dying aboard as a result of scanty milk from the shipboard cows. Borden set forth to condense milk. He concluded that milk was a living fluid, and as soon as milk came from the cow, it began to die and decompose. Inventors thought if milk was boiled, it wouldn't spoil. Milk cooked over a hot fire always became discolored, burnt, and still soured.

Borden's idea was to use a vacuum condenser, called a "vacuum pan," that **the Shakers of New Lebanon, New York** used to condense fruit juice. Inside Borden's vacuum pan was a heating coil that warmed the milk slowly and evenly, which allowed the milk to evaporate without burning. In 1856, Borden received a patient for his condenser he called "vacuo." Borden opened his canned condensed milk factory in Wassaic, New York, and sold his milk door-to-door. For the first time, his milk could be kept pure, germ free, and stored without refrigeration. At the same time it could travel long distances, thus replacing the shipboard cows. His milk business boomed. By the late 1860s Borden had changed the dairy business and his condensed milk made him rich, respected, and famous. The symbol for his milk, was Elsie the Cow.

Even at his death at the age of 72, many thought Borden was a genius, but at the same time thought he had a loose screw or two. Today the Borden business has grown into a three-billion dollar a year business. It all began with a series of crazy inventions and his most successful invention-- evaporated condensed milk.

EXTRACT: A concentration of liquid made from herbs, spices, and fruits used as flavorings, such as vanilla. Beef extract is another name for beef bouillon cubes.

EXTRUDED: Some food can be extruded, such as breakfast cereals (into the letters of the alphabet and stars), pasta, and corn appetizers, The process of forming long thin shapes by forcing the material such as dough or plastics through a fixed shape. Imagine a potato pushed through a French fry cutter as an example of "extruding."

EYES: Yes, it's true. Even eyeballs are considered in some cultures to be good food. If you are ever in the Middle East, don't faint if you are invited to eat a sheep's eye. The eyes of the giant catfish of the Mekong River do more than see. They provide Laotians diners a great treat. In Alaska, some of the Alaskan Natives prize fish heads, and it's always a fight who will get the eyes.

A SICILIAN FEAST
by Marie Prato

In Palermo, Sicily, skinned sheep heads, complete with eyeballs and tongue sit in the windows of the meat markets. Outside the stores, swinging in the tropical breeze, large pieces of white spongy tripe hang over the sidewalk, barely missing the heads of pedestrians. From hooks near the door, pink cow stomachs the size of hot water bottles jiggle whenever a customer walks into the store. On the sidewalk and in the store, shoppers inspect the delicacies with the same intensity as a jeweler picking out a diamond.

Tripe, the inner lining of a cow's stomach, is usually dipped in egg, breaded and then fried in olive oil until it is a deep golden brown. The empty stomachs form pouches to be stuffed with either a chopped meat or bread stuffing before baking. For a really special occasion, the good Sicilian host buys the sheep heads. After rubbing the outside with garlic and lemon, the entire head is placed on a rack in the oven to bake. After the meat is tender and juicy, the sheep's head is placed on a platter and set in the middle of the festive table. Then the feast begins. Forks fly as eyeballs are pulled from the sockets and the tongue is torn from the sheep's mouth. "*Mangia, mangia!*" says the proud host. "Eat, Eat."

Ff

FADGE: North Irish potato pancake.

FALAFEL: This Arab food is growing in popularity in America. It is a combination of garbanzo beans, yellow peas, bulgur, wheat germ, onions, garlic, cumin, coriander, pepper, salt, sesame seeds, soy sauce, baking powder, and parsley. The mix is combined with water, made into patties, and fried. Enjoy with yogurt or make a sandwich. Falafel is available at many supermarkets and health food stores. It is low in calories, fat, and a good source for protein. –*Virginia McNear*

FARCE: A French word for stuffing.

FARINA: A cereal grain where most of the bran and germ has been removed. Farina is a bland tasting breakfast cereal, and is the first solid most babies eat, because it easy to digest. It is also used in sweet puddings and a type of spoon bread. In English and Italian the word means simply "flour."

FARMS: Farms, the land and it's buildings where food is produced, come in all sizes and kinds. A family farm may have only a garden plot, a cow and some chickens. Or it may be thousands of acres of wheat farmed by one family with massive modern equipment.

MAKE YOUR NEXT VACATION ON A FARM

When European visitors first came to America, there were no inns like inns back home. The first inns were private homes which welcomed travelers, much like today's bed and breakfast inns. As the demand increased, hotels filled the need. In the 1930s and '40s came courtels, now called motels, for those driving across the country. For decades dude ranches offered greenhorn Easterners a vacation experience on a working cattle ranch. Most dude ranches were only a place to watch, not take an active part in the daily ranch duties. Today's dude ranches offer all kinds of recreation, from horseback riding to golf and tennis.

Today bed and breakfast inns have again become popular. Some of these inns are restored country inns, used by travelers a hundred or more years ago. Like the dude ranches, many bed and breakfast inns offer a variety of activities, from fishing to maybe a bike tour of the countryside.

Dude Farms

Now there are dude farms. The word "dude" originally referred to an Easterner who went west for a cattle ranch vacation. Eastern dude farms combine the idea of bed and breakfast with dude ranch experience. However, in the west, they call them "agri-farms."

Where Did this Idea Come From?

Many farmers today are not making enough profit from agriculture so they have opened up their roomy homes to vacationers. Unlike the dude ranches where it is "look and see," the farmers often use "dude" help in the planting, harvesting, or endless chores required.

Farm Fun

The farm can be a fun place. You can wake up early, pick some strawberries for breakfast or maybe harvest some blueberries to be added to your pancakes and muffins. After breakfast, you can help feed the chickens, gather eggs, and maybe milk a cow or a goat. There will still be time before lunch to tour the barn or an apple orchard. After the fall harvest, many of the corn fields will be turned into elaborate mazes, a great way to spend the afternoon. A hearty dinner is served either as a buffet or home-style, where it is necessary to say, "Please pass the potatoes."

Almost every farm has a pond for swimming, and maybe even a rope that you can swing on as you drop into the water. And probably the pond has fish, and with a little luck your catch might be your dinner. After dinner there may be a hayride or farm hands to entertain you with song and dance.

No Two Alike

Every farm is different, no two are alike. Some of the farms offer only day visits where you can harvest vegetables to take home. Others will also offer a lunch with fresh produce from the farm and an apple pie for dessert. Maybe you'll be offered afternoon tea with cake and cookies, and for the adults a wine tasting party.

Holiday Events

Enterprising farmers host special events throughout the year, such as on the 4th of July with fireworks displays, or Halloween fun in a big pumpkin patch. On holidays like Thanksgiving and Christmas, some farms offer seasonal feasts you will never experience in a restaurant. To find a participating farm, contact a chamber of commerce, a visitor bureau, farm bureau or the agriculture department of a university. Many regions have set up farm trails with maps and the best time to visit for harvesting. Whether your farm visit is just for the day, or the weekend, or maybe a week's vacation, you can find a new way of life that you will surely enjoy. You will not only see where your food is produced, you will receive a real-life, hands-on experience.

FARMER'S MARKETS: Open air markets where local farmers around the world bring their produce fresh from the farms in the warm months. Indoor versions of the market are open all year.

MARKET DAY IN ENGLAND
by Jean B. Seymour

Saturday was market day in Okehampton, Devonshire, England. Farmers came into town to sell their produce and to go to the cattle market. My mother took me to the indoor market where I would skip down the centre aisle, looking at the stall laden with fresh produce and home baked goods, chutneys and jams. Our target was a stall right at the end of the aisle, a long wooden trestle table covered by a white sheet. On it were two large enameled basins filled with double Devon cream., a thick yellow crust on top of each bowl. Beside the basins sat two large bowls of freshly laid brown eggs. Alongside lay a long slab with two squares of farm butter, covered by muslin cloth on a wire frame.

At the end of the trestle table stood a dozen white enameled buckets filled with summer blooms. There were dahlias of every hue imaginable, their velvet petals reaching upward toward the warm sunshine that filtered through the glass roof. The air near the table was heady with perfume from Michaelmas daisies, sweet williams, columbine, yellow daisies, marigolds and rich gladioli.

My mother gave me a mixed bunch of flowers to carry home, while she bough butter with a swam stamped on it, two dozen eggs, and double Devon cream. On the way home, we called at t the news agent where I spend my fourpenny weekly allowance. A penny spent on a chocolate bar, two halfpenny toffee bars, and a twopenny Enid Bylton Sunny Stories. My Sunday treat was nearly complete knowing that we would have homemade apple pie with Devon cream for supper. See DEVONSHIRE CREAM.

Even in a big city, chances are there's a farmer's market near you. Most of the produce sold at these markets is organic or **IPM** (see WHAT'S ORGANIC?). Other products you may find are honey, seafood and shellfish, poultry, jams and jellies, baked goods, and dairy products. All are grown, made, or raised by the farmers, who then sell directly to you! This means that the farmers don't have to go through retail stores first, which means they make a direct profit off of their products. Also, farmer's markets are a way to directly support the economy of your community. Markets are great ways to meet members of your

187

community and to talk directly to the people who grow your food. The farmers are happy to tell their customers about how their fruits and vegetables are grown, to give out samples of their food, or even let you visit their farms. Another advantage of shopping at the farmer's market is that all of the produce you buy is in season. It has been picked, often only hours before you buy it, at the peak of ripeness, which means it tastes better.

Commercial supermarkets often receive their produce from thousands of miles away, or even from other countries. This affects the flavor drastically. Produce imported from foreign counties such as Mexico, and South and Central **America** are sprayed with deadly pesticides that are banned in the United States. This is because those countries have no regulations concerning pesticide use. This is why it is not a good idea to buy any produce from those countries, and why you should try to buy produce in season.

The best reason to shop at your local farmer's market is you will get a chance to discover all kinds of unusual and delicious fruits, vegetables, herbs, and they offer recipes how to cook with them. Yes, the farmer's market is a fun place to be. To find a farmer's market near you, call your local chamber or commerce or tourism council. You can also log on to the internet: www.epicurious.com and click the city of your choice for a market's address and hours. The **U.S. Department of Agriculture** has a farmer's market directory, write to them: USDA/AMS/TMD/WAM, Box 96456, Room 2642, South Building, Washington, DC 20090-6456. – *Chef Laurel Miller*

FAT-TAIL SHEEP: These sheep of Afghanistan and other Middle Eastern areas look like small-headed beetles with very long legs. Some have tails that resemble enormous frying pans covered with wool. Others have long tails like a kangaroo's. The tail stores lanolin, acting like the hump of a camel, sustaining the sheep when food is scarce. Afghani nomads use this fat in cooking The fat is lighter and melts easier than regular fat so cooks like to use it. About 25 % of the world's sheep are fat-tailed. –*Virginia McNear*

FAUSTRIMEDINS: A man-made hybrid with green 2-inch long poor fruit. Grown mostly for root stock and grafting.

FEIJOA: (fay-hoa) Native to South America, better known as pineapple guava, produces a green fruit that is eaten fresh, made into jelly and preserves.

FEET: The feet of certain animals do get eaten. Ever heard of pickled pigs feet? Look in your grocer's shelves under specialties foods or with canned meats. They come in a glass jar. You owe it to your sense of adventure to try a jar and share it with friends. You'll find feet meat is more gristle than meat but hungry people will find a way to eat almost anything when the need arises. Mostly calves feet and pig together are boiled to provide gelatin. In **China** they make a tasty chicken feet soup and duck feet are boiled for their gelatin qualities. They don't have a lot of either in China. Uncooked pigs feet are available in many super and meat markets, and chicken feet are usually available in Chinese meat markets. The **Greeks** make a dish called *pihti,* aspic of pig's feet, as old as the ancient Greeks. Today we might still see pig's feet or pig's head on the Christmas table. See PICKLED PIG'S FEET.

PIGS FEET & PORRIDGE, A SWEDISH CHRISTMAS STORY
by Eva Holmes

A thick blanket of snow covered most parts of Sweden. Not in many years had the first Sunday of Advent brought such cold weather. Johan looked at his colorful Advent calendar's 24 "windows" to open until Christmas. He could barely wait. He found the first window right below Santa's green mitten. Inside was a picture of a lit candle.

"Johan, breakfast is ready," his mother called from the kitchen. Dad and *Mar-far* (grandpa) were already seated at the large kitchen table. Britta, his sister, was pouring steaming hot coffee into their ceramic cups. They all sat in silence as Mom lit the first candle on the Advent candelabra.

"Three more Sundays until Christmas," Britta sighed.

During the next few weeks the Renman family cleaned their large house from top to bottom. Britta was flying from room to room with pails of foaming soapsuds. Mom spent most of her time in the kitchen, preparing all kinds of food for the holidays. Added to the usual fare of meatballs and sausages, were seasonal specialties like *lutfish* (dried codfish) and Johan's favorite, jellied pigs feet. The whole house was filled with wonderful odors. Johan tried to be of as much help as he could but no matter where he turned he seemed to get into somebody's way. He preferred to help Dad and *Mar-far* out in the barn.

Night time fell early on the eve of Lucia. Johan took Mar-far's hand as they walked across the white barnyard.

"We better give the cows some extra feed tonight," said *Mar-far*. Johan turned and looked up at him. "You see," continued *Mar-far*, "this is the longest and darkest night of the year. If the cows get hungry, the trolls could lure them away from the farm.

"Have you ever seen them?" whispered Johan.

The old man laughed and shook his head.

The next morning Britta got out of bed well before daybreak. Johan opened the thirteenth window on his Advent calendar. It was to no great surprise that it had a Lucia bride picture inside. A little later Britta came up the stairs, singing the Saint Lucia song. She was dressed in a long white gown. A crown of lighted candles circled her head. She woke the family with coffee and *lussekatter* (saffron rolls). Then she sang a song about the darkness of winter, and the light that is about to return.

On the day before Christmas, Johan's mother called him to the kitchen. "Would you please take some food over to old Mr. Olson. We must not forget about others at this happy time of the year."

When Johan got there, Mr. Olson was out in his yard holding a sheaf of grain in his hand. He waved at Johan. "I want to get this feed out for the birds, but I'm not as limber as I used to be."

Johan climbed up the fence and tied the sheaf to a pole. Mr. Olson explained that many birds around the sheaf indicates a good harvest the following year. Johan handed the food basket to Mr. Olson, and wished him *God Jul* (Merry Christmas).

Johan raced back home. A sweet smell greeted him. Mom and Britta were baking *pepparkakor* (gingerbread cookies). Dad was setting up the tree in the living room. Together they brought the boxes of Christmas tree ornaments down from the attic.

Finally, Christmas Eve arrived. The whole family gathered around the glorious Christmas tree. After dinner Dad read aloud the story of the first Christmas. Afterwards Uncle Tore excused himself. Johan looked out the window. It was snowing heavily. He was wondering if Santa was going to make it. Just then Johan heard a knock on the door.

"It's Santa!"

"Are there any good children here? Santa asked. The voice sounded familiar, thought Johan, and doesn't Santa have the same watch as Uncle Tore?

When the last of the gifts have been handed out, it was time for more food. Mom had prepared a special rice porridge, served with sugar and cinnamon. Hidden in the porridge was a single almond.

"I got it! I got the almond!" Johan cried. His face sagged when Aunt Gerda told him that whoever gets the almond in their bowl will get married in the upcoming year. Everyone including Johan laughed.

"We better save some porridge for *Tomten* (a gnome)," said *Mor-far* and winked at Johan. The children all knew about the little people who were believed to live under the floor boards of the barn.

"Tell us a story about *Tomten*," begged Johan.

"*Mar-far* chuckled. "If he is honored, he is rather good-natured and will take good care of family and livestock. But I remember when I was just a lad, there was a *Tomten* living on a neighboring farm. One particular Christmas Eve, as he sat down to eat his porridge, he noticed that the honey on top was missing. He became furious that he struck the farmer's best milking cow dead. Afterward, *Tomten* sat down to finish the porridge only to find the honey at the bottom of the bowl. In a pang of guilt *Tomten* carried the dead creature to the nearest farm and traded it for an identical cow."

Later when the guests were gone. Johan sat down on the floor and pulled his boots on. Slowly, not to spill the porridge he walked across the starlit barnyard. It was very still in the barn. The cows were lying down, chewing their cud peacefully. Johan stroke one of them gently on the head. Suddenly there was a stir among the dark shadows of the barn. Johan held his breath as a small creature moved across the hay loft. Was it maybe the cat, or was it . . .?

"*God Jul, Tomten, God Jul*," whispered Johan as he placed the porridge bowl next to the ladder leading up to the loft.

FENNEL: It's native to the Mediterranean and a member of the carrot family. All parts of the plant are consumed. The leaves are cooked or used in salads, the shoots are cooked or eaten raw, and the seeds are used as a spice. Anise fennel has a mild licorice flavor, while sweet fennel has a mild celery taste. Fennel can be boiled, braised, or sautéd in butter until tender. **Nutrition facts** per ½ cup: 13 calories, zero fats, 22.6mg sodium (1%), 3.2g carbohydrates (1%), zero fiber,.5g protein (1%), 58 IU vitamin A (1%), 5mg vitamin C (9%), 21mg calcium (2%), and .3mg iron (2%).

FENUGREEK: Related to the pea family, this plant is grown for its irregularly shaped, yellow brown aromatic seeds with a taste of slightly burnt sugar. The seeds are used to make various spice blends which include curry. Fenugreek is also added to soups, stews, breads, and beans. The name means "Greek hay," and indeed, it does make good cattle fodder.

FERMENTATION: A chemical change caused by yeast or bacteria in food which produces a gas, generally carbon dioxide. Fermentation is used in leavening, such as in bread. It also converts fruit juice and grains into vinegar; milk into cultured milk, such as buttermilk and yogurt; and fruit and grains into wine and beer.

FESTIVALS: Food festivals abound across American and the world during harvest seasons. See also individual listings such as Apple, Cranberry and Oyster, for example.

FESTIVALS, WHERE THEY ENTERTAIN, COOK, AND EAT

For hundreds of years, folks have gathered in communities around the world to celebrate a harvest with crafts, dancing, entertainment, and lots of food.

Many of America's festivals started with our Native Americans, and were combined with celebrations by immigrants from Europe, Africa, and Asia. Music and dance take on the character of the region from the Eskimos in Alaska to the Cajuns in Louisiana. The best festivals have weeded-out imitators and have carefully documented authenticity for performances, crafts, and food.

FEBRUARY

Firehouse Art Center **Chocolate Festival**, Norman, Oklahoma*
Florida Citrus Festival, Winter Haven, Florida
Ice Worm Festival, Cordova, Alaska
National **Date** Festival, Indio, California*
Pancake Day, Liberal, Kansas

MARCH
Sweetwater **Rattlesnake** Round Up, Sweetwater, Texas*

APRIL
Catfish Festival, Belzoni, Mississippi
Chattahoochee **Trout** Festival, Helen, Florida
Jell-o Art Show, Eugene, Oregon
Salmon Bake Festival, Warm Springs, Oregon
Stockton **Asparagus** Festival, Stockton, California*
Tater Days, Benton, Kansas
Vermont **Maple** Festival, Saint Albans, Vermont*
World's Biggest **Fish Fry**, Paris, Tennessee

MAY
Apple Blossom Festival, Biglerville, Pennsylvania*
Crawfish Festival, Dormott, Arkansas
International **Horseradish** Festival, Collinsville, Illinois*
Isle of Eight Flags **Shrimp** Festival, Amelia Island, Florida*
Lower Keys **Food** Festival, Big Pine Key, Florida
Owensboro **Barbecue** Festival, Owensboro, Arkansas
Strawberry Festival, Bald Knob, Arkansas
Ramp Festival, Waynesville, North Carolina

Zellwood Street **Corn** Festival, Zellwood, Florida

JUNE
Alabama **Blueberry** Festival, Brewton, Alabama
Dairy Festival, Sulphur Springs, Texas*
Georgia **Peach** Festival, Fort Valley, Georgia*
Insectival, Athens, Georgia
Kutztown Fair, **Pennsylvania Dutch**, Kutztown, Pennsylvania
Nalukataq, **Whale**, A Blanket Tossing Festival, Barrow, Alaska*
New **Fish** Festival, Gloucester, Massachusetts
Okmulgee **Pecan** Festival, Okmulgee, Oklahoma
Putnam County **Dairy** Festival, Eatonton, Georgia*
Strawberry Festival, Handsome Lake, New York

JULY
Blackberry Jam Festival, Lowell, Oregon
Blueberry Festival, Chincoteague, Virginia
Central Maine **Egg** Festival, Pittsfield, Maine
Gilroy **Garlic** Festival, Gilroy, California
Heritage **Seafood** Festival, Wakefield, Rhode Island
Nebraska **Czech** Festival, Wilber, Nebraska*
Peach Festival, Gaffney, South Carolina
South Dakota State **Chili** Cook Off, White, South Dakota
Wild Blueberry Festival, Machias, Maine

AUGUST
Blueberry Arts Festival, Ketchikan, Alaska*
Gloucester **Waterfront** Festival, Gloucester, Massachusetts*
Hope **Watermelon** Festival, Hope, Arkansas
Huckleberry Feast, Warm Springs, Oregon
Northwest Ohio **Rib-Off**, Toledo, Ohio*
Shaker Kitchen Festival, Pittsfield, Massachusetts
Springfield **Filbert** Festival, Springfield, Oregon*
Tomato Festival, Lynchburg, Virginia
West Virginia **Chili** Cook Off, Jane Lew, West Virginia

SEPTEMBER
Apple Festival, Hendersonville, North Carolina*
Banana Festival, Fulton, Kentucky
Cajun Festival, Vinton, Louisiana
Country **Ham** Days, Lebanon, Kentucky
Harvest Festival, South Carver, Massachusetts
Essex **Clamfest**, Cape Ann, Massachusetts

Great **Insect** Fair, Erie, Pennsylvania
Johnny Appleseed Festival, Fort Wayne, Indiana
Louisiana **Shrimp** Festival, Morgan City, Louisiana
Minnesota **Renaissance** Festival, Shakopee, Minnesota*
National Hard **Crab** Derby, Crisfield, Maryland
Montana **Chokecherry** Festival, Lewistown, Montana*
Operation **T-Bone**, Audubon, Iowa*
Persimmon Festival, Mitchell, Indiana
Sheep and Fiber Arts Festival, Bethel, Missouri*
Warrens **Cranberry** Festival, Warrens, Wisconsin*
Watermelon Eating Contest, Pardeeville, Wisconsin

OCTOBER

Apple Butter Festival, Burton, Ohio
Arkansas **Rice** Festival, Weiner, Arkansas
Bayfield **Apple** Festival, Bayfield, Wisconsin
Chatsworth **Cranberry** Festival, Chatsworth, New Jersey
East Texas **Yamboree**, Gilmer, Texas*
Georgia **Peanut** Festival, Sylvester, Georgia
Kansas **Sampler** Festival, Pratt, Kansas*
Luckenbach Ladies **Chili** Bust, Luckenbach, Texas
National **Pecan** Festival, Albany, Florida
National **Shrimp** Festival, Gulf Shores, Alabama*
Norsk **Hostfest**, Minot, North Dakota*
Oyster Festival, Chincoteague, Virgina*
Pismo **Beach Clam** Festival, Pismo Beach, California*
Rice Festival, Crowley, Louisiana
Sorghum Festival, Grayson, Kentucky
South Hero **Applefest**, South Hero, Vermont
Sycamore **Pumpkin** Festival, Sycamore, Illinois
Whole **Enchilada** Fiesta, Las Cruces, New Mexico
World Championship **Chili** Cook Off, Rosamond, California

NOVEMBER

Chitlin' Strut, Salley, South Carolina
Festival of **Gingerbread**, Fort Wayne, Indiana*
Food and Feast, Williamsburg, Virginia
Sausage Festival, Tallahassee, Florida
Terlingua **Chili** Cookoff, Terlingua, Texas
Wurstfest, New Braunfels, Texas

DECEMBER

Apple Festival, Willcox, Arizona

Christmas Market, Georgetown, Colorado
Tamale Festival, Indio, California*

VARIOUS DATES AND LOCATIONS
Attend a **Bug** Festival*
Powwow Pabulum (**Native American Festivals**)*

* For additional information, these festivals will be found under that food. Example Firehouse Art Center **Chocolate Festival**, in the "C" chapter. Many festivals begin in one month and end in the next month, also festival dates will change from year to year. Check your own area chamber of commerce or **call your AAA travel service for information**. Always check to be sure.

** The following food festivals do not celebrate just one food but a variety: Kansas Sampler Festival; Minnesota Renaissance Festival; Nebraska Czech Festival; Norsk Hostfest; Powwow Pabulum.

TEXAS FOLKLIFE FESTIVAL

Would you like to "pig-out" on more than thirty varieties of ethic foods? How about samosa from Indian? Chin-chin from the Nigeria? Chicken adobo from the Philippines? Klobasniks from Czechoslovakia? Or Mexican gorditas? There are also foods from Africa, China, Greece, Italy, Lebanon, Norway, Poland, and lots of Tex-Mex foods as well. Texas is an ethic "melting-pot." Almost every community has their own ethic festival from the Danes in Danevang to the Yugoslavs in Galveston. And not to be left out are the Native Americans with a Thanksgiving fest with Don Juan de Oñate in El Paso to the National Championship Pow-Wow in Grand Prairie. The Institute of Texas Cultures brings them all together in one giant August event, the Texas Folklife Festival. In addition to the food, you will hear the sounds of bagpipes, zithers, dulcimers, mariachis, casanets, guitars, and not to be left out, the oompah bands of Germany. Additional fun events include the watermelon spitting content and climbing a Belgian pole. You can try your hand at branding, grind corn with a stone, learn about mesquite cooking, wood craving, and trick roping. For more information on August dates call the Institute at (210) 458-2390 or for a complete package on San Antonio write to the **Visitors Bureau**, 317 Alamo Plaza, San Antonio, TX 78205 or phone (210) 270-8748 or (800) 447-3372.TX 78205 or phone (210) 270-8748 or (800) 447-3372.

FETA CHEESE: Greek cheese made from sheep and goat's milk and eaten fresh or used for cooking. Great for topping salads. One of the richer cheeses, it's about 45% butterfat.

FIBER: Dietary fiber in food is important for proper bowel moments. Fiber is found in wheat bran, fruit pectin, fruit and vegetable cellulose, and legumes.

Everything You Wanted to Know about . . .
Dietary Fiber . . . but Were Afraid to Ask

In yesteryear, before foods were being overly refined, it was easy to receive plenty of dietary fiber. All breads were made with whole grains, not refined white flour. Fast foods were apples and oranges, not hamburgers and fries. And in many homes, high fiber fruit pies have been replaced with ice cream, which has no fiber.

Over the years, fiber had almost disappeared from our diets and just recently nutritionists have come to understand the importance of fiber in our diets. Once again, many are returning to eat whole foods.

What is Dietary Fiber?

Dietary fiber includes all food substances that your digestive enzymes **cannot break down and utilize** by the body as an energy source. Two type of fibers are **cellulose** (insoluble, meaning it does not dissolve), the major constituent of **plant fiber, and pectin** (soluble, meaning it does dissolve easily), the substance famous for its gelling properties, found in roots, stems, and fruits of plants.

Insoluble fiber found in foods such as bran, whole grains, and vegetables **stimulate the intestines**, keeping digested food moving, and so they take less time to travel through the bowels. That's good for regularity.

Soluble fiber (found in foods such as fruit, oats, and sea vegetables) **moves slower,** which lowers absorption of cholesterol, regulating blood sugar by slowing the absorption of sugar into the bloodstream, and absorbing and removing toxic metals and carcinogens from the body.

The United States Department of Agriculture has no recommendations for the amount of fiber needed. However, nutritionists suggest a range from 30 to 50 grams per day. A low fiber diet is less than 20 grams. If you fall into this lower range, you will need to control your intake of added fiber gradually, since your digestive system will need time to adjust for the extra fiber intake. You can begin by eating a bran muffin instead of a croissant, brown rice instead of white rice, and whole fruit instead of drinking fruit juice.

 Until your body adjusts to the additional fiber, you may experience flatulence and bloating. You can lessen this problem by adding fiber into your diet slowly, and by drinking at least eight cups of water daily.

Too much fiber can lead to mineral deficiencies, since fiber compounds bind with minerals to block absorption. The best way to counter this is by eating yeast-risen breads or by cooking high fiber cereals. A warning, if you have diabetes or elevated cholesterol, consult your physician before drastically increasing your fiber intake.

Some foods that have two or more grams of fiber include: one cup of oatmeal, one fresh banana, one medium raw carrot, one slice of whole wheat bread, one medium orange, one medium apple, 1 medium baked in skin potato, one cup of cooked broccoli, and one cup of cooked black beans. -- *Whole Foods Market*

FIDDLEHEAD: An edible fern found wild in northern New England along streams and lakes. The fronds are picked when young and tender. Fiddlehead is eaten raw in salads or steamed as a vegetable with salt, pepper, and butter. "When I was young, I would go camping in the Sierra Mountains and would find ferns growing along streams. I would pick the young fronds and fry them with bacon." – RSC

FIG: Figs are one of those foods we could talk about all day. There are more than 800 varieties of figs in varied shapes, sizes and colors, from almost white to black. Fresh figs are available during the summer to mid fall. Dried and canned figs are available year round. Fresh and dried figs are eaten raw, baked into bread, made into jam, and stewed for breakfast. Originally grown in Arabia in 2000 B.C. The fig is the first tree mentioned in the Bible (Genesis 3:7) and is the most talked about. Could it have been the forbidden fruit? Ancient Hebrews saw the fig tree as a symbol of peace and prosperity. Their Muslin neighbors called it the "Tree of Heaven." Romans sacrificed fig sap to their god Juno. In Africa, the tree is so sacred that its shade is used for ceremonial purposes.

The most popular of the dried figs are: **Calimyrna**, tender and nutlike flavor, best for eating out of hand; **Black Mission,** distinctive flavor, best for stewing and pies; and **Adriatic**, the most prolific of all varieties suited for stewing and baking. Best fig for canning is the **Kadota**, usually available fresh in season. Fig trees belong to the mulberry family and are especially sensitive to chemicals. Their tiny seeds aid in digestion. **Nutrition facts** per ½ cup: 74 calories, zero fats and sodium, 19.1g carbohydrates (6%), 3.3g fiber (13%), .8g protein (2%), 141 IU vitamin A (3%), 2mg vitamin C (3%), 35mg calcium (3%), and .4mg iron (2%). www.californiafigs.com; www.valleyfig.com.

FIG TRIVIA

- There was a fig tree in the **Garden of Eden**, "...the eyes of both of them were opened, and they knew that they were naked; and they sewed fig leaves together, and made themselves aprons."
- Figs were mentioned in a **Babylonian hymn book** about 2000 BC.
- Figs were so **revered** that Solon, the ruler of Attica (639-559 BC), made it illegal to export the fruit out of Greece, reserving figs solely for his citizens.
- As a token of honor, figs were used as a **training food by the early Olympic athletes**, and figs were also presented as laurels to the winners as the first Olympic "medal."
- Pliny the Elder, the Roman writer (52-113 AD) said, "Figs are restorative, they increase the strength of young people, preserve the elderly in better health and **make them look younger** with fewer wrinkles."
- The fig is reported to have been the **favorite fruit of Cleopatra**, with the asp that ended her life being brought to her in a basket of figs.

■Junipero Sierra first introduced figs to California, and fig trees were planted at each mission.
■While considered a fruit, the **fig is actually a flower** that is inverted into itself. The seeds are drupes or the real fruit. *--California Fig Advisory Board*

FIGGY PUDDING: According to the Oxford Companion to Food, the figgy pudding is "nowadays more sung about in the well-known Christmas carol, than eaten." The original may have been a "plum" pudding, while in early England could have been any dried fruit. In Cornwall, "figgy" still means raisins. Not only was the figgy pudding a Christmas necessity, it is still often eaten on Palm Sunday to remember the story of how Jesus condemned the unfruitful fig tree on that day.

FIJI APPLES: It is said a fuji apple is like fine wine, the flavor improves with age. Fuji's spicy, crisp sweetness makes it excellent out of hand, in a fruit salad, or made into applesauce. Fiji varies from yellow-green with red highlights to very red.

FIJIAN LONGAN: An Asian product; a small, greenish fruit with a leathery skin and translucent subacid flesh, eaten fresh. The longan is closely related to the lychee. www.thaifoods.com

FILBERT: Native to Europe where they are called hazelnuts, filbert nuts are round in shape and cream in color. They are drier than almonds, hence are easy to grind into meal. Filberts are available in shells, shelled, salted and unsalted, and eaten as is or added to baked goods such as cookies and cakes. Called by either name in this country, the hazelnut is enjoying great popularity today in coffee blends. **Nutrition facts** per 1/4 cup: 182 calories, 151 calories from fat, 18g total fat (28%), 1.3g saturated fat (7%), zero cholesterol and sodium, 4.4g carbohydrates (1%), 1.8g fiber (7%), 3.8g protein (8%), zero vitamins A and C, 54mg calcium (5%), and .9mg iron (5%).

SPRINGFIELD FILBERT FESTIVAL

In Oregon's Willamette's Valley, the filbert is commemorated in late August with a three day festival. All food booths must include filberts in their recipes, which includes filbert snow cones, filbert pizza, baked potatoes stuffed with filberts, filbert crusted chicken, and filbert pancakes topped with filbert syrup. You name it and it has filberts! Along with the filbert displays, the festival has top named entertainment, a fireworks shows, talent contests, puppet shows and storytellers. For more information, contact: **The Springfield Filbert Festival**, P.O. Box 480, Springfield, OR 97477 or phone (541) 744-1042 or 744-2628.

FILÉ: (fee-lay) It is made from dried sassafras leaves and used as a thickening agent in Creole cooking. Filé is a key ingredient for making gumbo. It is added gradually to boiling liquid, removed immediately from the heat, and stirring constantly until dish is thickened. Never boil again after filé has been added or it will turn stringy. The French name comes from *filé*, which means "to make into threads." They no doubt gave it the name after seeing how it turned stringy or thready when too hot. Before anyone knew about thickening with gelatin or cornstarch, they could use filé, thanks to the Choctaw Native Americans who once lived in Louisiana. Choctaw cooks shared their knowledge of sun dried sassafras leaves with French settlers.

FILLET: (fill-lay) (noun) French term for a strip of boneless, lean of fish or meat, especially the beef fillet steak, or *"fillet mignon,"* which is cut from the tenderloin, or most tender area. (verb) As a verb, it means to cut meat strips away from the bones.

FILLING: A mixture of ingredients to fill a pie crust and other baked goods such as cream puffs, cakes and cookies.

FILO (PHYLLO) (fie-low): The Greek pastry dough is rolled into paper thin layers. Although everyone thinks of it as Greek, the dough is really Turkish. For centuries, long before they had ovens, the Turks have made their layered breads. Do we know how they get it so thin? The word means "leaf" since that's about the thickness of the dough. When working with filo dough, we must work quickly and keep it covered to prevent the dough from drying.

FINES HERBES: (feen erbs) A French culinary term, a combination of two or more herbs used with meats, poultry, fish, eggs, and salads. The name comes from the herbs being chopped "fine," or tiny.

FINICKY EATERS: Is this you? If "finicky" describes you, or someone you know, you might want to share this article with your parents or school dietician.

Experience shows that kids hate mixtures of foods, as in casseroles and stews, and vegetables with strong flavors, such as turnips, Brussels sprouts, cauliflower and cabbage. They sometimes like these vegetables raw, thinly sliced and salted, but not with salad dressings or mayonnaise. Although some kids like gravy, most prefer meat plain, or perhaps with mustard or ketchup, and vegetables with only melted butter. Some like melted cheese on vegetables, but few children like any other kind of sauce. Tomato sauce on spaghetti and pizza are exceptions. Kids appreciate being given choices, right? They are more likely to eat even foods they don't like if they can choose among them.

Yuck, What Is It?

Cooks need to know color and texture are important to children. They don't like dark or grayish-colored foods. They hate lumps. They distrust foods if they don't know what their ingredients are - such as meat loaf or cranberry bread. They are more likely to eat a dish if they helped prepare it, or such foods as toaster waffles that they can cook by themselves. Most don't like foods with any amount of charring, unless they cook it themselves over a campfire.

Try a Dainty Morsel

Small portions of food, carefully separated on their plates or served separately in small dishes, are more likely to attract finicky eaters.

Will this Look Better by Candlelight?

Pleasant table conversation, not about food, is helpful for finicky eaters. If they become interest in conversation, they may eat their meal without thinking about it and then discover that it tasted all right. But it is a mistake, in that case, for a parent or sibling to comment on that result.

Listen Up, Parents!

The more parents fuss about the finicky eater, trying to tempt him or her, the more the problem will grow. Matter-of-fact acceptance of the child and his eating preferences is the best approach. Taking away uneaten food without comment but without offering substitutes at that time or allowing snacking can work. Scolding, forcing or shaming always exacerbate the problem.

Now the Bad News, Kids!

Allowing a child to substitute milk or fruit juice for other foods is not a good idea. Too much of either can cause digestive problems. It can also start a bad habit that can lead to serious medical trouble in teen and adult years and lead to nutritional deficiencies. Too much milk can also cause sleepiness at school. "Remembering that children do not need large quantities of food is helpful to the parents' state-of-mind." – *Joyce Ackermann*, **Former Finicky Eater**, Parent & Teacher

FISH: These cold blooded aquatic animals are divided into three groups: salt-water fish, such as bass, salmon, tuna, cod, halibut, and sole; fresh-water fresh, such as trout, catfish, perch; and shellfish, such as shrimp, crabs, lobster, clams, and abalone. Some fish can be cured, such as smoked salmon or pickled herring. And they can be salted, such as anchovies, cod, and caviar. Depending upon the fish (including shellfish), they can be pan-fried, deep fat fried, boiled, broiled, poached, steamed, baked, and char-broiled. Some fish are cooked with skin and/or bones, while others can be filleted with or without skin, or cut cross wise into steaks with both bones and skin. **Nutrition facts** vary, depending upon the fish, but generally fish is an excellent source of protein with varying amounts of vitamins and minerals.

BAYOU CORNE, FISH BALLS!
by Walter V. Barnett Jr.

I went to visit my grandpa on the Bayou Corne in southern Louisiana near the community of Belle Rose. People live in what they call camps. When they gossip about one another they talk about their neighbor's camps and whether or not they have insurance. Grandpa invited me to go fishing, my first time in the bayou country.

Grandpa's boat motor screamed as we skimmed across the bayou like a flat rock, in a flat bottom boat. We sliced through the Duckweed (a green blanket of leaf-like stuff covering the water), like a knife leaving a trail of waves on our way to Grandpa's favorite fishing spot. After skimming past hanging Spanish moss and slicing through duckweed, we reached open water. Grandpa let off the gas suddenly and I almost slipped off the seat.

"Boy," he said (he always calls me boy), "we are going to catch a lot of fish and make some fish balls. How about that?"

"Fish balls! What are fish balls, Grandpa?"

He cocked his "Alligator Store" ball cap on the back of his head and laughed, "You'll see." After catching a lot of different kinds of fish we headed back home. Grandpa cut the fish into fillets and put them into a large pan. I took the pan inside and washed the fish real good while Grandpa put the leftovers in the bayou for the raccoons and turtles.

"Where's the recipe?" I asked.

"There's no recipe," Grandpa replied. "No one has ever written it down, in fact all my neighbors each have a different way of making fish balls. We just work from memory."

I watched Grandpa make the fish balls and wrote down the recipe. I'm sure I made gastronomical history by putting this in writing.

GRANDPA'S FISH BALLS

3 pounds fish fillet (boneless meat)
½ large onion

Grandpa ground up the fish fillets with the onion in a food processor, and put it in a large bowl.

1 ½ cups potatoes, mashed without the skin
2 tablespoons butter, melted
1/4 cup evaporated milk
2 chicken eggs or 1 duck egg
(Grandpa used a duck egg)
1/4 teaspoon garlic powder

2. Mix all these ingredients with the fish and onion.

1 teaspoon yellow mustard
1 tablespoon salt
1 tablespoon black pepper
1 tablespoon Louisiana hot sauce

3. Mix the seasoning well in a small bowl and then mix with the fish.
4. Wash your hands and lightly coat them with peanut or olive oil.
5. With a tablespoon, scoop out some of the fish mixture and form a ball. Make sure to keep your hands coated with oil to prevent sticking.
6. After forming balls, place several fish balls in a deep fryer. Cook until golden brown. Stir with a wood spoon. Remove, drain on paper towels.

This recipe serves a whole bunch of folks. Grandpa put several fish balls on my plate with some tartar sauce, a scoop of cole slaw, and an ice cold soft drink (Grandpa drank ice tea). They were spicy, but good. Now I don't know if I got Grandpa's recipe right, but Grandpa says, "It'll do!"

KAH LITUYA AND THE EARTHQUAKE
by Richard S. Calhoun

A **True**–and **Amazing**–Fish Story

One rainy day in Alaska's panhandle, I had caught a red rock cod off our dock for lunch. "Richard, nice fish!," commented Dad. "You really like to fish, don't you?"

"Yes," I answered. "Dad, Willie asked me if I would like to go fishing with him and Benny near Yakutat. Okay?"

"How long with you be gone?" Dad asked.

"Three or four days. Willy heard from other fishermen there were large schools of fish everywhere.

"When?"

"Willie said he would pull out about three a.m. He wants me to sleep on board his boat tonight."

"Okay," Dad agreed.

After dinner, I grabbed a brown grocery sack and put in a change of clothes and took it down to the boat. Next morning I awoke at six. Benny and his dad, Willie, were already up and out on deck. My breakfast of fried eggs and herring with pilot bread waited on the table. Benny stuck his head in the door, "Fishing's great!"

Out on deck, Willie was pulling in one salmon after another. I grabbed a knife and helped Benny clean and ice the fish. By late afternoon, we pulled up the trolling poles and headed toward the mouth of a bay.

"Hey, Pop, where are you going?" yelled Benny.

"We'll anchor in Lituya Bay for the night," answered Willie.

"No, that not a good idea."

"No choice. Radio says a storm is coming. I don't want to be out in the open sea."

"But Pop, you know the spirit *Kah Lituya* is not too friendly. When Kah Lituya is at peace, the spirits of the trees and the rocks calm the waters. But, if *Kah Lituya* is disturbed, he will shake the mountains and create a big wave to wash us all away."

"Benny, where does *Kah Lituya* live?" I asked.

"He lives deep in an ocean cavern near the entrance," replied Benny.

Willie paid no attention to Benny and entered the bay. Benny went up to the bow. He was very quiet and nervous. I stayed with Willie in the wheel house. As we entered the bay, we saw two trollers, the *Sunmore* and the *Badger*, anchored beyond the sandbar to our port. Further in the bay, the Edrie was anchored to our starboard.

"Willie," I asked, "Is *Kah Lituya* a myth?"

"Some say it's true," answered Willie, "others say it's a myth. Benny was educated by his great-grandfather and follows all of the Tlingit Indian ways."

As we made our way deep into the bay, Benny pointed to an island and yelled, "Pop, look at the gulls and terns. I have never seen birds huddle together like that."

Willie looked and said, "They're silent. That's queer; they usually squawk when anyone gets near them. And look -- they are standing, instead of squatting and their feathers are ruffled."

201

"Pop," yelled Benny, "Let's get out of here. Those birds know someone has distirbed *Kah Lituya*."

Willie continued past the island. "Richard, have you seen a glacier?" asked Willie.

"No," I replied.

Benny came into the wheel house and said, "Pop, don't go any further or you will awake *Kah Lituya* and he will shake the mountains and throw ice at us."

"Benny, do you really believe that?" I asked.

"It's true," Benny answered. "Pop, tell Richard what happened about fifty years ago."

"Once there was a Tlinget village near the entrance of the bay," said Willie. "On one calm day, the men set out in their canoes to hunt for sea otters while the women walked south along the shore to pick berries. A roar came from the mountains. This scared the women so all but one old lady ran back to the village. Big chucks of ice broke away from the glaciers and caused a wave that flooded the village. All died, except the one old woman who had not returned to the village."

"Wow, what happened to the men?" I asked.

"When they heard the thunder, they paddled their canoes back to the village. Their village was gone. The trees were stripped from the ground and logs filled the bay. The one surviving woman ran to the canoes and told them what had happened. The Tlingets got back into their canoes and never returned to Lituya Bay."

"See Richard," said Benny, "even Pop knows all about *Kah Lituya*."

We cruised up the bay. It was filled with chunks of ice. Willie very carefully ran alongside of an iceberg.

"There's your glacier," said Willie. "If you want, lean over and touch the ice."

"Don't do it!" shouted Benny. "You will make *Kah Lituya* mad and he will throw ice at us."

I wanted to touch the iceberg, but I didn't want to upset Benny anymore than he already was. I thought it best to accept his superstition ways. At the same time, Willie had made this dangerous trip to let me touch an iceberg. Luckily, by the time I leaned over to touch the ice, we had drifted away from it. Black clouds were drifting in, but it was still twilight.

"We better anchor while there's still light," suggested Willie. "We will anchor near *Edrie*."

We cruised slowly toward the island. Suddenly the birds screamed and flew upward and out to sea. At the same time our boat started to vibrate violently. I looked back at the glacier and saw large chunks of ice catapulted high in the air. The ice came thundering into the bay and caused a wave. The wave looked like it was a thousand feet high as it rushed up the sides of the mountains. Willie saw the wave as well, and pushed the throttle wide open.

"Hang on!" Willie yelled.

I grabbed hold of a rail for dear life. The wave came toward us and lifted the boat higher and higher. The *Edrie* was caught in the same wave. Two seconds later the other two trollers headed over the sandbar. I saw the *Sunmore* roll over and disappear. The *Badger* looked like it was in trouble also, as several trees appeared to hit it. We reached the peak of the giant wave and fell behind it. The wave blocked the light from the west and all the sudden it became dark. I guess we went right over the top of the island and the giant wave pushed us right on out to sea.

Benny yelled, "*Kah Lituya* awoke and took revenge on us."

Willie was having a hard time steering the boat as more waves hit us. As each wave peaked, our boat would be on top of the wave and I could see the sky was still twilight. Then the boat would drop back into the trough and it would be pitch black again. I felt pain in my left arm. I hoped it wasn't broken. I wiggled my fingers. I was okay. I was glad I was in the wheel house, or I might have been washed overboard. The waves must have pushed us ten miles, maybe more, out to sea. To make matters worse, the storm had hit and rain poured down. Willie pointed the bow toward the south and gradually, about an hour later, we were out of the high wave action. By then it was pitch black and raining. Benny took the wheel as Willie checked out the boat. We had lost the trolling poles, the radio antenna, and taken on some water. But otherwise we were in good shape.

Two years ago I had ridden a roller coaster. That ride scared me to death. I vowed I would never ride another roller coaster. But the roller coaster was tame compared to riding the crest of the towering Lituya wave.

Late in the afternoon we arrived at the home dock. Dad came running down from the house and Mom was right behind him. Dad tied up Willie's boat. He asked, "Did you feel the earthquake?"

"Did we!" I answered. "We were in Lituya Bay and we rode on the crest of a wave miles out to sea."

"Did you get hurt?" Mom asked.

"Just bruised from being slammed around in the wheel house."

"*Kah Lituya* was disturbed," Benny said, "and he hurled large chucks of ice at us."

"Who is *Kah Lituya*?" Mom asked.

"Mom," I replied, "I will tell you all about it tomorrow. Right now I want to go to bed. None of us slept last night. We were too scared!"

Next morning Dad and Willie went to the woods and cut down two trolling poles. Benny repaired the radio antenna with a wire from a clothes hanger. I helped Benny strip bark from the poles. By noon Willie's boat was repaired and they headed out to sea. In the afternoon I read in *The Daily Alaska Empire*, Juneau's newspaper, all about the earthquake. The *Sunmore* was lost and the two aboard never found. The *Badger* made it over the sandbar, but sunk. The owner and his wife were saved. The *Edrie*, like us, had been swept out to sea. There was no mention about Willie's boat, because, I guess, no one knew we were there. That giant wave was actually bigger than I thought.

It stripped trees off the mountain sides up to 1700 feet in some places. That's more than four hundred feet higher than New York's Empire State Building! It was estimated the wave reached a hundred miles an hour. How we came through it, I will never know. I guess our boat was in the right place at the right time. –From *Cheechako*, 2001

Note: Though Richard didn't know it at the time, he lived through a natural phenomenon scientists now call the largest wave ever recorded. Giant waves are called Mega-Tsunamis, and this one is featured in an television special on the Discover Channel. The program is called **Mega-Tsunamis,** if you'd like to find out more about this and other giant waves.

FISH FUDDLE: In south Florida and abundant in the Keys, the plant produces pods that are dried and used to stupify fish.

FISH SAUCE: A sauce that appears in all southeast Asian cooking. The Cambodian name, *tuk trey*, literally means fish juice. It resembles Chinese soy sauce in the way it's made and used. Fish sauce is the liquid pressed out of the fermented fish paste (*pra hoc*), similar to the way olive oil is pressed. The first pressing is considered the best. Fish sauce does not have to be refrigerated. Oriental markets carry fish sauce in various brand names, The Phu Quoc brand comes from an island in Vietnam where it is made from anchovies. Fish sauce added to lime juice and seasonings makes a delightful salad dressing.

FIVE SPICES: A mixture of Chinese spices which generally include: star anise, cloves, fennel, cinnamon and pepper.

FLAGEOLET: (flaj-e- let.) A small European bean that are eaten fresh whole or puréed, or dried. Dried flageolets are cooked like any other dried bean.

FLAMBÉ: (flahm-bay) A French term that describes foods that are served flaming. Warm brandy is poured over food and just before serving, it is lighted. The alcohol burns off and a new flavor is added to the food. This is done with meats, desserts, and some beverages.

FLAN: A Spanish custard dessert. In France it also refers to quiche and other pastry-lined dishes with eggs as one of the main ingredients.

FLANK: A cut of meat between the ribs and hip.

FLANNEL CAKE: A thick pancake made the size of the pan.

FLAPJACK: Another name for pancakes.

FLATULENCE: (flach-u-lens)

THE LEGEND OF GENERAL FLATUS

by John M. Calhoun

FATHER: "Why, Johnny, you are picking at your dinner tonight. Are you not hungry?"
JOHNNY: "No, Father, I just don't want to produce flatus."
FATHER: "Isn't Flatus that Roman General in Biblical history . . .?"
JOHNNY: "Sure! General Flatus was always trying to conquer Greece and Turkey, and Sardinia, haha." (Johnny knew gastric distress is embarrassing.)

The Polite Terms

Intestinal gas will pass through your digestive system and be expelled as **flatus**. This is called **flatulence** which is a medical term for "gas" in the intestinal and bowel tract. In nice polite society, the discussion of flatulence is a no-no subject. In England they call it "wind." Your grandmother probably told you nice people don't talk about it at all.

If you eat a lot of beans, nuts, sweets, and large amounts of meats, fruits and vegetables, you'll pass gas. They should call it "laughing gas" because whenever you pass any noisy wind, nearly everybody laughs at you.

The Scientific Terms

1. **Nitrogen**: This is room air. The largest amount of intestinal gas comes from the air you swallow.
2. **Oxygen**: This also comes from the air you swallow.
3. **Carbon Dioxide**: This is formed in the small intestine as a by-product of digestion which is mixed with stomach and other acids. This also comes from lots of fatty foods and carbonated beverages.
4. **Hydrogen** is the gas used in balloons to make them float. In the lower bowels, which is the colon, fermentation causes the formation of the stink and foul gases by the action of the colonic bacteria on the undigested foodstuffs that have eluded absorption in the small upper bowl.
5. **Methane**: This is the gas in natural gas. This gas is mixed with hydrogen sulfide which releases the gas attack.

Gas Comes from Three Sources

1. The air you swallow;
2. Carbon dioxide built up in the beginning part of the small intestine as an outcome of chemical interaction between various acids, and
3. In the lower intestines by the action of bacteria upon undigested foodstuffs.

Between eating baked beans and the passage of massive bowel gas, you'll produce a hydrogen gas with a radical sulfide which stinks. But, don't fret, here's the answer. Eat lots of yogurt. The bacteria in yogurt will help to digest your foods and might bring your gas production to a halt.

Why Is Gas So Important?

After you have drunk a carbonated drink, you burped. Now, you felt great. If the gas doesn't come out of your mouth, it will find its way out the other end. Actually, in some countries, belching is a compliment to the cook. Gas is formed by foodstuffs in the digestive system and works its way through roughly twenty-seven feet of intestines; the gas keeps it from causing a tight and hard pile of food wastes. If these gases didn't pass through and free up the lumps of chow, there would be a mass of feces which any system on earth could not move. What a predicament! Therefore, the passing of gas is natural and normal. The less said about it the better.

When You Can't Avoid General Flatus

What do you do if you're at a gracious party with your folks and friends who are all well refined and all of the sudden you have the urge? Excuse yourself. Leave the room for a minute. Of course, your auntie will ask you, "Where are you going?" Don't answer. Keep going. You can make up something when you come back.

Gastric Distress Isn't Always Funny

Acute abdominal pain and constant passing of gas can indicate illness. Gas pains can be excruciating at times. This could indicate your bowels may be inflamed and as a result may be tender. If this is persistent, be sure to tell your parents.

Tips to Avoid General Flatus

Eat very slowly.
Play soft music. This will help you to slow down. What's your hurry, anyway?
Chew your food slowly with your mouth closed. Chewing with your mouth open won't make you sick, but it will your companions.
Do not talk when eating. No one wants to hear what you say with food in your mouth anyway.
Air is constantly swallowed as you eat, talk, and drink all at the same time.
Never overload your stomach.
Don't gulp fluids with your meals. Drinking through straws takes in a lot of air. The worst thing you can do is drink a carbonated drink with a meal.
Eliminate all desserts, especially whipped desserts. Whipped cream is full of air.
Don't suck on hard candies.
Do not chew gum.
Avoid foods you know cause problems for you. Not everyone is alike.

As you can see, it's impossible to avoid General Flatus all the time. Today there are enzyme products on the market to help prevent the worst case scenarios. Look for Beano and keep it near the salt and pepper. If you do embarrass yourself, just remember it happens to everyone sooner or later. Even kings and queens need **Beano**. We have it on the best authority **Prince Charles of England** himself warns against the danger of stubbing your face. In his book for children called *The Old Man of Lochnagar*, his Royal Highness wrote, "After the shoot the old man feasted on Loch-haggis and suffered terribly from wind afterwards." (*The Old Man of Lochnagar*, by H.R.H., the Prince of Wales, Farrar, Straus, Giroux, NY, 1980.)

FLAVOR: A food substance effecting taste when eaten. It also refers to the sense of smell. The flavor can be sweet, sour, salty, seasoned, spicy, or a combination of tastes and smells.

FLAVORING: A substance added to food, such as herbs, seeds, spices, and extracts.

FLOAT: A scoop of ice cream or sherbet on top of a beverage.

FLORENTINE: The French meaning is for any dish where spinach is one of the main ingredients. It was from the city of Florence in Italy that the French visitors learned to eat spinach. A dish of buttered spinach topped with boiled egg slices is called *a la florentine,* "in the manner of Florence."

FLORIDA CHERRY: Also known as Surinam cherry, produces a red to black 3/4-inch round and lobed fruit with a resinous flavor. Eaten fresh, made into jelly, used in salads, or excellent in sherbet.

FLOUNDER: A salt-water flat fish which includes sole, sand dabs, and fluke. The flesh is sweet and lean, and is available fresh the year round. Flounder is also available frozen plain, stuffed or seasoned. This tender fish can be pan-fried, broiled, baked, poached, or steamed. Cook until it flakes easy with a fork. Do not over cook. **Nutrition facts** per 3 ounces: 58 calories, 4 calories from fat, .4g total fat (1%), zero saturated fat and cholesterol, 47.6mg sodium (2%), zero carbohydrates and fiber, 12.7g protein(25%), zero vitamins A and C, 52mg calcium (5%), and .7mg iron (4%).

FLOUR: As a noun it means finely ground meal made from wheat, corn, rice and other grains. Flour should be stored in a cool, dark place, preferably in the refrigerator. Flour should be warmed to room temperature before baking. Also a verb meaning "to dust or coat food with flour." www.whitelily.com www.generalmills.com.

FLOWERS:

FLOWERS FOR FLAVOR AND FLARE
by Louise Ulmer

Ever taste a rose? Some taste as lovely as they smell. Flower lovers in Great Britain have been cooking with flowers since the **Middle Ages.** Roses were the most widely used, usually to make rose water flavoring for cakes, creams and beverages. As sugar became more available, rose petals were being crystallized for use as decoration or made into preserves for dessert. Other popular flowers of the day were apple blossoms, clove gillyflowers, and marigolds. The elder flowers were used in vinegars, wines, and fruit dishes. Marigolds were used to dye butter and cheese.

Today flowers can still be seen in fine restaurants in Europe and are gaining in popularity in America. Peppery tasting nasturtiums enliven salads, along with primroses, pansies, daisies, marigolds, and violets. Some flowers have little or no flavor but their addition lends so much beauty and appetite appeal that flavor can be left to the other foods. Picture real pink rosebuds on a wedding cake. Even a glass of water becomes a thing of beauty when served with ice cubes containing a tiny pansy.

Certain flowers have long been on the list of survival foods in scouting manuals. The problem is that some flowers are not safe to eat. Eat no flower unless you know for sure it is safe. Eat only those safe flowers which you are sure have not been treated with pesticides and harmful sprays. Do not eat flowers which have been growing along roadsides where they becomes contaminated with gas fumes and traffic contaminants. The safest way is to grow your own organic safe flowers for garnish and delightful dining. Shepherd's Garden Seeds has a collection of edible flower seeds, plus recipes. For information write: **Shepherd's Garden Seeds,** 30 Irene Street, Torrington, CT 06790-6658 or phone (860) 482-3638. www.shepherdseeds.com.

EDIBLE FLOWERS
by Virginia McNear

Yes, you really can eat some of them that are found in your garden. They must be free of herbicides and pesticides. If the flowers have been treated or if your neighbors sprayed their plants (chemicals can drift a long way on very little breeze), don't eat them, because such chemicals don't wash off easy. Some flowers are used as garnish, candied violets for instance, and some as part of a salad or appetizer. Others can be dipped in batter and fried. A few examples:

Nasturtiums originated from Peru. Both the leaves and the blossoms have a tangy taste similar to watercress with a hint of honey, sweet but mildly spicy. The Whirlybird variety come in tangerine, salmon, gold, mahogany, scarlet, and a cherry-rose. Mixed in with a salad, they bring bright colors to the dining table, and a surprise to your guests.

Hyssop is a member of the anise family. The entire plant is edible. Both the leaves and the blossoms have a naturally sweet licorice taste. The leaves make a wonderful tea, while the blossoms are added to baked goods and marinades. All can be added to Chinese stir-fry. For an extra treat, nibble on some blossoms and you will understand why it's called "the root beer plant."

Borage is an herb that grows up to 3 feet tall. It has silvery-green leaves and sky-blue blossoms. Plant and blossoms have a mild cucumber taste. The leaves blend well with dill, mint, and garlic, and a handful does wonders to homemade chicken soup. Add the blossoms to salads and fruit cups. Blossoms can be candied to cake decorations. Freeze some in ice and add to beverages.

Calendulas petals have a saffron-like taste. Add to rice, eggs, cheese spreads, breads, and salads.

Johnny-jump-ups have a mild wintergreen flavor. Add them to sliced fruit, garnish cheese plates, decorate cakes, or add to salads.

Chive blossoms have a mild onion flavor, add to salads. Rodale's Organic Gardening also lists the following: beebalm, daylily, English daisy, forget-me-not, fuchsia, geranium, hollyhock, impatiens, lavender, lilac, mint flower, pansy, portulaca, redbud, rose, snapdragon, squash blossom, violet, and zucchini blossoms (squash blossoms are especially nice for stuffing or frying). For information contact **Renee's Garden**, 888-880-7228, www.reneesgarden.com.

FLUMMERY: The word and the idea began as a Welch kind of oatmeal, boiled so thick you could cut it. Over several centuries, it came to mean a fancy jellied dessert made of whipping cream and almonds, molded in the manner of a blancmange. In American it came to mean a berry dessert thickened with cornstarch. It would be like cherry pie filling without the pie crust.

FLUTING: The act of trimming and **edging pie crusts** by pressing the top and bottom crusts together with a fork or pinching together with fingers so that juices will not escape. Fluting is also a process for **cutting grooves** in raw vegetables, such as a cucumber or cylinder-type summer squash. Fluting is done by scoring the skin with a fork, cutting deep grooves in the vegetable prior to slicing. The fluted vegetable is generally eaten raw, maybe topped on a cracker and served as a canapé.

FOIE GRAS: (foe-grah) A French term for a spread made from goose or duck livers. It is also eaten in salads, used to stuff meats, and cooked with vegetables. Foie gras in made in Europe, not in the United States, because it is considered cruel to the bird, which is fed to bursting in tight coops to prevent exercising.

FOLD: A means of mixing an ingredient (such as egg whites or whipped cream), gently without beating. Generally done with a rubber spatula.

FONDANT: A soft candy resembling firm marshmallows. Made by boiling sugar, water and corn syrup to the "soft ball" stage. It is used as a base for bonbons and chocolate creams.

FONDUE: (fon-doo) A French cooking process with a hot pot of melted cheese where pieces of bread are dipped before eating.

FOOD:

An Essay on Food and Language

WHEN FOOD ISN'T FOOD
by JoAn W. Martin

Language works in strange ways! It produces food terms that have nothing to do with food, but are useful in providing metaphors which everyone understands. Words dish up certain foods that have nothing to do with what we put in our mouths.

"Talking Turkey" originally meant "saying pleasant things" or "talking agreeably." But later these terms took on the meaning of speaking frankly, "talking tough" or "getting down to business." A journalist for the London Daily Express explained in 1928, "She talked cold turkey. **'Cold Turkey'**

means plain truth in America." This is also a term for stern treatment for a smoking or drug addiction, such as "quitting cold turkey."

We prove something is truly American by saying, "**As American as apple pie.**" But the idea of apple pie arrived in America on the Mayflower with the Pilgrims. These were favorite tarts, small pies that were brought to England by the French in 1066. Americans didn't invent pies, we just improved them. There is nothing orderly about a pie shell containing a jumble of cut apples, sugar, and spices. Yet the expression "**apple-pie-order**" means something is prim, proper and in order. This may be a corruption of the French phrase which means "folded linen" to describe the neatness of a well-made bed.

The "**big cheese**" means an important person, not something from the dairy case. "**Green cheese**" does not refer to its color, but to the fact that it's fresh, not dried. The notion that the moon is made of green cheese stems from an old expression that someone is so fresh and gullible as to believe in such a preposterous idea.

In a similar way, a "**chowderhead**" isn't a thick soup eater, but referred at first to a large, thick, clumsy-looking head on a person. Later chowderhead came to refer less to the person's outward appearance, than to how deficient the brain inside his head was. A "chowderhead" was a put-down, meaning the person wasn't very smart.

At Halloween the custom used to be "to egg" a house or car by throwing eggs and making a mess for someone to clean up. "**Egging**" with rotten eggs was the ultimate "trick" if the homeowner refused to grant a "treat." Closely connected may be the figurative expression indicating embarrassment, "**Egg on one's face.**" "Egg on" comes from an Old Norse word meaning to incite, suggesting the image of nudging someone with the edge of a sword. The expression has nothing to do with food. The "**egghead**," meaning a person with an over-sized brain, is an expression from the 1950s.

Likewise, a "**pea jacket**" isn't green like green peas. This heavy wool coat's name comes from a Dutch word for a jacket worn by sailors, a coat of coarse woolen material.

Way back in 1577, "fry" was extended from fish to humans, especially "insignificant beings." A small person, either in size or in power is a "**small fry.**" Nothing to do with cooking!

How did "peach," finds its way into "**impeachment?**" Hardly makes sense. But when we realize it comes not from the fruit but from the word that means to hinder, we understand that the "peach" in impeachment has no connection with the luscious fruit.

These English idioms seem to be food-related, but in fact they are not. It is fun to explore the nature of language and how we adapt and adopt names from history, culture and language. For additional reading on food and the language, see: *Ladyfingers & Nun's Tummies,* a lighthearted look at how foods got their names by Martha Barnette, Random House, 1997.

FUNNY FOODS
by Pamela Schmidt

Would you eat an elephant's ear? Well, how about some Mississippi Mud Pie, Dirty Rice, or Monkey Bread? You're not quite sure, you say? Well, if you think those dishes sound crazy, would you ever chow down on Britain's Bubble and Squeak or Ireland's Inky Pinky?

Many of the foods we eat have silly-sounding names, but actually taste quite delicious! In fact consider the hot dog. Fido's quite safe, but can you imagine a baseball game without a good-old-frank-on-a-bun-more commonly, the **hot dog**. We've been enjoying this American favorite since the early 1900's at New York's famous Coney Island.

I'll bet mom wouldn't object to digging into **Mississippi Mud Pie**. For dessert, that is. This delicious creation gets its name from the way it looks - just like the muddy Mississippi River, but there's no mud to be found here. You'll love the flavors of chocolate, butter, corn syrup, and sugar baked into a pie shell. Top the warm pie off with a scoop of vanilla ice cream, and you've got yourself a good, old-fashioned mud-pie mess!

Since we're on the subject of mud, how about some **Dirty Rice**? Actually, this southern dish is highly seasoned with red and black pepper, paprika, dry mustard, ground cumin, dried thyme, and dried oregano; then cooked with chicken, pork, onions, celery, green peppers, garlic, butter, and hicken stock. The blending of the seasonings, and other ingredients give the rice a "dirty" look.

Another great, southern-originated dish is called, "**Hush Puppies**." In the days before the Civil War when people cooked on open grills outdoors, the family dogs would gather around barking, tempted by the wonderful aromas. Their reward would be bits of the frying cornmeal batter accompanied by commands of, "hush, puppies!"

A sure favorite with every child would have to be **Elephant Ears**. These delectable cookies get their name from the size of the finished product, which is usually a large, round cookie about five to six inches large. They are flavored with cinnamon, butter, and nuts, and are lots of fun to make - even better to taste!

Bubble and Squeak is made with slices of beef cooked with potatoes and vegetables and emits a bubbling sound as it cooks. **Inky Pinky** can be created from finely chopped, leftover roast beef cooked with chopped carrots and onions.

Perhaps you've read Antoine de Saint-Exupéry's, *The Little Prince*. A familiar reference from this book is the **baobab tree**. It's a real tree, a native of Africa and India, having a thick trunk. Hiding inside these trees is a fruit quite similar to a gourd or a pumpkin that is a favorite of monkeys, commonly called, monkey bread. We can make our own version of monkey bread by joining current-filled balls of sweet dough and baking. The end result has the appearance of the knobby baobab tree. Food should bring pleasure and create wonderful memories. Everyone has to eat, why not make it fun? Sometimes, it can even bring luck. At least, that's the claim of **Hopping John**. Boil some black-eyed peas, with pork, and serve with rice. Eating it on New Year's Day, you'll be guaranteed good luck for the coming year.

FOOD AND DRUG ADMINISTRATION
Safeguarding America's Health

The Food and Drug Administration (FDA) touches your life every day, beginning with brushing your teeth in the morning to cooking your evening meal. It's the job of the FDA to oversee the food you eat, the shampoo you use, the medicines you take, the way you prepare and cook your foods and even feed for your pets and farm animals.

There are more than 7,000 FDA employees, all wearing different hats. It takes some 1,100 investigators to visit about 20,000 of the 100,000 FDA-regulated businesses each year. This includes checking wharfs for imported foods, vermin infestation of warehouses, proper labeling of food containers, the proper manufacturing of food products, and monitoring the recall of food and health products. When a company either can't or won't correct a health problem, it is the responsibility of the FDA to take that company to court, to force the company from selling that product, and to seize and destroy that product. The FDA finds almost 3,000 products a year that are unsafe, plus many imported products are unsafe and detained from entry to the United States. Two out of ten FDA employees are scientists and are involved in every avenue of research from removing dangerous chemicals in food to ways of treating diseases. These scientists are involved in the technology that includes biotechnology, microelectronics and magnetic resonance imaging. They must look at both the risks and the benefits of each food product and new medicines. This includes medicated feed for farm animals to make sure that antibiotics and other animal medicines are not passed on to humans.

To ensure the public, the FDA must spread the word to non-government companies and organizations about what is safe and what isn't. Yes, it's a big job, and everyone should be thankful we have the FDA to protect you and your family. www.fda.gov; www.ams.usda.gov/marketnews.htm

FOOD COLORING: Good food was a rare and wondrous thing in the Dark Ages when hunger was a way of life for most people. Little wonder some foods were thought to have magical properties. Color had symbolic connections and the rarest most wonderful was yellow. Like gold, it was most rare. For that reason, saffron, safflower and turmeric were precious spices. Saffron was the most rare and so most powerful. Today we use vegetable dyes. The most common are sold in tiny dropper bottles of red, blue, green and yellow in the baking section. Food dyes have to be approved and tested for safety even though they are used in small amounts since some people are highly allergic to substances from which dyes are obtained.

THE FOOD GUIDE PYRAMID

Originally the United States Department of Agriculture (USDA) designed the Food Guide Pyramid for adults. For the most part it works well from age ten through the teens. About the only difference is kids' calorie intake. Food labels are based on a 2,000 calories daily diet. If kids are inactive, 1,600 calories per day might be enough. On the other hand, for active kids 2,500 calories should be considered. If kids fall between these two groups, an average of 2,200 calories would probably be the best choice.

The Food Guide Pyramid points out what should be eaten in every group. In the grain group the USDA recommends 6 to 11 servings per day (on a 2,200 calories diet, that would be 9 servings). Might seem like a lot, but when you look at the serving sizes it is easy. A sandwich with two slices of bread is two servings, a plate of pasta could be four servings. The following chart will make it easy to figure out what is a serving:

GRAIN GROUP (6 to 11 serving):
1 slice of bread
1/2 English muffin, hamburger bun, or bagel
1/2 cup cooked rice, pasta or hot cereal
1 ounce (about 3/4 cup) dry cereal
1 cup popcorn
4 soda crackers

FRUIT GROUP (2 to 4 servings):
1 whole medium size fruit
1/2 grapefruit
1/2 cup berries
1/4 cup dried fruit
1/2 cup cooked or canned fruit
3/4 cup fruit juice

VEGETABLE GROUP (3 to 5 servings):
1/2 cup cooked vegetables
1/2 cup chopped raw vegetables
1 cup leafy raw vegetables
3/4 cup vegetable juice

DAIRY GROUP (2 to 3 servings):
1 cup whole, skim, or nonfat milk
1 cup whole or low-fat yogurt
1 1/2 ounces natural cheese
2 ounces process cheese
1/2 cup cottage cheese or 1/2 cup ice cream

MEAT GROUP (2 to 3 servings):
3 ounces lean and cooked meat, poultry or fish
2 eggs
1/2 cup cooked dry beans or peas
2 tablespoons peanut butter
1/3 cup nuts

OILS, FATS and SWEETS (use sparingly, but no more than 4 servings, especially if you are watching calories and fat): 4 teaspoons of butter, margarine or vegetable oil 12 teaspoons sugar

In addition, nutritionists recommend 8 to 10 glasses of water a day. Generally speaking, any liquid will fulfill this requirement such as milk, fruit and vegetable juices, most hot beverages, and most diet sodas.

FOOD QUIZ
by Joyce Ackermann

1. QUESTION: If you were invited to eat a mess of fish in a mess, would your reply
a) Yuck! No, thanks or b) Thanks, I'd love to come!

ANSWER:

You probably would be glad if you decided on (b) because you would enjoy a seafood dinner in a dining hall as the guest of military officers, served by waiters in short, white jackets. One definition of "mess" is a serving of food or prepared dish of a certain kind of food. A "mess" is also a group of people in the military assigned to eat together. The place where they eat is a "mess" or a "mess hall." They may be served by waiters in "mess jackets."

2. QUESTION:

A Welsh rabbit is a) A serving of melted cheese on toast or b) A bunny who lives in Wales

ANSWER:

(a) Welsh rabbit, also sometimes called Welsh rarebit, is melted cheese, mixed with butter, pepper and salt, poured over toast. This dish, probably named by the English, suggests that the Welsh were too poor to afford meat.

3. QUESTION:

What do all these foods have in common? 1) Mocha 2) Worcestershire sauce 3) Hamburger 4) Bologna 5) Cheddar cheese 6) Scotch broth. 7) Tabasco Sauce 8) Brunswick Stew 9) Cayenne pepper 10) Brussel's Sprouts 11) Hollandaise 12) Frankfurter.

ANSWER:

They are all named for places.
1. Coffee flavoring named for Mocha, a town in Yemen on the Red Sea.
2. Spicy sauce named for a county in England where it was refined to perfection.
3. Originally, "Hamburg steak" named for Hamburg, Germany.
4. A large smoked sausage originally from Bologna, Italy.
5. Originally made in Cheddar, England.
6. A soup of mutton and barley invented in Scotland.
7. Named for a state in Mexico.
8. A stew of chicken, corn, tomatoes, okra, beans and onions, named for the town of Brunswick, Georgia.
9. Named for a town in French Guiana.
10. A kind of baby cabbage named for Brussels, Belgium.
11. Creamy sauce named by the French for the country of Holland.
12. A smoked sausage named for Frankfurt, Germany.

Activity: Make your own food quizzes based on information found in this food book.

FOOD FESTIVALS: See FESTIVALS

FOOD HISTORY:

A HISTORY OF FOOD IN THE ANCIENT WORLD

Prehistoric - Hunting & Gathering

7000 - 5000 BC
- People hunted animals and gathered food from the wild.
- They began herding animals such as sheep and goats.
- Began to farm, growing barley and wheat. This enabled people to stop roaming and live on farms and in villages.
- In the Stone Age, circa 5000 BC, people made pottery from clay for cooking and learned to grind grain in stone bowls. They made wooden plows drawn by oxen.
- Farmers domesticated dogs, pigs, cattle and chickens.
- Chinese harvested millet and rice. In the Near East, people domesticated wheat and lentils.

First Civilizations:
Sumaria & Babylon - Farms & Wheels

5000 - 3000 BC
- Towns grew up along the rivers in the Near East. Along the Tigris and Euphrates Rivers, irrigation opened up farming by ox-drawn plows with wheels. Gardens flourished.
- By 500 - 600 BC the hanging gardens of Babylon were one of the seven wonders of the world.
- Foods became plentiful and rich.

Egyptian Empire - Imports & Exports

- About 3000 BC, cities flourished along the Nile River. Pharaohs built pyramids. Egyptian merchants brought foods and spices from North Africa and Arabia to trade as far north as Babylon.

Greek Empire - Oils & Wines

- Neighboring on the Mediterranean Sea, the early Greeks built roads and ships and traded with the Egyptians and Persians. Foods were mainly herded, fished, and farmed on small farms. Grapes were cultivated for wines.

Early China - Iron & the Spice Road

- Farming had been common in China from about 6000 BC. Rice was the favored grain for centuries in the East.
- The Chinese invented an iron furnace to forge tools and cooking pots about 100 BC.
- While Rome ruled the Western World, the Chinese ruled the East.

■ Caravans made regular runs with ginger, cinnamon and silk to Central Asia to exchange for gold, silver, grape wine, glassware, pottery, coral beads, and gems from the Roman world.
 By about 300 AD, even the humble Chinese peasants have tea, vegetable oil, and the iron wok.

Roman Empire - Supermarket to the World

■ From about 100 BC to 400 AD, Rome ruled the Mediterranean world. Its holdings spread from England to the Red Sea. The mighty Roman army conquered its enemies, built roads and waterways, policed cities and protected travelers. And the army had to be fed. Food was wealth.
■ Roman roads allowed far ranging free trade. Roman ships brought exotic fruits and vegetables from all parts of the known world. Roman farmers experimented with growing new trees and plants at home.
■ Roman banquet menus boasted fish, venison, lobsters, partridges, capons, swans, pheasants, quails, piglets, woodcocks, and spices from the East.
■ Poor Romans were given free grain. The ordinary household lived on grain made into gruel or bread, olives, some fish and wine.

Highlights of Food Development in History

500,000 BC: Humans learned how to create a permanent cooking place, a hearth.
18,000 BC: Middle Easterners domesticate and breed animals for food. The first were deer, antelope, and sheep.
8,000 BC: Egyptians master milling of grain by stone rollers to crush and grind grain into meal, thus creating flour.
5,000 BC: Chinese, Romans, and Greek domesticate pigs.
4,000 BC: Dairy farmers in the Middle East learn to make butter by churning milk.
2,500 BC: Egyptians domesticate geese, force-feeding them to make them bigger and better tasting when cooked.
2,000 BC: Egyptians learn fermentation in baking and cheese making. However, fermentation won't be understood for another 38 centuries. The breeding of goats, cattle, geese, chickens, and ducks begin replacing hunting.
500 BC: Europeans master the preservation of food by salting, which leads to the development of curing and pickling.
300 BC: Greeks develop grafting techniques, leading to the creation of orchards.
100 BC-400 AD: Roman Empire spread spices from India to Europe.
702 AD: Japanese wrote their first Code of Law. It included regulations and instructions to aristocrats for the production of dairy products (cheese and yogurt) and the preservation of foods with salt, vinegar, etc.
1191: Mongols and other northern peoples ate relatively little meat. Horses were too valuable for transportation and power. Rams were used for breeding, and ewes were the source of dairy products, mostly of the soured or fermented types. Yogurt, sour cream, sour cream cheese and *kumyss* were considered by the southern Chinese to be barbarian foods.
1200: The Crusaders spread Oriental foods to Europe.

1400: Candy is created in Europe when cooks dip fruits and berries into melted sugar.

1500-1700: Transfer of foods between Old World and New World by explorers.

1530: Spanish conquistador, Gonzalo Jimenez, discovered the potato in the Andes. After the potato, oca is the most important crop. In addition, the Incas eat the seeds of lupine, which is also called *tarw*i or *chocho*. Cultivated crops include *quinoa*, the Spanish call it "millet" or small rice. Millet thrives even in droughts that kill maize, and is used in soups and stews, along with potatoes and chili. Were maize is not grown, quinoa is used to make the fermented beverage, *chicha*.

1776: Steam-driven mill is invented in London, making flour milling the first modern food industry.

1810: The tin can was patented. "Here is the hammer and chisel. Please open these cans for me." This would have been a common request in the 1800's as the can opener wasn't invented for another 50 years.

1850: Horse-drawn reaping machines allow for large- scale farming across American's Great Plains. Soft drinks were invented in the United States by mixing fruit juice with sugar, carbonated water, and citric acid.

1861: Louis Pasteur develops pasteurization of milk.

1870: The navel orange is introduced into the United States from Brazil.

1900: The science of genetics is born.

1902: Drake Bakeries, founded by Newman E. Drake in New York, will produce mostly packaged sweet foods with names such as: "Devil Dogs," "Yankee Doodles," "Ring Dings," and "Yodels."

1904: Xerophthalmia is reported among Japanese infants whose diets are devoid of fats.

1906: Freeze-drying techniques are mastered in France.

1912: U.S. Biochemists Elmer Verner McCollum and Marguerite Davis discovered a fat soluble nutrient that would later be called vitamin A in butter and egg yolks. They established that it was a lack of this nutrient that caused C.A. Pekelharing's mice to die prematurely in

1905 when given no milk. Yale biochemists Thomas B. Osborne and Lafayette B. Mendel made a similar discovery.

1913: Home refrigerators are invented in the United States.

1917: Xerophthalmia is observed in Danish children whose diets are lacking in butterfats. Denmark has been exporting butter to the warring powers at the expense of their domestic needs. Dietary deficiency is endangering their children's eye sight.

1920: Charles Birdseye invents the process of deep- freezing foods.

1937: The Swiss invent instant coffee, which leads to the development of powdered foods.

1940: Microwave technology leads to the invention of the microwave oven.

1973: Biotechnology begins at Stanford University.

1981: Chinese scientists become the first to clone a fish, a gold carp.

1990: First food products modified by biotechnology, an enzyme used in cheese making, is approved for use in the United States; and a yeast used in baking, is approved for use in the United Kingdom.

Also see *FOOD CHRONOLOGY* by Trager. And International Food Information Council

Activity

FOOD MAGIC: Use a little bit of science to perform kitchen magic for your friends.

You will need:
3 clear glasses
1 ½ cups purple grape juice
1 tablespoon vinegar
2 tablespoons baking soda
Spoons or stirrers

Magic #1. Pour ½ cup of grape juice into the first glass. Add one tablespoon of vinegar (it's an acid) to the grape juice, stir, and see what happens. The grape juice turns redder.
Magic #2. Pour ½ cup of grape juice into the second glass. Add one tablespoon of baking soda (referred to as a base), stir, and see what happens. The grape juice will turn a deep blue or a deep green.
 Magic #3. Pour ½ cup of grape juice into the third glass. Pour half of the vinegar-treated grape juice (Magic #1) into the grape juice. Add one tablespoon of baking soda, stir, and see what happens. The solution will turn purple, then blue or green. The bubbles (gas) are from an acid-base reaction, the same reaction that makes a cake rise. -- *The Association for Dressings & Sauces*

FOOD MUSEUM:

While Thomas Hughes was teaching at the International School in Brussels, Belgian he started a student project on the humble potato. He felt the potato was treated with much snobbery, so he collected and preserved potato lore, forming his own museum in the Belgian village of Lanse-Maransart in 1975.

THE POTATO MUSEUM

"It's the world's most misunderstood food," Hughes said. "It has gotten a bum rap in the reporting of history. Historians . . . forget that the potato made possible the industrial revolution." It was not until the potato became accepted and provided a food surplus that the peasants could farm less and go to work in factories. Hughes decided the potato needed a proper place in history. In the 1980's, along with his wife, Meredith, he moved his Potato Museum to Washington, DC. Later it was expanded and renamed the **Food Museum** and relocated to Albuquerque, New Mexico.

The Food Museum focuses on how food influences and even makes history. The Museum began to take shape when the Smithsonian asked the Hugheses to write the potato script for "Seed of Change," to donate 120 items on the potato, and also contribute a section on corn.

Corn History

The exhibit on corn (also known as maize) included items from the American Midwest, buttons and postcards from the turn of the century, African fabrics, paper money and coins, corn starch products, Native American artifacts from the Southwest, housewares, and other items. The Food Museum has contributed to the Museum of the City of New York, "Gaelic Gotham - The Irish in New York." The Hugheses also collaborated with the Corpus Christi Museum of Science and History on a permanent exhibition of "Seeds of Change."

Food of the Americas

Another project was with students at the Navajo Pine High School in New Mexico. It was a three day undertaking to teach students on research, presentation techniques, as everyone worked together to produce an exhibit called "Magic Arrows - Foods the Americas Gave the World." Teenagers acting as interpreters guided students and adults through the exhibit. Information included nutrition, environmental issues, global food topics, healthy cooking and food history. "Foods of the Americas" is a new concept which will be a permanent exhibit and includes corn, potato, beans, squash, chocolate, tomatoes, avocados, pineapples, blueberries, peppers and other foods to the world.

Traveling Exhibits

The Food Museum also has traveling exhibits which go to schools and other museums to save money on expensive field trips while still providing the richness of a museum tour. Currently the Food Museum has twenty-four complete programs. Each program lasts between one to three hours and includes: science, math, global awareness, vocabulary building, poetry, music, arts, crafts, cooking, games, and books. The fun, hands-on program teaches kids and adults the essential facts about the food we eat.

For more information on the Food Museum, write: Thomas and Meredith Hughes, 908 La Paz N.W. Albuquerque, NM 87114 Or phone: (505) 898-0909 www.foodmuseum.com

FOOD ON THE TRAIL: See TRAIL FOOD

FOOD SAFETY:
SAFE HANDLING OF FRUITS & VEGETABLES

Although not commonly associated with food poisoning, fruits and vegetables can harbor disease-causing bacteria. Bacteria such as E.coli can be found in fresh apple cider, salmonella in melons, and shigella in a tossed salad, are three examples.

Their growth environment, such as soil, is a rich source of microbes. Poor agricultural practices, such as irrigation with unsanitary water, also may introduce bacteria. Poor storage and transportation practices can result in contamination, as can poor food handling by grocers and you in the home.

Industry practices, such as rinsing fresh fruit and vegetables with chlorinated water and transporting them in refrigerated cars, help reduce this risk. But, just as with other foods, safe handling of fruits and vegetables at home must be practiced. Here are a few pointers:

1. **Wash hands** with warm water and soap for at least 20 seconds before and after handling food.
2. **Rinse raw produce** in warm water only. Don't use soap or detergents, however, a little household bleach or peroxide can be added to the warm water, then thoroughly rinse in plain warm water. Some produce can be scrubbed with a small brush to remove surface dirt.
3. Use smooth, durable and **nonabsorbent cutting boards** that can be cleaned easily. Plastic boards are best, as they are not as porous as wood, making them less likely to harbor bacteria.
4. **Wash cutting boards** with hot water, soap and a scrub brush to remove food particles. Then sanitize the boards by putting them in the automatic dishwasher or rinsing them in a solution of 1 teaspoon of bleach to 1 quart of water. Always wash boards, as well as hands, after cutting raw meat, poultry or seafood and before cutting another food to prevent cross contamination.
5. Store cut, peeled and broken fruits and vegetables at **41 degrees** Fahrenheit in the refrigerator.
6. For those whose immune systems may be compromised, stick with pasteurized foods, especially juices, cider, and eggs.
7. When eating from a salad bar, **avoid** fruits and vegetables that look brownish, slimy or dried out. These are signs that the product has been held at an improper temperature.
8. Throw away the outer leaves of leafy vegetables, such as lettuce and cabbage, because they might contain **pesticides**.
9. **Peel and cook** when appropriate, although some nutrients and fiber may be lost when produce is peeled. – *Paula Kurtzweil*, A condensed article from FDA Consumer Magazine, December 1997 See FOOD AND DRUG ADMINISTRATION

FOOL: Have you ever heard the term "foolproof"? It means even a fool can't mess it up. That's the idea behind berry fool. Even the most inexperienced cook can fold cream into berries and make it look scrumptious. The name refers to the simplicity with which the dish is made, but it's really a very clever use of only berries and whipped cream. Berries can be swirled into whipped cream ahead of time and looks spectacular served in clear glassware.

FORCEMEAT: Finely chopped meat, potatoes, fruit or nuts that are used for stuffing poultry and fish. Forcemeat is also made into pâtés. Forcemeats are served hot or cold. Also see FARCE.

FORK: A table utensil with two or more prongs used for eating and serving food. Have you ever hear this exchange at the table? "Use your fork." "Why should I? Fingers were made before forks." That's true. Forks were not used in European society until the 1200s. At that time they were gold and only affordable by European aristocracy Until then everything was eaten with a knife or fingers. Forks were used in the Middle East and mentioned in the Bible long before. Forks were introduced to Venice by a Byzantine princess. Henry VIII made them popular in his court after being introduced to them by his friend Thomas Becket, who was famous for style and propriety at court.

FORBIDDEN FRUIT: Also known as *citrus paradisi*, it was discovered in 1750 on Barbados. We know it as grapefruit. It is thought to be a mutation or hybrid of *citrus grandis* which had been introduced there in the 1600s. There is another "Forbidden Fruit" which is from the Ceylonese tree *Tabernae montana dichotoma*. The seeds are narcotic.

FOWL: A edible wild or domestic bird or poultry.

FRANKFURTER: A German word, also known as hot dogs and wieners. They are made from ground meat, stuffed into casings, cooked by steam and quickly chilled. Some are also smoked, spiced and/or seasoned with garlic. Frankfurters are one of the easiest meats to prepare, since they can be barbecued, fried, boiled, steamed, or broiled. They also make great additions to recipes, such as beans, macaroni and cheese, rice, and corn.

FRAPPÉ: (frah-pay) A French beverage or dessert, partially frozen and stirred. Similar to a slusher or slushy. In Boston, it's what we'd call a milkshake.

FREEZE-DRY: Food is frozen, then placed in a vacuum chamber where the water (ice) is changed from a solid to a vapor and removed, but leaving the color and flavor of the food. This food is popular with campers and backpackers, since it is light weight and only water to reconstitute. This process is done with meat, fruit, vegetables, and cooked combinations such as stew.

FRENCH TOAST: Bread that has been soaked in egg and milk, than baked on a griddle or in the oven.

FRICASSEE: French term sometimes referred to as "hash." Generally less tender cuts of meat, slowly cooked, and served thickened with dumplings, rice, or potatoes. French fricassee today is likely to be white meat covered in cream sauce, as in chicken fricassee.

FRIED EGG TREE: Native of African, produces a round, hard shelled 2-inch fruit which is usually not eaten. The roots and leaves are used as medicine.

FRITTER: Chopped meat, fish, or fruit mixed with a flour batter and deep fat fried. Otherwise may be known as fried pies. See POCKET DOUGH

FROG: The frog has been called "the poor man's fish" though it is not cheap meat today. The **Aztec** emperors ate frogs sizzled in pimento sauce. The **Spanish**, who may have acquired the taste from the Aztecs by way of their explorers, considered the frogs "poor man's fish" because they were caught by gypsies and sold to make money. Frogs have always been eaten in times of need, but were prized as a great delicacy by the ancient **Chinese**. In Northern Spain they like the skin roasted. In other places, only the legs and part of the upper body are considered meaty enough to eat. According to superstition, frog tongues were poisonous, so no one ate the heads. Since it takes a frog five years to grow large enough to eat, stock is fairly scarce. In Spain, over consumption and shrinking habitat have made frog hunting illegal, although there are always poachers. Most frog legs sold there today come from **Thailand**. They are usually fried with garlic or stir fried with vegetables.

FROG LEGS: The hind legs are considered a delicacy in both the United States and Europe. They have a mild chicken flavor. The skins must be first removed, as well as the head and feet. Frog legs can be broiled, sautéd, or deep fat fried. **Nutrition facts**; Low in calories with good amounts of riboflavin and thiamin.

FRIZZLE: To pan fry until the edges curl.

FROMAGE: (fro-mazh) French word for cheese.

FROSTING: Same as icing. Generally cooked or uncooked sugar, moistened with water or milk, and flavorings used to spread on cake and cookies.

FRUCTOSE: (froo-toes) Extremely sweet sugar from fruit and honey.

FRUITCAKE: A cake made of mostly dried fruit and nuts with just enough batter to hold it together. Traditionally, a Christmas and holiday favorite. Probably it began as a creation of British cooks in the Middle Ages. It wasn't until the 1200s that dried fruits began to come into the British Isles. The first recipes for fruitcakes called for 4 pounds of flour, which would have made a huge cake. The fruits and nuts would have taken days to prepare. Only the wealthy upper class could have afforded them.

FRUMENTY: In England frumenty was a kind of wheat stew boiled with milk, cinnamon and sugar. It sounds like our modern cream of wheat. It was probably brought to England by Crusaders returning from the Middle East.

FRY: To pan cook meat, and some vegetables, in a small amount of fat or vegetable oil.

FUDGE: A candy made from milk and granulated sugar boiled to the "soft-ball" stage, then adding cocoa and butter. Nuts or raisins are optional. The hot fudge has to be cooled and set (thickened) before cutting into squares. The basic sugar and cocoa fudge recipe will be on the cocoa can. Easier recipes can be found on the marshmallow cream jars and bags. The old fashioned fudge on the cocoa cans required a period of boiling sugar and was difficult to get right without a candy thermometer. The new kinds require less cooking and call for shortcutting ingredients such as melted chocolate chips, marshmallows, and/or sweetened condensed milk. The old fudge has a grainy texture which the newer fudges do not have, but for nostalgia some people still prefer the old fashioned kind that Grandma used to make by the recipe on the tin.

223

Gg

GABON NUTS grow wild in West Africa. It is not related to the walnut, although its fruits resemble the walnut so much they are called "African walnuts." Eaten boiled or roasted, hey are also cooked to be processed into oil.

GALA APPLES: Sometimes referred to as "royal gala," this heart-shaped apple has distinctive yellow-orange skin with red striping. Gala is the perfect take-along-snack, any time.

GALANTINE: A French term for removing the bones from poultry, meat and fish, and then restuffing it to look like the original form. The meat is then cooked in a broth, chilled, sliced, and served cold.

GAME: A wild bird or animal, such as duck, quail, turkey, deer, opossum, beaver, or rabbit.

GAMBOGE: Native of southeast Asia, this medium sized, egg-shaped fruit, has yellow flesh, with an acid flavor. It is eaten fresh and made into preserves.

GARBANZO BEANS: See CHICKPEAS

GARDENS AND GROWING: GROW YOUR OWN NATIVE AMERICAN GARDEN

Native Americans grew corn, beans, and pumpkins in one plot. First the corn was planted, then the beans, finally the pumpkins. The beans used the corn stalks as poles to climb. The pumpkins shaded the ground to kept the moisture in the soil. The Natives also found that by adding fish to the soil, the plants had higher yields. While they didn't know it, fish added valuable nutriments and the beans supplied nitrogen to the earth. Would you like to grow a Native American garden? It's easy, just find a sunny location.

With a shovel, dig compost or aged manure into the soil. When the ground and the weather is warm, without chilly nights, it is time to plant the corn seeds. Plant each seed about one inch deep and five inches apart, in three rows about twelve inches apart. Firm the soil and water. When the seedlings come up, thin to ten inches apart. If you do not get a good stand (because of weather, birds or insects), replant. The new seedlings will quickly catch up. When the plants are about eight inches tall, feed with a high nitrogen fertilizer, and feed again at 18 inches tall.

When the corn is about 18 inches high, plant four or five bean seeds next to the sprouted corn. Wait for about two weeks and plant some pumpkin seeds in the middle of the corn patch. It is best to mulch just after the pumpkins start to sprout.

It is important to water frequently, especially as the tassels appear. Keep the garden weed free. Always save some seeds for next year's garden. *--RSC*

FLOWER POT GARDENING
by Alice Reeve

Do you like to dig in the dirt? Do you like to watch things grow? If you do, plant a garden of fruits and veggies. Flower pot farming is planting in a minimum of space. If you have a small back yard plat, fine. If not, you can plant these delightful midgets in the kitchen or your patio, porch, deck or in window boxes.

Midget veggies begin with baby carrots, tiny dill cucumbers, Tom Thumb lettuce with small, crispy heads and ornamental and yummy winter squash. Italian peppers are so mild, you can eat them raw. Yellow pear tomatoes are gooooood! Red Pixie tomatoes are about two inches wide and meaty. Pixies love a flower pot! Tiny Tim tomatoes come in both red and yellow. Little pumpkins have edible seeds.

Strawberries in hanging baskets, luscious and beautiful. In the melon line you find watermelons that tell you they are ripe by turning from green to yellow. Cantaloupes grow the size of a soft ball, sweet and firm with a small seed cavity. All these little darlings mature early, generally in 60 to 75 days. They are insect free and need only a shot of liquid fertilizer such as Miracle Grow. Start with herbs on the window sill. The herbs include: parsley, chives, basil, cress (called pepper grass) summer savory, alfalfa sprouts, wheat sprouts, and broccoli sprouts. All are good in salads, sandwiches, and for food flavoring. Some grow quite tall so you must trim them back.

Use scissors for "mowing." It won't hurt them, they'll grow back even thicker to be mowed again. You can purchase the seeds from seed houses by mail. Seed catalogs are sent free for the asking. Some supermarkets carry them as well as most nurseries. The seed packets will provide instructions on how to plant, type of soil, and any other information that might be required. Seeds can be started in tin cans, flower pots, milk cartons or paper cups. Punch holes in the sides and bottom of the containers, and place small rocks or marbles in the bottom for air circulation and drainage. Plants can grow indoors or outdoors, it's up to you. Pots can be moved around for change and display and are easily watered by spray or a pitcher. Here are the names of a few seed and planters suppliers:

Burgess Seed and Plant Co., Galesburg, MI 49053
Gurney Seed and Nursery Co., Yankton, SD 57078
Henry Field Seed and Nursery Co., Shenandoah, IA 51601
L.L. Old's Co., P.O. Box 1069, Madison, WI 53701
Renee's Garden, 7389 W. Zayante Road, Felton, CA 95018
Shephard's Seeds, 30 Irene St., Torrington, CT 06790

GARLIC: A member of the lily family, which also includes onions, leeks, chives, and shallots, this edible bulb is made up of small bulblets called "cloves." Garlic can be grown in almost any climate, and is an important crop in almost every country. www.crockettfarms.com

The ancients used garlic as medicine from everything from toothache pain to healing dog bites. Garlic was also used to catch birds. Garlic seeds would be sprinkled in the fields. The birds would eat the seeds, fall asleep, and be gathered by the farmer. And of course, garlic has been used to repel vampires. Even today, people around the world, including in the United States, wear garlic around their neck to ward off evil spirits and demons.

The main use for garlic is as a seasoning. It can be added to sauces, vegetables, meats, seasfoods, pastas, eggs, and of course garlic bread. It can be used as is, just peel and chop or press; or it can be made into a seasoning mixed with salt, pepper, and ginger.

Clemson University animal and veterinary researchers have been putting garlic powder in chicken feed and smelling the results. "It makes the poultry house smell like a pizzeria instead of manure," says professor Glenn Birrenkott.

Researchers noted another benefit. In taste tests, garlic-diet eggs tasted milder than others, possibly by reducing the sulfur content. Researchers are continuing the testing to see if it reduces cholesterol in eggs.

BROOM HILDA   By Russell Myers

Reprinted Courtesy of Tribute Media Services, Orlando, Florida

HOORAY FOR GARLIC!
by Diana Lowry

Do you think if you wore garlic around your neck you'd be able to keep disease away? In the past, some folks believed just that. Garlic has been around for thousands of years. This little bulbous herb of the lily family has been praised in folklore for the wonderful powers it was thought to have. Today doctors are starting to believe that some of those claims are true.

In 3758 B.C. the great pyramid of Cheops was being built. The workers went on strike. Why? Because their daily ration of garlic had been taken away, they were becoming too weak to perform their hard labor. When their masters returned the garlic, they were able to work again.

Greek gladiators and later, Roman soldiers and charioteers, depended on garlic to give them strength and courage,. Garlic has been associated with long-lasting youth and rejuvenation. The ancient Egyptians believed in life after death. When their pharaoh, King Tutankhamen, was buried, they placed garlic in the tomb with him to help him have everlasting youth and vigor. Garlic was also used to influence the gods of ancient Egyptians and to chase away evil spirits.

When people believed in and feared vampires, they hung clusters of garlic at their doors and rubbed garlic on windows.

In the Middle Ages the Russians revered garlic so much that the Siberians were permitted to pay part of their taxes in pounds of garlic. Do you think we could do that? Today in Russia many garlic-users live to be 100 years old or more. Some scientists say garlic gives the body immunity to life-threatening diseases.

How would you like to walk around with garlic in your socks? In the British Isles folks once used garlic to protect the wearer from infections.

Later, in American, it was believed the body could be detoxified from foot to head if garlic cloves were used on the soles of the feet. Ground garlic becomes the antibacterial agent allicin, so maybe they were right.

In the 1600s there was a terrible plague in Marseilles, France. Stories say that four thieves went from house to house stealing from the sick. When they were arrested, the four admitted that garlic had kept them from getting the disease too. After that, many citizens began eating garlic and thousands were spared the plague. Garlic contains vitamin C, which is needed to heal wounds. It was used during World War I for that purpose and also to prevent gangrene.

Today garlic is considered a respected medicine in Europe. It has been referred to as "Russian penicillin." In India a doctor used it to prevent heart attacks. It's said to lower blood pressure, perhaps because it contains potassium. Its value in treating cancer is under serious research, but it does contain selenium, a cancer fighter.

California produces most of the garlic used in the United States. It's in catsup, mustard, and pickles. It's sold as garlic powder and garlic salt. Other products are garlic tablets, capsules, and oil that are found in health food stores. Fresh garlic sales are about 40-million pounds per year.

Even cows like garlic. Unfortunately, it gives their milk an unpleasant taste and smell. If you like to eat garlic but don't want garlic-breath, eat an apple afterwards or rinse your mouth with lemon juice and water.

Although all the claims about the powers of garlic haven't all been scientifically proven yet, it's still a welcome addition to our diet. Garlic is great in stews, salad dressing, and meat. Garlic bread is a favorite. Try putting a peeled garlic clove in a bag of chips for a few hours before you eat them.

Who knows, maybe someday this little bulb will prove to be the cure-all it's been claimed to be for so many years?

GILROY GARLIC FESTIVAL

At Gourmet Alley chefs perform garlic magic over blazing fire pits. Watch famous chefs sizzle garlic calamari and other garlic creations in iron skillets the size of bicycle wheels. As you visit the 90 food booths, you can sample garlic stuffed mushrooms, garlic shrimp scampi with lobster butter, garlic bread, garlic pepper steak sandwiches, garlic ostrich meat on a stick, vegetarian garlic dishes, garlic shrimp fritters, garlic quesadillas with mango sauce, garlic popcorn, pickled garlic, wash it all down with garlic tea, and the delight you have been waiting for, garlic ice cream. If you have sampled each garlic delight, you can wear a badge with pride that reads, "I ate the WHOLE thing." On Saturday, finalists compete in the Great Garlic Cook-Off. The winner will take home $1,000 cash. If you have a garlic recipe, you could enter and be a winner as well.

In the Garlic Grove, garlic experts answer questions. Live entertainment blares from three stages, plus strolling musicians. Join a "twist and shout," sing-along with several thousand happy and crazy people. This is not just an adult festival, its for kids of all ages, with special kids' live entertainment, games, and dozens of "no garlic" food booths. The annual event takes place near the end of July in California's beautiful Santa Clara Valley. For more information write: **Gilroy Garlic Festival**, P.O. Box 2311, Gilroy, CA 95021-2311 or phone 1-408-842-1625. www.garlicsurvival.com

GARLIC SALT AND OTHER BLENDS: There are a variety of seasoned blends of salt, pepper, vegetables, and herbs. For those on a low salt diet, who still wish for the taste of salt, one of these blends might be an answer. A 1/4-teaspoon of salt provides 25% of your daily needs, which means if you consume a whole teaspoon of salt, that's 100%. With blends, the salt is reduced to any where between 3% to 10%, depending upon the manufacturer. To avoid more salt, try one of the many seasoned, saltless blends. Check the seasoning section of your supermarket.

GARNISH: Something added to a finished dish to make it more appealing.

GARNISHES, INSTANT PIZZAZ
by Louise Ulmer

Food doesn't have to be boring. A splash of color can make a dull dish interesting and it only takes a few extra minutes. Many garnishes you already have on hand most of the time. Others can be kept in the pantry. **Cherries:** The queen of garnishes is the maraschino cherry. Crown any ice cream dish or fruit cup with a long stemmed cherry, red or green. Add a cherry to a mound of cottage cheese. Serving fresh fruit in sections? With a toothpick, pin a cherry on each chunk. **Green Bits:** Don't throw out those tiny green celery leaves. Use them to add color and texture to the white dishes on your menu. The same goes for mint leaves, and other fresh herbs. **Flowers:** Daisies and baby roses can make salads sit up and sing. No cake decorations? Visit the garden and see what you can find. Garnishes don't have to be eaten; they only have to look pretty. **Candy Chips:** Don't throw out those hard candies no one likes. Smash them and sprinkle a few of them to brighten cakes, cupcakes, cookies, etc. If someone doesn't like them, they can be left on the plate. **Cookie Crumbs:** Colorful cookie crumbs can be used to put crunch in ice cream, top pies, brighten cake icings, and sprinkled on top of whipped cream. **Citrus Peels:** Before you use a lime or orange, shave some of the peel to use for garnish on pie toppings or whatever. **Citrus Slices:** in slices of citrus can add color to drink glasses, float in fruit punches, top salads, decorate gelatin salads, etc. **Shavings:** For delicious curls of chocolate, use a vegetable peeler on bar chocolate flavors. **Dribble:** Keep a few of those small cake decorating tubes in various colors in the spice pantry where you can write a quick message on the cake or the plate you serve it on.

GASTRONOME: A Greek word for a person who takes pleasure in food.

GASTRONOMY: A Greek word that means the art of good eating.

GÂTEAU: In French it refers to an elegant cake, especially a filled one, served at parties.

GAZPACHO: In Spain it is a cold soup mostly of tomatoes and cucumber with lots of garlic. It began as a hot soup brought to Spain by the Arabs, but tomatoes could not have been one of the ingredients as they were not known at that time.

GEFILTE FISH: This Jewish specialty is made with a pound each of whitefish, pike and carp. The fish is ground, mixed with eggs, seasonings, and matzo meal, then molded into small balls. The balls are simmered slowly in a vegetable or fish stock. Gefilte fish is served chilled with white or red horseradish. You may find it in jars in the specialty section of supermarkets.

GEL: Short for "gelatin." Cosmetic "gels" are used to style and hold hair in place.

GELATIN: A protein substance made from beef and veal animal tissues that's dissolved in a hot liquid and thickens when chilled. Gelatin is available plain and flavored. Transparent and colorless, it is sold in powder form. www.knoxge.com

HORSE HOOF DESSERT
by Eric Diesel

Would you make a treat that required two horse's hooves and all day to concoct? That's what you would have once had to go through to enjoy one of today's most popular treats: gelatin.

The Joys of Gel

Before the introduction in the late 1800s of mass-produced, boxed or canned foods, gelatin was reserved for the wealthy. Making it was expensive and time-consuming. In those days, common flavoring for home-made gelatin included fruit juices (especially citrus fruits), maple syrup, cream and even champagne. Mixing gelatin with champagne created a foamy, gooshy. This was ladled over iced grapes and served as the pre-dessert course at fancy Victorian dinner parties. Gelatin gently boiled with cream, honey, and raisins created a smooth alternative to ice cream that didn't require the then-newfangled luxury ice-box.

Humble Origins

But like so many fancy foods, gelatin had humbler beginnings. In the days when all food on the table was grown and harvested by the family, not one scrap was allowed to go to waste. For example, green beans were served with "snaps," or the vines that grew them. Bacon and sausage were the result of preserving every ounce of meat from an animal. Pioneer cooks - women who ran homesteads or men who cooked for work camps - discovered while curing animal hide that the hooves of pigs and horses, could be boiled to produce a rubbery substance. That thick goop added body and flavor to dishes from stews to jams. They did not know that they were separating the compounds of the animal's hooves to form collagen, that's the protein that makes an animal's hooves tough enough to walk on. They did not know that they were making food history. In true pioneer tradition, they were just trying to utilize their resources. What they did was to produce a food (gelatin) and a material (leather), without wasting an ounce of the slaughter.

A Cinderella Rise to Riches

Gelatin contains two key qualities that made it necessary in the days before mass refrigeration. Gelatin doesn't really require refrigeration to solidify, and on its own it is flavorless and colorless. For these reasons, gelatin was an important ingredient in the soda fountain fare. Soda fountains found their way into drug stores because, during that era, a pharmacist wasn't just someone who could make pills. The friendly pharmacist could concoct anything that required a knowledge of chemistry -even sweets! Such soda fountain staples as smooth ice cream sundaes, jewel-like dabs of puddings, bubbly sodas, and gummy fruit ices all owed their unique consistency to gelatin.

"Always Room for Jell-o®"

Gelatin today is made from protein by-products of the meat industry, chemical compounds that require no animal collagen. Strict guidance from the Food and Drug Administration (FDA) tries to assure that no cruelty to animals occurs. Gelatin's most popular brand-name, JELL-O®, ranks among the best-selling packaged foods of all time. To answer your next question, JELL-O's best-selling flavor is strawberry, and its worst flop was chocolate. **JELL-O®** is a register trademark of Kraft Foods, Inc.

Dessert Plate to Photo Plate

However, not all gelatin is eaten. Along with silver, it is the most important compound is another great American tradition: photography. Try making a soda fountain favorite treat of yesteryear.

CHERRY COLA COOLER

3 cups cola beverage
2 envelopes unflavored gelatin
1 jar maraschino cherries

1. Drain the cherries and lay the cherries on paper towels to absorb all excess liquid.
    IMPORTANT, if cherries are too wet, the gelatin will not set.
2. Dissolve the gelatin in the cola. This can take up to 4 minutes. Stir with a wire whisk or fork.
3. Stir in the cherries.
4. Chill until set. Scoop it out into a dish or in an ice cream cone, if desired

" My grandmother always had a jar of granules in the pantry. She said my grandfather scraped the granules from his horse's hooves. Grandmother made gelatin with these scraping. She never joked so I guess it was true. Or maybe my joking grandfather put gelatin in the jar and she didn't know."– *RSC*

GELATO: (jel-ah-to) In Italy every town has at least one *gelateria* where they congregate for their favorite frozen treat. In America, gelato is being introduced as a gourmet ice cream by the Häagan-Dazs company. It comes in cappuccino, chocolate, raspberry, coconut and hazelnut.

GENIP: Native of South America, this tree bears 4-inch long fruit, ripe when the skin becomes tan in color. It is made into a beverage. Genip is popular in Puerto Rico.:

GÉNOISE: A fine textured sponge cake made with melted butter, whole eggs, sugar and flour. .

GEODUCK (gooey-duck): No, these are not in the duck family. Geoducks are the world's largest burrowing clams. The odd name probably came from a Native American word. Geoducks are found along the Pacific coast from Vancouver Island to California. A large geoduck can weigh 11 pounds and be 15 years old. Geoducks are best made into chowder and one geoduck feeds a lot of people.

GHEE: Clarified and evaporated butter. Ghee has been used for 10,000 years in India because it stops butter from going rancid. Ghee is from the Hindi word, *ghi* for butter. Canned and commercial ghee is not recommended because of its rancid taste.

GHERKIN: (ger-kin) A small cucumber that grows up to 3-inches in length and is used to make both sweet and sour pickles.

GHIRARDELLI CHOCOLATE:

If your father was a famous chocolatier, would you want to leave home? In 1836, at the age of 19, Domingo Ghirardelli set out on his own from Italy to Peru where he set up his own candy business. Maybe he wanted to save the cost of importing all that cocoa from South America to Italy.

He apparently had a good head for business. While in Peru he made an American friend, James Lick, who set out for San Francisco with 600 pounds of Ghirardelli chocolate to sell. Lick had luck! He arrived in California 13 days before the famous Gold Rush at Sutter's Mill. Like so many, Domingo followed James Lick to California to pan for gold. However, it didn't take long for Domingo to see that selling chocolate was a lot easier than mining. He stayed on in the gold country running a general store until 1852. He moved back to San Francisco and setup his chocolate factory, which today is open for visitors, complete with some original equipment and a soda fountain. **Ghirardelli Chocolate** is available by calling 1-888-402-6262. www.ghirardelli.com.

GIANT GRANADILLA: (grah-nah-deel-yah) Native to tropical America, this passion flower vine produces egg-shaped, 8-inch greenish-yellow fruit, the largest of all the passion fruits. The subacid flavor is made into juice and the fruit is also cooked. *Granada* is Spanish for pomegranate.

GIBBONS, EUELL: (Yul Gibbons) American naturalist and cookbook writer.

WILD FOODS

"My greatest joy is opening young minds to nature's possibilities," Euell Gibbons said while he researched and rediscovered hundreds of wild plants and food in the American wilderness. As a child in his native Texas, Gibbons invented his first wild recipes - hackberry/ hickory nut candy bar.

"My lifelong passion," he said, "has been to seek out nature's bounty and subsist on it." Knowing which wild foods are safe to eat, a person would never starve to death in the American wilderness. His first rule remains. "Eat only what you absolutely know is safe."

For fascinating reading about the mysteries of wild foods, their history, and recent rediscovery, read *Stalking the Wild Asparagus* and other books by Euell Gibbons.

GIBLET: (jib-lit) Giblets are the heart, liver, and gizzard from poultry. Giblets are cooked, chopped and added to gravy. Boiled giblets provide stock for soup and gravy. They may also be made into a pate, or added to rice and noodles.

GIN: (jin) A clear alcoholic drink made of distilling grain mash with juniper berries. Tourists from Britain are surprised to find their national drink being made on the small Mediterranean island of Minorca. Minorcan gin is an island specialty under the name of Mahón gin. Gin is made in other countries, including the Netherlands and the United States.

GINGER: (jin-jer) A root that originated in southeastern Asia that is used as a spice. Ginger has long been used as a medicine, since it is believed it will prolong life. Ginger is still used as a digestion stimulant and reliever of motion sickness. Ginger can be eaten fresh, dried and ground into powder, or crystallized into sort of a candy. Fresh ginger can be added to soups, vegetables, meats, seafood, and made into a preserve. Dried ginger powder is used in all the above, plus used in baking cookies, cakes, and pies. Crystallized ginger can be eaten as candy (it's a bit hot!), or added to cooked fruits. Ginger is also added to make ginger ale soft drink and hot ginger tea. The ginger plant has been cultivated since ancient times in Southeast Asia and one of the "gems" traded from India to the Roman Empire. www.thaifoods.com.

GINGER ALE: A carbonated drink flavored with ginger.

GINGER BEER: A popular British drink made with ginger that has been fermented with yeast.

GINGERBREAD: A flat spicy cake made with brown sugar, molasses and spiced with ginger and other spices.

GINGERBREAD IN AMERICAN HISTORY

In the 1700s, the Brothers Grimm created the first gingerbread house by writing of *Hansel and Gretel* and a "house made of bread, with a roof of cake and windows of barley." Gingerbread had been around a long time before that house, however.

Ginger root has been treasured from antiquity for seasoning food and for its medicinal uses. Long before the Grimm Brothers, the ancient **Greeks** invented a hard gingerbread about 2000 BC and called it *melitates*. It was a hard layer made of honey combined with flour, ginger and spices. By the 14th century, **German cooks** had refined the hard lump into fanciful shapes, using carved wooden molds. It was the search for ginger, cinnamon and nutmeg, the spices that go into gingerbread that caused the early explorers to brave the unknown seas, always trying to find an ocean route to the spice islands in the South Pacific.

Pilgrims immigrating from the Old World to the New World brought their craving for gingerbread with them. Ginger wouldn't grow in American gardens, but clipper ships brought spices from the Far East to waiting colonial cooks. Sailors brought their bundles of spices back home then returned to sea, loaded with gingerbread to eat on the long voyage back.

In the early 1600s the French and English added eggs and honey. When molasses from the New World became available to the English, it was used for both softening and sweetening. As the popularity of gingerbread grew, the cry of the gingerbread hawker was heard in the streets.

England's Queen Elizabeth I is credited with inventing the first gingerbread men and served them to her guests. In Shakespeare's Day, fellow Elizabethans shared his love of gingerbread by enjoying the sweet spicy bread during feast days and country fairs. At Bartholomew Fair, children often ran after Joan Trash, the gingerbread woman, who filled her basket with gingerbread figures shaped like animals, men and women, and saints. **William Shakespeare** said, "Had I but one penny in the world, thou shouldst have it for gingerbread."

In the American colonies, traditionally, the first Tuesday in June was "Muster Day." The citizenry gathered with picnic baskets to view the local militia in training. Ladies served gingerbread as rewards for soldiers - and good children.

In the America South, gingerbread was used to bribe voters to elect certain candidates to the House of Burgesses. In some of the colonies on December 21st, the school boys made a game of "bar the master." Students would arrive at school early in the morning and make sure that the schoolmaster could not enter. After some half-hearted pleading and the offering of gingerbread as ransom, the teacher would give up and declare a holiday over Christmas. At New Year's time, parents gave their offspring gingerbread hornbooks (cookie style) so that they would be smart in the new year.

Half of the fun of gingerbread is its shape. In the Old World, artisans carved molds made of hard wood. Here in the New World, few artisans had time for such a minor job. Creative **tinsmiths devised cutters of tin** as a substitute and cookie cutters, as we know them today, were born.

By 1896, Fannie Farmer included eight different recipes for gingerbread in her famous American cookbook. A New England variety uses maple syrup instead of molasses.

And there's another old saying that "some things are eternal." American's love of gingerbread is one of those things. **Abe Lincoln said**, "I don't s'pose anybody on earth likes gingerbread better'n I do and gets less'n I do."

FESTIVAL OF GINGERBREAD

Beginning the day after Thanksgiving and running until mid- December, the Allen County, **Fort Wayne Historical Society** presents the Festival of Gingerbread in the Old City Hall Historical Museum. This festival features over a hundred gingerbread houses are exhibited by bakers of all ages, plus culinary students and professional bakers. In addition to the gingerbread house exhibit, you will visit the cookie house and treat yourself to a gingerbread cookie. Of special interest is the Money House, a gingerbread house filled and decorated with money, both coins and bills. If you can guess the amount of money without exceeding the exact amount, you win the house and the money.

Many of the gingerbread houses will be sold in silent auction. The highest bidder takes the house. Do you still believe in Santa? If so, bring your letters, cookies and milk, and visit with Santa and his elves. For more information, write to **The Historical Society**, 302 East Berry Street, Fort Wayne, IN 46802 or phone (219) 426-2882.

THE SECRET OF PERFECT GINGERBREAD MEN

To make perfect gingerbread men you need a few tips.

1. Use shiny or nonstick, cookie sheets. Avoid old ones which have been blackened by use. Blacking will cause overheating and sticking.
2. Use metal cookie cutters. Thin, plastic cutters don't cut deep enough to make a sharp edge and won't let go of the dough. Dough clings to thin cutters.
3. Use pan spray to prevent sticking. A light spray on metal cookie cutters will help prevent dough from sticking.
4. Chill dough before rolling and cutting. It will roll better and be less sticky.
5. Don't try to cut thin cookies and then place them on the pan. Do it backwards. Prepare your pan with a very light spray or dusting of flour. Then roll or press the dough about 1/4-inch thick on the pan. Cut the cookies out. Leave room for them to grow slightly without touching the others. When cookies are cut, remove the dough around the cookies. Save that part and chill it to make more.

TIPS ON BUILDING A GINGERBREAD HOUSE

Almost any gingerbread cookie recipe will work to make the walls and roof of your gingerbread house. Here are a few tips for the prefect house:
1. For a more sturdy gingerbread house, omit the soda and other leavening ingredients.
2. For walls and roofs, do not roll the dough too thin.
3. Bake just a little extra long and let the dough cool on the cookie sheet before lifting off.
4. For more even browning, bake smaller pieces on a different pan from larger ones.
5. Freeze cutout dough until hard, then bake immediately to retain shape.
6. If necessary, have an supervising adult involved during baking.
7. Before baking the gingerbread, plan your house design. You can find ideas and patterns in magazines, library books, and doll house patterns.
8. Gather all the edible decorations you will need. Do not use plastic and other non-edible decorations.
9. If you are helping a younger brother or sister, use graham crackers and cookies for walls and roof. This way there's no baking involved.
10. Use the following recipe for "gluing" the gingerbread house together:

3 egg whites at room temperature
1 pound powdered sugar
½ teaspoon cream of tartar

Combine all ingredients, beat at high speed for
7 to 10 minutes. This glue dries very fast, so
keep it covered with a damp cloth at all times.

11. If you plan to exhibit your gingerbread house at an event, bring along some of the above glue in case the house needs to be repaired. Also bring a few extra pieces of candy and other decorations as part of your repair kit.

THE GINGERBREAD LADY

Patti Hudson is the Gingerbread Lady of Lancaster, Pennsylvania. For many years she made gingerbread houses and sold them. Now she no longer sells them, but offers two-day gingerbread house classes for students of all ages. The first day she teaches how to make the dough, to roll it out and to bake it. The second day is for construction and decorating the houses. For those unable to attend her classes, she has books and videos available to purchase. The ***Gingerbread Ideas*** book contains 128 pages of recipes, patterns, step-by-step instructions and full color photographs. Three videos are available: *Gingerbread Land, The Joy of Gingerbread Housemaking* (also includes a Gingerbread Cookbook) and *The Gingerbread House*. The videos cover a wide range of gingerbread materials from gingerbread history in the 1800s to construction of not only the houses, but gingerbread furniture as well. For information on classes, books and videos, contact: **The Gingerbread Lady**, 2714 Royal Road, Lancaster, PA 17603, phone (717) 394-8220, or the web: www.gingerbreadland.com

GINGERSNAP: a small, crisp gingerbread cooky.

GLACÉ: A coating of sugar syrup on cakes, breads, and fruit. The syrup is cooked to the hard-crack stage.

GLASSE, HANNAH (1708-1770): Famous English cookery writer, author of *The Art of Cookery Made Plain and Simple* (1747), one of the first cookbooks in English.

GLAZE: (verb) To cover food with jells, sauces or syrups which form a smooth glossy surface, like very thin icing. (Noun) As a noun, it is the icing itself.

GLUTEN: (gloo-tin) A mixture of plant protein occurring in cereal grains. A tough, sticky substance remaining when flour grain is washed to remove the starch. Gluten flour is add to white flour which increases the leavening action for making bread. Additional gluten is added to bread recipes that contain heavy ingredients, such as raisins and nuts.

GNOCCHI: (g-noh chi) The word in Italian means lumps and that's a good likeness for the small dumpling of flour or potato dough. They are poached or baked.

GOAT: Goat meat is not on the top of the culinary list, even though it is lower in calories and fat as compared to other red meat. Goat meat is popular in the Middle East, West Africa, Italy, Caribbean, and Mexico. In Italy, a whole goat is roasted at Easter, and the Sofwa people in Africa make a goat stew to celebrate the birth of a child. While goat meat is not all that popular in the United States, goat milk has been enjoyed for centuries. From the milk is made yogurt, ice cream, fudge, and cheese. **Nutrition** facts per 3 ounces: 93 calories,19 calories from fat, 2g total fat (3%), .6g saturated fat (3%), 48.5mg cholesterol (16%), 69.7mg sodium (3%),zero carbohydrates and fiber, 17.5g protein (35%), zero vitamins A and C, 11mg calcium (1%), and 2.4mg iron (13%).

GOAT CHEESE: Lower than cow's milk cheese, goat milk cheeses are tasty, creamy, and of many flavors. Long a staple in the diet of Europeans, it is growing in popularity in American. In Northern California there are a number of small creameries and dairies which produce goat and sheep cheeses by hand, according to the traditional methods of Europe and Peru. Painstaking effort goes into the raising of the goats and the handcrafting of the cheese. bdgagoat@sonic.net.

Goat cheese is known by many names:

· **Chèvre** (French),satiny, salty.
· **Feta** (Greek), crumbly, tangy, salty.
· **Bleu** de bresse (French), mild, soft, creamy, blue.
· **Bûcheron** (French), soft, creamy, tangy.
· **Gorgonzola** (Italian), semisoft, sharp, pungent, blue.
· **Montrachet** (French), creamy, mild.

GOBSTOPPER is a British word for jawbreakers, the round sucker candy too big to chew.

GOLDEN DELICIOUS APPLES: A medium to large golden-yellow apple, sometimes russeted. They have a white or yellowish-white, crisp flesh, and are very sweet. Golden delicious can be used for any purpose, and retains its mellow flavor when baked or cooked. Skin is so tender and thin that it doesn't require peeling for most recipes.

GOLDEN SHOWER: Native to tropical Asia, the 12-inch bean pod has edible, sweetish, brown pulp used as a laxative.

GOOSE: There are both wild and domesticated geese, and different varieties of each. Wild geese have a tough, fishy tasting flesh, while the domesticated geese are tender and much milder in taste than their wild cousins. Geese are fat and it is important to cook out all the fat possible. The flesh is brown, and because of the fat, is quite rich. Stuffing the goose with a tart apple dressing will help reduce the richness. To remove some of the fishy taste in a wild goose, soak it in milk overnight. Geese have long been standard Christmas fare in many European countries. **Nutrition facts**: per 3 ounces: 137 calories, 57 calories from fat, 6.1g total fat (9%), 2.4g saturated fat (12%), 71.4mg cholesterol (24%), 74mg sodium (3%), zero carbohydrates and fiber, 19.4g protein (39%), 34 IU vitamin A (1%), 6mg vitamin C (10%), 11mg calcium (1%), and 2.2mg iron (12%).

GOOSEBERRY: Although cultivated, gooseberries still grow wild in northern climates. They look like round green grapes. Scholars disagree on the name. One dictionary credits the frequent use of the berry with roast goose. The tart berry went well with fatty goose meat. Possibly it came from the Scottish word "grost" berry where gooseberries have always been prized. The British love the berry so much they formed "Gooseberry Clubs" to hold competitions for growing best and biggest berries. Native Americans enjoyed gooseberries in all areas where they grew long before the English came to share them. **Nutrition facts** per ½ cup: 33 calories, 4 calories from fat, .4g total fat (1%), zero saturated fat and cholesterol, zero sodium, 7.6g carbohydrates (3%), 3.2g fiber (13%), .7g protein (1%), 217 IU vitamin (4%), 21mg vitamin C (35%), 19mg calcium (2%), and .2mg iron (1%).

GOOSEFOOT: A common green plant used in Europe as a green vegetable because it resembles spinach in taste. The name comes from its leaf's duck foot shape.

GOUDA CHEESE: (goo-dah or go-dah) A yellow cheese made from either whole or lowfat milk, semisoft. Flavor ranges from mild and creamy to slightly tart. It comes from Gouda in the Netherlands. .

GOURD FAMILY: A flowering vine in the *cucurbitaceae* family with more than 700 species. In the edible group are cucumbers, melons, pumpkins and squash. In the nonedible group is the bottle gourd. The hard walls of these dried gourds are used as containers in some cultures. The bottle gourd are used to carry water and to store grains Some of the smaller nonedible gourds are dried and used as baby rattles and rhythm-type musical instruments which are often decorated and painted. With a hold in the body, they make dandy birdhouses.

GORGEOUS GOURDS

Throughout the centuries the people of the Americas have used gourds for dishes and storage containers. Dried gourds were used as baby rattles, Native Americans used them in their dance, and Mexican musicians used them (maracas) as rhythm instruments. The gourds are often painted as works of art.

You too can decorate them to suit your tastes. You will need:
Variety of sun dried gourds, especially the long-necked kinds
Permanent markers, black and colors
Fabric colored paints
Spray shellac

1. Research pictures of African, Native American, Mexican, Central and South America art for ideas. Art and history books are good sources. African, Aztec, Mayan and Inca designs are not only interesting, but quite colorful.
2. You can draw or paint directly on the gourd, or if you wish, paint the entire gourd with white or a pastel color as the background. Let this background paint dry before you add the design.
3. Once you have found a design you like, paint it on a gourd. You can make your own design by combining your ideas with other designs. Be totally original by creating your own design.

Or, paint a picture of something you favor. 4. When the paint or ink dries, spray with shellac. The shellac will brighten and preserve your gorgeous gourds.

5. A small hole can be drilled near the end of the neck, a string inserted, tied in a loop. This way you can hang your gourd on the wall, as you would a picture.

DRINKING GOURD SONG

Gourds are mentioned in myths and legends the world over. In this legend, we know the part about the gourd is true, but the peg-legged sailor may be mythical. A peg-legged sailor supposedly made a number of trips through the southern United States, encouraging young Blacks to escape to the North. The sailor would teach the song to the Blacks and show them the marks left by his natural foot and the peg leg. Then he would go ahead of them and mark a trail of a foot and a round spot to represent the peg leg. In daytime they found other signs on trees. At night the Big Dipper showed they way North. The drinking gourd in the song represents the Big Dipper. The old man is the peg-legged sailor. The great big river is the Ohio.

When the sun come back,
When the firs' quail call,
Then the time is come
Foller the drinkin' gou'd.

The riva's bank am a very good road,
The dead trees show the way,
Lef' foot, peg foot goin' on,
Foller the drinkin' gou'd.

The riva ends a-tween two hills,
Foller the drinkin' gou'd.
'Nuther riva on the other side
Follers the drinkin' gou'd.

Wha the little riva
Meet the Grea' big un,
The ole man waits-
Foller the drinkin' gou'd.

Chorus:
Foller the drinkin' gou'd,
Foller the drinkin' gou'd;
For the ole man say,
"Foller the drinkin' gou'd."

GOULASH: (goo-lahsh) A thick Hungarian stew made with meat, vegetables, and paprika. In American, it's most often a dish with hamburger, macaroni and tomatoes seasoned with salt, pepper, and paprika.

GOURMAND: (gor-mahn) A French word for a hearty eater who enjoys luxurious food.

GOURMET: (gor-may) A French word for a connoisseur who knows fine wine and food.

GOVERNOR'S PLUM: Native to Madagascar, these round, red to black berries are eaten fresh and made into jelly.

GRAHAM CRACKER: Brown crackers made with graham flour.

GRAHAM FLOUR: In 1830 Presbyterian minister Sylvester Graham (1974-1851), a vegetarian, who believed white flour had been stripped of all nutrients, developed his own "graham" flour from unsifted whole-wheat flour that contains the rolled, product of the entire kernel. Graham developed a large following, but Americans were too fond of white flour to give it up. Later white flour was enriched by adding nutrients. There are imitations made with inferior grades of brown wheat flour mixed with bran that are hard to digest. Graham flour is used to make honey graham crackers. The cracker crumbs are used to make pie crusts and puddings. Two 2 ½-inch squares has about 55 calories.

GRAINS: All grains are grasses, which include **amaranth** (high in protein with a nutty flavor), **barley** (one of the earliest known cultivated grasses), **buckwheat** (not a true grain, but a grass), **millet** (rich in iron and amino acids), **oats, quinoa** (a supergrain from the Incan Empire, as it supplies all the nutrients to sustain life), **rice, rye** (high in protein, with a sour flavor), **sorghum** (mostly used for animal feed and molasses), **triticale** (a combination of rye and wheat), and **wheat** (more than 30,000 different varieties). All edible grains have four basic features:

· The **hull** which is generally not eaten and removed;
· The **bran** is the layer that is rich in vitamins and minerals, as well as fiber;
· The **germ** or the embryo that contains enzymes, minerals, and vitamins; and
· The **endosperm**, the starchy center, rich in carbohydrates.

Nutrition facts: When the whole grain is used, it will contain the most nutrients. When the grain is refined to only the starchy center, most of the nutrients are lost. White flour, unless it has been enriched, is made from the endosperm, and contains almost no nutrients. Bulgur, also called ala, is whole wheat which has been steamed, hull removed, and cracked, retaining all the nutrients.

GRANGE: An association of farmers, begun in the USA in 1867. It comes from Middle English (granary, a storage place for grain). In England it means a farm.

THE GRANGE-PATRONS OF HUSBANDRY

The Grange began as an association of farmers in the USA in 1862. Programs and projects offered in every local Grange reflect the varied interests and talents of its members with a special focus on family activities. The heart and soul of every Grange is community service, contributing a better way of life for all Americans. No project is too big or too small. The first USDA, Secretary of Agriculture, William Sauders, was a Grange member. One of his major projects was the designing of the Gettyburg Cemetery.

The **Grange fathered the 4-H and the Future Farmers of America** (FFA). However, not all members are involved in agriculture. Some join to better their public speaking, writing talents, participate in parades and fairs, and be active in community education and health care. Early Grange projects included the Rural Free Postal Delivery (RFD), Rural Electrification, and Land Grant Colleges. Granges fathered the current Cooperative Extension movement, and grandfathered the current Cooperative Marketing System.

Junior Granges

The Grange recognizes that one of the greatest needs of young families today is a place the family can go together, where kids are welcome. That place is the Grange. Most Granges have a meeting place called the Grange Hall. The Junior Grange program includes:
- Community service projects: for example, making tray favors for shut-ins; reading to a seriously ill child; sponsoring a holiday party for the kids of the community.
- Through the "One Earth Needs You" program, kids learn about recycling, conservation, and pollution control, as well as community beautification projects.
- In the "Small World International" project, kids study a different country and culture each year. Also a study is made on one of the 50 United Sates every year.
- Kids can also participate in the "Merit Badge Program" where they will earn recognition for completed project in a wide variety of subjects.
- Fun and fellowship are a big part of being a Junior Grange member, including taking part in camps, cooking, sports, games, crafts, talent contents, and more.

The Junior Grange program is open to boys and girls, ages 5 through 14. There are similar programs for teens and young adults. For information on a Grange in your community, contact: **National Grange**, 1616 H. Street, N.W.,, Washington, DC 20006-4999, phone (888) 4-GRANGE, or the internet: www.grange.org.

GRANITA: A frozen dessert made with fruit syrup.

GRANNY SMITH APPLES: A medium to large green apple, sometimes with a pink blush, with a crisp and crunchy texture. Granny Smith's are an all-purpose apple with a mouth watering tart taste. The tartness really comes through when baked or sautéd. Also, enjoy a Granny Smith out of hand or in a salad.

GRAPE: No one knows for sure when grapes were first cultivated by man. There is a reference in the Bible that Adam and Eve cultivated vines, but were they grapes? It is thought that grapes originated in Asia Minor, near the Caspian Sea. However, some varieties have been growing wild in temperate regions of Asia, Europe, Africa, and America since the beginning of time. There is evidence that grapes were enjoyed in Switzerland some 6,000 years ago.

Grapes have changed little since prehistoric times. In the natural state, the vine would creep along the ground, spreading further each year as new tendrils branched out. One vine can spread out more than 50 feet. The Romans found that these vines were susceptible to insects and animals. By elevating the vines, fruit loss was reduced. Today grape growers cultivate vines on a system of stakes and wires, which are heavily pruned each year.

Did you know that there are more than **8,000 grape varieties**? However, only about 20 varieties are grown for eating. The rest are made into juice and wine. Did you know that grapes are America's largest fruit industry and that grapes are grown in every state? California is by far the biggest producer, growing about 97% of the nation's table grapes.

Grapes are grown for eating, raisins, juice, and wine making. The most popular for eating are the light green Thompson and Red Flame, both seedless. Those grown in the United States are available from late spring into late fall. The same varieties are available from Chile and other southern hemisphere countries during our winter months.

Raisins are made from a variety of grapes, with muscats and saltanas the best for drying. Muscats are dried in the sun, while the sultanas are dehydrated indoors. Concord grapes are best for making juice, jellies, and jams. Thompson grapes are used to make white grape juice.

To keep grapes fresh, do not wash them until ready to eat and store them in the refrigerator. Before eating or using grapes in a recipe, rinse with cool water and drain. **Nutrition facts** for 1 cup: 98 calories, no fats or cholesterol, 14.7mg sodium (1%), 25.2g carbohydrates (8%), 2.5g fiber (10%), 1.2g protein (2%), 162 IU vitamin A (3%), 2mg vitamin C (4%), 25mg calcium (2%), 2.4mg iron (13%), and 262mg potassium. www.aalplum.com; www.cawg.org; www.cgtfl.com; www.nationalgrape.com. www.tablegrape.com.

GRAPEFRUIT: A member of the citrus family, it is almost considered an American fruit. It is thought to have originated as the shaddock in India prior to being imported to the West Indies. In any event, the grapefruit was developed from the pomelo in the Caribbean. Like all citrus, there are many varieties, sizes, and flesh colors. The most popular is the sweet pink grapefruit grown in Florida, Texas, Arizona, and California. Today the grapefruit is being introduced to the Europeans. They are not grown in Spain, Italy, and Greece. Many people of northern Europe still have not seen or heard of the grapefruit. Grapefruit can be eaten fresh, baked, or broiled. Fresh grapefruit is available most months of the year, with the peak season from mid fall to late spring. Grapefruit is also available canned, and frozen as concentrated juice. **Nutrition facts** per ½ cup: 38 calories, zero fats and sodium, 9.7g carbohydrates (3%), 1.3g fiber (5%), .8g protein (2%), zero vitamin A,

38mg vitamin C (64%), 14mg calcium (1%) an zero iron. Grapefruit web sites: www.bellsfarms.com; www.cacitrusmutual.com; www.engertfarms.com; www.stxogranics.com; www.sunkist.com www.texascitrusexhange.com; www.texasweet.com.

GROW A GRAPEFRUIT TREE
by Billie Jean Hepp

You will enjoy the very fragrant, green leaves from this citrus tree. You can grow orange and lemon trees the same way. You will need: Grapefruit seeds; Paper towels; Garden pot; Potting soil

1. Place several seeds on wet paper towels. Place more paper towels on top and wet.
2. Place towels on a saucer and keep the towels wet.
3. In several days the seeds will start to sprout.
4. Plant the sprouts, root end down, just under the surface of the soil.
5. Place in a sunny location, and keep the soil moist.
6. Soon the seed will sprout two small green leaves.
7. Once the tree gains some height, transplant into a larger pot so it doesn't get root bound.
8. Keep your grapefruit tree in a sunny location, and water when the soil dries out.

GRATE: (verb)To take hard food (carrots, cheese, etc.) and reduce it to smaller pieces or shreds by rubbing it on a indented surface, called a "grater." To shred.

GRATIN: (grah-tin) Baked and grilled oven dishes get a crispy brown crust on top. This is gratin. Chefs took advantage of this and enhanced it by topping it with cheese, crumbs, etc. Potatoes au gratin, for example, are scalloped potatoes topped with melted cheese baked to a crust on top.

GRAUDA: Native to the Amazon region, this shrub produces a small, dark red fruit with acid pulp. Tasty fresh and made into juice.

GRAV LACHS (also *gravlax* or *gravad lax*) is a Swedish specialty of raw salmon cured in a kosher salt, brown sugar, dill and lemon juice mixture and is generally served on a buffet table. *Grav lachs* is best when served on dark brown bread with lemon dill sauce. *Grav lachs* also makes a wonderful addition to a Caesar salad.

GRAVY: (gray-vee) A sauce made from fat, flour or cornstarch, and a liquid (water, milk, broth, etc.), thickened with flour or cornstarch and boiled until smooth and tasty.

GREASE: Animal fat that has been melted or cooked off the meat and bone.

GREAT NORTHERN BEANS: A large white bean used for baked bean dishes and Italian soups, and as a bean soup by themselves. .

GREENGAGE PLUMS: When these green plums are harvested, they should be tree ripe (they don't ripen well after picked), the flesh and juice quite sweet with just a little tang. These plums have more flavor than any other plum. The skin is green, and the flesh is a greenish-yellow. Often called the "dessert" plum, since they were served to French kings and queens in the early 16th century.

The fruit was **named after Sir William Gage**, an Englishman who transplanted the plum from France, where they are called Reine Claude, in honor French Queen Claude, wife of Francis I (1515-1547). King Francis held elaborate banquets, but Queen Claude probably didn't attend many of them. Believe it or not, during that period in the French court, fashionable ladies didn't eat in public festivals because the act of chewing spoiled their beauty. Peak season for greengage plums is during the early and mid summer months. They are also available canned in heavy syrup. **Nutrition facts**: One greengage plum has about 36 calories, no fat, some vitamin A and fiber, and a fair source for vitamin C.

GREENHOUSE FARMING: A greenhouse isn't green at all but glass. Plants grow well under glass because they can have the sun's rays and also the sun's warmth through glass. Many farmers and gardeners have small greenhouses where they start their plants from seeds before outdoor planting. There are giant commercial greenhouses which give tours to the public.

EPCOT'S LIVING LAND PAVILION

Squash plants hang suspended in thin air. See a living redwood tree that fits in the palm of your hand. Walt Disney World visitors at Epcot can encounter these and other wonders at The Land Pavilion. The Pavilion offers a fascinating look at our environment, the foods we eat, and creative ways to feed future generations. "Living With the Land," offers a narrated boat ride through four greenhouses. Visitors see crops from around the world and a "water garden", the amazing Aquacell. By boat, kids can glide into the following growing areas:

"The Tropics Greenhouse," growing crops native to Southeast Asia, Africa, Latin America and the southern United States. See squash that produces the loofah bath sponge. Learn how coffee is grown, as well as rice, sugar cane, bananas and a giant peach palm. All flourish under a 60-foot greenhouse dome.

"The Aguacell" showcases crops that swim: alligators, sturgeon, catfish, and more. More than 13,500 pounds of fish are raised for Walt Disney World restaurants in the Aquacell.

"The Temperate Greenhouse" features new ways of pest management and special methods to reduce waste and increase crops. Crops such as cotton and millet are grown in sand using underground irrigation.

In "**The Production Greenhouse,**" tons of tomatoes and other vegetables are grown for use in Epcot restaurants. Land scientists utilize growing systems that are kinder to the environment and improve productivity.

"**The Creative House**" shows hydroponics. Lettuce, squash and herbs thrive in growing systems that spray water and nutrients on the plants' roots without soil. Scientists are currently working at The Land to develop fruit with a longer shelf life. See HYDROPONICS

If you want a closer in-depth tour, the "**Behind the Seeds**" **Greenhouse Tour** is available. The Land scientists will take you on a tour of the growing areas and research labs. Here you can ask questions and take a closer look at environmentally friendly technologies.

You can visit the "**Pest Lab.**" Explore how predatory insects and parasitic wasps work as alternatives to chemicals for pest control. See wheat bran distributing predatory mites. In the Bio-tech lab, you will discover how plants are grown from tissue cultures instead of seeds. Watch genetic engineering improving food crops. By the end of this tour, you will be able to take home tips that you can apply to your home garden, and maybe a glimpse into your future. If you wish to spend more time at The Land, you can participate in the Epcot Youth Education Series half day "Harvests and Habitats" program. For more information on The Land, write to **Walt Disney World,** P.O. Box 10,000, Lake Buena Vista, FL 32830-1000.

GREENS: The leafy vegetable tops (lettuce, spinach, beets, chard, mustard, and watercress). They can be eaten raw or cooked; served as a vegetable. See COLLARD GREENS, MUSTARD GREENS and TURNIP GREENS Salad greens are the lettuces and raw green leafy vegetables.

GREEN SAPOTE: Native tree in Central America produces a small green fruit that turns yellow when ripe. It is eaten fresh and made into ice cream.

GRENADINE: A syrup made from pomegranates used as a flavoring for beverages and desserts. From the French, *grenade,* meaning pomegranate.

GRIDDLE CAKE: Same as a pancake.

GRILL: To cook by direct heat, such as a barbecue or broiling in the oven.

GRIND: To chop solid food into small uniform pieces.

GRITS: Corn grains hulled and coarsely ground. In the southern states, hominy grits are a popular food served as a hot cereal for breakfast with butter or as a vegetable with gravy. See HOMINY.

GROATS: Same as grits, but not as finely ground. In Britain the are likely to be crushed oats.

GROCER:

THE CORNER GROCERY STORE
by Richard S. Calhoun

People like to talk about the "good old days," a time when life was simple. A time when neighbors got together and held block parties. A time when you seldom locked your house. A time before TV, video games, and computers. A time where you only needed to walk a block or two for your food needs. One of my fondest memories was the neighborhood grocery store. This was a time before supermarkets. A time when we purchased our groceries on credit and no credit checks. A time of trust! And for those in need, there was always a helping hand.

"Betts Market" was the name of our neighborhood grocery store. Mr. Betts awoke early to purchased his produce at nearby farms. A couple times a week he would drive to Los Angeles to purchase bananas and other produce not grown locally. He opened at 7 a.m. sharp, rain or shine, seven days a week. He closed about 7 p.m. or when the last customer left the store. If you ran out of milk, bread or some other necessity after closing, you would call Mr. Betts on the phone and he would open the store. It was a family affair. Mrs. Betts collected the money. Mr. Betts did the butchering. Their two teenage sons stocked the shelves and delivery groceries to nearby homes.

A small store, Betts Market was about the same size as today's frozen food section. Street parking could hold only three or four cars, but seldom did anyone drive to Betts Market. The accordion front doors opened to expose four large tables mounded with fresh produce, two for vegetables and two for fruit. Walls on each side were stocked with canned and packaged products. Barrels of rice, beans, flour, sugar and other dry products filled the middle of the store. In the back of the store stood the meat counter. It was always an adventure to visit Betts Market. As you approached the store the odor of the fresh fruit filled the air. Smells differed day to day, depending upon what Mr. Betts could find at the farms and produce market. During summer afternoons the aroma of peaches and apricots filled the air.

I can still remember the different fragrances as I walked down the length of the store, past the produce to the fresh baked bread, on to the open bins of spices and the pungent pickle barrel. I can still hear the creaking sound of the wood floor as I walked down the aisles. Mom would send me with a grocery list almost daily. I handed the list to Mr. Betts and he filled the order. He would grind the hamburger fresh while you waited. If it was a chicken that Mom wanted, he would cut it fresh with a knife, not frozen with a band saw like today. The cut-up chicken always had three breasts, one had the wish bone in it. He would weight the sugar and flour as Mom ordered. After he pulled the cans from the shelf, he picked out the choices of fruits and vegetables. I could count on a free treat. Maybe a piece of candy or a dill pickle. I remember once Mr. Betts gave me a cinnamon stick. I asked, "Can I have a pickle?" "Give me a nickel, and I will give you a pickle," he answered.

I seldom had a nickel, so I would be happy with what ever he gave me. Mr. Betts had produce that is no longer available in the market today. One of my favorite vegetables was "salsify." It's also called "oyster plant," since some said it tasted like oysters. To me the flavor is the same as an artichoke. My favorite were the finger grapes. They were seedless and two to three inches long. Oh, so good!

During watermelon season, Mr. Betts would cut a plug out of two or three melons for us to taste so we would take the sweetest. When the order was filled, Mrs. Betts would write down the total in a book. On payday Mom would pay the balance. Sometimes she didn't have enough money and would only pay part. I remember once Mr. Betts called Mom and said he needed some money to pay for a delivery. Mom ran down to the store with whatever she had and gave it to Mr. Betts. In the mid 1930's, Ralph's opened a supermarket in the downtown area. The only time we went downtown was to shop for clothes. Why would anyone want to go all the way downtown to buy food? Plus the store was big and no one would help you. And there was no credit! I can remember Dad saying, "They won't make it. It's just a passing fancy!"

Five years later Safeway opened up the second supermarket. And in the mid 1940's Mr. Betts closed the corner store and retired. It was the end of our neighborhood store. The end of knowing that everything was fresh. An end of receiving individual service. It was the end of an era.

GROG: In America, it's a hot spiced tea drink spiked with rum. Originally, it was a name made to make fun of the watered-down rum served on board British Admiral Edward Vernon's ships to discourage drunkenness. George Washington named his house Mount Vernon, after his good friend Admiral Vernon, whose imports helped make the colonies rich. .

GROSELLA: Native to India, this medium sized fruit, high in vitamin C, is made into preserves and pies.

GROUPER: A salt water fish found in the warm Atlantic waters from Virginia to Brazil. They look similar to sea bass. Groupers can grow up to 50 pounds. Grouper can be baked, broiled, and pan-fried. **Nutrition facts** per 3 ounces: 78 calories, 8 calories from fat, .9g total fat (1%), .2g saturated fat (1%), 31.5mg cholesterol (10%), 45.1mg sodium (2%), zero carbohydrates and fiber,16.5g protein (33%), 122 IU vitamin A (2%), zero vitamin C, 23mg calcium (2%) and .8mg iron (4%).

GROUSE: They are related to the pheasant family and found only in the northern hemisphere. A grouse is the size of a small chicken, with flesh dark and rich. There are many kinds of grouse. One is a the prairie chicken, which is about the size of a hen. In the arctic regions, another grouse is the ptarmigan which has brown feathers in the summer and white feathers in the winter. Scotch grouse, said to be the finest, in highly prized by the British. Grouse can be cutup and pan fried, or roasted whole. The Native Americans would roast the grouse over an open fire, serve it with corn cakes and greens.

GRUEL is the ancient name for oatmeal or ground cereal grains, seldom used today because of the unappetizing sound of the name.

GRUMICHAMA: In its native Brazil, this shrub produces a small, orange-yellow, sweet fruit that is eaten fresh, made into jelly and jam, and sherbet.

GRUNION: This small salt-water fish is found along the California coast. At spawning time, on the high tide, the female grunion run up to the sandy beach, dig holes, and deposit their eggs. Male grunion follow to fertilize the eggs. The running of the grunion is forecast and people swoop down to the shore and gather them with their hands. Grunion can be boiled, sautéd, or deep fat fried. The taste is quite delicate and flavorful.

GRUNT: In America it is a dessert called "slump" in Colonial days. In England it's the name for several species of fish which make a grunting noise when they are in the water, especially when caught.

GUAJILOTE: Native to Central America, this tree grow fruit directly from the truck and branches. This fruit is about 1-inch in diameter and up to 6-inches long. This yellow, fibrous fruit is edible.

GUANABANA: (gwah-na-ba-na)) Also known as soursop, this small tree is native to tropical America. The large, green, fruit with soft spines is made into a drink and ice cream.

GUAVA: (gwah-va) There are several members of the Myrtle family. The various guavas are native from Mexico to Brazil. This small tree or shrub produces walnut to apple-sized, round, sweet and sour, aromatic, juicy fruit. The flesh can be red, green, or yellow. Guavas are eaten fresh, made into jelly, jam, preserves, paste, juice, and pies. Guavas are available fresh most of the year and canned whole or sliced. Guava leaves make a refreshing tea. **Nutrition facts** per ½ cup: 42 calories,4 calories from fat,.5g total fat (1%), .1g saturated fat (1%), zero cholesterol and sodium,9.8g carbohydrates(3%), 4.6g fiber (18%), .7g protein (1%), 654 IU vitamin A (13%), 152mg vitamin C (253%), 17mg calcium (2%) and .3mg iron (1%). www.thaifoods.com.

GUIANA CHESTNUT: (gih-ana) Native to both North and South America, this large tree produces football-shaped fruit up to 9-inches long. The seeds are cooked and eaten.

GUINEA FOWL; (gihn-ee) They originated in Guinea, Africa. Guinea fowl have been domesticated and are raised for food. The hen is better eating than the male. The taste is a bit gamy, and the meat is drier than most birds. They can be prepared as with any chicken recipe, but might take a little longer to cook. Mature hens should be stewed or braised with a little water. When roasting, since the meat is dry, top with uncooked bacon and/or baste with melted butter.

GUMBO: A thick Creole soup or stew made with seafood, meat, vegetables, rice, and thickened with okra or filé powder; highly seasoned.

GUMDROP: A soft jellied candy made in various shapes and covered with sugar crystals.

Hh

HABAÑERO PEPPER: According to the *Guinness Book of World Records*, the red savina *habañero* (ah-bah-nay'ro) pepper is the hottest chile known. The Chinese-lantern-shaped pepper is even hotter than the orange *habañero* A new *habañero* has been developed by botanist Frank Garcia, Jr. of Ventura County, California, the *fransica* (Frank Garcia, Jr. also developed the red savina). The advantage of the *fransica* is that it is larger than other *habañero* peppers, hence is safer to handle, because of the thicker walls and will keep longer–up to six weeks after being picked. The *habañero* originated in Mexico's Yucatan and grows best in areas with long hot summers. The pungent, smoky-fruity taste of *habañero* makes them ideal for fruit salsas and for topping grilled striped bass or salmon. (For a fruit salsa, purée *habanero* with mangoes or honeydew melon and a little fresh-squeezed lime, a clove of garlic and a handful of cilantro.) Both the *fransica* and the red savina are protected by the Plant Variety Protection Act. This means you can not sell these seeds. You can only grow them for your own use. Seeds, as well as *The Habañero Cookbook* are available from **Shepherd's Garden Seeds**, telephone (860) 482-3638 or on the internet www.shepherdseeds.com. www.starproduce.com;

HADDOCK: A salt-water fish, related to the cod, from the North Atlantic, which averages 2 to 6 pounds, and is one of the most important commercial food fish for the United States. The flesh is white, has a pleasant flavor, almost bland. When smoked, it is called "finnan haddie." Haddock can be cooked in any way desired. **Nutrition facts**: A 3-ounce serving has 74 calories, 6 calories from fat, .6g total fat (1%), .1g saturated fat (1%), 48.5mg cholesterol (16%), 57.8mg sodium (2%), no carbohydrates or fiber, 16.1g protein (32%), 47 IU vitamin A (1%), zero vitamin C, 28mg calcium (3%), .9mg iron (5%), and 265mg potassium. Smoked haddock has 99 calories, about same amount of fat, 648.9mg sodium (27%), and a little more protein, calcium and iron.

HAKE: A small fish, related to the cod, found in the north Pacific and Atlantic oceans. Hake weight from 1 to 4 pounds. The meat is white, a bit soft, and with a delicate flavor. It can be cooked as in any cod recipe.

HALF-AND-HALF: A mixture of half milk and half cream, sometimes called, "table cream." Substitute: 1 tablespoon melted butter plus 1 cup whole milk. **Nutrition facts** per tablespoon: 20 calories, 15 calories from fat, 1.7g total fat (3%), 1.1g saturated fat (5%), 5.6mg cholesterol (2%), zero sodium, zero carbohydrates and fiber, .5g protein (1%), 66 IU vitamin A (1%), zero vitamin C, 16mg calcium (2%) and zero iron.

HALIBUT: A cold-water fish found in all of the oceans of the world. This odd flat fish, with eyes both on the same side, and resembling the flounder, can weight up to 600 pounds. The smaller halibut, called "chickens," are the best eating. The flesh is snow white with a slightly sweet, mild, delicate flavor. The smaller halibut flesh has a fine texture, while the larger halibut is quite coarse. Halibut can be fried, broiled, baked, poached, and barbecued. It always maintain its firm texture and shape when cooked.

Halibut can be enhanced with herbs, seasonings or sauces that range from the simple addition of lemon to far more elegant preparations such as fruit-based salsas, vegetable purees, and garlic-flavored bread crumbs. **Nutrition facts**: A 3-ounce serving has 94 calories, 19 calories from fat, 2g total fat (3%), .3g saturated fat (1%), 27.2mg cholesterol (9%), 45.9mg sodium (2%), zero carbohydrates and fiber, 17.7g protein (35%),132 IU vitamin A (3%), zero vitamin C, 40mg calcium (4%), .7mg iron (4%), and 383mg potassium. www.alaskaseafood.org

HALIBUT TRIVIA

A 50 pound female halibut will lay about a **half-million eggs**, while a 250 pound female will lay more than four million eggs. The free-floating eggs are about three millimeters in diameter (about the size of a BB shot). The eggs are laid at a depth of about 1000 feet. The eggs hatch after about two weeks. As the newly-hatched larva develop, they slowly drift into shallower waters.

Once the larvae grow into a small fish, they **swim in an upright position** with an eye on each side of the head. When they are about an inch long, an **extraordinary transformation** occurs; the left eye moves over to the right side of the head and pigmentation on the left side fades to white.

When the fish are about six months old, they have developed into an adult form and then settle into about 400 feet of water with the grayest-black side up. With the **two eyes on both sides** of the head, they can see passing prey.

Very young halibut feed on plankton. After about one year old, they feed on small shrimp and fish. As the halibut increases in size, fish become their main food.

Halibut grow about three inches a year, and females grow faster than males. At age 10, a male averages about 10 pounds, while the female will be almost double that size. Females mature slower than males, where most males are mature at the age of eight, but it's closer to 12 years for a female to mature. --*University of Alaska Fairbanks, and The International Pacific Halibut Commission.*

CATCHING BIG BERTA
A True Story
by Richard S. Calhoun

Benny and I were sitting on the dock watching the fishing boats heading out of the bay. Benny's dad, Willie, walked up behind us and said, "Benny, why don't you and Clark catch some bottom fish? I would like to fry some red snappers for dinner tonight. You can use my skiff." Willie's skiff was powered with a ten horse Johnson outboard motor. Benny opened up the engine and we swiftly made our way into the middle of the bay. As usual in southeast Alaska, a light drizzle was falling and with the spray of the boat I was getting wet. I guess I should have worn my raincoat.

Once out in the middle of the bay, Benny tied several hooks on one line, baited them with herring, and tossed the line in the water. Benny tied the line around the bow post, leaned back in the skiff, pulled his cap over his eyes and said, "I'm going to take a nap. Wake me up if there's any action."

I sat in the bow, peering down the line into the water. I couldn't see the bottom. I noticed we were drifting toward a small island. Thirty minutes went by. I couldn't wait any longer and decided to pull up the line to see if there was anything on it. The line was heavy, like an anchor was on the end. "Benny, wake up. I think the line is stuck on the bottom."

Benny gave the line a jerk. He started the outboard, put in reverse, and headed for the island. He turned off the motor and tilted the propeller out of the water. He turned to me and said, "Jump out and pull the boat ashore."

I jumped into the knee deep water. I pulled on the stern until it touched the sandy shore. "Benny, I need help!"

Benny jumped overboard and the two of us pulled the skiff upon the shore. Benny untied the line from the bow and pulled on the line. "Help me pull," he ordered.

I grabbed the line and we pulled. The line was cutting into my hand. I took a handkerchief from my pocket and wrapped it around my hand. "What's on the line?" I asked.

"I don't know," Benny answered.

We continue to pull and soon a black object came into sight. "What is it?" I asked.

"It's a whale," Benny answered.

"A whale?" I questioned.

"It's a large halibut! It's looks like Big Berta! Help me pull her up on the beach."

"Big Berta?" I questioned. "Who's Big Berta?"

"She's my next door neighbor. She's big and flat, just like this halibut." Benny laughed.
I had never seem Benny's neighbor, so couldn't picture a big flat lady, but I laughed along with him. Benny removed his knife from his pocket, he cut back of the gills and removed the guts. It was a funny looking fish, black on one side and white on the other, with both eyes on one side of its head.

"That's a big fish! How much does it weight?"

Benny took a look, lifted the tail, and then the head, and said, "About two hundred pounds."

"Wow!" I remarked excitedly. "I didn't know they were that big."

"Halibut grow a lot bigger. Last year I saw one on our dock that was twice this size."

"You're putting me on, aren't you?"

"No," answered Benny. "Females are known to weight as much as seven hundred pounds."

"Wow! How big do the males get?"

"Males are small, seldom reach forty pounds."

"Really? That's strange that the female would grow so large and the male is so small. I thought it would be the other way around. What are we going to do with this fish?"

Benny pushed the skiff back into the water and said, "Help me get her in the skiff."

It was a struggle with Benny pulling on the tail, while I tried to lift the head. The skiff tilted on its side and started to fill with water. Benny tilted the skiff upright and the halibut slid into the skiff. I pushed the skiff away from the shore and jumped in. The skiff was overloaded with only about two inches between the water line and the top of the rail on the skiff.

"Benny, the skiff is sitting low in the water."

"You're right," Benny replied, "there should be about six inches of freeboard. It's the weight of the halibut and all this water in the boat." Benny took off his cap and started to bail water out of the skiff.

I grabbed my cap and within fifteen minutes we removed most of the water. Even at that there was only about three inches of freeboard. It would only take a six inch wave to swamp the skiff.

"Benny," I said, "Maybe I should stay on the island while you take the fish to the dock."

"No need to stay, the bay is calm, I'll take it slow." Benny started the outboard and we slowly made our way across the bay to the dock. Even though the halibut was gutted, it still had life, because the tail hammered the bottom of the skiff. I put my foot on the tail, hoping to stop the pounding, but the fish had more strength dead than I did alive. Now I was more worried that the fish would knock out the bottom of the boat than a wave swamping us.

Willie was waiting on the dock for us. "Where have you been?" he yelled. Then Willie looked into the skiff and asked, "Where did you find that whale?"

Benny pointed and answered, "We got her near that little island."

By this time other people on the dock came to see what was happening. It took five people to put the halibut on dock. Willie cut the halibut into steaks and handed them to those who helped. He gave me three large steaks. I walked home and into the kitchen door and said, "Mom, I brought home dinner."

Mom looked at the halibut steaks and calmly asked, "That's nice, where did you get them?"

"Benny and I went fishing, and we caught a two hundred pound halibut," I replied.

I don't think Mom believed me, as she took the steaks, washed them, and placed them in the refrigerator. I decided to go to Benny's house, as I wanted to see Berta, the big flat lady. Benny was sitting on the porch. Softly I asked, "Which is Berta's house?"

"That one over there," he pointed. "But she's not home, she works down at the cannery. If you want, we can go to the cannery and see her."

I thought for a moment, "No, I've done enough walking for today. I better go home and finish my homework for school tomorrow."

"Okay," Benny said, "See you tomorrow."

As I walked home a big lady came walking toward me. I wondered if that was Berta. Do I dare ask, I thought. Better not. She walked by, I smiled at her, she smiled back. She wasn't flat. I still can't picture a big flat lady. – From *Cheechako* by Richard S. Calhoun

HALVAH: In the Middle East sesame seeds are crushed and made into a delicious Turkish rich candy called "halvah."

HAM: The rear leg of a hog is called the ham. Ham is available both fresh and cured. Curing is done by salting and smoking. **Nutrition facts** per 3 ounces: 155 calories, 83 calories from fat, 9g total fat (14%), 2.9g saturated fat (14%), 48.5mg cholesterol (16%), 1120.1mg sodium (47%), 2.6g carbohydrates (1%), zero fiber, 14.9g protein (30%), zero vitamin A, 24mg vitamin C (39%), 6mg calcium (1%), and .8mg iron (5%).

AMAZING HAM HISTORY

Have you wondered why ham is served at Easter? This practice dates back to pagan times and has nothing to do with Christianity. Fresh meats were not always available in the spring, and since meat was a must for all feasts, the pagans buried fresh pork legs in the ocean sand in the late fall. The pork was marinated all winter by cold salt water, which preserved the meat. The meat would then be slow roasted over wood fires.

You have heard the term "He's a ham actor." Originally they were called "hamfatters." Since these actors were poor, they couldn't afford cold cream to removed makeup after their performance. Hence they used ham fat in place of cold cream. The term "big ham" also refers to those actors, since they were not experienced actors or second-rate. Such colorful terms came from the minstrel shows aboard showboats. Some bad actors were even called "showboaters," which is the same as a "big ham." Today "big" has been dropped. Now generally an amateur actor is referred to as a "ham."

Hams and How They Differ

Picking out a ham might bring confusion. First, a ham can be either fresh or cured, but a ham is always the hind leg of the pig. There are other portions of the pig that has been cured, such as the shoulder, loin, and the belly, but these cuts differ in how they are cured as compared to the hind leg. Most hams are labeled "water added." However, there are a large variety of hams without added water, and also various ways of curing the ham. Some of the hams you find will be labeled as follows:

Water Added Ham: These hams have been injected with water, which will increase their weight by about 10% from the point they went into the smokehouse.

Ham and Water Product: These hams can have as much as 35% of water and ham chunks added and come in a variety of shapes and sizes but are still 90% lean. This is generally a canned product with the added ham as chunks and formed into rounds, squares and other shapes.

Natural Juice Ham: No water is add to this ham. It comes out of the smokehouse the same weight as it went in.

Whole Boneless Ham: This ham has the bone removed, then trimmed of excess fat and reshaped into bags and pressed. There are also semi-boned hams treated much the same way.

Cooked Ham: Better called "boiled ham," because they are cooked in large vats of water until fully cooked.

Smoked Ham: This ham has been hung in a large smokehouse and is fully cooked with natural smoke from a variety of woods. Most will be labeled "hickory smoked." Beware, many cooked hams are treated with liquid smoke and have never seen a smoke house.

Dry Cured Ham: These hams are processed with salt or brine, sometimes with sugar, which draws out the moisture from the meat. They are then completed by smoking.

Hams also differ because of the pig's diet. Some are fed a diet of just one feed, such as acorns, peanuts, corn, apples or peaches. The smoking process differs with the wood used. Hickory, oak, and apple woods seem to be the most popular.

Ham curing varies around the world. In **Italy prosciuto** is dry cured, not smoked. Like many European hams, prosciuto is sliced paper thin. The Italians also make parma which is dry cured then aged for at least a year. The **Bayonne ham of France** is also dry cured, then aged. The **black forest ham from Germany** is smoked with pine wood then dipped in beef blood. The Germans also make **Westphalian ham** that is smoked with juniper berries and beechwood.

Imports

Many foreign processed hams cannot be imported into the United States, because they don't meet FDA health standards. Hence, some of the hams made in America, are similar to, but not exactly the same as those found in Europe. In America there are two well recognized hams, country and Smithfield. **Smithfield ham** begins as a pig that is peanut-fed. When treated, it is smoked and coated with black pepper only in the town of Smithfield, Virginia. Some of the pigs are raised in North Carolina, but must be processed in Smithfield. **Country hams** are dry-cured, and many are also smoked, but most are not cooked. Since all hams are not cooked, read the ham label for cooking instructions.

HAM HOCK: The last joint in the pigs hind quarter, which would be the same as the human ankle. The ham hock has been cured and smoked.

HAMBURGER: A term used for ground beef that contains no pork. The name came from Hamburg, a seaport in Germany. Originally hamburger was ground from less tender cuts, today it is available in tender cuts as well, and in a variety of fat contents. It can be fried, broiled, or barbecued. **Nutrition facts** per 3 ounces: 259 calories, 99 calories from fat, 11.2g total fat (17%), 3.9g saturated fat (20%), 33.2mg cholesterol (11%), 365.7mg sodium (15%), 28.8g carbohydrates (10%), zero fiber, 11.6g protein (23%), zero vitamins A and C, 60mg calcium (6%), and 2.3mg iron (13%).

HAMBURGERS

A hamburger is not a hamburger unless it is sandwiched between two buns. The same can be said for the hot dog. It must be a sandwich to carry that name. Both are true American inventions and seldom have they been copied successfully in other countries.

There's a misconception as to what is a hamburger. When the menu reads, "Diet Burger," you know it couldn't be a real hamburger. More likely it's a diet plate, with a piece of low-fat, ground, dried-up, almost burnt meat, with a side of cottage cheese on a lettuce leaf, and maybe a pineapple slice. That's not a hamburger, don't be fooled. Hamburgers must be juicy, a bit messy, with at least a trickle of ketchup running down the side of your mouth. Better still, if the juice is running down your arm all the way to your elbow, then you have the perfect burger.

Also a hamburger isn't a hamburger unless there are French fries and a cola drink with it. If you prefer a milk shake instead, that's okay, but never a fruit smoothie with a hamburger. What goes in between the buns with the ground meat is a matter of choice. Cheese, tomatoes, lettuce, pickles, onion (raw or grilled), plus a variety of dressings (such as mustard, mayonnaise, ketchup or, of course, your fast-food secret sauce) top the list.

You must take the hamburger seriously, especially when you travel. There are, of course, all the well known fast-food hamburger drive-ins. However, in various regions, you might want to try a local creation. In the West, there's the **chili burger** with grilled onions and crisp bacon. This is probably one of the messiest of all messy hamburgers, a real elbow pleaser.

In **Cajun** country, plan to have your taste buds damaged for the best part of the next day. Your eyes will water; you might choke on that first bite; and you will find it hard to breath! But for some unknown reason, you can hardy wait for that next bite. At the shore is the **sunshine burger**, which is best eaten on a sandy beach, and it should be dropped at least once to give it that gritty gourmet touch. Real surprises come when you visit an ethnic community.

Greek burgers will be topped with feta cheese and black olives. **German burgers** will have sauerkraut and melted cheese. **Italian burgers** will have garlic tomato sauce and Parmesan cheese. **Chinese burgers** are seasoned with soy sauce and topped with chop-suey. **Jewish burgers** are seasoned with cumin and topped with horseradish. Expect a latke potato cake on the side in place of the fries. **Hawaiian burgers** have ginger and topped with crushed pineapple. But in **Alaska** the beef will be replaced with ground walrus and lots and lots of ketchup. The worst hamburgers are **airport burgers**, impossible to describe. Don't bother! Avoid at all costs. *–RSC*

HAMBURGERS AND CHEESE
by Elizabeth Giles

Hamburgers and cheese
hamburgers and cheese
would somebody please
pass the hamburgers and cheese.

I do not need dill pickles
or catsup on my bun.
All I need is meat and cheese
and preparations done.

Now I get to eat it
and savor every bite.

Everything is wonderful-
There's cheeseburgers tonight!

SLUGBURGERS
by Cheryl L. Hoyer

Slugburger - a meat mixture containing beef and a breading extender, shaped into patties, deep-fried in hot oil and served on a toasted bun with mustard, pickle, and plenty of onions. Do you like hamburgers? Well, then you ought to try a crunchy, juicy slugburger. Have plenty of napkins handy, because slugburgers can be messy! In the extreme northeast corner of Mississippi sits the historic town of Corinth where the slugburger originated. This delicacy is featured in many local Mom and Pop diners in the Corinth area. It's been around for as long as the oldest living Corinthians can remember! As you pass through Corinth, stop in at a local diner and ask for a hamburger. "Beefburger or slugburger?" the waitress will ask.

Slugburgers should always be served hot and eaten right away. They aren't quite as tasty when they get cold! Where did the name "slugburger" come from? That's a matter of much debate. One of the most popular theories is that they were first called "slugburgers" because of the price. Many years ago, "slug" was a slang word for a nickel. Since the burgers then cost a nickel they became known as slugburgers! What? You thought they were made from that slimy, garden pest called a slug? No way! So go ahead, try one. Then you can tell your friends that you have eaten a slugburger. It'll be fun to see the looks on their faces! For even more fun, visit Corinth, Mississippi the second weekend of July and attend the **Slugburger Festival**, held on the Town Square.

BURGER RECOLLECTINGS
A Texas Tall Tale

Caddo-Lake-Area's "First-Ever, Almost-Annual and Historical Best Food Critic Awards"
by Author and Food Critic Lad Moore
And the nominees are...

Bubba's Burgers. My friend Jim Waters from Louisiana was a skeptic. He had to go to Bubba's place to see for himself. Now, I am afraid he will die there---situated permanently as he is, between the empty drink cases and the ammo box with the rubber rattlesnake in it. He's been holed up inside, eating burgers and yapping with old Woodcutter. Jimmy's wife of 36 years has gone on back to Louisiana without him. But she chose a burger to go.

Big Pines Lodge in Karnack, Texas: The specialty should be, and is catfish, and the menu allows you to "pitch with the fishes until you win." Way over in a small section of the menu is the select button for those who want instead to choose a burger. George hid it on the menu like that on purpose, so it would earn its own reputation. Well, it has. Try the Big Burger Basket with fries so limp from lard that you have to eat them like spaghetti. The Burger drips enough juice to run down to your elbows and puddle in your sleeves. Cleo Mullins, the three-times-defeated candidate for constable at Karnack says of them, *"Best uns' round."* Cleo is a man of few words---and it seems--

-fewer voters. In any case, I gave Big Pines nine stars out of ten for their burger. I would've made it ten, but I ate some of their startling Jalapeno hushpuppies while I waited, and got too full. Not George's fault, but I can't rate them all tens.

Moosie's. It might have been ten-star quality, but I had to withhold the prize altogether because Moosie died in 1970-something. But it would have been right up there. He cooked his onions *with* the patty, so you got caramelized onions. Two squirts of Tabasco on top of garlic-grilled buns, and a secret ranking of what condiment goes first. It might have been mustard before mayo, tomatoes under the lettuce, and cheese above the patty, but the secret is lost. The people who took time to dissect one to document the order and placement are all dead too. Well, it doesn't matter anyway. Moosie and his legend are up there in Greenwood Cemetery together. Before she died too, Mrs. Crain said that the secret, in his own handwriting, was sealed in a mayonnaise jar and rests in the pine box just east of Moosie's big toes. The tombstone writing says *"Gone But Not Forgotten."* It's absolutely true of the caramelized onions. It would've been good if the family had written something nice about Moosie, too.

Tiny Grill in Marshall had a burger that seemed almost as big as the inside of the shop, but the place was so small that two average-sized adults could never order at the same time, so it went out of business. But it had a good run while it lasted, tiny as it was. Oney McAfee said that the reason there were no flies in Tiny Grill was because of the risk of head-on collisions. To make sure you knew the burger was bigger, they fixed a patty larger than the bun by a half-inch around. You had to use both hands to pick it up, and three napkins and a sponge to catch the drippings, which were mostly mayonnaise-laced tomato juices---Tiny Grill only used vine-ripened ones.
But no matter what you thought about the food, the place was so small if you ate two burgers instead of one, you had to spend the night, because you couldn't get back through the door. Then when someone tried to compare it to other burgers, it could not be validated whether the burger was really that big, or if the place was just that small. It was marketing genius, but for reasons of unproven size, I could only grant it ten, *half-stars.*

Haddad's, in tiny Uncertain, Texas, fixed a burger that had fried onion rings on it instead of regular onions, and you got a basket of potatoes that were rolled in corn meal before he cooked them. The burger was exceptional, but it was smaller than all the competition, so I had to reluctantly gave it a three-star penalty---burgers are supposed to be big. Besides, if you caught Haddad on a day when he was tinkering on his Elgin outboard motor on the porch outside the kitchen, it might be a one-hour wait for the burger. Things could get worse---if he suddenly got it running he'd probably ramble off with his dog Quigley to do some crappie fishing over to Government Ditch.

My favorite then, (and glory it's still there today!), resides at **Fugler's Grocery Store and Dining Room-Laundromat, east of Harleton, Texas**, on State Highway 154. They have something fondly called a Bubba Burger, and it was around long before President Bill Clinton's brother, and long before it got its honorable mention as the best burger in the world on a network late-night television show. Someone said it was named for its middle girth and its endorsement by Bubba

Boozoo Cloninger---the 344-pound guard who made the all-state football team one time. I looked for it, but there is no newspaper account or even a hand-lettered sign certifying so. Therefore, the name might be just common old *lore*. You know, when ye run out of truth afore ye run out of words. It's less drippy than the one at Big Pines, because the locals say it has a wheelbarrow of chopped sirloin in it. Whatever the reason, it's my uncontested top choice, and by far the biggest of all the burgers I ever ate.

And the winner is...

 I presented Fugler's with ten stars the size of Aunt Flossie's Star of David quilt, and a one-year subscription to Caddo Lake *Digest*. CL *Digest* is the culinary magazine I sometimes think about publishing. Maybe I'll think about it again sometime after the next chili cook-off results at Marshall's *Fire Ant Festival*.

It was never actually documented for the record, but a friend of mine, Joey Lambert, once ordered a triple-meat version of the BB. It was the first time in Fugler's Bubba Burger history that anyone chanced a triple-meat, and it was the most newsworthy thing around here since the time Marshall spent three weeks as the state capital of Missouri. The story goes on to tell how old Woodcutter snapped a picture of the burger before Joey took his first bite--and the negative weighed four pounds.

HANGTOWN FRY: During California's Gold Rush says, a miner came down from the hills with a poke of gold dust to the community then known as Hangtown. (Now called Placerville.) Legend has it that he went into the Cary House Hotel and asked for the most expensive meal. The cook made him a dish from his two most expensive ingredients–eggs and oysters. Rather like an oyster omelet, the dish is still made today.

HARD CHEESE: Some cheeses are so hard they can not be sliced, but must be grated to be used. Grated hard cheese is used in cooking, especially sauces, and are also used as a topping on pasta and vegetables. Some hard cheeses are imported from Europe or South America. Most are made in the United States. Because hard cheese is dry, they will not melt without added moisture. Some of the more popular hard cheeses are:
Caciocavallo, Italian, beet shaped, made from either whole or skimmed milk, lightly smoked.
Gjetost, Scandinavian, made from goats' milk, chocolate in color, with a sweet taste.
Parmesan, Italian, made from partly skimmed milk that will keep indefinitely, sharp flavor, with either a green or black rind.
Provolone, Italian, round, netted cheese similar to caciocavallo, usually smoked, mild and sliceable when new, piquant and grated when aged.
Romano, Italian, a dry, salty cheese with a black coating.
Sapsago, Swiss, made from skim milk, green in color, flavored with aromatic clover leaves, is used as an appetizer or dessert.
Stilton, English, made from milk and cream, with green or blue mold, wrinkled or ridged skin, should be allowed to ripen for two years before being marketed.

HARD-COOKED: A term for hard-boiled eggs.

HARD SAUCE: A sauce made with sugar and butter and flavored with rum, brandy, wine, extracts, or spices. It is served with fruitcake, gingerbread, and plum puddings.

HARDTACK: A hard cracker or biscuit made with unsalted dough and dried after baking. It is also known as, "ship biscuit" and "pilot bread." It was developed for long sea voyages, where it wasn't possible to carry fresh bread. Hardtack is added to soups and stews, and sometimes softened with water to be eaten.

HARE: In Europe the rabbit is called a "hare." There is a difference between rabbits and hares. Rabbits are born blind and naked, while a hare has fur and open eyes. Also hares are bigger than rabbits. Hare is usually a wild game meat in Britain. Rabbits are raised domestically for food in America.

HASENPFEFFER: (ha-sin-fe-fur) A highly seasoned rabbit or hare stew that has been marinated for two days. Other game animals can be cooked the same way.

HASH: A mixture of chopped vegetables and meat or poultry, with corned-beef hash and roast-beef hash the more common. Made with fresh potatoes and onions. Hash is available canned. There's also a chilled dessert made with marshmallows and called, "heavenly hash."

HASTY PUDDING: HASTY OR SLOW

"Take the morning's milk and throw into it as much cornmeal as you can hold in the palm of your hand. Let the molasses drip . . ." This was the beginning instructions of an early recipe for making Hasty Pudding, a dish that today's cooks seldom make. What is a pudding to you? Is it a box mix you open, pour in some milk and whip it with an egg beater? Or, is it creamy baked egg custard? A dictionary describes it as "A thick, soft dessert, typically containing flour, milk, eggs, and sweetening." But that wasn't how it all began. There are three types of puddings: boiled, baked and steamed.

Boiled Pudding: Probably the first boiled puddings were made 5,000 BC, when early man stewed some grains together with maybe eggs or fruit. The basic boiled pudding is still America's favorite. But it wasn't until the 18th century that cookbooks presented a mind-boggling melange pudding with all kinds of ingredients.

Baked Pudding: Historians say that British puddings began as a medieval harvest dish, an unsweetened grain stew called *frumenty*. As the dish evolved, beef broth, bread, spices, raisins, currants and other ingredients were added. These elaborate puddings were usually served during the holidays. British puddings are more like fruitcake or nut bread and usually steamed. In England, Hasty Pudding was made with wheat and milk. In America there was no wheat. Native Americans showed the early settlers to make "pudding" with cornmeal, which they called *sappawn*. They combined cornmeal with water and maple sugar, then boiled it over an open fire.

Instant Pudding: Baked and steamed puddings take hours. Imagine what the early British cooks would have thought of making instant cream pudding out of a box in two minutes.

Hasty Pudding: The name, Hasty Pudding, comes from the simple ingredients and the ease to make it. Inventive cooks began adding other ingredients - spices, eggs, molasses - which make the pudding richer in flavor.

HAZELNUT: (hayzl nut) The word "hazel" comes from the Angle-Saxon word *haesil*, meaning headdress. The nut husk resembled a Roman headdress or helmet. Americans use the name hazelnuts for the wild variety and filberts (see FILBERT) for the cultivated kind. The small brown nut can usually be found in cans of mixed nuts. Hazelnuts are very popular as a coffee favoring. **Nutrition facts** per 1/4 cup: 182 calories, 151 calories from fat, 18g total fat (28%), 1.3g saturated fat (7%), zero cholesterol and sodium, 4.4g carbohydrates (1%), 1.8g fiber (7%), 3.8g protein (8%), zero vitamins A and C, 54mg calcium (5%) and .9mg iron (5%).

HEAD CHEESE: A lunch type meat made from the edible parts of a calf or a pig which can include: brains, tongues, snouts, cheeks and lips. Some head cheese also contains the heart and meat from the feet. At one time it did contain cheese, hence the name. Onions, carrots and other vegetables, plus spices are often added. After cooking, it is molded and pressed into a firm gelatin mass for slicing. Farm people the world over have their own version of head cheese. If the name isn't enough to put you off, the grey appearance might do it. It's one of those things people love or hate.

HEALTH ORGANIZATIONS: There are both private and government organizations that want to help you with health information. They have an abundance of printed information and much of it is available on the internet.

American Academy of Pediatrics (AAP) offers tips for feeding children ages one through five. P.O. Box 927, Elk Grove Village, IL 60009-0927, telephone (847) 981-7872, www.aap.org

American Dietetic Association (ADA), National Center for Nutrition & Dietetics features daily nutrition tips, home food safety and information on careers in dietetics: 216 West Jackson Blvd., Chicago, IL 60606-6995, telephones (312) 899-0040 or (800) 366-1655, www.eatright.org.

American Heart Association (AHA)presents a plan of healthy eating tips, 7272 Greenville Avenue, Dallas, TX 75231-4596, telephones (214) 373-6300, (800) 242-8721, www.amhrt.org

Food and Drug Administration (FDA) will help you take the guesswork out of good nutrition. 5600 Fishers Lane, Rockville, MD 20857, telephone (301) 443-3220, www.fda.gov

U.S. Department of Agriculture (USDA), Center for Nutrition Policy and Promotion provides information on the Food Guide Pyramid: 1120 20th St., NW, Suite 200, North Lobby, Washington, DC 20036, telephone (202) 720-7327, www.usda.gov

U.S. Environmental Protection Agency Office of Pesticide Programs (EPA), presents information government regulation on pesticides on foods, pesticide residue limits on foods and what kids can do who are sensitive to pesticides: 401 M Street, SW, Washington, DC 20460, telephone (800) 858-7378, www.epa.gov/pesticides/food.

HEART: The hearts of animals and poultry. Beef, pork, and lamb hearts can be stuffed and then braised for several hours. Poultry hearts are generally sold as giblets.

HEARTS OF PALM: See CABBAGE PALM

HEAVY CREAM: Generally, when a recipe calls for heavy cream, whipping cream is used. A heavy cream is obtained when all of the fat is removed from milk and this remaining fat is heavy cream. If heavy cream is not available for a recipe, a satisfactory substitute can be used in most cases. Over low heat, melt ½ cup of butter and mix it into 3/4 cup of milk. This will yield 1 cup of heavy cream. **Nutrition facts** per tablespoon: 51 calories, 48 calories from fat, 5.5g total fat (8%), 3.4g saturated fat (17%), 20.4mg cholesterol (7%), zero sodium, zero carbohydrates and fiber, .3g protein (15), 219 IU vitamin A (4%), zero vitamin C, 10mg calcium (1%) and zero iron.

HERB: (erb) An aromatic plant used to add flavor to meat and vegetable dishes. It can be the leafy part of the plant or the seeds. Some of the more popular herbs are: anise, basil, bay leaf, caraway, celery, chives, dill, fennel, horseradish, marjoram, mint, mustard, orégano, parsley, rosemary, sage, tarragon, thyme, and watercress. www.rosehill-herbs.com www.herbco.com

HOORAY FOR HERBS

Do you like to cook with herbs? Would you like to grow some herbs, but don't have any space? Did you know you can grow most herbs indoors, maybe right in your kitchen?

All you need:
■ Small plastic pots with drip catchers on the bottom. Plastic holds the moisture better than other materials,
■ Fast draining potting soil,
■ Bright, sunny location. Best is a west or east window, as a north window will not provide enough light, and a south window might burn the plants.
■ Plants need air circulation or pests may appear. In stuffy rooms, open a window or turn on a fan for a short period of time.

If space is at a premium, small two inch pots will work well to start. Plants can be planted from seeds or you can purchase small plants at your garden center. Plants are much easier. As the plants grow, it is important to pinch off the herbs regularly. This keeps them bushy and healthy. If an herb starts to bloom, immediately pinch off the blossom or your plant will stop making leaves and the flavor will change. Never pinch back more than half the plant, since in most cases, it's too much shock for the plant, and it could die.

To keep the plant healthy, it is important to turn the plant every few days, so that all sides of the plant receive light. Also it is necessary to fertilize monthly, or your plant will lack foliage. Once your plant becomes weak or leggy, replace. Water from the bottom since that's where the roots are. Add water to the drip catcher until its all soaked up then add again.

When purchasing seeds, follow package instructions. Some seeds, such as the hard parsley seeds, grow better if soaked overnight to soften them prior to planting. Once the seeds are planted, it is important to keep them moist until they germinate. To hold in the moisture, cover the pot with plastic wrap, but remove just as soon as they germinate.

Which Herbs Grow Best Indoors?

The smaller-leaved varieties usually make the best indoor plants. When purchasing your plant, look for compact healthy seedlings with a lot of bushy growth. Once a plant become root bound, you will need to replant in a larger pot or maybe even outdoors. All of the following herbs do well indoors, especially from seedlings: Basil, chives, cilantro, curled parsley, curly spearmint, dill, fennel, French tarragon, lemon grass, lemon thyme, oregano, rosemary, sweet marjoram, and thyme. Parsley has big roots so allow a fairly large pot.

 If your garden center doesn't have a good variety of seeds, there are several mail order sources: **Renee's Garden,** 7389 West Zayante Road, Felton, CA 95018, phone (888) 880-7228. **Shepherd's Garden Seeds**, 30 Irene Street, Torrington, CT 06790, phone (860) 482-3638.

COSMETIC HERBS FOR GIFT GIVING
by Anna V. Damiani-Becker

So what kind of jars are you going to use for your gifts? Have you a baby in the house? Baby food jars are the perfect size for herb and spice blends. Just paint the lids with spray paint or decorate them with stickers! To make a carrying case, paint a six pack holder or cardboard drink holder in bright colors. You can also add decorations to the cases or the jars. Tie a ribbon and make a card - viola a six pack of gifts!

Dried Flowers from Your Garden

The florals are always favorites for women. Rosebuds, Lavender, and Eucalyptus are wonderful scents. Try a few more of the exotics: Chamomile, Hibiscus, and Damiana. If not from your garden, most of these can be found in health foods stores and road side markets. Other favorites for men or women are as follows:

MEN: Ambergris, Ash, Gardenia, Ginger, Jasmine, Lavender, Musk, and Deerstongue.

WOMEN: Aster, Bay Leaves, Honeysuckle, Lilac, Musk, Patchouli, Rosemary, Stephanotis, Violet, and Vanilla.

Bath Herb Packets

Combine equal amounts of the following dried herbs: mint, rosemary, thyme, and lavender. For each packet fill a four-inch square muslin bag with the mixture and sew the open side shut. Attach the ends of a six-inch strip of ribbon to two corners of the packet to form a hanging loop. To use the bath herbs, hang the packet from faucet and let hot water flow through it. Then add the packet to the bath. Bath herbs are not reusable. Give a friend or family member about four to six muslin packs. The herb mixes can be given to men to use as well - so add some cinnamon or sassafras for them. Herbs and spices will stay fragrant about six months in the fabric, but can be boiled for use in a bath for up to a year. **Instructions for the sachet:** Put water in a one quart pot and bring to a slow boil. Place herb sachet into water for 20 minutes. Once boiled for 20 minutes, add to your bath water. Relax!

Herbs and Spices for Cosmetics

For these products you will boil the herb in either a metal or glass pot (Do not use Teflon coated pans!) and then allow to cool to room temperature. Once the herb mixture is cooled, remove the herbs with a strainer and pour the herb mixture into colored or clear jars. Jars with lids or corks will keep the herbs fresh for approximately four weeks.

Hair Rinses

Brew an herbal tea to use for hair rinse. Use amaranth, apple, fragrant, bedstraw, chamomile, club moss, coriander, damiana, heather, henna, marjoram, mint, rose, saffron and violets. You can pour these mixtures directly onto your hair after shampooing and then allow your hair to dry naturally to keep the fragrance.

Skin Treatments

FACE: Anise, avocado, catnip, cowslip, fern, flax, ginseng, maidenhair, myrtle, oatmeal, rosemary, thyme, vervain, witch hazel, and yerba santa. After boiling these herbs, mix the liquid with fragrance free baby lotion. To use immediately, mix with an egg white (no yolk) and apply directly to the skin. Rinse with cool water after about 15 minutes. Avocado and oatmeal can be made into a paste with a little water and applied directly to the face.

HANDS: Aloe, borage, columbine, hawthorn, lavender, lemon verbena, lovage, mesquite, pansy, passion flower, rose, and vanilla. In make hand lotions, you may boil the herbs and mix them with fragrance free baby lotion or petroleum jelly. You will place one herb mix (about 4 tablespoons - use your NOSE! to determine the potency of the fragrance) and 16 ounces of lotion into a blender and blend for about four minutes. If the consistency is too runny, add one tablespoon of petroleum jelly to the mix until you decide it is the right consistency. Place your lotion in colorful or clear jars. Tie the lids with pretty ribbons and perhaps a twig of the herb for decoration.

FEET: Anemone, ash, burdock, camphor, caraway, coriander, fern, geranium, juniper, mugwort, pine, and spearmint. These are simply boiled and then the person using them cools them down until they can place their hand or foot comfortable in the water. You place the herbed liquid into a foot soaking machine or a pan of warm water. The person then soaks their feet for about 10 to 20 minutes. You may want to bottle these mixes or also put them into muslin bags for gift giving. -- *Anna Damiani-Becker*

HERBS AND SPICES FOR COOKING

Adding an herb and/or a spice or two can bring new life a dish. Generally speaking one herb or one spice will do, but seldom more than three herbs and/or spices. Too many herbs or spices will over power the recipe. Some herbs are mild, such as parsley, hence a lot can be used. At the same time just a little oregano will do. The same can be said about spices, equal measures of cloves is several times stronger than the same amount of cinnamon. Pepper can also be a problem, as pepper intensifies as it cooks. Hence what might taste okay at the beginning of cooking, can be over powering when cooking is completed. Best to add a little of any one herb or spice, then increase to suit your tastes. --*Anna V. Damiani-Becker*

Beef Seasoning: Bay leaf, chives, cloves, cumin, garlic powder, black and white pepper, red pepper, marjoram, rosemary, savory, onion powder, tarragon, basil, anise, burnet, caraway, chervil, fenugreek, lovage, mustard, oregano, parsley, thyme, chili powder, mace, paprika, and curry.
Beverages: Burnet, fennel, cinnamon, nutmeg, and mint.
Bread Seasoning: Caraway, marjoram, oregano, poppy seed, rosemary, thyme, sesame seed, cardamon, savory, anise, basil, celery seed, sage, mint, parsley, allspice, cinnamon, cloves, ginger, mace, nutmeg, saffron, turmeric, and dill.
Cheese Seasoning: Basil, chervil, chives, curry, dill, fennel, garlic powder, marjoram, oregano, sage, anise, caraway, mint, mustard, rosemary, savory, paprika, red pepper, parsley, and thyme.
Dessert Seasonings: Anise, borage, basil, caraway, dill, fennel, mint, allspice, cinnamon, ginger, cloves, mace, saffron, turmeric, and thyme.
Egg Seasonings: Basil, caraway, chervil, sage, chives, fennel, marjoram, mustard, oregano, parsley, rosemary, savory, tarragon, allspice, nutmeg, paprika, black and white pepper, red pepper, turmeric, and thyme.
Fish Seasoning: Basil, bay leaf, tarragon, lemon peel, thyme, parsley, fennel, sage, savory, chervil, anise, celery seed, chives, marjoram, mint, mustard, oregano, rosemary, allspice, cloves, ginger, mace, paprika, black and white pepper, red pepper, saffron, turmeric, and dill.
Fruit Seasoning: Allspice, anise, basil, cinnamon, coriander, cloves, ginger, mint, and nutmeg.
Lamb Seasoning: Garlic powder, marjoram, mint, oregano, rosemary, thyme, black and white pepper, turmeric, and curry.

Pasta Seasoning: Black and white pepper, thyme, marjoram, garlic powder, bay leaf, onion powder, basil, oregano, paprika, parsley, lemon peel, sesame seeds, dill, tarragon, and nutmeg.

Pork Seasoning: Coriander, cumin, garlic powder, black and white pepper, red pepper, cloves, cinnamon, sage, savory, ginger, and thyme.

Poultry Seasoning: Dill, onion, caraway, garlic powder, saffron, sage, sesame seed, allspice, tarragon, thyme, paprika, nutmeg, paprika, black and white pepper, red pepper, saffron, turmeric, mustard, and rosemary.

Rice Seasoning: Onion powder, lemon peel, black and white pepper, red pepper, paprika, Parsley, mustard, curry, chili powder, cloves, garlic powder, caraway, cardamom, saffron, turmeric, and nutmeg.

Salad Seasoning: Basil, lovage, parsley, tarragon, borage, burnet, chives, garlic powder, dill, oregano, thyme, coriander, sesame seed, nutmeg paprika, black and white pepper, red pepper, onion powder, and poppy seed.

Sauce Seasoning: Basil, bay leaf, burnet, caraway, chervil, chives, sage, dill, fennel, marjoram, mint, oregano, parsley, rosemary, savory, tarragon, cloves, paprika, black and white pepper, red pepper, saffron, turmeric, mace and thyme.

Shellfish Seasoning: Bay leaves, curry, anise, basil, onion powder, oregano, tarragon, fennel, allspice, ginger, mace, paprika, black and white pepper, red pepper, turmeric, saffron, garlic powder, and dill.

Soup Seasoning: Bay leaves, chervil, tarragon, marjoram, parsley, savory, anise, borage, caraway, chives, sage, dill, lovage, mint, oregano, thyme, ginger, mace, paprika, black and white pepper, red pepper, saffron, and rosemary.

Vegetable Seasoning: Basil, parsley, savory, burnet, chervil, chives, dill, tarragon, marjoram, mint, pepper, cloves, ginger, mace, paprika, black and white pepper, red pepper, and thyme.

Green Beans: Dill, tarragon, basil, cloves, marjoram.

Tomatoes: Basil, oregano, tarragon, thyme, cloves, and marjoram.

Corn: Curry, chili powder, dill, and thyme.

Carrots: Ginger, allspice, mustard, onion, dill, cloves, and mint.

Spinach: Nutmeg, mace, onion, basil, mint, and mustard.

Peas: Mint, tarragon, dill, basil, and marjoram.

Potatoes: Dill, coriander, poppy seed, sesame seed, thyme, marjoram, onion, oregano, and parsley.

HERMIT: A spiced drop cookie often filled with nuts and dried fruits. They are also known as "snickerdoodles."

HERMIT CRAB: A species of crab considered a great delicacy but rarely eaten outside of France.

HERRING: A small salt-water fish related to the sardine, which lives in deep northern sea waters. In the spring, the herring arrive in large numbers and lay their eggs on rocks, seaweed, foliage hanging in the water, and on the sandy beaches. Herring are eaten fresh (fried), salted, smoked, kippered, and pickled. Kippered herring are large herring that have been salted, smoked, and baked. Salted herring must be soaked in water for 24 hours before they are cooked. Pickled herring are eaten as is without soaking or cooking. **Nutrition facts**: A 3-ounce serving has 134 calories, 71 calories from fat. 7.7g total fat (12%), 1.7g saturated fat (9%), 51mg cholesterol (17%), 76.6mg sodium (3%), zero carbohydrates and fiber, 15.3g protein (31%), 80 IU vitamin A (2%), 1mg vitamin C (1%), 48mg calcium (5%), .9mg iron (5%), and 278mg potassium. Pickled herring has almost twice the calories and fat, and 10 times the sodium.

HIBACHI: A small barbeque type iron grill.

HICKORY NUTS: Native to America, these thick-skinned nuts are in the same family as pecans and pignuts. Hickory nuts are mostly used in baking cakes, cookies, candies, and sweet breads. When a recipe calls for pecans, hickory nuts can be substituted. President Andrew Jackson (1828) was called "Old Hickory," a name he earned because he was as stubborn and tough as the extremely hard wood of the familiar hickory tree. Native Americans introduced settlers to the tasty hickory nutmeats. Florida natives made a milky hickory liquor they called "milk of nuts."
Nutrition facts: Hickory nuts are high in calories, fat, and rich in protein. Per 1/4 cup: 200 calories, 163 calories from fat, 20.1g total fat (31%), 2.2g saturated fat (11%), zero cholesterol and sodium, 5.7g carbohydrates (2%), 2g fiber (8%), 4g protein (8%), 41 IU vitamin A (1%), 1mg vitamin C (1%), 19mg calcium (2%) and .7mg iron (4%).

HIMALAYAN MULBERRY: In the Himalayas this tree produces slender green mulberries that are eaten fresh.

HOECAKE: A cornmeal cake cooked like a pancake. Such cakes were originally cooked on a hoe over the hot coals of an outdoor fire.

HOISIN SAUCE: A thick, dark brown sauce made from soybeans, flour, sugar, spices, garlic, chilies, and salt. It has a sweet, spicy flavor and used in many Chinese recipes. www.thaifoods.com.

HOLLANDAISE: A rich sauce made with egg yolks and butter to be served on eggs and vegetables.

HOMINY: Dried corn kernels with the germ removed is known as hominy. When the germ of corn kernels is soaked off in a weak wood lye solution, the starchy, swollen part that remains is hominy. After washing and boiling, it tastes like a whole new vegetable and looks more like popcorn. Dried hominy kept and traveled well for hard times. The name comes for this uniquely American food comes from the Algonquian Native Americans. To cook dried hominy, it must be soaked overnight, then simmered for up to 5 hours until tender. Today, hominy, both white and yellow, is readily available canned and only needs to be heated prior to serving. Try browning with onion and green peppers in bacon drippings. **Nutrition facts:** A ½ cup serving of canned hominy has 58 calories, 6 calories from fat. .7g total fat (1%), .1g saturated fat (1%), zero cholesterol, 168mg sodium (7%), 11.4g carbohydrates (4%), 2g fiber (8%), 1.2g protein (2%), zero vitamins A and C, 8mg calcium (1%), .5mg iron (3%), and 7g potassium. www.allencanning.com

HOMINY GRITS: Dried, ground hominy is called "grits," and is available in fine or coarse grinds. Some grits must be soaked for up to an hour prior to cooking. Fast-cooking grits are just poured into boiling water, and will be ready to eat in minutes. There are also "instant" grits in packets for microwave cooking. Grits need only butter, salt and pepper for seasoning when served as a side dish. For a hot breakfast cereal, top with milk and sugar. In the south, grits are often served with gravy or fried eggs. Try them with a spoon of peanut butter or cheese. **Nutrition facts** per ½ cup: 289 calories, 9 calories from fat, .9g total fat (1%), zero saturated fat cholesterol, zero sodium, 62.1g carbohydrates (21%), zero fiber, 6.9g protein (14%), 343 IU vitamin A (7%), zero vitamin C and calcium, 3.1mg iron (17%).

HOMOGENIZE: A process where the butter fat (cream) is mixed with the liquid (milk) so that the cream doesn't rise to the top of the milk, as it does normally. .

HONDAPARA: See ELEPHANT APPLES.

HONEY: This sweet sticky liquid made by honeybees is the oldest sweetener known to man. The bees suck the nectar from flowers and deposit this digested liquid in the hives made of a wax honeycomb. Honey is eaten fresh on baked goods, as a sweetener in beverages, and as a glaze for vegetables and ham. Honey has become a popular coating on breakfast cereals. Honey and its comb have many creative and medicinal purposes as well. www.nhb.org; www.honey.com; www.beebutter.com.   www.stroopebeeandhoney.com.

HONEY IN PLACE OF SUGAR

Honey can be used as a substitute for up to one-half of the sugar in baking recipes. It's easy!

To replace 1/4 cup of sugar with 1/4 cup of honey, reduce the liquid in the recipe by 1 tablespoon, and add 1/8 teaspoon of baking soda to the dry ingredients. Double for ½ cup, etc.

TIP: It will be necessary to reduce the oven temperature by 25° F to prevent over browning of baked goods. Honey adds a sweet, smooth and distinctive taste to recipes. Honey also absorbs and retains moisture. These qualities retard drying out and staling of baked goods.

TIP: For easy removal, spray measuring cups and spoons with vegetable cooking spray before measuring honey. **Nutrition facts**: One tablespoon has 64 calories (sugar has 48 calories per tablespoon), zero fat and sodium, 17.5g carbohydrates (6%), zero fiber and protein, zero vitamins A and C, zero calcium, and .1mg iron (1%).

Honey in Place of Stamps

Once when stationed in Korea, an 18 year old soldier, writing home to his mother found himself without stamps, except for one which had lost its stickiness in the humidity. The resourceful son went to the mess hall and glued his stamp with honey, which stayed stuck all the way from Korea to Arkansas. –LU

THE HONEYBEE SERVES OUR COMMUNITY
by Barbara Belknap

Humans are afraid of bees. Honeybees should be afraid of humans. The bee does not usually sting unless its hive or honey is threatened. Bees produce honey and beeswax, and they play an important role in agriculture by pollinating crops.

Pollen is the dust that is found in flowers. Bees carry pollen on their hairs and feet as they move from flower to flower. The pollen helps a plant produce fruit or seeds. This is called pollination.

The honeybee may do more for our planet than any other species in the animal kingdom. The United States Department of Agriculture believes that 3 ½ million acres of our nation's fruit, vegetable, legumes, and oil seed crops (soybean and corn), depend on insect pollination. An apiarist is a beekeeper. The apiarist will provide bees to farmers for pollination services. This means a beekeeper loads up his hives and trucks them to the farm where bees are needed. A farmer can see a 30 to 40 percent increase in his crops, such as apples, oranges, melons, or corn, when he uses the bee services of an apiarist.

Bees need help. There is trouble for bees. There are two types of parasitic mites (an organism living off another organism) that threaten the lives of the bees. But apiarists have found safe solutions to cope with the mites.

A bigger problem is the **misuse of pesticide**. A bee might tap a flower loaded with chemicals and die before making it back to the hive. Sometimes the poisons have not started to affect the bee when the guard bee lets him back into the hive. Then it is too late. The damage is done. The beehive is poisoned with a pesticide placed by careless humans.

We may lose our bees unless the use of pesticides is controlled quickly. The unselfish, industrious honeybee will no longer make the world a more food productive place.

HONEY CAKE: Long before refined sugar became available, cakes and breads were sweetened with honey. The name now covers any cake made with honey instead of sugar.

HONEYDEW MELON: The skin is a yellowish-white, and the flesh is green and quite sweet. It is believed the honeydew, like other muskmelons originated in Persian. Honeydews have been grown in the United States for almost 100 years. The fresh melons are served chilled for breakfast, added to a fresh fruit salads, and combined with citrus fruits for dessert. **Nutrition facts**: A 1/4 wedge has 113 calories, zero fat, 32.3mg sodium (1%), 29.6g carbohydrates (10%), 1.9g fiber (8%), 1.5g protein (3%), 129 IU vitamin A (3%), 80mg vitamin C (133%), 19mg calcium (2%), .2mg iron (1%), and 874mg potassium. www.duda.com; www.stxorganics.com

HONEY TANGERINE: See TANGORS

HOREHOUND: It's an herb, a member of the mint family, and in the raw state is quite bitter. The two main uses for horehound are making cough medicine and candy. Some cooks add the fresh leaves to braised beef dishes, plus some baked goods such as cakes and cookies. The plant is found is all parts of the world, except the tropics. Curiously, one scholar of ancient Rome advised putting out a dish of milk with horehound leaves to kill flies. Herbalists do say planting patches of horehound helps keep flying insects out of their gardens. The origin of the common name is unknown, but may come from the Anglo Saxon word *har*, meaning hairy. It may even have some connection to the early belief that the plant was an antidote to bites from mad dogs. Its generic name is *ballota* from the Greek. It is now little used by herbalists.

HORTICULTURE: The art and science of growing and cultivating flowers, fruits and vegetables. A person who performs these duties is called a "horticulturist." www.nwhort.org

HORS-D'OEUVRES: (or-derv) A French word meaning small appetizers or canapés and eaten as finger foods, served on a cracker, bread, pastry, or on a vegetable such as a piece of celery.

HORSE MACKEREL: See TUNA

HORSE MEAT: In Europe and Asia the meat of horses is eaten, but almost never in Britain and America where the horse is considered too noble to eat and the meat not tasty enough to compete with plentiful beef and pork.

HORSESHOE CRAB: See KING CRAB

HORSERADISH: Native to southeastern Europe, a member of the mustard family, and mentioned in the Bible as one of the five bitter herbs of the Jewish Passover used during the *seder* meal to remind them of the pain their ancestors suffered as Egyptian slaves. Horseradish is grown for its pungent roots, which are peeled and usually grated. When grated it is mixed with distilled vinegar to stabilize the "heat." Some processors also add spices, salt, sugar, cream or vegetable oil. Grinders wear a mask and rubber gloves. www.horseradish.org

Horseradish is served as a condiment for meats, seafood, and in sauces. Horseradish is available fresh, preserved in vinegar, mixed with beets, blended into bottled dressings and sauces, blended into mustard and relishes, and dehydrated.

The name horseradish comes from the mispronounced German word *meerrettich* which translates to "sea radish." The English pronounced "*meer*" as "mare" which was interpreted as "horse." Ancients recommended horseradish with its powerful taste and odor to clear nasal and sinus cavities, cure colds, coughs, and asthma. Not a favorite with children, fresh horseradish can reduce strong men to tears. The prefix "horse" is often used in English plant names to indicate that it's a strong or coarse kind, as in "strong as a horse." **Nutrition facts** per tablespoon: 7 calories, zero fats, 17.3mg sodium (1%), 1.7g carbohydrates (1%), .4g fiber (1%), zero protein and vitamin A, 4mg vitamin C (6%), 11mg calcium (1%), and .2mg iron (1%).

INTERNATIONAL HORSERADISH FESTIVAL

On the first Saturday of May in Collinsville, Illinois, the International Horseradish Festival is held. The day long event includes the Root Toss, Root Golf, and the ever popular horseradish recipe contest. --Jackie Kluthe

HOTCAKE: A name for pancakes.

HOT DOGS: The American name for wieners or frankfurters.

HOT DOGS

The hot dog is a close cousin to the hamburger, but there are rules. The bun must never be buttered. Toppings are a must and include mustard (the preferred choice), onion, pickle relish, chili, sauerkraut, melted cheese, and ketchup, or a combination of all. Hot dogs are best enjoyed at the ballpark with a cold beverage. They just don't taste the same anywhere else. Like the hamburger, there are some no-nos when it comes to hot dogs. Never fry a hot dog; they should be boiled or barbecued (some kids likes to pan broil hot dogs to a crisp, but never admit to this practice). Those movie theater hot dogs which are heated on a series of rotating rollers are a no-no, as this heat source only dries out the meat. Yuck! If you fry them, parboil first to get them done in the center.

Today some so called "healthy" hot dogs have been invented. These could contain chicken, turkey, or be made of all-vegetable products. Now manufacturers are even putting seaweed in hot dogs. It's just not right, to try to fool the public that they are eating a genuine hot dog unless it is made with beef and/or pork. Poultry and seaweed are just not hot dog substitutes. Real meat hot dogs are brown, not red. Be wary of reddish hot dogs.

Let's be frank (yes, that's a pun), these imitations and low fat hot dogs lack both the flavor and the texture of the old-fashioned variety. Some say once they're in the bun covered with mustard and relish, you will never know the difference, but you will. --*RSC*

HOT CROSS BUNS:

Hot Cross Buns

One-a-penny, two-penny
hot cross buns!
If you have no daughters
give them to your sons.

Hot cross buns begins as a bribe to get folks to go to church. According to legend which few dispute, hot cross buns originated in Europe during the Middle Ages when church attendance had fallen low. Monks came up with the idea of handing out warm buns as a reward for attendance on Easter Sunday. To remind the attendants that "man does not live by bread alone" each bun was marked by a cross.

In Charles Dickens' day, Good Friday morning echoed with the sound of boys calling "hot cross buns!" Thus began the various songs which have come down to us in nursery rhymes.

One-a-penny poker,
two-a-penny tongs,
One-a-penny, two-a-penny
hot cross buns!

HUBBARD SQUASH: This is the first cousin to the American pumpkin. It is available in many varieties, Green, Blue, and Golden Hubbard. This thick, hard, and warty- skinned winter squash can be stored for months in a dry, cool place. The flesh can be baked or boiled. **Nutrition facts:** A ½ cup serving has 23 calories, zero fat and sodium, 5.1g carbohydrates (2%), zero fiber, 1.2g protein (2%), 3,132 IU vitamin A (63%), 6mg vitamin C (11%), 8mg calcium (1%), .2mg iron (1%), and 186mg potassium.

HUCKLEBERRY: Often confused with the blueberry which belongs to a different family. The huckleberry is dark blue in color and grows from the tropics to near the Arctic. The huckleberry contains more acid than blueberries, and has 10 hard little seeds, whereas the blueberry has many seeds, so little they are not noticeable. Huckleberries can be served or cooked like any blueberry recipe.

HUMMUS: A mixture made basically with chick-peas, sesame, and garlic. Recipes vary. Greek and Arabic in origin, it is growing in popularity in America. Hummus is combined with water, olive oil, paprika, and parsley, and eaten as a dip or a spread.

HUMPBACKS: See SALMON

HUSK CHERRY: A native to South America, this small herb has ½-inch tomato-like fruit, encased with a paper-like husk, Eaten as a vegetable, it is made into sauces and jams.

HUSH PUPPIES: A cornmeal batter, dropped by small spoonfuls into hot fat, and fried until golden brown. Hush puppies, a necessity with fried fish, take their name from a time when the leftover batter from frying the batches of fish was cooked and given to the family dogs as they waited to be fed.

HYDROGENATE: A process of turning a liquid oil into a semisolid, such as shortening, margarine, and lard. See TRANS FATTY ACIDS

HYDROPONICS: In recent years, the word hydroponics has become familiar to those interested in growing plants. You have probably eaten hydroponic plants without even knowing it. If you ate bright red tomatoes last winter, they were probably hydroponically grown.

WHAT IS HYDROPONIC?

The term generally refers to the method of growing plants in water or, more correctly in a nutrient solution. The word hydroponic is derived from two Greek words, *hydro* meaning "water" and *ponos* meaning "to work." Put the two together, and it means **"working with water."**

Hydroponics in History

History records hydroponics as a growing method that was widely used in ancient times. The **Hanging Gardens of Babylon** is an example of a hydroponic growing system.

In South America, the natives and their forebears have used hydroponics with great success. They build rafts of loosely woven grasses, placing a thin layer of soil on the top and then planting seedlings in the soil. The rafts are then floated on rivers and lakes, and the roots of the plants grow through the loose weave into the water below.

In the 1800s, European scientists performed many experiments to discover the secrets of how and why plants grow and more importantly, to discover the secrets of what was contained within soil. By this time, scientists were confident that no other factors were involved beside the availability of water to plants. Eventually a simple experiment was to disprove this belief.

New Experiments

In one experiment, plants were grown with no soil, and only distilled water was provided to the root zone. The plants struggled for life and eventually succumbed to death by starvation. The experiment was repeated; however, this rime, rich soil was mixed with distilled water and the soil was allowed to settle. This time the plants prospered. From then on, great strides were made in scientific research, as different chemical elements were isolated and identified from the soil. Scientists concluded that it was **a cocktail of soil elements** that made the plants prosper.

During the early 1900s, many examples of hydroponic cultivation were documented. At the time, the costs involved in this new method of growing prevented any serious commercial exploitation.

New Methods

World War II gave hydroponics its first big break. The American forces built large hydroponic installations in the Pacific Islands, because the islanders used human waste to fertilize their crops, which put soldiers at risk for stomach disorders.

Commercial Attempts

Those early gardens were not fully understood. It wasn't until the 1970s that hydroponics was to become a commercial reality. Researchers were so convinced that hydroponics could be commercially viable that they began an intensive study into the subject. By the mid-1970's, a new system evolved out of this effort: nutrient flow technique or **NFT** (later the name was changed to nutrient film technique to better describe the process). Much has been learned in the following twenty years, and with this knowledge and working experience, systems and their control have been simplified so that today the competent conventional grower has no difficulty in adapting to hydroponic growing.

Hydroponic Farming Advantages

One of the best reasons for hydroponic farming is soil management. In hydroponic farming there is an **absence of soil-borne bacteria** (of which many are parasites). That plays an important part in plant health and yield. Soil sterilization is costly as compared to simple methods used to clean hydroponic systems.

The expected crop yields from hydroponic production **averages more than double of soil farming.** A tomato grower who normally grows in soil would produce about 11 pounds of fruit from one plant. With hydroponics the same plant could produce 22 pounds or more of tomatoes. Another advantage in hydroponic farming is the removal of the spent crop. Clean up, and preparation for new planting is measured in days, not weeks. Thus hydroponic gardening gives a greatly improved return for capital invested.

Finally, food grown in water produces a much cleaner product. The thought of growing plump strawberries, telegraph cucumbers, and rosy red tomatoes in the middle of the winter months is a strong encouragement for home gardeners to convert to hydroponics. For more information on how you can become a hydroponic grower at home, write to **New Moon**, P.O. Box 1027, Corvallis, OR 97339 or phone (800) 888-6785 or (541) 757-8477 for a list of books on the subject. They also publish *The GrowingEDGE magazine*. --Rob Smith, Managing director **Hydroponics International, New Zealand** --Condensed from *The GrowingEDGE*, November/December 1998

Ii

ICE: Frozen solid water. Water freezes at 32°F or 0°C. As a verb, "to ice" is to spread frosting.

ICES: Frozen desserts, such as frappés and fruit "ices" are made with juices, sugar, water and other ingredients. Ices are not frozen solid, but stirred to keep them soft-frozen to a slush. Frozen juice bars such as Popsicles may be called ices too.

ICE CREAM: Probably the most favorite dessert. It is made with milk, cream, sugar and a flavor such as fruit, fruit juice, extracts, and chocolate. Some ice creams contain eggs. Commercial ice cream can contain other ingredients not normally found in homemade ice cream, such as color, imitation flavors, gums, and preservatives. To be sure you are getting all natural ingredients, check the contents listing. If you can't pronounce an ingredient, you might not want to eat it.

ICE CREAM, FROM KINGS TO KIDS
By Bernice Erickson

Would you believe that Americans manufacture and eat more ice cream than any other country on earth, but ice cream wasn't created in America? The origins of ice cream actually go back to the first century BC.

From Roman Caesars to French Cafes

Nero, the Roman Emperor, had his slaves bring snow from the mountains, which Nero flavored with honey and fruit. This was the beginning of today's fruit ices.

When Marco Polo returned from his journey to the Orient, he brought back a recipe from the emperor for a frozen dessert that included milk and resembled sherbet. This recipe was popular in Asia for a thousand years.

By 1530, the young bride of the future King Henry II of France took the recipe with her from Italy and introduced their ices to the French people.

In the 16th century, ices had evolved into ice cream.. "Creme ice" was known and loved at the court of Charles I of England. He loved the taste of "creme ice" so much that he gave his chef, Gerrand Tissin, a pension of £20 so he wouldn't give the recipe to anyone else. After King Charles was beheaded in 1649, Tissin sold the recipe to a group of French men who owned the Café Napolitain in Paris, France. That name, curiously, has nothing to do with Napoleon, but was a misspelling of Neopolitan (referring to Naples).

First Ice Cream Parlors in Paris

Ice cream at that time was considered expensive, even for a king! It wasn't introduced to the general public until 1670. That was at the Café Procope in Paris where not only lemonades and coffee were served but "creme glacées" and sherbets. The café itself was a novel idea that year but by 1720 Paris had 300 cafes with frozen "glacées." By 1700, ice cream was so popular in France that a publication of 84 pages appeared under the title *L' Art de Faire Des Glacés*, which loosely means *fancy ways of making and serving ice cream*. The two first cookbooks by women (1747-1750) contained recipes for ice cream.

Ice Cream Takes America by Storm!

Who was responsible for bringing the recipe for making ice cream to the colonies we do not know. We do know ice cream made its way to America as early as 1700, when ice cream was served at a dinner party in the Annapolis home of William Bladen, Governor of Maryland.

Today, Independence Day just isn't right without ice cream, but in the year 1776, ice cream was an involved process, requiring lots of ice and much labor. The ice cream mixture needed vigorous beating in a pewter pan while at the same time the pan was shaken up and down in a larger pot of salt and ice. May 12, 1777, the first advertisement of ice cream appeared in the New York Gazette.

George Washington loved ice cream, and bought a "Cream Machine for Making Ice," and also two pewter pots. Martha Washington served ice cream at her dinner parties.

Thomas Jefferson not only loved ice cream, but invented an eighteen step process for its manufacture. Dolley Madison made it a White House speciality at state dinners.

By the beginning of the 19th century, ice cream was served to the general public in what was called Ice Cream Houses. The availability of ice cream led to the eventual birth of ice cream vendors. Ice cream was sold on the streets of New York in 1828.

First Home Freezer

In 1848, Nancy Johnson, a New Jersey woman who was handy with mechanical things, invented a hand crank freezer. By 1850, ice cream had become one of the necessities of American life. It was said that "A party without ice cream would be like a breakfast without bread or a dinner without roast."

Ice Cream Every Day in Every Way

As the people migrated west, they took the recipe for ice cream with them. It wasn't long before they had ice cream parlors and soda fountains where the people could sit at tables or counters to order and enjoy this king's delicacy. Today's kids would be the envy of kings because they can have ice cream every day.

ICE CREAM

Eating ice cream
in summers heat,
I can't think of
a nicer treat.

Make it caramel
or cherry chip,
French vanilla
or chocolate dip.

Raspberry swirl
or peppermint candy,
some of each
would sure be dandy.

Rocky road,
or lemon wish
I'll scoop it all
into my dish.
--*Elizabeth Giles*

ICE CREAM BEAN: Native to tropical America, this not-well-known tree produces bean pods up to 3-feet long. The pulp surrounding the beans is eaten fresh.

ICING: Same as frosting, as on cakes and cookies.

IDA RED APPLES: A large red apple, mildly tart and semi- firm. It's a good all-purpose apple.

ILAMA: Native to Mexico, this small tree produces large white or pink fruit that is eaten fresh and made into ice cream.

IMBE: Native to east Africa, the tree produces small, round, orange fruit with a large seed, eaten fresh.

INDIAN ATALANTIA: Native to India, the tree produces a 3/4-inch bitter fruit that is eaten fresh.

INDIAN BORAGE: The origin of this herb is unknown. The leaves of this plant are used to flavor food.

INDIAN JUJUBE: Native to India, this thorny tree produces a small oval, yellow or brown sweet fruit. It is eaten fresh, dried, made into jelly and candied.

INDIGESTION: The inability of the body to process food for nourishment and enjoyment. See FLATULENCE and BELCH.

INGA: Also know as Ice Cream Bean.

INSECTS: You may not want to eat a bug, but many cultures prefer insects over meat. Not all bugs are insects. To be an insect it must (1) breath air, (2) have its body divided into three parts, and (3) have three pairs of legs and usually two pairs of wings. This includes ants (usually wingless), grasshoppers, and termites. Worms, which are also eaten as an insect, are not insects, but larva, which may or may not undergo metamorphosis and eventually become an insect, such as a butterfly. In Africa, there are said to be folks who love earthworms.

For more about this subject, you'll find books to read under CRAWLING CUISINE.

HUNGRY? EAT A BUG!
By Professor Emeritus Gene R. DeFoliart

Insects have played an important part of human nutrition in many regions of the world. In North America, our Native Americans have enjoyed a variety of delights which include grasshoppers, caterpillars, beetle grubs and adults, winged termites, bees, wasps, ant brood (larvae and pupae), winged ants, cicadas, and a variety of aquatic insects.

Insects are not just used as emergency food to ward off starvation, but are ordinarily included as a planned part of the diet throughout the year or when seasonally available.

On the California-Nevada border are a number of alkaline lakes, the largest being Mono Lake. There lives a small fly that breeds in vast numbers in the alkaline waters. It's called *kutsavi* by the Paiutes. The fly pupae washes ashore in long windrows, depositing pupae about two feet deep and up to four feet wide that extends like a vast rim around the lake.

As the pupae attain locomotion, they creep up from the water and the natives gather them, dry them in the sun, mix them with acorns, berries, grass seeds, and make a conglomeration called *cuchaba*, which is kind of a bread, very nutritious and palatable. The worms are also eaten whole and undried. They are considered a delicacy fried in their own fat, and when done properly, resemble pork cracklins.

Crickets are another important insect food. The Shoshoni natives in Utah's Great Basin would gather them by the thousands, dry them, then grind them on the same mill used to grind pine nuts and grass seeds, making a fine flour. After grinding, the flour would be used to make a dark colored bread. Sometimes wild berries and currants were mixed in with the flour. Dried crickets were also made into soup and the flavor is like dried deer meat.

Today, there are many groups around the world who enjoy various insects. In Mexico there is a demand for *escamoles* (immature stages of the ant). Sold in some restaurants, it is fried in black butter (butter cooked over low heat until dark brown), or with onions and garlic. A new product, tequila-flavored lollipops, contain an embedded beetle grub.

In some regions of Colombia and Venezuela, the Yukpa people prefer insect foods to fresh meats. In South Africa, hundreds of tons of caterpillars are exported to other parts of Africa and play an important role in nutrition. When caterpillars are available, the sale of beef decreases.

In Asia, various insects are an important source for food. Two Asian insects are imported to the United States, the giant water bug from Thailand and silkworms pupae from South Korea. In Japan, grasshoppers are preserved by boiling them in soy sauce.

Insects are rich in protein, vitamins and minerals. Crickets are superior to soy protein. Insects vary in fat content, with caterpillars the highest in fat, as well as calories. Cholesterol levels in insects are generally low. Caterpillars are rich in iron, copper, zinc, thiamin and riboflavin. Winged termites are high in magnesium and copper. And grasshoppers are high in niacin.

Commercially grown insects are available to fanciers in the United States in some bait and pet food stores, and by mail order. They include crickets, mealworms, waxmoth larva, beetle grub, and honey bee pupae.

To purchase commercial insects, call:
Armstrong's Cricket Farm
(800) 345-8778
Bassetts Cricket Ranch
(800) 634-2445
Flukes Farms (chocolate covered crickets)
(800) 735-8537
Hot Lix (assorted insects to eat)
(800) EAT-WORMS

ENTERTAINING WITH INSECTS

One person's pest can be another's delicacy as people swarm to sample bugs. When it's a time to grub out, you will need the insect recipe book, *Entertaining With Insects*, by Ronald L Taylor and Barbara S. Carter. Order from Salutek Publishing Company, PO Box 696, Yorba Linda, CA 92885.

Prior to starting a recipe, all ingredients must be assembled, and the most important ingredient for these recipes is dry roasted insects. Head for your backyard or the open country and collect some ants, bees, crickets, grasshoppers, and termites.

AN ENTOMOLOGIST'S MENU
by Marjolaine Giroux

When entomologists get together, they start the party with wine, cheese, and an array of insect dishes. Some of the insects, especially waxworms and crickets, are eaten raw and alive. A sample menu could be as follows:

Hors d'oeuvres
Mealworm Canapes, A light and Savoury Spread
Crickets Rumaki, Marinated Crickets and Chestnuts
wrapped in a slice of Bacon
Crunchy Migratory Locusts, A Light Mexican Flavor
Waxworm Popcorn
Tenebrio Balls, made with Mealworms
Spicy Silkworm Bisque

Main Course
Bakuti, Bee Larvae, Napalese Style
Chien Tam Con, Chinese Fried Silkworm Pupae
Cricket Newburg
Chitoum Stew, Shea Butter Worms in Tomato Sauce

Desserts
Healthy Mealworm Cookies
Chocolate-Covered Crickets
Mealworm Lollipops

ATTEND A BUG FESTIVAL

Before you try your first bug recipe, you might like someone else to do the cooking. The best way is to attend an insect festival in your area. Some include (call for dates):

Annual Bug Fest, Garfield, Ohio (216) 341-3152
Incredible Edible Insects, Louisiana Nature Center,
New Orleans, Louisiana (504) 246-5672
Purdue University, Department of Entomology,
featuring Bug Café, Big Bug Bake Off, and Bug Bowl,
West Lafayette, Indiana (765) 494-4586
Insectival, Athens, Georgia, mid-June (706) 542-1244
Great Insect Fair, Pennsylvania State University,
featuring the Insect Deli in September,
Erie, Pennsylvania (814) 865-1895
L'Insectarium de Montreal, "Croque Insectes"
features the Bug Banquet in mid winter,
Montreal, Quebec, Canada (514) 872-8753

IRISH COFFEE: Coffee to which Irish whiskey and whipped cream has been added. Irish coffee was invented in the 1930s by Joe Sheridan, Chef at the Shannon Airport. Shannon wanted to fortify a hot drink to warm and cheer departing passengers as they walked the long runway to the planes.

IRISH MOSS: An edible seaweed, also called *carrageen*. Irish Moss varies in color from greenish yellow to purplish brown. This seaweed is found on the northeastern shores of the United States, Canada and the rocky shores of the British Isles. It was named after Carraghen, Ireland. The plant has many uses, mostly to clarify malt beverages. In New England it is made into a dessert, served with cream, sugar, and topped with fruit. In order to use, the seaweed is washed in salt water, dried on the beach (to bleach), washed and dried again several times. Irish moss is available at health-food stores.

IRISH STEW: Recognized as the national dish in Ireland from about 1800, it is basically neck mutton chops, potatoes and onions boiled together. Irish settlers in the American South made the same dish with pork or beef neck bones. The dish came from available ingredients and cooking over an open fire.

IRON:

IRON, THE POWERHOUSE MINERAL

Iron can make a big difference in how you learn and play. Iron is a part of the hemoglobin molecule in your blood that carries oxygen to your body's cells. Iron works in each cell to help you produce energy, such as your heart needs energy to serve as your body's blood pump.

When your blood level of iron is low, so is your energy level and you may feel tired or irritable. You may not be able to concentrate and may have trouble learning. Although iron is widespread in the food supply, it can be challenging to get enough of this essential mineral. Iron boosters include meat, fish and poultry. There are two forms of dietary iron: "heme" iron and "non-heme" iron. "Heme" iron is more efficiently absorbed. It is iron bound to hemoglobin. You don't need to know all the chemistry behind these thing to know that heme iron absorbs more easily and non-heme iron is absorbed better when you eat other foods with it. For example, iron in spinach salad will be much better absorbed if you eat meat, fish or poultry at the same meal. People who do not eat meat, fish or poultry will find it more difficult to meet their iron needs. Use the following tips:

Eat foods high in vitamin C to help absorb the non-heme iron in plant food. Example, drinking orange juice with a meal of iron-fortified breakfast cereal helps your body absorb the iron in the cereal.

These things interfere with iron absorption: Tea and coffee contain substance that interfere with iron absorption. Drink these beverages between meals or eat a steak with them. High fiber foods like bran reduce the absorption of iron. Some medications block the absorption of iron, such as antacids. Ask your doctor if there are other medications you are taking that might be interfering with iron absorption.

Best sources of heme iron (based on 3 ounce serving): **Liver**, 5mg; **Sirloin**, tenderloin or chuck pot roast, 3mg; **Extra lean ground beef**, 2mg; **Tuna**, 1.3mg; **Chicken or turkey**, 1mg; **Flounder, sole, salmon, or halibut**, less then 1mg.

Best sources of non-hem iron: Iron fortified cereals range 2 to 18mg per serving; **Lentils**, 1 cup, 6.5mg; **Cream of Wheat** or Malt or Meal, 1 envelope, 5mg; **Kidney beans**, 1 cup, 3.2mg; **Baked potato**, including skin, 3mg; **Split pea** or **black bean** soup, 1 cup, 2.5mg

Best sources of combination foods: Baked beans with pork and tomato sauce, 1 cup, 8mg; **Hamburger**, with tomato, 4 ounce beef patty at your favorite fast food restaurant, 6mg; **Chop suey** with beef and/or pork, 1 cup, 4.8mg; **Chili beans** with beef, 1 cup, 4.3mg; **Tuna salad** with spinach leaves sandwich, 2.8mg; **Lasagna** made with meat, 2 ½ inch square, 2.7mg

Yes, there were some surprises. That fast food burger on bun might not be all that bad after all, and, for most people, it beats the taste of liver. *--Washington State Dairy Council*

IRON COOKWARE

When the colonists came to the New World they brought cast iron cookware, the same type of simple cookware used during the Middle Ages. Yes, they're heavy, but except for some earthenware pots, that's all that was available. Blacksmiths in America used their skills to make new and better household tools, including many innovative tools for fireplace cooking. The favorite was the large, lidded cooking pot called a Dutch oven, in which food could be either boiled or baked over open fire. It was in Pennsylvania in 1762 that Dutch colonists began turning out cast iron cookstoves.

During modern times, aluminum, stainless steel and other metals made cooking easier, since the pots and pans were lighter, faster heating, and more convenient for the cook. Today, cast iron cookware is making a comeback. Many professional chefs are making iron cookware their first choice. The natural non-stick surface promotes healthy cooking. Lower heat is fuel efficient, and with proper care, cast iron will never wear out. Cast iron cookware comes in many sizes and shapes that includes a small 6 inch round skillet to 12 inch round ribbed grill pan, a 12 inch wok, an 18 inch griddle, sizzling steak and fajita pans, and various molded utensils from a muffin pan to corn bread molds.

Lower heat eliminates the need for excessive use of oils and grease in cooking. Because of the construction of cast iron cookware (the thickness of the bottom) the cookware will provide maximum heat conductivity. This makes for even browning and cooking to perfection, using less heat than other types of cookware.

The secret for a natural non-stick surface is in the seasoning (preparation) and once it is done correctly, will never have to be done again. It's simple. Here's how:

Wash new iron cookware thoroughly in warm, sudsy water. Use a scouring pad to remove all manufacturing residue and rough the surface for seasoning. Rinse thoroughly and dry completely. **Coat** the entire utensil inside and out with any vegetable oil. Place the iron cookware in a 300° F oven for about 1 hour.
Remove from oven, allow to thoroughly cool, and wipe excess oil from utensil with a paper towel.
Before each use, pre-heat the iron cookware for about 90 seconds over medium heat. This prepares the natural non-stick surface and allows the food to cook more evenly, with less sticking, from the moment you put food in the utensil. It's important to clean your iron cookware properly after each use to preserve the non-stick feature. For extra-hard-to-remove burned-on crusts, simply add water and boil the mess loose before washing.
Rinse the iron cookware in hot water. If necessary, use a mild dish soap.
Do not wash in a dishwasher. Harsh detergents will remove the seasoning.
Be sure to dry thoroughly to prevent rusting.
A light coating of vegetable oil with a paper towel can be applied occasionally to prevent rust and to maintain the non-stick feature.

After repeated use, your cookware will turn black. This is a sign of a durable, natural, non-stick surface. If your iron cookware begins to stick or starts to rust, it will be necessary for you to repeat the seasoning steps.

Cast Iron Dutch Oven

Many modern cooks still rate the Dutch oven among the most prized cooking utensils. A dutch oven is a cast iron pot for cooking over an open fire. It's the same vessel used by the Crusaders, pilgrims, chuckwagon cooks, and your great grandmother. It can bake anything from a whole turkey to a pan of biscuits.

Today's cast iron cookware has many improvements over those the new settlers brought to America. The inside bottom surface pans and griddles are available with grooves called ribs. Ribs allows the fat from meat to fall below the meat, providing less fat in your diet. A covered cast iron Dutch oven lets you cook beans, rice and other grains with less heat, for the same length of time as other cookware. If meat is placed on a small steamer rack, the fats drop to the bottom. The meat will be tender and juicy. Another big advantage of the Dutch oven is that it can be used on the stove top or baked in a 300°F oven.--*Benjamin & Medwin*

INTERNET FOOD INFORMATION:

As the wide-world internet continues to grow, more and more food products are on the web. Hence, if you are looking for additional history, recipes and activities on a certain food, the internet might be your answer. First start with:

THE ABC'S OF FOOD. This data base will continue to upgrade information as received, plus activities and recipes: www.abcs-of-food.com.

PRODUCE MARKETING ASSOCIATION. If it is produce information you are looking for, log on to: www.pma.com or www.aboutproduce.com

If you know what state is famous for the product you are looking for, log on to any of the following state department agriculture sites. Many of the states also list manufactured food products, most of which are something that can be ordered on line:

Also many products can be found with: www.(name of product).com or .org

Alabama: www.agri-ind-state.al.us
Alaska: www.dnr.state.ak.us/
Arizona: www.agriculture.state.az.us
California: www.cdfa.co.gov
Colorado: www.ag.state.co.us
Connecticut: www.state.ct.us/doug
Florida: www.doas.state.fl.us/

Georgia: www.agr.state.ga.us/
Hawaii: www.hawaiiag.org
Idaho: www.agri.state.id.us
Illinois: www.agr.state.il.us
Kentucky: www.lyagr.com
Maine: www.getrealmaine.com
Michigan: www.state.mi.us/audgren
Mississippi: www.mdac.state.ms.us
Missouri: www.mda.state.mo.us
Montana: www.agr.state.mt.us
Nevada: www.expandnevada.com
New Jersey: www.state.nj.us/agriculture
North Carolina: www.agr.state.nc.us
Ohio: www.state.oh.us/agr/
Pennsylvania: www.pda.state.pa.us
South Dakota: www.state.sd.usdoa.html
Texas: www.tdoa.state.tx.us
Virginia: vdacs.state.va.us
Washington: www.wa.gov/agr/
Wisconsin: www.datcp.state.wi.us

IRRADIATION: A process to make food safer by destroying harmful bacteria, fungi, and insects by radiation, similar to microwaving.

IVY GOURD: Native to Africa and Asia, this vine produces a 3-inch long, light green fruit that turns red when ripe. Only the immature fruits are eaten, as well as the leaves and the shoots.

Jj

JABOTICABA: A slow growing shrub, native to Brazil, with medium size, round, black, sweet fruit that is eaten fresh and made into wine.

JACK CHEESE: Jack cheese is sometimes called "Monterey" cheese or " Monterey Jack." Available made with whole to nonfat milk with a mild flavor. An aged dry Jack for grating is also produced. **Nutrition facts** per 1/4 cup: 105 calories, 76 calories from fat, 8.5g total fat (13%), 5.3g saturated fat (27%), 24.9mg cholesterol (8%), 150.2mg sodium (6%), zero carbohydrates and fiber, 6.9g protein (14%), 266 IU vitamin A (5%), zero vitamin C, 209mg calcium (21%) and .2mg iron (1%).

JACKFRUIT (JAKFRUIT): This large tree, originating in India, has very large elongated, segmented green to yellow fruit that is eaten fresh, cooked, dried, and the seeds are roasted. In India the fruit can weight as much as 80 pounds and is considered the world's largest tree fruit (more commonly about 30 pounds in Florida). The fruit is harder than breadfruit. Jakfruit has not gained in popularity in the United States because of its unpleasant odor. It is definitely an acquired taste. www.thaifoods.com

JALAPEÑO PEPPER: (hah-lah-payn-yo) On the chile scale from hot to mild, the popular jalapeño sits in the middle (the hottest is the habañero, the mildest is the paprika). Jalapeños make great salsa, hot pepper jelly, pickled peppers, and stuffed spicy appetizers. Those who enjoy these "popper" appetizers call them "Mexican popcorn." To make these poppers, char-roast the fresh chiles under the broiler to remove the skins, rub off the charred skin, stuff each chile with Monterey jack cheese, brush with slightly beaten egg white and bake in a 350°F for about 5 minutes or until the cheese is melted. When working with hot chiles, best to wear rubber gloves, and never, never put a chile coated finger in your eye. Wow! That's hot! **Nutrition Facts** per jalapeño pepper: 18 calories, zero fats and sodium, 4.3g carbohydrates (1%), .7g fiber (3%), .9g protein (2%),347 IU vitamin A (7%), 109mg vitamin C (182%), 8mg calcium (1%) and .5mg iron (3%). www.duda.com www.littleproduce.com www.starproduce.com

JAM: A jelled preserve of crushed fruit preserved in sugar, usually thickened with pectin and stored in glass jars. Jelly has the pulp strained out. Jam leaves the pulp in.

JAMAICA CHERRY: A small tree from tropical America that produces small yellow or red berries. The sweet, aromatic fruit is eaten fresh, made into jam and tarts.

JAMBALAYA: (jam-bo-lya) A highly seasoned Creole dish combining ham, sausage, shrimp (and other seafood) with tomatoes, onions and rice.

JAMBOLAN: Also known as Java Plum, it originated in southeast Asia. It produces a small plum-like, purple fruit that is usually very astringent. The fruit is made into jelly, juice and wine.

JARLBERG: A Norwegian semi-hard cheese. Named for a historic region said to be settled by the Vikings.

JELLIED: A dish containing gelatin, including aspics, molded salads, and gelatin desserts.

JELL-O: A registered brand name for an instant form of packaged gelatin dessert. The best thing about the invention of Jell-O was the way it opened up a world of quick and easy creativity for the housewife.

THE JELL-O GALLERY

LeRoy, New York is the birthplace of JELL-O, often called American's Most Famous Dessert. One of JELL-O's famous slogans: *There's Always Room for JELL-O* began there. In LeRoy you can see the JELL-O Gallery Exhibit. The museum is located in the 1822 Jacob LeRoy mansion. To honor the home of this gelatin dessert, The LeRoy Historical Society has put together his collection, along with a collection of JELL-O cookbooks and souvenirs. The LeRoy House was once the Ingham University, which was the first all female university in the United States. For a brochure, write: **JELL-O Gallery Exhibit**, 23 East Main Street, LeRoy, NY 14482 or phone (715) 768-7433.

JELLY: A preserve made with fruit juice, sugar, an acid (such as lemon juice) and pectin. The finished product should be bright-colored, clear and firm enough to hold its shape when cool. www.jelly.com. www.kraft.com.

JELLY BEAN: Also called jelly babies, they are a fruit or spice flavored candy bits made of flavored syrups and gelatin or pectin. The name comes from their bean size and shape.

JELLY BELLY:

THE JOY OF A JELLY BELLY
by Peter F. Cain

Two young brothers, **Gustav and Albert Goelitz**, left Germany for America and started making candy in 1869 in North Chicago. In the beginning, they sold their homemade candy from horsedrawn carts. Soon the candymaking family obtained a reputation for producing quality confections. In 1898 the brothers made **Candy Corn**, an invention by George Runniger at Wunderie Candy Company in Pennsylvania. This buttercream Halloween favorite was probably revolutionary at that time because of the difficulty of making the three colors of white, orange and yellow, all by hand.

In 1972 while Goelitz family members were driving across the Nevada desert, they came up with the idea for an elegant cool mint creme covered in rich dark chocolate and finished with a candy shell. The Dutch Mint became the company's first chocolate candy.

Four years later, the famed Jelly Belly candy was invented. Unlike other jelly beans, the new candy was made with natural ingredients such as chocolate, peanut butter, coconut, jalapeño, citrus oils, and fruit purees like strawberries and pears, as well as juice concentrates. The Jelly Belly was also smaller than other jelly beans and had more intense flavors with brilliant colors. Traditional jelly beans have no flavoring in the center, but the Jelly Belly starts with flavors in the heart of the bean and continues through the shell.

The eight original flavors were Very Cherry, Licorice, Lemon, Root Beer, Cream Soda, Grape, Green Apple and Orange. Within a year, 25 flavors were developed. Watermelon and Chocolate Pudding were the biggest hits for the public at that time. Today the company makes 40 different flavors, plus seasonal flavors such as Hot Chocolate, Gramma's Pumpkin Pie, Hot Cider, Egg Nog, and Cranberry.

The Jelly Belly gained fame when **President Ronald Reagan** was interviewed in 1980 by *Time* magazine and he expressed his fondness for Jelly Belly beans. He used them to help kick his pipe-smoking habit. During the 1981 Reagan inaugural, three and a half tons of red, white and blue beans were given out during the festivities. The blueberry flavor was invented just for this event.

In 1983, aboard the space shuttle *Challenger*, the Jelly Belly beans made their first space flight with Sally Ride. Jelly Belly beans are also the favorite of talk show host Larry King, entertainer Phil Collins, actor Mel Gibson and millions of others in 36 countries worldwide. While it is recommended to eat only one flavor at a time, many kids have come up with Jelly Belly recipes.

Examples: 2 Lemon + 2 Coconut = Lemon Meringue Pie; 2 Peanut Butter + 1 Grape = Peanut Butter & Jelly Sandwich; 2 Cotton Candy + 2 Lemon = Pink Lemonade. The combinations are endless. Why not create a recipe yourself? For a free Jelly Belly menu call (800) 522-3267. Or see www.jellybelly.com

Today there are two factories, one in Illinois and one in California. You can follow the Jelly Belly Candy Trail tour at both factories where you will see how the Dutch Mints, Jelly Belly beans, jawbreakers, and gummi creatures are made. For tour information in Chicago, call (847) 689-8950; in Fairfield, California (707) 428-2838. You can join the **Jelly Belly Taste Bud Club**. Members receive a quarterly newsletter and samples of new flavors. Obtain information for joining by calling toll free (888) 522-3267. For more information, write: **Herman Goelitz Candy** Company, 2400 North Watney Way, Fairfield, CA 94533.

JELLYFISH: Not used as food in the West, this ocean "seafood" is a delicacy in the Orient.

JERKY: The funny name comes from the Peruvian *charqui*, meaning dried meat. Spanish conquistadors liked the idea of drying meat in strips to carry along on their endless exploration trips on land and sea. Pioneers took jerky with them across America. The idea remains popular today. We can buy jerky or make it at home. See also PEMMICAN.

JERUSALEM ARTICHOKES: Believe it or not, they are not related to the globe artichoke, but to the sunflower. They are not native to Jerusalem, but to North America. Generally sold as **"sunchokes"** in the supermarkets and available during late fall and the winter months.

Sunchokes, as most people call them, were cultivated for centuries by Native Americans, and introduced to the French in 1616 by explorer Samuel de Champlain. Only the tubers are eaten, either raw or cooked. The tubers look similar to ginger root, with ivory-colored flesh. When raw it has a starchy, crunchy texture, with a taste similar to an artichoke. However, after being cooked, they are soft like a cooked potato. The tubers are also fed to livestock and are a source of fructose.

The name Jerusalem is derived from the Italian word *girasole*, meaning "turning toward the sun" or "sunflower." The word sounded like Jerusalem to the British who imported the plant from Italy. Jerusalem artichokes have about 60 calories per half cup, are rich in iron, and low in sodium. **Nutrition facts** per1/2 cup: 57 calories, zero fats and sodium, 13.1g carbohydrates (4%), 1.2g fiber

(5%), 1.5g protein (3%), zero vitamin A, 3mg vitamin C (5%), 10mg calcium (1%), and 2.6mg iron (14%).

JICAMA: (hee-kuh-muh) Also known as a "Mexican Turnip" and the "Yam Bean," it is a climbing vine grown for its edible tubers. Jicama is a member of the pea family, grown in most of Latin America, parts of California, China, and India. Jicama are found in the produce section of many supermarkets. Each vine produces several tubers. The tubers can be round like a beet or long like a carrot. A tuber can weight as much as two and one half pounds when harvested. Jicama has a brown skin and the white flesh is sweet. They are peeled, eaten raw, sometimes with a little salt or added to a salad. The crunch is similar to the crunch of a water chestnut. Some recipes add jicama to soup, generally cooked with yuca and beef. The stems, leaves, seeds, and seed pods are all toxic. They contain the chemical "rotenone," which is a natural insecticide, hence, jicama resists most insects. **Nutrition facts** per 1/4 cup: 11 calories, zero fats and sodium, 2.7g carbohydrates (1%), 1.5g fiber (6%), zero protein and vitamin A, 6mg vitamin C (10%), zero calcium, and .2mg iron (1%). www.frieda.com.

JOJOBA (ho-ho-ba): A shrub from northern Mexico. The seeds contain 50% oil, similar to sperm whale oil. Widely used in shampoos and other cosmetics.

JONAGOLD APPLES: A blend of Jonathan and Golden Delicious apples, offering a unique tangy-sweet flavor. With a yellow-green base and a blush stripe, Jonagold is excellent both for eating fresh and for cooking.

JONATHAN APPLES: Medium to small-sized apples with bright red color, Jonathans are crisp, with tart flavor and are good to use raw, in pies and for sauce.

JUICE: (noun) The liquid from any fruit or vegetable is called juice. (verb) As a verb, it means to squeeze a food until its liquids are separated from its solids. Or it can mean to turn the entire fruit or vegetable into juice by grinding it into a liquid. www.oceanspray.com

JUJUBE: There are a number of various jujubes all from Asian countries, that produce a small, yellow or brown fruit, somewhat bigger than an olive, that is eaten fresh, dried, candied, or made into jelly. They are also called Chinese dates. They are said to "taste vaguely like dates mixed with apples and chocolate," according to Clifford Wright in *A Mediterranean Feast*. American kids know Jujubes as a gumdrop candy. It's chief appeal is that it lasts a long time, making it a favorite to take to the movies. Made by Henry Heide, Inc. since 1869, now part of www.hersheys.com

JULEP: An alcoholic drink made with spirits, sugar, ice and mint. In Kentucky it is made with bourbon and in Georgia it is made with brandy.

JULIENNE (ju-lee-an): Vegetables, meat, or cheese that has been cut into thin strips.

JUNK FOOD: The common name for foods which contain little or no nutritive value.

article, and possibly do contain harmful ingredients. See NUTRITION and COLA.

Kk

KABOB or **KEBAB**: The word "kabob" means a small piece of meat. Kabob is also spelled "kebab" and often the word "shish" precedes the word, as in "shish kabob." The word "shish" comes from the Turkish and means "skewer." Hence: a "shish kabob" is small pieces of meat that have been threaded on to a skewer. The origin of kabob cuisine is the Near East, especially Turkey, Iran, Iraq, Lebanon and Syria. However, kabob is found in various forms around the world. The true shish kabob uses lamb as the meat, usually with the addition of fruits and vegetables. The meat is usually marinated, to help tenderize the meat so it will cook quickly. Marinade is a mixture of vegetable oil, fruit juices, spices and herbs. The skewered ingredients are usually roasted over an open fire. Brushing the meat with marinade during cooking helps improve the flavor.

Today, all kinds of meat are used, even shellfish. The skewers are not only made with metal, but with wood, such as bamboo. In America, the barbecue grill is the preferred method. However, the broiler works just as well. In some parts of Russia, a sword is used as a skewer and the meat is cooked over a campfire the way early warriors once did. Preferred vegetables to use are onions, green peppers, mushrooms, tomatoes, eggplant and zucchini squash. Some meats, such as chicken livers, are wrapped in bacon. Spices and herbs vary from country to country. Oils and juices in the marinade recipe differ according to region and tastes. Try some of the following meats and marinades:

Pork : A marinade of cayenne, cumin, brown sugar, peanut butter, lemon juice, and soy sauce.
Beef: A marinade of olive oil, minced garlic, honey, and soy sauce.
Lamb: A marinade of chopped onions, cayenne, coriander, and curry in orange juice.
Shrimp: Generally not marinated, but can be wrapped in bacon, skewered with chunks of pineapple, then dipped in melted butter just prior to cooking.
Scallops: Try a marinade of crushed garlic, minced ginger, soy sauce and sugar.
Chicken: Blend lemon juice, coriander, aniseed, chopped green chiles into yogurt.

In addition, tropical countries use a variety of tropical fruits, such as pineapple juice and coconut milk in their marinades. In the East, *sake* is often included in the marinade, while sherry and other wines are used in Western countries. Herbs and seeds include: bay leaves, parsley, dill weed, caraway, crushed red peppers, oregano, marjoram, turmeric, paprika, saffron and salt and pepper. Kabobs are generally served with rice or crushed wheat.

KAFFIR LIME: These limes are small, green and watery, with bitter rind and very sour juice. Cambodians use both for fragrance and flavor. In the US, most Asian markets carry only the leaves, which are ground and used like bay leaves to flavor broth. www.thaifoods.com.

KAFFIR PLUM: The small kaffir tree in South Africa produces a fruit with a thin skin, sweet flesh and a large seed. The plum-like fruit is eaten fresh.

KALE: A member of the cabbage family called by a number of names, "borecole," "cole," and "colewort." Kale leaves grows long, not in heads like some of the cabbages. Kale ranges in size from a dwarf variety to sizes as tall as celery, with big leaves that are smooth or curly-edged. Most varieties are dark green but there are purple (called "red") kinds which have purple in the stems and leaves. Kale is cooked the same as spinach, either with a little water or steamed. It's best to chop the large leaves to fit the pan and for easier eating. Kale is a good source of vitamins A and C, with some calcium and iron. Kale is so popular in Scotland that they don't ask if you have eaten today, they ask if you have had any kale. Kale in one of the most nutritious foods around, with superb health benefits. **Nutrition facts** per ½ cup: 17 calories, zero fats, 14.4mg sodium (1%), 3.4g carbohydrates (1%), .7g fiber (3%), 1.1g protein (2%), 2982 IU vitamin A (60%), 40mg vitamin C (67%), 45mg calcium (5%), and .6mg iron (3%).

KANSAS FOODS: KANSAS SAMPLER FESTIVAL

A Kansas October annual event that promotes items made or grown in rural Kansas. It is held in Pratt's Lemon Park with entertainment for all ages, exhibits of Kansas products and food, a living history exhibit, petting zoo. Roasted ears of corn, kettle popcorn, fresh cider slush, apple slices in a caramel sauce, barbecued ribs, a variety of Kansas made sausages, sauerkraut, and old-fashioned apple dumplings are featured. For dates and information, write: **Pratt Chamber of Commerce,** P.O. Box 469, Pratt, KS 67124 or phone toll free (888) 886-1164

KARANDA: In India, small purplish-black berries grow on a thorny shrub called Karanda. The acid berries are made into juice or jelly.

KARAYA TREE: The bark from this Himalayan tree is peeled and the brownish, gummy, vinegar smelling sap is collected. Once solidified, this hardened sap is a polysaccharide, a complex form of carbohydrates. When mixed with water, the granules swell to a hundred times their original size! Thus it becomes a natural bulk laxative. It is also used as a denture adhesive, resistant to both bacteria and enzymes in the mouth. The food industry uses it as a stabilizer for salad dressings, a binder for bologna, a gummy base for candy, and a thickener for meringue, ice cream, whipped creams and cheese spreads. It is also used in beauty products and manufacturing of tissue paper.

KASHA is the Russian word for hot cereal. The English would call the same thing groats or porridge. Russian kasha is a lot more versatile and less bland. Tasty variations can be served with any meal. Check the cereal sections of your grocer and health food stores.

KAVA: This green herb plant, referred to as "intoxicating pepper" by Fijians, is from the South Pacific. Used as an herb, it is made into a beverage in Fiji and served in a coconut shell in bars. Kava is sold in health food stores in capsule form and is supposed to promote calming and a soothing sense of well-being. www.herbco.com

KEDGEREE: An English dish borrowed from India. The original Indian dish was rice with onion, beans and eggs. The British added fish.

KEI APPLE: A shrub in South Africa produces both male and female medium sized, yellow fruit. The tart fruit is eaten fresh, made into jelly, preserves and sauce.

KETCHUP: A sauce that originated in China, called *ke-tsiap*, made from onions, garlic, vinegar, and spices. The Malayans adopted it, added mushrooms, and called it "kechup." The Americans added the tomatoes. When Henry Heinz in 1876 made his standard version, he labeled it "Blessed relief for Mother and the other women in the household!" Also spelled "catsup." www.heinz.com

KEY LIMES: This ball-shaped lime is about half the size of a Persian lime, paler, and only grown in southern Florida. When green, they are more acidic than the Persians, but ripened to yellow, they have a slightly sweet flavor. Floridians long ago found the key limes make the best pies, and there are as many recipes for this famous pie as there are cooks. Key limes are seldom available outside Florida but bottled juice is sold in stores. See PIES.

KID: This is meat from a young goat that has been slaughtered before being weaned. The meat is delicate but bland. It is prized in parts of Latin America and often served at Easter in place of lamb.

KIDNEY: This variety meat is an organ from beef, lamb, or veal. Kidneys can be served as a main meat dish, but more often are combined with other meats, stews and omelets. Kidneys can be braised or broiled. Avoid over-cooking, which toughens the meat. Kidneys are a good source of protein, iron, and vitamin A.

KIELBASA: A highly seasoned Polish sausage made with course ground pork or beef and flavored with garlic and spices. It is available fresh and smoked.

KIMCHI or KIMCHEE: Koreans developed a method of pickling and preserving foods by burying them in an earthenware jar outdoors during the long bitter winters. *Kimchi* is called Korean sauerkraut because it is made with Chinese Napa cabbage, packed in a jar and left to ferment (pickle) like sauerkraut. Unlike sauerkraut, kimchi contains vegetables such as daikon radishes, carrots, onions, garlic, ginger and Korean red pepper threads. Today most Koreans prefer to make their own kimchi, but they seldom bury it in the ground to preserve it. Korean markets sell kimchi in gallon jars. Kimchi is served with braised short ribs, stir-fried pork or salt fish. Koreans eat kimchi with every meal. www.kawa.or.kr.

KING CRAB: Often called the "King of Alaska," this crab is unmatched for its sweet flavored meat and rich, tender texture. The king crab is one of the world's largest in the crab family. They can weight up to 25 pounds and can measure six feet from claw to claw. The meat is eaten on the plate by cracking the legs and claws or it is added to any recipe calling for crab meat. King crab is used in salads, soup, pasta, rice, or oriental stir-fry recipes. **Nutrition facts** per 3 ounce serving: 82 calories, 1.3g total fat, 45mg cholesterol, 18g protein, zero carbohydrates, and contain all the essential amino acids, plus calcium, zinc, magnesium and iron. Sodium can vary from 100mg to 900mg depending upon the process used in preparing the crab for shipment. www.alaskaseafood.org

KING ORANGE: A member of the citrus family, this South Florida tree produces large, rough skinned fruit that is eaten fresh and squeezed into juice.

KING SALMON: See SALMON

KINNON: See TANGERINE

KIPPER: A fish, generally a herring, that has been cured with brine and then cold smoked. Beloved in Britain, kippers are mostly from Scotland and the Isle of Man.

KISS: A bite-size piece of candy.

KITCHEN:

KITCHEN HISTORY

The first "kitchens" were campfires. The first homes were tents, tepees, or huts built around or near the cooking fires.

The Earliest Ages

People learned to build open fires inside the huts and tents by leaving a vent hole in the roof. Smoke made a terrible mess and ruined the wall hangings, but it was warmer than cooking outdoors. The first kitchens had two basic things - **a table and a cauldron**. The table might be only a long board on trestle legs. The cauldron is a large boiling pot, under which a fire can be built. Water was usually kept boiling at all times for its multiple uses. Sometime around 7000 BC, someone clever learned to use **pottery** for kitchen use, rather than just for making idols and perfume bottles.

By the Neolithic Age, the first great Chinese culture, the Shang Period (beginning about 1700 BC) left behind wonderful **bronze, jade and ceramic vessels.** Tableware was on its way and kept getting better every millennium. By 500 BC, international trade and travel was such that Sicily became the garden spot of the Mediterranean world. Sicily gave us the world's first cooking school and first cookbook, *The Art of Cooking* by Mithaecus. As the Roman Empire grew, so did knowledge of food and cooking. However, it's interesting to note that in Rome, during the Roman Empire, poor family homes did not contain cooking facilities because the danger of fire was too great in crowded Roman streets. Cooking was done in designated areas with great ovens. In hard times, Rome's poor were doled out free bread. After Rome fell to the Visigoths in 410 AD, families had to go back to fending for themselves.

Medieval Times

Architectural advancements led to the permanent stone indoor fireplace. The well appointed medieval kitchen in Europe contained the following:

A table for chopping foods

Pots
Tripod with hook for hanging cauldron over fire
Mortar and pestle for crushing and grinding spices
Hatchet for chopping meat
Stirring sticks
Wooden bowl
Wooden platter called a trencher
Wooden pickle vat
Knife
Box for spices
Bread board
Sieve for sifting flour
Large spoon for removing foam and skimming fat

KITCHENS OF YESTERYEAR
by Greg Koos

Many historical museums have exhibits of yesteryear kitchens and a display of food products. One such museum is the McLean County Historical Museum in Bloomington, Illinois with six kitchen exhibits.

Wilderness Melting Pot

Shortly after the Revolutionary War, the area from Ohio to the Mississippi River was considered the western wilderness. In the young country's migration westward, settlers came to Illinois across from New England, north from Kentucky, and south from Canada and the Great Lakes region. In the 1800s, with so many immigrants pouring into the area, Chicago became a truly great "melting pot" of cultures. Homes had many things in common, but certain differences showed up clearly in the family kitchens.

The "Yankee" Kitchen in Illinois

When settlers arrived in McLean County, Illinois the New England "Yankees" (as they were called by the southern residents) built frame houses - with kitchens. Their prosperous kitchens featured newly invented cast iron cookstoves from Pennsylvania. In 1762, the Dutch iron workers at the Mary Ann Furnaces in the colony of Pennsylvania had cast the first iron cookstove. These stoves contained the fire that made possible a more varied cuisine than could be prepared at an open hearth. Yankee housewives were also adept at the art of preserving or "canning" fruit and vegetables. Upland Southerners, already in Illinois, mostly from Kentucky, scorned the Yankee as a "cow-milkin' set of men." The Yankee diet was very different from the neighboring Kentuckians'. Yankees relied on dairy products, especially milk and home-made butter. They preferred beef over pork. They loved fresh produce when available, welcomed "canned goods," and they wanted their breads and muffins baked from wheat flour, not corn. When a "Yankee" family sat down to eat, their meal was often served on imported decorative earthenware or porcelain dishes. Some of the items on exhibit are: 1870s wooden butter molds, 1840 waffle iron for stove top cooking, 1850 place setting with Lusterware, and an 1860 wooden butter churn with brass banding.

The Upland Southern Kitchen

Most southern cooking was still done over an open-hearth fire, using cumbersome iron utensils. Like her sisters in the South, these new settlers in Illinois prepared simple meals, largely based on roast, fried or boiled pork from free-ranging hogs. Corn came from the family patch. A cow provided dairy products, including the popular buttermilk. She manipulated heavy kettles, spiders (frying pans), and Dutch ovens around the fire; and while the pots were boiling and the meats roasting, she might cook a batch of "corn dodgers" in the waffle iron or bury her "ash cakes" right in the coals to bake. Plentiful corn allowed farmers to perfect the art of whiskey making.

The Anabaptist Kitchen

(Mennonite and Amish)

The Germanic ("Dutch") heritage and proud self- sufficiency of Anabaptists is reflected in their kitchens. In the early days of Anabaptist cooking, cooking was generally done "open-hearth." Displayed at the museum are an 1850 wooden handled iron meat-grinder and a handmade sausage stuffer. Both were used for preserving lesser parts of hunted game or butchered livestock. On display also is an 1880 wooden handled slaw-cutter for preparing the traditional cabbage dishes and sauerkraut. The utensils reflected the careful craftsmanship of growing eastern "Pennsylvania Dutch" cottage industries.

The Irish-American Kitchen

For Irish families, gardening was a "necessary hobby." Potatoes and other backyard vegetables and fruits could mean the difference between eating and going hungry during the winter. The Irish Americans needed no reminders of the famine from their homeland. Often men returned from a twelve-hour job only to toil late into the evening in their gardens. The women sweated through long summer days of canning the abundance that the gardens grew. Households generally raised pigs and cows, thus earning extra income by selling meat and milk. When the family sat down to dinner, they ate plain food on plain dishes - inexpensive 1850 English ironstone - and in the afternoon, time was made for tea and talk.

The African-American Kitchen

Peter Duff was part of the Black exodus from Kentucky northward after the Civil War and stayed because of opportunities for carpenters to build kitchens. His kitchens included wall cabinets, counters, pass-through doors to the dining room, cistern-pumps, and wall-hung sinks. The Duff kitchen reflects the African-American middle-class's desire to participate in "American progress" and technological innovation. The cuisine included traditional Afro-American foods with lots of greens and other vegetables from the family garden.

The German-American Kitchen

Like their rural Mennonite and Amish cousins, other central European and German-speaking immigrants loved the old-country national dish of sausage or pig knuckles and sauerkraut. But this was only the beginning of their cuisine. Making good coffee was important, but having quality beer and wine was essential. What the New England "Yankees" often considered luxuries - and sinful ones at that - the Germans insisted were staples of a healthy diet. Beer and wine were typically made at home, so the German kitchen would have all the utensils for brewing from fruit presses to bottle cappers. Almost every backyard had a vineyard, if only a simple grape arbor. With the fall harvest, began the winter-long round of winemaking: pressing, fermenting, aging and bottling. Spring brought the first sampling of the new wine - woodruff flavored "May wine," enjoyed with the season's first strawberries from the backyard garden.

Museum Gift Shop

The museum's gift shop has a fine collection of early day cookbooks, which includes a facsimile of 1776 *The First American Cookbook* by Amelia Simmons. The books are available by mail order. Write: **McLean County Historical Society**, 2200 North Main Street, Bloomington, IL 61701 for a list of currently available books. Telephone: (309) 827-0428

THE LOUISIANA KITCHEN
by Richard S. Calhoun

Have you ever wondered why early American colonists settled where they did? Most of the new settlers had been farmers in the "Old Country" and settled where they thought would be the best place to farm. They followed rivers, and old wagon trails until they found a promising spot. Others followed leaders to established communities of their same ethic heritage. Some places were chosen for good reasons, others made it only until their wagon broke down. Still others were placed without choice. New Orleans settlers came for all those reasons.

New Orleans was once a steamy bog between the Mississippi River and Lake Pontchartrain. To make the situation worse, alligators, snakes, and mosquitoes made the area a worthless swamp.

It began when **Robert Cavelier, sieur de LaSalle arrived in 1682**. At the time there were two small villages in what is now New Orleans, occupied by Quinipissa and Tangipahoa Native Americans. LaSalle erected a cross and claimed the land for France.

One of the first to attempt to colonize Louisiana was a group of **Germans**. They settled in Des Allemands, a few miles southwest of New Orleans. Within ten years almost half of the 8,000 settlers died from various epidemics. **France** decided that the land was not worth the expense and **gave**

New Orleans to Spain and other **parts of Louisiana to Great Britain.** The Spanish worked hard to develop the land, but they were not any more successful than the French.

In 1785, the **French from Acadia**, now known as Nova Scotia, were forced to leave. The British had doubts about Acadian loyalty and removed them from Canada. More than 1,500 Acadians migrated south to New Orleans, down the Mississippi River. The Acadians did not get along with the Spanish either, so they moved west of the Mississippi into the bayous near present day Lafayette.

Recipe for Immigrant Stew

During the American Revolution, many British fleeing the war migrated to New Orleans. In the 1790s more groups arrived from the Canary Islands to Saint Bernard Parish, Malagans to New Iberia, and Santo Domingans brought in blacks and mulattoes. In the 1800s still more nationalities arrived. During the great potato famine, 25,000 Irish arrived. Sicilians migrated to New Orleans and nearby Independence. All of these groups introduced their own recipes. Louisiana food started with **French** cuisine. The **Spanish** added spices. **Africans** contributed vegetables, the **Germans** brought pepper and pork. Potatoes came with the **Irish**. Garlic and tomatoes arrived with the **Italians**. More ideas and ingredients came from the **English, Swiss, and Dutch.**

Today's Two Types

These ideas have been combined into two basic types of cuisine, **Creole and Cajun**. Creole Cuisine originated in the French Quarter and used spices to disguise the wild taste of meat and fish. Cajun Cooking was born on the bayou and is more robust because of the many spices, but it still has roots from the French, Spanish and African cooking. Creole food is more refined because of the abundance of cream and butter. The Cajuns used roux (flour and fat cooked together until a dark brown), sausage and hot peppers. In addition, during those early years there was no refrigeration, so everything had to be eaten fresh. Today many of the Cajun and Creole dishes have been combined and the restaurants simply refer to it as "Louisiana Cooking," the best of each. Most dishes are quite time consuming with many ingredients. Impatience results in a loss of flavor.

KITCHEN SAFETY:
KIDS IN THE KITCHEN

Did you know that one-third of all kids over six years prepare their own breakfast and lunch? It's true, according to Noble Communication of Springfield, Missouri. Some kids have no choice, since working parents have no time to fix these meals. Cooking can be fun, that is if you are ready for it. It's very tempting for kids to just start right in, but it is much easier and safer if you follow these instructions:

Cooking is dangerous work, even with all the easy appliances to make cooking simpler. We cannot stress kitchen safety too much. Be careful at all times, especially when boiling and frying.

Avoid Disaster . . . Plan Ahead

1. **Request adult help** if you haven't been previously instructed. Make sure you know how to use the equipment and appliances called for. Never plug in electrical appliances with wet hands. This includes electric mixers. Can you use the microwave oven? Does the kitchen range have a timer and do you know how to set it?
2. **Read** through the entire recipe *first*.
3. **Get out all the equipment and ingredients** needed. There is nothing more annoying than finding out halfway through that an important ingredient is missing.
4. **Wash** your hands with water and soap before starting and dry them well.
5. Cooking means **clean-up**.
6. Be sure all appliances have been **turned off** when you leave the kitchen.

Make sure you understand the above rules before beginning a recipe. Safe cooking is fun cooking.

KITEMBILLA: Also known as Ceylon gooseberry, this shrub produces a sour tasting, small berry that is made into juice, jelly, and preserves.

KIWI FRUIT: Originally found in China by an English botanist in 1847. The kiwi vines are now grown in warm, temperate climates, mainly in New Zealand and California. In China they are called "Chinese gooseberries" or *yangtao*. About the size of a large lime, the homely fuzzy brown skin hides a brilliant green plup about the texture of a banana. Its tiny black seeds fan out like a sunburst. The kiwi has a refreshing sweet-tart favor. Kiwis can be cooked in cakes, pies, and preserves. Kiwi slices make lovely green "pinwheel" garnish. Kiwi juice enlivens lots of fruit punches. Kiwi can be peeled and sliced across or cut in half and scooped out with a spoon like a boiled egg. **Nutrition facts** per ½ cup: 62 calories, 4 calories from fat, .5g total fat (1%), zero saturated fat and cholesterol, zero sodium, 15.1g carbohydrates (5%),3.5g fiber (14%), 1g protein (2%), 178 IU vitamin A (4%), 100mg vitamin C (166%), 26mg calcium (3%), .4mg iron (2%). www.kiwifruit.org.

KNACKWURST: A German sausage, shorter and fatter than a frankfurter and with more garlic.

KNEAD: To mix yeast dough with the palms of the hands in a pushing and pulling motion to make the dough smooth and elastic. Flour is usually added at the same time. We usually think of bread dough as the only thing to knead, but fudge or taffy might be kneaded after it gets too thick to stir.

KNIFE: A cutting instrument with a handle and a blade made of steel. There are many types of cooking knives: dinner knives, butter knives, steak knives, and carving knives, to name a few. In the early days a man might have one knife, which he used to kill his food, skin it, roast it, and eat it. Such was the very most basic kitchen tool until the spoon and fork came along much later.

KOHLRABI: (kole-rahbi) A member of the cabbage family from northern Europe. The name is German, that means "cabbage turnip." The favorite part is a swelled stem just above the ground that grows about three inches in diameter. Kohlrabi are generally cut into strips and steamed. Kohlrabi can also be boiled, baked or fried, and eaten raw in a salad. When they are young and perfectly ripe, slice and serve raw with dip, like carrot sticks. The tender, young leaves that grow from the stem can be boiled. Kohlrabi is a good source of vitamin C and the leaves a good source for iron. **Nutrition fact**s per ½ cup: 19 calories, zero fats, 14mg sodium (1%), 4.3g carbohydrates (1%), 2.5g fiber (10%), 1.2g protein (2%), 25 IU vitamin A (1%), 43mg vitamin C (72%), 17mg calcium (2%), and .3mg iron (2%).

KOKANEE: See SOCKEYE SALMON.

KOLACKY: (Also spelled koláce, kolachy, or kolatchy.)

KOLACKY!
by Joyce Ackermann

What is it? Why shouldn't you be surprised to hear a robot say, "*Dobry den*!"? Because those words mean "Hello!" in the Czech language and the word "robot" was invented in the country now called the Czech Republic. Why might a Czech robot say, "*Chci kolacky!*"? Because that means, "Give me kolacky!" and people who live in the Czech Republic like kolacky as much as Americans like chocolate chip cookies. Famous Czechs who love kolacky are tennis stars, Ivan Lendl and Martina Navrátilová. Do you know the Christmas carol, *Good King Wenceslas?* Wenceslas is the patron saint of Bohemia, which is part of the Czech Republic.

Kolacky (pronouned "ko-lahtch-key) are cakes. Some are like coffee cakes topped with sliced pears, plums or apples. Others are like jelly rolls filled with sweetened ground poppy seeds. Others are like round cookies with centers of poppy seeds, apricot or prune filling. These are especially popular among people of Czech descent who live in the United States. Although the flavor of ground poppy seeds sweetened with syrup is not familiar to most Americans, those who try it usually like it. You can find kolacky in fancy food catalogs, especially at holiday time.

Activity
Plan a party and see how many kinds of cookies from other cultures you and your friends can find in local bakeries or get from ethnic friends to bring and share.

KOSHER: A Hebrew word meaning "pure." It applies to both food and utensils, and regulates the types of food which should or should not be eaten together and foods such as pork, rabbit, and shellfish which are not to be eaten at all. Dairy dishes must be cooked and eaten separately from meat dishes. Foods such as fish, eggs, fruits, and vegetables may be eaten with either meat or milk. Two sets of dishes, one for milk and one meat meals, are used, stored, and cleaned separately. And no cooking is permitted on the Sabbath, except for food prepared in advance that can simmer for a long time under a low flame, such as a stew. www.hebrewnational.com.

KUMQUAT: This tart, bright orange fruit is the smallest of the citrus family. Kumquats grow on a small tree native to Asia. The flesh is filled with tiny seeds and some juice, with a superb flavor. The kumquat can be cooked as part of a compote, a relish or a preserve. They can also be candied. Kumquats are a popular dessert in China, and growing in popularity in the United States, especially at Christmas time. Kumquats have been crossed with key limes and are called "limequats." Kumquats are found in some supermarkets during the winter months, and are also available on store shelves as a preserve. The secret to enjoying the dainty kumquat is to pop the whole thing in your mouth and chew. The sweet skin tempers the tart juice. Of course, if you wish, just eat the sweet skin. **Nutrition facts** per ½ cup: 69 calories, zero fats and sodium, 18.1g carbohydrates (6%), 7.2g fiber (29%), 1g protein (2%), 332 IU vitamin A (7%), 41mg vitamin C (69%), 48mg calcium (5%), and .4mg iron (2%).

KUWINI: An oval shaped fruit from southeast Asia, it has green skin and an orange flesh that surrounds a large seed.. The flesh has an objectionable odor and must be soaked in lime juice before eaten fresh. Kuwini is used to make curries, chutney and pickles.

KWAI MUK: In south China, this ornamental, small, round, yellow fruit is eaten fresh.

Ll

LABELS AND LABELING:

READ THE LABEL

They may not have the power of a Pulitzer prize-winning novel or the luridness of a supermarket tabloid, but federally required food labels still promise to make for good reading.

Food **labeling is not something new.** It started in 1906. But it wasn't until 1913 that contents were listed on some packages. New laws in 1924 regulated health claims. In 1938 the weight, and name and address of the company had to be listed. Over the years, various changes were made until 1990 when proposed new labeling suggested the listing of nutrition facts, standardizing serving sizes, and uniform use of health claims. This proposal went into effect on May 8, 1993. The Food and Drug Administration (FDA) and the United States Department of Agriculture (USDA) are still researching new labeling ideas to better protect you.

Problems in Labeling

At one time the wording "hydrolyzed proteins" was found on labels. Now this protein must be identified as either "vegetable protein" or "animal protein," and if animal protein from what source. Some religious groups do not permit milk and meat to be eaten at the same meal. Hence, if the animal protein is derived from milk, it cannot be added to canned meat, unless the label so states.

Some people are allergic to various ingredients, while others avoid them for religious reasons. Take a product that is listed as "nondairy." These products are presumed to be good for those allergic to dairy products. However, it was found that one of the ingredients listed was cassinate, which is a derivative from milk, and caused problems to some who were allergic to milk. Readers have to read with care and know the meaning of the words used.

Labels Must Be Specific and Clear

Sugar free has to have less than .5 grams per serving. If the label states, **"no sugar added,"** then no sugar can be added. However, these foods can be sweeten with fruit and fruit juice, which still contain calories and carbohydrates (carbohydrates are sugar). **Calorie free** must mean fewer than 5 calories per serving. If the serving seems small to you, you might eat ten times the suggested serving, and it may no longer be calorie free. **Low calorie** foods must be less than 40 calories per serving. Fat free is less than .5 grams of fat per serving. If the label reads low fat, it must have less than 3 grams of fat per serving.

Cholesterol free must have less than 2 milligrams per serving, and low cholesterol must be less than 20 milligrams per serving. **Sodium (salt) free** most be less than 5 milligrams per serving, and low sodium must be under 140 milligrams. **High fiber** labels means 5 grams or more per serving, and a package that reads **"Good source of fiber"** must have 2.5 grams or more per serving.

Additives
What are some of those strange ingredients listed, especially those that are hard to pronounce? Some additives are coloring, preservatives, and ingredients that are used for a number of other reasons, such as thickeners and flavor enhancers (see ADDITIVES).

Further, if the label reads "high," "rich in," or "excellent source" for a vitamin or a mineral, that food must contain 20% or more of that daily value. "Good source" must be 10% or higher. Labels are now often in more than one language, a tremendous help to non English speaking groups. Confusing reading? Not necessarily. It's just important to know what you are eating, and if the health claims are legit or not. *--Condensed from the FDA Consumer Magazine, May 1993*

LAMB: A sheep under the age of one is considered lamb. The meat from older sheep is called mutton. Spring lamb is meat from young sheep slaughtered during the spring and summer months. Sheep originated in Asia. They followed nomadic tribes as they spread west to the Mediterranean and throughout Europe. The Spanish first bought sheep to southwestern America. During Colonial days, sheep were smuggled into the eastern seaports by English sea captains, because importation was strictly forbidden.

Lamb in England is enjoyed with mint sauce. In the Middle East, lamb is the favorite meat, cooked in the same ways that Americans do their beef. The French like their lamb cooked rare with the meat pink. And in most countries, lamb is made into a stew with lots of vegetables. For a change of pace, try ground lamb on your next homemade burger. Lamb can be cooked in almost any style:

fried, boiled, braised. broiled, and roasted. **Nutrition facts** per 3 ounces: 175 calories,130 calories from fat, 14.1g total fat (22%), 6.2g saturated fat (31%), 47.2mg cholesterol (16%), 38mg sodium (2%), zero carbohydrates and fiber, 11.1g protein (22%), zero vitamins A and C, 8mg calcium (1%) and 1mg iron (6%)

LANGOSTINOS: A very small lobster crustacean found in the Adriatic Sea between Italy and Yugoslavia. Today they are farmed commercially in Chile. Langostinos have a delicate taste like lobster. Available only frozen in specialty seafood markets. Langostinos have no fat and less cholesterol than shrimp. See SCAMPI **Nutrition facts** per ½ cup: 60 calories, zero fats, 120mg cholesterol (40%), 42mg sodium (17%), zero carbohydrates and fiber, 14g protein (28%), 120 IU vitamin A (2%), 3mg vitamin C (2%), zero calcium, and 1.1mg iron (6%).

LARD: The fat from pork that has been rendered (melted) and clarified is called lard. Prior to vegetable oils and shortenings, lard was the main fat for cooking. It was the preferred fat for baking during Colonial days, and in some localities is still the fat of choice. Lard produces tender and flavorful pastry, because no other fat can beat lard in making pie crusts. Lard is still widely used south of the border, as well as in many European countries. Today's treated lard can be stored at room temperature, best in a cool dry place. Some lards require refrigeration. Read the label to be sure. When substituting lard for butter in cooking, use about 25% less lard than butter. For flaky biscuits, lard is best. For cake baking, use only hydrogenated lard, since other lards will make the cake flat with a sticky crust. Lard has no nutrition values, as all calories from lard are fat. Lard is high in saturated fat, lower in cholesterol than butter, and lard has no sodium.

LASAGNA (laz-an-ya) is an Italian casserole made with 2-inch wide noodles. The long noodles are first boiled, then layered in a baking dish between meat, cheese, spaghetti sauce. After the dish is assembled it is baked for about 30 minutes to melt cheese and blend the flavors.

LAVENDER: English lavender and spike lavender both originally came from the Mediterranean region and although used mainly in perfumery, they also has a place in food preparation. Lavender oil can flavor foods. The leaves and flowers are used by creature cooks to flavor or garnish salads, vinegars, jellies, ice creams and soft drinks. Dried lavender flowers make lovely confectionery decorations.

LAYER CAKES have two or more thin layers of cake, assembled with a thick frosting in between. Preserves and other filling can be used between the layers. After it is assembled, the cake is frosted on top and the sides.

LEATHER: Fruit leather was so called because fruit or berries and sugar were boiled until they formed a thick jell. Poured out and cooled, it was tough as leather. Today's equivalent is called fruit "roll up", or similar things.

LEAVENING AGENTS: The Latin word *levare* means "to raise." There are many substances which will lighten dough and batter to make it more palatable when baked. **Carbon dioxide** is a gas that comes from baking soda and baking powder when heated in the presence of moisture. **Yeast** is a living organism, and it too produces carbon dioxide in warm temperatures (too hot, the temperature will kill the yeast). Other leavening agents release gases within the dough, to make it rise. The main gas is carbon dioxide, while others are air and steam. **Air** can be incorporated into a batter by adding beaten egg whites, and to some degree by creaming fat and sugar. Angel food and similar cakes are leavened that way. **Steam** occurs when water is heated to a high temperature. It's steam that leavens popovers.

LEBKUCHEN is a popular German spice cake, usually made at holiday time with honey or molasses, candied fruit, and nuts. It is one of the many Christmas favorites at the traditional German Christmas fairs.

LEEKS: This bulb vegetable, which originated in the Mediterranean, is related to onions and garlic. The round stalk has a small bulb with dark green leaves. They look like a fat green onion. Leeks are used both for flavoring other vegetables and meats, and are also eaten as a vegetable by themselves. Except for the roots and the tough upper part of the leaves, all is used in cooking. Leeks can be boiled or braised, served with butter or a white sauce; and a flavoring for soups and salads. **Nutrition facts** for a ½ cup serving without butter or sauces: 32 calories, zero fat and sodium, 7.4g carbohydrates (2%), .9g fiber (4%), .8g protein (2%), 49 IU vitamin A (1%), 6mg vitamin C (10%), 31mg calcium (3%), 1.1mg iron (6%), and 94mg potassium.

LEFTOVERS are what we call food that is reserved from previous meals. Leftovers may be eaten as they are or recycled as ingredients in other recipes.

LEGUMES: Pods that open with two seams, having seeds on the inside are called legumes. Most such seeds are edible fresh, or can be dried for cooking later. Dried legumes can be stored for long periods of time in a dry, cool place. **Legumes include beans, peas, peanuts, lentils, and alfalfa.** Legumes are high in protein and are an essential food in countries where little meat is available. Legumes are also inexpensive, used in place of pasta, rice, and potatoes, and can be combined with other foods to stretch the more costly ones. After soaking, dried legumes can be cooked in a variety of ways. See BEANS.

LEMON: This fruit, believed to have originated in Malaysia, is a cousin of the citrus family. Lemon skin is yellow; the pulp is juicy and sour. There are many varieties of lemons, some better for juice, others prized for the skin for making candied peel, and oil. It takes about a thousand lemons to make a pound of oil. **Lemon oil** is made into an extract, used as a fragrant in cleaning products, in some medicines. Columbus brought lemon seedlings to the Caribbean on his second voyage. The plants were spread to Mexico, Florida, and the Spanish Franciscans carried them to California.

During those early days it was found that just an ounce of lemon juice prevented scurvy for the sailors on their long voyages. The lemon peel was also used to clean the teeth. Lemons add zest to meats and beverages, make marmalade, flavor pies and cakes, sauces, and create a basis for salad dressings and marinades. **Nutrition facts**, one ounce of lemon juice (about 2 tablespoons): 7

calories, zero fats and sodium, 2.5g carbohydrates (1%), zero fiber and protein, zero vitamin A, 13mg vitamin C (22%), and zero calcium and iron.

Lemon Juice Substitute

1 teaspoon lemon juice = 1/4 teaspoon cider vinegar in recipes
1 teaspoon lemon peel (zest) = ½ teaspoon lemon extract

LEMONADE is a chilled beverage made with lemon juice, sugar and water. Lemonade can be made with fresh lemons, frozen lemon concentrate, or powdered mix.

LEMON CURD is an English sauce made by mixing lemon juice with sugar, butter and eggs for a pie filling or as a spread on pastries. Look for it in the special jams section at the supermarket.

LEMON GRASS: A perennial grass with a lemony flavored stalk that can be used in cooking and flavoring. Grown and used all over the world, it is also called citronella or lemon balm.

LEMON VERBENA came to Britain from Chile in the 18th century. Though it belongs to the oregano family, the shrub has a lemony taste. It can be grown almost anywhere. The leaves put sparkle in drinks, salads and fruit dishes, anywhere lemon is called for.

LENTEN COOKERY, in the Christian religion, is food eaten during fasting in the Easter season. Some religions abstain from meat on certain days, especially Fridays, and replace meat with fish, cheese, or whole-grain breads. Some Christians also limit certain days to one full meal. Lent is the period of 40 days prior to Easter and is observed as a period of spiritual healing.

LENTIL: Lentils were probably one of the first legume seeds used as food during ancient times. Lentils originated in southwestern Asia. The seed is small and lens-shape, never eaten green, but dried and packaged. In the Old World, lentils are used in stews, in salads, and served in place of potatoes. In America, lentils are more often made into soup (see LEGUMES).

LETTUCE: There are hundreds of lettuce varieties. The first originated as a weed in southern Europe and western Asia. Lettuce came to America by way of the Caribbean. It is generally eaten raw in a salad; but can be cooked with vegetables, made into a soup, or a sauce. The most popular varieties are butterhead (also known as Bibb and Boston), romaine or cos, iceberg or crisphead, and leaf lettuce. The darker varieties contain more vitamins than the pale ones. **Nutrition facts** per ½ cup: 5 calories, zero fats and sodium, zero carbohydrates, .5g fiber (2%), .4g protein (1%), 539 IU vitamin A (11%), 5mg vitamin C (9%), 19mg calcium (2%) and .4mg iron (2%).

LIBRARY PASTE: No, it's not a food but where would the school library be without a way to repair all those books and cookbooks. If you have worn cookbooks at your house, you may want to preserve them for the next generation with the following safe and natural recipe. It also makes a nice all-around household glue.

1 cup flour
1 cup sugar
1 teaspoon alum
4 cups water

Mix all in a saucepan and cook until the mixture is clear and thick. Add several drops of wintergreen or oil of cloves for a nice smell. Store tightly covered. Apply with a paint brush.
–Virginia McNear

LICHENS are oddities. They are two plants in one–a fungus and also a green or blue algae. In many cold climates, they provide needed food. The two plants cooperate to grow on bare rocks where almost nothing else will grow. Using photosynthesis, they get food from the air. Iceland moss is used to feed arctic animals but also made into bread. *Iwatake* is the name of the "rock mushrooms" in Japan. Much scientific research is being done to find more uses for the wonderful lichen. Artistically speaking, lichen formations can be beautiful, resembling modern art paintings..

LICORICE: This herb, belonging to the pea family, is found wild in southern Europe and parts of Asia. It is now grown commercially in Spain and Italy. The roots are dried, made into an extract used to flavor beverages, candy, chewing gum, and medicines. The plant has feathery leaves and flowers of violet or blue. Like many spices, licorice was at first valued mainly for its medicinal properties. It was in remedies for cough, fever, toothache, and indigestion. Real licorice is hard to find in American products today. Most candies use anethole, an extract of the anise plant, instead of real licorice. In Europe, especially the Netherlands, they still use the real thing and specialize it licorice candies in charming shapes and varied textures. Licorice connoisseurs can discuss the subtleties of flavor the way a wine lover discusses wine. The most amazing thing about the licorice root is that it contains glycyrrhizic acid, a substance fifty times sweeter than ordinary sugar! Next time you bite into your favorite black candy, shock your friends with that bit of news.

LIMA BEANS: This native bean originated in Peru and was named after the capitol, Lima. By the time the European explorers arrive in the New World, the lima bean had spread throughout the Americas and were introduced to the new settlers by the Native Americans. Lima beans are available both fresh and dried. Fresh **varieties include the baby and the fordhook** (also called butter beans). Both are tender, white or green in color, with the fordhook the larger and plumper of the two. Fresh lima beans are available frozen and canned. Dried lima beans are white in color, generally in three sizes, small, medium, and large, and available packaged dried, or cooked and canned. Butter beans are a thumb sized, beige variety of lima, usually canned.

Lima beans take on the flavors of meat (especially smoked ham) and seasonings when cooked. Lima beans can be made into a soup, a casserole with pasta and vegetables (broccoli, onions, and tomatoes), mixed with green beans and marinated for a salad, and for the gourmet a bean soufflé will impress everyone at the dinner table. The most famous Native American recipe is succotash, limas cooked with corn. **Nutrition facts** for ½ cup frozen baby lima beans: 108 calories, 3 calories from fat, .4g total fat (1%), zero saturated fat and cholesterol, 42.7mg sodium (2%), 20.6g carbohydrates (7%), 3.5g fiber (14%), 6.2g protein (12%), 155 IU vitamin A (3%), 7mg vitamin C (11%), 29mg calcium (3%), 1.8mg iron (10%), and 371mg potassium.

GROW A LIMA BEAN PLANT IN YOUR POCKET

It's fun to do crazy things, like betting with your friends that you can grow a lima bean plant in your pocket. Of course your friends might think you are a bit odd, but once you show them how, they will be amused at your knowledge. Here's what you will need:

1 dried lima bean
1 paper towel
Water
1 small zip-type-lock plastic bag

1. Wet the paper towel, fold to fit the plastic bag.
2. Insert the paper towel in the plastic bag.
3. Place the dried lima bean on the paper towel so you can see it grow.
4. Zip up the bag.
5. Put the plastic bag containing the lima bean in your pocket.
Along with the wet towel and your body heat, the
bean will sprout in a few days.

After the lima bean sprouts its root and has two leaves,
carefully transplant it to a small pot filled with
potting soil. Place in a sunny location, keep the
soil moist, not soggy, and you'll have a nice house
plant. Plants are best watered from the bottom by setting
them in a dish of water. That way they will drink only as
much as needed.

LIMBURGER CHEESE: Made from whole milk, this semi-soft, creamy white cheese has a very robust flavor and a strong aromatic smell that makes it an acquired taste. Most kids think they would never acquire the taste for it. Try it for yourself. Some foods don't taste like their smell.

LIME: A green member of the citrus family that originated in southern Asia. The Portuguese brought it to the Caribbean in the 16th century. The small lemon-shape fruit is more sour than its sister, the lemon. The two main varieties found in America are **Persian and Key limes**. Key limes, smaller, yellow-green, and more acid than Persian, are grown in the Florida keys, and make a great pie. British sailors carried limes with them on their voyages, and received the nickname of "limeys." Lime juice is made into beverages, frozen desserts, and can be used in most recipes calling for lemons. Oil is extracted from the skin, and the rinds can be made into marmalade. Unlike lemons, limes have no seeds. Limes are interchangeable with lemons in most recipes, but you may need only half as much since limes are more acidic than lemons.

LIMEBERRY: A small shrub from India with small, red, thin skinned fruit that is eaten fresh and made into preserves.

LIMEQUAT: A hybrid citrus fruit, a cross between a key lime and a kumquat. Kumquats are one of the hardiest citrus fruits, so in 1909 Walter Tennyson Swingle made the first limequat. Limequats are of similar size, form and acidity to key lines, and could be good substitutes for limes. According to Mel Newman of Possum Pass Citrus of West Palm Beach (Florida), the few limequat trees he sells locally are bought as backyard plants. Dr. Carl Campbell, Emeritus Professor at the University of Florida (IFAS), says the limequat failed as a commercial crop because of the milky interior. It is not as clean as a lime and does not have as fine a flavor. Limequat trees grown in Florida and California are used mainly as ornamentals.–*Irene Squires*

LIMETT: (ly-METT) A tiny, dark green member of the lime family with a sharp tang, prized in cocktails. Grown mostly in Spain and India.

LINGARO: A weeping shrub of the Philippines with small red, sweet fruit that is eaten fresh and made into jelly.

LINGONBERRY: This Scandinavian tart berry is similar to the cranberry. It is used to make preserves and juice and always served with pancakes in Sweden.

LIQUEUR (li-KOOR) generally refers to liquids containing alcohol and made from grains, roots, or fruit, such as wine, brandy, rum, whiskey, gin, etc.

LITCHI NUTS (LICHEE or LYCHEE): This tropical fruit from Asia has been popular for more than 2,000 years in China. The round, rough shell is red, the inside flesh is white, with one single seed. The fruit resembles a white plum, juicy, with a slightly acid flavor, and mildly aromatic. It is available fresh in some Chinese markets, but more often is only found canned in the specialty section of major supermarkets. This delicate fruit is served as a dessert, but can also be added to a vegetable salad. Dried litchi nuts that look and taste like large raisins are used in Chinese recipes. www.thaifoods.com.

Activity
Lichee Eleganté

Spoon a few lichees over vanilla ice cream in colorful dessert bowls. For an elegant touch, use bowls with stems and add a maraschino cherry or citrus peel for garnish. Prepare an hour or so ahead and keep in the freezer until serving time. Lichees are especially nice after Oriental foods.

Lichee Compote

Not only will you enjoy the flavor of this fruit compote, it's also pretty. You can use more or less of the grapefruit sections to suit your taste. Serve in a clear glass bowl to show off the colors. Mix canned grapefruit sections, white or pink, and their juice with canned drained lichees. Add

Maraschino cherries, undrained. 1. Mix the fruits in a glass bowl. 2. Allow the flavors to blend for several hours. Lichees will turn pink. –LU

LIVER: When properly prepared, liver is delicious and nutritious. Best liver comes from young beef calves. However, lamb, pork, and poultry livers are also quite popular. In France, goose liver is made into the famous *pâtés de foie gras* spread. The Danish also make a *pâté* from pork liver with lots of spices. Liver can be cooked in a number of ways. The most famous way in America is fried liver with onions and bacon. Liver can also be boiled, broiled, braised, and deep fat fried. Once the liver is cooked it can be added to vegetables, pasta, or eggs. **Nutrition facts**, a **4 ounce serving of calves liver**: 152 calories, 46 calories from fat, 5g total fat (8%), 1.9g saturated fat (9%), 350.4mg cholesterol (117%), 70.3mg sodium (3%), 5.2g carbohydrates (2%), zero fiber, 20.3g protein (41%), 16,720 IU vitamin A (334%), 25mg vitamin C (42%), 10mg calcium (1%), 5.4mg iron (30%), and 331mg potassium. **NOTE:** Pork livers has about the same as calves liver, however, has the highest in iron (147%), and lamb liver is the highest in vitamin A (558%) and the lowest in vitamin C (8%). **Nutrition facts**, a 4 ounce serving of **chicken livers**: 142 calories, 41 calories from fat, 4.4g total fat (7%), 1.5g saturated fat (7%), 497.8mg cholesterol (166%), 89.6mg sodium (4%), 3.9g carbohydrates (1%), zero fiber, 20.4g protein (41%), 23,303 IU vitamin A (466%), 38mg vitamin C (64%), 12mg calcium (1%), 9.7mg iron (54%), and 259mg potassium.

LIVERWURST: Made from finely ground pork and pork liver, this sausage is ready to eat without cooking, but can be made into patties and fried, as well as made into a sauce with onions and tomatoes. The word *wurst* is a German word meaning "sausage." The most famous liverwurst comes from a German recipe called **Braunschweiger**, which was named after the town of Braunschweig. Liverwurst is boiled or smoked, the meat soft and pink. Some varieties have a firmer, darker meat. Like liver, it is high in iron and vitamin A.

LOBSTER: A crustacean, in the same family as shrimps and crabs, without spinal columns, but an outer skeleton shell. There are many varieties of lobsters found around the world. In American waters, the most prized is the New England lobster found in the northern Atlantic and having huge claws. The meat comes from the claws and tail. Early New England settlers found lobsters so plentiful they could be sold for a penny a piece. Dutch settlers around New Amsterdam (New York) reported catching lobsters as long as a tall man.

Continual fishing and pollutants have resulted in fewer, smaller lobsters worldwide. In the southern oceans, including the Gulf of Mexico, are rock lobsters, but they lack the large claws. Lobsters are best cooked whole, steamed, boiled, broiled, or baked. Coastal New England cooks buried lobsters in a pit covered with hot stones, right along with clams at their clambake. The meat is eaten as is, maybe dipped into a little melted butter; or the meat can be added to recipes such as stews, casseroles, chowders, and salads. **Nutrition facts**, one lobster tail: 255 calories, 24 calories from fat, 2.6g total fat (4%), .5g saturated fat (3%), 269.3mg cholesterol (90%), 839.2mg sodium (35%), zero carbohydrates and fiber, 53.3g protein (107%), 201 IU vitamin A (4%), zero vitamin C, 136mg calcium (14%), .9mg iron (5%), and 780mg potassium.

LOBSTER SAUCE: When a recipe calls for lobster sauce, what do you do? Buy it at the supermarket? No! Buy a lobster and make it yourself? No! Funny as it might sound, this Cantonese sauce contains no lobster. It's a simple sauce made with water, garlic, salted black beans, ginger root, sugar, soy sauce and thickened with cornstarch to be served with lobster, shrimp and other seafoods. Some cooks when they boil lobster will sometimes save the lobster water and use it in place of tap water.

LOGANBERRIES: Originating in California, they are named for the horticulturist James H. Logan. This berry resembles a blackberry, with the flavor like a raspberry. The red purple loganberry makes great pies, preserves, and eaten fresh. Fresh loganberries are available during the early summer, frozen and canned the year round. **Nutrition facts** per ½ cup, fresh: 40 calories, zero fats and sodium, 9.6g carbohydrates (3%), 3.6g fiber (14%), 1.1g protein (2%), 26 IU vitamin A (1%), 11mg vitamin C (19%), 19mg calcium (2%), .5mg iron (3%), and 107mg potassium.

LOLLIPOP: The name comes from the 18th century word "lolly" for "mouth." A lollipop was something to pop in one's mouth. In its first use, it did not necessarily mean a sucker on a stick but that's what it has come to mean in the United States.

LONGAN: A tree from China with small to medium, brown, sweet fruit that's eaten fresh, dried, or made into preserves. www.thai-food.com.

LOOFAH: A gourd vine from tropical Asia, sometimes called Chinese okra. It bears green cucumber-shaped-like vegetables up to 18 inches long. The very young are edible. The older ones are dried and the insides used as bath sponges. You may have one in your bathroom right now. It looks like a roll of beige mesh. Also grown in American gardens today. Arkansas gardeners jokingly called them "dishrag gourds" because they used the loofah sponges as kitchen scratch pads.

LOQUATS: A tropical fruit native to China, is now grown in California, the Gulf states, and Florida. The round, orange fruit contains several large black seeds and is juicy, with a slightly acid flavor. Is eaten fresh and made into preserves. Loquats grow on an evergreen tree of the rose family. **Nutrition facts**, per ½ cup, fresh: 34 calories, zero fats and sodium, 8.9g carbohydrates (3%), 1.3g fiber (5%), .3g protein (1%), 1,121 IU vitamin A (22%), 1mg vitamin C (1%), 12mg calcium (1%), .2mg iron (1%), and 195mg potassium.

LOVAGE: An herb, a member of the carrot family, resembles a celery plant. The green leaves have a celery flavor. The French call it "false celery." Lovage is native to southern Europe and Asia. Lovage came to American with the early colonists. All parts of the plants are used in cooking. The roots are blanched and used as celery. The roots are also candied or dried, powdered, and sold in health food stores. The leaves are used as an herb in many recipes, especially stews. The seeds are added to stews and fruit salad dressings

LOVE-IN-A-MIST: Also known as "wild winter lemon," a vine native to America with red to yellow edible fruit.

LOVI-LOVI: A small Malaya tree with bright, red, acid berries made into jelly and juice.

LUCMA: A South American tree with medium-sized oval fruit having a sweet pulp. The fruit is eaten fresh, with a taste similar to canistel or yellow sapote.

LUNCH is a light midday meal, usually consisting of soups, sandwiches, fruit and/or light sweets.

LUNCH BOXES:

PORTABLE LUNCH
by Louise Ulmer

The brown bag lunch goes to school tucked into backpacks everywhere. But once upon a time the school lunch rode in style. Lunch boxes wore the faces of celebrities such as Roy Rogers and Twiggie, Davy Crockett and Snoopy. Your dad's old lunch box gave him a certain status over the poor schmuck with the brown bag. The biggest manufacturers, **Aladdin and American Thermos,** began replacing their metal models with plastic ones in the mid-1900s when school officials complained that the metal types could cause injury. How they did this is not clear. Maybe kids fell on them or more likely, hit each other with them.

Granddad carried a black dome-topped box like his dad before him when countless lunch boxes went into the fields, factories, and mines. The first "lunch pail" was exactly that. Creative housewives sent their broods off into the world carrying empty lard or molasses pails, reused as roomy, weatherproof food containers. The pails had a lift- off top and wire handle and could carry leftovers as well as sandwiches. "Heat and eat" meant warming your pail on the pot-bellied stove in the classroom. The first lunch kits especially for kids appeared in 1920--a rectangular tin box with a leather handle from the same company--American Thermos--that since 1911 had made Dad's dome-topped models.

In the '30s, children also carried recycled biscuit (cookie) tins with lithographed flowers and nursery rhymes. Artist Robert O. Burton's Hopalong Cassidy metal lunch box by Aladdin Industries kicked off the celebrity trend in 1950. American Thermos carried it on with Roy Rogers and Dale Evans in 1953.

If you can find one of those early boxes, don't trash it. Find out its history. You may have a valuable antique. Even better, you may bring back a lot of fond memories for lunch box owners of the previous generation. For more information on lunch boxes, read *Pictorial Guide to Vinyl and Plastic Lunch Boxes*, by Larry Aikins, L-W Books, 1996, and *Lunch Box,* by Scott Bruce, Chronicle Books, 1988

LYONNAISE is a French term for dishes topped with sautéd onions. The term originated in the French city of Lyons. Basically, chopped or sliced onion are sautéd in butter until golden, or in the juices of fried meats, then served with the meat.

Mm

MABOLO: This unusual large fruit is native of the Philippines. Known as the "velvet apple" because of its reddish-brown hairs. It is eaten fresh.

MACADAMIA NUTS: The nut from Australia is also known as the "Queensland Nut," where it was always eaten by the Aborigines. It has a very hard shell with a white kernel. Kernels are eaten fresh and roasted. Macadamia nuts are now grown in many tropical regions. Hawaii now accounts for 90% of production. The nuts make fine oil and butter but the mild, coconutty taste goes too well in cookies and ice creams to have many left over for oil. Look for them in vacuum tins or jars in the grocery. A botanist, Dr. Hill, named the nuts in honor of his friend, Dr. John Macadam in 1857. The tree itself is so beautiful that it was once prized more for its ornamental beauty than for its hard-to-crack nuts. Modern machinery had solved the problem of dealing with the hard shell. **Nutrition facts** per 1/4 cup: 235 calories, 208 calories from fat, 24.7g total fat (38%), 3.7g saturated fat (19%), zero cholesterol and sodium, 4.6g carbohydrates (2%), 3.1g fiber (12%), 2.8g protein (6%), zero vitamins A and C, 23mg calcium (2%) and 8mg iron (5%).

MACARONI is a pasta made with semolina and water, dried, formed into tubes and cut into different lengths. Macaroni also comes in shells and other shapes. The name comes from the Italian word meaning "to pound," since the dough has to be rolled very thin. Makes great hot macaroni and cheese, or cool macaroni salad.

MACAROON is a small cake made with crushed almonds or almond paste, sugar, and egg whites. Other versions replace the almonds with coconut. Macaroon can also be a pudding with either almonds or coconut. Macaroons are at least as old as 791 AD when we know they were being made by Monks in Cormery. Legend says they were made in the shape of monk's navels. During the French Revolution, while hiding with citizens of Nancy, (non-see) France, two nuns who specialized in making macaroons continued to make them and the street became known as Macaroon Street. In 1952, the street was officially named after them and macaroons are still made there today. The name comes from Italian bakeries, especially in Venice.

MACE: (mays, rhymes with grace) A spice made from the outer layer of the nutmeg seed. Mace has a strong, sweet flavor, with the odor of nutmeg. Mace is not only used in baking, but adds spice to sauces, soups, meats, and vegetables. See NUTMEG.

MACÉDOINE (mah-say-dway) is a mixture of fruits made into a dessert, or a mixture of vegetables made into a salad. It comes from the French word, meaning "medley" or "mix."

MACKEREL: This salt-water fish is found in the north Atlantic Ocean from the United States to Norway, as far south as the Carolinas and Spain. Mackerel swim schools and are caught in nets. In very cold weather, the mackerel will sometimes migrate south into warmer waters. The long, slender fish averages about one foot long and weigh up to two pounds. Canned mackerel has a flavor much like tuna. Less expensive, it can be used like tuna in croquette recipes. **Nutrition facts**

per 4-ounce serving: 119 calories, 22 calories from fat, 2.3g total fat (3%), .4g saturated fat (2%), 60.1mg cholesterol (20%), 179.2mg sodium (7%), zero carbohydrates and fiber, 23g protein (46%), 824 IU vitamin A (16%), 2mg vitamin C (3%), 35mg calcium (4%), 2mg iron (11%), and 493mg potassium.

MADAGASCAR OLIVES: This tree produces 1 1/4 inch purple fruit that is edible.

MADELEINE (mada-lane) is a small cake, baked in shell-shape pans, with the taste of a butter cookie. The origin is attributed to various French chefs in the 1700s.

MADRILÉNE (madra-layne) is a clear soup made with tomato juice and served chilled. Used by the French to mean "in the manner of Madrid," perhaps because tomatoes were so popular in Spanish cookery.

MADRONO: A tropical America tree with medium size fruit. The rind is yellow, the flesh is white, the taste is slightly acidic, and eaten fresh.

MAHI-MAHI: In Hawaii and the South Pacific, this fish is known as mahi-mahi. Everywhere else it's known as dolphin, hence it wasn't a popular fish on American menus because many people thought they were "eating Flipper." Mahi- mahi, which means strong-strong in Hawaiian, is not related to the mammal dolphin. Mahi-mahi are found worldwide in most temperate waters, especially in the tropics. The taste is very delicate, sweet and moist, almost the same as swordfish, but not as dry. Mahi-mahi can be fried, grilled, broiled, braised, poached, and some eat it raw in *ceviche*. Because it is low in fat, many diners like to add Hollandaise sauce to give it a richer taste. **Nutrition facts** per 4-ounce serving: 96 calories, 8 calories from fat, .8g total fat (1%), .2g saturated fat (1%), 82.8mg cholesterol (28%), 99.8mg sodium (4%), zero carbohydrates and fiber, 21g protein (42%), 204 IU vitamin A (4%), zero vitamin C, 17mg calcium (2%), 1.3mg iron (7%), 472mg potassium.

MAIZE: A cereal grain, better known as corn. See CORN.

MALANGA: The herb from tropical America is grown mostly for its tubers. The young tender leaves can also be eaten. Both the leaves and tubers must be cooked.

MALAY APPLE: A large tree from southeast Asia, bearing large, red fruit that is sweet and watery, and eaten fresh or made into preserves. Two varieties are grown in Florida.

MALT: Malt is barley that has been processed for brewing or distilling alcoholic drinks. Malt is used in making beer, whiskey and vinegar. Added to ice cream, malt powder changes a milkshake into a "chocolate malt" or vanilla malted shake. In milk by itself, it makes a "malted milk" drink. Malt is also added to some baby foods, since its sugar is one of the easiest to digest.

MAMENY COLORADO: A large tree from Central America that produces a large reddish brown fruit that is eaten fresh, or made into ice cream and sherbert. This fruit is a member of the sapote family.

MAMMEE APPLE: From the West Indies, this tree bears 4 to 8 inch round, sweet to subacid fruit with a rough, brown skin. The fruit contains 1 to 4 large rough seeds. The fruit is eaten fresh and made into jam.

MAMMEE SAPOTE: The large tree produces egg-shaped, scruffy-skinned fruit with reddish flesh. Also known as the "marmalade tree," because the fruit is made into a marmalade type preserve. The finished preserve resembles orange peels.

MAMONCILLO: Also known as the "Spanish Lime," this large tree is native to tropical America. The medium size fruit has a green skin, whitish pulp with a subacid flavor that is eaten fresh. The Queen and Montgomery varieties are grown in the Florida Keys.

MANDARIN ORANGE: Mandarin is the family name for a group of citrus fruits which include Clementines and tangerines. Mandarin is the official language of the Chinese, from whom the small, bright, sweet oranges were first imported. The first thing you will notice about the Mandarin orange family is that they are smaller than regular oranges and second difference is how easy they are to peel. Tangerines are in the Mandarin family. Mandarin oranges are most popularly used in the canned variety today because they can go right from the can into a recipe without peeling. For eating fresh, look for the Clementine and tangerine. **Nutrition facts** per one: 106 calories, 4 calories from fat, .5g total fat (1%), zero saturated fat and cholesterol, zero sodium, 25g carbohydrates (8%), .5g fiber (2%), 1.2g protein (2%),1037 IU vitamin A (21%),77mg vitamin C (128%), 44mg calcium (4%), and .5mg iron (3%). www.sunkist.com

MANGABA: A Brazilian medium size fruit with red skin and sweet flesh that is eaten fresh.

MANGO: The mango tree originated 5000 years ago in the East Indies. India was cultivating it by 2000 BC. Portuguese traders in the 1600s carried the mango to Africa. From there it came to the Carribean in the last half of the 18th century. Mango was introduced to Hawaii by Captain John Meek. In 1833, the tree was planted in south Florida. Today it is grown in the tropical regions and some sub-tropics, such as southern Florida and California.

Called "the peach of the tropics," the distinctive acid flavor cannot be compared to any other fruit. The mango tree is related to both the cashew and the pistachio trees. The oblong green fruit turns yellow when ripe. The mango comes in other brilliant colors: purple, deep crimson and rose. The orange flesh surrounds a large oblong seed. They grow from the size of a plum to more than 5 pounds. Green mangoes are made into chutney and pickles, while ripe mango is made into jelly and jam. It is also used to flavor ice cream and other desserts. Mangoes are available fresh during the summer months, and canned the year round in supermarkets. Mango also makes a delicious nectar, sometimes combined with other fruits. **Nutrition facts** for ½ cup serving: 54 calories, zero fats and sodium, 14g carbohydrates (5%), 1.5g fiber (6%), .4g protein (1%), 3,214 IU vitamin A (64%), 23mg vitamin C (38%), 8mg calcium (1%), .1mg iron (1%), and 129mg potassium. www.thai-food.com

GROW A MANGO TREE
by Billie Jean Hepp

This tropical fruit tree will grow into a tall plant with long, glossy, dark green leaves. It's an indoor plant but it can be transplanted in southern California, south Florida, and along the southern Rio Grand river in Texas where prolonged frost doesn't occur.

You will need:1 mango seed; 1 8 inch garden pot; Potting soil;
1. Wash and dry the seed.
2. Fill the pot with potting soil.
3. Plant the seed, pointed end up, about 4 inches deep.
4. Keep the soil wet until it sprouts.
5. Place in a sunny location and water when the soil dries out.
6. As your plant grows, it will be necessary to transplant into a larger pot, as it will become root bound.

MANGOSTEEN: This soft, sweet oval shaped fruit originated in Indonesia. The pulp is eaten fresh.

MANICOTTI is a pasta tube, about the size of a roll of nickels. The tubes are boiled until tender, drained, filled with ricotta cheese, and baked with spaghetti sauce in a casserole dish. Manicotti can also be made by rolling up crepes.

MANIOC: (many ok) This tropical plant originated in South America and has been a staple food of many South and Central American tribes. Manioc is also known as cassava in the Caribbean, and when processed is used like flour for making thin bread cakes. In Central America, the sweet variety is called yuca and is boiled until tender. The shrub grows quite tall, up to nine feet in some areas. It's the tubers at the end of the roots which are used to produce flour. The sweet variety contains no poison and the roots are eaten like potatoes, with a chestnut-like flavor. Sweet manioc is available fresh or frozen, and sold as cassava or yuca in some Spanish food stores. The bitter variety tubers contain a poison related to prussic acid, but the poison is removed during processing. Tapioca is made from manioc flour. **Nutrition facts** per ½ cup serving: 142 calories, low in fats, zero sodium, 31.8g carbohydrates (11%), zero fiber, 3.7g protein (7%), zero vitamin A, 57mg vitamin C (95%), 108mg calcium (11%), 4.3mg iron (24%), and 904mg potassium.

MAPLE: There are more than a dozen maple tree species in North America. Only the sap from the sugar maple and the black maple trees are tapped to make syrup. Syrup, sugar, and maple butter are made by boiling the sap to various stages from soft to hard sugar temperatures, much like making candy.

When the Pilgrims arrived in America, it was the Native Americans who showed the colonists how to make syrup and sugar. It was used to sweeten some of their corn recipes. In February, a hole is tapped into the maple tree, a spout is inserted, and a bucket is hung to collect the sap. At first the sap flows slow, but as the days grow warmer, the sap flows more freely. To make maple butter, heat maple syrup to 232°F on a candy thermometer, cool rapidly on a dinner plate set over cracked ice to room temperature, then stir rapidly for 20 minutes. The heated syrup can also be poured on cracked ice to make a chewy candy called "sugar-on-snow" or "jack wax." To make maple sugar, heat the maple syrup to 240° F, stir immediately, than pack into molds or when cool, crumble into sugar. Maple sugar can be used as brown sugar in recipes.

MAPLE SYRUP:

THE SUGARMILL FARM

The visit to the **Sugarmill Farm in Barton, Vermont,** begins with a tour of the **Maple Museum**, a film history of sugar making, and a look at some of its unusual and changing traditions. Visitors can touch real tools used in sugaring, see a 1926 Model-T Ford used for three generations and then take a tour to the Sugarhouse and the maple orchards. The maple sap begins to flow in the spring.

The traditional sap buckets are no longer used. Today the 4,700 maple trees are connected by 25 miles of pipe that funnels the sap into the sugarhouse. Once the sap starts to flow, it comes into the sugarhouse at the rate of 25 to 30 gallons per minute. The maple trees produce about 1,200 gallons of syrup annually (it takes about 35 gallons of sap to make 1 gallon of syrup). The Augers Family finished product is sold in their store and by mail order.

A final stop is the Dairy Parlor where they feature Ben & Jerry's ice cream with their syrup in the "maple walnut" flavor. Maple syrup is not just a topping for pancakes and waffles, but is a flavoring in recipes. While Norman and Michael Auger and other members of the Auger family are busy with the operations of the farm, mother Jeanette Auger keeps things going at home with freshly cooked doughnuts dipped in maple syrup, sugar-on- snow and other maple specialties. Barton is a great place to vacation. The many lakes offer fishing, swimming, and boating and during the winter months ice skating. In the spring and summer months, try your luck hunting for wild mushrooms and herbs in the surrounding countryside. There also many farms which are open for visitors. For information on Sugarmill Farm phone 800-688-7978 or write Rt. 16 South, Box 26, Barton, VT 05822. *-- Barton Chamber of Commerce.*

VERMONT MAPLE FESTIVAL

To celebrate the maple harvest, Saint Albans has an annual maple festival every April. There are maple exhibits, a great place to sample foods made with maple syrup or maple sugar, maple cooking contests, and a pancake breakfast, served with what else but maple syrup. The festival also has antique and crafts shows, fiddler show, talent contest, a carnival and a huge parade. For more information, contact: **Vermont Maple Festival**, P.O. Box 255, Saint Albans, VT 05478 or phone (802) 524-5800.

MAPRANG: A medium sized tree from southeast Asia, bears a small oval-shaped fruit with a large seed. The subacid pulp is eaten fresh, cooked, and made into preservers.

MARASCHINO CHERRIES: This cherry is made from Royal Anns in the United States, which are bleached, pitted, soaked in sugar syrup, and re-colored red with food coloring. A touch of oil of bitter almonds is added to give that distinct taste. A green variety is also available, flavored with mint, using green food coloring. Three hundred years ago in Italy, where the cherry originated, a white cherry was soaked in a cordial called maraschino which was made from the marasca cherry. It was the French who first used sugar syrup to make them. Candied maraschino cherries are used in baked products, especially during Easter and Christmas, and candy. Maraschino cherries are added to fruit cocktails and salads, and in sweet sauces for ice cream and cake toppings. There's also a bottled syrup made from these cherries and called maraschino. That's what you use to make your own Cherry Coke and Cherry 7-Up! **Nutrition facts** per ½ cup: 146 calories, zero fats, 60.5mg sodium (3%), 37.1g carbohydrates (12%), 1.1g fiber (5%), .3g protein (1%), zero vitamins A and C, 19mg calcium (2%), and .4mg iron (2%).

MARBLE CAKE is two different colors of cake batter baked in the same pan so that the dark color streaks or swirls into the light color. The effect is achieved by putting the batters on top of each other and stirring only slightly just before baking.

MARBLED CHEESE: This cheese is delicately streaked throughout with blue or green veins (penicillium mold), usually with a strong salty flavor. It is used for desserts, salads, and salad dressings. Blue (bleu) is made with cow's milk and originated in Denmark and France. Today it is also produced in the United States. It is generally aged in limestone caves. **Roquefort**, a semi-hard cheese, originated in France, and is made with sheep's milk. The mold is produced by adding moldy bread. Other marbled cheeses include Gorgonzola from Italy and Stilton, which is ripened at least two years before being eaten.

MARGARINE is a spread to replace butter and made with hydrogenated vegetable oils without animal fats. Vitamins A and D are generally added, along with color, salt, and preservatives. Margarine has about the same calories and fat percentages as butter, but without the cholesterol. Almost any recipe calling for butter, can be acceptable with a margarine substitute. www.margarine.org

MARGARINE ISN'T JUST MARGARINE ANYMORE

The Emperor Louis Napoleon III offered a prize to anyone who could come up with a butter substitute. Butter was scarce, costly, and became rancid easily. The prize was won by Hippolyte Mège-Mouriez in 1869. He called it oleomargarine. This product was made by combining beef fat, margaric acid (a pearly fatty acid component isolated by chemist Michel Chevreaul 56 years earlier) and milk. In 1875, cottonseed oil was added to achieve a softer spread. While the product failed at first, the spread was still superior to poor butter in taste, odor and healthfulness. Finally margarine took hold in Europe. "Artificial butter," as it was called, cost about a third less than of butter.

Margarine Factories

In 1874, Mège-Mouriez's patent was purchased by the U.S. Dairy Company and the company licensed fifteen factories. These factories made both margarine oil (a liquid sold in casks) and margarine "butter," a soft spread made by churning oil with milk.

Many meatpacking houses started producing margarine as a secondary line of business, using animal fats. The market continue to grow, and many exporters shipped margarine as butter, and many retail stores replaced the margarine lids on barrels with one from a creamery. Because of this fraud, **labeling laws were enacted in 1877**. These laws stated that margarine must be labeled as oleomargarine, a name that stuck well into the twentieth century.

Because of intense competition, the dairy producers were able to convince law makers to imposed a tax on margarine and licenses for both manufacturers and retailers of margarine. By the turn of the century, yellow-colored **margarine was prohibited** in 32 states, and some states even required that margarine be colored pink. Taxes on margarine continued to rise, and non-taxed margarine could only be sold as white.

The Butter War

Interested parties in the dairy industry spread all kinds of slander and misinformation about margarine, claiming it was made in filthy factories or being made from diseased or dead dogs, and that margarine caused cancer and insanity. Slander caused almost two-thirds of the margarine companies to go out of business.

In 1915 came the birth of **hydrogenation** (hy-draw-jen-a-shun), a heating process, which meant that margarine could now stay solid at room temperature. It was still a vegetable-animal fat blend. In the late 1930s, manufacturers started to make an **all-vegetable oil** margarine using cottonseed and soybean oils and fortified it was vitamins A and D.

Color Matters

Margarine was still white. Chemists experimented with yellow oils, such as corn and mustard seed to give margarine a yellowish color to avoid taxation. It didn't work. The margarine industry designed a yellow color capsule that homemakers could use to color margarine yellow. The yellow coloring was mixed with in at home. **During World War II**, butter became scarce, and margarine became popular with homemakers, but the homemakers still had to color it with the new, improved "squeeze bag." This was a plastic bag with the color capsule inside and all the homemaker had to do was knead the bag to color the margarine. **This job went to kids** in the house. In the late 1940s, homemakers demonstrated against margarine taxation and the tax was rescinded by most states in 1940. In the 1960s and '70s, the popularity of margarine soared as health-conscious homemakers turned away from artery-clogging butter to cholesterol-free vegetable-oil spreads.

Hydrogenation Vs. New Heath Concerns

In 1994, Harvard researchers discovered that hydrogenation created **trans-fatty acids** that behave like dangerous saturated fat. Once again this raised health concerns for cholesterol and heart disease. Further, the researchers claimed these trans-fatty acids caused 30,000 U.S. deaths a year from heart disease. Because of this report, margarine sales dropped and butter sales increased. -- *National Association of Margarine Manufactures*

The Fat War Goes on

Margarine chemists are back to work on ways to improve margarine. Some European and American manufacturers now market trans-fatty-free margarine and U.S. manufacturers have introduced several kinds of low-fat spreads. However, these new spreads do not melt well and taste is inferior. Today, all-vegetable margarines have decreased the fat content. Many health associations recommend margarine instead of butter, especially the soft or liquid margarines. Other health experts argue that hydrogenating (heating) any oil makes it rancid and therefore dangerous to health. The question boils down to this. Are we safer eating butter which has cholesterol or processed margarines, which may be poisonous? What is next in the butter-margarine wars is anyone's guess? Stay tuned to the news for the latest results.

MARINADE: The liquid or sauce used to season meat by soaking before it is cooked. The soaking in juice is "to marinate." We "marinate" in a "marinade." www.lawrys.com.

MARINATE: (verb) To marinate is to soak vegetables and/or meat in a seasoned liquid mixture prior to cooking. Most marinates are associated with tough cuts of meat and used to tenderize them for an hour, overnight, or for several days. Marinating also allows absorption of flavors.

MARJORAM: An herb of the mint family with one inch long light-green oval leaves that have a sage-like flavor, but not as strong. There are different varieties of marjoram, some with milder flavors. Sweet marjoram is the most popular. Marjoram can be added to salads, vegetables, and meats. The herb came to America with the colonists, along with sage, savory, and pennyroyal. The housewife grew them in their gardens and dried the leaves in a reflector oven in front of an open fireplace then stored them in a dry place. Marjoram is available fresh and packaged dried.

MARMALADE is a preserve made with sweet or bitter citrus peels and sugar. Marmalade can also be made with peaches, quince, blueberries, and other fruits.

MARMALADE, SUNSHINE IN A JAR
by Louise Ulmer

Paddington Bear probably introduces more American children to marmalade than their parents do. Americans have been making marmalade since Colonial times, but no one loves marmalade more than the British. Breakfast is not breakfast in England without "sunshine in a jar." British marmalade may be flavored with ginger, cinnamon, lemon, or even brandy and whiskey. Any and all citrus fruits can be made into marmalade, alone or in combinations. In the jelly world, marmalade is defined as a jell which contains citrus rind. Variation can also be made by adding non-citrus fruits such as apricots. Adventurous cooks have made such concoctions as orange with carrot, lime with bell pepper, and orange with squash and ginger. The British are the world master of marmalade.

Marmalade History

History credits a British woman, **Janet Keiller**, with making the first commercial marmalade. One stormy night in 1796, a Spanish ship washed ashore in Scotland. Its cargo of Seville oranges was bought by Dundee grocer, James Keiller. When customers were in no hurry to buy the sour oranges, his wife Janet experimented with them until she made a delicious marmalade. Demand for Janet's new jam led to the founding of the James Keiller and Sons Marmalade Factory. About 1800, another Scot from Paisley went into the marmalade business. Instead of a dark, thickly shredded jelly, Roberts made a clear, thinly shredded jelly
.

Robertson's Golden Shred is still famous today. Imported British marmalades can be found alongside the popular bright yellow Smucker's types in American supermarkets. Many marmalade lovers prefer only Spanish Seville oranges for their marmalade, but Sevilles are also grown in California. Seville oranges were first planted around the city of Sacramento to provide sweet-smelling blossoms. Noticing the oranges were going to waste, Darrel Corti got permission to harvest some of the fruit. In his Capital Vintage Marmalade, it is the seeds instead of pectin, that provide the thickening for Corti Brothers Marmalade. The trees are still there. And the Corti family still makes its marmalade. Call Corti Brothers, 1-916-736-3800 www.cortibrother.com

Modern marmalades bear little resemblance to those in the Middle Ages. In those days, the Portuguese made a preserve of *marmelada* from fuzzy apple-shaped fruit, which came from a small tree that the French called *coings* and the English called quince. The English developed their own version of marmalade, substituting Seville oranges and other citrus for the quince. In 1524 England's King Henry VIII was presented a box of marmalade. By 1600 the term "marmalade eater" had come to mean "someone daintily brought up." Recipes for various marmalades appear in Martha Washington's ***Booke of Cookery*** and in the first published American cookbook, American Cooking, by Amelia Simmons, 1796. The best marmalades of all may be the ones you make yourself. See modern recipes and try it.

MARMALADE BOX: This South American tree produces 4 inch long fruit that becomes tan when ripe. It is made into a beverage.

MARROW is the fatty filling inside bones. The taste is rich and delicate, and easy to digest. In England, the bones are roasted, the marrow scooped out with long-handled spoons and eaten with salt and pepper. Marrow can also be poached, made into a soup, or into a sauce.

MARSHMALLOW is an American candy made with gelatin, sugar, corn syrup, and a flavoring such as vanilla. This mixture is whipped at high speeds for 15 minutes, poured into a pan coated with sugar and cornstarch, and allowed to set until firm. See MARSH MALLOW

MARSH MALLOW: An herb that is native to eastern Europe, a relative of the hollyhock.. It also grows wild in marshy areas from the east toward the west as far as Michigan and as far south as Arkansas. As a medicinal plant, it makes cough lozenges and syrups. A jelly-like substance come from the roots. The mucilage from the roots was once used to make a puffy confection called marshmallow, the forerunner of today's candy version. Notice the herb is spelled as two words but the candy is one word.

MARSHMALLOW CREME: Before it is processed into the pillowy candy, the sticky "cream" is bottled and sold for use in recipes or dip. Most often used in hot cocoa, cake icing, or cream fillings.

MARSH WOUNDWORT: Found in damp meadows, ditches and beside streams, marsh woundwort has an unpleasant smell with mottled pink-red to rose-purple flowers. The leaves are lance-shaped and usually lack a stalk. In the fall, it's the tubers people seek out that are eaten raw, boiled, baked, or pickled.

MARZIPAN is a candy made with almond paste, sugar, and egg whites. It can be colored, shaped into forms (fruit, animals, flowers, etc.), rolled thin for a cake covering, or molded into an infinite variety of decorative shapes to adorn other dishes. The word comes from the Italian word for a box of sweets. The most famous marzipan makers were the Ursuline nuns in France. See ALMOND.

MASK is a sauce that completely covers the food prior to serving.

MASTIC: This tree from south Florida has 1 inch yellow fruit that is eaten fresh. The very hard wood is also used to make boats and furniture.

MATASANO: Also known as the white sapote, it comes from Mexico. The large custard-like yellowish fruit is sweet and eaten fresh.

MATÉ: (mah-tay) This South American holly, thrives in the mountains of Paraguay, Argentina and Brazil. The leaves, unlike their northern holly relatives, are neither shiny or prickly. Commercial growers quickly smoke the leaves over small wood fires. The brittle remains are powdered, sacked and aged for a year or more. The powder is brewed into a tea. Maté is served in special cups and sipped through special straws which have a tiny strainer on the tip. The leaves are rich in caffeine.

MATZO refers to the Jewish unleavened bread eaten at the Passover meal. The flat cracker-like matzos are eaten in memory of the journey of the Children of Israel from slavery in Egypt (Exodus 12). Matzo meal is crumbled matzos to be used like any other bread crumbs. Matzo meal is also used to make pancakes, called *brie*. Since matzo is binding, it is not recommended for babies, the infirm or the elderly. In these cases, egg matzo is recommended, since it is easier to digest.

MAYA BREADNUT: A medium sized tree from Mexico with small orange skin fruit and a large starchy seed. The seeds are roasted and eaten.

MAYAN SPINACH: (see CHAYA).

MAYONNAISE is a cold spread made with eggs, oil, vinegar/lemon juice and seasonings. In 1756, the French defeated the British at Mahon, on the Isle of Minorca. Lacking cream for the victory dinner, the French chef used olive oil in the sauce and Duke de Richelieu named it "Mahonnaise," (native to Mahon). Hellman's is a refinement by the wife of NY deli owner Richard Hellman in 1906. *–Melissa Carter* www.bestfoods.com   www.dressings-sauces.org.

MAYPOP: A tropical American vine that produces edible fruit in the granadilla family.

MAXWELL HOUSE COFFEE: It was a practice in some parts of the country to give a boy a silver dollar, called the "freedom dollar," on his 21st birthday. It was a symbol of the boy's freedom to venture forth on his own--to pioneer.

In 1873 Joel Cheek received his freedom dollar. Leaving his family farm in Kentucky, he rafted down the Cumberland River to Nashville, Tennessee. There he got a job as a traveling salesman with a wholesale grocery firm. While on the road, Joel often thought about trying his hand at developing his own blend of coffee. He was sure he could improve on the blends he sold. Several years later and after many experiments, Joel Cheek found the blend of coffee that had fired his imagination. Cheek took his blend to the Maxwell House Hotel in Nashville and asked the management to try it on their guests. Soon the guests in the magnificent hotel were talking of the marvelous new coffee. "This Maxwell House coffee, sir," they said, "is superb!"

Many years later, Theodore Roosevelt was an honored guest at the Hermitage in Nashville, the old home of Andrew Jackson. The hostess asked Roosevelt if he would like another cup of Maxwell House coffee? "Will I have another?" he exclaimed. "Delighted! It's good to the last drop!" So a famous slogan was born. *--RSC*

McINTOSH APPLES: Medium to large apples with white flesh sometimes veined with red. Skin color may be greenish, deeply blushed with bright red. McIntosh apples are tender and slightly tart. They're good to eat out of hand or in pies or sauces.

MEAD is an ancient drink made of fermented honey and water.

MEAL has two meanings: 1. A time of day when food is served. 2. Grains, seeds, and legumes ground coarsely, such as cornmeal or oatmeal.

MEASURE (verb) in American cooking it means to use standard measuring devices, such as cups and spoons. In some countries, recipe measuring is done by weight with a scale.

MEATBALLS: Ground meat shaped into a ball prior to cooking. Meatballs can be fried, boiled, stewed, or cooked with other foods. In Italy, as well as American, spaghetti isn't spaghetti without meatballs. All cultures have their own versions.

MEAT LOAF is a mixture of ground meat and other ingredients, molded, and baked. Meat loaf can be served hot or cold. Meat loaf makes a great sandwich the next day.

MEDIEVAL FOODS: Throughout the history of the world, the story of food has been the story of feast or famine. In most of the world for most of history, it was mostly famine. The world's food supply depends upon the weather so a bad crop year can wipe out the food for a whole nation or region. Such were conditions in Europe in the early Middle Ages when an even worse catastrophe befell the population in the form of plague. In the 1300s, the Black Death killed so many people in that period that there were too few peasants to farm the land. With the farms going back to meadows and forests, wild animals multiplied and so the primary source of food became meat.

It took 200 years or more before there were enough people to till the land and raise grain enough to make it the main food. It was wheat the saved the peasant from starvation. The planting of grain in all its forms led to the cultivation of all kinds of garden vegetables. In good years, the poor had enough meat and grain to keep body and soul together. If the weather was kind and the land owners did not tax too heavily, families could survive and grow. But neither of these two things could be counted on so the peasant's life was always a daily struggle for food.

The feasts you read about could only happen to the rich and only in good years. Such feasts were recorded in detail because they were big news, great events worthy of recording for history. Remember that when you see the paintings of 16th century artists like Peter Bruegel. He painted peasants at harvest, peasants coming home from the hunt empty-handed, and a joyous peasant wedding. Bruegel is acting as the historian of his day, telling us what everyday life was life for the common people.

MEDIEVAL FEASTS
by Holly Martin

Medieval feasts were huge. At the feasts, there were always the king, queen, jesters and other noble families, rich and royal. Feasts were not possible without good harvests, so there would be speeches about the town, the crops, and how the food supply was holding up. There were also less welcome speeches about taxes. One reason to hold a feast was anytime soldiers came back from a crusade to the Holy Lands because they would bring back wonderful spices which could not be gotten anywhere else.

It was always a time for entertainment. Jesters would do that after or during the meals. Bards and storytellers kept everyone singing, dancing, and laughing. The famous "four and twenty blackbirds baked in a pie" is thought to be a stunt to make the ladies laugh when a huge pie was cut and live birds filled the air.

The castle kitchen hummed with activity. Cooks were cooking and servants served the food. The kitchens were extremely hot because food was cooked over an open fire A boy who stood by the fire and turned a roasting animal on a long pole over the fire was called a turnspit. His job was to see that the meat cooked all around and did not burn on one spot. With the incredible amounts of food needed at this enormous feasts, this kept a lot of boys working long hard hours. He'd have to roast all those whole pigs to serve with an apple in their mouths. Individual heraldic pies were served alongside the pigs and meats. Sweets and savouries were served together, not as meat courses and then dessert courses. And such courses they were! Food was highly colored with juices and seasonings.

The first course was brawn (pork), boar's head with trimmings, cygnets (young swans) capon (young roosters), pheasant, heron, and a subtlety. A subtlety is a sugar and marzipan model made by the cook in the shape of castles and animals.

The second course was served with venison, jelly (probably calve's foot) peacocks, cranes, bittern (a type of bird) fried brawn, tarts (little fruit pies) of all kinds, then a subtlety.

The third course was usually served with quinces (an apple-like fruit) egrets, curlews, partridges, quails, snipe and other small birds, large rabbits, fritters, iced eggs, and then another subtlety.

After the feast was done and everyone was finished eating and having festivities, the royals would retire to their chambers. The guests would return to their homes and the servants would work endlessly to clean up and prepare the castle for the next day's activities. (--*From a school report by Holly Martin in Grade 7*)

MINNESOTA RENAISSANCE FESTIVAL

The Renaissance actually came later than the Medieval period, but at these celebrations the two often overlap. A blend of lively entertainment, unusual foods, and costumed characters from simple peasants to ornate royalty, will transport you to the Renaissance of **16th century Europe**. Eleven stages continuously provide live comedy, music, mayhem, and storytellers with hilarious tales. See pirates as they perform, jousters on horseback in full armor, and men in kilts, throwing hammers and tossing heavy cabers. You can join in the grape stomp, press-a-wench, pumpkin bowling, be a ratcatcher, scale the Dragon's Tower wall, and search for a pot of gold. Afterwards chew on a smoked turkey leg, eat a Scotch egg (deep fried hard cooked egg covered with sausage) or savor an ostrich grilled steak. Other taste treats include chili seasoned fries, spinach pie, schnitzel fritters, shrimp and chips, English bangers (breaded sausage wrapped in egg), and sweet corn nuggets. For dessert enjoy a chocolate-filled cream puff (strawberry and caramel-filled also available) or a Greek baklava (phyllo dough filled with a nutting mixture and soaked in honey). The Minnesota Renaissance Festival is held in late summer to early fall and is one of the largest in the United States. For dates and other information, write: **Minnesota Renaissance Festival,** 1244 S. Canterburg Road #306, Shakopee, MN 55379 or phone (800) 966-8215. *--Michelle Nauertz*

DRAGON STEW
A Story
by Kellie McHugh

Beth darted up the front steps, flung the door open and plopped down on the couch. She was just in time to see the Adventurers. Beth picked up the remote and turned on the TV.

"Hey, Beth, how are things in the first grade?" asked her 14 year old brother, Michael. "Boring," replied Beth. "Nothing fun every happens to me."

"Well, I got something fun for us to do."

"What? A bicycle race? A skateboard show?"

"Nope, we're going to cook dinner," replied Michael.

"That isn't fun, that's work. What are we having anyway?"

"Dragon stew."

"DRAGON STEW?" asked Beth as Michael went into the kitchen.

Just then a loud noise came from the kitchen. Beth raced to investigate. "What was that noise?"

"I had to catch the dragon and put him in the pot. That's always the hardest part."

Beth looked at the stove and saw the shiny pot. She imagined a scaly green dragon, with wings, flaming yellow eyes and a pointed tail.

"There's a dragon in there?" quietly asked Beth.

"Of course, that's the most important ingredient in dragon stew. Beth, get some carrots, wash and peel them, and put them in the pot."

"Won't the dragon eat them?" asked Beth. She didn't want to go near the dragon.

"No, dragons don't like vegetables."

Beth stared at the pot as she cut carrots. The lid rattled and steam rose from the pot. Beth was sure the dragon was breathing as she carefully put in the carrots and slammed the lid down quickly. Michael added celery, salt, pepper, garlic, onions, and noodles.

"It's time to taste the dragon stew and see if it's done," Michael said. He stirred the stew and tasted it.

Beth was starving, but she didn't want to eat dragon stew. Michael spooned some stew into a bowl and handed it to Beth. Beth took the bowl and carefully stirred the stew. Beth closed her eyes, held her breath, and finally gulped down the first bite.

"Hey, there's no dragon in this stew," commented Beth, "it's vegetable stew. This stuff is really good.

"Do you know why?" asked Michael.

"No," answered Beth.

"Because we made it together. Fun things do happen around here."

"What was that noise I heard earlier from the kitchen?"

"That was me dragging out the stew pot from the cabinet."
Beth smiled and laughed as she hugged her brother.

MEDLAR: A member of the rose family, the medlar fruit is apple-like in appearance. Native to `Persia, it has a long history but is seldom heard of in American cooking. The Victorians favored the medlar pulp scraped out and sweetened with sugar and cream as a dessert. They even made a medlar "cheese" with eggs and butter, more like a thick sauce.

MELBA TOAST: César Ritz, the famous hotel owner, and August Escoffier became partners at the Grand Hotel in Monte Carlo. They later ran famous London hotels. César's wife, Marie Louise, complained that she could never get toast crisp enough so Chef Escoffier made it by toasting bread once, slicing it down the middle and toasting it again. He wanted to name it Toast Marie but she thought it should wait for something more advantageous to the hotel's promotion. Before long, he got a chance to show it off for Nellie Melba, the famous opera star and the one for whom he had named Peach Melba. Thus it was christened Melba Toast. See TOAST

MELONS: All melons originated in Asia and are a member of the gourd family. They include **cucumber, muskmelon** (both rough skin and smooth skin varieties), and **watermelon**. Rough skin muskmelons include **cantaloupe** and **Persian**. Smooth skin muskmelons include **casaba, crenshaw**, and **honeydew**. All melons grow on vines. See individual listings.

MELT (verb) It means to heat a solid until it becomes a liquid. Butter, cheese, and chocolate are three common things used in both solid and melted forms.

MENU is generally a list or choice of prepared recipes. In a restaurant, a menu is printed or given orally to the diner. Prior to preparing a meal, a menu is prepared listing the various courses.

MERINGUE is egg white beaten with sugar and used as a topping for pies and cakes. Can also be made into a pudding, cookies, or baked at a low temperature to make a pastry shell.

MESQUITE: The name applied to several small spiny trees or shrubs growing in the hot, dry regions of New Mexico and the Southwest United States. Native to the tropics and subtropics, especially in southwestern America, mesquite shrubs and trees produce bean pods related to legumes. The beans in the pods are a source of protein and highly nutritious with calcium, iron, potassium, and zinc. The dried beans are ground into flour which is available in many stores in the southwest. Cattle eat the leaves as forage. The flavor of the burning mesquite gives foods cooked over the mesquite heat a distinctive smoky flavor, greatly favored in barbecue cooking. Bags of mesquite chips are sold alongside the charcoal bags in some stores.

METTWURST: This German pork sausage is ground to a paste, seasoned with salt, pepper, coriander, then stuffed into a casing, cured, and smoked. It can be eaten without further cooking, and with the soft consistency makes an excellent spread for sandwiches. In Germany it is also known as **Schmierwurst**, a sausage that is smeared. **Nutrition facts** per 3 ounces: 264 calories,

211 calories from fat, 23.1g total fat (36%), 8.4g saturated fat (42%), 57mg cholesterol (19%), 915.1mg sodium (38%), 1.8g carbohydrates (1%), zero fiber and vitamin A, 18mg vitamin C (30%), 37mg calcium (4%), and 1.2mg iron (7%).

MICE:

MICE FOR DINNER
by Louise Ulmer

No, it's not a joke. Mice have always been a source of meat protein for rural tribes in Zambia, Africa. If you lived in Zambia, it might be your job to hunt for the delectable little mice for supper. Not just any mice will do and definitely not rats! Boys are trained to hunt for very specific breeds of burrowing, garden mice. Since the mice live with fifty or so to a hole, your job would not be too hard. If you happen to find a rat, you'd kill it, but certainly not to eat. Only the *mbeba* are eaten, which is only fair because the *mbeba* will eat up the people's crops if the *mbeba* are not eaten first. Since the mice eat only seeds, berries, corn, fruits and vegetables, they are nutritious and tasty. Mice are hunted during the dry season. Catching them requires tremendous skill, speed and patience. Boys learn from their fathers how to use short sticks to drive out the mice, hoping they do not mistakenly drive out dangerous wasps, scorpions, or poisonous snakes too.

The Zambian recipe for roast mice is simple. Mice are gutted, boiled in water for half an hour, then salted and dried over a low fire until crispy. While the boys have been hunting and cooking mice, the girls have been preparing the *masuku* fruit to go with their special supper of dried mice. In a country where beef costs over $100 a pound, and city people earn only about $50 a month, mice can look pretty tasty. Pound for pound, the mouse is a better bargain than beef in Zambia.

MICRO-BREWERY: All across the country micro-breweries are springing up. A micro-brewery is a brewery that produces less than 15,000 barrels for market distribution. Also a pub in a restaurant that brews only for their customers is considered a micro-brewery. These beers are handcrafted in small batches allowing a broad variety of ingredients to be used. This creates the deep, rich colors, aromas, and flavors that have made craft beers so popular. Most micro-breweries do not pasteurize their beer, hence refrigeration is a must to insure full freshness. Here is how the brewing process works: First, malted barley must be cracked to expose the starch. The cracked barley is mixed with hot water to form the mash. During mashing, natural enzymes convert into a rich, sticky, sugar called wort. Second, the sweet wort is lautered, this means it is clarified.

Third, the cleared wort is boiled for at least 90 minutes. During this time hops are added for flavor, aroma, and bitterness. Flavor builds during the boiling process, caramelization darkens the wort, and the wort is sterilized at the same time. Heavy proteins, called trub, clump together and settle to the bottom of kettle. Fourth, the wort is pumped into a whirlpool, which removes any leftover trub and other particles. Fifth, the wort is heated to 212°F and this hot wort is instantly chilled to 65°F, at which time sterile oxygen is added. Sixth, the wort is placed in the fermenter where fresh yeast is added. The yeast converts the wort sugar to alcohol and carbon dioxide. This takes three to five days. The contents is now beer. The dormant yeast settles to the bottom of the kettle and is removed. The beer is then aged for nine to eleven days, which further improves the flavor. Seventh, the beer is chilled to 35°F and is filtered to remove any fine particles of hops, trub and yeast, producing a bright, sparkling, crystal clear product. Finally, the beer is pressurized, carbonated, tested, and placed in kegs or bottled. Ales and lagers are made the same way, it all depends upon the aging. Ales are aged fourteen days, are darker, heavier and more bitter than beer. Lager is a dry and lighter beer, aged at least twenty one days, with some aged up to six months.– *Dave O'Brien*

MILK: (noun) A white, opaque liquid from the mammary glands of a female animal, which is most often from a cow or a goat in the United States; and from different animals in other countries such as sheep, camels, llamas, and zebras. Milk is a complete diet for animals of their own kind, hence, for humans, mother's milk is best for babies, since milk from other sources doesn't have the nutritive needs for the very young. After infancy, cow and other animal milk can be consumed, but some kids have lactose intolerance, which results in abdominal discomfort. This intolerance carries over to all milk products, which include cheese and ice cream.

Cow's milk is available pasteurized, homogenized, and fortified with nutriments. Pasteurized means the milk has been heated to kill harmful bacteria. In some rural areas, raw milk is available, but can be unsafe. Homogenized means that the milk has been treated to reduce the size of the milk fat so that this fat doesn't rise to the top to form cream. Fortified milk has essential nutrients added, such as vitamin D.

Today milk is available with less sodium, added potassium, and flavored with chocolate or cocoa. Milk is available with different butterfat percentages. Whole milk is 4% fat, low fat milk is 2% (also 1% and 1 1/2% is available in some markets), and skim or nonfat milk has less than .1% butterfat. Other milks include **buttermilk**, which today is cultured, not the leftover liquid from making butter (see BUTTERMILK); **acidophilus**, a form of buttermilk that has been sweeten; **evaporated** milk, where 60% of the water has been removed; **sweetened condensed** milk that is evaporated milk with added sugar; and **dried** milk, which is available as dry whole milk, dry skim milk, and dry buttermilk. **Nutrition facts** for an 8-ounce glass of **whole milk**: 139 calories, 68 calories from fat, 7.6g total fat (12%), 4.7g saturated fat (24%), 30.8mg cholesterol (10%), 111.1mg sodium (5%), 10.6g carbohydrates (4%), zero fiber, 7.5g protein (15%), 286 IU vitamin A (6%), 2mg vitamin C (4%), 271mg calcium (27%), .1mg iron (1%), and 344mg potassium.
Nutrition facts for an 8-ounce glass of **nonfat (skim) milk**: 79 calories, 4 calories from fat, .4g total fat (1%), .3g saturated fat (1%), 4.1mg cholesterol (1%), 116.8mg sodium (5%), 11g carbohydrates (4%), zero fiber, 7.7mg protein (15%), 463 IU vitamin A (9%), 2mg vitamin C (4%), 280mg calcium (28%), .1mg iron (1%), and 376mg potassium. **Nutrition facts** for an 8-ounce glass of **buttermilk**: 92 calories, 18 calories from fat, 2g total fat (3%), 1.2g saturated fat (6%), 7.9mg cholesterol (3%), 237.9mg sodium (10%), 10.9g carbohydrates (4%), zero fiber, 7.5g protein (15%), 75 IU vitamin A (1%), 2mg vitamin C (4%), 264mg calcium (26%), .1mg iron (1%), and 343mg potassium.

MILK THISTLE: Medieval nursing mothers once kept a special diet that included milk thistle. They believed that they would produce more milk, because the white veins on the leaves represented drops of the Virgin Mary's milk which had fallen when nursing baby Jesus. After removing the sharp spines from the leaves, milk thistle is not a problem to handle, since the French have eaten it for many years. Pliny, a Roman naturalist under the Caesars, recognized that it restores impaired liver function. It also supplies an antidote to the death cap mushroom, *amanita phalloides*, which kills by destroying liver cells. Milk thistle can be added to green salads and cooked as a vegetable.

MILKWEED: Native to America, it is also known as silkweed, Virginia silk, swallowort, and wild cotton. The Native Americans taught its medicinal properties to the English settlers. The name refers to the milky sap, which was, and still is occasionally, used to treat poison ivy, warts, ringworm, and other skin problems. The silk and cotton names refers to the fact that it was cultivated for the silky down from the seedpods. The down was used to stuff life jackets during World War II, as well as for stuffing for mattresses and pillows. The young shoots, flowers and seed pods may be boiled as vegetables, but not the roots, since they are poisonous.

MILLET: One of the cereal grasses, millet originated in eastern Asia more than 4,000 years ago. Now grown mostly in Asia and Africa, it is a staple for almost a third of the world's population. In the United States it is used mostly as forage and bird seed. Millet can be purchased in health food stores and makes an excellent porridge or replacement for rice in a millet pilaf. **Nutrition facts** for ½ cup serving of porridge without toppings: 143 calories, 11 calories from fat, 1.2g total fat (2%), .2g saturated fat (1%), zero cholesterol and sodium, 28.4g carbohydrates (9%), 1.6g fiber (6%), 4.2g protein (8%), zero vitamins A and C, zero calcium, .8mg iron (4%), and 74mg potassium.

MINCE (verb) is a method of cutting meat, vegetables, or fruit into very small pieces. Minced food retains some shape as compared to food that is ground.

MINCEMEAT is a mixture of cooked fruit, nuts, and spices, sometimes containing meat and/or suet, and often flavored with rum or brandy. Mincemeat can be made into a pie or added to cakes and cookies.

MINERALS:

Unfortunately, many kids grow up without the health benefits of enough minerals. While all are important, growing bodies especially need calcium, iron, magnesium, and potassium. Some minerals taken in excess can be toxic. Consult your family doctor if concerned.

Boron: Helps the body retain calcium, and magnesium, and helps to preserve bones. Best sources are fruit and vegetables.
Calcium: Builds bones, teeth, and is involved in muscle contraction and nerve function. Richest sources are dairy products (milk, cheese, yogurt, etc.), greens (collards, spinach, turnips, etc.), and calcium-fortified products (such as orange juice). Recommended minimum daily intake is 1300mg.
Chlorine which helps in the digestion of proteins, and is a stomach anti-parasitic. Salt is the main source along with fish. An excess of chlorine will destroy vitamin E.

Chromium: Helps regulate blood sugar by improving insulin function. Obtained from meat, eggs, and whole grains. Required amount has not been established, some nutritionists suggest 200mcg.

Copper: Helps the body make hemoglobin (which carries oxygen to red blood cells), iron absorption, and helps to make energy. Seafood (especially salmon), peanuts, and sunflower seeds are the best sources. Required amount has not been established; some nutritionists suggest 3mg daily. May be toxic at 10mg.

Iodine: Is necessary for normal function of the thyroid gland, healthy nails, and normal cell function. Iodine is obtained from iodized salt and dairy products. Recommended is 150mcg daily.

Iron: Essential part of hemoglobin which relays oxygen to the cells. Too little iron causes anemia, fatigue, dizziness, and reduced concentration. Best sources are liver, red meat, chicken, pumpkin seeds, beans, peas, green leafy vegetables, dried fruits, prune juice, and fortified breakfast cereals. Recommended is 15mg daily intake.

Magnesium: Aids in bone growth, regulates the function of nerves and muscles, and is thought to lower hypertension and headaches. Richest sources are tofu, raw spinach, pumpkin seeds, almonds, cashews, soybeans, bananas, apricots, beans, beet greens, high fiber cereals, oysters, and fish. Recommended 350mg daily.

Manganese: Essential for normal growth and bone formation, and is part of many enzyme systems. The best source is whole grains. Required amount has not been established; some nutritionists suggest 5mg daily.

Phosphorus: It generates energy in cells, a major component of bones and teeth, and most important, phosphorus will accelerate growth. Best sources are dairy products, fish, beans, and tofu. A sign for need is fatigue, weakness, and nervous system disorders. Recommended daily intake is 800 to 1200mg.

Potassium: If you suffer from insomnia, muscle weakness, you probably need potassium because it regulates heart beat, transfers nutrients to cells, and is even claimed to cure acne (might be a myth). Best sources are oranges, bananas, dried fruits, dried beans, peanut butter, potatoes, cocoa, yogurt, meat, and molasses. Potassium is so plentiful in a normal diet that minimum requirements have not been established. Most nutritionists recommend 3000mg daily.

Selenium: This mineral works with vitamin E to form an antioxidant complex which protects cells, helps to regulate water balance, and is known to lower fevers. Best sources are beef, chicken, turkey, seafood, tomatoes, garlic, wheat germ, and whole grains. Recommended is 70mcg. Might be toxic over 900mcg.

Sodium: The body needs some sodium daily to help in iron absorption, skin and cell growth. Sodium is naturally in most foods. Recommended is 3mg daily. Sodium is toxic to some individuals, even as little as 10mg.

Zinc: Essential for growth and wound healing; and helps the body use protein, carbohydrates, and fat. Best sources are oysters, crabmeat, beef liver, eggs, whole wheat bread, wheat germ, and zinc-fortified cereals. Recommended 15mg daily intake. Might be toxic over 150mg.

MINESTRONE is a thick Italian meatless, vegetable soup of pasta, beans, and herbs. The name means "big soup." It was a basic dish composed of whatever vegetables were in season, combined with rice or macaroni. Winter minestrone uses dried beans, peas, cabbage, etc. Summer minestrone has fresh tomatoes, beans, and garden vegetables. The best thing to happen to Europe, as far as food is concerned, were the Crusades. Thousands of Europeans walked to the Middle East and learned a whole new way of eating. They returned home with new ideas, seeds, rare spices, and an education in how and what to eat.

MINNEOLA: See TANGELO

MINT has a long history in both legend and cookery. Its uses, history, and the superstitions surrounding it all vary from culture to culture. For example, in ancient Greece, brides used to make bridal wreathes with mint. In Rome, Pliny the Elder said all students should wear mint to sharpen their minds– a kind of aromatherapy ahead of its time. The many variations of the mint family (*Mentha* genus) include water mint, peppermint, spearmint, gingermint, horsemint, red mint, and field mint. Long appreciated for its aid to digestion and fresh breath.

MINTS are small, sugary candies in the form of patties, lozenges, kisses, tablets, etc. flavored with mint.

MIRACLE FRUIT: From West Africa comes a small red, oval, sweet fruit that is eaten fresh, but more often added to made sour fruit taste sweet.

MIRAH: See AMARANTH LEAVES

MIREPOIX (meer-a-pwah) is equal parts of diced carrots, onions, and celery, sautéd in olive oil, the classic flavor base of French savoury cuisine. In American it might be sauted in butter or bacon grease and not called by any name.

MIX has two meanings: 1. (verb) To blend ingredients with a spoon, fork, beater, or blender. 2. (noun) A commercial or homemade mix of dry ingredients that eliminate steps in preparation of biscuits, pancakes, cakes, puddings, gelatins, etc.

MIZUNA: These deep green leaves with juicy, narrow, white central veins on one foot tall plants grow in a rosette form. They are very tolerant of a wide range of soil and weather conditions. The leaves which are slightly spicy, are especially good with peaches, nectarines, and flavorful cheeses. Mizuna is also good sautéd with garlic and onions or scallions (green onions) and served over rice or pasta.

MOCHA originally were coffee beans from Mocha, a city in Yemen. The area was once the center of the coffee trade. The name originally meant "superior coffee." Today the term mocha is used loosely as a flavoring of coffee and chocolate, which can be a beverage, or a flavoring for cake, pie, pudding, or ice cream sauce. .

MOISTEN (verb) means to add a liquid to dry ingredients, such as adding milk to a cake mix, where the ingredients are only slightly wet or moist.

MOJITO (mo-he-to) is called a South American julep, made with rum, lime, and fresh mint.

MOJO: (mo-HO) Latin American cuisine. a garlic vinaigrette sauce or marinade.

MOLASSES:

MOLASSES IN HISTORY

For centuries molasses was **sugar's ugly stepsister**. Refined sugar is also made from sugar cane, but molasses is produced after only one process, whereas refined sugar requires several. First the stalks are harvested, slashed, and pressed to extract the juices. The juices are then boiled down. Evaporation leaves sugar crystals and a thick dark syrup. The syrup is molasses. "First-strike" molasses, or light, table-quality syrup, is obtained during the initial evaporation. A subsequent evaporation produces "second-strike," or tangy dark, molasses. A residual "third-strike" syrup is the inky, viscous, and unpalatable "blackstrap," which is often fed to livestock or sold as a food supplement. Also a thick syrup made from maple sap is sometimes called maple molasses.

Molasses gives that old-time flavor of our forefathers to bread, cakes, doughtnuts, pies (Pennsylvania Dutch shoofly pie), and cookies (gingerbread); added to vegetables (Boston baked beans); puddings; meat sauces; and a topping for biscuits, pancakes, and waffles.

The molasses pitcher remained on the table until long after the Civil War. But by the end of the century, just as the invention of giant rolling mills made white bread cheaper, two other inventions lowered the price of sugar, quickly it replaced molasses. In 1840 a more efficient system of vacuum evaporation was invented in **New Orleans** by Norberto Rilleux. And the 1880s saw the development of the centrifuge, which could rapidly spin off sugar crystals, accelerating production while using less energy. Both the vacuum and the centrifuge are still used. Before the vacuum-centrifuge was developed, sugar-cane juice was simply boiled in open vats. Because the crystallization of sugar by this method was fairly inefficient, the molasses is said to have been extremely rich.

In many areas of the **Midwest, Appalachia,** and the **South,** fine molasses is still made this way, with antique presses and big kettles. In **England,** molasses is combined with sugar syrup and sold as "golden syrup" or treacle. Sorghum syrup, made from sorghum grain, is popular in parts of the South and Midwest. Bitter blackstrap molasses, is a tonic found in health-food stores. It cannot be used in place of sugar or regular molasses. In **Guatemala** molasses is used to pave back country roads to keep the dust down. Try walking across the road in the warm afternoon. You'll get stuck.

Molasses-making is celebrated in **Arnoldsburg, West Virginia with an early autumn festival** that attracts swarms of yellow jackets as well as hundreds of visitors eager to take home jars of fresh deep-amber molasses. The whole town turns out to help skim the vats and to sing, parade, square dance, play ball, and bake batches of sweetly fragrant old-fashioned breads, cakes, doughnuts, and cookies. *–RSC*

Molasses substitute: Use equal amounts of honey to replace the same amount of molasses. The taste will be different but the texture will be the same.

GREAT BOSTON MOLASSES FLOOD
by Louise Ulmer

One of the few times molasses ever made the headlines happened in Boston in 1919. On a mild January day about noontime, shoppers and merchants in Boston's downtown marketplace heard a blast that shook the city. Before they could imagine what it was, more than two million gallons of molasses came rolling down the cobblestone streets.

A huge tank filled to the top with molasses had burst apart, letting loose a sticky tidal wave higher than a house. The force of the blob pushed over buildings in its path until it gradually spread out, streaming down streets and alleys. The molasses flood poured over everything in its path, including horse-drawn carts, farm wagons, the few cars in town, and people.

A thick brown mass paralyzed the town. Anyone caught in it was glued in place. Molasses sucked the boots off the firefighters who tried to wash it away with hoses. Policemen who tried to rescue people got themselves stuck in the mess. It would have been funny if it hadn't taken the lives of twenty-one people and injured more than fifty others.

By late afternoon the molasses settled enough for people to attempt cleanup. Plain water wouldn't cut the syrup so firefighters used salt water to wash it down the sewers and into the harbor. It took months to clean all the sticky off that part of town. It is still remembered as one of the city's worst disasters. Next time you eat Boston Baked Beans, remember the great Molasses Flood of 1919.

MOLD has three meanings: 1. (noun) An utensil for shaping gelatins, cakes, etc. 2. (noun) Mold is a fungi that grows on food. It can be green, white, or blue, and thread-like. Some molds, such as found in blue cheese are okay, while others can be toxic. 3) (verb) To mold is to sculpt a shape as in molding dough or marzipan.

MOLE (mo-ahy): A Mexican sauce, it takes its name from the ancient Aztec word, *molli*. It meant any mix or blend, but today is more specifically a chocolate chili pepper sauce. Mole sauce also contains onions, almonds, peanuts, pumpkin seeds, sugar, anise seed, and cumin.

MOLLUSK: A shellfish, such as abalone, clams, cuttlefish, mussels, oysters, and sea snails, all with a hard shell. Land snails are also a mollusk. Crab, lobster, and shrimp, even though they have a shell are not in the mollusk family, but are in the crustacean family.

MOMBIN: A small fruit from tropical America that produces several varieties of colored, subacid fruit. The purple and red varieties are available from May to August, and the yellow variety from August to October. All are eaten fresh and made into jelly.

MONKFISH: For years American fishermen didn't take this ugly fish seriously, even though it was quite popular in Europe where it is known as "lotte." Monkfish, often referred to as the "poor man's lobster," has a mild, sweet, firm flesh, and is low in fat. Just the tail is eaten, which can weight up to 10 pounds. Today, monkfish are raised domestically and are available fresh or frozen in seafood markets. Some chefs use monkfish to extend lobster and scallops in some recipes. **Nutrition facts** for a 4-ounce serving: 86 calories, 16 calories from fat, 1.7g total fat (3%), .4g saturated fat (2%), 28.4mg cholesterol (9%), 20.4mg sodium (1%), zero carbohydrates and fiber, 16.4g protein (33%), 45 IU vitamin A (1%), 1mg vitamin C (1%), 9mg calcium (1%), .4mg iron (2%), and 454mg potassium.

MONOSODIUM GLUTAMATE (MSG) is a flavor and color enhancer for meats and vegetables. Originally made from seaweed, now is made from wheat and sugar beets. Some people are allergic to MSG which can cause headaches, dizziness, and other sensations. MSG is widely used by Chinese chefs.

MONOS PLUM: This shrub from Venezuela has round 3/4 inch yellow fruit that is eaten fresh.

MONSTERA: (see CERIMAN)

MOOSE: A member of the deer family, moose are found in the northern United States. In Europe they are called European elk. The meat can be used in any recipe calling for beef, whether it's ground for a hamburger or made into meatballs for pasta, a hind quarter roasted in a slow oven, or steaks or ribs barbecued over charcoal. Depending upon the cut, moose has less fat and higher protein than beef. **Nutrition facts** per 3 ounces: 87 calories, 6 calories from fat, .7g total fat (1%), .2g saturated fat (1%), 50.2mg cholesterol (18%), 55.3mg sodium (3%), zero carbohydrates and fiber, 18.9g protein (38%), zero vitamin A, 3mg vitamin C (5%), zero calcium, and 2.7mg iron (15%).

MOREL: While morel is a mushroom, it is not a fungi, but a member of the truffle family. It is one of the rarest of the mushrooms, seldom tasted by the average American, yet it is found growing wild in both the United States and Europe. Their brief season occurs in February in the South and in May in the North. So far, no one has been able to grow them commercially. It is a small mushroom, seldom more than six-inches tall. The hollow stem and spongy cap with irregular pits looks like a Christmas tree, though it is tan to rich brown in color. The morel is so rare that it seldom grows in the same place each year, and the entire season can be but a fortnight. Once gourmets have found this treasure, some will go on a binge like it is their last meal. Most of the mushrooms will be dried and saved for the year. Reconstituted, the morel retains it original flavor. Most morels are sautéd in butter; however, gourmet restaurants have found ways to stretch this costly mushroom in recipes.

MORNAY is a white, rich sauce made with Gruyere cheese and cream. It is credited to Chef Joseph Voiron. Probably named for Philip de Mornay, of the famous French noble family.

MORTADELLA: Originally this Italian smoked sausage was made only with pork. Mortadella was created in Bologna, and the town's name became a slang word for similar seasoned sausages, "boloney." In America, Mortadella is made with a combination of cured pork and beef, with added cubes of fat, lightly spiced, and smoked. A similar German-style sausage has added pistachios. Mortadella is available at most delicatessens and supermarkets. **Nutrition facts** per 3 ounces: 265 calories, 197 calories from fat, 21.6g total fat (33%), 8.1g saturated fat (40%), 47.6mg cholesterol (16%), 1059.7mg sodium (44%), 2.6g carbohydrates (1%), zero fiber, 13.9g protein (28%), zero vitamin A, 22mg vitamin C (37%), 15mg calcium (2%), and 1.2mg iron (7%).

MOUSSAKA (moo-sak-ka) is a recipe made with eggplant and meat in layers with sauces, cheese, and baked. The eggplant can be replaced with other vegetables such as asparagus, tomato, mushrooms, or a mixture of vegetables. Beef, lamb, and chicken can be used as the meat. Moussaka is enjoyed in many Middle Eastern countries. Authorities disagree over the origin of the dish, whether Greek or Turkish.

MOUSSE (French), pronounced "moose," is a light, spongy-like, rich dish, served either hot or chilled. Savory meat mousses can be made with fish, meat, poultry, vegetables, spices, herbs, and/or cheese, and are generally eaten with a fork. Sweet mousses are served as a dessert and made with chocolate, cheese, and/or fruit and eaten with a spoon. All mousses contain heavy cream.

MOUSSELINE (moos-aleen) (French) is similar to a mousse, but is made light and airy with the addition of whipped cream or beaten egg whites.

MOZZARELLA: (matz-a-rela) This cheese originated in Italy where it was made from ox milk. Today, most Italians make it with cow's milk, but it doesn't have quite the same flavor. In America it is made with whole milk, is white, semisoft, and mild. It is used for eating, and for cooking, especially in pizza, eggplant parmigiana, and other Italian recipes. **Nutrition facts** per 3 ounces: 271 calories, 189 calories from fat, 21g total fat (32%), 13.2 saturated fat (66%), 76mg cholesterol (25%), 353mg sodium (15%), 2.1g carbohydrates (1%), zero fiber, 18.4g protein (37%), 769 IU vitamin A (15%), zero vitamin C, 489mg calcium (49%), and .2mg iron (1%).
www.mozzco.com. www.kraft.com;

MUENSTER (MUNSTER): This cheese is made from whole milk, is semisoft, mild in flavor, and is yellow-white in color. It's a square, block cheese, with edible orange rind. It is used for both eating and cooking. Created in the 7th century by monks, the name is related to "monastery" (*monastère*). Modern Munster came from Munster in Northeast France, not Muenster in Germany. **Nutrition facts** per 3 ounces: 313 calories, 230 calories from fat, 25.6 total fat (39%), 16.3g saturated fat (81%), 81.3mg cholesterol (27%), 533.9mg sodium (22%), zero carbohydrates and fiber, 19.9g protein (40%), 953 IU vitamin A (19%), zero vitamin C, 610mg calcium (61%) and .4mg iron (2%).

MUESLI (moos-li) is the German word for mixture. Today it is a mix of cold cereals, dried fruits and nuts. Any variation is possible, even your own. A breakfast favorite, it was developed first by the Swiss nutritionists and now is popular everywhere.

MUFFINS are a small round breads, generally leavened with baking powder and/or baking soda. Muffins can also be leavened with yeast, such as an English muffin. In England, the muffin man once sold his fresh, grilled muffins on the streets, door to door. Originally muffins were leavened with eggs and yeast before soda was discovered and baking powder invented. During colonial times, refined potash and pearlash was used as a leavening with some success. The sweet, cake-like muffins are an American innovation. Variations are easy to make by adding to the basic batter.

MULL is a hot drink made with fruit juice, sugar, spices, eggs, and cider, wine, or beer.

MULBERRY: This edible berry is native to most mid-climate areas of the United States, as well as Europe and Asia. Mulberries look like a blackberry in shape and are found in white, red, and black colors. This bland tasting berry is mostly eaten raw, but also in desserts and preserves. Mulberries are not commercially cultivated. A mulberry tree in London is known to have lived 600 years. In India, mulberry leaves are used to wrap fish before cooking and the berries are made into a fruit drink. **Nutrition facts** for ½ cup: 30 calories, zero fats and sodium, 6.9g carbohydrates (2%), 1.2g fiber (5%), 1g protein (2%), zero vitamin A, 25mg vitamin C (42%), 27mg calcium (3%) and 1.3mg iron (7%).

MULLET: There are many species of mullets. In the United States they are found in the temperate waters of the Mississippi valley. They seldom grow larger than five pounds. The flesh is white, firm, and tender. Mullets have a delicate, sweet flavor. Mullets are also found in Mediterranean waters. Small mullets are best fried or broiled; the larger ones can be baked. **Nutrition facts** for 4-ounce serving: 133 calories, 41 calories from fat, 4.3g total fat (7%), 1.3g saturated fat (6%), 55.6mg cholesterol (19%), 73.7mg sodium (3%), zero carbohydrates and fiber, 22g protein (44%), 138 IU vitamin A (3%), 1mg vitamin C (2%), 46mg calcium (5%), 1.2mg iron (6%), and 405mg potassium.

MULLIGATAWNY is a peppery, clear Indian soup, seasoned with curry and pepper. Meat, chicken, rice, eggs, vegetables, and/or cream are sometimes added.

MUNG BEAN: You may not find mung beans in your grocery store under that name unless it's in the Chinese food section. Chinese and East Asian cooking use mung beans in interesting ways. It has always been animal food, but the bean can also be eaten like other legumes. The best way to see mung bean is in the cellophane noodles so popular with Asian cooking. Mung beans are also used to make bean sprouts.

MUNSTER CHEESE: See MUENSTER

MUNTINGIA: See JAMAICA CHERRY

MURLOTT: See TANGORS

MUSCADINE GRAPE: There are many varieties of this grape that originated in southeast United States. They are grown on a vine in clusters, are eaten fresh, made into wine and jelly.

MUSCAT: This grape is used for making raisins and wine, is white or black, and sweet with a musty flavor. They are grown in California, France, and Italy. The muscat is the grape used for making muscatel, a sweet, fruity, aromatic dessert wine.

MUSHROOMS: There are thousands of varieties of mushrooms, in as many shapes and sizes, and in a variety of colors from white to black. The cap may be as small as pin head or as large as a basketball. Mushrooms can be round, like most from the supermarket, cone shaped, or like a piece of coral. The outside can be smooth or pitted and most are spongy to the feel. The flavor can be anything from bland to peppery to nutty to sweet.

Many wild mushrooms have a very short life; they can be up at dawn but gone at noon. Also some mushrooms, such as the morel, have a short life after they are picked, since the cap can dissolve into fluid. Most important of all, **wild mushrooms can be dangerously poisonous** and can even cause death. Mushrooms like to grow in a dark, damp place, such as under a shade tree, in the cellar of your home, or in some deep dark cave. Commercially they are grown in special dark houses. Mushrooms are available fresh, canned, and dried. Mushrooms can be eaten raw, sautéd, made into soup, and added to stews, casseroles, and salads. **Nutrition facts** for ½ cup serving, raw; 9 calories, zero fats and sodium 1.6g carbohydrates (1%), .4g fiber (2%), .7g protein (15%), zero vitamin A, 1mg vitamin C (2%), zero calcium, .4mg iron (2%), and 130mg potassium. www.americanmushroominst.com; www.mushroomcouncil.org;

ALMOST EVERYTHING
YOU NEED TO KNOW ABOUT MUSHROOMS

Like all life, there's no beginning and no end. "Which came first the chicken or the egg?" The same can be asked for the mushroom. Which came first, the mushroom or the seed? The seed in this case is a spore.

What Is a Mushroom?

The mushroom is in a plant group called fungi (fungi is the plural word for fungus). The word doesn't sound very appetizing, does it? However, you do eat some form of fungi everyday. "No," you say! Do you eat bread? Bread rises because of yeast, and yeast is a fungus. Do you like blue cheese dressing on your salad? The blue mold in the cheese is also a fungus. Now back to what came first, the mushroom or the spore? No one can answer that question, but we do know where the spores come from today. They come from under the caps of the mushroom.

A Close Look at the Cap

The cap is the upper part of the plant. Under the cap are the gills. These gills can only be seen when the mushroom is mature. Prior to maturing, the gills are covered with a membrane called the veil. Within the cap, millions of spores are being developed. When the veil breaks and the gills of the cap open up, these spores spray out. This is known as the flush. A spore is so small, they can only be seen under a microscope. Even a million spores close together only looks like dust. One mushroom cap can produce 500 million spores in 24 hours. Yes, that's a billion spores in two days. Sounds like science fiction, doesn't it? Alien spores evading earth from outer space!

A Close Look at Spores

These spores are collected and placed in a sterile environment. They are then used to inoculate sterile grain seeds to produce a product called spawn. This spawn is similar to a seed that you would plant in the garden, only in this case, the spawn is worked into compost, and from the spawn, a mushroom will soon appear as a white pin-like-head and pushes its way up through the compost.

The collection of spores is done in a laboratory, not on the farm as you might think. The spores are so tiny that they cannot be handled by just anyone. It takes trained laboratory personnel to gather, inoculate sterile cereal grains with the spores, and incubate them. When these grains become spawn they can be sown like seed. It takes two to four weeks to make compost. This is done outdoors and then followed by indoor pasteurization (pas-chew-rize-a-shen) to kill any pests that are present in the compost. The compost is placed in trays, the spawn is sown, and peat moss is placed on top. The mushrooms you purchase at the supermarket are grown in trays, in rooms that are temperature and humidity controlled. The grower, called a farmer, orders the spawn and from the beginning of preparing the compost and planting the spawn, it takes nine to twelve weeks to harvest, and to your market.

Mushrooms are difficult to grow. Mushroom farms today are also highly technical operations, complete with computerized systems to monitor each point in production. The mushroom capital of the United States is in Kennett Square, Pennsylvania where 47% of edible mushrooms are grown. California is second, followed closely by Florida. As a cold weather crop, mushrooms were only available in the winter and springs months. Today with technological advances, mushrooms are now available the year-round. -- *Mushroom Council & the American Mushroom Institute* www.mushrooms.com

THE MUSHROOM MUSEUM

In the heart of Pennsylvania's Brandywine Valley is the Mushroom Museum at Phillips Place. The museum fully explains the history, lore and mystique of mushrooms with motion pictures, dioramas, slide presentations and exhibits where you can see shiitake, portabella, crimini and oyster mushrooms growing at all stages of their development. The gift shop offers fresh mushrooms, mushroom delicacies, mushroom gift packs and other gourmet items. For hours of admissions, write: **Mushroom Museum at Phillips Place**, 909 East U.S. Route 1, Kennett Square, PA 19348 or phone (215) 388-6082. www.mushroommuseum.com

MUSKELLUNGE: Commonly called musky in the America's Great Lakes, this fresh water fish is a member of the pike family and can weight up to forty pounds. A great fighting fish, fisherman love to catch them. The meat is lean, firm, white, and delicious. They can be fried, broiled, and baked stuffed or not. Seldom are they found in fish markets.

MUSK OX: An Arctic animal similar to a large goat or sheep, it provides meat for the Inuit people and for Arctic wolves.

MUSSEL: This shellfish is found in both fresh and saltwaters, world-wide. The shell is black, with a hairy beard, and must be harvested alive. The meat is yellow and sweet. Can be eaten raw, but better cooked. Mussels can be fried or steamed. They are used in curries, sauces, and soups. Best to purchase at a seafood market, because if they are harvested during a "red tide" period they are poisonous. **Nutrition facts** per 3 ounces: 73 calories, 28 calories from fat, 1.9g total fat (3%), .4g saturated fat (2%), 24.8mg cholesterol (8%), 243.2mg sodium (10%), 3.1g carbohydrates (1%), zero fiber, 10.2g protein (20%), 136 IU vitamin A (3%), 7mg vitamin C (12%), 22mg calcium (2%), and 3.3mg iron (18%).

MUSTARD: The yellow hot dog spread you use is a simple sauce of vinegar, ground and/or whole mustard seed, turmeric for the color, paprika, and garlic powder. It has been an American favorite since it was introduced at the 1904 World's Fair. The British, French and German countries all have their own favorite forms of mustard. Different meat dishes require different mustards to enhance their flavors. **Grey Poupon** gets its name from the owner named Grey, not from its dull color. Grey Poupon has come out with a yellow version for those who don't like gray food. **Dijon** is from the French city of the same name. You can make your own simple prepared mustard by mixing ½ teaspoon of ground mustard to 2 teaspoons of vinegar.

MUSTARD GREENS: Applies to one of several herbs which are cultivated for its leaves and seeds; a member of the cabbage family. The leaves are used as a vegetable, have a peppery flavor, and are boiled in salt water. Best when cooked with salt pork or bacon. Leaves can also be added raw to a salad. Mustard leaves are also used in mustard baths and as a poultice, long believed to relieve chest congestion. **Nutrition facts**: A ½ cup serving has: 7 calories, zero fats and sodium, zero carbohydrates, .6g fiber (2%), .8g protein (2%), 1,484 IU vitamin A (30%), 20mg vitamin C (33%), 29mg calcium (3%), .4mg iron (2%), and 99mg potassium. www.allencanning.com

MUSTARD SEED: These seeds come from the white and black mustard plants. Black seeds are smaller and sharper in taste than the white seeds. Whole seeds are used in pickling, are boiled with vegetables and fish, and are added to salads, especially good in a potato salad. The seeds are crushed into a powder and used in sauces, gravies, creamed meats and fish, vegetables, some baked goods (such as cookies), and egg dishes. The powdered mustard seed is also added with vinegar and other ingredients to make a prepared spread, and is great on hot dogs and hamburgers. The black mustard seed mentioned in the Bible was cultivated in Palestine and its use is thought to be throughout the Middle East since ancient times.

MUTTON: In the United States, true mutton is hard to find (found in Canada and England). Most mutton found in the United States does not have the taste of true mutton, and even the smell is bad. True mutton are sheep fed a special diet, slaughtered, aged for tenderness and flavor, and excess fat trimmed. One of the favorite cuts is the mutton chop, cut thick, and rolled around the kidney. The chop is best broiled or roasted, and cooked while the meat is still pink, for a juicy and tender delight. Mutton leg is roasted on the raw side for the best flavor. Mutton can also be boiled, stewed, and braised. Lamb can be substituted for mutton in recipes.

MYROBALAN: (see EMBLIC)

MYSORE RASPBERRY: A small bush from India offers a small, black, sweet berry that is eaten fresh, made into juice and ice cream.

Nn

NAAN: An Indian teardrop shaped bread.

NACHOS:(nah-choze) Small, fried tortilla chips are topped with melted cheese and/or a chili pepper sauce and placed in a hot oven or microwave for a few minutes to melt together.

NAMNAM: A small tree from southeast Asia produces 2 to 4 inch pods with subacid pulp that is eaten fresh.

NANCE: Also known as "golden spoon," this Central America tree grows small, sweet, aromatic, yellow fruit that is eaten fresh, made into beverages or into brown dye for cotton textiles.

NAPA CABBAGE: Also known as Chinese cabbage, it looks like a cross between celery and romaine lettuce. The young, inside tender leaves can be eaten fresh mixed into a salad, or any part of it can be cooked. Great in stir-fry recipes. **Nutrition facts** per 1 cup: 9 calories, zero fats, 45.5mg sodium (2%), 1.5g carbohydrates (1%), .7g fiber (3%), 1.1g protein (2%), 2100 IU vitamin A (42%), 32mg vitamin C (53%), 73mg calcium (7%), and .6mg iron (3%).

NAPKIN: Used at the table to wipe the mouth and fingers when eating food. Napkins can be made of fine linen, cotton, or paper. Napkin comes from a Latin word *mappa*. The French replaced the M with the N and napkins were called nappy until the English added the suffix kin.

NAPOLEON: A dessert originated by the French where layers of puff pastry are filled with a rich cream custard pudding. The best napoleons are made by experienced bakers, using lots of fresh butter and rich creams. The top can be sprinkled with confectioner's sugar or iced. The Napoleon pastries have nothing to do with the Emperor Napoleon. The name is a result of the French

Napolitain, meaning "in the manner of Naples." *Neopolitan* means the same thing and became the standard spelling.

NARANJILLA: (nah-ran-hell-yah) A shrub from Ecuador produces an orange skinned fruit that covers hairy green flesh and is made into juice.

NASTURTIUM: (nas-tur-shum) An herb from the Peruvian Andes used in a variety of ways. The young leaves go in salads, larger leaves in sandwiches. Blossoms combine with cheese for a spread, the unripened green seeds substitute for capers, and even a single seed added to tea is delicious. The seeds can also be pickled.

NATAL PLUM: (nay-tal plum) A shrub from South Africa that has red fruit that produces a milky juice and is eaten fresh, added to salads, made into a sauce and juice.

NATURAL FOODS:

WHAT ARE "NATURAL" FOODS?

Generally speaking, natural foods are foods that have not been processed, keeping all their natural vitamins and minerals, containing no preservatives, nor any additives of any kind, and having nothing artificial. Unless you live on a farm, grow your own fruits and vegetables, raise chicken and cattle, most foods you purchase are not natural. Even fresh fruits in the market could be waxed. That's an additive that doesn't wash off easily. Also the fruit and vegetables might have been sprayed with a pesticide; that's not natural.

Most canned foods have additives, sugar in fruit, salt in vegetables, to name just two. If the sugar was raw, that might be considered a natural ingredient, but since refined sugar is generally used, it's considered an additive. Canned fruits packed in their own juices are generally okay. Some say sea salt is natural, but that is questionable by some health experts. Some frozen vegetables contain sugar, salt or some other additive. Read the package ingredients if you want natural vegetables. When it comes to dairy products, only raw milk is natural. But it is not always legally available, because it has been found unsafe from time to time. Cereal grains used in making bread, pasta, breakfast cereals, and other products are generally made with enriched flours. Natural grains are those that retain the whole grain such as stone-ground whole-wheat, brown rice, and whole oats. Be careful. Some products made with whole grains will have additives.

Yes, there are few available natural foods found in your local supermarket, so it is up to you to pick and choose what is the healthiest. Pick fruits and vegetables high in vitamins and minerals. Eat meat that is low in fat. And avoid non-whole-grain flour products, especially baked products with lots of refined sugar. It is impossible to avoid food additives, but don't worry, a little won't hurt. And some additives, such as in enriched flour, are good for you. See ADDITIVES.

NEAPOLITAN: An English word from a French phase meaning "in the manner of Naples." The term is loosely used in culinary circles for dishes that are layered with pasta, vegetables, meats, and/or sauces. In desserts, it is generally referring to three different flavors of ice cream in layers. It could also be a cookie layer with different colors of dough. Originally in Naples, Italy, it was an antipasto salad made with fish, vegetables, olives and Italian dressing made with olive oil and wine vinegar.

NECTAR: A Greek word with two meanings. One meaning was a drink made for the gods on Mount Olympus. Second meaning, a sweet liquid from plants, such as bees gathering nectar to make honey. Have you even sucked on the end of a flower for a sweet taste? That's nectar. Today this could be any beverage made from fresh fruit (usually a thick mixture) or fruit made into wine.

NECTARINE: It has been said this fruit is a cross between a peach and plum. This is not true. It is a member of the rose family, thought to have evolved from the almond, and is one of the oldest known fruits. The skin ranges from yellow to orange and sometimes red. The flesh is sweet and juicy, can be the same color as the skin. There is also a white variety. Nectarines are best eaten fresh. Also used raw in fruit salads, ice cream, sherbet or as a garnish. Cooking destroys the flavor. If used in a pie, it is best that the pie shell be made, and just prior to serving, the raw nectarines added, either as is or in a custard sauce and top with whipped cream. **Nutrition facts** per nectarine: 67 calories, 5 calories from fat, .6g total fat (1%), zero saturated fat and cholesterol, zero sodium, 16g carbohydrates (5%), 2.2g fiber (9%), 1.3g protein (3%), 1001 IU vitamin A (20%), 7mg vitamin C (12%), 7mg calcium (1%), .2mg iron (1%), and 288mg potassium.

NESSELRODE: Nesselrode's name lends itself to several elegant dishes such as a rich soup thickened with eggs and cream, a small bird stuffed with truffles, but best known as an elegant dessert pudding. This rich pudding is made with egg yolks, cream, dried fruit, candied fruit and peel, and a liquor such as brandy or rum or a liqueur. The dish was named for Count Nesselrode, foreign minister to the Czars of Russia, at the French court in the 1800s. The primary ingredient then was chestnuts. It was an "iced pudding" created by Nesserode's chef during the Congress of Vienna in 1814.

NETTLES: Stinging nettles are gathered wild and used as a green vegetable in many parts of the world. Only the young shoots on top are used. Nettles are also used to make nettle and ginger beer. The Scottish version of nettle soup is nettle *kail*, served on Shrove Tuesday or to celebrate the arrival of spring. *Kail* is their word for kale or any green soup. In Asia, so the story goes, a Tibetan poet and saint, lived on nettle soup for years until he turned green. What happened after that, we aren't told. Presumably, he ate something else then.

NEUFCHATEL CHEESE: (nuff-shah-tell) A soft white mild cheese made with whole or skim milk for eating. You'll find it in the dairy case beside the Philadelphia Cream Cheese.

NEWBURG: A sauce made with cream, egg yolks, and wine or brandy used with seafood, generally lobster and shrimps. Created by Mr. Wenberg, a former head chef at Delmonico's restaurant in New York City. The letters were transposed from Wenberg to Newburg.

NEW ZEALAND SPINACH: A small herb from New Zealand with edible leaves. It was discovered for Europeans by Captain Cook in 1770.

NIGHT-BLOOMING CERUS: This shrub from South America produces a pod with tasteless white pulp flecked with black seeds. However, it's pleasant chilled. The nocturnal flowers are quite spectacular.

NISPERO: (nees-pay-ro) Native of southern Mexico, the tree bears a large brown fruit with sweet tan flesh that is eaten fresh and made into sherbet.

NITRATES: See SODIUM

NOODLE: A generally narrow dough strip cooked in soup. The word can also apply to all forms of pasta, Western and Oriental. In the West, noodles are almost always wheat based. In Asia, noodles are more often made with rice flour. Oriental cooks also make noodles of vegetable starch, potato starch, and cornstarch. *Yang fen* is seaweed noodles similar to mung bean vermicelli but thinner. See PASTA.

NOODLE EATING TIPS

I eat my spaghetti
without any sauce,
just noodles alone you see.
'Cause I eat with my fingers
not with a fork.
Sauce is too messy for me.

I pick up a noodle
swirl it twice
then pull it right in with my lips.
This is just one
from a long list of many,
noooooooodle eating tips.
--Elizabeth Giles

NOODLES, HOMEMADE: Anyone can make egg noodles. All you need are egg yolks, flour, and salt. Break 2 or 3 eggs yolks into a large bowl. Beat until fluffy. Add 1/4 teaspoon salt. Beat flour into the egg yolk until it forms a stiff dough. Using extra flour to prevent sticking. Roll out the dough flat on a bread board. Cut into strips about an inch wide. Drop strips into a meat broth or salted boiling water until they are cooked through, about 5 to 10 minutes. Take out to test for doneness.

NOUGAT: (noo gat or nugget) A candy made with nuts (most often almonds), sugar, and egg whites that originated in the Moorish region of northwest Africa. Nougat candy can be hard or soft, chewy or brittle. Nougats are quite popular at Christmas time. See TURRON

NOUVELLE CUISINE: (noo-vel qwiz-ine) Modern style of cookery avoiding heaviness and emphasizing pleasing presentation. It's the opposite of rich, grand gourmet cooking.

NUT: Generally a nut is a single seed enclosed in a shell, such as walnuts, pecans, almonds, and hazelnuts. Shells may be either hard and soft, depending upon the variety, as in the case of almonds and pecans. Not all nuts are nuts, many are legumes, such as the peanut. Other nuts grow inside pods. A good example is the Brazil nut, whose pod will have a dozen to two dozen nuts. Some nuts can be eaten raw; others are dried prior to eating, and some must be roasted. Nuts also have a variety of uses. They may be ground to make a beverage like coffee, substituted for flour, and added to butter to make a butter-nut spread. See individual names for more information.

NUT BUTTER: A spread where nuts are ground into a paste, generally with a little salt. Peanut butter is one of the most popular spreads, but almonds and cashews make great butters as well. Ground nuts can also be combined with butter, sometimes with a little honey and/or spices. Nut butters are high in fats and a good source for protein.

NUTMEG: A native tree of the East Indies and Indonesia, now grown in the West Indies and tropical America. The nutmeg is covered with a hard shell that is split open. The nutmeg is removed, and the outer layer is dried and made into mace. The remaining seed is the nutmeg, a sweet spice used in baking, added to vegetables such as spinach, cream sauces, fruit desserts, and topping for eggnog. For the best flavor, purchase whole nutmegs, and grate as needed. Nutmeg is also available ground. The search for the nutmeg touched off most of the great sea voyages in the 1500s, since Columbus was only one of the great explorers searching for a way to the Spice Islands. Nutmeg was thought to be a cure for the plagues that ravaged Europe from time to time. Its history could fill more than one book. One of the most recent is *NATHANIEL'S NUTMEG, The True and Incredible Adventures of the Spice Trader Who Changed the Course of History* by Giles Milton, published by Farrar, Straus and Giroux, NY, 2000.

NUTRITION:

LIKE MONEY IN THE BANK
by Mary Eddy Stewart

Snack cakes, fruit treats, donuts, and chips were stacked haphazardly in the boy's shopping cart. I watch as he made progress toward the cashier in the supermarket. The cashier added up the price of the items. "Sorry," the cashier said. "Your bill is $18.75. I only count $15.10 here. Can you decide what you don't need?" That's easy, I thought. What he needs is his fifteen dollars back and a fresh start with an empty shopping cart.

341

Food is Like Money

Eating right is like putting money into the bank for a CD player or the gifts you want to buy next Christmas. Banking your money means it will be there when you need it. The food we put into our body now not only makes for a healthy, happy future but also pays rich dividends immediately. Did you know what you eat helps you to avoid the common cold, cancer, and mental illness? It helps you see clearly, heal quickly, and develop healthy skin and bones? How about the energy you need to play, dance, and concentrate on your studies or do your job well? The food you eat--or don't eat--plays a big role in the story of your life.

Food on Deposit Goes to Work Like Money on Deposit

Remember what you were taught about digestion in school? Your mouth begins to water at the sight of the red delicious apple you chose for your snack. You take a bite and chew slowly. The sweet juice mixes with the saliva in your mouth and digestion begins. You swallow and the partially digested apples travels to your stomach where more digestion occurs. From there it goes to the small intestine. Here it is broken down into nutrients (vitamins and minerals) that pass through the intestine wall and into the blood vessels. You know what happens next!

Your Body is Food Bank

- The blood takes the nutrients to every part of your body.
- It feeds the trillions of cells that make up your brain and muscles, your teeth and toe nails.
- And this allows these cells to do what they were intended to do: grow, reproduce new cells and repair the damaged ones. The apple nutrients that haven't passed into the blood steam from the small intestine travel into the large intestine where, again, some pass into the blood to feed your cells. The material left from your apple may be fiber that doesn't dissolve and so passes out of your body as waste.

No Deposit - No Return

The food which filled the boy's cart in the supermarket isn't called "junk" food for nothing. Such food
- is processed with lots of salt and sodium, fat and sugar;
- escapes into the blood steam, to line the walls of the blood vessels with a fatty substance,
- increases the blood pressure flow through the veins and arteries,
- and trick us into thinking we've had plenty to eat.

In reality our cells are crying out, "Feed me...I'm starving for nutrients!"

Rich Rewards

The nutrients our body needs daily don't exactly read like a grocery shopping list.

- Carbohydrates for energy,
- Proteins to build and repair cells,
- Vitamins for brain power, a healthy nervous system etc.,
- Minerals for bones, teeth and overall good health,
- enough fat to carry four important vitamins throughout the body,
- and lots of water.

Ninety percent of the blood is water, so it is this that carries food to the cells and waste from the body. Water is what keeps our bodies the right temperature. Luckily, others have done the hard work of figuring out which foods contain necessary nutrients. We have only to look at the Food Guide Pyramid to see what we need to eat each day.

MORE NUTRIMENTS FOR BETTER HEALTH

Are you receiving the most vitamins and minerals from your fruit and vegetables? Here are a few tips for keeping most of the nutriments intact:

1. **Leave edible skins on** fruits and vegetables. Most vitamins and minerals are found in the outer layers and the area just below the skin, not the center.
2. Cook vegetables and fruits in a small amount of water or even better, none at all. **Steam or microwave** them instead of boiling. Also avoid soaking them as you wash, since some vitamins dissolve in water.
3. Cut vegetables into **larger pieces**. With larger pieces, fewer surfaces are exposed, and fewer vitamins are lost.
4. **Eat vegetables and fruit raw.** If you must cook them, do so quickly, since B and C vitamins are easily destroyed by heat.
5. **Eat fresh produce soon** rather than keeping it in storage for days.

WHERE DOES IT ALL FIT
In the Five Major Food Groups?

"Okay, I know I need to eat a variety of foods, but what about my favorite foods?" This often-asked question is asked when the five major food groups are examined.

Dried Beans or Meat?

You need both dried beans and meat for protein, since each has something the other doesn't have. Dried beans have fiber, meat doesn't. Iron in meat is better absorbed in the body than dried beans. However, eating meat with dried beans, your body will absorb more iron found in dried beans. An important vitamin B-12 is not found in dried beans, only in meat. See, it's a toss up.

What about Nuts?

Like dried beans, nuts have no cholesterol, but they are higher in fat and calories than meat. Two tablespoons of peanut butter has 16 grams of fat, as compared to 3 grams of fat in an one ounce serving of lean pork. And that peanut butter, again compared with the meat, has 190 calories to the 60 calories in the meat. The question is, how much peanut butter do you eat as compared to pork? Most people eat about two tablespoons of peanut butter on a sandwich, as compared to five to seven ounces of meat, which makes calories in meat higher than the peanut butter, with about the same amount of fat in both. If you compared the peanut butter with halibut, then the fish would be the best choice, but if you compared peanut butter with an egg, stick with the peanut butter. It's a matter of comparing something with something else. It's your choice.

I like Ice Cream!

All dairy products provide a good source of calcium. If ice cream was nothing but frozen flavored milk, it would be okay. But ice cream has added sugar and is higher in fat than a glass of milk. Let's compare: One-half cup of ice cream has about the same amount of calcium as 1/3 cup of milk. However, the same amount of frozen yogurt has the same amount at the same size of milk. So, if you want a frozen dessert, yogurt is a better choice. If you want ice cream, that's okay, just cut out other sweets and fats that day.

Where Do Tacos Fit?

Take a moment and figure it out. Tacos contain both meat and vegetables. And the tortilla shell belongs to the bread group, and when topped with cheese, you're in the dairy group as well. The only negative is that the taco shells are fried, which means added fat. By and large, a taco covers four bases. Don't skip on the lettuce and tomatoes. The same can be said for spaghetti with meatballs and tomato sauce. Pizzas topped with cheese, tomato sauce, and meat have supplied you in four of the five groups. So eat some fruit for dessert and you're covered.

What's the Bottom Line?

Sugar is a carbohydrate, as are starches. The body needs carbohydrates to supply energy. Fats also provide your body with energy, and fats carry fat-soluble vitamins to your cells. Calories are not nutriments. Calories are just a measure of heat needed for energy. Even if you are sitting still, your body needs energy calories for your digestion, heartbeat, and breathing. Calories in excess of what your body needs are stored in the body as fat. Water is not covered with the Food Guide Pyramid, and is often called the "forgotten nutrient." Water is needed to replace body water lost in urine and sweat. Water helps to transport nutrients, to remove wastes, and to regulate your body temperature. You need more than forty different nutrients for good health - protein, fat, carbohydrates, water, vitamins and minerals. A variety of foods can provide all these nutrients. No one food supples all you need. Eat a variety of foods for good health.

Oo

OATS: A grain from one of the cereal grasses that has a hard outer shell with a soft interior. Oats grow best in a cool, damp climate. That is why they grow so well in Ireland and Scotland. The oats are kiln-dried to help loosen the hull that also develops the oats nutty flavor. The grains are cleaned and the hulls removed. **Oat bran** is made from the hulls. Packaged oats found in the supermarket are the grains with the hulls removed and flattened between heated rollers. Flattened oats, also called **rolled oats**, are made into hot cereal and added to baking recipes. Some oat grains are steel cut into granules rather than flattened. **Steel cut oats** take longer to cook than the rolled variety. Steel cut oats are not used in baking unless precooked.

Hulled oats are also ground into flour and called oatmeal. The term "oatmeal" is loosely used for the hot cereal, but this is incorrect. Oats are not "mealy." Bread made from oatmeal flour doesn't have the gluten to make the bread rise, hence, oatmeal must be mixed with wheat flour to make a satisfactory loaf of bread. Rolled oats can be added to breads, cookies, and some cakes. Oats contain fat, proteins and minerals, and are considered an energy food for active people. Oats are a good source for thiamine, with some riboflavin and vitamin E. In the olden days, oats were called gruel. **Nutrition facts** per ½ cup cooked: 73 calories, 10 calories from fat, 1.2g total fat(2%), .2g saturated fat (1%), zero cholesterol and sodium, 12.6g carbohydrates (4%), 2g fiber (8%), 3g protein (6%), zero vitamins A and C, 9mg calcium (1%) and .8mg iron (4%).

GRUEL AND UNUSUAL PUNISHMENT
by Louise Ulmer

One morning I woke with the feeling I just couldn't face another day of school. Mom was already gone to work but Dad was home. "I know what will fix you right up," he said. "I'll make you some of my special oatmeal."

That sounded good. When he set the bowl in front of me, I began to have doubts. The spoon stood straight up in it. When I lifted the spoon, the whole thing came up with it in a beige blob.

"Dad!" I said, holding the blob up for him to see.

"How much sugar do you want?" he asked, looking at the oatmeal-on-a-stick as if that were normal. "Here's milk, but I wish we had real cream."

I put the blob back in its bowl and began to work sugar into it. Milk was something else. It didn't soak in but kind of ran around the solid oatmeal lump. Two raisins stared up at me. I figured it was as good a time as any to try a bit. It didn't taste bad, once you got it off the spoon.

Dad said, "Good, eh? Did you know that oatmeal in the olden days was called gruel?"

"As in "gruel and unusual punishment'?" I asked, trying to smile. Now I knew what they meant when someone said he had a lump in his throat.

"I'm feeling better already, Dad," I said. "I think I better hurry to school now." When he wasn't looking I let the disposal have the rest of my gruel.

The following week Mom offered me oatmeal for breakfast. "I don't think I like oatmeal, " I said. "Dad made it for me last week."

"Oh," she said. "Don't judge by the stuff your father makes. Let me give you some real oatmeal."

When she set the steaming bowl in front of me, it looked like the oatmeal I remembered. The spoon lay on the side. You could see each individual flake. The milk stirred in bathed each little fluffy oat. You could pick it up one spoon at a time.

Mom laughed. "Your father doesn't make oatmeal; he makes wallpaper paste. I'm surprised you lived to tell about it. Did he slice it or give it to you in a glop?"

We had a good laugh at poor ole Dad's expense.

"He makes it the way his mother made it, and I make it the way my mother made it. So be careful what you say or could insult someone's whole family."

Mom took the time to explain it all came down to two different cooking methods. For fluffy oatmeal, you start with boiling water and then put the oatmeal in, and stir only a few times. After about three minutes, turn off the heat and cover the pot to steam about five minutes. That way the oatmeal never overcooks. Mom showed me right on the oats box the recipes for two kinds. One they call "creamier" and the other "chewier."

The one called creamy is the one you start out by pouring the oats in cold water and bringing it all to a boil. That one you stir constantly, which makes the flakes smaller. I think Dad must have got carried away because he didn't have any flakes left. I also noticed on the oatmeal box that there are instructions for doing it in the microwave - one for creamy and one for chewy. That way all kids can make their own oatmeal one way or the other.

My advice is to use the microwave and avoid gruel and unusual punishment. Give it a try and prepare both kinds and give each a taste test.

OCA (oh-cah): In the Andes region of South America, oca is second only to potatoes as a root vegetable. Oco tolerates poor soil and high altitudes. Its spinach-like leaves, can be eaten as well as the roots. The roots look like short wrinkled carrots. They range in color from white to red and vary in flavor from slightly acid to sweet-enough-to-pass-as-a-fruit. Oca plants were introduced to Europe but didn't flourish there. Oca does flourish in New Zealand. Oca can be prepared any way the potato can. In Mexico they like it raw and seasoned hot.

OCTOPUS: While the octopus can grow to several hundred pounds, the ones found in seafood market will range from one to three pounds. The flesh, raw or cooked, is tough and tasteless. The Japanese like them, as do some Greeks and Portuguese, but the rest of the world seldom adds them to their menus. **Nutrition facts** for 3 ounces: 68 calories, 9 calories from fat, .9g total fat (2%), .2g saturated fat (1%), 40.8mg cholesterol (27%), 195.6mg sodium (8%), zero carbohydrates and fiber, 12.7g protein (25%), 127 IU vitamin A (3%), 5mg vitamin C (7%), 45mg calcium (5%), and 5mg iron (28%)

OFFAL: In butchering, offal is the edible internal organs of an animal. White offal includes brain, bone marrow, stomach, and head. Red offal is the heart, liver, tongue, lungs, spleen and kidneys. Regarded an inferior meats, they are nevertheless eaten in various ways. In America, red offal is often found in potted meat spreads.

OIL: Food cooking oils that are made from plants include: almonds, canola, coconuts, cottonseed, corn, olives, peanuts, poppy seed, rapeseeds, safflower seed, sesame seed, soybeans, sunflower seed, walnuts, and others. Oils from animals are better known as fats. Milk contains butter fats. Oils and fats used in cooking help to prevent food from sticking to pans. More importantly they add flavor to food. Biscuits and cakes are made tender by oils and pie crusts become flaky. New lower fat and nonfat oils are also available.

OIL PALM: A tree from Africa that produces large bunches of reddish to blackish fruit with clusters up to 200 fruits. This very important crop in the tropics is the source for palm oil that is extracted from the seeds. Sap is also made into wine and is rich in vitamin A.

OITI: A Brazilian tree that produces three-inch-long, yellow, edible fruit. A medicinal oil is made from the large seed.

OKARI NUT: The four inch fruit has a 3/4-inch kernel that is edible.

OKRA: This green seed pod vegetable is popular in southern recipes originated in tropical Africa. A member of the mallow family, okra is best when young and very tender. Old or large okra, has seeds that can be ground and used as a coffee substitute. When cooked by itself, the interior of the pod is gooey and slimy. When sliced and added to stews, such as gumbo, it is used as a thickener. Okra is available fresh the year round in the southern states, in the north during the summer months. It is also available canned, pickled and frozen. Okra can be boiled, or breaded and fried. Okra is most prized in all African continental cooking for its thickening properties. In Africa, even the slime is appreciated. There is a saying that wherever okra grows, Africans have been there. It is known to have reached Brazil by 1658. Okra is an African name, and so is **gumbo**, the other name for okra. It's okra, or gumbo, which gives the name to the Creole and Cajun "gumbo" soups. Okra has a fair source for vitamins A and C and is low in calories. Usually pods are green but there are red varieties. **Nutrition facts** for ½ cup: 19 calories, zero fats and sodium, 3.8g carbohydrates (1%), 1.3g fiber (2%), 330 IU vitamin A (7%), 11mg vitamin C (18%), 41mg calcium (4%), and .4mg iron (2%).

OLD WORLD GRAPE: Originating in Europe, this vine produces bunches of grapes that are eaten fresh, made into preserves, and wine.

OLEASTER: Known as the ancestor of the olive, the Mediterranean fruit is about the size of an olive but after drying looks more like dates.

OLIVES: This evergreen tree originated in the ancient Middle East. Since fat is essential in every diet, it is doubtful man could have lived in the arid areas where dairy products were not available, if it were not for the olive and the oil obtained from it. It takes eight years for an olive tree to produce, hence, having an olive tree during ancient times was a sign of wealth. In fact, it was a crime to cut down an olive tree, partly because it was also a sign of peace. There are many references to olives in the Bible, the most famous is Psalm 23, verse 5: "Thou preparest a table before me in the presence of mine enemies; thou anointest my head with oil; my cup runneth over." The olive tree was bought to Mexico in the 17th century by missionaries, who also brought them to California where today they flourish.

Fresh olives cannot be eaten because they are very bitter. This bitterness is removed during a long process of soaking in lye, washing, then soaking in a salt solution. All this takes up to a year. The green olives are also fermented by adding sugar to the solution from time to time. Ripe olives are sometimes just aged in a salt solution which removes some of the bitter taste and leaves them wrinkled.

GLOSSARY OF OLIVES

Olives comes in all shapes, sizes, and colors. They come whole with the seeds, pitted, cracked, and stuffed with pimientos, garlic, onions, almonds, hazelnuts, hot peppers and anchovies.

■ **Calabrest**: A green, medium sized Italian olive with a lively flavor.

■ **Cerignola**: One of the larger Italian olives, with a gentle flavor, less salty than most varieties. They are also called "Christmas" olives because during the holidays these olives are dyed red and green.

■ **Green Cracked**: The olive is cracked slightly to allow the marinade to penetrate the flesh. You can purchase green olives, crack them yourself and place in a marinade of your choice, such as an Italian salad dressing.

■ **Kalamata**: from Greece come black olives that are brine and vinegar cured. They have a strong flavor, and work well in recipes, especially salads.

■ **Ligurian**: A brownish-black (sometimes gray) olive from Northern Italy. These salt-brine cured olives have a lively flavor.

■ **Moroccan**: These wrinkled black olives are dry-cured in salt, rubbed with oil and have a slightly bitter flavor, which mellows out with age.

■ **Naflion**: A Greek green, cracked, mild olive that has been brine-cured and then packed in olive oil.

■ **Nicoise**: From the French town of Nice comes a small, brownish-black brine-cured olive. They are the key ingredient in a salad made with tuna, potatoes and green beans.

■ **Picholine**: A mild green olive from France that is cured in salt brine and has a rich delicate flavor. These high priced olives are best eaten out of hand or you can marinated them for added flavor.

■ **Provencal**: Same as picholine olives, except they are marinated with herbs.

OLIVE OIL: The longer the olive is left on the tree, the more oil can be pressed from it. The oil is washed and refined. The best oil is golden-yellow. Olive oils that are green in color are inferior. There are many variations of olive oil from extra virgin to extra light. The extra light is mild tasting, while the extra virgin has a more distinctive flavor. Olive oil is used in salad dressings, low heat sautéing, and can replace any vegetable oil in baking, though you'd want to use one with no taste to speak of. Olive oil should be stored away from light and heat, since both will make it fade. Olive oil should not be stored in the refrigerator because it will separate. **Nutrition facts** per tablespoon: 119 calories, 119 calories from fat, 13.5g total fat (21%), 1.8g saturated fat (9%), zero cholesterol, sodium, carbohydrates, fiber, protein, vitamins A and C, calcium and iron.

OLOSAPO: From Central America comes a tree that produces small to medium sized, elliptical, (oval) edible fruit. The skin is rough; the flesh is soft.

OMELET: (ohm-let) A combination of eggs, water or milk, and seasonings, beaten, and cooked in a skillet either stove top or in the oven. Puffy omelets are made by separating the eggs from the whites, the whites beaten separately and folded into the mixture. Omelets can also be filled with an infinite variety of meats, cheese, and/or vegetables. Dessert omelets are filled with nuts, fruit and/or cream cheese.

ONE GREEN WORLD is an organization dedicated to introducing to the United States fruit trees, shrubs, and vines found in Russia and Eastern Europe. Founded by Jim Gilbert in Molalla, Oregon, the purpose is to share horticultural information in the interest of better food for all. Write to One Green World, 28696 S. Cramer Rd, Molalla, OR 97038. Free catalog available. www.onegreenworld.com

ONIONS: A member of the lily family, wild onions are found worldwide and have been eaten since prehistoric times. Most of the cultivated onions known today originated in western Asia. In the onion family are leeks, garlic, chives, and shallots, and all have variations. The pungent smell and taste comes from the plant's oil that is rich in sulphur. Onions grown in a cooler climate are hotter than the milder, sweet varieties grown in a warmer climate. There are many folk medical uses for onions. It is said to stop the pain of a bee sting by applying a slice of onion for a minute or two. Onions also are claimed to cure colds, earaches, lower fever, laryngitis, and warts. To avoid tears, onions can be peeled under water, but when it comes to chopping and slicing, nothing can prevent tears with the hotter varieties. Onions can be eaten raw, boiled, fried, baked, and braised. Onions are low in calories with some vitamin C. The top green parts have some vitamin A. **Nutrition facts** per ½ cup: 15 calories, zero fats, 296.8mg sodium (12%), 3.2g carbohydrates (1%),1g fiber (4%), .7g protein (1%), zero vitamin A, 3mg vitamin C (6%), 36mg calcium (4%), and .1mg iron (1%). www.onions-usa.org; www.web-tec.com/vow.jtm; www.bmi.net/onions

Onion substitute: 1 teaspoon onion powder or 1 Tablespoon of dried minced onions can replace 1 small onion.

WHY DO ONIONS MAKE US CRY?

When onions are cut, the cells are crushed and air goes to work with the enzymes in the onion to release something called allicin. Sounds like a pretty girl's name, doesn't it? You can remember it that way but that's the stuff that irritates your eyes to make you weep. To cut down on the potency of the allicin, you can cut the onion under water, but that also washes away the onion bits. Someone thought of chilling the onion before cutting it. That works better since cold reduces the allicin's ability to travel in the air. Sweet onions tend to cause fewer tears, but don't count on it. One thing is certain, lemon juice will take the smell out of your hands when you are through cutting and crying.

Onion types: It's impossible to pin down all the varieties of onions. Here are a few common types you'll see in the market.
Spanish: Large, on the milder side, yellow skinned.
Bermuda: Varieties include red, white and yellow.
Vidalia: Large, sweet, hybrid named for the Georgia town where it grows.
Walla Walla: Large, named for the Washington town where it grows. It came from Corsica in the 20th century.
Maui: Named for the Hawaiian island whose volcanic soil give it sweetness.

OPOSSUM: This small animal found in the United States is about the size of a cat. Some cultures eat it as food, usually roasted. It has a taste similar to pork. American settlers ate it, along with other wild game such as raccoon and squirrel.

ORACHE: An herb from Asia is known by many names. It is prepared like spinach. The arrow-shaped, crimped leaves range from a yellow green to a dark red, and the plant grows up to six feet tall. It is grown as a potherb in France where it is known as French spinach. In England it is called "fat hen."

ORANGES: This evergreen tree originated in China. There are three basic varieties: sweet, loose-skinned, and sour. The sweet orange is best to eat of which there are many varieties, the Valencia and the seedless navel the most popular. Loose-skin oranges are better known as tangerines with the mandarins and temples the most popular. The sour oranges are used mostly for cooking, especially marmalade. Oranges came with Columbus to Haiti in 1492.

Oranges first came to Florida by accident. When Ponce de Leon was searching for the Fountain of Youth in Saint Augustine, Florida, he and his men were eating oranges and dropped the seeds. The seeds sprouted and produced sour orange trees, so the story goes. The Seminoles ate these oranges with wild honey. Oranges are mostly eaten raw or made into juice, but are also found in many meat, poultry, seafood, and vegetable recipes. Oranges also cooked with rice and other grains, made into puddings, cakes, pies, and sherbets. The California Orange industry began originally in 1793 when missionaries began to grow oranges in lower California, now part of Mexico. Texas grows its share of oranges too. Other great orange importing countries are Australia, Spain, and Israel. Oranges are an excellent source of vitamin C, with some vitamin A. **Nutrition facts** per orange: 62 calories, zero fats and sodium, 15.4g carbohydrates (5%), 3.1g fiber (13%), 1.2g protein (2%), 269 IU vitamin A (5%), 70mg vitamin C (116%), 52mg calcium (5%), and .1mg iron (1%). See MANDARIN www.sunkist.com

ORANGEADE: A cold beverage made with orange juice, water, sugar and sometimes lemon juice Malt powder is added to some commercial orangeades, such as the **Orange Julius**. Make it just like lemonade but with less sugar and serve over ice.

ORANGE TRIVIA

Benjamin Franklin had a special recipe for orange shrub which was mostly rum, the rest orange juice and sugar. He was so fond of it, he even made a device to skim the dregs to the last drop.

Thomas Jefferson tried to grow orange trees imported from Italy.

Oranges cannot tolerate frost, as Jefferson soon found out.

Orange pickers have to wear gloves to prevent bruising the fruit.

Many oranges are picked green and dyed to give them that sunny golden color we love.

Texas raises some of the best tasting and least known-about oranges in the world.

The best way to serve oranges is to slice them across into pinwheels and then cut the pinwheel in half. They look beautiful and inviting and this method cuts down the mess of having to peel them.

The Tarocco, one of the red oranges, is named for its resemblance to a child's toy top.

The first mention of the sweet orange in Europe is thought to be in the archives of Savona, in Italy, in 1471. Probably the seeds had come through the Genoese trade route, which had connections with the far East.

The name "orange" comes from an Indian word "Narange" (fruit like elephants). Just how they thought it reminded them of elephants is anyone's guess.

The sour orange traveled to Europe about 500 years faster than the sweet variety.

It was the Portuguese explorer, Vasco de Gama, who brought the sweet orange back to Portugal after discovering his trade sea route to India around the Cape of Good Hope. In 1498, the Portuguese grew a sweet orange that was said to be directly from "China." That name got applied to all the sweet oranges after that.

Thus, the "China oranges" so popular in England after the 16th century were actually from Portugal.

Blood (red) oranges take their name from the red color, which happened by some sort of mutation in Sicily in the 17th century. Sicily remains the best place for blood oranges because of the soil and the cold nights and warm days.

Navel oranges are seedless and have to be propagated by cuttings.

Oriental women rub orange peel on their skin for perfume.

OREGANO: An herb that is native to the Mediterranean and a member of the mint family. Oregano is bitter and pungent and is best used sparely. The leaves can be used fresh or dried in sauces and dressings, added to meat recipes, and to flavor vegetables. Oregano is widely used in Mexican and Italian recipes. Also known as marjoram.

ORGANIC FOOD:

WHAT'S ORGANIC
By Chef Laurel K. Miller

Organic is a term for food grown or raised without the use of chemical, such as pesticides, herbicides or fertilizers. In the case of livestock such as cattle, not only does the animal's food source need to be organically grown, but the animals themselves need to be raised without the use of hormones (to make them bigger or fatter), or antibiotics. If a sick animal needs to be treated with antibiotics, it cannot be used for human consumption.

Sustainable Agriculture

"Sustainable agriculture" is used to describe farming methods that are environmentally friendly. Farmers who grow food organically are said to be practicing sustainable agriculture.

Crop Rotation

Crop rotation means that organic farmers grow different types of crops on the land according to the seasons. This helps to prevent the soil from being depleted of certain nutrients. It also helps to reduce the number of pests, which means less pesticide use.

Clean Water

Not using harmful chemicals means that our water supply stays cleaner and safer. In many parts of the United States and around the world, wildlife and fish are being born with genetic mutations and birth defects as a result of toxic pesticide residues in the water. One scientific study showed that pesticides might be responsible for an extra four million cancer cases among Americans every year. If pesticides are designed to kill insect pests, then they can't be healthy for humans!

Transitional Farms

Sometimes some chemical use is necessary to combat plant diseases or insect that would otherwise destroy crops. Some firms, known as "transitional farms" practice IPM (integrated pest management). This means that the farmers may resort to using chemicals, BUT only during certain phases of the plant's growth, such as when fruits are in bloom, but not on the actual fruit. Or it many mean that synthetic pesticides have not been used, but commercial, petroleum-based fertilizers have. For a farm to be certified organic, no synthetic pesticides or fertilizers may have been applied to the land in the last three years. California currently has the strictest organic regulations in the world.

From Farmland to City Streets

In the 20th century, the United States has gone from being a mostly farm-based society to being a mostly city, technology-based society. Nevertheless, modern farming methods rely heavily on today's advanced technology. society. But what happens when we pave over all the farmland? Where will we grow and raise food? Scientists and astronauts are working hard to develop ways to grow food in space, but is that really the answers? (see BIOTECHNOLOGY and HYDROPONICS) Do we really want to live on a planet that is wall-to-wall cars, houses and people.

You Can Help

Maybe there is something you can do to help save American's vanishing farmland. By arranging field trips to and visiting organic farms, dairies and farmers' markets, you are helping to support local farmers. Visiting these places is the best way to make a connection between food and it's origins. Talking to farmers will teach you more about how food is grown and processed. You will also learn how sustainable agricultural works to protect our environment from pesticide residues and soil depletion. Organic farms are not subsidized, or supported financially, by the government the way big, commercial (agribusiness) farms are. Organic farmers must make their living by selling produce at farmers' markets and to stores and restaurants who sell organic produce.

ORGANIC HOME GARDENING

Have you ever wondered how a forest or meadow grows and thrives with no added fertilizer? The answer is that natural ecosystems make their own fertilizers though the decay of dead animals, insects, and plants. Organic gardening works the same way. Instead of using commercial fertilizers, you save all the dead plants and weeds and make a compost pile. Rotting vegetables, peelings, and egg shells are also good. Save any garbage that will decay.

In the spring, spread compost on the ground used for gardening. Then plow the ground under. Next, mix the compost with the soil. If your garden plot is large, ask someone to use their rotating cultivator for you. Now you are ready to plant. A lot of work is put into this project because you can't use poisons to kill the weeds. You have to pull them out by hand. It takes about four years before ground can be truly be called "organic."

Many gardeners choose the organic method because they want to be good stewards of the environment. They are concerned about pollution of the air, water, soil, and the health of their families, and communities. They know that using synthetic pesticides can destroy wildlife, bees, and other beneficial insects, and may have an effect on food quality and safety. Tending an organic garden connects them with the soil and make them feel close to nature. --*Bernice Erickson*

Visit an Organic Farm

There's probably an organic farm near you. The easiest way to find one is on the Internet. The following organization has links to organic farms all over the country, organic growing information and lots more: www.caff.org Also you can just type in "organic farms" in the search category that have educational tours. In Northern California, Eatwell Farm in Davis has information on their Internet: www.organic@eatwell.com Also try: www.umass.edu/umext/CSA Recipes: www.epicurious.com Nutrition: www.navigator.tufts.edu *–Chef Laurel Miller*

ORGEAT: An Arab syrup originally made from barley, now made with almonds, sugar and rosewater or orange-flower water. The syrup is used to make a beverage that is favored by Latin countries of the Mediterranean area.

ORLANDO: See TANGELO

ORTOLAN: A small southern European bird, now almost extinct, was once a gourmet delicacy. At one time, they were caught in nets, domesticated and fattened, then roasted.

OSSOBUCO: In Italian it means "hollow bone," and is a dish made with veal shanks or knuckles, simmered with white wine, olive oil, tomatoes, and anchovies, and served with saffron rice.

OSTRICH: The world's biggest bird and its eggs have been eaten since before recorded history in Africa, home of the long-legged bird. While on one of his voyages in the *Beagle,* Charles Darwin wrote home about eating ostrich dumplings. Even though the ostrich is a bird, it doesn't taste at all like chicken or duck. The taste is similar to lean beef. Ostrich meat is found in some supermarkets, but has not gained in popularity in the United States as yet. This might change, because the flesh is low in calories, fat, and cholesterol. Ostrich eggs can weight three pounds, and it would take at least 45 minutes to hard cook one. Ostrich meat is forbidden under Hebraic law and in other religious dietary codes. Ostrich eggs do not fry like chicken eggs . They are most useful in dried or powdered form for cake baking and such. The creamy white eggs are about the size of a baby's head. www.ostrichstuff.com.

THERE'S NOTHING CHICKEN ABOUT AN OSTRICH
by Marie Prato

Canada is a great place to sample exotic fare. If horsemeat doesn't grab your taste buds, there are always snails, elk, caribou and goose to fill up on. But, for a real taste treat, I recommend ostrich.

My first experience with this dish was a shock. When the waiter brought my meal to the table, I thought he had made a mistake. No, he assured me, this is what I had ordered--ostrich.

Looking at the dish before me, I had my doubts. I thought the meat of a bird, even a flightless one like the ostrich, would resemble something that came from one of our more common feathered friends.

Expecting the dark, solid-looking meat to be gamy or stringy or both, I hesitantly raised a forkful of sliced ostrich to my mouth. To my surprise, the ostrich meat, cooked in a ginger sauce, was as tender as an expensive steak and twice as tasty! Not only that, but with less fat than chicken and not a threat to my cholesterol count, I could order a second helping without feeling even a twinge of guilt. Why haven't we discovered ostrich meat in the United States?

On my return to New York, I learned that many farmers in the United States are raising ostriches. But, though the meat is heavenly, the ostriches and the problems with commercially processing them are keeping the birds from appearing in our supermarkets.

Some of the problems in raising ostriches are a result of the birds' nature. Unlike docile cows and sheep that can be easily herded and maneuvered around the farm, ostriches are dangerous. In its native Africa, ostriches kill and maim more people than both alligators and lions combined. Striking with their two-toed feet, the huge birds are capable of ripping open their opponents with one swift strike.

In addition to the danger involved in handling the birds, the cost of the food the ostriches require is high. Some farmers feed a fish based food but the Bronx Zoo feeds a kale and grain mixture. The biggest drawback to the birds is the problem of processing the meat. In order to sell ostrich meat to the public, it has to be processed in a government-approved plant. For many of the farmers, who embarked on raising ostriches, the plants are too far away and the cost of building a processing station of their own is too prohibitive. Instead of the lucrative business adventure many had envisioned, the expensive ostrich flocks have plunged many farmers into serious financial difficulties.

Someday, however, when more Americans like myself have their first taste of ostrich meat and clamor for more, we may yet be able to add this delicious, healthy meat to our diet.

OTAHEITE APPLE: From the South Pacific a large tree produces large oval yellow fruit, with sweet flesh, and a spiny seed. The flesh is eaten fresh, made into preserves and jelly.

OTAHEITE GOOSEBERRY: Native of Madagascar this tree produces medium size six-lobed, pale green, sour fruit that is made into preserves and pies. Fruit is high in vitamin C.

OUTDOOR EATING: Food tastes better outdoors, whether it is on a backyard barbecue, on a sandy beach near a lake or river, sitting on a log besides a camp fire high in the mountains, or under a canopy at an outdoor restaurant, food just tastes better outdoors. Why food taste better outdoors, no one knows. Maybe it's the fresh air, or maybe its just doing something a little adventurous that brings out the flavor. The nice thing about eating outdoors, food can be either cooked on site or brought from home in a picnic basket. Picnic foods range from a bologna sandwich to a casserole to a deep dish cobbler. It all tastes better outdoors!

OVALTINE:

REMEMBERING OVALTINE

In the late 1930s, kids would race home from school, turn on the radio and tune in to hear the latest adventures of Little Orphan Annie. The program wasn't a musical like the current stage show and movies, but an exciting fifteen minute program that always ended with a cliff hanger, as well as a secret coded message. In order to decode the message you had to have a Little Orphan Annie decoder badge. To receive a decoder it was necessary to send the inner seal from a jar of Ovaltine plus postage to the Ovaltine company. The problem, Ovaltine was expensive, and not all families could afford that luxury. Also, Ovaltine was sold as a vitamin drink and was only available in some drug stores. **Today**, vitamin enriched Ovatine is available at most supermarkets. However, it's not the same drink as back in the 1930s. The European-made Ovatine of yesteryear was a high-energy, vitamin packed chocolate malted drink. The drink also contained less sugar and more barley malt extract than today's American version. The European version is still available, but generally only by mail order. If you would like to experience the original old-time favor, write to: **Vermont Country Store**, P.O. Box 3000, Manchester, VT 05255. They will send you a catalogue filled with lots of products from yesterday.

OVEN: A box that cooks food by fire, gas, electricity, or microwave. Today most ovens are part of the kitchen range, have one or two doors with racks and the heat controlled with a thermostat. Some ovens also broil foods. Microwave ovens cook food using electromagnetic microwaves that penetrate food, generating heat within the food to cook it in a very short time.

OXEN: A large castrated bull; not generally considered good eating since the meat is tough.

OXFORD SAUCE: Also known as Cumberland sauce, is an English sauce made with shallots, oranges, lemons, red current jelly and port wine, served with cold venison and other game meats.

OXTAIL: A beef tail weighing up to two pounds that can be braised or used for soup.

OXTAIL SOUP: Beef tail is now used to flavor soup in countries where ox is no longer eaten. Ask for your soup bones at the butcher counter by the popular name of "oxtail." The classic English soup probably was introduced to England by the French refugees during the French Revolution in the late 1700s.

OYSTER: A shellfish found in the shallow waters of oceans worldwide, except the polar regions. The shells are two part and irregular in shape. They open and close like a puppet's mouth. Wild oysters in the United States are found on both Atlantic and Pacific coasts. The eastern variety are generally larger. Oysters are also commercially cultivated. Oysters are available fresh from fall to spring. For centuries it was said that oysters should only be eaten during the months containing the letter "R" (September through April). Modern refrigerated transport makes that unnecessary today. Red tides and other toxins can make the oysters poisonous. Oysters are also available canned and frozen. When buying fresh oysters, they must be alive with tightly closed shells. Oysters are eaten raw, fried, and stewed. Oysters are a good source for protein, high in calcium and iron, and low in fat. **Nutrition facts** per 3 ounces: 58 calories, 19 calories from fat, 2.1g total fat (3%), .7g saturated fat (4%), 45.1mg cholesterol (15%), 179.5mg sodium (8%), 6.4g carbohydrates (1%), zero fiber, 6g protein (12%), 85 IU vitamin A (2%), 3mg vitamin C (5%), 38mg calcium (4%) and 5.7mg iron (32%).

Chinoteague is world famous for its oyster beds and clam shoals. During the early days, residents seldom used money in their business transactions, paying with oysters instead. This demand was so great by 1915 the oysters were almost depleted. Now with protected seasons, the oysters are back and plentiful. Annually on Saturday during the October Columbus Day weekend the Chinoteague Island Oyster Festival is celebrated with an all-you-can-eat seafood feast. Unlike most food festivals where you pay for food as you go, here you pay-one- price for all the seafood you can eat. Oysters are served on the half-shell, steamed, single-fried, and fritters. Other seafood offered is clam chowder, clam fritters and steamed crabs. Additional food includes hot dogs, hush puppies, salads, and beverages. A dessert booth is offered for those with a sweet tooth. All desserts are sold with the proceeds going to the Oyster and Maritime Museum. This day event is held rain or shine at Maddox Family Park. Along with the food, entertainment is provided. Tickets are limited and sell out early. For cost and other information contact: **Chincoteague Chamber of Commerce**, P.O. Box 258, Chincoteague, VA 23336 or phone (757) 336- 6161. Chinoteague also hosts a Blueberry Festival in July, *--Jacklyn Russell*

OYSTER MUSHROOMS: These unique, oyster-shell-shaped mushrooms range from a soft brown to smokey gray in color. They have a delicate, briny flavor when cooked. Cooked, they can be used in any mushroom recipe. Sautéing with butter and onions brings out their full flavor.

OYSTER PLANT: This southern European herb is also known as salsify. It is cultivated for the root and eaten as a vegetable. The yellow-gray root can grow to a foot long and two inches in diameter. Some say the flavor is that of an oyster, but others say it tastes like an artichoke. The young leaves can be added to a salad. The roots can be cooked like carrots, peeled or scraped, boiled or fried. **Nutrition facts** pr ½ cup: 55 calories, zero fats, 13.3mg sodium (1%), 12.4g carbohydrates (4%), 2.2g fiber (9%), 2.2g protein (4%), zero vitamin A, 5mg vitamin C (9%), 40mg calcium (4%), and .5mg iron (3%).

OYSTER SAUCE: A thick brown sauce made with oysters, soy sauce, and brine. It has very little fish flavor, used only to intensify other flavors.

OZARK FOOD: Settlers of the Ozark Hills were mostly transplanted pioneers from the Appalachian Mountain area. The mountain folk brought their seeds, farming knowledge, and cooking ideas with them. They found that cleared Ozark land produced abundant corn, potatoes and beans. Their pigs, who will eat almost anything, grew fat on the plentiful wild acorns, nuts and fruits. With a small farm, a few oxen or mules to work the land, a cow and some pigs and chickens to provide food year round, the Ozarkians could live well. They knew how to supplement their diets with the varied greens, fruits and nuts growing wild in the mild climate.

Most Ozark families have grandparents who tell about eating squirrel and dumplings, possum stew, baked corn, fried rabbit and deer steaks. Corn provided fresh corn, dried corn, popcorn, and feed corn, as well as hominy and hominy grits. Corn husks made mattresses, dolls, decorative crafts and brooms. Pork was the main meat on the Ozark farm. Hog butchering became a social occasion with neighbors butchering several at a time. The meat was dressed, salted, and preserved by smoking over hickory wood in the smokehouse. Ozarkians wasted nothing and bragged about using all of the pig but the squeal. Poke greens, dock and watercress no more than raised their heads in the springtime than Ozark cooks picked them and brought them to the table.

Everyone had a garden from spring until late fall, beginning with spring peas, onions, beans and ending with potatoes, cabbage, turnips, squash and pumpkins. Most farms had a cane patch for making sorghum molasses. Ozark farm folk could be pretty well self-sufficient. A ride to the nearest village trading post would get them salt, flour, and sugar, but wild honey and molasses provided much of their sweetening needs. Fall brought apple butter time and the making of hominy. Both kept the huge black wash kettle busy over the open fire for days at a time. While women stirred the kettles, the men filled the root cellars with everything that could be kept over the winter months in the cool, dark underground. Children gathered nuts and piled them up for cracking later when the winter winds kept everyone indoors instead of planting and harvesting. Keeping food on the table was an endless job for the whole family.

Some of the Ozark farming and cooking methods were still in use as recently as the Great Depression of the 1930s and had changed very little from the days when American pioneers were still settling the wild West. The Great Depression caused a migration of families from the Ozarks to California where food promised to be more plentiful. But the Ozarks have long recovered and still retain much of their unique regional flavor. Later newcomers discovered the Ozarks had ideal soil for growing grapes and a small but growing wine industry began. Ozark peaches and strawberries rank with the best in the world. Blueberry farmers recently replaced strawberries fields in popularity. Specialty shops abound where lovers of fine food can buy smoked Ozark meats, local jams and jellies, and take home fresh produce from farmer's markets. Many restaurants still feature Ozark mountain home cooking. All summer long you can find harvest festivals to celebrate the incoming crops, beginning with strawberries and ending with apples. *–Louise Ulmer*

Pp

PAELLA: (pah-el-yah) A Spanish rice casserole that originated in Valencia, Spain, made with a combination of meats (salt pork, chicken, sausage, fish, shellfish, etc.) and vegetables (tomatoes, onions, green peppers, etc.).

PALAQUIUM: A large tree from the Philippines has one-inch, reddish-brown fruit with a similar taste to sapodilla.

PALM: A variety of evergreen trees from the tropics and sub-tropics. The cabbage palm provides (1) tender young leaves eaten like greens and (2) palm fronds (heart of palm). From the oil palm we get palm oil and palm nuts. The coconut palm gives both coconut and its milk. The sugar palm yields a sap made into a drink. See also DATES, which come from desert palms.

PALM GRASS: Also called the hummingbird flower, it originated in tropical Asia and produces two-inch long pods that are not eaten. Only the large flowers are eaten.

PANAMA BERRY: See JAMAICA CHERRY.

PANBROIL: A stovetop method of cooking meat, chicken, or fish in a heavy skillet over medium heat.

PANCAKE: A bread made by pouring a thin batter on a hot griddle, turning once to brown each side. Various flours can be used, wheat, rice, buckwheat, and corn. Some of the more famous pancakes are: sourdough from Alaska, egg rolls from China, cannelloni from Italy, blini from Russia, and crêpes Suzette from France. Jewish pancakes are called blintzes. German pancakes are filled with apples. Pancakes can be leavened with either baking powder or yeast. Pancakes are served at breakfast topped with syrup, or rolled and stuffed with meat for lunch, or served with a hot sweet sauce for dessert.

WORLD'S LARGEST PANCAKE BREAKFAST

To celebrate the 1636 founding of Springfield, Massachusetts, the community offers an annual breakfast in the month of May. A team from the International House of Pancakes whips up enough batter to make 130,000 country griddle cakes. It is made with 2,100 pounds of a secret blend of **Cream of Wheat** buttermilk prepared mix, 900 pounds of eggs, 210 pounds of butter and mixed by hand with 250 gallons of water. The flapjacks are topped with 400 gallons of maple syrup. In addition to the pancakes, 1,100 gallons of milk, 1,100 gallons of orange juice and 3,360 gallons of Maxwell House coffee are served. For more information, contact: **Spirit of Springfield,** Inc., 101 State Street, Suite 220, Springfield, MA 01103-2006 or phone (413) 733-3800.

PANDANUS: Also known as the screw pine, this tree from Madagascar has round yellow fruit growing in clusters. The fruit is edible when cooked.

PANDOWDY is an old recipe for a deep dish fruit pie or cobbler that was usually sweetened with molasses. It differs in that about halfway through baking, the top crust is pressed down into the fruit to absorb the juice. The process is called "dowdying." As the cobbler continues to bake, a crispy crust is formed. Some cooks also stir both the bottom and top crusts into the fruit juices.

PANFRY: A form of cooking meat and vegetables with a little fat in a heavy skillet.

PANETTONE: (pana-tonee) A high, light Italian yeast cake or bread (*pane*) that originated in Milan. Containing dried and candied orange peel and nuts, it is served at family celebrations. Watch for it in the special foods sections of the supermarkets at Christmas time. It comes boxed for gift giving. Delicious warmed and buttered. On the Panetonne box from Real Torino is the following: *For centuries the Italian Panettone cake has been the most famous of desserts on the Italian holiday table. The Panettone comes from a famous recipe of "Pasticerria Pertici" in Torino, Italy.*

The Panettone, a cultural symbol of all Italian festivities, is a delicate cake, which fills the room with a fresh baked aroma. Within the last few years, the popularity of Italian Panettone has grown due to its flavor and acceptance as an everyday dessert throughout the world, as well as special occasions.

PANIALA: This shrub from India produces dark red berries that are eaten fresh and made into jelly.

PAPAW (PAWPAW): Also known as the custard apple, this tree is native to southern North America. The fruit is banana shaped, two to six inches long with a dark brown skin and a soft creamy yellow flesh with many seeds. This sweet, custard-like fruit is not available commercially. The somewhat aromatic fruit is eaten raw. www.onegreenworld.com

PAPAYA: This small tropical tree originated in the West Indies or Mexico, with fruit resembling a melon. The skin and flesh is a yellow-orange, with a sweet musky flavor, a cross between a peach and crenshaw melon. Papayas are now grown in most tropical countries. Papayas come in all sizes and shapes, from one pound and the size and shape of a large pear, to 20 pounds the size and shape of a watermelon. It's the smaller variety from Hawaii that is mostly found in supermarkets. It's easy to eat. Slice in half, scoop out the seeds, and eat the flesh with a spoon. The larger varieties from Mexico are best skinned, seeded, and cubed. A squeeze of lime juice helps mellow the flavor.

Papayas are generally eaten raw, especially at breakfast. Papayas are added to fruit salads. It makes a wonderful summer cold soup, can be baked with other fruit, barbecued as a kabob with ham and shrimp, and made into bread. Overripe papaya can be made into salsa, a marinade for chicken, and sherbet.

For a special dessert, fill the center with a scoop of strawberry ice cream or pineapple sherbet, top with meringue and bake in 450°F oven until meringue is lightly brown. Instead of an apple a day, it might be better to eat a papaya a day to keep the doctor away, as papaya has more vitamin C (157%) and fiber (25 grams) than an apple. **Nutrition facts** per ½ cup: 27 calories, zero fats and sodium, 6.9g carbohydrates (2%), 1.3g fiber (5%), .4g protein (1%), 199 IU vitamin A (4%), 43mg vitamin C (72%), 17mg calcium (2%), .1mg iron (1%). www.planet-hawaii.com/papaya

PAPILLOTE:(pah-pee-yote) A French culinary term meaning "wrapped in paper." Paper or parchment was once used, now aluminum foil is more widely used. The wrapping holds in the juices during cooking. Recipes include meat, fish, and vegetables. In short, it's cooking in paper.

PAPRIKA: A spice made by grinding dried pods and seeds of a certain kinds of red bell pepper. Paprika is usually used for nonsweet dishes, especially meats and poultry. Hungarian goulash is probably the most famous paprika recipe, however, this spice is used in Spanish, Mexican and Turkish cookery. The spice is available sweet to pungent. Must be stored in a dry cool place. Paprika is most highly developed in Hungary, where the peppers were brought from the East by Bulgarians, who brought them from Turkey. In 1604, they were called "Turkish pepper." They weren't called "paprika" until about 1775. The name derived from the Latin "piper" (pepper). Most paprika is mild but there are hot varieties. Spanish paprika is sweeter and called *Pimenton.* Szegred, Hungary is famous for the best paprika, a "pink" that has no bitter aftertaste.

PARAFFIN: A wax made from petroleum used to coat the top of jams, jellies, and preserves to keep the air from spoiling the jarred product. Paraffin is added to chocolate candies to prevent the candy from melting quickly in hot weather. Grocers also use paraffin to coast perishable vegetable and fruits to help prevent spoilage. You might have noticed the waxy coating on cucumber and certain apples. Paraffin can be bought in supermarkets with the canning supplies. It is also the main material in making candles. Before paraffin became available, cooks relied on beeswax when they needed wax.

PARBOIL: Means to cook vegetables for a short time in boiling water so that they are partially cooked. Some people parboil chicken before putting on outdoor grill to speed cooking time. Also used to prepare vegetables for freezing. When cooking a dish with varied vegetables, the harder ones can be parboiled so that when combined vegetables all can be tender at the same time.

PARCH: Food cooked by dry heat, usually by the sun, over long periods of time to where there is little moisture left in the food.

PARE: (verb) To peel. To remove the skin or surface of fruit and vegetables.

PARFAIT (par-fay): A French word, meaning "perfect." A dessert parfait consists of layered ice cream, fruit, sauces, and/or whipped cream in a tall glass.

PARKER HOUSE ROLLS: Named for a famous hotel restaurant where they originated. A yeast dinner roll cut with a 2 ½ inch biscuit cutter then folded one side on top of the other. After baking, the fold pulls apart easily to insert butter.

PARMESAN CHEESE: (par-me-zhan) A sharp, hard, aged cheese made with lowfat milk with a green or black rind. The English name applies both to a specific brand of Italian cheese, *Parmigiano,* and also to a group of Italian grating cheeses. The only true Parmesan is *Parmesan-Reggiano*, an aged cow's milk cheese molded into 80 pound wheels from the region of Emelia. *Parmigiano-Reggiano* was beloved by Napoleon and the author Moliere would have nothing else on his deathbed tray. Use grated on pasta and added to recipes. **Nutrition facts** per tablespoon: 23 calories, 14 calories fat fat, 1.5g total fat (2%), 1g saturated fat (5%), 3.9mg cholesterol (1%), 93.1mg sodium (4%), zero carbohydrates and fiber, 2.1g protein (4%), 35 IU vitamin A (1%), zero vitamin C, 69mg calcium (7%) and zero iron.

PARROT: Although Australian cookbooks in early times did contain recipes for parrot pie, the eating of parrots has never been taken seriously. Not that it couldn't happen in desperate circumstances, but it has never been common.

PARSLEY: This herb from southern Europe with more than 30 varieties, is the most widely used herb worldwide. The word parsley comes from the Greek word *petroselinon* that means, "celery growing among the rocks." Some varieties are grown just for their green leaves, while others are enjoyed for their roots that are cooked like any other root vegetable. Parsley is added to sauces, gravies, eggs, meat, and vegetables. By itself, it can be made into soup, salad and fried. Parsley is available fresh and dried. When eaten in large amounts, parsley is a good source for vitamins A and C. **Nutrition facts** per tablespoon: 10 calories, zero fats, 17mg sodium (1%), 1.9g carbohydrates (1%), .4g fiber (2%), .8g protein (2%), 875 IU vitamin A (18%), 5mg vitamin C (8%), 55mg calcium (6%) and 3.7mg iron (20%).

PARSNIP: The English name, parsnip, comes from the French, *pastinica*. The "nip" on the end meant it resembled the turnip, though more in texture than in shape or taste. In Medieval times, the sweet, starchy parsnip grew in every kitchen garden because it was just as good sweetened when eaten as a vegetable. It went well with honey and spice, rather like our sweet potato pie. Another bonus for the parsnip grower was its ability to stay in the ground after the frost, so it could stay there until needed. This was a very helpful thing in cold European climates.

A white or yellow member of the carrot family, this edible root is cooked like most root vegetables. It's considered a winter vegetable, since the true flavor doesn't come out until after the first frost when the starch changes to sugar. Parsnips can be boiled with a little sugar to improve the flavor, baked and mashed with a little orange rind, and they can be sautéd with a little black pepper. **Nutrition facts** pr ½ cup: 50 calories, zero fats and sodium, 12g carbohydrates (4%), 3.3g fiber (13%), .8g fiber (2%), zero vitamin A, 11mg vitamin C (19%), 24mg calcium (2%), and .4mg iron (2%).

PARTRIDGE: An Old World bird, the partridge has been propagated in the United States. There are birds in the United States called American partridge, but these are not a true partridge. They are native ruffed grouse. It takes at least one partridge per serving, since they weight only about three quarters of a pound. Partridge meat is low in fat, hence many cooks will wrap them in bacon before roasting them. Frozen and canned partridges are available in some specialty food stores. Children today hear about the partridge in a pear tree in the old English Christmas carol: "The Twelve Days of Christmas," though they are unlikely to ever eat one.

PASKHA is a cheesecake or a pudding made in Russia at Easter time. Paskha means Easter.

PASSION FRUIT: Better known by its Spanish name of *granadilla*, passion fruit is native to tropical Brazil. The name comes from the look of the flower, as it appears like the crown of thorns worn by Christ. In Hawaii, passion fruit is known as *lilikoe* and was brought to the Islands by Eugene Delmar from Australia in 1880. A much larger, yellow variety was introduced in 1923. The sweet-acid flavor is eaten fresh, and made into beverages. The purple variety is found in many supermarkets. It is ripe and the pulp (mostly seeds) is ready to eat when the skin is wrinkled. **Nutrition facts** per ½ cup: 60 calories, 4 calories from fat, .4g total fat (1%), zero saturated fat,

17.2mg sodium (1%), 14.4g carbohydrates (5%),6.4g fiber (26%), 1.4g protein (3%), 431 IU vitamin A (9%), 18mg vitamin C (31%), 7mg calcium (1%), and 1mg iron (5%). www.ogw.com

PASTA: A mixture of flour and water, sometimes eggs and vegetable juices, made into a thick dough that is rolled out thin to made noodles, or extruded to make spaghetti, stars, hearts, and letters. Pasta is available fresh, frozen, dried, and canned. Pasta is served both hot with sauces or cold in salads, added to casseroles with meat and/or vegetables and cheese, and with a cheese sauce for dessert. www.ilovepasta.org; www.goldengrain-mission.com; www.americanbeauty.com

PASTA, IS IT ITALIAN?

The Chinese have enjoyed noodles since 1100 BC. Since pasta is a simple mixture of flour and liquid, quite similar to bread, it's possible people of many lands made pasta, but didn't call it that. n Cerveteri, there's a stucco relief on an Etruscan tomb that depicts kitchen utensils for making pasta. Those same tools from circa 400 BC are still in use today. Latin writers Horace (65-8 BC) and Cicero (106-43 BC) both expressed a fondness for pasta. However, most historians give credit to the Italian explorer, **Marco Polo** for bringing pasta to Italy from China in 1292 AD.

Legends abound. One tells of a Chinese maiden, who while making bread, was lured from her chores by a sailor from the Marco Polo expedition. Wind blew leaves into the bread dough. The sailor attempted to save the dough by straining it through a wicker basket. The thin strands of dough dried in the sun. When the sailor departed on his ship, the maiden gave him the dried dough. Later he boiled the dried dough and it soon became a favorite food not only by the crew, but of Marco Polo himself. This legend gives shared credit to Chinese and Italian cooks, thus saving diplomatic relations. There are many references to pasta in Italian literature. In the short story "Calandrino," author Boccaccio (1313-1375) speaks of macaroni and cheese.

Another legend says that an Italian ruler gave **macaroni** its name when he was served the dish for the first time. He said, "*Ma caroni*" which translates "How very dear!"

The word pasta comes from the Italian word "*paste*." Most pasta is made from durum hard wheat called "semolina," derived from the Italian word "*semola*," meaning bran. Whole durum wheat is unrefined flour, high in protein and has not been stripped of its nutrients. It makes a firmer pasta than the softer wheats. Semolina is more used in Europe than in the United States. There are more than 100 varieties and shapes of pasta, as well as colored pastas made from spinach and beet juice. Pasta with egg yolks is usually called egg noodles. --*RSC*

Tip: If you are one of the many people who are allergic to wheat, rice can be substituted for pasta with many of the great pasta sauces. Try spaghetti sauce over rice, rice goulash, pizza sauce and cheese on rice cakes. You might even learn to like it as well or better than pasta.

PASTA FACTS, TIPS & TRICKS

Make mealtime more enjoyable by serving different, fun pasta shapes. There are stars, letters, wheels, and the all time favorite, spaghetti. Pasta is low in calories, but supplies low-fat energy you need for bicycling, running, and other fun activities.

The Food Guide Pyramid recommends 6 to 11 servings of grains. Might sound like a lot, but it's possible you are already eating that many. A slice of bread counts as one, as does a ½ cup of cooked or ready-to-eat cereal, ½ cup of rice, and ½ cup of pasta. You probably eat more than one serving, especially when it comes to cereals and pasta. Most kids can down two cups of pasta easily, and with a sandwich for lunch, that's two servings (pasta and a sandwich totals six servings).

Picking the right sauce for the pasta choice is easy. A thin sauce for thin pasta such as angel hair. A thicker pasta such as fettuccine requires a heavier sauce. When there are nooks and crannies, such as macaroni, a chunky sauce with bits of meat is perfect.

Tips: Pasta **can be made in advance** and refrigerated. Cook pasta, but undercook it 1 to 2 minutes. Rinse in cool tap water, stir in a little vegetable oil to prevent sticking. When it is time to reheat, drop pasta into boiling water for about a minute, drain well, and it's ready for the sauce. If you have a recipe that calls for baking, such as macaroni and cheese, undercook the pasta by one-third, since it will continue to cook in the oven.

Leftover pasta has many uses. Can be added to salads with your favorite dressing, added to soup and stews at the last minute of cooking, and added to vegetables with a cream sauce.

How much to cook is always a question. Two ounces of uncooked pasta (about ½ cup) equals about 1 cup of cooked pasta. Expect it to double in bulk when cooked.

Directions

To cook pasta, first bring the water to a boil, add pasta, and stir occasionally. A pound of pasta requires at least four cups of water; six cups are preferred. Cook as per package instructions, usually 5 to 10 minutes, maybe longer for thicker pasta. Never overcook, because it will be gummy. To test pasta, cut it with a fork or cool a piece and take a bite. It should be slightly undercooked, as it will continue to cook while draining. Dry pasta can be stored for up to a year if it is kept dry in an air-tight container and in a cool place. *--National Pasta Association*

PASTA OR PASTRY CLOTH: A cloth for rolling out pasta and pastry dough. The rolling pin is generally covered in a stockinet cloth, and all are rubbed with flour to prevent sticking.

PLEASURABLE PASTA
A True Story
by Livia F. Sparagna

Several years ago I visited my cousin, Francisco, in La Spezia, Italy. Francisco was the District Attorney for the town, he also taught law, and had his own law office. One morning, before leaving for his office, he asked me to join him. Walking along with him was a great pleasure. He knew and greeted everybody and he had their respect. His office turned out to be well suited for his image. It was elegant, lined with books, a beautiful desk in the center of a paneled room, and he sat at the desk in a large leather upholstered armchair. Sitting across from him we talked on topics of scholarly interest.

He answered the telephone several times and looked through his mail while talking. He impressed me as a person under pressure who was capable of making serious decisions quickly and efficiently. As the time came close to noon, Francisco slowly opened the long center drawer to his desk. He started to look intently in the open drawer. Then smiling he said, "Livia, come and see." I walked around the desk and looked over his shoulder.

To my surprise, lining the drawer was a chart of pasta shapes. With a little chuckle, he told me that at this time everyday he selected the pasta he wanted for dinner (Italians have their main meal at noontime). He suddenly appeared like a little boy as he viewed the pasta, enjoying the name given to different shapes. Surrounded by law books, he had found a way to relieve the stress his position imposed upon him. He called home and said, "Today, I would like capellini." Maybe this is one of the reasons the manufacturers of pasta produce shapes with descriptive names attached. I think pasta shapes were created for our enjoyment. Here are a few of the pasta shapes I remember from his desk drawer:

Alphabets, used for soups.
Capellini, also known as angel hair, meaning "fine hairs."
Conchiglie, meaning "shells." Shells come in several sizes from small to large.
Ditalini, meaning "little thimbles."
Egg Noodles, from the German word "*nudel*," meaning "to paste with egg." Noodles come in many sizes from fine to extra large.
Farfalle, also known as bow ties, meaning "butterflies."
Fettuccine, meaning "small ribbons."
Fusilli, meaning "twisted spaghetti."
Lasagne, from the latin word "*lasanum*," meaning "pot."
Linguine, meaning "little tongues."
Macaroni, refers to "dumpling.
Manicotti, meaning "small muffs."
Mostaccioli or *Penne*, meaning "small mustaches" and "quills" respectively.
Orzo, an Italian word for "barley."
Radiatore, meaning "radiators."
Rigatoni, meaning "large grooved."
Rotini, meaning "spirals" or "twists."
Ruote, also known as wagon wheels, meaning "wheels."
Spaghetti, meaning "a length of cord."
Vermicelli, meaning "little worms."
Ziti, meaning "bridegrooms."

PASTRAMI: This preserved meat originated in eastern Europe by dry curing it with salt and saltpeter. It is made from various cuts of beef, usually brisket and round. After curing, the meat is rubbed with a mixture of spices that includes pepper, cinnamon, cloves, and garlic. It is then smoked and cooked. It is available in some supermarkets, but the best is found in Jewish delicatessens. It can be eaten hot or cold, in sandwiches or on a plate with potatoes. Today, pastrami is also made with the dark flesh of turkey and is lower in fat when compared to beef.

PASTEURIZE: (pass-chu-ryz) A method to kill harmful bacteria in milk and other liquids, including eggs, by heating to certain temperatures. This process was invented by the famous French scientist, Louis Pasteur in 1876.

PASTILLE: (pas-teel) A French confection made with sugar, water, and flavoring. They are called "drops" in the United States, as in a lemon drop.

PASTRY: A dough made with flour, shortening, salt, and water used to make pies, pasties, tarts, and appetizers. When eggs are added, it creates a puff pastry used to make cream puffs and éclairs that are filled with a puddling-like cream or whipped cream.

PASTY: A baked turnover pie filled with meat and vegetables, or fruit. Cornish miners in England took their pasty recipes with them when they migrated to America. Today they are still common fare in Michigan. The pasty has a long and colorful history in England. Medieval pasties might contain a whole bird.

PATÉ: (pat-tay) A paste made from pureed meat, vegetables or fruit. The most famous *pâtés* from goose liver are called *pâté de foie gras*. Pâté is a French word meaning "pie."

PATTY: A small, round, flat piece of food, such as ground meat made into hamburger, or potatoes made into a potato cake. A patty can be fried or baked.

PATTYPAN SQUASH: This flat-topped squash with a ruffle around the edge has delicate flavor, almost none until cooked. Most are pale green. The sunburst variety are yellow with a buttery taste. Pattypan can be eaten raw in salads, steamed or sautéd. Pattypans are especially good sautéd with sweet onions and bell peppers. Look for the smaller pattypans (less than 1 ½ inches across), since the larger one's skins will be tough. For an appetizer, pick one-inch squash, hollow out the top part, then steam for a couple of minutes. Fill with your favorite cheese and bake in a 350°F oven until the cheese is melted.

PAUCHOUSE: A French name for a fresh water fish soup, usually made with five different kinds of fish, with salt pork, wine, and cream.

PAUPIETTE: (paw-pi-ay) In the United States it is called a "bird." It is a thin slice of meat or fish rolled up with forcemeat or other stuffing.

PAVLOVA: An Australian meringue dessert topped with fruit and whipped cream.

PEA: Originating in western Asia, this legume is now cultivated world wide. They grow best in cool moist climates, usually during the spring and fall months. There are many varieties. Some have edible pods, while in others only the seeds are eaten. Some seeds are dried and are available whole or split. Peas are available fresh, frozen, and canned. Fresh peas are cooked in a little salted water, while dried peas are cooked like their cousins, the bean, by soaking and simmering for a long time. Cooked dried peas are mostly made into soup, but can also be mashed and served as a vegetable. Fresh peas make wonderful partners with rice, onions, and corn. Fresh peas can be creamed, minted, and spiced. **Nutrition facts** per ½ cup: 59 calories, zero fats and sodium, 10.5g carbohydrates (3%), 3.7g fiber (15%), 3.9g protein (8%), 454 IU vitamin A (9%), 29mg vitamin C (48%), 18mg calcium (2%) and 1,1mg iron (6%).

SLIMY LITTLE BALLS OF GREEN MUSH
by Roberta Greenwald

Once upon a time in the 20th century, a boy named Darin gave a disgruntled sigh. Once again, his mother has served him those slimy little balls of green mush. Do your taste buds say chalky and mushy when canned green peas appear on your dinner plate? Consider how this came to be.

Poor peasants living in Italy during the 1700s were first to unearth green peas. Since food was scarce, they tried the taste of wild green peas. Then, they improved on the taste when they gardened their own green peas, resulting in bigger and better varieties. Over time, news of the green peas popularity spread to France and England. Expensive as they were, kings of the Old World discovered green peas' secrets first. King Louis XIV of France "almost stuffed himself to death with them." After eating peas for dinner, he would have them waiting in his room to eat before going to bed.

About the same time, William III ruled England. The story is told that King William grabbed green peas and wolfed them down before anyone else could get them. Other parts of the world caught wind of how green peas had gained favor. In Peking, China, boys and girls would listen for the pea vendor's bell much as you listen today for the ice cream vendor. Children watched as vendors cooked and ladled peas into their outstretched bowls.

The benefits of green peas became apparent to kings and peasants alike. Peas were accepted as a complete food. Gentlemen approved of the rosy cheeks of ladies whose diets included green peas. Tips for proper eating of green peas appeared. Tips like: "Eat with a little honey to keep peas from rolling off your knife." Kids were also quick to learn on their own that mashed potatoes work well for holding peas on their silverware. Today, you know what kings did not know about green peas.

You know that peas add "fiber" to your diet. You know peas give you energy for more vigorous play time by adding vitamins B and C to your diet. And yet, peas can be a replacement for meat because they contain protein. Green peas are usually bought from supermarkets. They are available dried, suitable for eating in summer and winter. Appearing most often on 20th century tables are frozen green peas. Almost never do supermarkets have fresh ripe peas in their pods. You may wonder if somewhere there is a William III who grabs and wolfs down fresh podded peas.

The true taste of green peas fresh from their pods can only be found when we return to the peasant's garden. Farmers today grow green peas in fields. A Farmer's Market is a great source of fresh, crisp podded peas. In the country, a roadside stand is a possible place for new peas. Of all sources, the best lies in the green gardens of the midwestern United States. A springtime morning wet with dew will yield bright green peas, juicy, crisp with plump velvety pods hanging from the greenery. Peas are so good they can be eaten raw. Pop one into your mouth just for the fun of it! The flavor of new peas is like no other. So if you don't like canned peas, ask your mom to find fresh peas, not canned.

Amelia Simmons who wrote the first American Cookbook, *American Cookery in 1796*, advises "Peas should be picked carefully from the vines as soon as the dew is off, shelled and cleaned without water and boiled immediately; thus they are the richest flavor." Green peas, cooked at their very freshest, will be a flavor forever a part of your memory.

PEACH: Native to China, now the third most important fruit crop in the United States, this fruit tree was bought to the New World by the Spanish. A cousin to the apricot, plum, cherry and almond, the peach has a fuzzy skin, rosy yellow when ripe. Peach flesh may be orange, like the apricot, or it may be look almost as "red" as a plum or a pale almond yellow. Fresh peaches are available almost the year round, with the United States crop during the summer months, and those from Chile arriving here during our winter. Peaches are available fresh, canned, dried, and in nectar. Peaches are eaten fresh, stewed, and cooked with meat, vegetables, made into pie, cakes and a variety of desserts. Because of their beautiful blossoms and taste, the peach has long been a favorite of poets and artists as well as chefs. **Nutrition facts** per ½ cup: 37 calories, zero fats and sodium, 9.4g carbohydrates (3%), 1.7g fiber (7%), .6g protein (1%), 455 IU vitamin A) 9%), 6mg vitamin C (9%), zero calcium, and .1mg iron (1%) www.calpeach.com; www.onegreenworld.com www.state.nj.us/agriculture

PEACH TRIVIA

Because of its flavor and culinary uses, the peach ranks near the top as a favorite fruit. To tell a lady she has a "peaches-and-cream" complexion is a great compliment. Less subtle, but still flattering, is to describe a lady as a "peach."

The Chinese endowed the peach with rich symbolism.. Some early Chinese writers described it as the tree of life; others as the tree of death. The peach blossom in ancient China has its share of myth and old wives tales. It was once thought to make young girls overly romantic. Fathers were warned never to plant a peach tree near their daughter's bedroom window.

The Spaniards were the first to plant peaches in the New World, first in Saint Augustine, Florida. They were followed by the French in Louisiana and the English in Jamestown. The Native Americans carried the peach far inland in advance of the white settlers.

The 19th century Pennsylvania Dutch were said to employ a number of bizarre practices to assure good crops: They supposedly painted hex signs on barns for fertility. They held pow-wows to exorcize curses on fields. On Good Friday, before breakfast, farmers horsewhipped their trees to guarantee a good harvest. --*Dr. Donald H. Petersen, Pennsylvania State University*

GEORGIA PEACH FESTIVAL

Everything is "just peachy" in Fort Valley during this three day June event. It all starts with a pancake breakfast, followed with a peach dessert contest, peach hat contest (hats decorated with peaches), peachy pooch parade, peach bin races, and a free bite of the World's Largest Peach Cobbler. There are all kinds of activities for kids. First, meet Peaches the Bear; next, paint peaches on downtown streets. Try your skill climbing a 24-foot rock, visit the Peach Clown Town, play softball, feed a goat in the petting zoo, and there are free balloons for everyone. Fun never stops with street parties, square dancing, nightly fireworks, road races, and the Georgia Peach Queen Pageant with Tiny Miss Peach, Little Miss Peach and Junior Miss Peach awards. For more information write: **Georgia Peach Festival**, P.O. Box 2001, Fort Valley, GA 31030, or phone toll free 1-87-PEACHES-1.

PEACH MELBA: Who was Peach Melba? It's not a "who," but a "what." Peach Melba is a sundae made with vanilla ice cream over peaches and raspberries. It is believed this Victorian dessert was named by Chef Escoffier for the famous opera singer Nellie Melba (real name Helen Porter Mitchell). Nellie Melba developed her stage name, Melba, in 1887 in Brussels, from her home town of Melbourne. There are a number of versions of peach melba. Most contain rum or brandy. Here's an easy one without the alcohol. Chef Escoffier served his masterpiece on a silver dish between the wings of a swan carved in ice.

Raspberries, fresh or frozen, thawed, puréed
Peaches, fresh or canned, halved
Vanilla ice cream

1. Place a peach halve in the bottom of a dessert dish.
2. Top the peach with a scoop of vanilla ice cream.
3. Top ice cream with the raspberry purée

PEACH PALM: From Central America comes red and yellow 1 ½ inch fruits that grow in clusters. The yellow fruit is eaten fresh. The red fruit is made into preserves.

PEACOCK: While not today's everyday fare, at one time an English or a Roman banquet was not a banquet unless peacock was served. The peacock, cousin of the turkey, would be carefully skinned, stuffed with herbs and spices, roasted, and the skin with the feathers placed back on the peacock. The tail would be carefully spread, the claws and beak gilded in bright gold, and the peacock served on a gold or silver platter. Sometimes spirit-soaked cotton would be placed into the beak, and set aflame when served. For very important guests, sometimes the whole bird was gilded. King Arthur supposedly carved peacock for 500 guests, but after all he did rule in mythical Camelot.

PEANUT: Native to South America, probably Brazil, the peanut is not really a nut. It is a legume with pods that split open. The plant looks like a pea plant, hence the name. The peanut pods grow underground, and are called groundnuts and ground peas in some regions of the world. Another name, goober, comes from the African word for peanut, *nguba*. The pods grow up to two inches long, and can contain from one to three seeds, with two seeds the most common. There are different varieties of peanuts, hence the seed can be round (Spanish variety) or oblong (Virginia variety), and are covered with a thin paper-like skin that ranges from red to white.

Both the shell and the seeds are used as animal feed. In Africa a peanut soup is common; in Jamaica the peanut is cooked with chicken; in Java a hot chili sauce is made; and in Mexico peanuts are added to cabbage coleslaw. Peanuts are also used to make breads, cake, cookies, muffins and candy. **Nutrition facts** 1/4 cup unsalted: 209 calories, 149 calories from fat, 17.8g total fat (27%), 2.5g saturated fat (12%), zero cholesterol and sodium, 6.8g carbohydrates (2%), 3.3g fiber (13%), 9.5g protein (1%), zero vitamins A and C, 32mg calcium (3%) and .7mg iron (4%).

PEANUT HISTORY IN A NUTSHELL

How do you like your peanut butter? Did you know by the time you graduate from high school, you will have eaten fifteen hundred peanut butter sandwiches? That's true, if you're an average kid.

In the 1600s European explorers of the New World, found peanuts in South America and took them home where they were further transported to Africa and Asia. In the 1800s immigrants and slave traders brought peanuts back to American for planting. During the early 1800s, peanuts were mainly used as a source for oil, as basic food, and a substitute for cocoa. The Civil War increased the uses for peanuts as both the Yankees and Confederate soldiers ate what was then called "goober peas." After the war, vendors sold hot roasted peanuts on the street, at ball games and at the circus.

"The Peanut Man"

George Washington Carver will always be known as "the Peanut Man." A Black scientist in Alabama, he developed more than 300 products from peanuts. Not only did he create peanut soup, salad, bread, cookies, and ice cream, but - believe it or not - bleach, axle grease, shoe polish, wood stains, and plastics! His peanut soup eventually became peanut butter. Would you believe you can remove that sticky stuff left behind when you peel off a price sticker by rubbing it off with peanut butter? It's true.

Creamy or Oily?

Peanut butter was invented for kids, right? Wrong! It was **invented for grandparents**. In 1890 a Saint Louis doctor whipped up some peanut purée as a health dish for his elderly patients who had no teeth. From cranking an ordinary kitchen grinder to the development of Dr. Staub's patented peanut butter machine only took thirteen years. By the 1914 Saint Louis World's Fair the public couldn't get enough peanut butter. Back then, peanut butter was all natural - just peanuts, peanut oil and salt. Oil tends to float to the top. In 1923 J.L. Rosefied changed that by adding hydrogenated oils (trans fatty acids) to get that familiar creamy look. Today we can still get the all natural kinds and with food processors, kids can make their own. The country oldest brands, Peter Pan and Skippy added a sweetener. By law, peanut butter must be at least 90% peanuts, the rest a combination of salt, sweeteners, and stabilizers.

Good news! Pound for pound, peanut butter has more protein, minerals and vitamins than beef liver! And it only takes two tablespoons to supply your daily needs for protein! Two peanut butter sandwiches, an apple, and a glass of milk provides one third of your daily nutrition requirements. In short, peanut butter is one of the best vegetables sources for protein around.

Now for **the bad news**. Peanut butter contains calories and fat. There are 95 calories in a tablespoon of fat, almost as much as butter, and 38 of those calories come from fat. But there is good news. Peanut butter is mostly unsaturated fat, no cholesterol, and is high in monounsaturate fats, which will reduce your cholesterol.

FESTIVALS

Every year there are peanut festivals in the south from Virginia to Texas. There are many events from a peanut butter sculpture contest to all kinds of food made from peanuts that might include peanut butter soup and peanut butter pie. Would you like to learn more about the no-nut peanut?

Yes, the peanut is not a nut. It's a legume and belongs to the pea family. For peanut history, geography, nutrition, poetry, songs, and recipes? Contact: **American Peanut Council**, P.O. Box 845, Nashville, NC 27856-0845 or phone (919) 459-7396.

FAMOUS PEANUT BUTTER LOVERS

Everyone likes peanut butter! Billionaire **Malcolm Forbes** calls it "beloved tan ambrosia" and eats in on buttered toast with crisp bacon, lettuce and mayonnaise.
President Gerald Ford spreads it on an English muffin and called it "a power breakfast."
Journalist George Will relishes it in sandwiches with sweet pickles. Singer **Weird Al Yankovic** pairs in with broccoli. **Comedian Phyllis Diller** loves in on white bread with mayonnaise. Singer **Elvis Presley** ate in on white bread with sliced bananas, honey and fried in butter. Olympic gold-metal speed skater **Bonny Blair** eats a peanut butter and jelly sandwich before competition. Actress **Liz Taylor** likes hers on whole-wheat bread.

PEANUT BUTTER, NATURAL: Pure peanut butter is ground peanuts, nothing else. Most commercial peanut butters also include salt, sugar and/or vegetable shortening.

MOTHER AND THE PEANUT BUTTER SONG
by Richard S. Calhoun

During my youth and when I made a peanut butter and jelly sandwich, Mother would sing the peanut butter song to the tune of Polly Wolly Doodle. She would pat her chest when the word "flutter" was sung and blow an imaginary horn when the words "toot" were sounded.

 Yes, when I was young I enjoyed Mother singing this little ditty, but by the time I was in my early teens, it became annoying to the point I would never make a peanut butter sandwich when she was around. Now that she has gone, I wish she was back, so I could join her in the lyrics to the tune of Polly Wolly Doodle . . .

A peanut sat on a railroad track;
his heart all a flutter;
'Round the bend came number ten.
TOOT! TOOT!
Peanut butter!

PEANUT FLOUR: Made from ground peanuts from which most of the oil has been removed. In Europe the flour is used in breads. Peanut flour is available in most health food stores.

PEANUT OIL: By cold pressing peanuts, oil is obtained. This colorless oil is used for cooking and table use.

PEAR: A member of the rose family and native to an area stretching from central Europe to western Asia. There are more than 5,000 varieties of pears making at least one variety fresh off the tree during most months. **Bartlett** pear season is July to October, followed with **Anjou** pears October to March, and **Winter** from February to May. Pears are one of the few fruits where the flavor improves as it ripens, even after it is picked. Most pears become soft when ripe, but at least one small green variety remains firm and crunchy when ripe and sweet. You just have to cut one to taste and see. Depending upon the variety, the skin can be green, yellow, brownish yellow, or red. The flesh is white, the taste ranges from sweet to spicy. Pears are available fresh, dried, and canned. Almost any recipe calling for apples, pears can be substituted. Pears make a great pie, can be baked stuff with raisins and nuts, and made into jams and preserves. **Nutrition facts** for one pear: 98 calories, 5 calories from fat, .7g total fat (1%), zero saturated fat, cholesterol, and sodium, 25.1g carbohydrates (8%), 4g fiber (16), .7g protein (1%), 33 IU vitamin A (1%), 7mg vitamin C (11%), 18mg calcium (2%), .4mg iron (2%), and 208mg potassium. www.ca/pear.com; www.enzafruit.com www.usapears.com www.wastatefruit.com www.onegreenworld.com

PEASE PORRIDGE: Porridge generally refers to a hot cereal such as oatmeal. In England dried peas were made into a porridge, and as the old nursery rhyme goes, "pease porridge hot, pease porridge cold" is the way the English ate peas as a basic stable diet for centuries. The word "pease" was the plural archaic spelling for "peas."

PECAN: A tall native tree of North America, pecans were often the sole food of the Gulf Coast Native Americans for months at a time, when no other food was available. The trees grew wild along the rivers of Southern United States in what is now referred to as the "pecan belt," an area extending from South Carolina to Arizona. There are both hard and soft shell varieties, but even the hard shell variety has a thin shell and are easy to crack. The meat has a higher content of fat than any vegetable. Southern cooking includes pecans in many recipes, from a simple garnish to a major ingredient. Pecans are available in the shell, shelled, salted and unsalted. Fresh pecans mostly available in winter. Can be frozen and kept year round. **Nutrition facts** per1/4 cup unsalted pecans: 180 calories, 154 calories from fat, 18.3g total fat (28%, 1.5g saturated fat (7%), zero cholesterol and sodium, 4.9g carbohydrates (2%), 2.1g fiber (8%), 2. 1g protein (4%), 25 IU vitamin A (1%), 1mg vitamin C (1%), 10mg calcium (1%), .6mg iron (1%), and 106mg potassium www.ilovepecans.org www.tuckerpecans.com

PECTIN: A substance found in citrus, apples, and sugar beets used to firm jam and jellies. Using pectin provide larger yields and less cooking time. Without pectin, jellies have to be boiled a very long time to reduce the water and thicken.

PEEL: (noun) The outer skin of fruit and vegetables. (verb) When used as a verb, it means to remove the skin with knife or vegetable peeler.

PEJIBAYE: Same as PEACH PALM.

PELLAGRA:

THE "LEPROSY" OF THE POOR
by Louise Ulmer

Pellagra is a disease seldom heard about today but during the early 1900s the deadly disease ran rampant in the American South, killing or disfiguring thousands. No one knew what caused it, and no one knew a cure. Victims were treated like lepers, for it was feared to be contagious. The Latin word means "rough skin." But it also causes severe diarrhea and dementia.

Pellagra was written about in history but not always under that name. People didn't always diagnose it but could describe the symptoms and it always turned up where diet was extremely poor. The disease remained a medical mystery. The only clue doctors could see was that the disease was somehow associated with corn. In those days medical science had only barely begun to understand germs and microbes. Their first suggestion was contaminated corn.

The most misunderstood clue was that it was a disease of the poor. Poverty and ignorance always make matters worse. In their ignorance, medical people isolated victims. Victims would rather die than admit they had the dreaded disease.

The Sherlock Holmes who discovered the cause was Dr. Joseph Goldberger, working for the United State Public Health Service and Marine Hospital. Goldberger had already made medical history when he went south to battle pellagra. Dr. Goldberger was one of the greatest research doctors in all of history.

The first thing Dr. Goldberger noticed in the poor rural South was that people existed on meal, molasses and meat. Make that cornmeal, molasses, and salt pork. No one else in the country ate this way so Goldberger had his first set of clues. Poor people ate these things because they were available, cheap and kept well over the winter when all fresh food had long been eaten. Since wealthy people never got pellagra, Dr. Goldberger ruled out infection as a possible cause.

In the end, the brilliant doctor demonstrated it was not what the poor people ate that cause pellagra but *what they did not eat.* The victims were dying for lack of vitamins. It was a long hard road and many years later that Dr. Goldberger could announce that the cure for pellagra was brewer's yeast. His discovery was ridiculed in medical circles but in 1927 when floods caused widespread pellagra, the American Red Cross distributed six tons of brewer's yeast and cures happened in a few weeks. It was not until 1937 that another doctor, Dr. Conrad Elvehjem at the University of Wisconsin identified nicotinic acid, a B complex vitamin as the deficiency that causes pellagra.

Dr. Goldberger died in 1929 of cancer, but he died knowing medical history so he had hope. His experience was typical. In 1793, James Lind had reported that two oranges and a lemon a day would cure scurvy (Vitamin C deficiency) but British Naval powers waited 43 years to adopt his findings. It took 10 years for medical authorities to believe that whole grain rice would cure beri-beri. Dr. Goldberger's hopes were not in vain. Starting in World War II, commercially made bread was enriched with "niacin" (nicotinic acid). Pellagra faded into history.

PEMMICAN: A meat that has been dried, sometimes smoked, pounded into meal, mixed with fat and herbs, and made into little cakes. Originally made by Native Americans with buffalo, deer or other game meat. It's a form of jerky.

PENUCHE: (penoosh) A fudge made from brown sugar and sometimes containing nuts. The name comes from the Mexican word *panocha,* meaning "raw sugar."

PENGUIN: No, you won't find penguin meat in the supermarket, but if you were hungry and ice bound in the Antarctic, penguin just might be your meat of choice. Penguins have no fear of humans. While great swimmers, on land they waddle awkwardly, so to catch one is simple. The meat is low in fat, rather tasteless, with a fishy shrimp flavor.

PEPPER (Capsicum): Better known as red and green peppers, capsicum peppers are native to tropical America and have been part of the human diet for more than 7,000 years. They contain high amounts of vitamins, in fact a green chile pepper has more vitamin C than an orange. There are both hot and sweet peppers. The hot ones will range in color from green to red, and from one-half inch to seven or more inches. Sweet green peppers will turn red if left to ripen. Paprika is made from drying and grinding one of the red variety of mild capsicums. Other sweet pepper colors are yellow, orange, ivory, purple, and chocolate brown. The hottest pepper is the *habañero*, which are red or orange. A medium hot variety is the jalapeño. Tips: When working with hot peppers, wear rubber gloves. It's the seeds and veins which contains most of the heat, so to make a hot sauce hotter, throw in a few seeds. To put the fire out in your mouth, don't drink water, as the chili oils and water do not mix. Eat or drink something with fat, such as whole milk or a banana.
www.state.nj.us/agriculture

PEPPER (Piper nigrum): A vine from southwestern India grows pepper berries. Pepper is the most popular spice of all. The dried pepper berries produces both white and black pepper. The black berries are picked when unripe, dried and smoked. White pepper is the ripened berries, fermented and water soaked. Black pepper is more pungent than white pepper. Pepper is available whole, cracked, coarse ground or fine ground. Sometimes the black and white are ground together to obtain various degrees of hotness. Whole pepper will keep its flavor for a long time. Once ground, it should be used within a month or two, since it will lose its flavor quickly. The main use for white pepper is when black specks are undesireable, such as in mashed potatoes and white sauces. Green pepper berries are picked when unripe and still green, then dehydrated and freeze-dried. The pink peppercorn is not a pepper, but is a dried berry from a tropical rose. Pepper should be stored in glass, not plastic, which lets in air to rob flavor.

Pepper was once as valuable as gold. During the last days of the Roman Empire, Alaric the Goth was said to demand 3000 pounds of pepper as part of a ransom for Rome. By the Middle Ages, pepper was common enough in England to be used as a commodity of taxation. The London Guild of Pepperers dates back to at least 1180. In Antwerp, Belgium in the 1500s, the price of pepper served as an indication of business health. Today Singapore is the center of pepper trade around the world. The first self-made millionaire in the United States was Elias Haskett Derby. He made his fortune importing black pepper from the East Indies. Derby used his profits to endow Yale University.

Pepper in Surprising Places

Black peppercorns are a spice that can be used in many desserts. With just the right amount, only a pinch in most cases, the sweetness of fresh ground pepper brings out aromatic flavors in baked goods like ginger, cinnamon and cardamom, and heightens mellow flavors such as fruit, honey, and almonds. Use a mortar and pestle or a rolling pin to coarsely crush the peppercorns. The fresher the peppercorns, the sweeter the taste. Try adding 1/4 teaspoon of fresh ground black pepper to your next gingerbread recipe.

PEPPERGRASS: An annual herb with a flavor similar to watercress that is used as a garnish and in salads.

PEPPERMINT: An herb, *mentha piperita*, found growing wild in damp lowland areas of the United States, Asia, and Europe. The leaves have a cool refreshing flavor when added to citrus beverages. Throw in a few leaves into vegetables (such as peas and green beans) as they cook. Southeast Asian cooks serve fresh mint in hot soups and stir fries to add a refreshing flavor lift. Oil is extracted for candy and chewing gum. The extract is also used in pies, cakes, ice creams, jellies, and puddings. Peppermint is available fresh and dried.

PEPPERMINT SOAP
by Marie Prato

Peppermint has other uses besides flavoring gum and making your mouth tingle. There's nothing like the thrill of having a puppy of your very own! But parents hate the accidents and soiled rugs.

Rule #1: *Never use anything that contains ammonia to clean up a mess if you have dogs.* This will guarantee another mess in the same spot because there is ammonia in urine. Cleaners containing ammonia and to Rover the ammonia smells like urine. Rover will think you not only don't mind him soiling the area, but you're using the same area yourself!

Rule #2: A capful of liquid peppermint castile soap in a quart of warm water should be kept handy. Pour the mixture on a sponge, go over the entire spot, then rinse the sponge and repeat the process. No rinsing is necessary. This will neutralize the ammonia odor and remove the stain. It will leave a fresh natural smell in its place.

Besides cleaning rugs, two or three capfuls of peppermint soap in a bucket of water is great for cleaning messes on linoleum and no-wax floors. A capful in the final rinse when washing dog blankets cleans and deodorizes them and helps to repel fleas. And bathing the puppy with liquid peppermint will leave its coat shiny and smelling nice longer than special dog shampoos and cost a lot less. Liquid peppermint castile soap is sold at most health food stores.

PEPPERONI: An Italian dry sausage made with beef and/or pork and highly spiced with pepper, cayenne, and garlic. Every kid knows it as the red circles of meat on top of pizza.

PERCH: A freshwater fish found in parts of the mid west and eastern United States. Also known as a yellow perch, which is distinctive with black and yellow bands along the side, and reddish fins. True perch should not be confused with white perch; it's a member of the bass family. The pike perch is related, but unlike the yellow perch that lives in brackish waters, the pike lives in clear waters. Perch are available fresh in some markets, frozen in most markets. Perch has a mild flavor. Perch can be broiled, sautéed, deep fried, baked, poached, and steamed. **Nutrition facts** per 3 ounces: 77 calories, 8 calories from fat, .8g total fat (1%), .2g saturated fat (1%), 76.5mg cholesterol (26%), 52.7mg sodium (2%), zero carbohydrates and fiber, 17g protein (33%), zero vitamin A, 2mg vitamin C (3%), 68mg calcium (7%), and .8mg iron (5%).

PERCOLATOR: A 3-part type of coffee maker that brews coffee by dripping boiling water through ground coffee. The water sits in the bottom section, the coffee grounds in a metal basket on top, and a hollow tube holds the basket above the water. The bottom section sits on the stove burner and forces boiling water (by the bubbling action) up the hollow stem into the basket holding ground coffee. The boiling water bubbles over the tube and runs back down though the coffee to the water below. The water "perks" in this way until the desired strength of coffee is obtained. The longer the water boils, the darker the coffee becomes. The percolator is usually clear glass so the person making coffee can turn it off when the coffee looks the shade of brown he/she likes. Before the glass ones were invented, metal percolators made the brewing a lot more difficult since it was hard to guess what color the coffee had become. There are also electric version with preset timers that turn off automatically. All are considered antiques today, replaced by the automatic electric coffee brewers, most of which require hot water to be poured over the ground coffee.

PERSIAN MELON: A bit larger than a cantaloupe, with a green netted skin. The flesh is orange with a mild sweet taste. Available from mid-summer to mid-fall.

PERSIMMON: There are basically two main species of persimmons. The American variety is native to the warmer areas of eastern United States from Connecticut and Iowa south to Florida and the Gulf. The oriental persimmon is native to China and Korea, and has been introduced to the United States mostly in California and Florida. The fruit somewhat resembles a tomato in size, with an orange skin, reddish orange pulp. The taste is sweet with some tartness. Ripe persimmons are eaten fresh, added to fruit salads, and made into puddings. Unripe persimmons are not edible. Persimmon season starts in mid fall and ends in mid winter. **Nutrition facts** per ½ cup: 123 calories, 3 calories from fat, .4g total fat (1%), zero saturated fat and sodium, 32.5g carbohydrates (11%), zero fiber, .8g protein (2%), zero vitamin A, 64mg vitamin C (107%), 26mg calcium (3%), and iron (14%).

PESTICIDES are chemicals used to prevent contamination of foods. Pesticides are used to protect food from pests, such as insects, rodents, weeds, mold, and bacteria. It is believed chemical pesticides do more harm to food, people, water and wildlife than they do good. These same pesticides also make their way into processed foods. More research is being made by government agencies, universities, and private groups to better control and to eliminate pesticides.

What You Need to Know

To protect your health, the Environmental Protection Agency (EPA) has set standards on the amount of pesticides that may remain on food.

Kids Are More Vulnerable to Pesticide Exposure

Since your internal organs are still developing and maturing, you are at a higher risk from pesticides than adults. Because of your growing body, kids generally eat and drink more than adults, again increasing your exposure to pesticides, not only in food, but water as well. Even your outdoor activities present a problem. Playing on lawns and fields, can increase your exposure to pesticides.

Healthy, Sensible Food Practices

As you know, health professionals recommend that you eat at least five servings of fruits and vegetables every day. So how do you protect yourself from pesticides used in fruit and vegetable farming? First, wash and scrub all fresh fruits and vegetables thoroughly under running water. Running water has an abrasive effect that soaking does not provide. Washing helps to remove bacteria and trace chemicals from the surface and crevices.

Second, peel fruits and vegetables when possible to reduce dirt, bacteria, and pesticides, since washing will not remove all pesticide residues. Remove outer leaves of leafy vegetables. Trim fat from meat and remove skin from poultry and fish, because pesticides collect in fat and on the skin.

Third, select a variety of foods from a variety of sources. Not only will this give you a better mix of nutrients, it will reduce your likelihood of being exposed to a single pesticide.

What about Organic Grown Foods?

Some grocers will stock organically grown foods, and while they are safer, they can still provide some pesticides. Some pesticides can be used on a limited basis with organic growing. Also pesticides from nearby fields can be carried by the wind to the organic fields. Even organic foods must be washed well. Peel those you are uncertain about. For more details, contact: U.S. Environmental Protection Agency Office of Pesticide Programs Communication Services Branch (7506C), 401 M Street SW, Washington, DC 20460   Phone (800) 858-7378. Also visit the Internet: www.epa.gov/pesticides/food This website has information on how the government regulates pesticides, what are the pesticide residue limits on food, why you may be especially sensitive to pesticides, and just what organically grown foods means.

PET FOOD: Feeding pets table scraps has been replaced by dietitians who have researched pet needs. People food contains too much fat for animals to digest. Even a saucer of milk high in lactose can cause cat digestion problems. Food designed for dogs is generally not good for cats, since dog foods contain less protein that cat food. Just like humans, animals need a balanced diet of protein, fat, fiber, moisture, vitamins, and minerals. www.purina.com

PETITE MARMITE: Means a complete meal in a bowl of soup. Served in French restaurants, it is make with beef, poultry giblets and lots of different kinds of vegetables.

PETIT FOUR: A French term, *petit* means "small," and four means "oven." Hence, a petit four is a little baked something. Petit fours are usually little layered cakes, about one inch square and iced in different colors. They can also be cut in various shapes, diamonds, triangles, circles, etc.

PHALSA: This tropical tree produces ½ inch purple fruit that is eat fresh, made into a beverage, sherbet, and jam.

PFEFFERNÜSSE: (fef-fer-noos) It means "pepper nut" in German and is a highly spiced Christmas cookie that includes black pepper as one of the spices. These easy to make German cookies uses just a pinch of pepper.

2 tablespoons butter
2 cups sugar
4 teaspoons cinnamon
2 teaspoons cloves
2 teaspoons nutmeg
Pinch of black pepper
4 eggs
3 cups flour
2 teaspoons baking powder
1 cup walnuts or pecans, chopped

1. In a large bowl, cream butter with the sugar.
2. Add the spices.
3. Beat in the eggs.
4. In another bowl, mix flour and baking powder.
5. With a wooden spoon, mix in the flour mixture.
6. Stir in the nuts.
7. Drop by round tablespoons on ungreased cookie sheets.
8. Bake at 350oF for 12 minutes for soft cookies or 15 minutes for harder cookies.

PHEASANT: Native of Asia, closely related to the partridge, this handsome game bird has an unusual, succulent flavor, sort of a cross between chicken and venison. Wild pheasant is still hunted in several American states. Small pheasants can be roasted, but large birds should be braised because they can be quite tough. Wild pheasants do not have much fat and are usually cooked with bacon or salt pork. **Nutrition facts** per 3 ounces: 132 calories, 64 calories from fat, 6.8g total fat (11%), 2g saturated fat (10%), 56.8mg cholesterol (38%), 29.2mg sodium (1%), zero carbohydrates and fiber, 16.6g protein (33%), 130 IU vitamin A (3%), 4mg vitamin C (7%), 9mg calcium (1%) and .8mg iron (4%).

PHILI NUT: A tree native to tropical Southeast Asia has 2 ½ inch long nuts that are pointed at both ends, hard to crack, and are eaten fresh and roasted. It has the highest oil content of any nut (70%). The texture and flavor resemble the almond. It is greatly favored in Filipino cooking.

PHILIPPINE FIG: A shrub where only the tender young foliage is edible.

PHILIPPINE TEA: The leaves of this shrub are used to make tea.

PHYLLO DOUGH: See FILO

PHYTOCHEMICALS : Found in a variety of foods, phytochemicals (fie-to-kimi-cals) are beneficial nutrients whose uses are just being explored. Unlike minerals, phytochemicals are not basic elements. And unlike vitamins, they have not been proven to be essential to human life. However, nutritionists believe they seem to promote health and hold great promise for the future. Phytochemicals include such substances as **isoflavones** (ice-o-flay-vowns), found in soy foods; **bioflavonoids**, found in many fruits and vegetables; and **indoles**, found in **cruciferious** (krew-sif-er-i-ous) vegetables like broccoli, cauliflower, Brussels sprouts and cabbage. It is believe these substances have anti-oxidant effects and they may mimic hormones.

PICCALILLI: (pika-lily) Originating in the East Indies, it's a pickled relish made from combinations of green tomatoes, corn, peppers, onions and pickled with sugar, vinegar and spices. Cabbage is sometimes added.

PICKLE: Generally a pickle is a cucumber preserved in salt, vinegar, and spices. Other vegetables such as carrots, green tomatoes, onions, and cauliflower, plus some fruits, such as watermelon rind, peaches and pears are also pickled. Depending upon the spices, herbs and sugar used, pickles can be sweet or sour, hot or mild. Even boiled eggs are delicious when pickled with or without the addition of red beets.

A GLOSSARY OF PICKLES

Dill: One of the most common pickles, it gets its name from the predominate taste of the dill in the mix.
Kosher Dill: Kosher dills are just dills with garlic added.
Polish Dill: The Polish is a basic dill with more garlic and seasonings.
Zesty Dill: The same as Kosher or Polish dills but with more peppery heat.
Bread and Butter: A mixture of sweet and tart.
Sweet: To get the taste, they first have to be marinated in sugar, often with a hint of spice, such as cloves or ginger.
Gherkin: These are sweet pickles made with the smallest cucumbers. A favorite with kids.
Kosher Deli: Packed fresh, they need to be kept chilled. Look for them in the refrigerated section of most markets.

OTHER PICKLED FOODS

If you thought cucumbers were the only things to pickle, you should walk down the pickle aisle of your nearest supermarket. In specialty stores, you may find even stranger things pickled in jars.

Pickling is one of the oldest ways of preserving foods, but sometimes cooks pickle things just for the taste. The food may get eaten so quickly there is no need to preserve it. Pickled beets with boiled eggs never last more than a few days around my house but in Alaska they pickle eggs to keep them through the long winter when the hens aren't laying so well.

> Bread and butter without a pickle
> Is like an itch without a tickle.
> –author unkown

Did you ever wonder where "bread and butter" pickles got their name? Perhaps it came from the days when pickles were commonly served with nearly every meal. Or perhaps the name got attached to this kind of pickle because it goes great when all you have is bread and butter.

Pickling often involves boiling water and syrups, which are dangerous. **We do not recommend pickling without adult supervision.**

Pickled Fruits

Among the recipes in the *Amana Colony Recipes* cookbook of 1948 are recipes for pickled fruits. Here's one that fits a variety of fruits.

> 7 lbs. prepared fruit (pears, apples, citron, plums, apricots, or cherries)
> 3 ½ pounds sugar
> 1 pint vinegar
> 1 stick cinnamon
> 6 whole cloves

Boil all ingredients together until fruit is tender. (It will make its own juice.) Skim out fruit and boil syrup 20 minutes. Return fruit to syrup, let simmer several minutes longer. Fill into sterilized jars and seal. Or, if you plan to eat the fruits in the next few days, just keep them in the refrigerator.

Americans first made picked watermelon rinds. It's pretty much like the pickled fruits above. You can find recipes in standard cookbooks.

Pickled Veggies

Would you believe dilly green bean pickles? Onion pickles? Green tomato pickles? Carrot pickles? Or yes–it had to happen–zucchini pickles? You can find all of these and more in *Woman's Day Encyclopedia of Cookery* and other cookbooks.

Pickled Fish? Why not?

Yes, you can even find pickled fish! Pickled herring has been around for a very long time and is still a great favorite in Europe. The recipe is simple, not a lot of spices go into it. It's mostly vinegar, salt and pepper. Some recipes call for onion and sour cream.   Pickled salmon is another example. Salmon fillets, boned and skinned, get the full pickling spice treatment.

Activity
You Can Make Your Own Pickle Relish

Relish is nothing but chopped pickles. If you need relish for hot dogs, for example, and don't have any on hand, make your own. All you need is dill pickles and juice. Chop 1 and ½ cups of pickles in a blender with enough juice to keep them moving around.   For **hamburger relish,** mix in 1/3 cup of catsup. For **hot dog relish,** mix in 1/4 cup of mustard.

PICKLED PIGS FEET & OTHER CUTS: The Europeans learned how to pickle meats before refrigeration. Especially the Germans liked to pickle pork hocks and other cuts to cook with their sauerkraut. There are many pickling methods. Feet and other cuts are simmered with onions, spices, herbs, vinegar and water for several hours. A longer time method is called "corning." When pork is corned, the results are similar to corned beef, but pork flavor is much richer. Corning is done with water, pickling salt, saltpeter and pork. These ingredients are soaked for one to two weeks. The liquid is drained, fresh water added, plus vegetables, herbs and spices to be simmered for two to three hours or until tender. The Germans also pickled beef, which is better known as "sauerbraten."

PICKLE FRUIT: From Malaya, this small tree produces sour greenish-yellow fruit that is made into pickles and preserves.

PICKLING SPICES: A blend of herbs, seeds, and spices which could include cloves, dill weed and seeds, ginger, mustard seeds, black pepper, chilies, celery seed, cinnamon, and allspice. Depending upon the mixture, they can be used to preserve vegetables, fruits, and meats. Pickling spices are also added to stews, sauces, and gravies.

PICNIC: Food served informally outdoors.

INDOOR-MIDDLE-OF-THE-WINTER or RAINY-DAY PICNIC
by Pamela Schmidt

Do you like to do things out-of-the-ordinary? Especially when it means to break a few rules and get away from the norm. How about an indoor picnic? If Mom goes for it, pitch in and help set up a fun meal. It goes something like this:
●Clear away or push back extra furniture.
●Lay a picnic tablecloth, blanket or a sheet on the floor.

- Set out a picnic basket if you have one (otherwise improvise), filled with paper plates, napkins, cups, forks, spoons, and knives.
- Have a cooler filled with ice, sodas, juice, or your own favorite picnic drinks.
- Set up a battery operated cassette player with Nat King Cole's *Those Lazy-Hazy-Crazy Days of Summer* blasting away. That's for your Mom, later play what you like.
- Even in the dead of winter, turn up the heat, and have everyone wear shorts and T-shirts.
- Tie a couple of helium balloons to the picnic basket.
- Plan indoor-safe games, such as, putting golf balls into paper cups, hot potato.

Menu could include: deviled eggs, good old-fashioned potato salad, ground baloney sandwiches, brownies and ice cream for dessert. If you have an indoor gas grill, hamburgers and hot dogs are also great picnic fare.

- If you want to do the indoor picnic again, clean up the mess, and put all furniture back the way you found it. – from her cookbook, *Standing Ovations*

PICNIC FOOD SAFETY
by Vickie Mabry

During the picnic season, you and your friends will be packing coolers for a fun time outdoors. Whether you're ordering food to go or bringing food you made at home, there are several important facts to remember about food safety. There's a concern about mayonnaise. Despite what you have heard, mayonnaise does not increase the chances of food poisoning. In fact, commercially prepared mayonnaise actually contain ingredients that protect against bacteria, such as vinegar, lemon juice, and salt. It's **homemade mayonnaise** that uses unpasteurized eggs that gave birth to the myth that mayonnaise causes food poisoning. You probably wonder what sometimes makes you sick from eating prepared salads made with potatoes and meats? It could be the potatoes, chicken, ham, and other low-acid ingredients that could account for the growth of food poisoning bacteria.

Practice Cleanliness

Wash your hands, utensils, and other food contact surfaces using soap and water after contact with raw meat or poultry, before contact with the same food when cooked. Make sure all sandwich and salad ingredients are fresh and properly washed, keeping foods separate to avoid cross-contamination. When you're at the picnic grounds and running water is not available, take along disposable, wet hand-wipes or the new hand sanitizers that don't require water to clean hands before and after working with food.

Keep Hot Foods Hot and Cold Foods Cold

Cook all foods to the proper done temperatures and store promptly. When traveling with food, keep all perishables in a cooler with ice or freeze-pack inserts until serving time. Frozen juice boxes and frozen individual size water bottles can also serve double-time as ice packs until they melt for drinking water. . Make sure that food is cold or frozen to the touch before placing it in the cooler or cold thermos jug. Use a Thermos designed for hot foods to keep soup, chili, and stews at a safe high temperature for several hours. Refrigerate leftovers within two hours when the temperature in the food serving area is below 90°F, within one hour when the temperature is about 90°F. Have a food-safe and fun picnic.

PIE: Almost any food baked with a top flaky flour crust is considered a pie. Dinner pies contain meat, vegetables, or a combination. Dessert pies contain fruit, custard and other fillings. Some pies have both a top and bottom crust, others are topped with mashed potatoes (Shepherd's pie), an egg white meringue (lemon pie), and some have no top crust (pumpkin pie).

HOW MUCH DO YOU KNOW ABOUT PIES?
by Louise Ulmer

If you can bake a good pie, you probably think that's about all there is to know about pies. Take a look at the pie history you probably did not know.

"Four and Twenty Blackbirds Baked in a Pie"

Did you think that was just a silly little rhyme to amuse toddlers? Wrong! It really was a custom in the Middle Ages. Medieval cooks had lots of fun with food. Great chefs not only made blackbird pies to amuse kings, they also made frogs to leap out of pies and frighten the ladies. The blackbird pies were sort of like the modern birthday cakes from which a girl pops out to shout "Happy Birthday."

What Do You Know about the Early Pies?

Not counting the blackbird pies, early pies in England were more like fried pies or turnovers. In France the pie was a small fruit tart. It took Americans to make pie as we know it. Americans tend to do everything in a big way. With large families to feed and little time to make desserts, the large pie became practical. With fruits and berries in abundance, the two-crust pie could be made and served much easier than several small ones. Cream and custard pies were called pudding pies.

Was Pumpkin Pie Invented for Thanksgiving?

That's questionable. It is known the pumpkin pie was invented by colonial cooks, perhaps for Thanksgiving, but we don't know exactly when. The pilgrims appreciated the Native Americans for showing them how to grow and cook pumpkins and other squashes but pumpkins were first baked and eaten right out of their shells. As always, someone came up with a better way and the pumpkin pie was born. Naturally, it wasn't long before the pie crust was also used for berries and fruits too.

Did the Shakers Invent Lemon Pie?

The Shakers, a religious community in the 1800s, lived on large farms and the cooks fed several hundred people at a meal. They did invent lots of work-saving devices and made wonderful lemon pies. But the pie they invented was an onion pie. The bacon-onion-egg pie was served for breakfast and the leftovers carried out to the fields for lunch. Lemons, being a great treat in those days, were saved for holidays.

Was the Funeral Pie Named for its Color?

Funeral pie is raisin pie, but it got its name for other reasons. The name comes from another early American religious sect, the Amish. It is believed the name comes from the fact that raisin pies carry well and thus were easy to take to funerals or be carried to eat on the long trip home. We are sure that raisins were kept for special occasions and it was customary in the Amish farm communities to gather and share food when one of the members passed away. Perhaps it was just a handy pie to fix quickly and take along in an emergency.

Shoofly Pie Is Not Really a Pie, but a Cake

Surprised? The shoofly pie is really a descendant of the German molasses crumb cake baked in a crust. Making much of little (mostly molasses and flour), the pie filling puffs up in the oven and settles down when it cools to form a top crust. The molasses mixture sinks to form a "wet bottom." Sticky molasses peeping through the topping attracted flies, hence the name.

Which Pie Originated in the South?

If you guessed, pecan pie, you were right. Pecans are native to America, first found in the southeastern United States and Mexico, The pie probably originated in Louisiana where cane sugar is plentiful. Long associated with southern cooking and traditions, pecans are grown commercially now as far north as Indiana and Virginia, though mostly in Texas and Oklahoma.

What Yellow Pie Is More Popular in the South than Pumpkin?

Sweet potato pie was to the South what pumpkin was to the Northeast. Milder and somewhat richer than pumpkin, it is truly regional. Think of it as a marriage between Native American sweet potatoes and English pasty crust.

What Kind of Apple Pie Never Sees an Apple?

Wartime scarcity makes for colorful substitutions. Mock apple pie came out of the Civil War, returning again during the 1930s Great Depression, and once more in the middle of World War II when people were willing to believe that Ritz Crackers and cinnamon could substitute for apples.

Does Key Lime Pie Receive its Color from Green Limes?

No, key limes are actually yellow, the color comes from green food coloring. Key lime pie got its start when a Florida pie maker tried to cut the sweetness of condensed milk by adding the juice of limes. This was another wartime favorite. We know for certain that the invention of condensed milk in the 1850s was a godsend to the South, where dairy products could not be kept in subtropical climates without refrigeration.

How Do You Think Chess Pie Got its Name?

Do you think it requires great strategy to make? No, the name is a mistake. "Chess" meant cheese when the small cheese tarts were popular in England five hundred years ago. The filling, like out modern cheesecake, became just as tasty without the cheese when the recipe came across the ocean. Southern colonial cooks left out the cheese but kept the name, which has caused all the confusion every since. Similar to chess pie is "meal pie," another southern favorite made with cornmeal, milk and egg, which thickens as it bakes in the shell.

What is Mincemeat?

No, it isn't mainly chopped meat. It did begin that way since adding spices helped to preserve meat, but today's mincemeat contains little or not meat. It's mostly raisins, chopped apples and lots of cinnamon, cloves, and nutmeg. Mincemeat is one of the oldest pies, having been made in Europe for centuries.

What Would Be the Easiest Pie for You to Make?

It's an ice cream pie. You start with a graham cracker crust from the supermarket and then add your favorite softened ice cream, and freeze. For a chocolate pie, use a chocolate cookie crumb crust with chocolate or chocolate chip ice cream. For an added treat, soften a half gallon of vanilla ice cream and mix in a six-ounce can of frozen lemonade. Mix and fold the ice cream into the pie shell. Re-freeze and enjoy.

Pie to Die for

Food police have always been around. At the end of the 1800s, American were just as concerned about eating the right things as they are today. And the advice they heard was just as confusing. Food reformers decided the best way to make immigrants into true Americans was to change their eating habits. Out with borscht and boiled cabbage that stinks up the whole neighborhood. Pitch those potato peels and pumpernickel. In the words of reformer C.W. Gesner, "We are fond of pies . . . we cry for pies . . . pies kill us finally. How can a person with a pound of green apples and fat dough in his stomach feel at ease?" Maybe Mr. Gesner just needed a better cook. Americans went right on eating their pies. Since colonial days, Americans have made pies, which in England were merely fruit tarts or fried "pockets" with meat and chopped vegetables. Americans made the European "pie" something bigger and better. As fruits and berries grew bigger and more juicy, so did the pies made from them.

PIE TIN: A round, flat bottomed pan with short, sloping sides for making pie crusts and pies. The sides slope so the pie can be lifted out without spilling the contents.

FLYING PIE TINS

Have you every wondered how the "**Frisbee**" got its name? A baker, William Russell Frisbie, in Bridgeport, Connecticut started the **Frisbie Pie Company** in 1871. Yale students purchased these pies and used the empty tins to toss to one another and would yell, "Frisbie!" A west coast inventor, Walter Morrison invented a plastic flying disc in 1948 that was mass produced by the Wham-O company in 1957. Wham-O executive heard about the Yale tradition of flying pie tins and students shouting out, "Frisbee" and so named their product Frisbee. Now stop and think. Was it only Yale students who threw pie tins? Maybe students at other universities also threw pie tins, and if so what did they cry out? Today restaurants across the country sell their pies to take home in metal pans. If today students just started to toss pie tins, would they yell, "Denny's," Eppies" or "Brookfields?" Just doesn't sound right, does it? The next time you visit an antique store, see if they have an old Frisbie pie tin. They're still around and sell for $50 or more. –LU

PIG: When the term pig is used in cookery, it generally means a 12-pound-or-so suckling pig that has not been weaned from its mother and is roasted whole. (see PORK)

PIGEON: There are more than 300 different species of wild pigeons. Some that have been domesticated when full grown are too tough to eat. Only the young, known as squabs are eaten, as well as doves which are sometimes sold as pigeon. The famous Moroccan Pigeon Pie, called *Bastila*, is reserved for high holidays. The handmade dough is even thinner than phyllo dough, if that's possible. Pigeons are raised there for eating, the way chickens are here. The pie would be famous for its size alone. The recipe in *A Mediterranean Feast* takes 5 pounds of pigeon, 5 pounds of chicken, 2 Cornish hens, 1 pheasant, and a turkey thigh. It takes a 16 inch round pie pan to hold it. **Nutrition facts** per 3 ounces: 197 calories, 143 calories from fat, 15.6g total fat (24%), 5.5g saturated fat (28%), 62.2mg cholesterol (21%), 35.3mg sodium (2%), zero carbohydrates and fiber, 12.1g protein (24%), 159 IU vitamin A (3%), 4mg vitamin C (6%), 8mg calcium (1%), and 2.3mg iron (13%).

PIGEON GRAPE: The vine, native to south Florida, produces 3/8 inch fruit in clusters that is eaten fresh and made into jelly.

PIGEON PEA: From tropical Africa, the shrub produces small bean pods that are eaten green and dried. Over 90% of the world's crop now comes from India. The immature green peas are eaten as peas. The whole young pods are eaten like green beans.

PIG NUTS: See HICKORY NUTS

PIKE: A fresh-water fish from North America is an important game fish for fishermen. The two main varieties are the pickerels and much smaller than the muskellunge, which is the largest of the pike family. Fishermen have caught them up to sixty pounds, but seldom are larger than ten pounds in the market. Pickerels seldom get larger than eight pounds and average a lot less. Pike can be broiled, baked, fried, and braised.

FISHING FOR NORTHERN PIKE
by Bernice Erickson

My friend and I went fishing for Northern Pike one day. We took our rods and reels with 40 pound test line. I had my 14 foot boat with a 15 horse power motor, and a depth finder. We were on the lake about a half-hour, when we came to a location with the right sort of bottom for this type of ishing. I turned the motor off, and dropped anchor. We baited our hooks with artificial bait, and started casting, and reeling in. We were there about an hour and only had a few strikes. My friend caught one that was too small and threw it back.

As we were sitting, talking, and fishing, all at once I had a good strike. I gave my pole a jerk to set the hook, and the fish took off toward the middle of the lake. I started reeling in, and my fish headed for the bottom of the lake, then came to the top and repeated the process, over and over, until he became tired enough to let me reel him in. When I got him next to the boat, and ready to net him, all at once a huge Muskellunge (muskie) came swimming along the side of the boat, grabbed my Northern, and took off. I cut the line, because we guessed the muskie to be almost five feet long. It covered at least one-third of the boat. All in a day's fishing in the lakes of Northern Wisconsin! We had a pretty good day fishing even so. We took six Pikes home, and had a good fish story to tell.

PILAF: A fluffy, seasoned rice dish in which the grains are never mushy, but well cooked and separated. Meats, poultry, fish, shellfish, vegetables, and seasonings can also be added.

PIMENTO: Slices of a small red bell pepper packed in cans or jars for garnishing purposes. These are also the little red slivers you see in stuffed green olives. From the Spanish, *pimiento*. See PEPPER, CAPSICUM

PINEAPPLE: No, pineapples were not native to Hawaii, but to northern South America, where still some of the best pineapples are grown. The English gave it the name because it resembled a pine cone. The Spanish followed suit with *piña*, a Spanish word meaning "pine cone." In other European countries, its name is *ananas*. They took from a Paraguayan native word *nana*, meaning "excellent fruit." Spanish mariners brought the pineapple to Hawaii in 1790 where today most of the world's pineapple is produced. Pineapple now grows in almost all tropical countries. Much of the fresh pineapple eaten in the United States comes from Puerto Rico and Mexico. Pineapple is best eaten fresh, but can be cooked in sweet and sour sauces, with rice, beans, and made into pie, cake, sherbet and other desserts. Pineapples are available fresh, frozen, canned, candied, juice, and preserves. **Nutrition facts** per ½ cup: 38 calories, 3 calories from fat, .3g total fat (1%), zero saturated fat and sodium, 9.6g carbohydrates (3%), .9g fiber (4%), .3g protein (1%), zero vitamin A, 12mg vitamin C (20%), 5mg calcium (1%), and .3mg iron (2%). www.dole.com

Tip: What's the world's healthiest frozen pop? Any fruit slice you keep in the freezer and ready to eat, such as pineapple slices individually wrapped.

GROW A PINEAPPLE PLANT
by Billie Jean Hepp

Tropical plants are beautiful and many can be grown in indoor pots at home. Pineapple plants will grow into gorgeous plants and may even produce a pineapple.

Your will need: 1 pineapple; Garden pot; Potting soil
1. Twist off the top of a fresh pineapple. Do not cut, as it won't work.
2. Dry the top for a couple of days.
3. Push the bottom end of the top into potting soil.
4. Water and wait. 5. Keep the soil moist.
6. Once it starts to grow, transplant into a larger pot,
keep in a sunny location, and water when the soil dries out.
7. In a year round warm climate, the plant can be transplanted into the ground.

PINCH: A loose term where just a little salt, pepper, spices, herbs and other seasonings are added to a recipe. It is generally less than an eighth teaspoon.

PINDO PALM: Also known as the jelly palm, this tree from Brazil produces yellow clusters of fruit that are eaten fresh and made into jelly.

PINE NUTS: A small oblong seed extracted from certain pine cones. In the United States they are found in the Rocky mountains and along the Pacific coast. In Europe they are found in the Mediterranean. Pine nuts are used in many recipes in the Near East countries, especially in Arab lands. Pine nuts are also sold as *piñons* the United States. When pine nuts are labeled *pignolias,* they have been imported from Italy. Pine nuts are eaten fresh, added to meat recipes, and make wonderful cookies. **Nutrition facts** per 1/4 cup: 206 calories, 154 calories from fat, 20.3g total fat (31%), 3.1g saturated fat (16%), zero cholesterol and sodium, 5.7g carbohydrates (2%), 1.8g fiber (7%), 9.6g protein (19%), zero vitamin A, 1mg vitamin C (1%), 10mg calcium (1%), and 3.7mg iron (20%).

PINK BEANS: 1) another name for pinto beans, or 2) baby kidney beans.

PINK SALMON: The smallest of all the salmon, are also known as humpbacks or regionally as humpies. Available fresh, frozen and canned. Their pink, tender texture, delicate flavor and lower fat content requires care to prevent overcooking. Consider using canned pink salmon in chowders, soups, sandwiches, pasta recipes, casseroles or salads.

PINTO BEANS: Also known as pink beans, are colored a very pale pink with lots of brown specks. There is a variety without the brown specks. Pinto beans turn a brown-red when cooked.. **Nutrition facts** per ½ cup cooked: 117 calories, 4 calories from fat, .5g total fat (1%), .1g saturated fat (1%), zero cholesterol and sodium, 21.9g carbohydrates (7%), 7.4g fiber (29%), 7g protein (14%), zero vitamin A, 2mg vitamin C (3%), 41mg calcium (4%), and 2.2mg iron (12%).

PIONEER FOOD: See COLONIAL COOKING.

Activity:

Cities across our great land celebrate the birth of their community. You can have your own pioneer day celebration at home with family and friends. Dress in period costume and cook pioneer and ethnic foods of your region.

PIPÉRADE: Originating in Basque area on the border of Spain and France, it is a combination of tomatoes, sweet peppers and onions cooked until tender. Then eggs are added and cooked to a frothy puree.

PIPSISEWA: Also know as "ground holly," "prince's pine," and "wintergreen," pipissewa was popular with the Native Americans, who taught the settlers how to use it. Pipsissewa extract is used for flavoring candy (wintergreen mints) and soft drinks (especially root beer).

PIROG (peer ohg) is the Russian name for pie. In Russia, meat pies are as common as hamburgers are in the United States. Spellings vary. The larger pies are called *pirogi*. See POCKET DOUGH and PIROZHKI. www.milliespierogies.com

PIROZHKI: (PIEROGI or PIROGUES) These little Russian and Polish pastries are popular throughout Eastern Europe. They are both served as an appetizer and as a light dinner usually with a bowl of hot cabbage soup or borscht. Pirozhki come in a variety of shapes and are either fried or baked. Fillings vary. Some are stuffed with mashed potatoes, others with ground meat. The pastry is similar to pie crust. The fat is generally butter and the liquid used is sour cream. Pirozhki/pirogi are found in the frozen food section of many supermarkets. In cities where there are strong Russian and other Eastern Europe cultural groups, chances are we can find a bakery or deli that make pirozhki fresh. See POCKET DOUGH. www.pierogiplace.com.

PISTACHIO: Native to central Asia, although some nonedible, related species have been found growing wild in California and Mexico and other parts of the world. Today 98% of pistachios are grown in California for United States consumption and California is second in world production. Iran is number one. Pistachios grow in grape-like clusters, each nut encased in an outer hull. When ripe, the hull turns pink and the shell within splits naturally. The nuts are roasted in the shell, the majority salted, and some dyed red for those who prefer a colorful shell.. The nut meat is a light green and has a delicate flavor. Pistachios are most commonly eaten as a snack and can be used in any recipe calling for nuts. Pistachios are a good source of potassium, calcium, iron, and vitamin A. **Nutrition facts** per 1-ounce serving (that's 47 nuts, according to the USDA): 170 calories, 31 calories from fat, 13g total fat (20%), 1.5g saturated fat (8%), zero cholesterol; sodium 190mg; 9g carbohydrates (3%), 3g fiber (12%), 6g protein (12%), 151 IU vitamin A (4%), 1mg vitamin C (2%), 31mg calcium (4%), and 1.2mg iron (6%). www.pistachios.org

PISTACHIO ICE CREAM: The next time you purchase pistachio ice cream, check the ingredients. Except for the more pricey brands like Ben & Jerry's, most have no pistachio nuts. They might trick you with other nuts and with green food coloring (real pistachio ice cream has no coloring, but is a creamy white). One of the ingredients found in the imitation pistachio ice cream is turnips. Yes, turnip! Since when does a turnip taste like a pistachio? Also check the ingredients on pistachio pudding mixes. Again, most have no pistachios. Donna Gavello from the **California Pistachio Commission** suggests to make your own pistachio ice cream. from this recipe, which is both low in fat and cholesterol, plus a good source for vitamin C:

½ cup pistachios, chopped
12 ounce can of low-fat evaporated milk
1 envelope plain gelatin
1 cup sugar
1 cup nonfat plain yogurt
2 cups pureed fresh fruit
(strawberries, peaches, nectarines, apricots or bananas)

1. Spread pistachios in a shallow pan and roast at 400°F for
3 minutes or until roasted and fragrant; cool.
2. Combine milk with gelatin in saucepan; stir over medium
heat until dissolved.
3. Add yogurt and pureed fruit, blend.
4. Turn into ice cream maker that holds 2 quarts and follow
manufacturer's directions until frozen.
4. Stir in pistachios; freeze until firm.
Makes 12 servings.

Nutrition facts per ½ cup made with strawberries: 135 calories, 24 calories from fat, 2.8g total fat (4%), .4g saturated fat (2%), zero cholesterol, 47.8mg sodium (2%), 24.4g carbohydrates (8%), 1.2g fiber (5%), 4.5g protein (9%), 132 IU vitamin A (3%), 15mg vitamin C (25%), 131mg calcium (13%) and .6mg iron (3%). For more recipes log on to: www.pistachios.org.

PITANGA: See FLORIDA CHERRY.

PITOMBA: This shrub from Brazil has small, yellow-orange, sweet fruit that is eaten fresh, made into jam, jelly and sherbet.

PIZZA: Best described as an open face pie, topped with tomato sauce, cheese, vegetables, and/or meats. The original Italian pizza was fried bread dough dipped into tomato sauce with no other toppings. American pizzas are a good source for protein, calcium, and many vitamins and minerals, especially vitamin C. The pizza presumably began in Naples, but even in Naples historians can't agree on what that first pizza was like. Basically, it must have been crust, tomato, garlic, oil and oregano–the same as today. Mozzarella cheese topping came along later. A famous quote comes from Burton Anderson: "If Naples had managed to patent the pizza, it would now be among Italy's richest cities instead of one of the poorest."

PIZZELLE: These wafer-like round cookies, they are sold commercially. They look and taste like thin waffles.

PLANK: (noun) A thick piece of wood that has been soaked in water for 12 or more hours, seasoned with oil, heated in a slow oven prior to placing a steak or a fish on it. (verb) To plank a steak is to finished cooking it in the oven on a plank then serve it with vegetables and garnish on the same board. Thus prepared, the plank can be used for serving steaks or fish.

PLANTAIN: A member of the banana family and native to southeast Asia, plantains are much larger, about a foot long, less sweet, and quite starchy. They must be cooked to be edible. They can be baked, fried, or boiled. Green plantains can be sliced thin, fried and made into chips. Ripe plantains can be boiled in their skins until tender, cut into one inch slices and sautéd in butter, brown sugar, and cinnamon and served for dessert. When baked in the skin until tender, plantains can be split open, stuffed with beans and served in place of potatoes. Plantains are rich in vitamin A and potassium, low in sodium, and fair source for vitamin C. **Nutrition facts** per ½ cup: 137 calories, 3 calories from fat, .4g total fat (1%0, zero saturated fat and sodium, 35.9g carbohydrates (12%), 2.6g fiber (10%), 1.5g protein (3%), 1267 IU vitamin A (25%), 21mg vitamin C (34%), zero calcium and .7mg iron (4%).

PLANTAIN PLANT: A name given to a group of small, leafy greens. From the Anglo-Saxon *wegbreed,* meaning "growing by the wayside." Mostly it is found in Italy and Europe.

PLASTIC FOOD: Ever wonder why the burger on your plate doesn't look like the one in the poster over the counter? Did the cake you made have the same dazzle as the one in the magazine picture? If it didn't, there's a reason. The perfect food in the picture is probably plastic.

That's right! The old rubber chicken has been around a long time, starting with the theater. Yes, plastic is the reason people in the movies always leave all that food on their plates. The more delectable it looks, the more likely it is to be fake. Why? Real food looks faded and melts under hot lights.

With the rise of color photography in the 1920s, the Japanese developed fake foods called *"sampuru"* to use in show display and restaurant windows. Today many Tokyo companies hire artists who specialize in imitation food. Would you like to be a food artist and use a hot air gun to make cherries jubilee? That hamburger you admire so much on the poster has vinyl cheese and cloth lettuce. And don't worry about spilling the drink. It's solid glycerine.

You can see samples of fake food in the toy section of your favorite store, but toy food won't fool you like the photographable wonders of the real *sampuru* artist. If you're thinking of a career in food but don't like to wash dishes and eat leftovers, give food art a thought. But don't plan on fast advancement. It takes a Japanese artist about ten years to be able to make the most challenging food of all--fake fish. The faux salmon sells for over $1,000 and is a truly artistic creation. *--LU*

PLAY DOUGH: Make a batch of play dough for the preschoolers in your family. Also take a fresh batch when you babysit. The ingredients are kid friendly, just in case someone takes a bite, but don't encourage eating play dough.

1 cup flour
½ cup salt
1 teaspoon cream of tartar
1 cup water
1 teaspoon vegetable oil

1. Combine dry ingredients in a large bowl.
2. Add the water and oil; stir.
3. Pour mixture into a sauce pan, heat over medium
heat, stirring with a wooden spoon.
4. When mixture become dry and doughy, turn it out on
waxed paper or a bread board to cool.
5. Store in closed container.

PLUM: Native plums have been found in Europe, Asia, and North America. Plums are in the same family as almonds, apricots, cherries, and peaches. Japanese plums, probably originating China, and came to American in 1870. Beach plums grow wild along the Atlantic coast from Canada to Virginia. The blue-purple, small beach plums are too tart to eat raw, but are delicious in jams. Plums can be round or oval, have a smooth skin in various colors of red, purple, yellow, green, and blue. Plums are both sweet and tart, with a thick, juicy flesh. Plums are eaten fresh, stewed, dried (prunes), and made into desserts. Plums are available fresh and canned, or as preserves. America's growing season is early summer to mid fall, and from Chile plums arrive in January and last until April. **Nutrition facts** per 1 plum: 36 calories, 3 calories from fat. .4g total fat (1%), zero saturated fat and sodium 8.6g carbohydrates (3%),1g fiber (4%), .5g protein (1%), 213 IU vitamin A (4%), 6mg vitamin C (10%), zero calcium and iron.

PLUM PUDDING: Strange as it might seem, there are no plums in English plum pudding. It is made with suet, raisins, citrus peels and spices, and comes out looking like a mincemeat cake that is either steamed or boiled. Served as a dessert during the Christmas holidays with hard sauce.

POACH: (pohch) A method of cooking foods in simmering water. Eggs, fish, chicken and vegetables are simmered slowly in a small amount of water so they retain their shape. Vinegar, spices, and herbs can be added to the water for additional flavor.

POCKET DOUGH: Many foods are baked, fried, or boiled inside a "pocket" or pouch formed by dough. The stuffed pocket resembles a small mound or pillow.

LITTLE PILLOWS STUFFED WITH GOODNESS

Lay down a piece of pastry dough on your bread board. Take a dollop of something you like and top the dough. Now take another piece of dough and place it on top. Finally seal the edges and cook it. What do you have? You would have a little filled pillow that you would enjoy to eat. These pillows are found in various forms all around the world. The **Chinese** would have *cha yun t'un,* the filling would be shrimp, chopped water chestnuts and sliced green onions. In **Vietnam** they're called *bon-bow* and filled with hamburger and onions. The **Mexicans** make *empanadas* that are filled with either apples or meat. To the south of Mexico, in **El Salvador** the filling would be pineapple. In **India** they're called *samosas* and are filled with cooked lamb or beef, onion and potato. Their neighbors in **Pakistan** make *paratha* and stuff them with potatoes and green peppers. The American Southwest has sopaidillas (soft pillows) with chili and salsa.

Most European countries also make stuffed pillows. In **Denmark** they're called *spandauers* and filled with raspberry jam. The **Austrians** fill *germkodel* with plum preserves. The Jews in **Israel** make *knishes* with potato, onion and cheese. In **Greece** they enjoy *tiropetes* made with feta cheese, eggs and chives. The **Russians** make *pirozhki* with ground beef, onion and hard boiled eggs. And in **Poland** their *pierogy* is stuffed with sauerkraut and mushrooms, while the **American** version contains mashed potatoes and meat. The most famous stuffed pillows of all, which no doubt you have enjoyed many times, are **Italian** ravioli, and can be stuffed with beef, cheese and/or spinach, usually a blend of two main ingredients.

Each country makes a different kind of pastry. Some with flour and egg, while others tend to make them sweet with a little sugar. The choice of liquid to make the dough ranges from water to sour cream. Some use prepared dough such as filo leaves or wonton skins. Cooking of the stuffed pillows varies. They can be boiled in water, some are baked, while others are deep fat fried. Some are used for dipping, most are topped with a sauce. Still others are added to a clear soup.

Would You like to Make a Stuffed Pillow?

It's easy with your choice of prepared ingredients. For the dough, use wonton skins. Here's how you can do it.

1. Lay down a wonton skin.(store bought)
2. Top it with a teaspoon of your favorite filling.
   If using meat, cook and chop it first.
3. Lay a second wonton skin on the top.
4. Moisten the edges with a little water. Next fold
   over all the edges and seal with a little more water.
5. Drop your filled wonton skin in boiling water.
   Cook until tender about 10 minutes.

What you do next will depend upon your filling. If it is a meat, vegetable or cheese filling, you can top your cooked pillows with tomato sauce. If it is a sweet filling, and you would like them a little crisp, fry them and top with powdered sugar. You can also make your own pastry dough. Just follow the directions from your cookbook on how to make the dough and the best way to cook your pillows. One of the easiest pastries is pie dough which can be baked or fried. Or you can make a pasta dough with egg and cook them by dropping them in boiling water. And don't forget to add a little extra to the filling, such as your choice of spice to canned fruit pie filling or herbs to meat and vegetable fillings.

RAISIN-FILLED SUGAR COOKIES

If you like raisins and sugar cookies, make a sugar cookie dough recipe and fill cookie with raisin pie filling. Roll out the sugar cookie dough flat, about an eight of an inch thick, cut a round about the size of a one pound coffee can lid. Add some raisin pie filling to the top of the cookie and top with another cookie. Now pinch the edges together and baked in 350°F oven for about 15 minutes or until slightly brown.

Some like their pillows sweet and eat them for dessert like a cookie. While others use them as an appetizer. But mostly you will find pillows as the main course for dinner topped with your favorite sauce. What is your favorite stuffed pillow?

Fifties comedian Buddy Hackett likes his food spicy, peppery hot. As he says, "They're so hot, they burned the lint out of my navel." Now that's hot!

POI: To make poi, starchy taro roots are cooked, pounded, then kneaded until smooth. Taro then is mixed with water to make a grayish-white bland flavored paste called poi. Poi is eaten with the fingers. Poi can be eaten immediately or allowed to ferment for several days. Lactic acid bacteria invade it and cause the fermentation. Poi is a staple in the Hawaiian Islands. Visitors can't wait to get a taste of it as a curiosity but seldom ask for it twice. www.luauking.com.

POISONOUS PLANTS: Most of the following plants are found in the southern sections of the United States. Others, like poison ivy, are found also throughout the East and poison oak in the West. There are many others. For a complete listing, you'll need a book on the subject.

Akee: The fruit is edible, but over-ripe or under-ripe fruit can be toxic. Captain Bligh introduced this to Jamaica, and while akee is a popular dish, many people have died from eating it.

Angel's Trumpet: All parts of this plant are poisonous. The seeds have been used to murder people. Even the fragrance can cause dizziness.

Balsam Pear (also known as bitter melon): Eating the mature orange fruit can cause vomiting. The leaves can be cooked and eaten at a vegetable. Bitter melon is an important ingredient in Oriental cooking, but has to be carefully prepared to reduce bitterness.

Black Nightshade: Both the leaves and the berries are toxic. However, when the berries are completely ripe and turn black, they are often eaten. Luther Burbank developed a variety called "wonderberry," but care must be taken, and only the very ripe fruits should be eaten.

Brazilian Pepper: These colorful red clusters of berries are not pepper. With the red skins removed, the seed looks like black peppercorns, but are not, and should never be used in cooking. This tree is related to poison ivy.

Caladium: All parts of this plant will cause burning in the mouth, tongue, and throat.

Candelabra Cactus: The sap is toxic internally, and irritating to the skin and eyes.

Carolina Jessamine: While the flowers are fragrant, eating the plant can cause death to both animals and humans.

Cashew Apple: While the fruit and nuts can be eaten, the husk around the nut is toxic, and must be roasted before it is peeled and eaten.

Cassava: The popular root found in some supermarkets is somewhat toxic. A sweet form is cooked and eaten like a potato. A bitter variety is processed into tapioca.

Castor Bean: While a source for castor oil (the toxins are removed during processing), just a couple of seeds eaten will cause death.

Century Plant: The sap will cause a rash on the skin, and burning in the eyes.

Chili Pepper: While not poisonous, it is highly irritating to skin, eyes, and mucous membranes. When handling, wear rubber gloves.

Coontie: The root of this fern once used to make starch by the Miccosukee Native Americans was also made into bread. All parts of this plant are toxic. Now it is believed this starch produces cancer.

Dumbcane: Although a popular house plant, the juice is irritating to the skin and will cause blisters. If the juice is swallowed, the juice will cause dangerous swelling and will restrict your speech. Hence the name, "dumbcane."

Lantana: A common flowering shrub is fatally poisonous to young children.

Lime: Lime oil will irritate the skin of some people and will cause brown patches.

Manchineel: The fruit looks like a small green apple, but if eaten, can be fatal.

Mayan Spinach (also known as chaya): The leaves are quite nutritious when cooked in two changes of water, but the fresh leaves will sting, and irritate the skin.

Night-blooming Jessamine: The fragrance can cause headaches and nausea, and the fruit is poisonous.

Oleander: All parts are highly toxic and if eaten can be fatal. The smoking from burning plants is also poisonous.

Oyster Plant (also known as salsify): The juice causes a rash. The plant can be cooked and eaten without a problem.

Physic Nut: The seeds are quite delicious, but will cause vomiting within minutes, followed by death.

Pokeweed: The tender young leaves are used to make "poke salad." In order to use, the leaves must be boiled twice in two changes of water, but can still be fatal.

Rosary Pea: The seeds were once strung for rosaries. If the seeds are swallowed whole, they may not have an effect, however, if crushed they can be fatal.

Tread-softly: While the roots can be eaten safely after being cooked, the leaves will cause a stinging rash. Don't eat any plant unless you know it is safe.

POKE: A wild spring green, also known as pokegreens, pokeweed, skoke, garget, and pigeonberry. The passenger pigeons, before they became extinct, loved the deep purple berries that ripen in late summer. The whole plant is poison except for the tender green shoots and leaves in early spring. Native Americans put the berries to use in making pink dyes, and in cures for arthritis and cancer. **Nutrition facts** per ½ cup pokeberry shoots: 18 calories, zero fats, 18.4mg sodium (1%), 3g carbohydrates (1%), 1.4g fiber (5%), 2.1g protein (4%), 6960 IU vitamin A (133%), 109mg vitamin C (181%), 42mg calcium (4%), and 1.4mg iron (8%).

POLENTA: An Italian word for cornmeal. The cornmeal is made into cornmeal mush by constantly stirred the mixture until a crust forms around the edge of the pan. It is then sliced and eaten in place of bread, usually with tomato sauce. Its history goes back to when maize (corn) was introduced to Northern Italy from America in the 1600s.

POLLOCK: A saltwater fish of the cod family is found in both the northern Atlantic and Pacific waters. No other white flesh fish matches pollock in its mild, delicate flavor that is similar to haddock. Most of the Pacific pollock is used to make *surimi* seafood, while the Atlantic variety is used for fish and chips. Pollock is becoming more popular for home consumers because it can be baked, sautéd, poached, and simmered in stews and chowders. **Nutrition facts** per 3 ounces: 69 calories, 7 calories from fat, .7g total fat (1%), .2g saturated fat (1%), 60.4mg cholesterol (20%), 84.2mg sodium (4%), zero carbohydrates and fiber, 14.6g protein (29%), 56 IU vitamin A (1%), zero vitamin C, 5mg calcium (1%) and .2mg iron (1%).

POMANDER: A bag or box of aromatic substances to sweeten the air. An air freshener made of citrus and spices. The simplest pomander is an orange into which clove spices have been stuck. Make one yourself.

POMEGRANATE: About the size of an orange with a red leathery skin, the pomegranate is filled with tart tasting red seeds. Originating in Persia, it is grown best in hot dry climates. The seeds are eaten fresh and made into juice. "When you eat the pomegranate...each seed in a person's stomach lights up his heart and silences the whispering devil for forty days." That is the reverence with which the pomegranate was held by Abdullah Ibn Abbas, a cousin of the prophet Muhammad at the beginning of the 17th century. According to legend, the fruit was said to have been watered by drops of water from Paradise. From the Latin into the French, *pome*, meaning fleshy fruit.

Cathegian sailors, it is believed, brought the fruit to Spain 3000 years ago. Jews and Arabs cultivated them in Andalusia. The Arab name is *gharnata*. It shouldn't be surprising to learn that the city of Granada in Spain is named after the pomegranate and the symbol of the city is the pomegranate. The beautiful red color makes lovely drinks and flavors other dishes. **Nutrition facts** per ½ cup seeds: 45 calories, zero fats and sodium, 11.4g carbohydrates (4%), .4g fiber (2%), .6g protein (1%), zero vitamin A, 4mg vitamin C (7%), zero calcium, and .2mg iron (1%). www.pomegranatecouncil.org

POMELO: The original name for "grapefruit." It's possible the word "pomelo" is a misspelling of "pummelo," which is not a true grapefruit. The grapefruit is a cross of pummelo and the sweet orange. **Nutrition facts** per ½ cup: 45 calories, zero fats and sodium, 11.4g carbohydrates (4%), .4g fiber (2%), .6g protein (1%), zero vitamin A, 4mg vitamin C (7%), zero calcium, and .2mg iron (1%). www.sunkist.com

POMPANO: A salt water fish found along the western Atlantic coast from New England to Brazil. The pompano, related to jacks, are found in quantity in the waters of Florida. Pompano has a delicate flavor and can be cooked by any method, with broiling the most successful. In New Orleans it is cooked in a paper bag with shrimp and crab. **Nutrition facts** per 3 ounces: 139 calories, 75 calories from fat, 8.1g total fat (13%), 3g saturated fat (15%), 42.5mg cholesterol (14%), 55.3mg sodium (3%), zero carbohydrates and fiber, 15.7g protein (32%), 94 IU vitamin A (2%), zero vitamin C, 18mg calcium (2%), and .5mg iron (3%).

POND APPLE: From the West Indies and south Florida, this small tree produces large, yellow, barely edible fruit that is eaten fresh, mostly as a survival food.

POPCORN: A variety of corn with small kernels that is dried and later popped inside out. The unpopped kernels are either white or yellow. The white when popped is smaller and sweeter than the yellow. The kernels can be popped up to 20 times their original size in oil, or by dry heat. **Nutrition facts** per 1 cup air-popped without butter: 31 calories, 3 calories from fat, .3g total fat (1%), zero saturated fat and sodium, 6.2g carbohydrates (2%), 1.2g fiber (5%), 1g protein (2%), zero vitamins A and C and Calcium, .2mg iron (1%) www.jollytime.com

THE ALL-AMERICAN EXPLOSION

Did you know you can make a gigantic explosion in your kitchen with a common ingredient found in most pantries? Did you know it is perfectly legal? Most parents not only say it is okay, in fact they would rather have you blow up this element than to have them do it for you.

The pressure from this blast generally exceeds 2,000 pounds per square inch. Sounds dangerous, doesn't it? But with care, there is no risk at all. Of course if you use too much, you could blow the lid off of a pot, causing a mess on the kitchen stove. The good news, it is easy to clean up after the big bang.

Did You Guess the Ingredient? No? Here Are a Few Clues:

It's in the grass family. The Aztecs in Mexico cultivated this grass more than 7,000 years ago. This grass can grow taller than six feet. The original name was *zee mays everta*, which is also known by our Native Americans as *maize*.

- It was unknown in the Old World before the European explorers came to America.
- The Arawak and Carib natives first presented it to Columbus and his crew.
- Cortes got his first sight of the All-American Explosion, when he invaded Mexico.
- The pilgrims received it as a gift from the Wampanoags during the Thanksgiving feast.

By Now You Have Guessed It. Yes, it Is Corn.

More precisely it is popcorn. The mystery is, **why does this seed blowup**? The popcorn seed contains a starchy substance where water is stored. When the kernel is heated the water inside boils and creates steam. The outside of the grain is a hard enamel-like cover which tries to contain the steam. When the pressure is too great, you guessed it, it blows up! Then it turns the kernel inside-out to about twenty times the original size.

When you pop corn, there always seems to be a few kernels which did not explode. They are called "old maids." These seeds have less than thirteen percent of water. This happens with some inexpensive brands of popcorn, or maybe the kernels have been kept too long on the pantry shelf and have dried out. You can avoid this problem by soaking the kernels prior to popping for a few minutes in ice water. While it will reduce the population of the old maids, some will still not rip apart, no matter how long they are soaked.

There are basically two kinds of popcorn, white and yellow. The white is sweeter, but the yellow pops bigger. To make a sweeter, bigger popcorn the two species have been combined to make a hybrid, usually referred to as "gourmet popcorn."

Popcorn Is One of the Good-for-You Snack Foods

When the kernel is popped without oil, a small bowl (about a pint) without added butter or salt contains only sixty calories, of which six calories come from fat. This means it is low in fat and has no cholesterol, as well as no sodium. More good news: It is high in carbohydrates, which provides the body with energy. And, popcorn contains more protein and iron than potato chips. When the popped popcorn becomes old and stale, don't throw it out. The unbuttered and unsalted popped kernels have many uses. You can string them with thread for the holiday tree. You can glue them on plastic balls and cones to make festive decorations. Old popcorn also makes great packing material for shipping fragile items in place of styrofoam and it is environmentally sound. --*RSC*

PERFECT POPPED POPCORN GRANDMA'S WAY
Tips to Make Every Kernel Pop

1. Keep popcorn stored in freezer or refrigerator so it won't dry out.
2. Check instructions on the package for variations or additional tips and amounts to be popped.
3. Use a heavy or copper bottomed, deep pan. Do not use a thin pan.
4. Find a glass lid, if possible, with a good fit on the pan.
5. Over medium heat, heat vegetable oil in the pan. Do not use butter or margarine because it burns.
6. When the oil is hot, throw in two or three kernels to see if they pop. When a test kernel pops, add enough popcorn to form a thin layer on the bottom.
7. Cover and keep the heat even. Do not shake pan or remove lid.
8. Watch through the glass lid and listen for the popping to slow down. As the pan fills, the popping should begin to slow down. When it almost stops, turn off the heat. Wait for the last few grains to pop. When popping stops, quickly remove pan from the burner.
9. Pour popcorn into large, roomy bowl.
10. Melt butter or margarine in pan while still hot and drizzle it over popcorn. Salt to taste. Do not salt until popcorn is popped. Salt makes the corn tough while popping. . –LU

POPOVER: A bread that is steam leavened. Made with eggs, popover batter is similar to pancake batter, baked in muffin pans or custard cups in a hot over. Their name comes from their tendency to swell out over the sides of the pan while baking.

POPPY SEEDS: Tiny black seeds from large poppy flowers. The crunchy, nutty flavor is baked into breads, cakes, cookies, and pasties. Poppy seeds are also added to pasta dishes and salads.

POPSICLE: A frozen juice bar made with water, sugar, real and/or imitation flavors, and coloring. A trademark of Popsicle Industries, Inc.

PORGY: There are a number of porgy varieties of fish found in Atlantic and Mediterranean waters. The ones found along America's Atlantic coast are better known as scup. Porgy is generally baked or broiled whole, and when cooked the bones can easily be lifted and removed. Porgy will lose much of its good flavor quickly after being caught.

PORK: The flesh of the swine, more commonly called pig or hog. The meat is a light pink, white when cooked, and is often referred to as "the other white meat," but is technically considered red meat. Depending upon the cut, pork can be fried, roasted, broiled, braised and barbecued. Pork is also smoked, and while many call this smoked ham, ham is really the rear leg cuts. Ham is available both fresh and cured. Pork is made into sausage, smoked or unsmoked, with a variety of spices and herbs. **Nutrition facts** per 3 ounces: 193 calories, 128 calories from fat, 14g total fat (22%), 4.9g saturated (25%), 58.7mg cholesterol (20%), 45.8mg sodium (2%), zero carbohydrates and fiber, 16g protein (31%), zero vitamin A, 1mg vitamin C (1%), 13mg calcium (1%) and .7mg iron (4%). www.nppc.org

PORK AND BEANS: Dried beans that are slow cooked with pork and usually sweetened with brown sugar. Pork used can be fresh, salt pork or ham.

PORK PIE: The favorite meat pie in Britain, it is similar to ham and veal pies. First made in medieval times, it has changed little since. The filling is made of fresh pork and seasonings, especially sage.

PORRIDGE: A hot cereal made with grains and water, the most common made with oats. Porridge is also a thick soup made with vegetables. Porridge is the staple that for centuries kept poor people from starvation when other foods were scarce or unaffordable.

PORRINGER: A shallow dish with or without a handle used for soup or porridge.

PORT: A sweet wine from Portugal generally served as an after dinner beverage. Port is made from a variety of grapes and as it ages brandy is added to the fermentation. Port is aged up to twenty years in both bottles and casks. The color can be either red or white, depending upon the grapes used.

PORTABELLA MUSHROOMS: A large-cap variety of agaricus and crimini that can range up to six inches in diameter. Their long growing period gives portabellas a very rich flavor. Portabellas are served fresh, whole or sliced; grilled, baked and fried. Stuffed, it makes a great meat substitute for sandwiches. www.mushroommuseum.com

POSSOM: See O'POSSOM.

POSSET: Hot milk that has been curdled with wine or lemon juice, sweetened and sometimes thickened. It goes back to the 15th century where it began as drink for invalids.

POTATO: When Spanish conquistador Francisco Pizarro went searching for gold in the New World, he found Peruvian Quechua natives feasting on strange tuberous roots and took back samples to Europe where it was received with reactions ranging from fear to distrust. The same was said of tomatoes and other New World fruits and vegetables.

Now the potato is often called "The Eighth Wonder of the World," but it took almost 200 years before it was accepted in Europe. Part of the problem, no one knew what part of the plant was edible. One royal chef was fired for feeding Queen Elizabeth I the leaves. Luckily, not all Europe feared the potato.

Sir Walter Raleigh took the tuber to Ireland and it became a staple of the Irish diet. When the 1840s blight hit, Irishmen migrated to New Hampshire bringing the potato with them. Even today, the white potato is commonly known as the Irish potato.

In France it took Antoine Aususte Parmentier to trick people into acceptance. During the day, Parmentier stationed guards around his mysterious field. At night the garden was deliberately left without the guards and the French peasants began to pilfer the crop. Soon potatoes, like forbidden fruit, became a rage throughout the country. The Quechua's called the potato *papa*; the Spanish called them *patata* which developed into today's spelling. The original spelling would have been a lot easier to remember, don't you agree?

The potato is the fourth most cultivated crop in the world. They can be grown both below sea level and high in the Himalayas, from the Arctic Circle to south in the Strait of Magellan, and in the hot desserts of Africa. The only place potatoes do not grow well is in the sultry jungles where humidity encourages diseases. Potatoes can be boiled, baked, pan roasted, and fried. Potatoes can be served at all meals and in any way the cook can dream up. **Nutrition facts** for one baked potato without toppings: 88 calories, zero fats and sodium, 20.1g carbohydrates (7%), 1.8g fiber (7%), 2.3g protein (5%), zero vitamin A, 22mg vitamin C (37%), 8mg calcium (1%), .9mg iron (5%), and 608mg potassium. www.potatoes.com; www.idahopotatoes.com; www.oregonspuds.com; www.mainepotatoes.com

THE AMAZING POTATO

■ The average annual crop in 1990 (about 300 million tons) could cover a four lane superhighway circling the world six times.
■ The potato is so nutritious that a man in Scandinavia lived healthily for 300 days on only potatoes and a little margarine.
■ Gangster John Dillinger is said to have carved a pistol from a potato, dyed it with iodine and used it to escape from prison.

- The spud yields more good food more quickly on less land and in harsher climates than wheat, corn, or rice.
- A single potato can supply almost half a person's daily vitamin C needs.
- If a captain and crew were cast away on an island with a bushel of potatoes, they could grow a ton of food within a year and survive.
- One acre of potatoes can yield 1,200 gallons of ethyl alcohol for auto fuel.
- Farmers in the Andes Mountains cultivate as many as 3000 of the 5000 potato varieties and have named each one.
- Andean farmers grow a long, black potato they call "pig droppings."
- Prussia and Austria, in 1779, had to call off a war (The Potato War) when neither could find enough potatoes to feed the armies.
- In Ireland six years of potato famine led to a million deaths from starvation.
- The Emperor Napoleon's favorite dish was fried potatoes with onion.

POTATOES

I love to eat potatoes
boiled, mashed or fried.
I fix them in a salad
with pickles on the side.
I like them baked, or scalloped,
hash browns or french fries,
potato chips with onion dip,
or cheese potato pies.
--Elizabeth Giles

POTATO CHIPS: Thinly sliced, fresh potatoes, deep fat fried. The potato chip was supposedly invented in Saratoga Springs, New York in 1853 by a short-order cook, Native American George Crum, when a customer complained about his thick potato slices.

POTATO FLOUR: Potatoes are ground to a pulp and all liquid is removed. The result is dried into a very fine flour that can be used for thickening sauces and gravies. In America cornstarch is preferred, while in Germany and the Scandinavian counties potato flour is their choice. Potato flour is also used during Passover in place of wheat flour. Potato flour can be used in place of wheat flour in some recipes, such as cookies. It cannot be used by itself to make bread, because it doesn't have the gluten power to make bread rise.

POTATO TREE: A small tree with 2-inch, green fruit, not edible.

POT-AU-FEU: A French phase meaning "pot of fire." It's a boiled dinner made with meat and vegetables.

POT CHEESE is cottage cheese that has had the liquid drained out of it, causing a dry, firm cheese. This makes it useful in cheesecake because of its texture and sour flavor. Farmer cheese is pot cheese to which cream has been added.

POT HERBS: Certain herbs can be cooked as a vegetable with the leaves and stems like spinach, and the roots like carrots. The most common cooking herbs are: borage, chervil, chicory, lovage, sorrel, sweet cicely and rampion.

POT LIQUOR: The liquid left over after cooking meats and vegetables. Most of the broth comes from cooking greens, such as collards and turnip greens. In the southeast it is called "pot likker." This liquid is served as a broth or saved for cooking.

POTLUCK: A gathering of people where each brings a prepared dish. The name comes from not knowing what kind of variety will be on the table.

POT PIE: A meat and/or vegetable recipe that is baked in a pot with a pie or biscuit top crust, sometimes both top and bottom crusts.

POTPOURRI: (popo-ree) An air freshener made with dried flowers, herbs, and spices. The word means mixture or assortment.

POT ROAST: Generally less tender cuts of meat that are cooked slowly in a small amount of water, called "braising" on top of the stove or in a slow cooker.

POTTAGE: The word comes from the French, *potage,* meaning something cooked in a pot.

POTTED: Meat that has been ground into a fine paste and lightly seasoned. Also made with poultry, fish, vegetables and cheese.

POULTRY: A term used when referring to domesticated birds, such as chicken, ducks, and turkeys (see individual birds, CHICKEN, GOOSE, etc.).

POULTRY SEASONING: A blend of ground herbs usually consisting of sage, thyme, marjoram and savory. This seasoning is used not only for poultry, but for other meats, stuffings, and quick breads such as biscuits.

POUND CAKE: A cake made with a pound of flour, a pound of eggs, a pound of butter, and a pound of sugar, without addition of liquids or leavening ingredients. This produces a compact, fine-grained, and easy-to-slice cake that will keep for long periods of time. Endless variation have developed from the basic recipe. Cooks in the American South have adopted it for their own and enriched both the recipe and the endless ways it can be served.

POUND CAKE

Today, Southerners claim pound cake as a regional specialty, but the original recipe probably arrived with early British settlers. Hannah Glasse's *The Art of Cookery Made Plain and Easy,* published in 1747 England, states that the pound cake may have evolved from the almond cake of Renaissance Italy and Spain. The first American cookbook, *Amelia Simmons's American Cookery,* published in 1796 in Hartford, Connecticut, included two recipes for the cake. With no leavening agents, a cook had to rely on whipped egg whites and a strong arm to beat the necessary air into the batter, since those early cookbooks instructed, "Beat it all well together for about an hour with your hand, or a great wooden spoon." Pound cake is still popular. Traditionally, it consists of a pound each of butter, sugar, flour, and eggs. Today the list has endless variations developed over the years.

The Basic Pound Cake

Today, few cooks weigh the ingredients, and many add baking soda or baking powder as a leavening. Try making it the original way with just butter, eggs, sugar, and flour. It is important to have all ingredients at room temperature. Don't let the butter get too soft, because it will cause the cake to flatten. Flour should not be sifted, but gently spooned into the measuring cup.

1 cup butter, soften (do not melt)
1 cup sugar
1 cup eggs (about 4 eggs)
2 ½ cups flour
1/4 teaspoon salt

1. Cream butter and sugar, gradually, beating until light and fluffy.
2. Add the eggs, one at a time, beating well.
3. Slowly add the flour and salt. Mix only until blended after each addition.
Do not over beat.
6. Grease and flour a 9 x 5 x 3-inch loaf pan or spray with nonstick spray.
7. Pour batter into the loaf pan.
8. Bake in a preheated 275°F oven about 1 3/4 hours until a crack forms.
This crack occurs when the outside of he cake is done, and the inside if still soft.
It's also best to test with a wooden toothpick for doneness in the middle.
9. Cool in pan for 5 minutes. Turn out on a wire rack to cool completely before slicing.
Makes 16 slices.

VARIATIONS

Lemon: Add 2 teaspoons lemon extract and 2 teaspoons grated lemon rind to the batter.
Chocolate: Combine 1/4 cup cocoa to the flour mixture.
Praline: Replace sugar with brown sugar and fold in 1 cup of chopped pecans to the batter.
Marble: Melt 2 ounces of semi-sweet chocolate and blend it into about 1/3 of the batter. Alternate by dropping tablespoons of each batter in the loaf pan.
Vanilla: Add 2 teaspoons vanilla extract.

Spice: Add 1/4 teaspoon mace, 1/4 teaspoon nutmeg, or ½ teaspoon cinnamon.
Blueberry: Fold in ½ cup fresh or frozen blueberries into the batter.
Poppy Seed: Combine 2 tablespoons poppy seeds in the flour mixture.

Pound cakes can be served plain, topped with a fruit sauce, coated with sugar glaze, pudding, hot fudge sauce, ice cream, or fresh fruit and/or berries. Some people like to crumble the cake before adding a topping. For more information contact pound cake specialists in Elmore City, Oklahoma at MariDee's Country Kitchen Cakes at 800-798-7730.

POWWOW PABULUM:

What is "pabulum?" It's another word for food, not to be confused with Pablum®, the brand name baby cereal. What is a powwow? It's a gathering of people. It could be a meeting or a conference, a ceremony to cure the sick, a war victory celebration, an observance for spring planting, an autumn harvest feast, or a religious event. The word comes to us from the Native Americans, who held powwows for all those reasons. There were many reasons in yesteryear to hold a native powwow. It could be . . .

> Iroquois game of lacrosse,
> Chippewa smoking of the "pipe-of-battle" with a feast of dog meat,
> Arapaho sun dances,
> Sioux rainmakers,
> Pawnee sacrifice to the morning star,
> Shoshoni taking of scalps,
> Navajo fire dance,
> Hopi snake dance,
> Pueblo corn dance,
> Hupa ushering in the new year,
> Wintun dance from October to May to save the world from disintegration, or
> Tlinget potlatch.

Today's powwows are also food festivals held mostly as an tourist event, even through the powwow might reflect an event of yesteryear. The powwow has been modernized to meet the enjoyment of today's visitors. Dances, games and entertainment play a big part in the modern powwows, as does food. The main food item found at most powwows is fry bread. Fry bread is made with wheat flour, yeast or baking powder, and fried in deep fat. Another favorite is the Navajo taco, which is fry bread topped with a variety of ingredients: beans, tomatoes, lettuce, meat and cheese. The Navajo taco is served at many non-Navajo powwows. Native American foods at powwows reflect and help preserve their heritage by using traditional ingredients. In **Massachusetts** the Mashpee offer a clam bake, clam fritters, and succotash served with corn bread. The Nanticoke in **Delaware** also highlight their powwow with succotash. In south **Florida**, the Miccosukee include fried catfish, frog legs, and pumpkin bread. They also roll cooked ground beef in fry bread dough and deep fry it. In **Tennessee**, the Chucalissa offer a hominy stew, and for the kids snowballs, better known as snow cones. The powwow at Black River Falls in **Wisconsin**, offers corn and squash soup, wild rice and blanket dogs (a hot dog rolled in fry bread dough and deep fried). In **Illinois** at the Black Hawk War site, corn, beans and squash highlight the food, along with fish. The Cherokees in **Oklahoma** make bean bread with cornmeal, and offer it with fried pork and corn-on-the-cob. In **New Mexico**, the Navajos serve red chile stew, mutton stew, hot pickles, posole (hominy and pork cooked with red chiles), and of course Navajo tacos. On the Warm Springs Reveration in **Oregon**, they have almost a dozen powwows a year. A salmon bake is the main course in April along with various root vegetables, and in August it's a huckleberry feast with alder smoked salmon, fresh salad greens, wild rice, fry bread with huckleberry jam, and for dessert, huckleberry pie. Not all powwows offer tradition Native American food, since the powwows are open to non-Native American venders who sell hamburgers, hot dogs, pizzas, cotton candy, and soft drinks. --*RSC* www.powwow.org

PRALINE: Originally a candy made of sugared almonds. Today other nuts are used, especially pecans in the southern United States. Depending on where you live it is pronounced either "pray-lean" or "prah-lean."

PRALINES

It seems, neither food historians nor southern cooks can agree on just what a praline should be. Every praline maker swears by a different recipe, and every recipe has a story. Moreover, the very word praline is a catch-all term. The sugared nut that Savannah residents call pralines are a far cry from the pecan-studded wheels of caramel favored in West Texas.

Sugars used differ, too. Light and dark-brown sugar, refined sugar, corn syrup, and molasses all show up in different recipes. . Also, pralines are pronounced different from region to region, in Dallas they are *prahleens,* while in other parts of Texas they are called *prayleens.*

.

The French inspired the **Savannah praline,** which is closest to the original 17th century sugared almonds by that name. The Savannah praline remains faithful to its Gaelic origins, celebrating the purity of the roasted nut and holding sugaring to a simple glaze. The further west it goes, the more the praline changes. **The New Orleans or Creole praline** emphasizes the Delta's wealth of sugar cane by embedding pecan halves in a hearty penuche-like base. The Creole praline is firm and opaque, creamy, not grainy, and incredibly rich.

Texas is home to two kinds of praline. One is the massive **Texas chewy.** The other is the thinner, flatter Mexican praline. The **Mexican praline** is a sugar-and-water confection, resembling a thin piece of fudge in texture and lacking the cream and butter of the caramel-like chewy. Mexican-style pralines are best when they are still faintly warm from the skillet. A well-crafted Mexican praline will snap neatly in two. Try that on a chewy and you're in serious trouble.–LU

PRAWNS: No, a prawn is not a large shrimp, although it is part of the crustacean family. Prawns have longer legs and more slender bodies than shrimps. Like shrimp, prawns are found in both salt and fresh water. In the market there is confusion, because large shrimp are often sold as prawns and prawns are sold as shrimp. There are also some small lobsters that are sold as prawns. Prawns found in temperate waters average about 1 ½ inches. Those found in warmer water will grow up to 2 feet and may be sold as a lobster.

PREHEAT: To heat a skillet or an oven prior to adding the food to be cooked in it.

PRESERVE: Foods that have been processed to be saved for future use. Some, such as fruit are made into jams and jellies with sugar. Meats are preserved with salt and other ingredients. Preserving can also be done by canning, freezing, dehydration, and other methods.

PRESERVATIVES FOR FOOD: Unless you grow all your food in your own garden and prepare all your meals from scratch, it's almost impossible to eat food without preservatives added by manufacturers during processing. Without such preservatives, food safety problems would get out of hand, to say nothing of your grocery bills. Bread would get moldy, and salad oil would go rancid before it's used up.

Ingredient labels should contain what is within. You'll see calcium propionate (pro-pea-on-ate) on most bread labels, disodium (die-so-de-um) EDTA on canned kidney beans, and BHA on shortening, just to name a few. Even snack foods, such as dried fruit, potato chips, and trail mix contain sulfur based preservatives.

Preservatives Allowed

Manufacturers add preservatives mostly to prevent spoilage during the time it takes to transport foods over long distances to stores and then to your kitchen. It's not unusual for sourdough bread baked in California to be shipped to Maine, or for olive oil processed in Spain to be used on your salad. Rapid transport systems and ideal storage conditions help keep foods fresh and nutritionally stable. But breads, cooking oils, and other products usually need help.

Preservatives serve as either **antimicrobials** (an-ty-my-crow-bee-als) or antioxidants (an-ty-oxy-dents) or both. As antimicrobials, they prevent the growth of molds, yeasts and bacteria. As antioxidants, they keep foods from becoming rancid, browning, or developing black spots. Rancid food may not make you sick, but they smell and taste bad. Antioxidants suppress the reaction that occurs when foods combine with oxygen in the presence of light, heat, and some metals. Antioxidants also minimize the damage to some essential amino acids and the loss of some vitamins.

Preservatives Not Allowed

Nitrites are used in combination with salt and serve as antimicrobials in meat to inhibit the growth of bacterial spores that cause botulism. Nitrites are regulated by the FDA, because an over-use of nitrites is believed to cause cancer. Scientists are still at work to prove or disprove this theory. **Bha** (butylated hydroxyanisole) and **BHT** (butylated hydroxytoluene) have been used for years, mostly in foods that are high in fats and oils. They slow the development of off-flavors, odors, and color changes caused by oxidation. BHA is also used as a preservative for dry foods, such as cereals. Like nitrites, it is believed that high amounts of BHA could cause tumors. Preservatives may not be used to deceive you by changing the color of food. For example, sulfites are prohibited on meats because they restore the red color, giving meat a false appearance of freshness.

Sulfites are used primarily as antioxidants to prevent or reduce discoloration of light-colored fruits and vegetables, such as dried apples and dehydrated potatoes. Sulfites are used in other ways, such as for bleaching food starches and as preventives against rust and scale in water used to making steam that will come in contact with food. Also some sulfites are used in cellophane for good packaging. FDA prohibits the used of sulfites in foods that are important sources of thiamin, such as enriched flour, because sulfites destroy the nutrient.

Sensitive to Preservatives

Some people are sensitive to sulfites, but the label is not always obvious, so those who are sensitive should look for the following names: **sulfur dioxide, sodium sulfite, sodium and potassium bisulfite, and sodium and potassium metabisulfite**. They are often used in baked goods, some beverages, imitation dairy products, shrimp and lobster (both fresh and frozen), dried and dehydrated fruits and vegetables, gelatins, grain products, sugar and molasses, and various sauces and syrups. If you have difficulty breathing, stomachache, or hives after eating, it just might be the sulfites.

READ THE LABEL

Potato chips might state "BHA and BHT are added to help protect flavor." Potato chips are cooked in lard and the added BHA and BHT is to slow or prevent oxidation. Lard is high in fat and oxidation could cause the fat to spoil and give the potatoes an off-flavor if these preservatives weren't added. Sodium nitrite and salt are added to processed meats, such as ham and lunch meats, to inhibit the growth of bacteria.

Maraschino cherries have three preservatives; **potassium sorbate, sodium benzoate, and sulfur dioxide**. If you are sensitive to sulfur dioxide, pass on the maraschino cherries. Bottled lemon juice contains **sodium bisulfite**, so stay with fresh lemon juice to avoid any problems.

Many labels contain **monosodium glutamate** (MSG), it is not a preservative, but a flavor enhancer, but some are sensitive to MSG which is often added to Chinese food in restaurants. You can avoid health problems by reading the labels. Choose foods with minimal preservatives. Avoid entirely those to which you are sensitive. Even in a restaurant you can ask the waiter what preservatives are used, especially with potato products and canned foods.

FDA scientists continue to carefully evaluate all research presented on new preservatives to ensure that substances added to food to preserve quality and safety are themselves safe. – *Judith E. Foulke, condensed from an article in FDA Consumer Magazine*, April 1997

PRESERVING:
FRUITS AND VEGETABLES

What are your thoughts when it comes to preserves? Do you picture jars of jams and jellies at the supermarket? Or, maybe you think it's something your grandmother did many years ago? Prior to the invention of the metal can, many home-makers, especially those in rural areas, put up jarred preserves of local produce to last through the winter months. When you purchase canned fruit and vegetables in the supermarket, those are preserves, along with the jams and jellies.

Anyone Can Make Homemade Preserves

Fruit preserves come from a process of replacing some of the water in fruit with a sugar syrup. There are 2 methods: 1) one by which glass jars are processed in a hot water bath, and 2) by freezing.

Cooked Method–The Hard Way

Basically, this is what you'd be getting into. Canning is dangerous. Kids should not try it without an adult present. Follow directions from a cookbook.

First, the fruits are boiled in water and/or sugar for five to ten minutes.. It is important that the fruit remain plump, yet be tender and bright in color. Fruit boiled too long turns dark. Once tender, the liquid is drained, and sugar syrup is added to finish the boiling process. Instead of boiling, some cooks like to "plump" the fruit. Plumped fruit is heated only until it bubbles. The fruit is then set aside at room temperature for several hours or overnight. Plumping lets the fruit absorb more syrup. The fruit is reheated once again. Once the fruit is ready to be canned, the fruit will be sealed in glass jars. After the jars are filled, the jars are placed in boiling water. This final process prevents bacteria and mold growth. Heat causes the lids to seal. It is important that all jars, rubber rings, caps, spoons and other utensils be sterilized in boiling water. If you open a sealed jar, and if even a little bit of mold is present, toss it out.

Freezer Method: The Easy Way

Before freezing, the fruits are washed, peeled, pitted, sliced (as desired), and placed in plastic cartons. To prevent darkening of the fruit, a fruit protector made of a mixture of ascorbic acid (vitamin C) and other ingredients are added to the sugar syrup. After the syrup is added to the fruit, the fruit can be poured in the cartons, then sealed and frozen. After the fruit is frozen, remove the lid, add enough syrup to cover the fruit, or the exposed fruit on top will darken. Fruit can be frozen without sugar syrup, just in plain water, but be sure to add the fruit protector to prevent darkening of the fruit. Berries can be frozen separately on a tray and then put in plastic bags to prevent clumping together.

PRESS: A device that squeezes the liquid from a food, such as juice from fruit. A similar but different device is used to compress food to make it compact. A pressed duck is a good example of compacted food.

PRESSURE COOKER: A large pot with a tight cover used in canning and cooking foods for a shorter time by keeping most of the steam inside the pot, forcing steam pressure on the food. The advantages of using a pressure cooker, are in saving time and it also "locks in" the nutrients and flavor in food. The disadvantage is the danger involved in accidental explosions when the cooker's directions are not followed perfectly. Definitely not recommended for use by children.

PRETZEL: Traditionally a bread dough shaped almost like the letter "B." The word pretzel comes from the Latin word *bracciatello* which means "little arms." Pretzels can be either soft or hard, salted or unsalted, and made into various shapes.

THE RIDDLE OF THE PRETZEL
by Louise Ulmer

What is fat or thin, long or short, round or straight, hot or cold, soft or hard? Of course, you know the answer is a pretzel, which comes in all those forms and more. You can have your pretzels salted or unsalted, white or whole wheat. Don't even be surprised to see them dipped in chocolate, yogurt or cheese. Pretzels themselves pose a riddle.

Nobody knows exactly where the first pretzel came from, but according to one story, the traditional twisted ones were invented by an Italian monk about 610 A.D. He got the idea to twist his dough into the shapes of arms folded in prayer and then used his tasty twists as a reward for pupils who memorized their daily prayers. The Latin word, *pretiole* means "little gift," and the word for pretzel in Italian means "small arms."

In the Middle Ages pretzels were more like the soft, freshly baked ones we see today at street venders and carnivals. In Germany they have been called *brezel* about 1200 A.D. when someone brought the recipe from Italy.

Pretzels have been popular in America since the pilgrims settled here. The first pretzel bakery was tarted in Lititz, Pennsylvania by Julius Sturgis just eight years after the Revolutionary War. The same baking company still makes about 1,000 pounds of pretzels every day. Other large bread and snack companies make tons of pretzels every years, but some bakers still make their pretzels by hand. Either way, the pretzel is a mixture of flour, water, yeast, and oil -- about the same ingredients of light bread. Pretzel dough has to be shaped into its form before it rises. A special dip or spray adds the shiny brown crust and helps the salt stick.

Pretzels are good for nearly everyone, including people on low fat or low calorie diets. They are easy to store and keep so well that they can be packed for long journeys. Homesteaders carried them Westward as a staple survival food. If the pretzel is more popular in New England, it's no wonder. More pretzel bakers live in the Philadelphia area than anywhere else, mostly because of the many German immigrant bakers who settled there.

The main problem with pretzels is making a choice. Would you like yours hot, soft, twisted, salted, and dipped in mustard? Or how about long, hard, golden sticks? With soft drink or ice cream? Don't worry; sooner or later you can get around to trying them all! No matter which way you like your pretzel, remember when you see the folded arms that they are sending you a message.

PRICKLY PEARS: Also known as cactus apples, the pears are edible fruit of some cactus plants. The pear shaped fruit has thorns, and is yellow to red in color. They can be eaten fresh and made into jelly and preserves. The fruit is peeled, sliced and chilled. and generally served with lemon juice and sugar. Some enjoy it with cream and sugar. **Nutrition facts** per ½ cup: 36 calories, 4 calories from fat, .5g total fat (1%), zero saturated fat and sodium, 8.5g carbohydrates (3%), 3.2g fiber (13%), .7g protein (1%), 45 IU vitamin A (1%), 12mg vitamin C (21%), 50mg calcium (5%) and .3mg iron (1%).

PROCIMEQUAT: A man-made hybrid produces ½ inch orange citrus fruits grown mostly for ornamental purposes.

PRODUCE: A term for fresh fruits and vegetables as a group.

PRODUCE MARKETING ASSOCIATION

The Produce Marketing Association (PMA) was founded in 1949. This non-profit trade organization, with 2,500 members, participates in the marketing of fresh fruits, vegetables, and floral products worldwide. These members are involved in the production, distribution, retail, and food service sections of this industry.

PMA hosts two web sites, their own, one for those in the produce trade:
www.pma.com

and one for consumers, which provides information on the produce industry, along with recipes and health information:
www.aboutproduce.com

PMA can be reached by writing:
Produce Marketing Association
P.O. Box 6036
Newark, DE 19714-6036

THE PRODUCE FOR BETTER HEALTH FOUNDATION

The Produce for Better Health Foundation (PBHF) is an incentive project creating a Healthier America through increased consumption of fruit and vegetables. The nonprofit organization works with the National Cancer Institute (NCI) and sponsors the national "5 A Day" project for better health. The "5 A Day" goal is to increase the consumption of fruits and vegetables to an average of five or more servings per day to improve the health of all Americans. More than 1,800 organizations across the nation promote the 5 A Day message, which makes this the nations largest public/private educational program. In addition, more than 35,000 retail stores participate in promoting 5 A Day in heir supermarkets. The PBHF has two web sites: www.5aday.com; www.aboutproduce.com The "aboutproduce.com" web site provides healthy benefits of fruits, vegetables, nuts, and herbs. The site includes not only information, but recipes, food events, serving suggestions, food and nutrition dictionary, plus an E-mail Club where you can send PBHF recipes to your friends. For more information on the PBHD, write: **Produce for Better Health Foundation** 5301 Limestone Road, Suite 101, Wilmington, DE 19808-1249

PROFITEROLE: The smaller version of a cream-puff, filled with meat and cheese mixtures, or custard or whipped cream filled.

PROSCIUTTO: Means "ham" in Italian. In Italy there are two versions: *cotto* that has been cooked and lightly smoked, and *crudo* that is raw, air-dried and has been smoked.

PROVOLONE CHEESE: Made from whole milk, this Italian cheese is pale yellow in color. Smoking gives it flavor when fresh, piquant when aged. Tasty in sandwiches and it melts well in cooking. Originally it came from Campania, Italy where it was made from buffalo's (ox) milk. It starts out as a sliceable cheese, but when aged and hard it can be grated. **Nutrition facts** per ½ cup: 199 calories, 136 calories from fat, 15.1g total fat (22%), 9.7g saturated fat (48%), 39.1 cholesterol (13%), 496.4mg sodium (21%), zero carbohydrates and fiber, 15.5 protein (29%), 462 IU vitamin A (9%), zero vitamin C, 429mg calcium (43%), and .3mg iron (2%).

PRUNES: Prune is the French word for plum. Specifically, it's the dried fruit of the plum. Not all plums can become prunes. The choicest plum for drying is the blue- purple Freestone. At one time plums were sun dried. Now commercially they are dehydration to control the moisture so that they remain soft. Prunes are eaten fresh, stewed, added to dessert recipes. You will find prunes in the stores today under the name of "dried plums." Some are flavored with lemon or orange. **Nutrition facts** per ½ cup: 193 calories, 3 calories from fat, .4g total fat (1%), zero saturated fat and sodium, 50.7g carbohydrates (17%), 5.8g fiber (23%), 2.1g protein (4%), 1605 IU vitamin A (32%), 3mg vitamin C (4%), 41mg calcium (4%), and 2mg iron (11%). www.prunes.org www.sunsweet.com; www.prunebargaining.com.

PUCHERO: A Spanish stew that is quite popular in Latin American countries made with several meats, chick-peas, cabbage and other vegetables.

PUDDING: A term used to describe a variety of foods that can be baked, boiled or steamed and served hot or cold. It could be an egg custard made with or without vegetables, a sweetened cream dessert with or without fruit, or a suet based cake-like dessert.

PUDDINGS, AMERICAN OR BRITISH

American children reading British stories may scurry for their dictionaries to see what on earth could be a "flaming" pudding. Or puddings being carried in a cloth! Sometimes poor kids get beaten about the ears with a pudding. Surely pudding in England can't be the same as it is in American, can it? No one over here would think of setting fire to a dish of Chocolate Instant Pudding and Pie Filling. No, in Britain pudding is not the same as pie filling.

Pudding as Dessert

In Britain "pudding" has come to mean "dessert," any dessert. Children ask, "What's for pudding, Mum?" On holidays, the answer might be "Plum pudding, dear." However, the plum pudding probably never saw a plum but has nuts and raisins, prunes or currants. The English have separate words for raisins and other dried fruits, but they tend to lump them all under one word, "plum." They do much the same with "pudding." Their meat "pudding," we would call a sausage. That's the one a naughty boy might get whacked with! A flaming pudding is the crowning glory of the British Christmas feast. It's a mound of steamed fruit and nut cake, drizzled with brandy and set aflame before being carried to the table to make a grand entrance. -- *LU*

PUFF: A light hollow pastry that is filled with cream and called a "cream puff."

PUFF PASTE: A flaky, tender, crisp pastry used to make cream filled desserts such as Napoleons.

PULISAN: A large tree from Malaysia has small, oval, red-skinned fruit with translucent, sweet flesh called pulisan. It is eaten fresh.

PUMMELO: Better known as Chinese grapefruit, larger than grapefruit with a thick yellow skin with very sweet white or pink flesh. The pummelo was crossed with the sweet orange to create the grapefruit.

PUMPKIN: Native to Central America, the pumpkin had migrated to North American long before the European settlers arrived. It was the Native Americans who showed the colonists how to prepare pumpkin. They boiled it for soup, baked it for a vegetable, dried it and ground it into meal for making bread and puddings. The first pumpkin pie was made by slicing off the top of a whole pumpkin, scooping out the seeds, and filling the hollow with milk and spices to be baked. Today eggs and sweeteners (maple syrup, sugars, or molasses) are added. The name pumpkin came from the Greek word *pepon*, meaning large melon. The French converted it to *popon* and later to pompon. The English went with *pumpion*. It was the American colonists who added "kin" to finalize today's spelling.

Legends abound worldwide. The most famous in America is *The Legend of Sleepy Hollow*, in which the ghost lifts his pumpkin head from the pommel of his saddle and hurls it at the fleeing Ichabod Crane. Fairy tales have Cinderella's coach made of a giant pumpkin, and Peter the Pumpkin Eater confined his wandering wife in a pumpkin shell and there he kept her very well.. And what would Halloween be without craving a pumpkin into a scary jack-o'-lantern?

Pumpkins are not just large in fairy tales, but have been recorded weighing more than 600 pounds.
Pumpkin vines grow long, some up to 2,000 feet.
Pumpkins are available fresh during the fall months and canned the year round.
Pumpkin pies are available frozen. Pumpkin seeds are dried, shelled, and salted.
Puréed pumpkin can be added to breads, pancakes, muffins, cakes, and cookie recipes.

THE HUMBLE PUMPKIN

The Native Americans first used them for rattles, since they were small like gourds. As the pumpkins grew sweeter and larger, they soon became a staple food for the Native Americans. When the English settlers arrive in America, they were introduced to the pumpkin.

At first the pumpkin was baked on ashes around the campfires, then mashed, eaten as baked squash or made into a soup. Pumpkins kept many settlers from staving to death during the first winters. Soon the colonists learned how to preserve the pumpkin by drying rings of it by the open fires. Many of their recipes contained pumpkin combined with beans, peas and corn all simmered together in a stew. And along the way, the colonists even learned to make pumpkin beer.

Tales abound around the world. In India there's a legend where a devote father used a huge pumpkin as a tomb for his only son. In time the pumpkin was found to be filled with water in which swam a large fish. Intent on taking the fish, four brothers lifted the pumpkin to carry it away but became frightened and dropped it. The resulting cracks in the shell flooded the earth with water, thus creating our oceans.

Pumpkin vines can grow fast, which has spurred another tale. A young boy named Jack mounted his horse on a warm spring day to plant pumpkins. Even though the horse galloped at top speed and as he dropped the seeds in the prepared hills, he was unable to keep ahead of the fast-growing vines. A more modern story was told by Dr. Haseman of the University of Missouri where he grow a vine for 173 days with an over-all growth of 1,986 feet and produced enough pumpkins to make 500 pies.

Believe it or not, the pumpkin is not a vegetable but a fruit. In fact, it is a berry belonging to the genus *Cucurbita*, which includes a range of pumpkins from giant to the small New English pie pumpkin, also called a sugar pumpkin.

There are many varieties of pumpkins. Some grown for human food, others for animal food. There are pumpkins bred especially for carving so they will have nice round body, giving more thought to outer beauty than inner taste. These are best for Halloween's jack-o'-lanterns. Giant pumpkins can grow up to fifteen pounds a day are mainly grown for contests and not for eating. The "cheese" pumpkin gets its name because of its flattened top and bottom, but it's a good pie maker.

Easy to Grow Your Own

If you have space in your yard, even a small space, you could grow your own crop. You will need a well drained soil, because pumpkins will not tolerate wet soil, since the seeds could decay before they germinate. Best to mix some organic matter into the soil, which will help retain the moisture, and if the soil is slightly acid, so much the better. Your nursery supplier can test your soil and advise you what your soil might require. Delay the planting until after the last frost and the soil has warmed up. If your space is small, purchase bush or small-vine variety. If you plan to eat the, pick the ones that say either "sugar" or "pie" or "sweet" in the name. Plant only one variety, or cross-pollination could occur, creating a different kind of pumpkin than what you want.
Once your pumpkins are ready to be harvested in October, save some for Halloween, but try your hand at making a pumpkin pie, bread, muffins, pudding, custards, a stuffing for meats and vegetables, a side dish as you would for squash, or as they do in Europe, make a delicious soup with carrots, onions, celery, parsley, etc.

An easier, and less dangerous way than cutting raw pumpkin, is to place cleaned out pumpkin on a cookie sheet and heat in 250°F oven for at least half an hour. It may take an hour or more, depending on the size and thickness of the pumpkin. As the pumpkin cooks, the shell sides begin to cave in. That means the inside is getting soft. When it looks like all the air had been let out of it, the pumpkin is done. Carefully remove the cookie sheet with the warm pumpkin on it and let it cool enough to touch. With a large, long spoon, scrape soft pumpkin from shell. Discard shell. You now have pumpkin ready to use in a pie recipe.

A 17th-century verse:

Our pumpkins and parsnips are common supplies;
We have pumpkins at morning and pumpkins at noon.
If it was not for pumpkins we should be undoon.

PUMPKIN HEAD

In New Haven, Connecticut, a law once required men to cut their hair in a round cap-like shape. Often empty pumpkin shells were sometimes used as a guide during the barbering. Thus the townspeople earned the name, "pumpkin heads."

Guy Wetmore Carryl, a turn-of-the century writer, observed:

How imposing it would be,
If pumpkins grew upon a tree.

Henry David Thoreau once said: "I would rather sit on a pumpkin and have the seat all to myself than be crowded on a velvet cushion."

PUMPKIN SHELL USES

Peter Peter, pumpkin eater
Had a wife and couldn't keep her
Put her in a pumpkin shell
and there he kept her very well
– *English Nursery Rhyme*

The shell, lined with foil, can be used as a serving container for a harvest picnic.
A foil lined shell, can also be filled with fruit, nuts, or popcorn for a table centerpiece.
A large pumpkin can serve as a punch bowl filled with icy cold cider for an autumn buffet.
A pumpkin can be used as a vase to hold chrysanthemums, marigolds, etc.

Activities

PUMPKIN CENTERPIECE

Pumpkins can be used for more than jack-o-lanterns. Bring out the beauty of fall with a pumpkin vase for your flowers.

You need:
Medium sized pumpkin with a flat bottom
Assortment of fall flowers (real, dried, or silk), berries and pods on steams, such as bittersweet
Florist foam (check at home before buying, as some may have been saved from florist arrangements)
Dinner candles, long and thin, varying sized (prefer smokeless or dripless kind)
Ribbon for bows in fall colors
Twigs about as long as a new pencil

Directions:
1. Cut a large hole in the top of the pumpkin, and clean out the seeds. Save the seeds to clean and dry for other decorating ideas or to roast and eat.
2. Fill the empty pumpkin shell with florist foam.
3. Anchor 2 or 3 candles in the foam so they sit up straight.
4. Arrange flowers around the candles. If using live flowers, dampen the foam with water. .
5. Tie bows on twigs and insert them in the flower arrangement.
6. Place the pumpkin arrangement in table center on a plate or placemat.
7. Surround pumpkin with more bows, berries, flower heads, pods, or nuts. –LU

PRETTY PETITE PUMPKINS

Tiny ornamental pumpkins and their gourd cousins can be made into hanging decoration or spicy balls called pomanders. The idea is to decorate your rounded pumpkins like Christmas balls or like those orange pomanders with whole cloves sticking out.

You will need:
Several assorted **miniature pumpkins** and/or gourds
Thin decorative **ribbon** in holiday colors, no wider than 1 inch
Several yards of very thin ribbons for the hangers
Thumbtacks or push pins
Quick drying **craft glue**
Spices: Whole cloves, Cinnamon sticks, Fresh sprigs of herbs
Sewing pins with big colorful heads
Large flat-headed nail or small pointed **screw driver**

Directions:

1. Start by putting your ribbon hanger in place. Cut the thinnest ribbon about 2 feet long. Lay the ribbon flat. Set the pumpkin in the middle.

2. Anchor the ribbon to the bottom center of the pumpkin with a thumbtack.

3. Bring the ribbons ends up and tie at the top center.

4. Anchor the knot with a thumbtack.

5. Bring the loose ends back to tie again at the bottom. The loose end will now be your hanging ribbon. Tie a knot at the end.

Options:

1. With a nail or screwdriver, punch holes in the pumpkin skin so you can insert the cloves into the holes so that the clove heads stick out.

2. Tie or glue cinnamon sticks or fresh herbs up where ribbon crisscrosses.

3. Push sewing pins in up to their heads for dots of color in rows or at random.

4. Finish off your ornament by tying a sweetheart bow to the hanging ribbon down close to the pumpkin's top.

5. Use your imagination to add sparkle with sequins, tassels, bells, etc.

PUMPERNICKEL BREAD is a dark brown bread made with whole rye.

PUMPERNICKEL

A group of young language specialists from the University of Pennsylvania met to discuss "names;" in particular, the origins of certain names. Since the word "pumpernickel" did not have a history of how it originated, they made up a history, and this is what they said: It probably comes to us from the time of **Napoleon**. Napoleon and his French army did a great deal of traveling across Europe. One evening, while marching through Germany, they stopped at an inn to rest for the night. Now, the name of Napoleon's horse was Nicole. During dinner, a freshly baked, very coarse, black bread was served. Napoleon had never seen bread of this texture before. French bread and pastry were always white and of the finest and most delicate quality. He turned to his assistant and asked, "What is this?" The innkeeper, overhearing the question, spoke up, "Why it is bread, Sire." Napoleon examined more closely the morsel of bread and with a quick wave of his hand, commanded his assistant, **"Bon per Nicole."** That means "fit for Nicole." Since the German innkeeper had no name for the bread, and since he regarded the French emperor as an authority on everything in Europe, he misunderstood the name of the bread to be "pumpernickel." And so it remained. --Livia F. Sparagna

Actually, the truth is more interesting. The bread was originally a whole grain rye from Westphalia in Germany, leavened by sourdough. It was known as *schwatzbrat* because of the dark color which results from the caramelization of starches in the rye grain during the long, slow baking. According to the *Oxford English Dictionary*, pumpernickel originally meant "lout" or "stinker" and then by transference got applied to the bread, which was notorious for producing flatulence. *Pumpern* meant "breaking wind." *Nickle* meant a goblin. Put the two together and what is your translation?

PUMPKIN PIE SPICE: A blend of spices, usually cinnamon, cloves, and ginger that have been ground together and left to marry. Pumpkin pie spices are used in pies, cookies, gingerbreads, winter squash, and sweet potato recipes.

½ cup cinnamon
½ cup ginger
2 Tablespoons nutmeg
2 Tablespoons ground clovers

PUMPKIN SEEDS can be eaten after drying and roasting.

PUMPKIN SEEDS
by Elizabeth Giles

Pumpkin muffins
and pumpkin pie,
now the seeds
you need to try.

Cut the pumpkin.
Scoop the seeds.
Use a spoon.
That's all it needs.

Wash 'em, rinse 'em,
drain 'em too.
Spread in pan.
That's all you do.

Cook in oven
medium heat
'bout five minutes,
cool, then eat.

PUNCH: A beverage made with a blend of fruit juices, with or without alcoholic spirits. The name comes from the Hindi word panch meaning "five." English sailors brought the idea back from their voyages East to find spices. This was one of many new food ideas they found when they stopped at ports along the coast of India. Traditionally punch was made with five ingredients: alcoholic beverage, water, sugar, lemon juice and spices. Today the most famous alcoholic punches are made with champagne or white wine. Rum and other spirits are also used. Non-alcohol punches are a blend of fruit juices and carbonated beverages. Punch needed to be made in the biggest bowl possible so the need for a punch bowl arose and beautiful punch bowls were being manufactured by 1692.

PUNCH BOWL: Punch bowls were originally the biggest bowls anyone could find for making punch or wassail to serve a large number. The biggest punch bowl in on display at Pittsburgh's Carnegie Museum. It is four and a half feet tall, 150 pounds of cut glass, made by H.C. Fry of Rochester, Pennsylvania in 1905. Punch bowls are collectible treasures of yesteryear, sometimes costing a small fortune because of their rarity, beauty, design and costly materials.

PURÉE: A mixture of raw or cooked food pressed through a food mill or a blender to a smooth paste. The word comes from the French which means to cleanse or to remove all impurities.

PURSLANE: A herb with edible leaves and stems, considered a common weed in South Africa along the coastal regions. It is one of the herbs considered good for prostate health.

PYREX: A heat resistant glassware used for cooking and a trademark of Corning Ware. www.corning.com.

Qq

QUABLI: A recipe from northern Iran made with peas, carrots, raisins that are layered with seasoned beef and rice. Irani immigrants living in Minnesota serve this at the Jewish fall festival of Sakkot, which commemorates the huts that housed the Jews in the desert after their exodus from Egypt.

QUAIL: (kwayl) This American game bird is about the size of a small plump chicken. The flesh is white and has a delicate flavor. The young quail can be fried, broiled, or roasted. The tough older birds are best pot-roasted. Quail are available frozen in some supermarkets, smoked and canned in specialty food stores, along with quail eggs. Quail is experiencing a comeback on the restaurant scene and farm-grown quail is a growing industry. Turkey, like the quail, was once a game bird until demand made it popular and profitable to raise commercially. Quail eggs are yellow-green with brown markings. They may be served hard boiled. Hard boiled quail eggs are pickled as a cocktail snack. **Nutrition facts** per 3 ounces: 105 calories, 24 calories from fat, 2.5g total fat (4%), .8g saturated fat (4%), 49.39mg cholesterol (17%), 46.8mg sodium (2%), zero carbohydrates and fiber, 19.2g protein (38%), zero IU vitamin A, 5mg vitamin C (7%), 8mg calcium (%), and 2mg iron (11%).

QUARK: (kwark) A mixture of yogurt, sour cream, sugar, and spices used as a spread or a topping. In Germany, a kind of low fat curd cheese. In Pennsylvania, a mixture of ingredients used as a spread or a topping is called "quark." Try mixing quark with your favorite breakfast cereal, especially granola. Also it makes a great dip for fruit.

QUART: A standard measurement, two pints to a quart; four cups to a quart. A dry quart equals 1.1 liters. A liquid quart equals 0.946 liters. One liter equals 1.05 quarts.

QUASSIA: A tropical shrub in America the wood of which produces juice for tonics. Quassine, the bitter extract, flavors fizzy drinks and bitters.

QUEEN PALM: From South America, this tree produces one-inch, yellow, sweet fruit that is eaten fresh. The young palms are also used to make palm heart. The unripened seeds are poisonous.

QUEENSLAND ARROWROOT: An herb from South America. The root is used to make starch. It is grown commercially in Australia. The leaves are fed to livestock.

QUEENSLAND NUT: Better known as macadamia nuts, they originated in Australia. See MACADAMIA.

QUENCH: (verb) To put an end to or satisfy a thirst with a liquid.

QUENELLE: A boiled dumpling made with spiced meat, fish or poultry forcemeat formed into a sausage or egg shape and served with butter, either as a garnish or a main dish. Originally, it came from the German word for dumpling.

QUERN: (Old English origin) A hand mill for grinding corn.

QUESADILLA: (kay-sa-dee-ah) It was originally a cheesecake made in El Salvador. In the United States, it is a cheese sandwiched between two flour tortillas. Many Mexican restaurants are making an art form from this delicious tortilla cheese sandwich.

QUESO: (kay-so) Spanish word for "cheese." In Mexico there are a variety of white cheeses, from soft to firm. When called "*queso anejo*" it means it is "aged," but not necessarily a hard cheese. When called "*queso fresco*" it means "fresh," or not aged, similar to cream cheese.

QUETSCHE: (kwet-cha) A mauve skinned plum with yellow flesh, grown mostly in Alcase, from where it gets its original German name (*zwetsche*). Best known in a brandy, it is also a favorite for tarts and jam.

QUICHE: (keesh) A mixture of eggs, vegetables, fruit, cheese, meat, fish and/or poultry baked in a pie type plate with or without a bottom crust. The crust can be a pastry crust or a crust made with cooked pasta. Best know is the "quiche Lorraine" made with cream, cheese, eggs and bacon. Quiche are always served hot. The crust is generally made from pastry. The crust can also be made with cooked cornmeal, grits, potatoes, pasta or beans.

QUILLAJA SAPONARIA: Better known as "soap bark" in Peru and Chile were it grows. It contains quilliac acid, quillajasapin, sucrose and tannin. It is used as a natural flavor in foods, as well as to make foams for various products.

QUINCE: (kwins) Native to Asia, they came to the Mediterranean by Arab traders. The quince in medieval times symbolized love, joy, and harmony. Shaped similar to an apple, the quince has the color and texture of a hard pear. Quinces can be eaten fresh off the tree if cut in thin slices, but they are hard to digest and taste better when stewed, baked, made into a sauce or preserves and added with apples to a pie. "If an apple can do it, a quince can do it."

LONG HISTORY IN EUROPE

Believe it or not, some people think it was the quince that got Adam and Eve in trouble. In Athens, Greece, the wedding party tossed quinces into the bridal chariot for luck. The Romans believed it protected them from the "Evil Eye," so they painted quinces and their leaves all over the place. If a Roman gave a quince to a person of the opposite sex, it was considered to be the same as an engagement ring. Borrowing from Rome, Emperor Charlemagne planted a hedge of flowering quince around his palace. In France in the Middle Ages, it was a quince, and not oranges, which first went into the making of marmalade. The Germans make a quince pie. The English make quince honey. The Italians make a quince sauce for meat. In Turkey they cook quince with chicken. The Spanish make it into a sweet paste and eat it with cheese.

Quince has a delicate, floral flavor, and a tantalizing aroma. The blossoms are used to make perfume and the fruit to make hair dye.

POMPEY'S HONEY APPLE DUMPLING

Pompey the Great (108-48 BC), contemporary of Julius Caesar, introduced the quince fruit to the Roman people in 65 BC. After conquering most of the coastal regions from Rome to Lebanon, Pompey visited the island of Crete, a Greek island about 80 miles from the Greek mainland and tasted the quince. The name quince come from the Greek *kydonion malon,* meaning "apple of" or "from Cydonia," a town on Crete. Pompey also brought back a Greek recipe for cooking them. The core of the quince was filled with honey, wrapped in a sweet pie crust dough, and baked until the quince is tender and until the crust is golden brown, similar to an apple dumpling.

Quince in America

No sooner did the first pilgrims land than they sent back lists of things future pilgrims should bring with them, which included quince seeds. By 1700 nearly every New England yard had a quince tree. Easier to grow than apples or pears, the quince can be used in all the same ways. The little crooked tree puts forth gorgeous hot pink blossoms and apple sized fruit. But there are smaller, plum-sized quinces that grow on bushes called flowering quince. These bush quince are only good for jellies. Little wonder the pilgrims wanted quinces for their yards and gardens.

The quince seed was said to grow so well it could bear fruit in three years, even in cool New England.

Luther Burbank, developed the "pineapple" quince, a large smooth skinned yellow quince, but by then (1890), apples had replaced the quince in the favor of cooks. Quince are available today, and still beloved by those who know heir unique charm. **Nutrition facts** ½ cup: 41 calories, zero fats and sodium, 11g carbohydrates (4%), 1.4g fiber (5%), .3g protein (1%), 29 IU vitamin A (1%), 11mg vitamin C (18%), 8mg calcium (1%), and .5mg iron (3%).

Activity

PLANT A QUINCE TREE

While some nurseries offer quince trees, try your luck at planting one from seed. Obtain some seeds from the pineapple quince and refrigerate them for three months. You can buy a quince to eat from the market and save the seeds. Start in pots. Plant seedlings in moist, well draining soil. Only one tree is required to bear fruit and can grow up to twenty feet tall. Quinces can be trimmed like a shrub or a hedge. Once established, trim the long branches and prune the broken and diseased laterals. Do not use a high nitrogen fertilizer, 5-10-10 is best. Your tree will bloom with white or pink blossoms in the spring, will bear fruit in about three years. The quince is harvested in the early fall, and the fruit will keep fresh for months if kept in a cool, dry place or refrigerated.

QUININE WATER: (kwy-nyne) A bitter alkaloid obtained from the bark of the cinchona tree from South America, medicinally used to treat malaria. Small amounts are used in the flavoring of some soft drinks, such as tonic water and Canada Dry Bitter Lemon.

QUINOA:(kee-no-ah or keen-wah) A tasty grain native to South America's Andes mountains. This ancient yellow grain was called the "mother grain" by the Incas and was one of their chief foods. Quinoa came to the United States in 1980 and is cultivated in the higher elevations of Colorado, Oregon, and Washington. Quinoa stalks grow tall, topped with large clusters of small seeds. The seeds must be cooked and are generally eaten like rice. You'll find it packaged as a breakfast cereal in health food stores and at major supermarkets. Quinoa is also ground into flour to make bread, tortillas and pasta. The seeds can be popped, like popcorn, or added to soup. The leaves, shaped like goose feet, are eaten like spinach. If purchased in bulk, and to make quinoa as a cereal, it must be washed several times. Then mix one part quinoa to two parts water, cover, bring to a boil. Simmer for about 15 minutes. Guinoa is greatly prized for its nutritional value, which is roughly akin to milk, due to high amino acid content. Quinoa is one of those grains most hopeful for feeding a hungry planet. **Nutrition facts** for 1/2 cup serving: 318 calories, 44 calories from fat, 4.9g total fat (8%), .5g saturated fat (3%), zero cholesterol, 17.9mg sodium (1%), 58.6g carbohydrates (20%), 5g fiber (20%), 11.1g protein (22%), zero vitamins A and C, 51mg calcium (5%), 7.9mg iron (44%), and 629mg potassium.

Rr

RABBIT: This small furry animal is a member of the rodent family, long a member of wild game cookery. The meat is almost all white, very lean and mild flavored, similar to chicken. Young rabbits are best pan fried, but can also be broiled or roasted. Older rabbits are best braised or stewed. Domesticated rabbit meat is available in many supermarkets, mainly in the South and Midwest. **Nutrition facts** per 3 ounces: 115 calories, 45 calories from fat, 4.7g total fat (8%), 1.4g saturated fat (7%), 49mg cholesterol (16%), 45mg sodium (2%), zero carbohydrates and fiber, 17g protein (34%),, zero vitamins A and C, 11mg calcium (1%), and 1.4mg iron (8%).

RACCOON: Native to North American, they are found throughout the United States and along the Pacific coast to South America. Raccoons are also known as "coons." Raccoons saved many pioneers from starvation and the dark meat is still enjoyed by many. The fat is both strong in taste and in odor. Young raccoons are best roasted, while older ones need to find their way to a stew pot to be tenderized.

RADICCHIO (ra-dicky-o) is a purple-red chicory (endive) with white stems and a loose-leafed head. The dark wine color of the leaves can be added to green salads, creating a crunchy, mildly bitter flavor. The Italians shred radicchio, sauté it with garlic in olive oil until tender, then add it to rice with grated hard cheese.

RADISH: This root vegetable comes in many colors from white to red to black, and with a pungent flavor from mild to hot. A native of Asia, radishes range in size from a half inch rounds to more than a foot long. The young radishes are eaten fresh, generally in a salad. Older, large radishes are best cooked or pickled. They resemble tiny red turnips in the USA. White radishes are larger and carrot shaped. Black radishes are common in Spain and Eastern Europe. They have been grown in China for over 3000 years. **Oriental radishes** are known by other names: *daikon* in Japan and *mooli* in India. Oriental radishes are so different they are actually considered a different vegetable from the radishes we know. **Nutrition facts** radish: 1 calorie, zero fats, sodium carbohydrates, fiber and protein, zero vitamin A, 1mg vitamin C (2%), and zero calcium and iron.

RAFFALD, ELIZABETH (1733 - 1781): Author of *The Experienced English Housekeeper*, one of the first and finest cookbooks in English. It sold well into the 1800s.

RAGOUT: (ragoo) A well seasoned French stew made with meat, poultry or fish and with or without vegetables. Served in a rich brown sauce. The word comes from the classical French and originally meant anything that woke the appetite.

RAGU is the brand name of a commercial line of sauces, mostly for spaghetti and pasta.

RAISE: A culinary term to make food light, such as a yeast bread dough "rises" and creates a porous bread when baked.

RAISINS: Sun dried grapes are called raisins. They can also be dried with artificial heat. When grapes are dried, they have a higher sugar content and a different flavor from grapes. The darker variety of raisins, usually muscats, are best sun dried. The golden variety made from sultanas are dehydrated indoors and receive a sulfur treatment to preserve the color. Raisins are eaten out of hand, mixed with other fruits and/or nuts for a relish, made into pies, baked in bread, cookies and other sweet doughs. To plump raisins, boil them in an equal amount of water about five minutes. Plumped raisins are juicier and they mix better with other ingredients.

An often asked question, "Why is a raisin called a 'raise-in' when it's really shrunken?" Like many English terms, it originated from Latin words, in this case *racémus,* which meant a "bunch of grapes." From here it went to the French and they used today's spelling, which meant "grape." When the English received the word they used it to mean "dried grape." **Nutrition facts** per ½ cup: 217 calories, 3 calories from fat, .3g total fat (1%), .1g saturated fat (1%), zero cholesterol and sodium, 57.4g carbohydrates (19%), 2.9g fiber (12%), 2.3g protein (5%), zero vitamin A, 2mg vitamin C (4%), 36mg calcium (4%), and 1.5mg iron (8%).

Activity
RACING RAISINS

At your next party, ask if your friends if they would like to play with their food? You will need:

Drinking glasses
Club soda or lemon-lime soda
Raisins

Fill each glass with the soda, being carefully not to let it fizz. At the same time, have each friend drop a raisin in their glass. The raisin will drop to the bottom, then rise to the top, where it will fall and repeat this process two or more times. Whose raisin makes the first round trip? Which raisin makes the most round trips and how many? The scientific principle has nothing to do with the raisin, it deals with buoyancy. The bubbles (carbon dioxide gas) gather on the raisin so the raisin becomes buoyant and floats to the surface. Once on the surface, the bubbles burst, the raisin loses its buoyancy and sinks to the bottom of the glass.

RAMBEH: A tree from southeast Asia, producing small, yellowish clusters of white, sweet fruit, eaten fresh.

RAMBUTAN is a member of the lichee family. A medium sized, juicy fruit with a delicate scent and flavor, found in Southeast Asia from Thailand to Malaysia. They are eaten fresh and made into preserves. They look like big peanuts growing hair. Picture tiny red hedgehogs. The colorful shell opens to a creamy fruit like a peeled white grape.

RAMEKIN: There are two meanings:1) a cheese tart and 2) a baking dish that holds only enough for one person. Today's ramekin is a pastry filled with a cheese and egg mixture and baked in a small dish that resembles a very small soufflé dish.

RAMONTCHI: From Madagascar, it is a shrub producing red to black berries that are eaten fresh and made into jelly. It's also called "governor's plum" in India.

RAMP: A member of the onion family, this sharp tasting, raw vegetable leaves the odor on one's breath for at least a week after eating one. Most ramps are scrambled with eggs or meat loaf. Ramps grow wild in East Tennessee where they hold an annual ramp festival the first week in May near Gatlinburg. Contact Cosby Ramp Festival at www.cockecounty.com

RAMPION: A wild European vegetable whose young leaves are added raw in salads or cooked like spinach. The foot-long root is edible if cooked like turnips. .

RANCID: (ran-sid) Staleness. Fats turn rancid by exposure to light, heat, metallic contamination or age.

RANGPUR LIME: Better known as lemons.

RAPESEED: See CANOLA OIL

RAREBIT: A cheese dish, better known as "Welsh rabbit."

RASPBERRIES are still found wild in the woods in many parts of the world, and are cultivated in the Americas from Alaska to Chile.

In one version of the mythical tales of ancient Greece, a young nymph named Ida went up to gather some white raspberries to soothe the cries of baby Zeus. She scratched herself on the thorns of a raspberry bush, and the once-white raspberries became tinted with her blood. The botanical name for raspberry is *rubus idaeus*, rubus meaning "red" and *idaeus* meaning "belonging to Ida." Raspberries are a member of the rose family.

Raspberries look like a red bubble made up of many tiny bubbles. Today raspberries are either red, purple, black or amber in color. They are eaten out of hand, used to made jams, jellies, preserves, puddings, cakes, pies, and vinegar. Raspberries can be used in almost every recipe calling for strawberries. Fresh raspberries deteriorate rapidly and must be used promptly. When buying fresh packaged berries, if there is a stain on the bottom of the package, don't buy, because they are probably overripe. Raspberries are also available frozen and canned. **Nutrition facts** per ½ cup:30 calories, 2 calories from fat, .3g total fat (1%), zero saturated fat and sodium, 7.1g carbohydrates (2%), 4.2g fiber (17%), .6g protein (1%), 80 IU vitamin A (2%), 15mg vitamin C (25%), 14mg calcium (1%), and .4mg iron (2%).

RATATOUILLE: (ra-ta-too-wee) A richly seasoned French vegetable stew usually made with eggplant, zucchini and green peppers, and sometimes with meat. In French, *"touiller"* means to mix or stir.

RATTLESNAKE MEAT: Wherever rattlesnakes grow, they are also hunted and eaten. The meat is said to be quite tasty. Several states hold Rattlesnake Roundups.

SWEETWATER RATTLESNAKE ROUND UP

While you might not like heading out to the countryside and rounding up rattlesnakes, you could enjoy many of their food events and sampling made-on-site chili, beans, pork ribs, chicken, beef brisket, and rattlesnake meat cooked in a number of ways. This Texas event is held annually in mid-March. It's a day of sampling. At 10 AM you can sample beans, at 11 AM it's chicken, noontime it's chili, 1:30 PM it's the ribs, brisket at 3 PM, and the main event, rattlesnake at 4 PM. Hundreds of cooks come for each event, so if you like chili, for example, you can taste several different kinds, and at least one will be made with rattlesnake meat. Two other cooking events are the Salsa Challenge and the Dessert Contest. All food must be prepared on site. Awards are given in ten divisions for salsa, and almost that many in the dessert contest including cakes, cobblers, ice cream, pies, and candies. Only electricity is be provided, all entrants must bring tables, ingredients, utensils, and appliances. In the rattlesnake event, rattlesnake meat will be provided. In addition to the food is great country entertainment, gun and knife show, a carnival, and arts and crafts. For more information, write: **Sweetwater Chamber of Commerce**, P.O. Box 1148, Sweetwater, TX 79556 or phone (915) 235-5488.

RAVIGOTE: A highly seasoned French sauce with lots of herbs, served with hot or cold meats, fish, poultry and vegetables.

RAVE: A French term of vegetable snobbery, with certain root vegetables falling into the lower class. Among the "peasant class" of foods would be kohlrabi, turnips, swedes and black radishes. The upper class would be herbs and green leafy vegetables.

RAVIOLI are noodle dough shells (like envelopes) filled with various ingredients from meat to cheese to vegetables. While the ravioli is an Italian dish, similar noodle-filled recipes are made by the Chinese, Jews, and Russians. Today Americans fill ravioli shells with almost anything, including smoked salmon. Ravioli can be served with either a tomato or a white cream sauce. Presumably, it was invented in Liguria as a way of using up leftovers. *Rabiole* means bits and pieces. See POCKETS.

REBOUX, PAUL (1877 - 1963): French author of several recipe books.

RECIPE: A formula and instructions for making a prepared dish. The old English word was "receipt."

RED BAY: A tree from Florida whose leaves are used like bay leaves for seasoning.

RED DELICIOUS APPLES: A medium to large bright red apple, sometimes showing a striped appearance. The fine white flesh is sweet and mellow. It's great eaten out of hand or in salads. Not a good cooking apple. The red delicious was discovered as a chance seedling in Iowa in 1850.

REDFISH: Norway haddock.

RED PEPPER: See CAPSICUM and CAYENNE PEPPER and PEPPERS.

RED SNAPPER: A salt water fish found in the south Atlantic and the Gulf of Mexico. This fish should not be confused with the red snapper found in north Pacific waters, which are really rockfish, but markets sometimes sell them as red snapper. Red snapper can be cooked in almost any method, from frying to poaching, but are best when baked whole. **Nutrition facts** per 3 ounces: 85 calories, 11 calories from fat, 1.1g total fat (2%), .3g saturated fat (1%), 31.5mg cholesterol (10%), 54.5mg sodium (3%), zero carbohydrates and fiber, 17.5g protein (35%), 85 IU vitamin A (3%), 2mg vitamin C (2%), 27mg calcium (3%), and .1mg iron.(1%)

RED SALMON: See SALMON.

REDUCE: A process of cooking by evaporation a liquid until a given amount is boiled or simmered away. This applies to sauces, syrups, and some stews.

REFRIED BEANS: The name is confusing because they are not fried and then refried. The explanation is in their Spanish origin. The Mexicans use "re" as a prefix to words for emphasis. "*Retebien*" means "very good." "*Refrito*" is where we get the English word "refried." Actually the beans have been boiled and then "fried" or reheated in a skillet. Refried beans are perfect with Mexican meat tacos, salads, etc.

REINDEER: Prized in Scandinavian countries, reindeer have been domesticated and not only used as a source of food but as draft animals as well. The meat has excellent flavor, both fresh and smoked. The meat can be tough, and is best marinated for several days, then pot roasted. Reindeer meat has been imported and is available in some specialty foods, fresh, frozen and canned.

RELISH: Simply it means to "enjoy," but as a culinary term it is loosely used to mean vegetables or fruits that have been chopped, pickled and preserved. Coming from India, it closely resembles chutney but is more highly spiced, more sweet-and-sour, as in pickle relish for your hot dogs. See CHUTNEY.

RÉMOULADE: (rim-oo-lahd) A French, highly seasoned sauce made with mustard and vinegar served with cold seafood, meat, poultry, and vegetables.

RENDER: A method to remove fat from meat by cooking with low heat. The rendered (melted) fat cools and becomes firm. It is stored cool to be used later for cooking. The remaining bits are called cracklings.

RENNET: A substance obtained from the stomach membranes of young animals is primarily used to coagulate milk to make cheese. Rennet is also used to make custard-like pudding. These desserts are easy to digest, so are often served to children and invalids. Vegetable rennets are obtained from certain plants such as the cardoon. In the French countryside many cheeses are made this way.

REUBEN SANDWICH: The most common version of the famous sandwich is a pound of pastrami on rye bread with kraut and Swiss cheese melted on top. Authorities disagree on the origin of the name. Some assume it came from New York City's famous Reuben's Restaurant and Deli, created by the cook and named for the founder Arnold Reuben. Reuben's son says one of the chefs made it for him when he was a child in 1928 to induce him to eat fewer hamburgers. Reuben's daughter tells another story. A sandwich in Omaha, Nebraska, most similar to the one we know today, won the National Sandwich Contest in 1956 and gained instant national fame. The Omaha version is made of corned beef, sauerkraut, and Swiss cheese on rye. The concoction was made by a poker player by the name of Schimmel, who also operated the Blackstone Hotel and sold it on the hotel menu. It could be that all the stories are true, Patricia Bunning Stevens says in *Rare Bits: Unusual Origins of Popular Recipes*. When you are dealing with food recipes, things naturally get "invented" more often than once.

RHUBARB: Its popularity for pies has earned it the nickname of "pieplant." Rhubarb originally came from Mongolia, but today it is grown in Europe and America. Rhubarb belongs to the buckwheat family. Although rhubarb is technically a vegetable, it is used as a fruit for desserts and sauces, pies, jams, puddings, beverages, and chutneys. Early varieties were green with red in the stems. Today's varieties are bright red with a much sweeter taste. Supermarkets sell rhubarb fresh, frozen and canned. Rhubarb lends a tart, lemony taste that combines well with strawberries. Rhubarb can be stewed or baked but, because of its tartness, sugar or sweeteners are always added.
Nutrition facts per ½ cup: 13 calories, zero fats and sodium, 2.8g carbohydrates (1%), 1.1g fiber (4%), .6g protein (1%), 61 IU vitamin A (1%), 5mg vitamin C (8%), 53mg calcium (5%), and .1mg iron (1%).

A Chinese Medicinal Remedy

The early Chinese had several uses for the plant. The Chinese use *rheum officinale*, the tap root, called *da-huang*, as a toothache remedy. The root and leaves are poisonous. Rhubarb contains at least six pain relieving elements. Another rhubarb, *rheum palmatum*, was included in Chinese herbal books more than 2,000 years ago. It was called *tahuang*, or "great yellow" from the color of the roots, which were used as a laxative.

WILD RHUBARB

There is also wild rhubarb, *cañaigre*, called "wild pieplant" and "tanner's dock." Health food stores have products labeled "wild red American ginseng" and "wild red desert ginseng." These are not ginseng, but are an unrelated, wild rhubarb plant. You can easily tell the *cañaigre* from true rhubarb. Wild rhubarb likes sandy/dry soil and is native to southwest America. The leaves are long, narrow, lance-shaped, with wavy edges, and a noticeable central vein. Those of garden rhubarb are big and fan shaped, and large enough to be used as a place mat! **Do not eat the leaves,** because they contain poisonous oxalic acid salts.

The English first brought rhubarb to the kitchen. Until the 18th century it was used only for its medical properties. Its smell while cooking is so uninviting it is easy to see why. But it tastes nothing like it smells.

The Navajos use wild rhubarb as a yellow dye for wool. Herbalists use the roots to make tea for diarrhea, and a gargle. Native Americans have also used the roots to soften their buckskins, which accounts for the "tanner's dock" name.

Rhubarb plants produce many seeds, but plants from the seeds are not always like the parent plant. Growers plant pieces of the big storage root that have several buds from which new plants grow. Each plant last 5 to 8 years. Rhubarb is relatively free from insect attack and suffers from few diseases.--*Bernice Erickson and Virginia H. McNear*

Activity
GROWING A PIE PLANT
by Virginia McNear

Garden rhubarb, also known as "pieplant," is an easy plant to grow. If you don't want to eat it, your birds will. The pieplant does prefer cool summers and freezing winters, but will grow almost anywhere that has rich, loamy soil.

A friend may give you a piece of root, or you may buy a plant from a nursery. If you have just a piece of root, plant it about two inches deep. If planting a whole plant, place it at the depth it was growing. Plant in the spring in cold weather climates, spring or early fall for the rest of the country. Space the plants two to three feet apart, since it forms a large yellow root system with a mass of feeder roots.

Do you have some flower beds at your house, but no space for a rhubarb garden? Think again, rhubarb can not only be grown with flowers, but also makes a great addition to the bed. It can go in front, for easy pulling and makes a great accent plant, with its fountain shape, and rosy stalks.

Pieplant for Birdseed

If you forget to remove the flower stalk, let those whitish, bubbly flowers ripen into seeds. The birds will love you. The seed stalks tower about six feet tall. After the birds have feasted, the brown stalks look good in dried flower arrangements. Rhubarb is as hungry as a teenager. Manure or compost should be heaped on each plant each fall. Spring would be a good time to add more around, but not on, each plant.

Harvesting Pieplant

The first year, plants must be left to grow untouched. The second year, take a paring knife into the garden with you. Grasp the stalk at ground level, and twist- pull to remove it. Do not cut it. Rhubarb stalks should never be cut - always pulled. The cut end lets disease and decay set in. If the stalk breaks, pull the rest of it, the broken end can lead to decay too. Use the knife to cut off the entire leaf, since it is **poisonous** with oxalic acid salts. Put the leaf back under the plant to nourish the soil. Never remove more than half of the stalks at a time; the remainder are needed to nourish the plant. That second year, only pull stalks until the first of June. In later years, you can pull until July first.

LITTLE DREAMER'S HIDE-A-WAY
by T. Marie Smith

I sneaked out the back door and headed for the rhubarb patch.

"I'm only eight years old," I said aloud. "Why do I always have to help with the dishes? Chuck and Darrell are fun brothers but they never have to do any housework." I scowled in self-pity.

It was a warm June afternoon and a gentle breeze was blowing across the high North Dakota sky. I had no intentions of staying inside all day.

"Marie!" My older sister was calling me to dry and put away the dishes.
I knew I would be in trouble when Mamma came home, but without answering, I broke into a fast run and dove into the rhubarb patch.

"She'll never find me here!" I said as I stroked a thick, red rhubarb stem. My touch prompted a little green frog to hop out of my reach. His plump body and gangly legs created a perfect silhouette as the bright sun penetrated the umbrella-like leaf.

"Marie! Get in this house right now!"

I bit into one the rhubarb stems. The cool, sour juice squirted into my mouth. I screwed up my face and felt a little shiver as the strong, red liquid dripped to my chin. Lying flat, I scooted from plant to plant until I reached my very special one. It was much larger than the others. I could easily sit under it without being seen. Today, as usual, I would lie on the soft, cool dirt and dream about how I would someday become a great artist, painting rhubarb, and trees, and fluffy white clouds, and maybe even beautiful women.

Dishes? They could wait . . . as usual!

RIBS: A series of curved bones attached to the spine that covers the chest of an animal. The most popular are pork ribs, available in various cuts: spare ribs, back ribs, country-style ribs, etc. Also good are beef ribs, especially the hard-to-find baby beef ribs. Other ribs include veal, lamb and wild game such as deer, elk and moose. Ribs are best barbecued, but can be slow roasted in the oven.

NORTHWEST OHIO RIB-OFF

A three day August event is promoted as "Toledo's Biggest Family Picnic" with continuous music, and more than seventeen choices of ribs. There are other festival foods, but it's the ribs with all the different secret sauces that highlight this event. There's a small charge for each sample and when you find the one you like best, you can purchase half or full slabs of ribs for your picnic dinner. Awards are given for the Peoples Choice and the Golden Rib competition on Sunday, the last day of the event. There's a kids area with arts and crafts, and games. For information on Toledo area ethic food festivals, write to: **Greater Toledo Visitors Bureau,** 401 Jefferson Avenue, Toledo, OH 43604-1005 or phone (800) 243-4667 or (419) 321-6404. *--Melissa Gregg*

RICE: Native to India and southeast Asia, this ancient grain is now the chief source of food for half the world's population. It grows best in semi-marsh areas, but will grow in lesser qualities on land with a good rainfall. One advantage of rice over other grains, is that it takes less milling prior to being eaten. Only the husks need to be removed for brown rice. Further milling to make white rice removes some of the important nutrients, especially the B and E vitamins and minerals.

Brown rice (whole rice) has a nutty flavor. **White rice** is brown rice from which the germ and outer layers have been removed. **Polished rice** is white rice further refined to remove any flour clinging to the grains. There are long, medium and short grain rice. **Long grain** is best for light and fluffy rice, since the grains tend not to stick together when cooked. **Medium grain** is more tender than long grain. **Short grain** rice is the most tender and has a tendency to stick together, hence is best used for rice puddings. One of the most fragrant, aromatic rices is long grain **basmati** rice, originally from India and Pakistan, now grown also in Texas. **Converted and instant** rice have been precooked, then dried to seal in vitamins, and the taste can be disappointing.

Rice can be cooked stovetop in water and other liquids, steamed, or baked in a slow oven. American wild rice is not a member of the Asian rice; it is a marsh grass. **Nutrition facts** for ½ cup **cooked brown rice**; 109 calories, 7 calories from fat, .8g total fat (1%), .2g saturated fat (1%), zero cholesterol and sodium, 22.9g carbohydrates (8%), zero fiber, 2.3g protein (5%), zero vitamins A and C, 10mg calcium (1%), .5mg iron (3%), and 77mg potassium. **Nutrition facts** for ½ cup **cooked white rice**: 132 calories, zero fats and sodium, 28.6g carbohydrates (10%), .4g fiber (2%), 2.8g protein (6%), zero vitamins A and C, 11mg calcium (1%), .2mg iron (1%), and 40mg potassium. www.successrice.com; www.mahatmarice.com; www.carolinarice.com

A BIT OF RICE HISTORY

The English word "rice" comes originally from the Arabic word *ruz* by way of the Greek and Latin *oryza* and, finally, the French *ris*. It is believed that rice grew wild in the deltas of the Ganges in Indian, the Yangtze in China, and the Tigris and Euphrates in what is now Iraq. However, because rice has been cultivated since the beginning of historical times, the wild form cannot now be distinguished from the thousands of varieties that are grown for food in subtropical regions, world-wide.

In the classical language of China, the words for agriculture and for the cultivation of rice are interchangeable. That fact suggests that rice was the principal crop in China when the language was developing more than 4,000 years ago. In some other languages in the East, the word meaning "rice" is the same as the word meaning "food." Rice was so important in the life of people of the Orient in ancient times that religious ceremonies grew up around its planting and harvesting, and the rice grain and plant were used in decorative art.

Rice was being grown in the Po Valley of Italy by 1475 and also in Spain. Known to the Romans, it was not grown by them. Once they had water enough for irrigation, it was grown in the Islamic world in swamps and flooded river plains. This would be along the Nile and Euphrates rivers from about 800 AD.

Rice was brought to the American colonies in the middle of the 17th century. It was first grown in the low country of South Carolina. Later it became an important crop in Arkansas, Louisiana, Texas and California. Irrigation is used in those areas where rainfall is not adequate.

Although the United States produces enough rice to export to Europe, South America and the West Indies, almost 90 percent of the rice in the world is grown and eaten in China, India and Japan.
–Joyce Ackermann

HOW TO MAKE PERFECT RICE

Fast cooking or instant rices are easy to cook. Just follow directions on the box. But the taste of brown and Oriental rices, cooked slowly in the time honored way can't be found in a box. Cooking rice only takes 20 minutes, so don't be put off from trying it. Take are. Boiling is dangerous.

1) Measure the amount of rice and liquid exactly. Use a pan with plenty of room for rice to expand. It will double in size. Follow directions on the package.
2) Time the cooking with a timer. Don't guess at it.
3) Keep lid on during simmering to prevent steam from escaping. Stir occasionally. Very important!
4) At the end of cooking time, remove lid and test a few grains for doneness. If rice is not quite tender or liquid not absorbed, cook another 2-4 minutes longer.
5) When rice is done, stir once more, then turn it out into serving bowls.
6) When serving, rice should be fluffed with a fork to allow steam to escape.

RICE FLOUR: Ground rice flour is generally not used to make bread, but is added to cakes, cookies, ice cream, and candy. Rice flour is helpful to people allergic to wheat.

RICE PILAF is rice seasoned with a variety of seasonings.

RICE PUDDING: A sweet dessert made by baking milk, egg, vanilla and cinnamon into cooked rice. Often served with raisins or raisin sauce. Gentle on the tummy, it has been used since early Roman times as a dish for invalids.

RICER: A utensil that presses vegetables through a sieve to rice-like pellets. The process is called "to rice." The ricer works best for potatoes, and makes them fluffy. Today the ricer is seldom used with the advent of the electric mixer

RICOTTA CHEESE: (rik-ahta) Ricottta was originally a goat cheese made as a byproduct of making provolone cheese. Today in American it is made wit cow milk. It is the recooked whey. *Ricotta* means "recooked" in Italian. Ricotta is soft, like cottage cheese but less lumpy and is used both for eating and cooking. Mainly you'll see it in lasagna and cheesecake. Ricotta cheese has little taste of its own, which makes it blend well for many uses. Generally believe to be Sicilian in origin, it probably came from the days when the Arabs ruled Sicily (827-1091 AD). **Nutrition facts** per ½ cup: 214 calories, 144 calories from fat, 16g total fat (25%), 10.2g saturated fat (51%), 62.2mg cholesterol (21%), 103.5mg sodium (4%), 3.1g carbohydrates(1%), zero fiber, 13.9g protein (28%), 603 IU vitamin A (12%), zero vitamin C, 255mg calcium (25%), and .5mg iron (3%).

Activity
From India comes this tasty, easy recipe. Simply sweeten Ricotta with sugar and add almond flavoring to taste. Stir and chill. Experiment with other flavorings.

ROAST: Generally the same meaning as "bake," a method of cooking by dry heat either in an enclosed oven or over an open fire. Recipes will usually distinguish between oven roasting, split roasting, flame roasting, etc.

ROCK CORNISH HEN: Also known as Cornish game hens, are a small fowl with all white meat and weighing about a pound. They can be fried or broiled, but are best stuffed and roasted. **Nutrition facts** 3 ounces: 151 calories, 80 calories from fat, 8.7g total fat (14%), 2.4g saturated fat (12%), 55.8mg cholesterol (19%), 196.5mg sodium (8%), zero carbohydrates and fiber, 17.3g protein (35%), 102 IU vitamin A (2%), zero vitamin C, 10mg calcium (1%) and .8mg iron (5%).

ROCKFISH: A name for various salt water fish found along the Pacific coast from Alaska to California. The white, flaky meat has a crab texture and flavor, and is often used in salads and sauces in place of crab meat. Rockfish can be fried, broiled, and steamed, but are best baked whole. Rockfish can be used an any recipe calling for red snapper and are often sold as red snapper. **Nutrition facts** per 3 ounces: 80 calories, 12 calories from fat, 1.3g total fat (2%), .3g saturated fat (2%), 29.7mg cholesterol (10%), 51.1mg sodium (2%), zero carbohydrates and fiber, 17g protein (32%), 315 IU vitamin A (3%), zero vitamin C, 8mg calcium (1%) and .4mg iron (2%).

ROCK LOBSTER: A species of lobster found in the Gulf of Mexico and the Caribbean. While related to America's North Atlantic lobster, they lack the meaty claws. See LOBSTER.

ROE: Fish eggs, also referred to as caviar (which is roe that has been salted). Roe must be cooked slowly by poaching, broiling or baking. Shad roe is the most popular in this country. Roe is available fresh and canned. Roe has as much protein as fish. Fishermen who find roe in pregnant fish usually fry the roe right along with the fish and enjoy it.

ROEBUCK: A small deer in Eurasian forests whose tender red meat is growing in popularity, especially in Germany where it lives in abundance.

ROLL: This term has several meanings. (Noun) A roll is a small muffin-size bread to be eaten at meals in place of loaf bread. Roll-up means to roll something up, like a jelly roll. (verb) To roll, means to flatten out dough, such as a pie crust.

ROMAINE LETTUCE: Also knows as cos lettuce, it has long green leaves that are darker on the outside, light green on the inside, and almost white in the center. The crisp leaves store well, generally for longer periods than other lettuces and best mixed with other lettuce in salads. **Nutrition facts**½ cup: 5 calories, zero fats and sodium, zero carbohydrates, .7g fiber (3%), .5g protein (1%), 737 IU vitamin A (15%), 7mg vitamin C (11%), 10mg calcium (1%), and .3mg iron (2%).

ROMANO CHEESE: This grating cheese can be made from either cow or goat milk. When cured, it has a black surface, white on the inside, with a sharp, salty flavor. It originated in Italy. **Nutrition facts**½ cup: 217 calories, 137 calories from fat, 15.1g total fat (23%), 9.6g saturated fat (48%), 58.2mg cholesterol (19%), 672mg sodium (28%), 2g carbohydrates (1%), zero fiber, 17.8g protein (36%) 320 IU vitamin A (6%), zero vitamin C, 596mg calcium (60%), and .4mg iron (2%).

ROOT BEER: Originally a non-alcoholic beverage made with a combination of roots, barks and herbs. The beverage contains sugar, carbonated water, sometimes coloring and natural or artificial flavorings. Two of the most popular flavorings are sarsaparilla and ginger. Today, most root beers are made with artificial flavorings. Early root beer contained blends of sarsaparilla, sassafras, spruce, wild cherry, spikenard, wintergreen, and ginger.

ROOT CELLAR: A cool, dry place to store potatoes, beets, turnips and other root vegetables, winter squash, and fruit such as apples and pears. Depending upon the produce, the cellar can keep food for a month or longer.

ROQUEFORT CHEESE: (rowk-fert): The trademark name for a cheese made with ewe's milk and ripened in caves. **Nutrition facts** ½ cup: 207 calories, 154 calories from fat, 17.2g total fat (26%), 18.8g saturated fat (54%), 50.4mg cholesterol (17%), 1012mg sodium (42%), zero carbohydrates and fiber, 12.1g protein (24%), 586 IU vitamin A (12%), zero vitamin C, 371mg calcium (37%) and .2mg iron (2%).

ROSE: The flower that smells so delicious has been eaten and used for flavoring forever. Rose petals have always garnished dishes and been eaten as salad by themselves. Rose petal jam is popular in the Middle East. The Persians made rose wine as early as 2000 years ago. Look for rose jellies, candied rose petals, and rose water in specialty stores. See GARNISHES and ROSE WATER and ROSE HIPS.

ROSE APPLES: Native to the East Indies, there are three different varieties: pale yellow, rose-pink, and white. Rose apples grow in clusters, pear shaped, about three inches long, with a sweet aromatic flavor similar to apples. Rose apples are full of seeds, and have a wooly texture. The are eaten fresh, candied, and made into preserves. The Indian name is *jambu*. The English name is misleading, since the fruit has little to do with roses or apples.

ROSEFISH: Also called redfish, this fatty fish is often sold as ocean perch, and with its bland flavor works well in sauces.

ROSE HIPS: At the base of the rose flower and above the stem is a round red capsule that is filled with seeds. These are the rose hips. Rich in vitamin C, hips are sold in concentration by health food stores. Wild rose hips have more vitamin C than domesticated roses. Rose hips can also be made into jelly and jam.

ROSELLE: Known as the Florida cranberry. It originated in the Old World Tropics, has a sour taste like cranberries, and it is made into a sauce and a beverage.

ROSEMARY: An herb from southern Europe, now grown throughout Europe and the United States. The herb is used to season almost everything from eggs to vegetables and all kinds of meat, poultry and fish. Like all herbs, rosemary is best used fresh, and only takes a little to season food. When used dried, it is best to crush to release the full rosemary flavor. Rosemary has a long fascinating history as an herbal tea and healing remedy.

ROSETTE: A type of waffle iron that is heated, dipped into a batter, then deep fat fried. When the batter becomes crisp, the batter removes itself from the iron and continues to fry until crisp and golden brown. Rosette iron comes in many sizes and shapes, with the butterfly one of the most popular. After cooked, the waffle is dusted with powdered sugar and cinnamon and eaten as a cookie. The waffles are also filled with diced fruit or berries, sometimes mixed with cream cheese and/or topped with whipped cream. .

ROSEWATER: An ancient flavoring made from rose petals that is used like baking extracts, such as vanilla. Still very popular in Europe and the Near East to India. It is available imported from France in specialty food stores.

ROTISSERIE: A cooking appliance that rotates food over flame as it cooks. Manual rotating is one of the oldest methods of cooking when primitive man cooked food over an open fire. Turning ensures even cooking.

ROUGH LEMON: From India, this tree has three-inch, yellow fruit, some used like lemons, but grown mostly for seeds to be used for root stock.

ROUX: (roo) A mixture of flour and fat cooked together for several minutes to brown the flour, and stirred constantly because it burns easily. Roux is one of the basic ways to make gravy. Cooking the flour in fat before adding liquid gives the flour a "brown" or cooked taste. Once a roux has been browned, it is ready to become gravy by the addition of water, milk, or meat stock. Created by the French, roux is a key ingredient in Cajun recipes, where they use a chocolate colored roux. The French use mostly white or blond colored roux. Roux is used to thicken soups, stews, and sauces.

ROYAL MANDARINS: See TANGORS.

ROYAL PALM: Native of Cuba, grown for high quality heart of palm.

RUE: This little-used bitter herb is added to meat stews, and used in Eastern European meat stuffings in very small amounts and in soft cheeses and salad dressings. Care must be given when picking the leaves, because it can cause a rash. Some Europeans makes rue leaf sandwiches on buttered brown bread. In Italy it is used to flavor a brandy. An old expression, "You will rue the deed you have done" means that you will regret or feel bitter about the deed.

RUKAM: From Malaysia, a shrub with dark purple berries made into jelly.

RUM: An alcoholic beverage made from sugar cane. Rum is used in mixed drinks and a flavoring in recipes. The most famous rum drink is a rum punch and one of the more popular recipes containing rum is an Italian rum cake. See SUGAR CANE and MOLASSES.

RUMP STEAK: A cut of beef taken from below the sirloin, less tender but more flavorful then the sirloin. .

RUSSIAN DRESSING: A salad topping made with mayonnaise, chili sauce, and chopped dill pickles. It's probably an American invention. As easy version any child can make is to begin with a cup of mayonnaise and add 1/4 cup each of diced onion, pickle relish, and ketchup.

RUTABAGA: While a member of the mustard family, it is also related to cabbage. Shaped like a turnip, but a bit larger, it has either a yellow or white flesh, and a sweet flavor. Rutabagas can be used in place of turnips in most recipes. Eaten as a vegetable, they are generally boiled in salted water with a little sugar added, and served with butter, salt and pepper. Rutabagas are also good raw. Slice it thin, cut into sticks, soak in salt water for several hours, and serve it with a veggie dip, with carrot sticks, celery, etc. **Nutrition facts** ½ cup: 25 calories, zero fats,14mg sodium (1%), 5.7g carbohydrates (2%), 1.8g fiber (7%), 1.8g fiber (7%), .8g protein (2%), 406 IU vitamin A (8%), 18mg vitamin C (29%), 33mg calcium (3%), .4mg iron (2%).

RYE: A cereal grass used to make rye flour and alcoholic liquors. To make bread, rye flour is mixed with wheat flour, as rye flour doesn't have the gluten to make bread rise. Breads made with all, or almost all, rye flour as quite heavy and can be moist. Rye flour is popular in northern European regions, because it can grow in colder climates than wheat. Rye flour is also used to make crackers and cookies. When the new settlers arrived they first used corn as the flour of choice. When wheat didn't do well, they planted rye and mixed the rye flour with corn flour and this bread was known as "rye'n'Injun." Rye grass was a boon to mankind because it will grow in Nordic regions, in mountains, and on poor soil. Rye is also used in some kinds of vodka and whiskey.

Ss

SABAL PALM. This, the state tree of Florida, is also known as the palmetto. It produces clusters of 1/4-inch edible fruits. The terminal bud is eaten fresh or cooked like cabbage.

SABAYON: A French dessert, similar to the Italian *zabaglione* dessert made with wine, eggs, sugar and citrus juice. *Sabayon* is also served as a dessert sauce.

SABLEFISH: This saltwater fish, also known as black cod, though it's not in the cod family, is found in northern Pacific waters. Sablefish has white flesh, is quite rich with oil. It is best smoked or barbecued. **Nutrition facts** 3 ounces: 166 calories, 120 calories from fat, 26g total fat (40%), 5.4g saturated fat (14%), 41.7mg cholesterol (14%), 47.6mg sodium (2%), zero carbohydrates and fiber, 11.4g protein (23%), 253 IU vitamin A (5%), zero vitamin C, 15mg calcium (2%), and 1.1mg iron (6%). www.alaskaseafood.org

SACCHARIN: (sak-rin) An artificial sweetener made without sugar and having no calories.

SADDLE: A meat cut taken from between the last of the ribs to the hind quarter for roasting. It includes the two joined loins (shaped like a saddle). A saddle of rabbit is from the lower rib to the tail on both sides.

SAFFLOWER: An herb native to the East Indies. Oil is cold-pressed from the white seeds. This bland oil is used to make salad oil, margarine, and marinades. It's a good frying oil and is available at most supermarkets and health food stores. Now cultivated in the South of France and other areas.. The flower petals are sometimes used as a substitute for saffron, though the taste is more bitter. In Jamaica, safflower oil is used as a spice combined with chili peppers and cloves.

SAFFRON: A purple flower of the crocus plant. In the center of the flower are three tiny, fuzzy yellow filaments that are dried to make a pungent flavoring. These filaments are so small, it takes more than 4,000 to make an ounce. While the purchase price is high, the good news is it only takes a little for both flavoring and yellow coloring. Saffron is used to flavor meats and breads, as well as soups, sauces, rice and potatoes. Since the cost is high, many budget-wise chefs will substitute turmeric in saffron recipes. In the Middle Ages, a pound of saffron cost as much as a horse, which was something the common man could not even own. The best saffron still comes from Valencia, Spain. Safflower and turmeric are sometimes substituted for the expensive saffron.

SAGE: (sayj) There are hundreds of varieties of this leafy herb found around the world. The pungent, grey-green sage leaves, either fresh or dried, are used in flavoring. The name came from the French word *sauge*, from the Latin *salvia*, meaning the "healing" plant. Sage is used to flavor poultry, stuffings, and meat, especially pork sausage. Sage is also added to vegetables, such as eggplant, onions, and tomatoes. One of the most imported and most used sages is the mild *daimatian* from Yugoslavia. Pineapple sage, native to Mexico, smells like pineapple and makes an excellent garnish to salads and iced tea. The unrelated western sagebrush or purple sage is not used in recipes.

SAGO: (say-go) A starch made from the sago palm of the southwest Pacific, is used in the United States as a thickening agent for soups, sauces and puddings. Known in Europe since the Renaissance, it was a popular starch for thickening. In Indonesia sago paste is used with coconut milk for making fritters, cakes and desserts. In India they make a dessert out of it.

SAINT JOHN'S BREAD: This Mediterranean tree is known as the tree that produces carob bean pods. The pods are used to make syrup, dehydrated and added to breakfast foods. The dried carob powder is used as a substitute for cocoa.

SAKE: (SAH-kee)An alcoholic Japanese beverage made from fermented rice. Sake is clear and colorless, sweet but with a bitter aftertaste and very potent.

SALAD: A Latin word meaning salt. Originally salads were preserved vegetables. Today, it is a loose term for mixed (mostly raw) vegetables or fruits served with a dressing.

RED PEPPERS MAKE GREAT LIPS

The **Association for Dressings and Sauces** and the **Produce for Better Health Foundation** annually conducts the National Salad Head Competition. Using fruits, vegetables, and salad dressing as their medium, elementary students from across the country turn classrooms into produce stands every fall to create the ultimate Salad Head. To enter, schools must submit a color photograph of their Salad Head made from salad ingredient. All entries must include a lesson description; school and teacher contact names; names and ages of student participants; and a list of ingredients. This activity will show you how to explore new foods and tastes, as you learn the basics of good nutrition, and have great fun doing it. In the end, you will find out that not only do red peppers taste good, they make great lips. For contest rules, deadlines, and prizes, send a self-addressed, stamped, business-size envelope to: **National 5 A Day Salad Head Competition**, 5775-G Peachtree-Dunwoody Road, Atlanta, GA 30342.-- *Robb Enright*

SALAD DRESSING: Any mix of oils and vinegars blended with seasonings to enhance the flavor of salad greens. The simplest of all is a splash of olive oil and vinegar rubbed through the greens and sprinkled with salt and pepper. Variations of that basic recipe abound.

SALAK PALM: From Java, the palm produces sweet to tart pulp used fresh and in preserves.

SALAMANDER: An iron kitchen tool that is heated to glaze and brown the top of cooked foods. Today the home oven broiler has replace the salamander. Chef sometimes even use a blow torch in their kitchens for quick browning. In professional kitchens, the salamander is an oven that heats only from the roof of the oven so that it glazes or browns food already cooked. It gets its name from the animal, which according to legend, was fireproof.

SALAMI: Originally a cooked Italian sausage now made in other countries. The meat can be beef, pork or poultry, with salt, spices and garlic added. There are two kinds of salami, soft and hard. Soft is better for sandwiches.

SALERATUS: Refined potash used before baking powder was invented. See COLONIAL COOKING and BAKING POWDER.

SALLY LUNN: You can believe either the British legend that says Sally Lunn was a London baker in the city of Bath and that she sold these tall cakes on the street - or the likelihood that the name comes into English from the French word *Salilune* or *Sael Leme* for an identical brioche-style bun. Characters in Charles Dickens's novels ate Sally Lunn buns, so we know they go back at least to1800.

SALLY LUNN IN AMERICA

In the American colonies, sally lunn became a tall, spectacular cake, more like a sweet bread that was leavened with yeast. Traditionally sally lunn is baked in a tube pan, while you could use tall juice cans, you will probably have better success to make buns in muffin tins. The name was once capitalized but now has become a common noun and is not capitalized when it refers to the food and not the woman. Some cookbooks still capitalize it for either use.

SALMAGUNDI: In France, it's a traditional stew made with leftover meats, seasoned with pickles, vinegar and/or wine. Also, it can be an elaborate salad made on a platter, arranged with colons in concentric circles.

SALMI: A dish made from partially cooked poultry and finished cooking at the dinner table in a chafing dish.

SALMON: Basically a saltwater fish found in the northern Pacific and Atlantic oceans. Fresh water varieties are found in rivers and lakes that also include trout and steelhead. www.alaskaseafood.org

Pacific Varieties: Five varieties are found in the Pacific Ocean: king, sockeye, silver, pink, and chum.

Kings, also known as chinook salmon, are the largest in the Pacific, sometimes weighing up to 130 pounds. The flesh has a high fat content, can be colored from red to white. Most king salmon are smoked, but are available fresh and a few are canned. **Nutrition facts** 3 ounces king salmon: 153 calories, 82 calories from fat, 8.9g total fat (14%), 2.1g saturated fat (10%), 56.2mg cholesterol (19%), 40mg sodium (2%), zero carbohydrates and fiber, 17g protein (34%), 387 IU vitamin A (8%), 4mg vitamin C (6%), 19mg calcium (2%), and .6mg iron(4%). www.smoked.fish.com

Sockeyes, also known as red salmon, can weight up to 15 pounds. Sockeyes have a bright red flesh, and mostly are canned. Sockeyes that have become landlocked in lakes are known as *kokanee*.. **Nutrition facts** 3 ounces sockeye salmon: 98 calories, 28 calories from fat, 3g total fat (5%), .5g saturated fat (3%), 44.2mg cholesterol (15%), 57mg sodium (3%), zero carbohydrates and fiber, 16.9g protein (34%), 100 IU vitamin A (2%), zero vitamin C, 11mg calcium (1%), 1.7mg iron (4%).

Silvers, also called coho salmon, average about 12 pounds, but have been caught up to 35 pounds. Silvers are generally eaten fresh. Most flesh is red. While rare, a white flesh variety does exist. **Nutrition facts** 3 ounces silver salmon: 124 calories, 43 calories from fat, 5.1g total fat (8%), 1.1g saturated fat (6%), 38.3mg cholesterol (13%), 39.2mg sodium (2%), zero carbohydrates and fiber, 18.4g protein (37%), 85 IU vitamin A (2%), 1mg vitamin C (1%), 30mg calcium (3%), and .9mg iron (3%).

Pinks, or "humpbacks," are the smallest, seldom over four pounds. They have the lowest fat content, and are mostly canned. Some are sold fresh and are best barbecued. **Nutrition facts** 3 ounces pink salmon: same as sockeye salmon.

Chums, also known as dog salmon, are a bit larger than the pinks. Generally sold canned or smoked. Fresh salmon can be fried, baked, broiled, barbecued, steamed, or poached. Canned salmon can be served chilled with a sauce or in salads. Salmon is also salted, dried, pickled and kippered. Fresh salmon is flown to major markets in the United States, as well as Europe and Japan. Most fresh salmon is frozen, then glazed with a thin layer of ice to provide drying. **Nutrition facts** 3 ounces chum salmon: 102 calories, 30 calories from fat, 3.2g total fat (5%), .7g saturated fat (4%), 67.8mg cholesterol (21%), 47.5mg sodium (2%), zero carbohydrates and fiber, 17.2g protein (35%), 74 IU vitamin A (2%), zero vitamin C, 10mg calcium (1%), .5mg iron (3%).

Atlantic: Unlike the Pacific Ocean, the Atlantic Ocean only has one species of salmon. Atlantic salmon are found in the northern waters from North America to Europe. Atlantic salmon, unlike the Pacific salmon, steam up stream to spawn two or more times. **Nutrition facts** 3 ounces: 121 calories, 50 calories from fat, 5.4g total fat (9%), .9g saturated fat (4%), 46.8mg cholesterol (16%), 37.4mg sodium (2%), zero carbohydrates and fiber, 16.8g protein (34%), zero vitamin A and C, 10mg calcium (1%), and .7mg iron (4%). www.smoked.fish.com

Salmon Spawning:

Spawning is the fish birth cycle. Spawning salmon found in fresh water are generally not commercially fished. Fishermen don't want to kill the fish before they make more fish. When the salmon first enter the river, they are edible. But by the time they swim upstream to their spawning grounds, they have been beaten so badly by the rocks in the rapids, the flesh is like mush. Pacific salmon die soon after spawning. Atlantic salmon will live and spawn two or more times. Salmon are known to swim amazing distances to the spawning grounds. Kings will sometimes swim more than 2,000 miles up the Yukon river just to spawn. Kings are the first to spawn, followed in the same order as listed.

FINN McCOOL & THE SALMON OF KNOWLEDGE
An Irish Legend
retold by Louise Ulmer

From the mists of time came many legends of Ireland's Finn McCool, warrior and wizard.

When Finn was only a boy of seven, he chanced upon an ancient seer named Finneigeas (fini-gus). On the bonnie banks of the Boyne River, they sat for a wee chat. Old Finneigeas had been fishing and on he went with it until he happened to catch the fish of his dreams. He could barely contain himself as he hauled and hustled and pulled in the large salmon, which wasn't just any salmon but the Salmon of Knowledge. According to ancient legend, the first to taste this salmon would become the world's wisest man.

"Gather sticks. boy," he said to young Finn. "I must cook and eat this fish as fast as ever I can for I am famished near unto death."

Finn didn't think the wizard looked all that famished, having pulled in a right smart salmon all of a sudden, but he did as he was told and soon had a fire going for the old wizard.

When Finn was working on the fire, old Finneigeas hurried to get the fish ready to eat for he knew the legend and had been seeking wisdom all his life. After all, that is what it means to be a seer - a wise man. He said to the fish, "I'll have you now, my good fish, and the blessing that you bring will be mine. I shall be the first to taste your meat and thereby I shall gain all the world's knowledge, for such is the promise of old."

When the fire smoldered low in the coals, just right for roasting a fish, the old man set the fish on a turning spit over the heat and waited for the fire to do its work.

"Watch that fish with all your wits, boy," said the old seer. "But remember it's my catch and you're not to have so much as a morsel until I have had mine." With that the tired old man fell asleep watching the fire.

By and by, the fish began to brown and looked ready to eat. As all good cooks do, young Finn pressed on the fish's side with his thumb to test if the juices had cooked dry.

"Ow!" said Finn when the hot juices burned him, and he popped his thumb into his mouth. When he did this, he became the first to taste the Salmon of Knowledge and thus the prophecy was fulfilled.

The old seer felt the earth tremble with the magic and woke. There stood the boy with his thumb still in his mouth. But instead of looking stupid, as you might expect, Finn had the light of wisdom shining in his eyes.

"Aye, what a fool I've been," cried the seer. "The prize that I waited for has gone to a lad while I lay sleeping."

Now most people look foolish, and then some, with their thumbs plugging their mouths but such was never the case with Finn McCool, for from that day on whenever he needed wisdom he had but to put his thumb in his mouth and think. And as the old wizard said when he shared the fish with his young friend, "Perhaps it was meant to be so."

SALSA: A zesty red sauce made with chopped tomatoes, peppers and onions, which can either be peppery hot or mild. Similar to relish or chutney, it goes with all kinds of meats, in bean salads, and as a dip for snacks and veggies.

SALSIFY: See OYSTER PLANT www.frieda.com

SALT: The chemical name is sodium chloride. It is found naturally in oceans, and some lakes like the Dead Sea and the Great Salt Lake. Salt is obtained by evaporation of the salty water or by mining where long ago seas dried up and left salt behind. **Salt is essential** for good health because it helps to regulate the balance of bodily fluids and plays an important role in muscle contractions, especially the heart muscle. Salt also helps the transmission of electrical nerve impulses Salt is used to season and to preserve food. And where would be the old fashioned hand-cranked ice cream freezer be without rock salt in the ice? Seasoned salt contains fine grained salt and ingredients such as sugar, spices, and herbs. www.unitedsalt.com.

USE SALT IN MODERATION

When you hear the word "salt" what do you think of? Most people think of table salt, a seasoning found in every kitchen. Table salt is made of sodium and chloride. Some salt in your diet is needed for good health. The term **"salt" does not mean the same as "sodium"** because salt is only forty percent sodium. Most health professional believe it is wise for people to consume less salt (and sodium). High blood pressure is related to diets containing high levels of sodium. We need much less than we usually consume.

Sodium is important because it helps to regulate body fluids and helps maintain normal blood volume. Sodium is also needed for the normal function of nerves and muscles. The National Academy of Sciences **suggests 500 milligrams** of sodium a day as a safe minimum intake. That's less than a fourth teaspoon. The average American consumes between 4,000 to 6,000 milligrams of sodium daily.

The fact is, that no one really knows how much sodium you should consume. Some health authorities now suggest limiting the amount of sodium to 2,400 milligram a day. One level teaspoon of salt contain 2,335 milligrams of sodium. Sodium content is listed on all canned and packaged foods, which makes it easy to count. But foods in their natural state also have sodium. You need a handy chart if you are counting all sodium intake. It's not always possible to tell how much sodium is in food from the taste. Most recipes can be made either with less salt or no salt.

How do you spice up a food without salt? Herbs, seeds, and spices are great replacements. A few examples: In a meat loaf, use allspice, garlic, marjoram, and/or thyme. Beans taste great with dill and/or rosemary. In cabbage, use caraway seeds and/or curry powder. Try pasta with poppy seeds and/or savory. And basil, curry, onion powder and/or turmeric works wonders with grains such as rice and bulgur.

When using packaged foods, read the labels to be sure. And when dining in a fast food restaurant, beware! Most fast foods are loaded with sodium. The good news: those salted french fries have less sodium than a plain hamburger. Make "sodium-smart" recipes. In Oriental cooking, use low sodium soy sauce. In seasoned crumb coating replace, salt with herbs and l vegetable powders. In meat marinades just eliminate the salt and use more herbs. It might take a little time to experiment with amounts of these substitutes. Just go easy at first and increase as you think necessary.
--*Human Nutrition Information Service*

23 SALTY FACTS YOU PROBABLY DIDN'T KNOW

- Salt - sodium chloride (NaCl) - is necessary to the health of every living creature on the planet.
- In ancient days salt was worth twice as much as gold.
- Tibetans used salt cakes as money.
- Civilizations rose in Africa, China, India and the Middle East near abundant salt deposits. Need for salt sent camel caravans into the African deserts and along the Silk Road.
- Salt revenues helped build kingdoms throughout Europe and Asia. Salt taxes also spurred revolutions, such as in France where "Salt for everyone" became a cry for democracy.
- Nations have fought wars over salt and salt mines. During the American Civil War, northern generals set out to capture southern salt mines as soon as possible.
- In India, Mahatma Gandhi in 1930 set out on a 200-mile march to the sea to protest Britain's salt tax.
- Prehistoric peoples gathered salty "powder" left behind on ocean rocks and in dry tidal pools. Julius Caesar showed the conquered British how to boil ocean brine for salt, as the Romans had been doing for centuries.
- Rome's Via Salaria (Salt Road) was built to carry salt to the city from other Mediterranean areas and Asia Minor.
- One Utah salt farm produces about half a million tons a year.
- Salt beds, formed from dried oceans, occur in New York, Oklahoma, New Mexico, Kansas, Texas, and Louisiana.
- Table salt accounts for only four percent of all salt production. Most goes for road salt and water conditioning.
- Morton salt makes 400 different kinds of salt products.
- The oldest salt mine in the country is on Avery Island, off southwestern Louisiana. Most of its 2 ½ million tons of rock salt go north to de-ice winter roads.
- Adding salt to water makes dishes sparkle, hair shine, soap suds up better, clothes come out cleaner and more supple, nozzles less clogged and prevents mineral build up in pipes.

- Ancient Jewish temples included a salt chamber because Jews were required to offer God ten percent of their salt.
- Roman Catholic priests once placed a pinch of salt on a baby's tongue during baptism, saying, "Receive the salt of wisdom."
- Arabs made peace and declared friendship with the phrase "There is salt between us."
- Swiss grooms would put bread in one pocket and salt in the other to assure married happiness.
- A German bride would put salt in her shoe for good luck.
- Goiter, a disfiguring disorder caused by iodine deficiency, was cured worldwide by the simple addition of iodine to table salt.
- People have been bathing in mineral salts and salt soaks for healthy benefits for who knows how long. In the 1800s and 1900s it was fashionable to "take the waters" at famous mineral spring spas for rest and recuperation.

OTHER USES FOR SALT

Salt has many uses around the house.

Peel eggs: Put a pinch or two of salt in the water before hardboiling eggs. The shells will come right off. **Remove tea stains** from tea cups by scrubbing with a damp sponge, sprinkled with salt. If the stains persist, rub with equal parts of vinegar and salt. **Stop candle drip** by soaking candles in a solution of two to three tablespoons salt to two cups water. Dry candles well. When candles burn, they won't drip. Are **water rings** on furniture a problem? Put a pinch of salt on a damp rag and gently rub the stain until it fades away. Wipe off salt, than rub area with furniture polish. **Deodorize plastic** containers by filling with warm warn and a few teaspoons of salt. Let the mixture sit for an hour or more, then wash with soap and warm water.

SALT FISH:

SALT FISH IN THE 1800s

Americans once ate dried fish about as often as bread. In Europe an endless need for fish brought fishermen to the New World. In order to preserve and transport the fish, the abundant cod was dressed and salted right aboard the ships. New Englanders soon led the world in cod fishery. Salt cod became an important element in world trade.

On an American visit in 1820, a European lady wrote home about American food with disdain. "In eating, the Americans mix (strange) things together. I have seen eggs and oysters eaten together; ham with apple sauce; beef steak with peaches; and salt fish with raw or fried onions." In her 19th century cookbook, Mrs. Putnam wrote, "Garnish (salt fish) with eggs boiled hard and cut into slices with boiled beets. Beets should always be served with salt fish." Perhaps it was to add color to the meal. Sounds like a good idea anyway.

Fish for Breakfast

In an 1886 Boston cookbook titled *What to Get for Breakfast*, it was suggested, "Serve salt fish balls for breakfast accompanied by cracked wheat, brown bread toast, spiced peaches, coffee and ripe fruit."

Fish for Thanksgiving

In *Observations of a British Consul*, 1839-1846, Thomas Colley Grattan wrote, "The national taste certainly runs on pork, salt fish, tough poultry and little birds of all descriptions." Salt fish replaced turkey at times. In early Rhode Island, salt cod was mashed with potatoes, diced raw onions, and cracklings from fried salt pork and known as "Block Island Turkey." In nearby Massachusetts, a whole salt codfish was freshed, simmered, and served with vegetables and an egg sauce and known as "Cape Cod Turkey."

How Do You Desalt Salt Fish?

How did they desalt and prepare salt fish, you ask? We consulted Jennie June's *Cook Book of 1886*. "Put your salted codfish in to soak the night before; pick if off in shreds the next morning and scald it in a saucepan, pouring off the water just before it comes to a boil; this will freshen it (remove salt) sufficiently. Put in then a little more water, a small piece of butter and a few shakes of pepper and let cook till it is tender. When it is done, thicken it with a beaten egg, but don't allow it to boil. Mix it with double its bulk in potatoes, mashed finely with milk, and season with pepper and a little salt. Pile up as near like a haystack as possible. Pour over the whole some good egg sauce and garnish with parsley and egg rings." Sounds like mashed potatoes flavored with a can of tuna to modern ears. American children may wonder why we should include such old fashioned advice, but there are many places around the world where salt fish is still eaten.

North Atlantic Salt Fish Still Available

Salting is till used to preserve fish where other methods are not convenient. If you are not familiar with salt fish, it generally comes in a little wooden box, now from Nova Scotia, Canada, and is available in many fish markets, some supermarkets, and in stores specializing in Portuguese and Caribbean foods.

SALTINES: A salted soda cracker.

SALT PORK: A fat side of a pig, less lean than bacon, and cured with salt, but not smoked. Salt pork is used as a flavoring in beans, soups, and stews.

SAMPHIRE: A perennial herb found along the rocky coasts of northwestern Europe. Also known as parsley pert and Saint Peter's herb. The crisp aromatic leaves are added to salads. Rich in iodine, the leaves also flavor soups and pickles.

SANKA:
WORLD'S FIRST DECAFFEINATED COFFEE
In 1903 Dr. Ludwig Roselius, head of a large European coffee business, shipped a load of coffee to Europe. During the voyage, sea water deluged the cargo and the coffee was ruined. The beans were turned over to researchers for experimentation. It was discovered the brine-soaked coffee

beans removed part of the caffeine With more experimentation and new techniques, the researchers were able to remove 97% of the caffeine without injuring the delicate coffee flavor.

The product was first introduced in France with the name of Sanka (a contraction of the French phrase *sans caffeine*, which means "without caffeine. Sanka came to the United States in 1923. General Foods began distribution of Sanka in 1928 and purchased the product and the patents four years later. *--Kraft General Foods, Inc.*

SAND DAB: A small flounder found in the Pacific Ocean from California to Alaska. Seldom weighing more than two pounds, most sand dabs found in fish markets are about half a pound. The flesh is white, tender, with a delicate sweet flavor. Sand Dabs are generally sautéd quickly in a little butter.

SANDWICH: The modern, ubiquitous sandwich is named after John Montague, the fourth Earl of Sandwich who placed food between two pieces of bread. The fillings range from peanut butter to a variety of meats and cheeses. In parts of Europe, the sandwich has only one slice of bread, an "open face" sandwich, and is generally eaten with a knife and fork. Over here, we have the hot roast beef (or turkey or chicken) sandwich with one slice of bread topped with mashed potatoes and gravy, which is also called an open faced hot sandwich.

SANTOL: From Southeast Asia, this tree produces a juicy fruit that is eaten fresh.

SAPODILLA: (sappa-deeya) Native to tropical America, the Aztecs used it as a source of *chiki*, our "chicle" gum. The Spaniards carried it to the Philippines. It looks like a small apple with a thin, golden brown skin, with the texture of a pear but sweeter. Sapodilla is eaten fresh and made into sherbet.

SAPOTE: (sa-POH-tee) There are many varieties of sapotes: black, green, white, yellow. All originated in tropical South American. This sweet, custard-like fruit is mostly eaten fresh but it is used to make desserts, especially ice cream.

SARDINES: This tiny, fatty fish is found in most oceans around the world and in an assorted varieties. They swim in the millions around the island of Sardina, hence the name. Sardines weight ounces, not pounds. Mostly you'll see sardines salted, smoked and in small flat cans. Most are packed in olive oil, others in tomato sauce, or mustard sauce. Fresh sardines are generally deep fat fried. Canned sardines can be eaten on a cracker, made into a cocktail, minced into a sandwich spread, and added to salads. Sardines are an excellent source of protein, with some calcium and iron. **Nutrition facts** 3 ounces: 177 calories, 90 calories from fat, 9.9g total fat (15%), 1.3mg saturated fat (7%), 120.7mg cholesterol (41%), 428mg sodium (18%), zero carbohydrates and fiber, 20.8g protein (42%), 190 IU vitamin A (4%), zero vitamin C, 325mg calcium (33%), and 3mg iron (14%).

Activity: Have a tasting party. It won't cost much if everyone in the group brings just one or two items from the list of "weird" foods you have never tried. Cut them into bits and serve with toothpicks so each one can have only a taste.

SARSAPARILLA: (sass-pa-rilla)An extract from a tropical bramble vine from Central and South America, whose dried roots are used as a flavoring, especially in beverages. The name comes from two Spanish words meaning bramble and vine. The Spanish found it already being used on Native American tonics. Once used in soft drinks, its use is rare today.

SASSAFRAS: Sassafras root is what root beer was originally made from. The tree grew wild from Canada to Florida in the East. French settlers probably took the name from Native Americans who were familiar with it. Sassafras is a small tree that can grow to be 100 feet tall. Sassafras is also call "ague tree" and "tea tree." Lore: A shipload of sassafras root leaving Virginia for London in 1609 was North America's first export. Sassafras was used as a cure for a long list of ailments. We do know it to be a weak antiseptic. Today the flavor has been made artificially to use in soft drinks, toothpastes, medicines and soaps. The leaves are dried and ground for their mucilage. It's the main ingredient in filé powder, a thickening and flavoring agent for Louisiana gumbo. We no longer prepare sassafras tea from the roots and drink it for the blood every spring as our forefathers did, though some people still make the tea because the like the taste. In the spring, we can buy it in many southern markets in little stick bundles in the produce department. Today we know the whole tree should be used with caution because it's part of the laurel family, which contains many poisonous plants. The taste can also be found in jellies.

SATIN LEAF: From the West Indies comes a 1-inch, purple fruit that's eaten fresh and made into jelly and preserves.

SATSUMA: A pale orange in the Mandarin family with a baggy loose skin, easy to peel. www.frieda.com

SAUCE: A thick liquid made with fat, flour, and water or milk. Sauces can also contain meat juices, puréed vegetables. There are two basic white sauces: *béchamel* and *velouté*. *Béchamel* is made with milk, flour and butter. *Velouté* uses veal or chicken broth in place of the milk. Both these sauces are generally used to make other sauces, such as mornay, a cheese sauce. Other sauces include salad dressings, barbecue, butter, vegetable, and dessert sauces.

SAUERBRATEN: (sour-brah-tin) In Germany, it means "sour roast." Beef sauerbraten is prepared in a spicy marinade that tenderizes the meat, while adding flavor. Sauerbraten is usually a tough cut, such as brisket or rump, requiring slow cooking. Sauerbraten is generally served with a gravy made with sour cream and wine. Some recipes get a distinctive zip by using gingersnap cookies to flavor.

SAUERKRAUT, (sour-krowt) as we know it, originated in German. Sauerkraut is shredded, pickled cabbage that has fermented in a brine of salt. Pickling vegetables we common before kraut was made.. The unique thing about sauerkraut was the way it was dry salted. The only water comes from the cabbage itself. Romans dry salted their cattle feed but did not do the same for vegetables. They did preserve and pickle in sour wine or vinegar. At its simplest, kraut is only two things–cabbage and salt. Food with vitamin C were a tremendous boon to sailors at sea who had been suffering and dying on long voyages for lack of vitamin C, the cause of scurvy, a disease that kills slowly and horribly. Sauerkraut is mentioned in James Hind's famous *Treatise of the Scurvy* in 1772. They didn't know why but they knew the pickled cabbage helped prevent scurvy The acidity helped retain the vitamin C in the cabbage. It was a long time before scientists learned why it worked. Captain Cook persuaded his sailors to eat it by pretending it was too good for the common sailor and only something the upper class should have. Naturally, then the sailors wanted it. After that, no ship would sail without their kraut and citrus fruits but the kraut kept longer than the fruits.

SAUSAGE: A meat made with ground meat, salt and spices. Can be fresh or cooked, and stuffed into a casing. There are several hundred different kinds of sausages found worldwide. Some of the better known sausages are frankfurters, bratwurst, liverwurst, salami, bologna, pepperoni, and chorizo. America contributed country sausage, made with fresh pork, which can be purchased in bulk or stuffed in casings. Some of the stuffed sausages are also smoked. www.jimmydean.com

J.L. Herring wrote a series of stories of old wiregrass Georgia in a book called, *Saturday Night Sketches* and published by the Sunny South Press at the Georgia Agrirama. The following is a condensed version of how he made sausage as a young boy.

HELPING AUNT MARY MAKE SAUSAGE
by J.L. Herring

The sausage Aunt Mary made tasted just a little better than any other in the world. There was a combination of meats and condiments and art in grinding, mixing, stuffing and smoking that produced a harmony of flavors to tempt the most capricious appetite. On a cold morning, a few days after hog-killing, and after the early breakfast, the Boy was out to help Aunt Mary with the sausage. Close by the log smokehouse the sausage grinder, of cast iron, had been screwed fast to the end of the meat bench, on which the year's supply of ham, shoulders and bacon had been salted down the day before. To the other end the stuffer, also of cast iron, had been fastened. These two useful machines were neighborhood property, passing from family to family during the hog-killing season.

The meat was the trimmings from the pork, before salt had been applied. The tenderloins, strips of lean from the joints, and bits of fat from the flanks; just the right proportion of each. Cut into strips, there were fed into the grinder, the Boy furnishing the steam power; lean and fat alternating, until the meat exuding from the small aperture in the bottom of the grinder was a reddish gray. After several hours' grinding - the Boy meanwhile having frequently "hollered for the calfrope" for relief at the crank - the meat nearly filled the cedar tub used as a receptacle. Then Aunt Mary's skill came into play.

Carefully pulverized by beating in a coarse cloth with a mallet, was the sage - which had been gathered the summer before from the bushes by the garden fence, dried in the sun and put away for the occasion. Pulverized also were the pods of brilliant red pepper, then the salt, and other seasonings -just the right amounts, for therein lay the secret of Aunt Mary's success. Then came the stuffing. The iron box of the long stuffer was filled with meat, and over the tin tube on the end the casing was drawn. Always, the Boy wanted to turn the stuffer, and always he turned too fast until a

warning cry stopped him. Then came the smoking, for Aunt Mary's skill didn't stop with sausage making. Just the right kind of dry, pine sap, or oak, and the smudged fire was kept going, day and night, until those sausages were cured just as she wanted them.
And the result?

> When the mists of dawn are flying
> Before the rising God of Day;
> Just to smell those sausage frying
> In the kitchen, 'cross the way.
> On the table, dark brown, luscious;
> Pile the dish up, full and high
> Bring a hoe-cake, one for just us;
> Give elbow room and let'er fly!
> Oh, ye gods of things delicious!
> Avaunt, Lucullus, of fabled shade!
> Of all the best of childhood's dishes,
> Give us the sausage Aunt Mary made!

Gone are the sausage with other good things of childhood and youth. Remains only memory, but thank God for memory!

Do you remember how they tasted Sunday morning for breakfast, with hot, beaten biscuit, and brindled gravy? Or, did you ever come in from a long tramp, cold and hungry, in mid-afternoon, stop by the smokehouse and purloin a few precious links; then broil them on the coals of a smouldering fire and eat them with a chunk of cold cornbread? If you did neither, then it is no use to talk longer.

Activity
Make a batch of sausage the way they did in 1898 and one the modern way. Compare and rate for taste, convenience and satisfaction.

HOME-MADE SAUSAGE IN 1898

Sausage making was one way of preserving meat for later use. This recipe is from *The Enterprising Housekeeeeper* cookbook of 1898. In this recipe, the butcher used cotton bags, instead of casings. Today, some butchers still prefer cotton bags for aging the sausage. There are instructions at the end of this recipe so that you can make sausage a more modern way.

> 2 pounds lean fresh pork
> 1 pound fat fresh pork
> 3 teaspoons ground sage
> 3 teaspoons salt
> 2 teaspoons white pepper
> 1/4 teaspoon allspice

449

1898 INSTRUCTIONS:

1. Make cotton bags the desired shape and length;
dip them in a strong brine and dry.
2. Chop the meat and fat very fine together and mix
thoroughly with seasonings.
3. Attach the sausage stuffer to the meat chopper.
Press the meat into the bags as closely as possible;
tie the bags tightly and hang in a cool place.
4. When using the sausage from the bags, the end should
be turned back after the desired amount has been cut off,
and tie closely again.
5. Cut the sausage into slices and fry until brown.
--Anabaptist Kitchen

TODAY'S INSTRUCTIONS: You will need:

Ingredients as listed
Food processor
Wax paper
Aluminum foil

1. While you can chop the meat in a food processor, best to have the butcher do it at the meat market. If you still have an old fashioned hand crank meat grinder, you can, of course, grind the pork the way they did in 1898.
2. Combine meat with the seasonings.
3. On a board, lay down a 3-foot sheet of aluminum foil. Lay 3-foot sheet of wax paper on top of the foil.
4. Make a rope from the ground meat, about 1-inch in diameter. Lay it on the edge of the wax paper.
5. Roll up the meat in the wax paper. Roll the aluminum foil around the rolled-up wax paper.
6. Continue rolling until all the meat is used.
7. Age in the refrigerator at least 24 hours before using. Will keep in the refrigerator for several weeks, or it can be frozen.

SAUSAGE CASINGS: Until recently casings were generally the intestines of animals. Sheep and pig casings were plentiful, but also used were ox and beef. The casings have to be soaked and washed and washed to be fit for use. Today there are machines to do that. Artificial casings are common today, mostly made from collagen (obtained from boiled hide) or cellulose, a plant material.

SAUSAGE SEASONINGS: A blend of spices and herbs used to make sausage. Sausage seasonings are also used to season meat loaves and other meat dishes. Basically, sage, allspice and pepper.

SAUSAGE TREE: An African tree that produces 24-inch long fruits that have no particular use.

SAUTÉ: (saw-tay) To cook food in an open shallow pan with butter over low to medium-low heat. Some chefs use margarine and other fats and call it sautéd, but only butter makes it a true sautéd food. Clarified butter is best because it doesn't have the solids that burn easily, and the food is less likely to stick with clarified butter.

SAUTERNES: (so-tern) A sweet, golden colored wine, high in alcohol, from France, and generally served chilled with dessert.

SAVARIN: A yeast-risen dessert cake made with little or no sugar, rich in eggs and butter, a variation of the baba cake, with or without raisins and filled with Chantilly cream. Named to honor the famous writer, Brillat-Savarin, some time before 1860. Created by the Julien brothers, Parisian pastry cooks.

SAVOURY: A nonsweet after dinner treat, such as a slice of cheese, to cleanse the taste buds of a sweet dessert prior to enjoying a glass of after-dinner wine.

SAVORY (herb): There's both a summer and winter savory and they all belong to the mint family, and both have about the same mild flavor. The aromatic leaves are used for seasoning, especially in beans as it is often called the "bean herb." Summer savory is also added to vegetable juices, meats, soups and sauces. Savory leaves are available dried, either minced or ground in most supermarkets. The perennial winter savory is mostly used to flavor goat and ewe's milk cheese in Provence, France.

SCALD: To heat a liquid to almost boiling, such as "scalding" milk. "Scalding"also means to heat water to pour over utensils and food to kill organisms.

SCALLION: A skinny member of the onion family, often called green onions. Green onions are those picked before the bulb has time to grow large and round, in other words, simply new or young onions. The tender part of the green stems can be eaten as well as the white onion part. The word "scallion" is regional, used mostly in the Northeast. Scallions are used the same as any onion but have milder flavor. Scallions are low in calories, less than 25 calories per half cup. **Nutrition facts** ½ cup: 16 calories, zero fats and sodium, 3.7g carbohydrates (1%), 1.3g fiber (5%), .9g protein (2%), 192 IU vitamin A (4%), 9mg vitamin C (16%), 36mg calcium (4%) and .8mg iron (4%).

SCALLOP: A baking dish shaped like a scallop shell that contains a casserole type recipe with some type of a sauce, often topped with crumbs

SCALLOPS: A mollusk found in Atlantic waters from the United States to Europe. There are two varieties found in seafood markets, the small bay scallops, and the large deep- sea variety. In the United States only the muscle is eaten. In Europe, the whole scallop is eaten, including the orange roe. Bay scallops are sweeter and more tender then the deep-sea scallop. Scallops are available fresh and frozen. Scallops can be sautéd, breaded and fried, broiled, and baked. **Nutrition facts** 3 ounces: 75 calories, 7 calories from fat, .7g total fat (1%), zero saturated fat, 28.1mg cholesterol (10%),

136.8mg sodium (6%), zero carbohydrates and fiber, 14.3g protein (29%), 43 IU vitamin A (1%), 3mg vitamin C (5%), 21mg calcium (2%) and .3mg iron (2%).

SCALLOPINE: An Italian word for thin slices of meat, usually veal, flattened, and cooked in a seasoned sauce.

SCANDANAVIAN FOODS:

NORSK HOSTFEST

North America's Largest Scandinavian Festival is held in mid-October. The Festival promotes family traditions that hold families together. Food is highlighted as famous chefs, mainly from Scandinavia, prepare native dishes from Norway, Denmark, Sweden, Finland, and Iceland. Some of the food served at past festivals included: fish soup, fish cakes, liver paté with pickled beets, almond tortes, smoked trout, and venison with juniper sauce. Local cooks also get into the act with all kinds of pastries, open face sandwiches and Scandinavian beverages. Events include "The Strongest Men" contest, where in the past one man pulled seven semi-tractors at once. There are also other pull contests, arm wrestling, power lifting, and more. Entertainment is provided for all ages, music from country to classical, with dances nightly. For more information, write: **Minot Visitors Bureau**, P.O. Box 2066, Minot, ND 58702; or **Norsk Hostfest Association**, P.O. Box 1347, Minot, ND 58702, or phone (701) 852-2368.

SCHNITZEL: A floured veal cutlet that has been browned in a combination of vegetable oil and lard, then cooked in a sauce with various other ingredients until tender. The Austrian wiener schnitzel differs where it is breaded and deep fat fried similar to the Texas chicken fried steak. Cordon bleu is made with veal, ham and Swiss cheese, folded, breaded and deep fat fried. Other schnitzels could include salted or smoked fish, various kinds of cheese, vegetables, and topped with a variety of sauces, such as a paprika or curry sauce.

SCONE: The Scottish forerunner of the American biscuit is a sweet biscuit tea cake from Scotland that can be cooked on a griddle or baked in the oven. Scones are generally one large, flat round, cut in pie shape wedges.

SCORE: To slash less tender cuts of meat with a knife prior to cooking. By cutting the long fibers in a flank steak, an example, it helps to tenderizes it.

SCRAMBLE: (verb) To mix foods, the way eggs are beaten prior to cooking, with seasonings and other ingredients added. (noun) It is also the name given to foods cooked while mixing, such as scrambled eggs or sausage scramble.

SCRAPPLE: Cornmeal mush combined with pork and pork by-products, molded in a bread pan, refrigerated overnight, and in the morning sliced and fried in shortening until crisp. Scrapple is the invention of thrifty Pennsylvania Dutch who wasted nothing.

SCREW PINE: A palm-like tree from Madagascar that produces clusters of round, yellow fruit edible after cooking.

SCROD: A term used to describe a small young cod or haddock from the northern Atlantic and Pacific oceans.

SCULPIN: A small fish found in both salt and fresh waters of the northern hemisphere. Because of the many bones, it is not fished commercially except for one species found in California waters, are generally sold whole and are best baked.

SCURVY: A deadly disease due to the lack of vitamin C in the body. Scurvy was common among early sailors aboard ship when their fresh food supplies ran out on long voyages. In 1747. British Naval surgeon James Lind, 31, conducted experiments with 12 scurvy victims on board the HMS *Salisbury*. His tests proved that patients given two oranges and a lemon each day recovered in no time. His findings were largely ignored by the Royal Navy but in 1774 Captain James Cook returned to England from the Pacific with all but one of his crew alive and well thanks to sauerkraut. He was awarded a medal for curing scurvy. They had also had citrus juices on board but they were not fresh and did not work. It wasn't until 1795 that the Royal Navy ordered lime juice rations for all sailors after the fifth week at sea, following another confirmation of Lind's theory the year before, the same year of Lind's death. It took the navy 48 years to accept Lind's simple cure for scurvy.

SCURVY GRASS: Because of a lack of vitamin C, many early day sailors developed deadly scurvy on long voyages. Captain James Cook (1728-1779) carried a supply of scurvy grass on his three voyages to the South Pacific. Scurvy grass is an excellent source of vitamin C. Native to northern Europe, the young leaves and steams can be eaten raw, in a salad, or cooked. The taste compares with its relatives - watercress, sea kale, and horseradish. All are in the mustard family. See SCURVY.

SEAFOOD: A term that applies to any fish or shellfish, but more often used when referring to shellfish.

SEAFOOD IS BRAIN FOOD

It's well known that full-flavored fish, such as salmon, contains high levels of omega-3 fatty acids, which reduce the risk of heart disease and cancer later in life. Recent studies show that one of these omega-3s, linolenic acid, can also work wonders on our gray matter by helping our bodies to make docosahexaenoic acid (DHA), the brain's primary structured fatty acid. Scientists once though that DHA was only crucial to brain development before birth and during infancy, but now reports have linked a deficiency of DHA to depression, dyslexia, and attention-deficit disorder (ADF) in kids, as well as adults. Of course, DHA is just one nutritional bonus that comes from eating fish, which is also rich in high quality protein, calcium, zinc, and vitamins B and D. Need more reasons to put some fish on your plate? Consider this: even the richest fish contains only fifteen percent fat. You can lower total fat and saturated fat in your diet significantly with a weekly serving of salmon, halibut, or cod. To reduce fat when cooking, consider poaching your fish just until it is flaky. Then enjoy it hot or chilled, maybe added to a salad. Second best methods are to broil or barbecue until cooked crispy on each side.

GLOUCESTER WATERFRONT FESTIVAL

Ever been to a lobster bake? If not, place an August visit to Cape Ann in Gloucester, Massachusetts. The two-day event features seafood, shows, arts, crafts and a pancake breakfast. Sunday, from noon to 5 PM, is the big lobster bake. Just to watch the lobsters baking is a thrill, but just wait till you take your first bite. The Cape Ann area has other seafood festivals. In June, it's the New Fish Festival, a buffet dinner presenting new ways to cook seafood. In September are three festivals. The **Gloucester Seafood Festival** and **The Gloucester Schooner Festival** boast schooner races, deck tours, marine activities, and a fish fry. **Essex Clamfest** has a chowder contest and more seafood.. For information, contract: **Cape Ann Chamber of Commerce**, 33 Commercial Street, Gloucester, MA 01930 or phone (978) 283-1601. *--Tracy Arabian*

SEAGRAPES: From South Florida come these white to purple fruits used to make jelly.

SEAR: A cooking term for browning meat over high heat to seal in the juices. After searing, the food is cooked at a lower temperature.

SEASONING: Any ingredient that is added to food to improve the taste, such as salt, pepper, herbs, and spices.

SEAWEED: Also known as sea vegetables, they are rich in minerals, low in fat and calories. They bring a salty flavor when combined with other foods. Available fresh in some markets, but generally found dehydrated. Soaking rehydrates them. Some of the most common are:
Arame, a very mild-flavored sea vegetable rich in calcium, iodine, and potassium. This is a good choice for those new to eating seaweed. Rinse through, soak for 10 minutes prior to cooking, and simmer for 20 minutes. Great when simmered with lemon juice, rice wine and sprinkled with toasted sesame seeds. Arame can be served as a side dish with fish or added to stir-fry dishes. **Nutrition facts ½ cup arame:** 31 calories, zero fats and sodium, 8g carbohydrates (3%), .6g fiber (2%), .6g protein (1%), zero vitamins A and C, 64mg calcium (6%) and 2.2mg iron (12%).
Wakame, a mild and tender sea vegetable that is often added to soup. After rehydrated, it makes a refreshing salad with orange slices or combined with marinated vegetables. Try it in split pea soup and other bean dishes. **Nutrition facts ½ cup wakame:** 53 calories, 6 calories from fat (1%), .8gr total fat (1%), saturated fat (1%), zero cholesterol, 1031.5mg sodium (43%), 10.g carbohydrates (4%), 6g fibre (3%), 3.6g protein (7%), 426 IU vitamin A (9%), 4mg vitamin C (6%), 177mg calcium (18%), and 2,6mg iron (14%). **Hijiki**, is full-flavored. Soak for 10 minutes, then simmer for up to 45 minutes. Hijiki is served as a side dish with vinegar or lemon juice, and can also be added to a clear soup. **Kombu** contains glutamic acid, a natural flavor enhancer, an alternative to MSG. Kombu is often simmered (without prior soaking) with beans and grains to enhance the flavor, and can be added to vegetable stews. www.luauking.com.

SEEDS: The part of a plant capable of becoming another such plant is called the seed. Many seeds are eaten. Beans, peanuts, nuts, and coffee beans are all seeds. Herbs and flowers produce edible seeds like caraway and poppy. From grain seeds we get wheat, barley, rice, and oats.

SEDER: Passover is a Jewish festival commemorating the exodus of the Israelites from Egypt and their safe flight across the Red Sea. The festival name is *pesah*, meaning "protection." The Jews marked their dwellings with lambs's blood so that God could identify and thus pass over or protect them. The week-long festival is celebrated about the same time as the vernal equinox and usually the same time as Easter. On the first day **the Seder meal** is prepared. These foods symbolize the ordeal undergone by the Hebrew enslavement in Egypt.

The Seder Plate

Zeroah: A roasted shank bone, symbolizes the lamb sacrificed on Passover eve. **Betzah**: A roasted egg, signifies eternal life. **Haroset**: A mixture of chopped nuts and apples in wine, inspired by the mortar used to build Pharaoh's cities. **Matzoth**: Jews must abstain from eating leavened bread during Passover. They substitute, usually in the form of a cracker or flat bread. The unleavened bread is eaten because there was no time during their flight to prepare raised bread. **Karpas**: A vegetable dipped in salt water commemorates spring. **Horseradish**: A reminder of the bitterness of life in slavery. Orthodox Jewish tradition prescribes that Passover meals must be prepared and served using sets of utensils and dishes reserved only for that festival.

SELTZER: A bubbling water containing carbon dioxide, either naturally or artificial.

SEMOLINA: It's the fine particles remaining in the bolting machine after the wheat is ground into flour. Semolina is used for making pasta, and as a thickening agent for puddings. Easily digestible it makes a flaky baby cereal.

SESAME SEEDS: The sesame plant, an herb, grows as high as a kitchen chair. It produces white or black seeds with a nutty flavor. When the seeds are mixed with grains and beans, they help to increase the protein content. Sesame seeds are best roasted in a 325°F oven for about five minutes to bring out the full flavor. That's why they can be toasted on top of baked rolls and breads to enhance the flavor of both seed and bread. Sesame seeds can be added to stir-fry dishes, cooked greens, noodle salads, and tossed on rice dishes. When the sesame seeds are pressed, they produce a salad-type oil. Sesame seed paste is a spread called *tahiti*. *Halvah* is a sugar and almond treat made of ground sesame seed base. Sesame oil is plentiful used in Chinese, Japanese, and Arab cooking.

SESBANIA: From tropical Asia, the tree produces large flowers and bean pods. In a strange twist, the large flowers are edible, but the beans are not.

SET: (adjective) When a liquid, such as gelatin, becomes firm, it has "set" or "set up." (verb) During food preparation, one phase might be "set aside" while the next phase is prepared. For example, chopped nuts might be set aside while we mix the cake batter.

SEVILLE ORANGE: Originally from Southeast Asia, this tree is cultivated widely in Spain and California and used in the making of marmalade. Known as "sour orange." See ORANGES.

SHAD: Related to the herring, shad are larger than herring, with American shad weighing ten pounds or more. Shad are found naturally in the coastal waters of the north Atlantic and the Mediterranean. They were transplanted to our Pacific coast in the late 1870s. Shad flesh is tender; so it is better to leave the skin on when cooking. Shad is very bony, so it takes an expert to remove the bones. Shad, like salmon, swim up rivers to spawn, and this is generally when they are fished commercially. Shad is available fresh during the winter to mid spring. Buy canned shad the year round. Shad can be sautéd, baked, broiled, and planked. **Nutrition facts** 3 ounces: 167 calories, 108 calories from fat, 11.7g total fat (18%), 3.8g saturated fat (19%), 63.8mg cholesterol (22%), 43.4mg sodium (2%), zero carbohydrates and fiber, 14.4g protein (29%), 94 IU vitamin A (2%), zero vitamin C, 40mg calcium (4%) and .8mg iron (5%).

SHADDOCK: Also known as pummelo, it is native to the East Indies. Believed to be the Chinese ancestor of grapefruit, the shaddock can grow up to the size of a watermelon! It has a thick and aromatic rind, but bitter flesh. Still popular in China, but not grown commercially in the United States. The peel can be candied.

SHAKER COOKING: Many books exist on the Shakers. The Shakers are a religious community that flourished in the 1800s, now open as living museums. See TABLE MANNERS and PIES.

SHALLOT: A member of the onion family, very popular for its mild flavor, it is primarily used in cooking meat and vegetables, especially French recipes. Eaten raw in salads. Shallots are available fresh during the spring and dried during the fall and winter months. Fresh shallots are perishable and must be refrigerated. Dried shallots can be stored in a dry, cool place for up to six months. **Nutrition facts** ½ cup: 58 calories, zero fats and sodium, 13.5g carbohydrates (4%), zero fiber, 2g protein (4%), 9987 IU vitamin A (200%), 6mg vitamin C (11%), 30mg calcium (3%) 1mg iron..

SHARK: Yes, Jaws is good food. The meat is flavorful, boneless, and nutritious. Fresh shark meat should have a slightly fresh metallic smell. If there is an ammonia smell, discard it, because sharks carry urea in their tissues and blood. If not properly chilled after caught, this ammonia can build up. Shark is available fresh in seafood markets the year round. In Asia, white shark fins and tails are desired and are sold for around $100 a pound. **Nutrition facts** 3 ounces: 110 calories, 36 calories from fat. 3.8g total fat (6%), .8g saturated fat (4%), 43.4mg cholesterol (15%), 6.7mg sodium (3%), zero carbohydrates and fiber, 17.6g protein (35%), 198 IU vitamin A (4%), zero vitamin C, 29mg calcium (3%) and .7mg iron (4%).

SHEA BUTTER: An oil obtained from the kernel of the African tree *butyrospermum parkii*. It is used as cooking fat. Recently it has also found a place in many cosmetics as a skin softener.

SHEEP: If the sheep is less than a year old, the flesh is sold as lamb. Older sheep are sold as mutton.

WORLD SHEEP AND FIBER ARTS FESTIVAL

This September festival in Bethel, Missouri includes: Sheep Knowledge Contest; Sheep Dog Demonstrations; Sheep Shearing Contests; Exotic and Colored Sheep Sale; Angora Goat Show; Spinning Relay Competition; Fiber Arts Competition; Fiber to Shawl Competition; Angora Rabbit Wool Competition; Alpaca Show.

This is not just a festival for adults. Many youth activities include: National Youth Sheep Knowledge Contest; Junior Lamb Show; Wool Judging Contest; Wool and Mohair Rainbow Dying; Sheep Fitting and Showing Demonstration; Sheep Spelling Bee; and Youth Art Show. In the **Learning Center** you will learn how to spin wool and cotton, how to cook with lamb, and how to make goat cheese. Within the **Sheep Festival** is also the **National Wildflower and Herb Festival.** For information write: **World Sheep Festival**, Route 1, Box 206, Shelbyville, MO 63469.

SHEEPSHEAD: Related to the porgy, this fish is found along the Atlantic coast and the Gulf of Mexico. There is also a freshwater sheepshead, but the two are not related. Sheepshead are generally only available fresh along the Atlantic coast the year round. Sheepshead are usually pan fried. The freshwater varieties are best in chowders and fish stews. **Nutrition facts** 3 ounces: 92 calories, 20 calories from fat, 2.1g total fat (3%), .5g saturated fat (3%), 42.5mg cholesterol (14%), 60.4mg sodium (3%), zero carbohydrates and fiber, 17.2g protein (35%), 85 IU vitamin A (3%), zero vitamin C, 18mg calcium (2%) and .4mg iron (2%).

SHEKWASHA: From Taiwan, this small fruit is better know as mandarins. They are eaten fresh.

SHELLFISH: A marine animal without interior bones, but covered with a shell, either a thick shell or a thin shell. There are two classifications: **Mollusks** have hard shells, with the body within one or two shells. Mollusks include abalone, clams, oysters, etc. **Crustaceans** have softer shells and segmented (sectioned) bodies: crabs, shrimps, lobsters, and their like.

SHELLOUTS: See CRANBERRY BEANS

SHEPHERD'S PURSE: A common Eurasian weed having small white flowers and flat heart-shaped fruit. Shepherd's purse is also known as "mother's-heart," and a member of the mustard family. The peppery young leaves are eaten like spinach, and used to season stews. The seeds can substitute for mustard seed. The name comes from its pouch-like pods which resemble the purses carried by shepherds.

SHERBET: A frozen dessert containing fruit juice and fruit puree, sweetener, water and/or milk, and sometimes a soft thickening agent such as egg whites or gelatin. Resembles ice cream but more fruity.

SHERRY: Originally a wine from southern Spain, now made in California and New York too. Sherry is colored amber to brown, and can be either dry or sweet. After the grapes are pressed, they are allowed to ferment, then blended with brandy. Sherry is used for cooking in sauces and as a dessert wine. Cooking sherry is not a drinking sherry since it contains salt.

SHIP'S BISCUITS: See HARDTACK.

SHIRR: A method of baking seasoned eggs in a light cream.

SHISH KEBAB: Meat, vegetables and/or fruits placed on a skewer, usually after marinating and cooked under a broiler or barbecued. Early warriors in southern Russia started the trend by threading chunks of meat on their swords and cooking the meat over open fires.

SHIITAKE MUSHROOMS: These mushrooms are characterized by broad, umbrella shaped caps, wide open veils and tan gills that radiate on the underside of the cap. Shiitakes range from tan to dark brown in color, have a rich and woodsy flavor, a meaty texture and are best sautéd or grilled. Can be added to stir-fries, pastas, soups, or as a main course in place of meat. In Japan they are also known as *donko* and *koshin* mushrooms, which has more to do with the look and shape. A *hana-donko* shiitake develops cracks on the cap due to temperature changes, creating a pretty pattern, known as a "flower." The larger *hana-donko* mushrooms are preferred, hence are also the most expensive. A *ju-donko* shiitake does not have this pattern. *Koshin* shiitakes have a slightly different configuration from *donko*. They are larger, thicker, more opened and quite impressive and are called *dai ju atsu*, meaning large, thick and tall. Shiitake mushrooms will keep for a long time, if kept in a cool, dry dark place and well sealed. Smaller shiitakes can be used as is. However, for the larger ones, it is recommended to soak overnight in cold water.

SHORT: A very flaky pastry that contains a lot of shortening or butter.

SHORTBREAD: A tender cookie that contains a large amount of butter or shortening.

SHORTCAKE: A flat, biscuit-like dough made slightly sweeter and more cake-like, to be eaten with fruit or berries and topped with ice cream and/or whipped cream. Some people actually use their own favorite biscuit recipe unsweetened. The name is also used to apply to the entire dessert, cake, berries, topping and all, as in strawberry shortcake.

SHORTENING: Any cooking fat, oil, butter, lard, or margarine.

SHORT-LEAF FIG: Native to south Florida, the 3/4-inch purple wild fruits are eaten raw.

SHOULDER: A cut of meat from the front section of an animal, usually called chuck. It is a less tender cut as compared to the hind section, or the rump.

SHRED: Instead of cutting food, such as meat, into small pieces, it is torn apart in strips. This works well for hot sandwiches. Bake a London Broil or lean roast, then shred the meat. Add barbecue sauce or ketchup and serve on buns.

SHRIMP: This crustacean is found in ocean waters world wide and is known by several names. Jumbo shrimp are often sold as prawns; however, while prawns are in the same family as shrimp, they are not shrimp. Some medium size shrimp are called scampi. True scampi are not shrimp, but langostinos. Colored from brownish red to a grey, all turn pink when cooked. Shrimp can be cooked by almost any method, frying or boiling the most popular. Larger shrimp can be skewered and broiled or barbecued. Shrimp are available fresh near the oceans. Frozen or canned you can have them the year round. To shell shrimp, hold the tail by one hand and remove most of the shell by the other hand. Then pull the shrimp out of the tail. Large shrimp need to be deveined. That means cutting along the curved outside to remove the black vein. It's generally not necessary to devein small shrimp. Shrimp can be served hot or chilled. **Nutrition facts** 4 ounce serving: 112 calories, 12 calories from fat, 1.3g total fat (2%), .4g saturated fat (2%), 221.1mg cholesterol (74%), 254mg sodium (11%), zero carbohydrates and fiber, 23.7g protein (47%), 248 IU vitamin A (5%), 2mg vitamin C (4%), 44mg calcium (4%), 3.5mg iron (19%), and 206mg potassium. www.alaskaseafood.org

DANGER! SHRIMP AHEAD!
A True Story by Marie Prato

My mother was always very territorial when it came to cooking food for the family. She was, however, more than willing to share the washing of the dishes and pots afterwards. I was a young teen and visiting in South Carolina, before I finally got a chance to prepare a meal. I was thrilled with the prospect of planning and cooking dinner.

This was to be no ordinary meal! While everyone else went out for the day, I hurried to the food store. I could hardly contain my excitement as I put shrimp, fresh spinach, rice, and ice cream into my cart. Back at the house, I put the spinach in a strainer and cleaned the leaves. Then I cut gloves of garlic into small pieces, took out the bread crumbs, beat an egg and began to shell the shrimp.

After all the shells were removed, I went to the cabinet to take out the pots and pans I would need. That's when I noticed the funny feeling in my hands - they itched and felt numb at the same time. Trying to move my fingers, they took on a claw-like shape. Then my eyes began to burn. I stumbled to the bathroom and washed my hands and threw water in my face. Looking through watery eyes into the mirror, I could see what looked like blisters on my eyeballs! Panicking, I ran to the next door neighbor. One look at my eyes and she took me by the arm and led me to her car. At the hospital, after being given shots and medicine, I was told I had an allergy to shellfish! Yet, I had eaten shrimp from as far back as I could remember with never a problem.

Millions of people like me suffer from shellfish allergies. Shrimp, lobster and crabs are the most common culprits. The first reaction is often relatively mild, but if the person persists in eating

459

shellfish, reactions worsen, effect breathing, and could be fatal. Even with the doctor's warning, being a Doubting Thomas, I tried to eat different types of shellfish. I'm allergic to shrimp, I reasoned, but that doesn't mean lobster will bother me.

After feasting on a lobster I looked down at my hands. No problems there. Just as I was about to congratulate myself, I noticed the strange feeling in my mouth. Going into the bathroom, I opened wide and peered into the mirror. Black blood blisters had formed inside my mouth and on my tongue! My face swelled up and my eyes closed. I looked like the loser of a bar fight for the next two days. Now, the only place I want to see shellfish is in an aquarium with a nice thick piece of glass between us. If you have any reaction to shellfish, rush to get medical help.

THE ANNUAL NATIONAL SHRIMP FESTIVAL

To honor the succulent shrimp, Gulf Shores, Alabama has an annual shrimp festival. It is held on a white sand beach every October. The festival features shrimp cooked in about every style you can think of: blackened (highly spiced), fried, boil, *etouffé* (a Cajun rice dish), gumbo (a seafood stew), and shrimp po-boy sandwiches. Fish and other seafoods are also prepared in a number of ways like the shrimp, plus there's alligator, hot dogs, onion blossoms, curly fries, funnel cakes and more. Along with the food there's entertainers providing a variety of music for all ages and musical interests, an arts and crafts fair, and a sandcastle contest. For more information write: **Alabama Gulf Coast Visitors Bureau,** P.O. Drawer 457, Gulf Shores, AL 36547 or phone (800) 982-8562 or (334) 974-1510. *--Bebe Gauntt*

ISLE OF EIGHT FLAGS SHRIMP FESTIVAL

The Shrimp Festival is held in early May on Florida's Amelia Island, which has been ruled under eight flags (French, Spanish, English, Patriots, Green Cross of Florida, Mexican Rebel, United States and Confederate). The festival begins with a pirate parade, followed by the invasion of pirates, shrimp boat tours, and the blessing of the fleet. More than 35 food booths, feature shrimp and other seafood delicacies. Along with the pirate theme, there are pirate costume contests for both kids (ages 4 to 15) and adults, along with a beard contest. For information write to: **Isle of Eight Flags Shrimp Festival**, P.O. Box 6146, Fernandian Beach, FL 32035- 6146, phone (800) 2-AMELIA, (904) 261-3248, or see their website at www.shrimpfestival.com.

SHRUB: A beverage, either alcoholic or nonalcoholic, made from fruit juice and sugar, and aged in a crock for several days, then strained, served over ice, and sometimes with carbonated water. Shrub is an old term from the Colonial days, sometimes also called **bounces** or **flips**. Today it would be a called fruit punch.

SHUCK: To remove the husk or shell, the outer covering of corn, nuts, shellfish, etc.

SIDE: A cut of meat from the sides of an animal, such as bacon, also referred to as side meat.

SIFT: A placing of dry ingredients, such as flour, powdered sugar, and baking powder. through a fine screen to add air and to remove large particles.

SILVER SALMON: See SALMON

SIMMER: A method of cooking food and liquid just under the boiling point.

SINGE: A method to remove hair and pin feathers from animal and poultry skin by holding the plucked bird over a flame.

SKATE: Yes, it's a fish, not a rollerblade. A member of the ray family, this flat-bodied fish has wing-like fins. Skates are found in both the Pacific and Atlantic oceans. Skates are known to grow up to 100 pounds. The body is bony; it's the flesh in the fins that is eaten. Skate is available during the fall and winter months at some seafood markets. The fins must be skinned and can be sautéd or poached. It is important to first soak the fins in salted water for three hours prior to cooking. Skate flesh has its own distinctive flavor.

SKEWER: A metal or wooden rod used to thread meat, vegetables and/or fruit for cooking over direct heat, such as a shish kebab roasting on a grill.

SKILLET: A flat-bottomed, long handled pan for frying food.

SKIM: To remove the top layer of a liquid, such as the cream off the top of milk. The fat should be skimmed off the top of a meat stock. Removing the froth while cooking jam is also skimming.

SKIN: It's the outer layer of an animal, poultry or fish. Also refers to the peel of potatoes, apples and other vegetables and fruits. "To skin" means to remove the skin.

SLAW: A term for finely shredded or sliced vegetables, such as cabbage and other greens to make into a salad. Also "slaw" is short for "coleslaw".

SLICE: (verb) "To slice" is to cut food thin, such as a slice of bread, or lunch meat is sliced. (noun) A slice is a thin portion of food.

SLIVER: A small, thin slice of food, such as almond slivers.

SLOE: In the United States, it's the small fruit of a native plum, red to yellow in color, used to make jelly and jam. In Great Britain and France, it's the fruit of the blackthorn and is used to make a liquor, sloe gin. During the Depression it was also used to make gin in this country. The name comes from an Old English term for plum, *slah*.

SLOW COOKER: Another name for an electric crock pot.

SLOW FOOD: The term given to food which is made the time honored way without hurry, given in reaction to "fast" food.

SLOW FOOD MOVEMENT

When it comes to food, some people are not in a hurry. An Italian organization led by food writer **Carlo Petrini**, began as a protest to the opening of a McDonald's fast-food restaurant in Rome in 1985. Now grown worldwide, "slow food" numbers 100,000 chefs, food writers, winemakers, and hungry public members.

The group treasurers the old recipes, such as cave-ripened cheeses, mountain-cured hams. They intend to give a voice to down home cooking styles and small-time food producers. It celebrates products that rely on time to create, to ripen, to ferment, to develop slowly. It celebrates calories! Members promote sausages, foie gras, triple-cream cheeses, and real ice cream. Some great foods can only be made at home. Maybe it takes a wood burning, smoky stove to make a wonderful tasting pizza. Sometimes 40 egg yolks are needed to make a perfect pasta. There are people willing to wait a whole season for just the right moment to pick the perfect fruit.

The Slow Food Movement began in Europe where dining slowly is a pleasure. Fast food is an American thing. Conventions held in both Europe and the United States have tasting workshops, food seminars, and dinners with as many as ten different meats. Between the conventions, members meet with pot-luck dinners, picnics, barbecues, vegetarian feasts, and costume party buffets. Trips are offered to farmers' markets, oyster farms, food bookstores. There are cooking classes, lectures, and workshops for kids.

As part of their manifesto: *We are enslaved by speed and have succumbed to the same insidious virus: Fast Life, which disrupts our habits, pervades the privacy of our homes and forces us to eat Fast Food.*

Our defense should begin at the table with Slow Food. Let us rediscover the flavors and savors of regional cooking and banish the degrading effects of Fast Food. For information on upcoming conventions, activities, publications, slow food products and membership write: **The Slow Food International Office,** Via della Mendicita Istruita 14 12042 Bra (CN) Italy. Or you can contact them by email: international@slowfood.it, or by the internet: www.slowfood.com, or telephone toll free 1-877-756-9366.

SLOW FOOD FAIR
"Noah's Ark for Taste"

"Taste is the highest expression of the identity of a people," says Carlo Petrini, who presided over an assembly of international food experts at the Slow Food Fair in 1998 at Turin, Italy. A vast assembly hall held samples of the world's best food creations, representing about 50 counties and every region of Italy. *The Salon de Gusto* which means **The Hall of Taste**, honored slow, sensuous cooking: breads, cheeses, cured meats, oils, wines and confections. Nearly all items on display were handcrafted treasures of their respective regions, in keeping with the Slow Food mission of safeguarding traditional food heritage.

At the biennial event, guests sampled horse meat, goat, Buffalo's Milk Mozzarella, 100 year old Chinese eggs, and even a pasta sauce made of salted plums. Croatia and Israel sent goose liver; Australia served kangaroo ragout, just for two interesting examples. Italy out did everyone with tons of salamis, cheeses, aged vinegars, candied chestnuts, gelatin, olives and who knows what else. The Americans displayed beer and wines to go with the 2,500 wines represented from 24 countries. Beneath the fun lay a deep purpose. "The core idea," said Chef Petrini, "is getting back respect for the taste in food" - and away from uniform fast foods. "The organization is trying to be a Noah's Ark for taste," said Giovanni Garomno, Turin maker of fruit preserves. "Over the centuries, little by little, we have lost some flavors and now we are trying to preserve them." He showed an example of pears that had once been grown all over Italy and now grow only in one place.

"Slow Food is about the idea that things should not taste the same the world over," said the editor of *Slow Magazine*. Americans at the Slow Food affair agreed. Spokesman for the American members of Slow Food said American local cooking styles such as Tex-Mex and Cajun need to be preserved. Plans were underway **to create such curriculum for U.S. cooking schools.** For information on **Slow Food in the U.S.** call (877) 756- 9366 or go to www.slowfood.com.

SLUGBURGERS: See Hamburgers

SMELT: The flesh is rich with oil, in fact, so much oil, that our Native Americans would dry them, then use them as candles for light! They called them "candle fish." Smelt can be fried or broiled. Smelts are available fresh from fall to spring, frozen and canned the year round. Found in both the Pacific and Atlantic oceans. Like salmon, smelt swim up rivers to spawn. **Nutrition facts** 3 ounces: 183 calories, 20 calories from fat, 2.1g total fat (3%), .4g saturated fat (2%), 60.1mg cholesterol (20%), 51.1mg sodium (2%), zero carbohydrates and fiber, 15g protein (30%), 43 IU vitamin A (1%), zero vitamin C, 51g calcium (5%) and .8mg iron (5%).

SMETANA: A Russian word for sour cream, also refers to food cooked in sour cream.

SMOKE: A way to preserve meat, poultry and fish by dry smoke heat. Today many smoked foods are not smoked at all, but an artificial smoke ingredient is added to give food a smoky flavor.

SMÖRGÅSBORD: A Swedish buffet, but originally it referred to a sandwich. *Smör* means butter, *gås* means goose, and *bord* means table. However, when combining *smör* and *gås*, it means bread and butter or an open face sandwich. The Americanized term, is a long table filled with food, starting with soup and ending with dessert. Not all smorgasbords (in the United States the word is used without the accents) use Swedish recipes.

SNACKS: A light, between meal food to temporarily satisfy the appetite.

SNAILS: They are quite popular in parts of Europe, not so much in the United States. Snails have very little taste. It's the garlic butter that makes them a delight. The easiest way to prepare them is to stuff some garlic butter into the previously boiled shells, then baked them in a hot oven for a few minutes. Serve hot. Remove the meat with a small fork, and dip into some more garlic butter. **Nutrition facts** 3 ounces: 68 calories, 14 calories from fat, 1.7g total fat (3%), zero saturated fat and cholesterol, zero sodium, zero carbohydrates and fiber, 14.2g protein (27%), zero vitamins A and C, zero calcium and 3.4mg iron (19%). For snail farming see www.Frescargot.com .

SNAP BEANS: They are native to the New World, now grown world wide. Better known in supermarkets as string beans or green beans. Snaps are available year round. There's a yellow variety called wax beans. Fresh snap beans are best boiled or steamed in a small amount of water from 15 to 30 minutes or until tender crisp. Snap beans are also available canned and frozen. **Nutrition facts** cup: 17 calories, zero fats and sodium, 3.9g carbohydrates (1%), 1.9g fiber (7%), 1g protein (2%), 367 IU vitamin A (7%), 9mg vitamin C (15%), 20mg calcium (2%) and .6mg iron (3%).

SNIPE: See WOODCOCK

SNOWBALL: Made commercially, it is a round cake, iced with marshmallow and topped with coconut. A snowball can also be a scoop of ice cream rolled in coconut or a round cookie.

SNOW CRABS: They are harvested from the clear, cold waters of Alaska's Bering Sea. Snow crabs have a sweet, delicate flavor, snow-white meat and tender texture. Snow crabs make great appetizers with your favorite sauce. They can be added to salads, soups, a main entre, pasta, or stir fry. For a special treat, make a sandwich. Snow crabs come fully cooked. Can be eaten chilled, or heated by steaming, in the oven, or in the microwave.

SNOW PEAS: Peas like to grow in cold weather. Crops are sown in the early spring for an early summer harvest. Snow peas should be harvested while the pods are still flat, before the seeds begin to swell. Add fresh crisp snow peas to salads, sauté them quickly in a little butter, or add them at the last moment to stir-fry recipes. Fresh snow peas are available in supermarkets in the early summer and frozen the year round. **Nutrition facts** 1/2 cup: 32 calories, zero fats, 178.1mg sodium (7%), 5.3g carbohydrates (2%), 2.1g fiber (8%), 2.5g protein (5%), 99 IU vitamin A (2%), 36mg vitamin C (60%), 32mg calcium (3%) and 1.5mg iron (8%).

SOCKEYE SALMON: Also known as red, blueback, and Spring-run. Sockeyes average 3 to 8 pounds, are best when baked, broiled or poached. Sockeye has the highest amount of omega-3 fatty acids of any fish. **Nutrition Facts**: 2.7 grams per 100 gram portion. 98 calories, 28 calories from fat, 3g total fat (5%), .5g saturated fat (3%), 44.2mg cholesterol (15%), 57mg sodium (3%), zero carbohydrates and fiber, 16.9g protein (34%), 100 IU vitamin A (2%), zero vitamin C, 11mg calcium (1%), 1.7mg iron (4%).

SODA: Same as baking soda, a sodium compound used as a baking leavening agent. A fountain "soda" is flavored carbonated water mixed with a scoop of ice cream.

SODA CRACKER: A thin, flaky baked bread, either salted or unsalted, with soda as the leavening agent.

SODA FOUNTAINS

SODA FOUNTAINS OF YESTERYEAR
by Louise Ulmer

On a hot day, what tastes better than a tall chocolate soda, served in a frosted mug, topped with a mountain of whipped cream and a cherry on top? Sadly for all soda lovers, the soda fountain has almost become a thing of the past. As American's cities grew up, the soda fountain took its place inside the drug and variety stores across the nation. With the closing of **Woolworth**'s and other "five and dime stores" in the last decade, the soda fountain has joined the ranks of vanishing Americana. Yes, ice cream sodas are still around but that grand counter where you could climb a tall, spinning bar stool and sip a frothy ice cream masterpiece remains only in a few tourist attractions. And a soda in a paper cup is just not the same thing!

The **inventor of the soda fountain** was an Englishman, John Matthews, who learned as an apprentice how to make carbonic acid gas, better known today as seltzer. At age twenty-two, he set out for American, where he hoped to find people less dedicated to tea drinking.

Natural carbonated waters have been bubbling up out of the earth since time began, and it's only fair to mention some of the other "seltzer" discovers. **Chemist Joseph Priestly**, the same man who discovered oxygen, pioneered carbonated water in 1767. That was before the American Revolutionary War when everyone was too busy to care much. But then life settled down again, and in 1806 carbonated water became available for sale in bottles by a Yale professor, Benjamin Silliman. No one seemed to know what to do with the bubbly waters except to flavor it and dispense it as a cure for obesity. That is where John Matthews came in.

Matthews set himself up in the business of manufacturing his bubbling waters to retail stores in small tanks. To be able to do that, he could thank the use of cast- iron boxes lined with lead where carbonic acid gas was formed by the action of sulphuric acid on chalk or whiting. Matthews didn't have much of either in New York City, but he found something better -- marble.

Matthews could thank heaven that **Saint Patrick's Cathedral** was being built and his firm bought all their leftover marble chips. Those chips supplied nearly 25 million gallons before the church was built and the supply of marble chips ran out. The two most interesting things about Matthews process were the "rocking" and the safety valve. The newly formed gas had to be purified by passing it through water and conducting it into a tank partially filled with cool water. An employee had to rock the tank for up to half an hour to make the tank bubbly.

Pressure is always a problem in gas manufacturing and there were many explosions among Matthews competitors, but Matthews had **a secret safety device.** Pressure had to be kept from rising above 150 pounds. Matthew's safety valve was a man named Ben Austen, an ex-slave. When a batch of soda water needed measuring, the task belonged to Ben, who put his powerful thumb over the pressure cock. When the pressure blew Ben's thumb away from the cock, they estimated the pressure must be 150 pounds and the water fully charged. When the Civil War draft riots broke out, angry Irish mobs roamed the streets, punishing any Negro they could find. To save Ben's life, Matthews had him shipped out of town in a box like a seltzer order.

With convenient seltzer supplies available, a Frenchman in his **Philadelphia perfume store** began adding flavors to his soda water and selling it to customers. Soon Matthews and his competitors all began keeping favored syrups on hand too. Some people even added sweet cream. But the addition appreciated most the world over came in **1874 when Robert M. Green ran out of cream** and in desperation threw in vanilla ice cream. This happened at the Franklin Institute's 50th celebration in Philadelphia. And the public went wild for it! Thus the ice cream soda, and behind the counter in a clean starched white jacket and a white cap, the **"soda jerk"** were born.

Soda fountains soon became a permanent fixture in drug stores everywhere. Small wonder it was in drug stores that Coca-Cola was invented to cure headaches. Soon the local soda fountain became everyone's favorite social spot, especially for kids like you. Early soda fountains had only six glasses which could be washed quickly with no thought to germs, which had not been discovered yet. Later fountains were elegantly decorated with rows of fancy glassware, washed to a shine in hot water, since germs had become a recent major concern.

John Matthews was called **"the Father of American Soda Water"** but he hated the title because there is no soda in his water. He preferred to call it "aerated water." John Matthews' only memorial can be seen in Greenwood Cemetery, Brooklyn, New York, and quite a monument it is too, telling much of the history of his life in its statuary. Many people think a memorial to the man who made ice cream sodas available should have a grander national monument. But we can be reminded of him every time we enjoy an ice cream soda.

If your town no longer has an old fashioned soda fountain, you can see them in scads of old movies or you might travel to one of the restored soda fountains around the country.

SODA POP: A flavored beverage made with carbonated water, also called a "soft drink." It was called "soft" in comparison to "hard" liquor drinks.

SODA WATER: A water made with carbon dioxide that can be added to beverages to give it that special cooling fizz.

SODIUM: A metallic element that oxidizes rapidly in moist air and is found in nature only as a combined element.
- Sodium bicarbonate, also called "baking powder."

- Sodium chloride is salt.
- Sodium nitrate, also known as "saltpeter," is used as a food preservative, especially in meat.
- Sodium alginate is a powdery crystalline compound used as a food thickener and stabilizer.

SOFT DRINK

SOFT DRINKS IN AMERICA

When the pioneers of America's soft drink industry began experimenting with "soda water" in the 1700s, they had no idea what they were starting.

Soda Pop for the Bath Tub

The forerunners of soft drinks began more than 2,000 years ago when a Greek named **Hippocrates,** also known as the "Father of Medicine," first suspected that mineral waters were good for people. Hippocrates didn't envision drinking the effervescent mineral waters bubbling from the earth's crust. Instead, the Greeks and Romans used them for bathing, like a natural Jacuzzi. It took more than a thousand years before these waters became soda pop.

American immigrants discover the natural springs in New York state. Many myths developed about these mysterious waters. Scientists flocked to study the tiny fizzing bubbles. Eventually, in the 1700s the fizz was given its scientific name, carbon dioxide. Soon thereafter a New Yorker found a way to make this water artificially.

Dandelion Cola Anyone?

By the 1830s, both artificial and natural mineral waters were considered healthful and refreshing. Pharmacists, believing they could improve upon water's curative properties, experimented with a multitude of ingredients. Flavors from birch bark to dandelions, resulted in some interesting flavors. Ginger ale, root beer, sarsaparilla, lemon and strawberry were among the most popular of the early flavors.

Cola to Go!

For many years, the local drug store soda fountain was the social hot spot. Gradually a demand grew for soft drinks to be consumed in the home. Bottling the product proved difficult, since the pressure from the carbon dioxide forced corks right out of the bottles. It took years to try out more than 1,500 different corks, caps and lids for soft drink bottles.

In 1892, the "crown cap" was invented. Tiny in design, the crown completely revolutionized the soft drink industry by preventing the escape of carbon dioxide from bottled beverages. Home consumption grew and the corner drugstore fountains began to dwindle. Many pharmacists abandoned their trade to become full-time soft drink bottlers. Ever improving machinery increased the production of soft drinks. By the time "The Great Depression" of the 1930s hit, carbonated beverages were well established as part of the American way of life. Consumers were unwilling to give up soft drinks, the one small pleasure they could still afford to enjoy. The Depression actually created new soft drink brands and containers.

There's an endless search for new varieties to go with the 450 flavors we already have. Some are produced by small companies and are only sold locally. That's why you probably can't name more than five big national brands. See how many you can name. Watch for new colas to try when you are traveling the country. *-National Soft Drink Association*

WHAT IS IN SOFT DRINKS

Soft drinks begin with the creation of a flavored syrup. This syrup is a combination of ingredients along with a sweetener. Many soft drinks use natural flavors from spices, natural extract and oils. Fruit-flavored drinks, such as strawberry, cherry, orange, lemon and lime, often contain natural fruit extracts. Other flavors such as colas, root beer and ginger ale contain flavoring made from nuts, herbs and spices. Other soft drinks are made artificially.

Flavor syrups are then added to water. Regular soft drinks are 90 percent water, while diet drink have 99 percent water. Next carbon dioxide gas is added for bubbles just before the soft drink container is sealed. Even though brand name syrup recipes are a closely guarded company secret, all ingredients are regulated by the U.S. Food and Drug Administration. These ingredients include colors, caffeine, acidulants, preservatives, and sweeteners. **Nutrition facts:** a popular cola has 93 calories in an eight ounce glass, 23.6 grams of carbohydrates (8%), some calcium (1%), and 22.7 milligrams of caffeine. Most other soft drinks, such as root beer have no caffeine. There are no health benefits from soft drinks, only enjoyment. *–RSC*

SOFT DRINK HISTORY AT A GLANCE

1798: The term "soda water" was first introduced as a beverage. Actually, soda drinks have no soda in them and are fizzed with carbon dioxide. Over the years other names were introduced that included: "marble water," "syrup water," and "aerated water" for those who thought soda drinks contained baking soda or sodium. The term "soft drink" was used to separate from "hard" liquor drinks.
1809: First U.S. patent issued for the manufacture of imitation mineral waters.
1815: The first soda fountain is patented.
1835: Bottled soda water first produced in the U.S.
1850: Corking device is first used for bottling soda water.
1851: Ginger ale is introduced in Ireland.

1861: Soft drinks were referred to as "pop."

1874: The first ice cream soda is served.

1876: Root beer is produced in quantity for public sale.

1881: First cola flavored beverage is introduced.

1892: Invention of the crown bottle cap.

1899: First patent for glass blowing machine, used to produce glass bottles.

1913: Motor trucks begin to replace horse drawn carriages as delivery vehicles.

1920: There were by then 5,000 bottlers in the U.S.

Early 1920s: Automated soft drink vending machines begin to dispense sodas in cups.

1923: Introduction of six-pack cartons called "Hom-Paks."

1934: First colored labels used on soda drinks.

1946: First diet soft drink introduced.

1957: First aluminum cans are introduced.

1962: Easy opening pull-ring tabs are first available.

1965: Soft drinks in cans appear in vending machines.

1970: Plastic bottles are first used for soft drinks.

1973: Creation of the polyethylene terephthalte (PET) bottles, which were developed but were not used until 1991 for soft drinks.

1974: The stay-on tab is invented.

1981: Talking vending machines are invented.

Mid 80's: Caffeine-free and low-sodium soft drinks gain in popularity.

Early 90's: Clear colas are manufactured.

Today: About 700 bottling companies produce more than 450 variations of soft drinks.

Activity

How much of this cola history have you witnessed personally? Ask older friends and relatives how much they remember of this history. How many remember their first and favorite soft drinks? How many events would you add to this history in recent years, such as the furor over Coke which resulted in Classic Coke in the 80s?

SOLE: True sole is only found in European waters, with Dover sole the best variety. Various small flat fishes found in United States oceans are sold as sole, but are not true sole. Dover sole is imported from England, but at a high price.

Dover Sole: Fillets average 5-10 ounces, have mild delicate flavor, and are moist and flaky.

Flathead Sole: These thin fillets average 2-6 ounces, have mild flavor, dry and flaky.

Rex Sole: Slender fillets average 3-8 ounces, have sweet flavor, and a fine delicate texture.

Rock Sole: Fillets average 2-7 ounces. Sweet and slightly rich, the texture is firm and succulent.

Yellowfin Sole: The smallest sole at 1-3 ounces; mild, sweet, with a soft and fine flakey texture.

Nutrition facts 3 ounces: 58 calories, zero fats and cholesterol, 47.7mg sodium (2%), zero carbohydrates and fiber, 12.7g protein (25%), zero vitamins A and C, 52mg calcium (5%) and .7mg iron (4%).

SONCOYA: From Mexico, this small tree produces large, brown skinned, sweet and aromatic fruit with orangey pulp which is eaten fresh.

SORBET: A French frozen dessert made with fruit juice, fruit puree, sugar and sometimes egg whites, but never any dairy products unlike sherbet. Sorbets are also served as an appetizer as well as between courses to freshen the palate.

SORGHUM: A cereal grass resembling corn used to make a syrup and molasses.

SORREL: An herb, also called sourgrass and dock, is available in eastern markets almost the year round. It grows wild everywhere. There are many varieties, all are sour in various degrees. The name comes from an old French word meaning sour. The milder variety can be added to salads. Others are cooked like spinach and can replace spinach in most recipes. Safe to eat in small quantities, but large amounts can be poisonous. The sour taste almost guarantees it will not be overeaten. Once the flowers blooms, sorrel leaves are too tough to eat. Sorrel is rich in vitamin C.

SOSUMBER: Used as a vegetable, the ½-inch yellow berries are cooked like eggplant in Southeast Asia and Jamaica.

SOUFFLE: (soo-flay) A dish made with separated, beaten eggs and other ingredients such as cheese, vegetable puree, meat and fish. Souffles can be served as a main course, or sweet as a dessert. The souffle rises during cooking because air is trapped in the egg white and expands the volume. If not served while hot, the air cools and the souffle falls.

SOUL FOOD: A loose term for down-home country cooking, fresh ingredients from the land like free range chickens, grits, boiled wild greens, sweet potato pie, and other Southern type cooking. First applied to the traditional foods of American Black cooks.

SOUL FOOD
by Eric Diesel

Imagine that you are walking the earthy paths of a southern bayou. Spanish moss drapes the willows like a shawl around Grandma's shoulders. The moon spins above the trees in a silver dance. Owls watch through the trees as a dark-skinned woman bustles around a one room cabin lit by kerosene and moonlight. Rich blooming smells guide you through the night air: tomato, onion, pepper, sugar, pork. The woman cooking in the cabin is someone's ancestor, a slave's descendant. One of the ways she cherishes her culture is through her artistry in the kitchen.

Soul Food did not become a recognizable term until the 1920s, but anyone who has eaten fried chicken, cornbread, okra, ham and beans, coconut cake, or any of the dozen of dishes also known as "Southern Cooking" has eaten soul food. The term itself comes from the antebellum South, when slaves preserved their culture through every means at their disposal: song, dance, even food.

Preserving their culture was their method of surviving their circumstances. It was their way of preserving their "soul."

The Caucasians who ran the plantations discovered that they liked the food that the kitchen slaves prepared. To be acceptable to white society, "soul food" was rechristened "Southern cooking." **After the Civil War,** when food was scarce in all areas of the South, "soul" food took on added importance, since it was a method of making meager staples taste good. Think about it: Classic Soul Food dishes are the easiest to prepare. What is simpler fare than a plate of rice and beans? What better use for a slaughtered pig's shoulder blade (its "hock") than to flavor beans? Who better than an individual whose ancestors lived off the land in Africa to know the goodness of turnip, collard, or mustard greens? Slave cooks who worked the sugar cane plantations used the readily available sugar syrups and beat them with cream to produce glossy caramel, a candy which delights babies of all races and ages?

After Reconstruction, the former slaves who moved north began flavoring American culture with African spice. **During the Harlem Renaissance,** which peaked during the 1920s, African culture exerted profound influence on American pop culture. This happened in big cities and tiny hamlets, anywhere there was a population of people with African heritage. Every area with a population of African- Americans has a roadhouse where jazz and dancing counterpoint steaming platters of ribs, smothered chicken, fried pork chops.

Soul food today tells the story of African culture as expressed through transplantation to American. Today's African-Americans are the descendants of people who brought vivid joy and unquenchable spirit to unspeakable circumstance. Soul food is literally history you can eat.

SOUP: Soup is a broad categorical name for any flavored liquid, with or without solid ingredients such as meat, poultry, and vegetables. **Clear soup** can be a broth, also known as bouillon or consommé. **Bisque** is a soup with meat, poultry, seafood and/or vegetables, usually with cream. Italian minestrone and seafood chowders are examples of thick soups. Thin soups are usually served as an appetizer, while the other soups can be a complete meal or the main course. There are chilled and jellied soups that are ideal during the hot summer months. The Scandinavians also offer a chilled fruit soup that can be eaten as a dessert or used as a topping for ice cream and cakes. The Vietnamese make a fruity thin dessert of mung bean base they call "cold, sweet soup."
www.campbellsoup.com; www.progresso.com

SOUP IT UP!

Soup, a good hearty soup, can be made quickly and can be a complete meal. While "quickly" doesn't work for all soups, some of the best soups will take all day, and a crockpot is one of the best ways to make such a soup. Soup making can be an art. It means starting with a base and then adding various ingredients at just the right time.

SOUP BASICS

To make soup you need to have on hand a variety of ingredients:

Chicken and beef stock or broth
Fresh or canned stewed tomatoes
Canned or cooked beans
Rice
Pasta
Herbs
Seasonings
A variety of fresh vegetables
Meat, poultry and fish

Generally soup starts by sautéing meat in a large pot. Once the meat is browned, it is removed to be re-added later. Next, add some cut up seasoning vegetables, such as onions, and celery and sauté them in the meat juices. Cook until the liquid is reduced. Add meat stock or broth, the previously browned meat, and rice, then simmer slowly until meat is tender and the rice is soft. Now add the cut up vegetables in the order of their cooking times. Example, fresh green beans could take up to thirty minutes, while cabbage only takes five minutes. Most cookbooks have vegetable timing cooking charts to help you in timing.

International Favorites

The **French** make a thick soup, by combining a variety of vegetables in a broth and simmering all day. Then they cool it, place it in a blender and set aside. In the evening, another soup is started with broth, and various ingredients. Just before serving, when the vegetables are tender crisp, the cooled blender mixture is added to thicken the soup. As you travel in the many ethnic kitchens, you will find some cultures lean toward specialty soups. The French also savor a mushroom soup **Scandinavians** like cauliflower soup. In **China,** it's wontons. The **Japanese** like a clear soup. In **East Africa** an avocado broth is preferred. **Mexicans** add tortillas to their soup. In **Greece**, it's an egg soup. The **Spanish** like a chilled vegetable soup, as do the people of the **Middle East**, made with cucumbers and yogurt.

For a complete meal soup, try hearty **Italian** vegetable soups called minestrone. In Italy the soups will vary from region to region. In Southern Italy, garlic, tomato and olive oil are the main ingredients. In Central Italy beans play the important role. In the north, rice is the essential ingredient; and along the Riviera lots of fresh herbs are a must. During the summer, these Italian soups are often served chilled, taking a lesson from the Spanish and their popular gazpacho chilled soups. **Pennsylvania Italians** boil a beef roast and small chicken together and then use the stock as a starter for vegetable soups.

The **Russians** favor cabbage soups. Another hearty soup is a Russian beet soup called borscht. While beets are one of the main ingredients, this hearty soup also contains beans, beef, potatoes, cabbage and is topped with sour cream. Borscht, like gazpacho is often served chilled. However, it is a much lighter soup with fewer ingredients.

In **India** a soup is made with lamb (the British make the same soup, but with chicken) and is called **mulligatawny.** This soup is first made as a meat broth with lots of spices. Then the chopped vegetables and apples are added about ten minutes before serving.

In **Latin America,** fish soup (sopa de pescados) is quite popular, again with lots of vegetables, a couple pounds of fish, and all simmered in a chicken broth.

Bean Soups

A robust bean soup made with **garbanzos** is a favorite in Spain. The soup also contains ham, lots of vegetables, including a whole head of cabbage. It is served as a complete meal with crusty bread and a caramel custard for dessert. The Italians also make a bean soup with pasta (*pasta e fagioli*) that is served with Italian bread and fresh fruit, a nourishing winter soup supper.
Other bean soups include the Dutch made with **green split-peas;** the Swedes favor **yellow split-peas.** In the Middle East the favored beans are **lentils** and in the Caribbean it's **black beans**. All these been soups are hearty and great for that first autumn night meal. In the Southern United States., expect **pinto** and **great northern** bean soup anytime.

Any Leftovers? Try Vegetable Soup.

If you have the basic meat stock or vegetable juices, you can add browned onion and celery, seasonings and whatever veggies you have on hand, fresh or left over. Canned or left over cooked veggie (such as peas, carrots, corn, potatoes, turnips) may be added and just simmer to a boil. With bread and butter, this makes a nice meal. – *Erville Allen*

Activity
Make a cornucopia centerpiece out of a variety of colorful vegetables. Then, after the meal, use them in a soup with any soup starter or meat broth. Works especially well after turkey dinner, using turkey leftovers.

SOUR CREAM: Originally sour cream was made with unpasteurized, heavy sweet cream left in a warm area to set. Today, commercially made sour cream is treated with an acid bacteria resulting in a thick, mild tangy flavor.

SOURDOUGH: You might think sourdough started with the Alaskan gold miners. Actually a form of sourdough has been used since bread was first made. Sourdough was not only used in the home but was taken on long journeys, such as aboard the ships of early European explorers. At least one of the first three Spanish ships to America carried sourdough starter, which is called "pot." Today there is an exceptionally nice wet sourdough starter which must be kept in the refrigeration. You can't buy it since it is passed from friend to friend, sometimes called "friendship bread." The starter is kept in a glass jar and fed sugar to keep it growing. If someone offers you this kind, you'd be wise to take it.

The bread recipe does not have to be kneaded, which makes it wonderfully easy to use and the bread is high, light and delicious.

Sourdough played an important part in the California Gold Rush of 1849 prior to moving to Alaska. Prospectors carried a sourdough pot with them to make fresh bread, biscuits and pancakes. Many of these miners carried the sourdough starter in the middle of a sack of flour. During cold winter months, it was necessary to keep the sourdough starter warm, so it went to bed with them and during the day was carried under their shirts, next to their bodies. The loss of starter meant having no baked goods for several months. Many considered their starter more important than a poke of gold.

Activity

One modern sourdough starter is made with one package of yeast and two cups each of flour and water. Mix this and store it in a non-metallic bowl, jar, or crock, covered with cheese cloth. Let it age for two or three days for the bacteria to grow. When used, about a half cup is saved before adding two cups each of flour and water to make a batch of bread. In other words, always save half and use half. Once made, the starter will last as long as it's kept under the right conditions. King Author's Flour Company offers in their catalogue a starter that is 250 years old. There are other kinds of sourdough starters in bread books for those who have the patience. It can be started with nothing but flour and water, although the books we checked were unclear about exactly how or why this works. –LU www.sourdoughbread.com

SOUR MILK: Originally sour milk was made with unpasteurized milk left at room temperature. If left long enough, it would form curds and whey. Pasteurized milk will not sour naturally, but will only spoil. If a recipe calls for sour milk, buttermilk is a good substitute. Or you can add one tablespoon of white vinegar or lemon juice to one cup of sweet milk and let it stand for five minutes. The vinegar flavor will not be tasted in the cooked product.

SOUR ORANGE: See SEVILLE ORANGE

SOURSOP: See GUANBANA

SOYBEANS: Are known by many similar names, soya, soy peas, shoyu, soja, and soi. Native to Asia, soybeans are beloved by vegetarians since they are served as a meat substitute. Soybeans provide moderate calories, high fiber and protein, moderate fat, low sodium, and no starch. Soybeans are available fresh and frozen in pods, or just as beans in some health food stores. Cook fresh soybeans as you would peas, either in or out of the pods. Most soybeans are dried, and must be soaked and cooked like navy beans. Soybeans are used to make soy oil, soy flour, soy milk and soy sauce, as well as margarine (Jeff Smith, in *The Frugal Gourmet*, refers to margarine as plastic butter), plastic and soap. Soybean sprouts can be eaten raw in salads or cooked. **Nutrition facts** for ½ cup serving of fresh or frozen **green soybeans**: 188 calories, 73 calories from fat, 8.7g total fat (13%), 1g saturated fat (5%), zero cholesterol, 19.2mg sodium (1%), 14.2g carbohydrates (5%), 5.4g fiber (22%), 16.6 protein (33%), 230 IU vitamin A (5%), 37mg vitamin C (62%), 252mg calcium (25%), 4.6mg iron (25%), 794mg potassium, and a good source for many B vitamins.

Nutrition facts for ½ cup cooked **dried soybeans**: 149 calories, 64 calories from fat, 7.7g total fat (12%), 1.1g saturated fat (6%), zero cholesterol and sodium, 8.5g carbohydrates (3%), 5.2g fiber (21%), 14.3g protein (29%), zero vitamin A, 1mg vitamin C (2%), 88mg calcium (9%), 4.4mg iron (25%), and 443mg potassium.

EATING HEALTHY WITH SOY

Americans are now eating more meatless meals than ever before. One meat substitute is soy. Soy foods are rich in protein, calcium and iron, as well as many of the B vitamins. Soy is high in fiber, cholesterol-free and low in saturated fats as compared to meat, eggs and dairy foods.

Did you know it takes **an acre of grass to feed one cow** that produces only 58 pounds of meat? That's two and half months of protein for one person. If soybeans are grown on this same land, the soybeans will produce enough protein to sustain that same person for seven years. Wow! So not only do soybeans provide you with better nutrition, but also help save our precious resources.

There are more than 2,000 soy products produced which include milk, cheese, lunch meats, yogurt, ice cream and a variety of meat substitutes, such as ground meat and hot dogs. When soy products were placed on the market a couple of decades ago, the public rejected them, mainly because of taste and lack of knowledge how to use them. Today the soy producers have not only improved the taste, but offer recipes on how to use their products. If you haven't eaten a soy product, try making your favorite pasta sauce with soy sausages. See TOFU. TEMPEH and VEGGIE BURGER.

SOY CHEESE is made from soy milk and can be used in place of dairy cheese in most recipes.

SOY FLOUR is roasted soybeans ground into flour. Soy flour is mostly used to add protein to wheat flour recipes. While it can replace wheat flour, however, it doesn't have gluten for making bread.

SOY MILK: Soymilk is made by grinding, cooking and draining soybeans. This produces a rich, light and creamy product that can be used as a beverage and in many recipes calling for milk. Soymilk is a good replacement for those allergic to lactose.

SOY SAUCE: A sauce made by adding salt to cooked soy beans and letting the beans ferment. A staple in Chinese cooking, it gives stir fries that distinctive Chinese taste.

SPACE FOOD:
DINING WITH THE ASTRONAUTS

WANTED: Astronauts; picky eaters need not apply. John Glenn, America's first man to eat anything in the near-weightless environment of Earth orbit, found the task of eating fairly easy, but oh, the food! Mercury astronauts had to endure bite-sized cubes, freeze-dried powders, and semi-liquids stuffed in aluminum "toothpaste-like" tubes. All agreed the foods were unappetizing. Also freeze-dried foods were hard to dehydrate and crumbs could cause a problem by fouling instruments.

Gemini missions food improved somewhat. The first things to go were the squeeze tubes. Bite-size cubes were coated with gelatin to reduce crumbling, and the freeze- dried foods were encased in special plastic containers making reconstituting easier. Gemini astronauts had such food choices as shrimp cocktail, chicken and vegetables, butterscotch pudding, and apple sauce. Apollo astronauts were first to have hot water, which made rehydrating foods easier and improved the food's taste. These astronauts were the first to use the "spoon bowl," a plastic container that could be opened and the contents eaten with a spoon.

A big boost came with Skylab; it featured a dining table. Footholds allowed the astronauts to "sit" to eat with knife, fork, and a spoon, plus a pair of scissors for cutting the plastic seals. Also the Skylab had a menu of 72 different food items, plus a freezer and refrigerator.

GOOD TASTE IN OUTER SPACE

Space Shuttle astronauts now have an astonishing array of food to choose from, many that are also available on supermarket shelves. Shuttle astronauts can design their own menus. However, a dietitian checks the menu to ensure that astronauts consume a balanced diet of nutrients. On the Space Shuttle, food is prepared at a galley that contains a water dispenser used to rehydrate foods, and an oven for warming foods to proper serving temperatures. It's almost like eating at home with a special tray attached to your lap by a strap. This tray allows the astronaut to choose from several foods at once. Without the tray, the contents would go floating away in the microgravity. Lunch and dinner menus now include chicken and rice soup, macaroni and cheese, spaghetti with meatballs, hot dogs with mustard, hamburgers with catsup, fresh vegetables such as carrots and celery, peanut butter and jelly sandwiches, flour tortillas, puddings, brownies, fresh fruits such as apples and bananas, and a wide array of beverages including fruit drinks and cocoa. Breakfast includes scrambled eggs, sweet rolls, fresh bread, oatmeal with raisins, a large variety of cold cereals, and for those who like grits, it is served with hot butter. All this can be washed down with hot coffee, hot tea, or chilled juice.

For the semi-gourmet astronaut, there's a wide choice of foods which include: barbecued beef, beef stroganoff with noodles, chicken cacciatore. turkey tetrazini, green beans with mushrooms, potatoes au gratin, and peach ambrosia for dessert. And there are all kinds of snacks: candy coated peanuts, Snickers, chewing gum, chocolate covered cookies, graham crackers, trail mix, granola bars, and yogurt.

"VOMIT COMET"

Foods flown on space missions are researched and developed at the Food Systems Engineering Facility at the National Aeronautics and Space Administration Johnson Space Center in Houston, Texas. It is staffed by food scientists, dietitians and engineers. Foods are analyzed through nutritional analysis, sensory evaluation, freeze drying, rehydration, storage studies, packaging evaluation, and many other methods. All foods are tested in zero-gravity aboard the KC-135 airplane, affectionately known as the "Vomit Comet," to see how the food will react in micro-gravity.

Currently all foods are designed for the short duration of the Space Shuttle. New foods and long-term storage containers must be redesigned for deep space missions, such as to the planet Mars, and beyond. It will almost be like starting over again, as with John Glenn's first flight. Then there was time to experiment between space missions, but on a long deep space flight there will be no time to experiment. It must be perfect the first time. *--National Aeronautics and Space Administration (NASA)*

SPAGHETTI: This Italian word, *spago*, means "string," and best describes this favorite pasta product. Spaghetti is made with semolina and water, the slender solid rods comes in thin, medium, and thick sizes. www.obpasta.com

SPAGHETTI SAUCE: Sauces for spaghetti come in many variations, but basically they are tomato, seasoned with olive oil, garlic, onion, basil, and rosemary. From there, other recipes begin to add things like thyme, green peppers, grated cheese, mushrooms, meat, and hot peppers. Every cook has his or her personal favorite combination. www.ragu.com www.eat.com

SPANISH BAYONET: Native to Florida, it produces up to 5-inch green, cucumber shaped fruits. The fruits are rubbery but edible. The flowers are more commonly eaten raw, sometimes cooked.

SPANISH CHERRY: The 5/8-inch yellow fruits are edible, as are the seeds. The bark is used to make a tonic.

SPANISH LIME: See MAMONCILLO.

SPARERIBS: The bones and meat from the lower portion of the rib cage of animals. Spareribs generally refer to pork ribs, but lamb and beef ribs can be just as succulent as pork, especially baby beef ribs.

SPEARMINT: When the herb mint is called for in a recipe, spearmint is usually the cook's choice. This herb is native to both Europe and Asia, and is now grown in temperate regions of the United States. Spearmint is available fresh, dried, and as an extract.

SPELT BERRIES: This variety of wheat has a delicious, light and nutty flavor. It contains 30% more protein than most wheat and can be substituted for wheat in any recipe. Spelt berries are more tolerated by those sensitive to wheat. Use in pilaf or salads. Great when combined with bulgur, millet and barley in soups. Widely used in Europe until the 20th century, it is comparatively rare today.

SPICE: A loose term that applies to a pungent and/or an aromatic substance of vegetable origin that includes leaves, seeds, bark, nuts, roots, etc., and is used as a seasoning to add flavor to food. Examples: bay and basil (leaves), caraway and pepper (seeds), cinnamon (bark), nutmeg (nut), and ginger (roots). Most spices come from the tropics. www.fiestaspices.com; www.chefpaul.com

SPICE BLENDS YOU CAN MAKE

You will find most of the basic spices in your kitchen. Just mix, age a few days, use or give them as gifts. Some recipes can be cut in half, or doubled to meet your needs. Use the blends as requested in recipes. Place the blends in a tightly closed jar and store in a dark, cool place. All ingredients listed are dried, ground or crushed spices and herbs.

PUMPKIN PIE SPICE

½ cup cinnamon
1/4 cup ginger
2 tablespoons nutmeg
1 to 2 tablespoons cloves

APPLE PIE SPICE

½ cup cinnamon
1 tablespoon nutmeg
1 tablespoon allspice
1 tablespoon cloves
½ teaspoon ginger

TACO SEASONING MIX

1/4 cup instant minced onion flakes
3 tablespoons chili powder
2 tablespoons cumin
2 tablespoon salt
1 tablespoon red pepper flakes, crushed
1 tablespoon garlic powder
1 tablespoon cornstarch
1 tablespoon oregano, crushed

SAUSAGE BLEND (add to 2 pounds lean ground beef or pork)

½ teaspoon sage or thyme
1 each teaspoon salt and pepper
1/8 teaspoon ginger, nutmeg, cumin, allspice

CREOLE MILD SPICE BLEND

2 tablespoons paprika
2 tablespoons garlic powder
2 tablespoons salt
1 tablespoon black pepper
1 tablespoon thyme
1 tablespoon oregano
1 teaspoon cayenne red pepper

CAJUN HOT SPICE BLEND

As above, but double both the black pepper and cayenne red pepper.
Great for blackened fish, shrimp, and chicken. Both Creole and Cajun
blends make an excellent flavoring for beans and rice.

A QUICK GUIDE TO SPICES AND FLAVORINGS

Allspice is a berry of an evergreen tree native to the Western Hemisphere. The name comes from its flavor which is similar to a combination of nutmeg, cinnamon and cloves. Used in many quick bread recipes.

Anise Seed was used by the Egyptians, Greeks and Romans. It was a commodity taxed to pay for the repair of the London Bridge. This licorice-like flavor tastes great in the core of a baked apples and other baked goods.

Black Pepper has always been the most important spice in the world. It is the dried, unripened fruit of the peppervine.

Caraway Seed, a native to Europe, was recorded in papers as early as 1552 BC. It was used by the Ancient Greeks and Romans and was enjoyed with baked apples in Elizabethan England. Sprinkle in bread dough, especially rye bread before baking.

Cardamon, native to India, is the Queen of Spices. It is richly perfumed with a sweet refreshing flavor. Used in some bread recipes.

Cinnamon, the bark of a tree, is one of the oldest spices known. Arab traders brought it from China to the Middle East. It is the most popular spice for baking. Try a dash of cinnamon in a cup of coffee.

Cloves are the bud of a tree. Marco Polo brought them back from China. They became the object of a trade war between the Portuguese and the Dutch. Use sparely.

Coriander Seed is said to be the color of manna, "the bread from heaven." It has a slight lemon flavor and is used both whole and ground in baked goods, especially good in bread puddings.

Cumin Seeds, sometimes called Comino, is an ancient seed dating back to the Old Testament. It is popular in Mexican dishes.

Fennel Seeds has been used for centuries. The Puritans called it "meeting seed" and nibbled it during church service. This slight licorice flavor is added to breads before baking.

Ginger is one of the earliest Oriental spices known to Europeans. It is the essential spice for gingerbread. Ginger is available fresh as a root, dried and ground for mixing in baking, and crystalized. Crystalized ginger can be minced and mixed into cream cheese as a spread for fruit bread.

Mace and nutmeg comes from the same fruit. Mace is the lacy covering of the nutmeg. Orange in color, mace has a sweet, warm spicy flavor. Mace can be interchanged with nutmeg in most recipes.

Nutmeg comes from the East Indies. It has a warm, sweet, spicy flavor that can be used in baking recipes, as well as sprinkled on fresh as a topping.

Poppy Seeds are from the opium poppy, but have no narcotic properties. Poppy seeds and poppy seed oil have been used since 1500 BC. Sprinkle on bread, rolls and coffee cakes before baking.

Red Pepper is a New World spice and comes from the Capsicum pepper, sometimes called Cayenne pepper. It is made from the dried pods.

Saffron is the most expensive spice in the world. The thread-like stigma comes from the crocus. It takes 225,000 hand-picked stigmas to make one pound. It requires only a few stigmas to flavor baked goods.

Sesame Seed is the first recorded seasoning. Assyrians wrote of it in 3,000 BC. Sometimes called bene seed, it has a nutty flavor when toasted. Sprinkle on bread and coffee cakes before baking. To toast, bake at 350oF for about 15 minutes.

Vanilla Beans are the fruit of an orchid and native to Mexico. Add a bean to a jar of sugar to keep vanilla sugar on hand.

White Pepper comes from the same vine as black pepper. The berries are picked ripe and the outer hull removed. The berry turns white when dried. *--McCormick/Schilling*

SPICES, EAST AND WEST
by Louise Ulmer

When children of ancient China day-dreamed of adventure the way you and I might dream of taking a rocket to the moon, they imagined riding a camel on **the Silk Road**. The ancient Silk Road gets its name from the silk trade, but it could just as easily have been called the Spice Road. Along with the bundles of silk carried on camelback from China to the Middle East came bags of herbs and spices.

Where were those silks and spices going? They met welcoming traders from Persia, Egypt, Palestine, and Arabia. In exchange for Oriental fabrics and foods, Chinese merchants took back home other spices from North Africa, South Arabia, and the coast of North India. The Silk Road brought East and West together. That is how a mother in Egypt could serve tea to her family and a mother in China could burn frankincense to purify her home.

It's true that most spices do come from the Far East. However, there were **spices in the Bible** world and Arabian lands–frankincense, myrrh, cancanum, and tarum. But by 500 AD, most of the Arab grown spices had died off the market. Either they failed to be cultivated well, disappeared, or were being grown successfully in other lands. Coriander and cumin grew wild along the banks of the Nile. We seldom hear about the spices mentioned in the Bible today.

For centuries the Arabs were in the best position to act as spice merchants between the distant countries. Civilizations rise and fall. With the fall of the Mongol Empire, new routes had to be found. Looking to the South, merchants found Syria and Egypt where Muslim merchants were already in the habit of traveling in caravans on pilgrimages to Mecca in Arabia. As the Greeks came to power, things changed and their armies opened new roads and built grander cities than ever before. By the 1500s, spices could be brought by ships as well as by camel caravan. The world grew bigger each passing century. And the spice trade grew with it. Transporting perishable goods was always slow and expensive, made all the more dangerous by the value of the cargo itself. Pirating and theft, bad weather, regional wars and bad luck made traders rich if they lived to enjoy it.

SPINACH: The cartoon character, Popeye, really didn't receive his strength from the iron in spinach as you were lead to believe, but did receive a good source of vitamin A which might have improved his eyesight. This herb originated in southwestern Asia and is grown for its green leaves. Available fresh, frozen and canned. Fresh spinach must be washed thoroughly, as the leaves seem to gather sand and dirt from both the soil and the wind. Fresh spinach can be eaten raw in a salad or cooked as other green vegetables. Whenever you see a recipe with the word "Florentine" it will contain spinach. Kids who don't like spinach cooked should be encouraged to try it raw in salads where it has virtually no taste. **Nutrition facts** ½ cup serving: 6 calories, zero fats, 22.1mg sodium (1%), zero c carbohydrates, .8g fiber (3%), .7g protein (2%), 1880 IU vitamin A (38%), 8mg vitamin C (13%), 28mg calcium (3%), .8mg iron (4%), and 156mg potassium.

SPINELESS YUCCA: From Central America, the flowers are eaten as a vegetable.

SPOILED FOOD: Generally, any food that is overripe, decayed, rotten or contaminated is spoiled. If it looks bad and smells bad, it is bad.

SPOILED OR JUST GROSS?

If buttermilk is spoiled, how do you know, since it's already sour? What about plain yogurt? Can it get any worse? Here's a list of foods and how you can know if one is too far gone to eat.

Apple: Soft with brown places inside and Out. **Beans:** Green beans will be limp and spotty or won't snap when broken. **Broccoli:** Limp or buds turned yellow. **Buttermilk** and Yogurt: Read the dates on the package and the if they smell more sour than usual or look separated, throw it out. If it just a little past the expired date and smells okay, you can still use it in cooking. **Carrots:** Limp and lifeless. **Cauliflower**: Looks dull and has little black spots on its flowers. **Celery:** Limp and dull. **Corn:** Has husks that are dry or spotty, kernels look shriveled. **Fish:** Watch for cloudy eyes or greyish gills. **Mushrooms:** Look spotty and dark. **Meat:** Has a grey color or feels slimy to touch; smells awful. **Milk:** Smells sour. Looks curdly around the opening. **Pineapple**: Don't even try it if it's been in the refrigerator for more than two days. **Potatoes**: Wrinkled and sprouting or green skinned. **Spinach:** Has yellow leaves or slimy edges. **Strawberries**: Look mushy and have 'things' growing on them.

Beware of **dented cans**. Throw out any can you open that spews at you or smells odd or looks off color. **When in doubt throw it out.**

SPONGECAKE: A light airy cake leavened with egg whites. The yolks and whites are beaten separately, the whites folded in last, creating an airy batter. Spongecakes were made before baking powder and soda were used in cakes, since the only other known leavening was yeast.

SPOON: (noun) The spoon is an ancient scooping device. The spoon is as old as the knife. Forks were invented much later. Spoons are used for cooking and measuring, even where chopsticks and fingers are preferred for table use. There are all kinds of spoons, depending on the purpose for which they are needed. Measuring spoons come in sizes of 1/8, 1/4, ½, 1 teaspoon, and 1 tablespoon sized for precision baking and cooking. There are even small spoons just for collecting. (verb) "To spoon" means to add or remove ingredients by the spoonful. One might "spoon" strawberries over cake.

Activity

How many kinds of spoons can you name? See how many you can locate to show as a collection and give a demonstration of their uses. A good place to look is in flea markets and thrift stores. Rare collector spoons can be profitable to sell or trade.

SPOON BREAD: A type of corn bread, usually cooked in a single size baking dish and served with a spoon, rather than cut with a knife. This of it as a kind of cornbread souffle'. It's that light and creamy! The elegant little dish came from African American cooks playing with French influence. The light texture comes from using beaten egg whites as the leavening agent, as with chiffon cake.

SPORES THAT SPOIL:
Grow Your Own Mold Garden

You've seen mold on bread and other foods. Want to see how it looks up close? When mold spoils food, it isn't pretty, but it can be fascinating to see under a microscope. You will need:

Bread
Paper towel
A plate
A clear glass jar
Microscope

Directions:
1. Fold a paper towel twice to make a pad. Wet the pad slightly, not dripping.
2. Place pad on the plate.
3. Take about 1/4 of a slice of bread and rub it on a dusty surface. The floor usually has enough dust to make it work.

4. Place the bread square, dusty side up on the damp pad. Cover the bread with the upside down glass jar.

5. Store the "mold garden" in a cabinet or closet.

6. Check the bread daily. In a few days, you will see little white threads through your microscope on the bread. Those threads are alive and growing. Gradually you will see little white dots too. These dots are balls on the ends of the threads. Soon the balls will become colored. Each tiny ball contains more tiny balls. The balls are called spores. When the balls ripen, they will break and send thousands of new spores out into the air.

7. Keep a daily record of what you see on the bread as it goes through the stages to become mold and spreads to cover the bread.

SPORTS NUTRITION

The most asked question about sports nutrition is, **"What is the best diet for an athlete?"** It's important that an athlete's diet provide the right amount of energy, the 50-plus nutrients the body needs and adequate water. No single food or supplement can do this. A variety of foods are needed every day. Whether you are a competitive athlete or just an individual who exercises for better health, both of you need the same nutrients. However, athletes, because of intensive training, do require more calories and fluids. This means that all foods and fluids must be increased by the same percentage amounts.

Nutrition professionals recommend that 55% to 60% of the calories in your diet come from carbohydrates, no more than 30% from fat and the remaining 10% to 15% from protein.

"How many calories do I need a day?" That depends upon your age, body size, sport and training program. For example, a 250-pound weight lifter needs more calories than a 98-pound gymnast. Extensive training can increase your calorie need by 1000 to 1500 calories per day. It is necessary to consult a nutritionist or a physician to determine your daily calorie intake.

How Much Water?

Fluids are most important. As your body sweats, you lose water. You must maintain your body's fluid level, this means you must drink fluids before, during, and after a workout. The fluids can be water or a sports drink, it's a matter of choice. However, if your workout last for more than 90 minutes, you may benefit from the carbohydrates provided by sports drinks. It is important that the sports drink have 15 to 18 grams of carbohydrates per eight ounces. Higher carbohydrate content will delay the absorption of water and could cause dehydration, cramps, nausea and/or diarrhea. **You can make your own sports drink.** To eight ounces of water add four teaspoons of sugar, a fourth teaspoon of salt and a teaspoon of lemon juice or other flavoring.

What about Carbs?

"What are carbohydrates?" you might ask. Carbohydrates are sugars and starches found in foods like bread, cereals, fruits, vegetables, pasta, milk, honey, syrups, and sports. The origin of the carbohydrates are not important, because the body breaks them down into glucose and your blood carries glucose to cells to be used for energy.

Carbohydrates are important during a workout, since you lose some glycogen, and this loss results in fatigue. When to consume these carbohydrates differs from person to person. Some athletes eat two to four hours before a workout. Others perform best with a small amount 30 minutes before. Still others eat nothing for six hours beforehand. Some athletes load up on carbohydrates days before an event, but this has been found not necessary. A simple diet that derives more than half of its calories from carbohydrates will do.

If you eat 1,800 balanced calories per day, you probably need few vitamin and mineral supplements. However, if you're a vegetarian or avoid any one food group, you may need those supplements that are not supplied by food. Always obtain professional advice for your specific needs.

MINERALS ARE ESSENTIAL

Iron is important because it is part of your hemoglobin. Hemoglobin carries oxygen from the lungs to all parts of your body, including your muscles and your muscles need oxygen to produce energy. A blood test might be necessary if you fatigue easily, become dizzy or have headaches during your workout. Taking an iron supplement will not improve your performance unless you are iron deficient. Too much iron can cause constipation or diarrhea and can interfere with the absorption of other nutrients. Calcium is important for strong bones and proper muscle function. Dairy foods are the best source for calcium. In some events, it might be necessary to cut back your weight, and many athletes then cut out dairy products. If you do not receive enough calcium, there is danger of stress fractures and later when you are older, osteoporosis. Teens, especially females, need about 1,300 milligrams of calcium per day.

The best foods to eat before a workout are those that break down quickly to provide glucose to the muscles, such as bananas, breads, and fruit juices. During the workout, you need cool liquids, at least a half a cup every twenty minutes. After the workout, you need to replenish your body with foods and liquids high in carbohydrates that include grains, pastas, potatoes, vegetables and fruits. A teaspoon of sugar can be added to increase taste appeal. This information is not a substitute for professional medical care, only an insight of your needs as an athlete.-- *The President's Council on Physical Fitness and Sports, produced by The Sugar Association, Inc.*

SPRAT: A small herring found in Europe. Some sprats are sold as Norwegian sardines or anchovies. Imported sprats come from France and Denmark and are found in specialty food stores.

SPREADS are usually something applied to a slice of bread, such as butter, margarine, mayonnaise, etc. Typical sandwich spreads are chopped ham, cream cheese, chopped corned beef and deviled eggs. There are hot spreads such as garlic in butter on French bread, heated under the broiler.

SPRITZ: A type of shortbread cookie that is squeezed out of a cookie press in different patterns. The word spritz comes from the German wording, meaning "to squirt."

SPROUTS: Fresh sprouts are grown from a variety of seeds which only take a week to grow. The easiest to grow are alfalfa, lentil, mung, sunflower and wheat seeds. Sprouts can be grown at home, but it is important to purchase seeds that have not been treated with chemicals, such as fungicides. You can find alfalfa sprouts in the produce department still growing in clear packs.

You can make them at home with seeds, water, and a nonmetallic opaque container. Just follow these easy steps:
1. Rinse about a half cup of seeds several times in a strainer.
2. In a bowl, mix the seeds with two cups of water and soak overnight. The seeds will double in size.
3. Place the swelled seeds in a two-quart opaque container. Glass is best, but unglazed pots work just as well. Soak three paper towels in water and place on top of the seeds. Cover with a plate.
4. Set aside at room temperature. Remoisten the paper towels in about four hours.
5. The next day, fill the container with warm water, cover, and turn upside down to drain. Gently stir the bottom seeds to the top. Turn container right side up. Replace with moist paper towels, and remoisten four hours later.
6. Continue as per instruction number five for the next few days until the sprouts are about one inch long.

The secret is to keep the sprouts warm and moist. All of the sprout is edible. Some prefer to wash away the shell, but this isn't necessary. You can refrigerate the sprouts up to a week to a week and a half, but keep moist with a paper towel. Many vitamins, especially vitamin C, will increase during refrigeration. Sprouts can be eaten fresh, in salads and sandwiches; added to soups just before serving, great in scrambled eggs, sautéd in butter for about five minutes and eaten as a vegetable. Sprouts can be ground in a food processor and added to breads, muffins and other baked goods, as well as pancakes and waffles.

SPUMONI: An Italian ice cream of various flavors molded together. Spumoni usually contains an outer layer of custard, a layer of candied fruit and nuts, and brandy or rum flavored ice cream in the center.

SQUAB: A young pigeon that has not been allowed to fly is a squab. During early times when chickens were not always tender, squabs were the choice at fine dinner parties. Squabs are available on some specialty food stores. Allow one squab per person. Best roasted whole or split in half and broiled. Can be cut up in smaller pieces and sautéd. **Nutrition facts** 3 ounces: 114 calories, 37 calories from fat, 3.9g total fat (6%), 1g saturated fat (5%), 76.6mg cholesterol (26%), 46.8mg sodium (2%), zero carbohydrates and fiber, 18g protein (37%), 49 IU vitamin A (1%), 5mg vitamin C (7%), 9mg calcium (1%) and 2mg iron (11%).

SQUASH: Native to Peru, the name came from the Inca word *askutasquash*, that means "green thing." There are two main varieties, summer and winter, and many varieties of each. Summer squash are best harvested when young and eaten fresh, whereas, winter squash should be left on the vine until fully matured. www.state.nj.us/agriculture; www.perryandsons.com

SUMMER SQUASH VARIETIES

- **Chayote**, pear size and shaped green squash.
- **Crookneck**, best while the skin is a pale yellow. There is also a straightneck variety.
- **Scallop**, diskshape and best when a pale green. When white, it is too mature,
- **Zucchini**, a cylinder shape and and dark green in color, some are lighter green with stripes.

Summer squash is generally cut up in bite size pieces, boiled in a small amount of water and seasoned with salt, pepper, and butter. Also, great in stir-fries. By parboiling summer squash, it can be baked, broiled, and barbecued. Cooking shish kabob style is common too.

WINTER SQUASH VARIETIES

- Acorn, dark green and acorn shaped, it will turn orange in storage.
- Banana, one to two feet long, four to eight inches in diameter and grey-white in color.
- Butternut, light bulb shape with a brown skin.
- Hubbards, globe-shape with pointed ends, with a skin color ranging from green to orange.
- Pumpkin, round and generally with bright orange skin. There are red, green and white varieties.

The flesh of winter squash ranges from yellow to orange. Winter squash is best baked. Smaller ones should be cut in half. Longer ones need to be cut into pieces to remove the seeds. Winter squash can be peeled and boiled. See ZUCCHINI.

SQUASH MARMALADE and FLORIDA APPLE PIE

In June of **1835, the Florida Herald** reported a shortage of small fruits. Imagine Florida 100 years before all the fruit orchards! The newspaper suggested to homemakers that green squash could be used as a substitute. Here are two recipes just as written in the newspaper,

Florida Apple Pie: "*First buy at Market, or gather from your garden, about a dozen of young green squashes, pare them, quarter and take out the seed, cut into slices as nearly resembling apples as possible, have ready your paste, put a layer of fruit in the bottom of the dish, then sugar, then fruit till sufficient, a gill of water, 6 cloves bruised fine, juice of a lemon and the grated rind. Bake as usual.*"

Squash Marmalade: *"Pare as for the former recipe, boil in clear water till quite tender, then drain and lay in a deep dish, pour over a mixture of milk, sugar, nutmeg, lemon juice &c. to the taste; Eats very like codled apples. N.B. The juice of sour oranges or lemon Syrup is a good substitute for the lemon." –RSC*

SQUID: In the octopus family, it has a long slender body and ten arms or tentacles. Squids are found in all the oceans worldwide. Generally, only the arms are eaten with some parts of the body, but not the head. The arms are best when cut into rings, breaded and fried. Squid can also be baked. **Nutrition facts** 3 ounces: 78 calories, 11 calories from fat, 1.2g total fat (2%), .3g saturated fat (2%), 198.3mg cholesterol (66%), 37.4mg sodium (2%), 1.3g carbohydrates (1%), zero fiber, 13.3g protein (27%), zero vitamin A, 4mg vitamin C (7%), 27mg calcium (3%) and .6g iron (3%),

SQUIRREL: This rodent has a pleasing taste, not as gamey as other wild game and can be prepared the same as rabbit. Once common on American frontier tables, it has been replaced in popularity by supermarket meats. **Nutrition facts** 3 ounces: 102 calories, 26 calories from fat, 2.8g total fat (4%), .4g saturated fat (2%), 70.6mg cholesterol (24%), 87.6mg sodium (4), zero carbohydrates and fiber, 18.1g protein (36%), zero vitamins A and C, zero calcium, 4mg iron (22%)

STAR APPLE: See CAMITO

STARCH: A thickener made from some grains (wheat, corn), vegetables (potatoes), or roots (arrowroot).

STAR FRUIT: See CARAMBOLA. www.frieda.com

STAYMAN APPLES: A red apple, flesh is sometimes tinged with yellow and has a semi-firm texture. Stayman apples are tart in flavor, are good eaten raw, or cooked in pies and sauces.

STEAK: Generally a steak is a slice of meat from animals and fish, such as a T-bone steak, or a salmon steak with the bone in the middle. Ground meat, such as hamburger can be molded into a large patty and called a steak, such as a "Salisbury steak" or "chicken fried steak." .

STEVIA: A small green plant from Paraguay that has leaves 400 times sweeter than processed sugar and provides no calories because the body cannot break down the glycosides. It is used in cooking because heat doesn't break them down either. Stevia is usually ound in health food stores.

STEAK: Prime or best cut of lean meat or fish, usually a one portion size (6 - 16 ounces).

STEAM: A method of cooking by vapor (steam), above boiling water. This quick method helps to retain the nutrients, as well as the flavor. Vegetables stay crisper than when boiled. Most foods take 15 to 20 minutes after the steam begins. Foods that can be steamed are: bread, dried fruit, fish, rice, and vegetables. A pressure cooker basically cooks by steam. Certain British "puddings" (like the

Christmas or figgy puddings) are cakes or breads made by slow steaming over several hours. It makes a very moist cake. The method was more popular before every home had ovens.

STERILIZE: A process of heating foods and liquids, as well as utensils, with high heat or boiling water, to kill microorganisms (germs). There is also chemical sterilization, such as preserving meat with salt. Radiation method is still being perfected but is costly and raises some health concerns.

STEW: (verb) A process to cook meat and vegetables in a covered pot slowly with only enough water to cover. Some fruits, especially dried fruits are also cooked in this manner. (noun) Any thick, chunky soup.

STICKY GROUND CHERRY: Native to south Florida, this herb produces ½-inch golden fruit covered with paper-like husks. Eaten fresh and made into sauce.

STINGING NETTLE: Prior to mass transportation, there was a shortage of green vegetables, especially in the winter months. Since scurvy was a problem, stinging nettle stalks were boiled to remove the "sting," and then eaten as a tonic. The boiled stalks are rich in protein, iron, and vitamins A and C. At one time, the Scottish people cultivated stinging nettles for their fibers, which was made into a durable linen-like cloth. Today the plant is a commercial source for chlorpophyll and green dye.

STIR: To mix or blend foods with a spoon or a whisk, moving the food in a circle motion. This helps to prevent food from sticking and burning. Some recipes will state "stir occasionally," while other recipes request "stirred constantly." Believe it. Stirring also helps to reduce lumps in sauces.

STIR FRY: A method of cooking foods over high heat by constant stirring. Many Oriental recipes are cooked this way in a wok (a round bottomed skillet).

STOCK: It's the liquid left over from cooking foods, such as boiling a chicken. The liquid, or broth, is referred to as chicken stock. Stocks are made from meat, fish, poultry, and vegetables. The liquid is cooled and the fat removed. Some meat stocks turn into a gelatin when cooled.

STOLLEN: (stoe-lyn) A type of coffee cake made with yeast dough. Fruit and nut filled stollens are served as part of the Christmas breakfast in Germany.

STOUT: A strong, dark Irish and English beer. Some roasted barley gives it a distinctive flavor.

STRAIN: This means to pour food and liquid through the holes of a sieve where it separates the solid from the liquid. The liquid might be saved as stock. "To strain" also refers to pressing cooked food through the holes of a sieve, such as in making applesauce.

STRAWBERRIES: Wild strawberries are found worldwide in the temperate zones. Today's cultivated strawberries are a cross from wild strawberries found in Virginia and Chile. Oddly enough, both were taken to Europe to be crossed by horticulturists. The strawberry is a member of the rose family, a family that also includes apples and many other fruits. Wild strawberries are the most tasteful and fragrant of all the fruits. Strawberries range in size from the size of a hazelnut to as large as an apple. Strawberries are eaten raw, sometimes with a little sugar and cream, added to gelatin salads, made into ice cream, jams and jellies, pies, cakes, and puddings. Delightful as a topping for shortcake with whipped cream. Strawberries are generally found fresh the year round, also frozen individually, frozen in syrup, and canned. Strawberries are an excellent source of vitamin C. **Nutrition facts** ½ cup: 22 calories, zero fats and sodium, 5.2g carbohydrates (2%), 1.7g fiber (7%), .5g protein (1%), zero vitamins A, 42mg vitamin C (70%), 10mg calcium (1%) and .3mg iron (2%). www.calstrawberry.com

STROGANOV: Most books credit this dish to Court Paul Stroganov in Russia or to his chef. The recipe contains sliced of beef braised with onions and mushrooms in a sour cream sauce. According to Patricia Stevens in *Rare Bits*, the recipe is much older than that, having appeared in a cookbook published in 1871. Most likely the dish had been in the family for years and came to popularity through the genial Count Stroganov's lavish entertaining. Czar Alexander III often dined with him so the recipe no doubt traveled through the aristocratic kitchens of day. Russians eat their Beef Stroganov over fried potatoes, very much like our french fries. Americans serve it over flat noodles.

STRUDEL: (stroo-dle) An Austrian pastry made with several layers of thin dough and fruit or cheese filling. The baked strudel is crisp and the dough almost transparent. Strudel is difficult to make, hence some bakers use Greek filo dough, normally used to make baklava, but the end result is not the same as strudel dough. Strudels are generally served as a dessert, but do find their way to the breakfast table.

STUFF: (verb) This culinary term describes the act of filling a hollow or pocket with other foods, such as the inside of a fowl is stuffed with dressing. Other meats, such as flank steak (rolled up or hollowed-out, can be stuffed. Thick chops can be split open like a pocket and filled with vegetables or stuffing.

STUFFING: A mixture of ingredients used to stuff meat, fish, and poultry. It could be a combination of bread, fruit, meat, nuts, seafood, seeds, vegetables, and seasonings.

STURGEON: A prized delicacy, sturgeon are found in both fresh and salt waters of the north temperate zone. Many sturgeon spend most of their life in salt water and swim up river to spawn. There are varieties that spend their entire life in fresh water. Sturgeon caught in the rivers range from about three feet and have been caught up to an amazing twenty-five feet long. To get an idea how long twenty-five looks, take twenty-five steps. These large sturgeons can weigh more than a ton, and it takes a block and tackle to catch and land. Unfortunately, most of the sturgeon have been fished out of American rivers and the Great Lakes. While expensive, sturgeon is sold as steaks and smoked. The biggest prize is the roe, better known as caviar. **Nutrition facts** 3 ounces: 89 calories, 32 calories from fat, 3.5g total fat (6%), .8g saturated fat (4%), 51.1mg cholesterol (17%),

45.9mg sodium (2%), zero carbohydrates and fiber, 13.3g protein (28%), 595 IU vitamin A (12%), zero vitamin C, 11mg calcium (1%) and .6mg iron (4%).

SUBMARINE SANDWICH

SUB OR HOAGIE?

Legend says hoagies have been around since before the Great Depression. Back then workmen in the Philadelphia area carried their lunches out to a place called Hog Island. The "hogie" lunch began when someone split a loaf of Italian bread and filled it with last night's leftovers and salad. Other workmen, envious of such a whole meal in a roll, started making their own "hogies." Whether it all started in New York, New Orleans or other cities which claim credit for the idea, they all agree it has a history with Italian laborers.

"Hogie" somehow became "hoagie" as the idea spread and began to be sold. In the '50s, the hoagie's torpedo or submarine shape gave it a new name. In Eastern cities, enterprising sandwich makers began specializing in "submarines." In Williamsport, Pennsylvania, a typical "sub shop" raised the sub sandwich to a work of art. Cillini's Sub House opened in 1955 and made a sub so tasty that it lives locally in memory as the very best. Members of the Cellini family are still in the business.

The classic sub was made on a foot long roll, crisp on the outside, cloud light on the inside. A bed of shredded lettuce laid the groundwork for layers of real chopped ham, pepper loaf, old fashioned loaf, and hard salami. Provolone cheese crowned all that meat. Onion and tomato slices added color and vitamin A, not that anyone eating a sub cared about vitamins at the moment. A seasoned Italian oil flavors the whole creation.

Today's subs, or hoagies, appear around the country by other names and many variations. In Tennessee, it is called a "poorboy." In Vermont, you might ask for a "grinder." Blimpie, Miami Subs, and SubWay sandwich shops allow customers to choose their own ingredients on rolls made fresh right in the shop. Subs allow you a healthful choice of ingredients, many without all that fat and salt found in most fast-food restaurants. The Italian sub is very salty and fat, while the turkey sub is lean. What do they call subs in your town? Why? --*LU*

SUBSTITUTION CHART
What to use when you don't have what a recipe calls for.

Baking Powder: ½ teaspoon cream of tartar + 1/4 teaspoon baking soda = 1 teaspoon of baking powder.
Biscuit Mix: mix together 1 cup flour, 1 ½ teaspoons baking powder, ½ teaspoon salt in a bowl, than cut in 1 tablespoon of shortening = 1 cup of Biscuit mix.
Buttermilk: 1 teaspoon lemon juice or 1 teaspoon vinegar + enough milk to measure 1 cup (stir, let sit 5 minutes) = 1 cup of buttermilk.
Chocolate (semi-sweet): 3 tablespoons semi-sweet chocolate chips = 1 square of semi-sweet chocolate. Also 1 square of unsweetened chocolate can replace 1 square of semi-sweet chocolate.

Chocolate (sweet): 1/3 cup chocolate ships = 2 squares of sweet chocolate.

Chocolate (unsweetened): 3 tablespoons cocoa + 1 tablespoon melted butter or 1 tablespoon melted shortening = 1 square unsweetened chocolate.

Cornstarch: 2 tablespoons all-purpose flour = 1 tablespoon of cornstarch. If used as a thickening agent, 1 tablespoon of tapioca = 1 tablespoon of cornstarch.

Corn Syrup (light): 3/4 cup sugar + 1/4 cup water = 1 cup of light corn syrup

Corn Syrup (dark): 3/4 cup light corn syrup + 1/4 cup molasses = 1 cup dark corn syrup. Also dark corn syrup can be replaced with light corn syrup.

Cracker Crumbs: 1 cup dry bread crumbs = 3/4 cup of cracker crumbs.

Cream (coffee cream): 7/8 cup of milk = 3 tablespoons melted butter = 1 cup of coffee cream.

Cream (half & half): 1 tablespoon melted butter + 1 cup whole milk = 1 cup half & half.

Cream (heavy or whipping cream): 1/3 cup melted butter + 3/4 cup whole milk = 1 cup heavy cream (mixture can not be whipped).

Cream (sour): 1 cup plain yogurt = 1 cup sour cream.

Flour (cake): 1 cup all-purpose flour - 2 tablespoons = 1 cup of cake flour.

Flour (self-rising) 1 cup all-purpose flour + 1/4 teaspoon salt + 1 ½ teaspoons baking powder = 1 cup self-rising flour.

Flour (replacement because of allergy): 1 cup corn flour, or 1 cup rye flour, or 3/4 cup coarse cornmeal, or 5/8 cup potato flour, or 1 ½ cups ground rolled oats, or 7/8 cup rice flour = 1 cup all-purpose flour. Replacement flours can not be used to make bread, as they do not have the gluten to make bread rise.

Garlic: 1/8 teaspoon garlic powder = 1 garlic clove.

Garlic salt: 1/8 teaspoon garlic powder + 7/8 teaspoon salt = 1 teaspoon garlic salt.

Honey: 1 to 1 1/4 cup sugar + 1/4 cup water = 1 cup of honey.

Lemon Juice: 1/4 teaspoon cider vinegar = 1 teaspoon of lemon juice.

Lemon Peel (zest): ½ teaspoon lemon extract = 1 teaspoon lemon peel.

Milk (sour): 1 teaspoon lemon juice or 1 teaspoon vinegar + enough milk to make 1 cup (stir, let set for 5 minutes) = 1 cup sour milk.

Milk (whole or 4%): 1 cup reconstituted nonfat dry milk mixed according to package directions + 2 teaspoons melted butter = 1 cup of whole milk.

Molasses: 1 cup honey = 1 cup molasses.

Mustard (prepared): ½ teaspoon ground mustard powder + 2 teaspoons vinegar = 1 tablespoon prepared mustard.

Onion (chopped): 1 teaspoon onion powder or 1 tablespoon dried minced onion = 1 small chopped onion.

Sugar: 1 cup packed brown sugar, or 2 cups sifted confectioners powdered sugar, or 1 cup maple syrup + 1/4 cup corn syrup (reduce recipe's liquid by1/4cup), or 1 cup honey (reduce recipe's liquid by 1/4 cup) = 1 cup sugar.

Tapioca: 1 tablespoon all-purpose flour = 2 teaspoons of tapioca.

Tomato Juice: ½ cup tomato sauce + ½ cup water = 1 cup of tomato juice.

Tomato Paste: 1 tablespoon catsup = 1 tablespoon of tomato paste.

Tomato Puree: 2 tablespoons tomato paste + water to make 1 cup = 1 cup of tomato puree.

Tomato Sauce: 3/4 cup tomato paste + 1 cup water = 2cups tomato sauce.

Yeast (cake): 1 1/4 ounce package of dry yeast or 2 teaspoon of active dry yeast = 1 yeast cake.

SUCKER: A type of carp found in fresh water streams. Suckers live and feed on the bottom, and are easy to catch. Suckers can be cooked like any other fish and are best when served with tartar sauce.

SUCCOTASH: An early Native American dish with corn and lima beans cooked separately, then combined.

SUET: The firm fat around animal kidney and loins used as a fat in cooking and in recipes. The British use suet to make pastries and steamed bread puddings. Suet may also be an ingredient in minced meat.

Activity

MAKE A SUET BIRD FEEDER

Certain birds eat protein in the form of insects and worms. In the winter, they can't get insects so we can help them with suet. Save the grease from frying hamburger. When it cools, save only the white part. Place the thick, white grease onto an aluminum pie pan. The kind you can throw away is best so you can keep the feed on it when you put it outside. Stir bird seed into the grease until it forms a ball. Place the pan out on the snow or ice where the birds can find it. Do not make during warm weather since it will attract ants and other insects and the suet will melt.

SUGAR: These sweet crystals are made from sugar cane and sugar beets. Sweeteners are also made from corn and maple sap, usually in a liquid syrup form. Sugar has only calories and no nutrition values. White granulated sugar is for general use. Superfine sugar (also called powdered sugar) is used for quick dissolving. Confectioner's sugar (also called powdered sugar) is a combination of superfine and corn starch. Brown sugar is granulated sugar combined with molasses, available in light and dark. www.sugar.com

Sugar Facts

Sugar is present in almost every fruit and some vegetables. When looking at the nutritional values of a food or a recipe, it's the carbohydrates that indicate sugar and starches. Sugar is a combination of carbon, hydrogen and oxygen. Raw sugar is not really raw, it just hasn't been fully refined and is no better for you than white sugar.

Types of Sugar

Fructose: An extremely sweet sugar found in fruit and honey. Also known as levulose.
Glucose: Fruit sugar with about one half the sweetness of granulated sugar.
Lactose: A sweet, white, crystalline substance found in milk.
Maltose: A sugar formed by the action of an enzyme on starch. Hence, a starchy food can turn to sugar within the body.

Sucrose: Sugar obtained from sugar cane and sugar beets. Sugar beets have a white root and can be shaped like a beet or a carrot.

SUGAR FROM CANE TO CANDY

5000 BC: South Sea Islanders discover and enjoy wild sugar cane.

3000 BC: Sugar cane, along with certain spices, came to **India** by traders from the South Sea Islands. India's wet climate made sugar cane easy to grow. Indian farmers pressed sugar juices from the end for sweetening.

700 BC: Arab traders supply **Persia and the Mediterranean** lands with sugar from India. Arab chemists improved the refining process.

800 BC: Talented Persian cooks made **marzipan**, probably the world's oldest candy that is still made today. Marzipan was used as much for decorating foods as for eating.

100 BC: Sugar and spices sold East to West, thanks to safe travel in the **Roman Empire**. Sugar was introduced into Sicily by the Arabs, where they established a thriving industry until the 13th century. The Arabs had several sugar factories throughout the Middle East.

900 AD: Spanish and French farmers learn to grow sugar cane in their warm, southern regions.

1200: European Crusaders marched from France and England to capture the Holy Land from the Arabs. They did not take the Holy Land but **Crusaders** brought home a world of sugar and spices and the scientific knowledge of how to use them.

1400: Venetians import vast quantities of sugar from Arabia and refine it even more. They sold it in conical loaves to the rich all over Europe. Candy making began in apothecary shops. Pharmacists used sugar to mask the taste of bitter remedies. The first hard candies were probably cough drops.

1500: Sugar remains valuable as gold. Spanish explorers introduced sugar cane to **the New World** where it could be cultivated abundantly in the islands.

1600: Sugar production flourishes in the New World and makes sugar **available to the common people** all over Europe.

1650: Lemonade invented in Paris as sugar and lemons become affordable. First London chocolate drink shop opens.

1700: English Parliament opens the slave trade to British merchants whose Trading will become a triangular route as they carry New England rum to African slavers in exchange for slaves to sell in the West Indies and then return to New England with West Indies sugar and molasses to make more rum. Sugar is **now in worldwide demand** for tea, coffee, and cocoa and cooking.

1775: British heavy taxation of sugar, molasses, and tea goads colonists into War for American Independence. Americans find their own way of refining sugar.

1800: Sugar cane grown in **Louisiana;** sugar production adds to the growing slave trade in America .

1900: Milton **Hershey** makes chocolate candy bars cheap enough for everyone in America.

SUGAR SUBSTITUTES

Aspartame: Is made from two amino acids, is low in calories, and is 200 times sweeter than sugar. It will lose its sweetness when heated, but with care can be added successfully at the end of the recipe process.
Acesulfame-k: About 200 times sweeter than sugar, it contains no calories, and can be used in baking.
Saccharin: Made from petroleum and about 300 times sweeter than sugar. A teaspoon has about one eighth of a calorie. Usually bitter when heated.
Splenda: A no-calorie sweetener made from sugar for cooking and baking.

SUGAR APPLE: From tropical American, a small tree produces large, heart-shaped, segmented, fruit that is creamy white and sweet enough to eat fresh or make into ice cream.

SUGAR BEET: An herb in the same family as the garden beet. The sugar beet is a source of about two-fifths of the world's supply of sugar. Unlike sugar cane, sugar beets grow in a cooler climate with a mean temperature of 70 degrees. The sugar beet looks like a white carrot.

SUGAR CANE: An herb in the grass family that is cultivated in tropical and subtropical countries throughout the world. The grass grows to a height of 8 to 20 feet at time of harvest. The cane is cut near the surface, stripped of its leaves, then ground, which extracts the juice. Sugar is made from this juice. See SUGAR.

SUGAR PALM: See BLACK SUGAR PALM.

SUGARPLUM: A small, round piece of candy.

SUGAR SNAP PEAS: These tasty peas are eaten pod and all when the pod walls are thick, sweet and juicy, and when the seeds are fully developed and round in the pods. Since they are more heat tolerant than snow peas, they are harvested well into the warmer summer months. Fresh sugar snap peas are great for dipping. Or, pull off the strings and sauté them in a little butter until they turn dark green (also great with a little fresh ginger and soy sauce). Steam them as you would string beans. Fresh sugar snap peas are available most of the summer months, or frozen the year round.

SUMAC BARK: A rust colored herb from the Middle East with a tangy flavor used in Arab recipes. Rich in tannins, it is also used in tanning leather.

SUNCHOKES are native to Canada. They look like a knobby potato and taste like an artichoke heart. **See** JERUSALEM ARTICHOKES. www.frieda.com

SUNDAE: A dessert made with ice cream, sauce toppings, fruit, nuts, and/or whipped cream. There is no set single recipe A sundae only takes your imagination. Sundaes were once served only on Sundays, which is how they got their name. Now available any day of the week.

SUNFISH: A large group of fresh water fish that include bluegills, calico bass, and crappies. They are good fighters and make a good game fish for fishermen. Sunfish are generally not available in fish markets. Sunfish can be panfried or broiled. Sunfish are prized for their taste, but watch out for bones. **Nutrition facts** 3 ounces: 75 calories, 6 calories from fat, .6g total fat (1%), zero saturated fa, 57mg cholesterol (19%), 68.1mg sodium (3%), zero carbohydrates and fiber, 16g protein (33%), 43 IU vitamin A (1%), 1mg vitamin C (1%), 68mg calcium (7%) and 1mg iron (5%).

SUNFLOWER SEEDS: The sunflower plant produces large, edible nutlike seeds. The outer black shell has to be removed to reveal a grey "nut" the size of a rice kernel. The tall annual plant comes from Mexico and Peru. Sunflower seeds are available fresh, unhulled and hulled, and roasted salted or unsalted. Most sunflowers seeds are raised for bird food.

Fresh hulled sunflower seeds can be used as a grain to make a pilaf and served as a vegetable side dish. To dry roast, spread unhulled seeds on a cookie sheet and roast in a 325°F oven for about five minutes. Or they can be lightly browned in a skillet over low heat, shake the pan often to prevent scorching. Roasted sunflower seeds are great snacks, can be added to breakfast cereals, made into trail mixes, and used as bacon bits substitute.

Fresh, unhulled sunflower seeds can be used for sprouts and are ready in about three days when the sprouts are about one-half inch long. Eat raw or in stir-fries. Sunflower seeds have a nutty flavor, lots of potassium and protein. The seeds also produce a rich, healthful **sunflower oil** for cooking and salad dressings. **Nutrition facts** ½ cup: 410 calories, 299 calories from fat, 35.7g total fat (55%), 3.7g saturated fat (19%), zero cholesterol and sodium, 13.5g carbohydrates (5%), 7.6g fiber (30%), 16.4g protein (33%), 36 IU vitamin A (1%), 1mg vitamin C (2%), 84mg calcium (8%), 4.9mg iron (27%).

Activity: Plant a row of sunflower seeds for your own eating or feed them to the birds next winter.

SURIMI: Best known as imitation seafood, usually made with a mild white fish such as pollock and flavored with crab, lobster, or shrimp, then molded into crab legs, lobster chunks, and shrimp shapes, also available shredded. Surimi can be added to stir-fry recipes, pasta, salads, made into cakes, and sauces.

SURINAM CHERRY: See FLORIDA CHERRY.

SUSHI: A Japanese recipe made with vinegar-seasoned rice rolled around raw fish and wrapped in seaweed. Americanized versions include vegetables along with raw and cooked fish, shellfish, fish roe, and condiments.

SUSHI SECRETS

Sushi, a Japanese finger food, usually made with raw fish, vinegar rice and wrapped in seaweed. Yuck! Doesn't raw fish have harmful bacteria? True, some of the fish is raw, and true it can have bacteria, even parasites. But don't worry, most sushi is made safe, or those who make it won't stay in business very long. Sushi has been around in one form or another since the 7th century. In the beginning, most ingredients were fermented as a preservative. Present day sushi, with raw fish, has been made for more than 100 years in Japan. It came to California not too many years ago, and these tasty morsels are fast gaining appreciation across America. As to the fish, it may be raw, more likely pickled, cooked or smoked. The raw fish is first selected for freshness, flavor, texture and color. Second, the raw fish is frozen at four degrees below zero, a temperature below what your home refrigerator freezer can attain. This deep freeze kills all parasites and bacteria. Most of the raw fish used is tuna, salmon or flounder.

SWEETBREADS: Are the pancreas and thymus glands of a young calf or lamb (boiled with lemon juice). Once precooked, the sweetbreads can be broiled or breaded and sauteed. Sweetbreads should be white when you buy them and soaked for an hour in cold water before cooking. Considered a great delicacy in some cultures, they are sold only in specialty butcher shops.

SWEET CICELY: Both the leaves and seeds are eaten. The leaves of this herb are added to salads and stews, and have a anise flavor. The seeds are eaten fresh as a snack, added to fruit salads and mixed fruit cocktail.

SWEET CUP: See CONCH APPLE.

SWEET GUM: Native to North American, sweet gum trees grow from Connecticut west to southeast Missouri and eastern Texas, and southward through Mexico and into Central America. The Aztecs used sweet gum as a flavoring for tobacco. When dried, sweet gum is called "storax" and used as an expectorant and antiseptic. The food industry uses sweet gum for a flavoring.

SWEETMARY: See COSTMARY.

SWEETMEAT: A highly sweetened delicacy, such as candy, cake, or preserved fruits.

SWEET ONION: No bite, no tears, that's a sweet onion. Sweet onions are low in sulfur content, about half that of an ordinary yellow onion, and contains about ninety percent water. The soil they are grown in results in a sweet onion, especially in a mild climate. Sweet onions are best eaten raw, but can be used for cooking in most recipes. **Nutrition facts** ½ cup: 26 calories, zero fats, 12.8mg sodium (1%), 5.9g carbohydrates (2%), 2.1g fiber (8%), 1.5g protein (3%), 308 IU vitamin A (6%), 15mg vitamin C (25%), 58mg calcium (6%), and 1.2mg iron (7%). See VIDALIA ONIONS. www.wallawalla.com; www.vidaliaonion.com.

SWEET POTATO: Don't confuse the sweet potato with the yam. They are two different species. However, they can be interchanged in recipes. The sweet potato originated in tropical America and was cultivated by the Native Americans long before the Europeans arrived. Most sweet potatoes have an orange flesh. However, there is a white variety. Sweet potatoes can be sweet, though some are no sweeter than an Irish potato. Sweet potatoes come in all shapes and sizes, long and slender to round, beet-sized. Sweet potatoes are available fresh year round, canned, and frozen. Best when baked, but can be boiled in their skins, peeled, then mashed. To roast, peel and parboil for about ten minutes, then roast with meat for about an hour before serving. Sweet potatoes can be made into a soup, candied, added to pancake batter, puddings, and pies. See YAMS. **Nutrition facts** ½ cup serving: 68 calories, zero fat and sodium, 15.8g carbohydrates (5%), 2g fiber (8%) 1.1g protein (2%), 13041 IU vitamin A (261%), 15mg vitamin C (25%), 14mg calcium (1%), .4mg iron (2%), and 133mg potassium. www.nesweetpotatoes.com

THE SWEET POTATO

The American scientist George Washington Carver created 118 products and numerous recipes from the sweet potato. Sweet potatoes contain high amounts of carbohydrates and vitamins A and C. They are available fresh, canned, frozen or dried. Sweet potatoes are used for animal feed, alcohol, and starch.

The flesh and skin of sweet potatoes vary in color from purple to white. The most common flesh colors are orange and yellow. Some sweet potatoes, such as Porto Rico and jewel varieties, have moist flesh. Others, including the Jersey and Triumph varieties, have dry flesh. Sweet potato plants are commonly grown from roots placed in moist, warm, sandy soil or sawdust in green houses or hotbeds. About four to six weeks before planting time, the roots produce sprouts called slips. The slips are cut from the roots and transplanted to fields. In tropical regions, the plants are grown from vine cuttings rather than from slips.

In tropical areas where frost is not a problem, sweet potatoes may remain in the soil for as long as 7 to 12 months. In colder regions, however, sweet potato crops are harvested in the early fall, before the first killing frost. Immediately after harvesting, the potatoes are cured (partially dried) and stored at temperatures from 55 to 66 degrees (13 to 16 C). Curing and storing the roots help keep them in good condition for marketing during the winter and spring.

If you think you don't like sweet potatoes because you've only had them candied, try baking one with the skin on. Shed the skin and eat with salt and pepper exactly like a white potato.

How to Start a Sweet Potato Vine

Take one small sweet potato, and cut it in half-- across, not lengthwise. Insert a toothpick about halfway down on each side. Take a glass jar or plastic container and fill it about 2/3 full of water. Place the sweet potato in the glass so the tooth picks rest on the edge of the top, holding the potato half out of the water. The pretty vine grows quickly. When the potato gets roots, it can be planted in a flowerpot like any houseplant. --*Bernice Erickson*

SWEETSOP: Sometimes known as sugar apples, this sweet pulpy fruit came from the American tropics. The custard-like flesh is similar to the cherimoya and has many black seeds. Can be eaten raw, better used in desserts. They are grown in southern Florida and California and are available in mid-summer to early winter in specialty food stores.

SWISS CHARD: See CHARD. www.frieda.com

SWISS CHEESE: Known as *emmentaler* cheese in Switzerland, this cheese is also made in the United States. It has a mild, flavor, is light yellow in color, has holes when cured, and is made from whole milk. **Nutrition facts** ½ cup: 213 calories, 141 calories from fat, 15.6g total fat (24%), 10.1g saturated fat (50%), 52mg cholesterol (17%), 147.4mg sodium (6%), 1.5g carbohydrates (1%), zero fiber, 16.1g protein (32%), 479 IU vitamin A (10%), zero vitamin C, 545mg calcium (54%) and .1mg iron (1%) www.kraft.com.

SWORDFISH: This salt water fish is found in temperate and tropical waters round the world. It has a sword-like upper jaw. The swordfish has strong muscles, making it one of the best game fishes. Swordfish are also fished commercially and available fresh in fish markets from early summer to mid-fall, and frozen the year round. The flesh is red and a good source for protein and vitamin A. Swordfish steaks can be sautéd, broiled, and baked. **Nutrition facts** 3 ounces: 103 calories, 32 calories from fat, 3.4g total fat (5%), 9.5g saturated fat (5%), 33.2mg cholesterol (11%), 76.5mg sodium (3%), zero carbohydrates and fiber, 16.9g protein (34%), 101 IU vitamin A (2%), 1mg vitamin C (1%), zero calcium and .7mg iron (4%).

SYLLABUB: It is wine or hard cider put into cream.   The wine turns the cream to a soft curd. The name comes from Champagne country of Sill or Silli and the "bub" is an English slang for any bubbly drink. Spellings vary over the centuries from about 1600 to now. Sometimes egg whites are added, but this is not a true syllabub. A similar drink is called a "posset," a 15th century drink for invalids made by putting wine or ale into hot milk. The milk curdles and it can be spiced to improve the flavor.

SYNTHETIC FOOD: Generally, synthetic foods are foods made from other foods to look like the original food. Examples: bacon made from soybeans, hamburger made from mushrooms, juice from a powder, cream made from non-dairy products, sugar and salt substitutes, milk made from rice, decaffeinated coffee, and ice cream made from seaweed. Always read the label when purchasing synthetic foods, as generally they do not contain the nutritional qualities of the "real" food. To top it off, many of these fake foods are cooked in a microwave with fake heat. See PLASTIC FOOD.

SYRUP: Early day syrups were made from corn and sugar cane. These syrups were available in bulk at the corner grocer and were ladled out to consumers. Maple syrup at that time was too expensive for the average consumer, hence maple and cane syrups were combined, of which Log Cabin Syrup was one of the first such name brand blends. www.spices-and-seasonings.com

COMMERCIALLY MADE SYRUPS

■ **Cane Syrup**: This syrup is made from sugar cane. The juice is extracted from the cane, then boiled down to a syrup by evaporation. Pure cane syrup has nothing added or nothing extracted, and while it isn't as   concentrated as molasses, it has more total sugars than molasses.
■ **Corn Syrup**: This syrup is made from cornstarch in two grades: light and dark. The light corn syrup has been clarified and decolorized, while the dark has not and has a stronger flavor. Corn syrup contains glucose mixed with dextrine and maltose.
■ **Fruit Syrups**: Fruit and berry juices, such as blueberries, are blended with corn and/or cane syrup.
■ **Honey**: The only known natural sweetener that needs no additional refining or processing to be utilized. Its flavor is attributable to the floral source from which the honey bees gather nectar.
■ **Maple Syrup**: Pure maple syrup is made from the sap of maple trees. The sap is boiled down to the syrup stage. Further boiling produces maple butter and maple sugar. Maple syrup is also blended with corn and/or syrup and is usually labeled as "maple flavored" syrup.
■ **Molasses**: A heavy-bodied liquid derived from sugar cane and is available in a number of grades from a light to a very dark called blackstrap. Some molasses contains sulphur dioxide and is used to artificially bleach and clarify the liquid.
■ **Sorghum**: A tall grass resembling corn. Its sweet juice from the tall stalks is boiled down into syrup. Sorghum syrup is still popular in the southern United States where it is used in place of molasses.

HOME-MADE SYRUPS

You can make a variety of syrups at home. Here are two examples:
■ **Brown Sugar Syrup**: Made with equal amounts of brown sugar and liquid boiled for several minutes. Liquid can be water or apple juice. A little cornstarch can be added as a thickener.
■ **Simple Sugar Syrup**: Made with two parts of sugar with one part of water that is boiled for about 10 minutes without stirring. An essence, such as almond, lemon, maple, orange, or vanilla extracts can be added to the slightly cooled syrup.

In 1911 a heavy freeze hit the southern Louisiana sugar cane crop. One farmer, C.S. Steen had a crop of 600 tons of frozen cane and no way to get it to the sugar refinery in time before it spoiled. He purchased a small mill from a local hardware store and ground what cane he thought was acceptable. That produced three barrels of putrid, thick, sour syrup.

Not dismayed, Steen planted more sugar cane. With the cooperation of the elements, he ground his cane crop, producing a very appetizing product. When he wasn't able to meet the supply from his own cane fields, he purchased from neighboring farmers who normally sold to the sugar mills. By the time of his death in 1936, his mill was processing about 10,000 tons of cane into syrup annually.

Today the mill is still under the guidance of the Steen family. They extract the juice from the cane which is cooked in large rectangular pans. It boils only on one end, forcing the impurities to flow toward the cool end in the form of a scum that is skimmed. The juice then drains through fine screens which further clarifies the liquid. The juice is then cooked down in the evaporation stage until it reaches the right temperature and consistency. The taste is similar to a very light molasses and makes an excellent syrup or can be used as an ingredient in recipes. The finished product is available throughout the United States.

Tt

TABASCO: The brand name for America's hottest sauce made from chili peppers marinated in vinegar and salt. Tabasco peppers are a small, yellow member of the Capsicum family. The company has been in business in Avery Island, Louisiana since 1868. www.tabasco.com

TABLE MANNERS: :

TABLE MANNERS

Many books have been written about table manners: Basically, the rules are concerned with:
- Which fork to use for what (appetizer, salad, dinner, and dessert forks);
- How to cut with a knife (in Europe use your right hand to cut and eat with a fork in your left hand, in America use your right hand to both cut and eat);
- What can be eaten with your hands (finger foods, small meats with a bone in, fried chicken, pizza, corn on the cob, artichokes, and sandwiches,) and,
- What not to eat with your hands (spaghetti, gelatin salads and ice cream, unless its in a cone).
- Do not pick your teeth with the tip of a knife at the table (or with anything else);
- Do not wipe your eating utensils on the table cloth unless instructed to do so;
- Do not cut up all of your food at one time, lest you appear to be in a rush, but only as you intend to eat it; and do not eat it in a rush.
- Never eat the whole meal with a spoon.
- At a party, when the host leaves the table, consider the meal finished.
- For proper etiquette, serve the dessert in another room (the way it use to be).

SHAKER TABLE MANNERS FOR CHILDREN

First in the morning when you rise,
Give thanks to God, who well supplies
Our various wants, and gives us food,
Wholesome, nutritious, sweet and good.
Then to some proper place repair,
To wash your hands and face with care;
And never the table once disgrace
With dirty hands or dirty face.

When at the table you sit down,
Sit straight and trim, nor laugh or frown.
Of bread then take a decent piece,
Nor splash about with fat and grease;
But cut your meat both neat and square,
And take of both an equal share.
Also of bones you'll take your due,
For bones and meat together grew.

Potatoes, cabbage, turnip, beet,
And every kind of thing you eat,
Must neatly on your plate be laid.
Before you eat with pliant blade:
Nor ever - 'tis an awkward matter,
To eat or sip out of the platter.

When bread or pie you cut or break,
Touch only what you mean to take.
And have no prints of fingers seen
On that that's left - nay, if they're clean.

Clean your knife; don't lick it, pray!
It is a nasty, shameful way - ,
But wipe it on a piece of bread,
Which snugly by your plate is laid.
Thus clean your knife, before you pass
It into plum or apple sas,
Or butter, which you must cut nice,
Both square and true as polished dice.

And always take your equal share
Of coarse as well as luscious fare.

Don't pick your teeth, or ears or nose,
Nor scratch your head,
Nor tonk your toes;
Nor belch nor sniff, nor jest nor pun,
Nor have the least of play or fun.
If you're obliged to cough or sneeze,
Your handkerchief you'll quickly seize,
And timely shun the foul disgrace
Of splattering either food or face.

And when you've finished your repast
Clean plate, knife, fork - then at the last
Upon your plate lay knife and fork,
And pile your bones of beef and pork:
But if no plate, you may as well
Lay knife and fork both parallel.
Pick up your crumbs and where you eat
Keep all things decent, clean and neat.

Then rise and kneel in thankfulness
To Him who does your portion bless;
Then straightly from the table walk,
Nor stop to handle things and talk.
If we mean never to offend
To every gift we must attend,
Respecting meetings, work or food,
And doing all things as we should.
Thus joy and comfort we shall find,
Love, quietness, and peace of mind.
Pure heavenly Union will increase,
And every evil work will cease.
– Shaker Advice to Children C. 1800
www.ShakerVillageKY.org   www.ShakerMuseumandLibrary.org

TABOULI SALAD: (TABBOULEH) (ta-boo-lee) A mixture of bulgur wheat, parsley, olive oil, mint, salt, onion, garlic, herbs, spices, and chopped tomato served cold on a bed of lettuce. The Lebanese gave the world tabbouleh.

TACO: A folded corn tortilla filled with meat or poultry, cheese, lettuce, tomato, and salsa. The corn tortilla shell can be deep fat fried crisp or warmed a little and served soft. A taco is a sandwich, sometimes called the "Mexican hamburger."

Bread can be made in a number of ways, baked, grilled, and fried in deep hot fat. Many Native Americans make what is commonly called "Indian Fried Bread." This by no means means that it's a Native American creation. Or is it? It's possible that a tribe in prehistoric America made the first fried doughnuts, since archaeologists have unearthed petrified fried cakes in the Southwest. Various forms of deep fried corn cakes are found throughout America and it is believed our Native Americans slowly replaced the corn with wheat as the new settlers migrated across America.

The Native Americans also make tacos with the fried bread. There are two basic versions, both you can make at home. In one, the bread is deep fried, then topped with beans, meat, cheese, tomatoes, lettuce and a sauce. In the second way, the dough is filled with meat, cheese, and/or beans, made like a turnover and then deep fat fried. They can also be filled with apples and other fruit for an after dinner sweet.

TAFFY: An old-fashioned candy that is made by pulling the sugar mixture apart to make it light and fluffy. The pulling can be done with hands, more fun with two kids, or by machine. Taffy and toffee once meant the same thing. The English preferred to say toffee. That may have come from "tafia" a cheap rum apparently used as the flavoring. Originally, molasses flavored, taffy now comes in all kinds of flavors. www.fralingers.com. Recipes www.spices-and-seasonings.com

TAHINI is a sesame seed paste popular in Mediterranean cuisine.

TAMALE: No, this is not just Mexican food. Tamales are made throughout the Americas. In America's southwest and Mexico, most tamales are meat or poultry filled in cornmeal *masa* and wrapped in a corn husk. In Central America the tamale is wrapped in a banana leaf. Both the corn husk and banana leaves give the two tamales different flavors. In Texas the tamales are small, about an inch in diameter and about five inches long. In California they are much larger, almost double the size. In Cuba, the filling is not in the middle, but thoroughly mixed with the *masa*. In Central America, sugar is added to the *masa*, and the tamales are filled with meat or poultry, or fruit and served at breakfast.

THE TAMALE FESTIVAL

During the first week of December, in Indio, California, there is a two-day festival celebrating the holiday season. The festival honors the tamale that was originated by the Aztecs prior to the arrival of the Spanish conquistadors. Tamales are highlighted, since they are traditionally served on Christmas Eve in Mexico and Central America. There are more than 50 different kinds of tamales featured. Each is filled with highly spiced, finely chopped pork, chicken, beef or vegetables, wrapped in cornmeal dough called *masa*. Many of the tamale cooks also enter their tamales in a contest and are judged for the best tasting and appearance in traditional and gourmet categories. A festival highlight is the cooking demonstration of tamales by famous chefs. Along with all the food comes entertainment by local bands, dances, a fun area for kids called TamaleLand, carnival, parades, and 5K and 10K runs. For more information, write: **Indio Chamber of Commerce,** 82-503 Highway 111, Indio, CA 92201 or phone (800) 44-INDIO or (760) 347-0676.

TAMARA: A combination of spices used in Italian cooking, such as aniseed, fennel seed, cinnamon, cloves, and/or coriander. Tamara can be found in Italian markets.

TAMARIND: A native tree from Africa's upper Nile region, now grown in most tropical areas. It produces edible leaves, flowers, and bean-like pods. Pulp is scraped out of the pods and is used to make beverages, preserves, chutney, curries, and for pickling fish. Tamarind is available in specialty food stores, fresh and frozen. The juice is available as frozen concentrate and canned. As a beverage it does have a mild laxative effect. Tamarind pulp is high in sugar and calcium. Chinese cooks use candied tamarind as a garnish.

TANGELO: A hybrid of the tangerine and grapefruit. The name comes from a combination of "tangerine" and "pomelo" (another name for grapefruit). There are two varieties, "*minneola*" and "*orlando*." Minneolas are pear shaped, almost seedless, with thick rind, easy to peel, and quite juicy. The orlando is round and smaller than the minneola but has a more grapefruity tang. Tangelos are eaten fresh and added to salads. **Nutrition facts** per tangelo: 92 calories, zero fats and sodium, 22.9g carbohydrates (8%), 4.7g fiber (18%), 1.8g protein (4%), 400 IU vitamin A (8%), 104mg vitamin C (173%), 78mg calcium (8%), and .2mg iron (1%). www.sunkist.com

TANGERINE: A descendant of the Chinese mandarin orange, tangerines are named after the African city of Tangiers. It was there the Europeans tasted them for the first time. In the Orient, they are still called Mandarins. There are three varieties: clementine, dancy, and kinnow. The **Clementines** are small, seedless, juicy, peel easily, and mostly imported from Spain. **Dancy** are quite seedy with a seet, low acid juice. The peel is so loose it almost falls off. There are a dozen varieties of the dancy tangerine. **Kinnow** has some seeds, a mild flavor and, like all tangerines, peels easily. Tangerines are eaten fresh, added to salads and gelatins, and made into juice. Tangerines are available from December until April, and many a tangerine has found its way into a Christmas stocking. Tangerines are also canned and labeled as mandarin oranges, the family name. **Nutrition facts per** tangerine: 37 calories, zero fats and sodium, 9.4g carbohydrates (3%), 1.9g fiber (8%), .5g protein (1%), 773 IU vitamin A (15%), 26mg vitamin C (43%), 12mg calcium (1%), and zero iron. www.sunkist.com

TANGORS: There are two varieties of this cross between a mandarin and a sweet orange. **Murcott**, better known as "honey tangerines," are seedy, easy to peel, very juicy and high in vitamin C. **Temples** are also know as Royal Mandarins, have some seeds, a pebbly skin that peels easily, and a sweet taste. Tangors are available from early winter to mid-spring.

TANSY: A camphor scented herb with fern-like green leaves and yellow "button" flowers, used for seasoning omelets and sausages. Because large amounts can be poisonous, it is not widely used. Common in the British Isles, tansy flavoring is used to make a traditional English Easter cake. Widely used by monks in the Middle Ages. Once widely used to repel insects and to rid animals of internal parasites. Tansy tea or powder can be applied to swellings and bruises. Tansy is the herb which flavors Irish sausage made of sheep's blood and milk.

TAPIOCA: A food starch made from manioc roots used to thicken pies, puddings, soups, and gravies. True tapioca comes from Guyana, Brazil and the West Indies. Tapioca comes in various sizes from the size of a pearl (also called pearl tapioca) to the size of a grain of sand. The smaller size is used for quick cooking, while pearl tapioca must be soaked for at least an hour and cooked longer. Tapioca is also made into flour and is available at most health food stores.

TARO: This tuber, with elephant-sized, heart-shaped leaves, symbolizes everlasting life and historically holds an honored distinction in many tropical countries. It is believed that taro originated in ancient Egypt. Being from Egypt, this prized plant was considered legendary by the Hawaiians. During the Hawaiian monarchy period, the taro leaf design motif was restricted to royalty for it symbolized the origin of the Hawaiian people. Taro has a high starch content and is used much like potatoes. Easy to digest, the roots can be boiled, fried, or baked.

Taro is an ingredient added to cakes, breads, muffins, pancakes, puddings, stews, casseroles and salads. When sliced thin and deep fried, they make excellent chips. The leaves are also eaten when young and are known as "Hawaiian spinach." In the Pacific islands, taro root is used to make poi. A variety of Taro, dasheens, are grown in the southern United States and are eaten as a substitute for potatoes. Taro has a wide variety of **medicinal uses** from treating insect bites and bee strings. It has the ability to stop a wound from bleeding, and is believed to even reduce fever. **The Terra Chips** company makes tasty chips from taro, yuca, batata, parsnips, and sweet potatoes in one bag, sold at health food stores. The taro chip is the beige one with purple streaks through it. **Nutrition facts** ½ cup: 56 calories, zero fats and sodium, 13.8g carbohydrates (5%), 2.1g fiber (9%), .8g protein (2%), zero vitamin A, 2mg vitamin C (4%), 22mg calcium (2%), and .3mg iron (2%).

TARRAGON: This all-around herb has a slightly anise flavor, is available fresh and dried. Its flavor gives a lift to poultry, fish, meats, salads, soups, sauces, salad dressings, and egg recipes. Tarragon originated in Central Asia. Tarragon may come from Latin and Greek word for dragon. The plant was supposed to cure venomous bites and stings from animals. It grows all over the Northern hemisphere. For home canning and pickling, no home should be without tarragon. Tarragon vinegar is easily made by steeping fresh leaves (just before flowering) in a good white wine vinegar for two weeks. www.herbco.com

TART: (noun) A small pastry shell filled a variety of ingredients. Sweet tarts can be filled with puddling-like cream, fresh fruit, fruit preserves, nuts, and/or whipped cream and served as a dessert. Nonsweet tarts are filled with meat, poultry, fish, cheese, eggs, and/or vegetables and usually served as an appetizer. (adjective) "Tart taste" means having a sharp or slightly sour taste.

TARTARE: It comes from an early way of cooking meats covered in bread crumbs, grilled and served with sauce. Somehow it came to mean the sauce or a raw meat dish. Tartare is a French word and refers to one of the early Turco-Mongol peoples of Central Asia, the Tartars. Tartars were fierce nomadic tribes. How this connects with the grilled or raw meat dish we are not sure but we can imagine the Tartars used grills and perhaps had a taste for rare meat.

TARTAR SAUCE: A mayonnaise with boiled eggs, onion, and chives served to accompany fish.

TASTE: On your tongue are taste buds that can give you the sensation if a food is bitter, salty, sour or sweet. The smell of food also adds to and enhances the taste of food. In cooking, taste is the most important element. No matter how good it looks, if the food doesn't taste good, it's not going to be eaten or enjoyed. Always taste before you serve any dish.

TATSOI: Also known as *tah tsai*, is easy to grow and is a standard ingredient in baby salad called mesciun. Baby salad is so named because all the salad leaves are tiny and young. Tatsoi has shiny, deep green, spoon-shaped leaves which grow in a flat rosette. Very hardy, it can be used even when lightly snow covered. Tatsoi can be added to stir-fry recipes, and can be sautéed in butter or olive oil and served with chicken.

TEA: The tea plant is native to China and now grown throughout the Orient and parts of Africa. There are three basic teas: black, green, and oolong. Tea is a member of the *camellia* genus. Black tea is the most popular, followed by almost a dozen varieties such as Ceylon, Earl Grey (a blend), and Sumatra. The best teas are grown above 6500 feet in the mountains in hot, humid regions with mild winters. For more history go to www.tetley.com

Black teas are labeled pekoe, orange pekoe, fanning, and other names that refer to the size of the leaf. Fanning, for example, are small broken leaves used in tea bags since the small leaves brew faster than the larger leaves. Orange pekoe is made from only the top two newest leaves on the bush. The **Green teas** comes from Japan and have a delicate light flavor. Green teas have added antioxidants to fight diseases. **Oolong** teas, such as Formosa tea is semi-fermented, and **jasmine** tea is scented with white jasmine flowers. There is also **white** tea made when tea leaves are dried and steamed briefly without rolling or oxidization, making it the least processed of all teas. Its red-orange brew is delicate, smooth, and soothing. Tea is available as loose leaves, in tea bags and as instant tea in jars and vacuum-sealed foil packages. Teas can be flavored with citrus, sweetened with sugar or sugar substitutes, and can be served hot or cold.

Tea type beverages are also made from other leaves and herbs, such as mint. Specialty teas of many kinds can be found around the world. Dim Sum Herb tea is made by adding pure chrysanthemum blossoms to black tea. Lichee black tea contains the pure juice of the lichee fruit. *—Foojoy Tea Company*, PO Box 7848, Alhambra, CA 91802   www.tetley.com

To Make Perfect Tea

There are many methods of making tea. However, the only approved method, especially by the English, has to be brewed in a china pot, never in a tea cup. The water must be boiling, the pot must have a lid, and the tea must steep for at least five minutes. Some English add milk to their tea, some will add a slice of lemon and/or a little sugar. Iced tea is the favored drink of the American South, brewed bold, sweetened and with a slice of lemon or a leaf of mint. Whole volumes have been written on tea and tea history.

Tea Grown in America

The only tea grown in America is about 20 miles off Charleston, South Carolina on Wadmalow Island at Charleston Tea Plantation. Tea does not improve with age, so if you want fresh tea, order from **Charleston Tea Plantation,** 6617, Maybank Hwy, Wadmalo Island, SC 29487 or call 1-800-443-5987.

TEAPOT TRIVIA

Anna, Duchess of Bedford (1788 - 1861) instituted the custom of afternoon tea around 1840 in England. Then, as now in British countries, the upper class ate dinner around 8:00 in the evening. For an afternoon pick-me-up, Anna would slip into her boudoir for tea and something light to eat. When invited to join her, friends so enjoyed the tea party that it became all the rage and lasted from that day to this.

When sweetening for tea became available in the 17th century, people needed sugar bowls and little tongs to handle the sugar lumps, which were chipped off a sugar block or "loaf." In 1877 sugar merchant Henry Tate introduced sugar in neat precut cubes. In the 1920s fashionable hostesses decorated their sugar cubes with tiny frosting flowers.

In the 1770s, with the coming of world trade by way of sailing ships, Europe became entranced with Chinese and Japanese arts. Europeans had to have beautiful tea services to go with their imported Chinese tea.

A **gawain** is a traditional Chinese "covered cup"--a small, decorated china bowl with lid and saucer. In the Oriental tea service, the cup is warmed and the tea brewed right in the cup.

High society loved the **tea dance**, an afternoon social occasion from the 1900s until about 1940. In the 1920s and '30s, everyone needed a dance frock for the 5:00 gatherings to take tea and flirt through the waltz, the foxtrot, and the charleston. The coming of World War II brought an end to the carefree social whirl inspired by teatime.

It was at a tea dance in London that the tango migrated from Buenos Aries to fashionable European salons. After that, the naughty tango, very risque for the time, helped usher in the Roaring Twenties.

The first **"Cosy" teapot** was invented in 1922 at Abram Allwar Ltd. Of Bristol, England. The new design eliminated the spout, added a built in strainer and patented the dripless "Cosy" pot lid. The new design allowed drips from the pouring spout in the lid to run back into the pot.

Tea napkins are the hostess's fanciest dainty napkins reserved for tea guests. Originally used at the court of Louis XIV when coffee and chocolate were served, tea napkins were just part of the perfect hostess's collection of fine linen cloths and doilies reserved for company.

Happy birthday teas delighted Victorian children. They had everyday tea with plain cakes but for birthdays the fancy tea things came out. Victorian cooks gave the birthday teas the best frostings and jams.

Children have from the 1700s had **tiny tea sets** for their dollhouses and similar miniatures for display and collecting.

"Tea for two" originally came from a London tea shop. J. Lyon's shop motto was "a good pot of tea for tuppence." Tuppence was two cents. Later "Tea for Two" became the name of a romantic song.

Tea in Morroco had been an elaborate tradition since the 1850s when it was introduced by British merchants bringing their Chinese green tea. The Moroccans favor sweet mint tea. Every household shows off its lovely silver tea service with ornate glasses, Gunpowder tea, and fresh spearmint leaves.

Gunpowder tea is so called because it is rolled into tiny pellets that pop when hit by boiling water.

Tea "artists" like to pour tea from the pot held at least a foot above the glass to circulate the aroma.

Jane Austen ordered her tea from Twinings, her china from Wedgewood.

Josiah **Wedgewood** perfected Japanware in 1776 and by 1795 hostesses demanded it on both sides of the Atlantic. Wedgewood's china production made Europeans less dependent on china from the Orient.

All that tea drinking inspired cooks to bake wonderful breads and cakes such as Bath buns, Sally Lunns, brioche, and gingerbread. *–information from The Collectible Teapot and Tea Calendar for 2000 by Joni Miller, Workman Publishing.* www.workmanweb.com

TEABERRY: A popular ice cream flavor in the North East United States. Most people know it as teaberry gum. See WINTERGREEN

TEFF BERRIES: A cereal grass that makes a great morning cereal with a light creamy-sticky -crunchy texture and a molasses flavor. Flavor from a naturally occurring yeast that ferments when moist. Can be lightly toasted before cooking for a richer flavor. Teff berries are also made into a gluten free flour used in quick breads, pancakes and waffles. For a leavened bread, use five parts of wheat flour to one part of teff. Use teff flour to thicken stews, soups and sauces. Teff flour has a sweet malty flavor. Teff is rich in calcium, protein, and twice as much iron as wheat and barley.

TEMPLE ORANGES: See TANGORS

TEQUILA: (te-keela) A Mexican liquor made from the century plant.

TERRINE: A loose term with many meanings. Generally it is a food prepared and served in the same dish. A large bowl with a matching lid is called a terrine.

TETRAZYGIA: A shrub found in south Florida with round, blue, 3-inch berries that grow in clusters and are eaten fresh.

TETRAZZINI: An Italian main meal recipe cooked with poultry and pasta (usually spaghetti) in a rich cream sauce.

THANKSGIVING:

AMERICA'S FIRST THANKSGIVING
by Richard S. Calhoun

In **1598**, colonizer Don Juan de Oñate in Santa Barbara, Mexico, put together a group of 400 brave Spaniards (130 of them had families travel with them), 83 wagons and carts, and 7,000 head of livestock (cattle, sheep, goats, plus burros and horses) and formed a 4-mile long procession as they headed north across the unmapped **Chihuahua Desert**. Oñate choose this route instead of the well traveled Rio Conchos route, because he figured it would save months of travel time. This route closely follows Mexico's Route 45 through present day Chihuahua.

While this route did save them months of travel, on the four-month trip they experienced many difficulties. At one point in their travels, it rained for seven days and the wagons sank in the mud up to the frames. This event was followed by a drought, and then they ran out of food and were forced to eat roots, berries, and weeds, and to drink water from occasional water holes and from cactus. The group broke up into several parties and while they went searching for water, the main group prayed for rain, and their prayers were answered, it rained. They also found it slow going through the sand dunes south of Samalayuca, just 30 miles south of the Rio Grande River.

Shortly before reaching the Rio Grande, the horses could smell the water and raced to drink. Two horses drowned in the swift current, while other horses drank until their bellies burst. The people also drank too much water and lay down on the ground with swollen stomachs. Oñate named this spot for San Elizario, "Elysian Fields of Happiness," a place of supreme delight on April 20, 1598. For 10 days they swam in the deep cool waters, rested in the shade of the cottonwood trees, hunted, fished, and ate as they had not eaten in months.

They crossed the river and went west to present day Socorro where they met the Pueblo people. The Pueblo name , which means "town," was given to the Native Americans by the Spaniards. Here Oñate ordered everyone to put on their best clothes and gather for a thanksgiving feast on April 30, 1598, in celebration of the 350 mile expedition across the Chihuahua desert. The Spaniards roasted geese, duck, and fish over an open bonfire. The horticulturist Pueblos brought to the feast some of

509

their dried winter provisions, corn, beans, squash, along with some wild foods (mesquite beans, screw beans, yucca, agave, and the fruit of the saguaro cactus). They made a bread called "*piki*" from cornmeal mixed with water and wood-ash lye, patted into a thin paste and baked on hot stone slabs. These thin crisp wafers are similar to tortillas.

After the feast, Oñate gave a speech, beginning, "In the name of the most Holy Trinity, and of the eternal Unity, Deity and Majesty, God the Father, the Son, and the Holy Ghost . . ." and closed by taking possession of the land for King Phillip II of Spain. The soldiers fired their weapons and the colonists gave a throaty shout. Oñate's day of thanks was held 23 years before the Pilgrim's festivities in Plymouth, Massachusetts. This **Texas event is still celebrated on the last Sunday in April by El Paso history buffs**. Local El Pasoans, dressed in full costume, re-enact the event on the grassy slopes of the **Chamizal National Memorial**. Some of the food that Oñate's group enjoyed is still served at this annual event. For the 400th anniversary (1998) the event was moved to Socorro where lots of fun and games, entertainment, and refreshments were offered.

THICKEN: In culinary terms, it means to make a sauce or a gravy denser in consistency. Thickening can be done with flour, cornstarch, tapioca, grated potato, egg yolks, or bread crumbs.

THYME: (time)   Kids may be surprised to know that thyme is one of the herbs that gives spaghetti and pizza sauce that special flavor. Garden varieties of this Eurasian herb all have one thing in common: the pungent and fragrant sweet leaves can be added to almost any meat, fish, poultry or vegetable recipe. Thyme is available fresh and dried. You may find thyme in strange places. Look for it on labels of toothpaste, mouthwashes, gargles, deodorants and cosmetics. Herbalists have long used thyme in compounds to treat lung disease and stomach disorders. www.herbco.com

TI-ES FRUIT: See CANISTEL

TIGER NUT is an ancient tuber. We know because it has been found in 6000-year-old Egyptian tombs. Not widely used around the world, it was always in Spain known as *chufa*, where they made tiger nut milk called *horchata*. The brown tiger nut grows like a potato underground. Its taste is like an almond and chestnut. The nut is extremely healthful and nourishing. *Horchata* is also made with melon seeds, pumpkin seeds, and almonds.

TILAPIA: Native to Africa's Nile River, tilapia has recently been introduce to the American market. They are farm grown from Canada to South America. This small fish is similar in size and the mild taste to perch. Some Bible scholars claim it was the fish caught by Peter and Jesus multiplied them, hence some seafood markets sell tilapia as Saint Peter's Fish.

TIMBALE: A small mold for cooking custard desserts, cheese and meats. Timbale foods can be served in the mold or unmolded. Timbales can be made of metal or glass. Edible timbales are made with pastry or pasta. Timbales come in all shapes and sizes. The Scandinavians make their timbales with a heated iron dipped in a pancake-like batter, fried in deep oil, and then filled with creamed mixtures or fruit. See ROSETTE.

TIME: When cooking and marinating food, it must be measured in seconds, minutes, hours, and even days. Most foods require accurate timing, so as not to undercook, overcook or burn food. This is why it is important to use the electric timer on the back of your stove or buy one that rings a warning bell. It's too easy to become distracted and forget. Also timing takes the guesswork and worry out of cooking. Cooking is a science, so accurate timing is a must.

TINT: A way to color food with natural or artificial food colors. The juice of a beet can color food red naturally. Artificial food coloring can be purchased to use in tinting. It only takes a drop at a time. Tinting is used mostly in sweets, such as frostings and candies. Some natural coloring is added to pasta, such as spinach juice. (My mother's secret ingredient for turning her giblet gravy an inviting yellow instead of "gravy grey" is a drop of yellow food coloring. *–LU*

TOAD TREE: It has small, irregular-shaped fruits eaten fresh.

TOAD IN THE HOLE: A British breakfast dish in which the sausage link peeps out from the surrounding eggs and toast.

TOAST: (verb) A method of browning bread by heat, such as in an electric toaster or under a broiler. Melba toast is bread cut very thin, then baked in a slow oven until crisp and a light brown. The phase, "to toast," is to honor a person or an event by the drinking of a glass of good cheer. Usually glasses are clinked and the toast master says something like, "We drink to the good health and long life of the bride and groom." The toast comes from the Anglo-Saxon in the 5th century. Their custom was to seal a pledge with a drink between friends. *Waes-heil*, (be well), in Old English. One person would say *"Waes-heil,"* to which the other would respond "drink-heil" (drink well). Often pieces of bread floated on the top of the drink. The drink and the custom became called a toast. See WASSAIL.

TODDY: A hot or cold alcoholic drink, usually with sugar and spices.

TOFFEE: A candy cooked to the hard-crack stage, so that it is both brittle and chewy. The basic ingredients are molasses, brown sugar and butter. www.brown-haley.com

TOFU: One of the first soy products was tofu. Tofu was developed by the Chinese about 200 BC. Tofu is made by adding mineral salt to soy milk, which then solidifies into a white, semi-soft cake. Tofu is added to soups, to main courses, even desserts. Tofu, which is tasteless, takes on the flavor of the other ingredients with it. See SOY and article EATING HEALTHY WITH SOY.

TOMATILLOS: The green-fleshed fruit looks like a large, green cherry tomato, except for the green paper-thin, outer husk hugging it. Tomatillos have a sweet-tart flavor that makes them exceptionally good for salsa.

TOMATOES:

"TOMMY'S TOES"

by Karon G. Booth

Have you ever eaten "Tommy's Toes?" Were they good? Did you eat them cooked or raw? Probably you ate them both ways and you didn't have to remove the toenail. As a matter of fact, lots of people eat "Tommy's Toes" all the time. Tommy Toes is an old Victorian word for tomatoes. Who is this Tommy? His real name is *Tomatl*, who migrated from the Incas in the Andean Mountains into Mexico about 700 AD with the Aztecs before Columbus came to call. With the arrival of the visitors from Europe, Tamatl moved in with the Catholic Priests and went home with them to southern Europe in the 1500s.

Tomatl was adored as the *pomodoro* or "golden apple" by the Italians. Oh how they delighted in turning him into sauce to toss with their spaghetti, mashing him into paste to smear on their pizza and cooking him with layers of cheese between lasagna pasta. The romantic French proclaimed him *pomme d'amour*, the "apple of love." Never had passions swelled so over the candlelit tables of France. The Germans called him "the Apple of Paradise." His slightly acid taste, mixed with the sweet sugar of love, turned supper time into a festival of earthly delights.

Alas, then something happened! *Tomatl* journeyed into the cold lands of the North. There he was arrested for murder. Yes! Pleading innocent, he railed at his two cousins for bearing false witness against him. What a cruel fate. Just because he shared some neurotoxin solanine in his leaves and roots, like Belladonna and Nightshade, he was accused of causing his victims to die in convulsions. That is how his poisonous kinfolks had killed Europeans for centuries. Rather than face a life sentence as an ornamental flower, *Tomatl* fled and returned to America.

At Home in American Gardens

There he became a proud plant in Thomas Jefferson's garden at Monticello, Virginia in 1781. It had taken him some 300 years to travel from South American to North America. But then, he too the long way around. Once *Tomatl* became an American citizen, he revealed his true identity. In the land that proclaimed the right to be yourself, he announced that he was not a vegetable and indeed had never been one. He was a fruit. Yes, a fruit, a berry to be exact. He's made up of segments full of tiny seeds floating in a pulp crammed full of vitamins A and C, as well as some minerals.

There was no stopping Tommy now. No place in the world took to him like his fellow citizens. Americans raise some 67-million short tons (61-million metric tons) of him and his siblings every year, with California leading the way with 13,754,000,000 pounds (6,239,000,000 kilograms) a year. And his volume keeps increasing. Not satisfied with just plain ole Tommy, he found himself bred into more than 4,000 varieties. Sometimes he was a girl as Big Girl or Early Girl Imp, sometimes he was a boy called Better Boy or Lemon Boy. Then sometimes he just had a name all to his own; Starshot, Earliroughe, Glamour, and Beefsteak.

There was no end to the tricks Tommy could pull either. From a cherry-size tomato, Sunray, to a whopping three-pounder, fittingly named the Ponderosa, he could gain or lose weight. Shape shifting was just as easy. On one vine he can be a long rangy LaRoma or become Fantastic, the globe-shaped wonder of the garden. Red, orange, yellow, pink, even green and purple, he can change his color as well.

Was that a yellow pepper plant? No, it was Tommy in disguise. If you don't like his acidic nature, try a type that is low acid. He accommodates your needs if you want juice, beefsteak style slices, or just bite size treats for salads. "Toe," flower, fruit, berry - delicious or poisonous - how many things can one tomato be? The next time you dip your french fry into scarlet catsup just remember all the happy confusion one little plant has caused.

You can add to the fun by having your friends guess what berry they are eating when they pass the bottle of catsup. Once they have eaten a bite, you can tell them how they have all been poisoned, or so people once thought. There is no end to the adventures that you and Tommy can have. Vine ripened tomatoes have the best flavor. However, most tomatoes arrive at the supermarket unripe. Tomatoes will ripen in a few days at room temperature. Never refrigerate a tomato, even ripened ones. They will lose their flavor and become mushy. Eat and enjoy as quickly as possible. Never put a tomato in direct sunlight, since light will destroy the ripening process. Tomato ripening can be hastened but put them in a brown paper bag. As the tomato ripens, it emits ethylene gas, and this gas speeds up the ripening process.

The tomato is a fruit, but eaten as a vegetable. The structure that develops from the plant's ovary after fertilization occurs as a berry, since it is fleshy and contains seeds. Most tomatoes are red in color, come in a variety of sizes from the size of an olive to almost grapefruit size, and in color of green and yellow. Tomatoes are available the year round from both California and Florida, and during the summer months everywhere. Tomatoes can be boiled, stewed, broiled, baked, and microwaved. Green tomatoes can be fried, with or without breading. As to the seeds, most chefs remove them. However, the seeds have significant nutitional value and generally will not effect the recipe. **Nutrition facts** ½ cup: 19 calories, zero fat and sodium, 4.2g carbohydrates (1%), 1g fiber (4%), .8g protein (2%), 561 IU vitamin A (11%), 17mg vitamin C (29%), zero calcium, and .4mg iron (2%). www.tomato.org; www.floridatomatoes.org; www.jerseytomato.com

A SUN WARMED TOMATO

A tomato
still warm from the sun
is best if eaten
immediately.
So I do.
Warm juice
drips from my chin
as I close my eyes
and enjoy
my tomato.
– *Elizabeth Giles*

HOW TO PEEL

The easiest way to skin a tomato is to dip it briefly in boiling water, about 30 seconds. Then immediately into cold water, and then you can slide the skin right off. When slicing (and to retain the juice) it is better to slice lengthwise, rather then crosswise.

USES

Tomatoes are also available canned as whole, stewed, paste, and pickled. Tomatoes are also canned and made into soup, sauces, preserves, and bottled as catsup and chili sauce. Dehydrated and sun dried tomatoes are also available. Tomatoes can be frozen, but must be stewed when thawed. Tomatoes are eaten fresh, out of hand like an apple, cut up for salads, stuffed with tuna or chicken salad, marinated with red onion rings in Italian salad dressing, and made into fresh salsa peppers and onions. A fresh medium size tomato has about 35 calories, provides 40% of the daily allowance of vitamin C and 20% of vitamin A, and low in fat and sodium.

TOMATOES IN HISTORY

THE JUDGE TAKES A BITE OUT OF DEATH
by Josephine Jaquett

Everyone knew that the tomato was poisonous. Tomatoes were grown in America's gardens as ornamentals, but few dared to eat them. Historians credit Judge Colonel Robert G. Johnson of Salem, New Jersey as the one responsible for the public acceptance of the tomato, at least in that part of New Jersey. To prove his point, Colonel Johnson made an announcement that he planned to eat a tomato on the court house steps.

In July 1820, a large crowd gathered, complete with first aid equipment, a doctor, and a cleared path to the hospital. The judge walked out of the courthouse. On the top step, he removed a bright red tomato out of a bushel basket. The crowd gasped in horror as he took that first bite. When he finished the tomato, he took out another from the basket and continued eating until the basket was empty. Colonel Johnson was never worried that he would die. He knew that many Europeans were enjoying them, as well as South Americans. He also had an 1812 cookbook with a recipe for "love-apple (tomato) catsup."

Tomatoes had been sold in Philadelphia years prior to this event, but generally only purchased by the French and Italians. Even in the late 1700s, Thomas Jefferson, who made a hobby of growing exotic foods, planted and ate them at Montecello. With this research, the colonel had no fear. After his lunch of a bushel basket of tomatoes, the judge didn't "bite-the-dust" as everyone thought he would. He returned to the court house and continued to hear cases, just as he had done that morning. Because of Colonel Johnson, the tomato eventually became a major crop in New Jersey. Thirty tomato canning factories appeared by 1900, including the H.J. Heinz catsup factory in the Colonel's home town of Salem.

The recipe for **love-apple catsup** in the 1812 book Archives of Useful Knowledge, was as follows:

"Slice the apple thin and over every layer
sprinkle a little salt; cover them and let
them stand for 24 hours; then beat them well
and simmer them half an hour in a bell-metal
kettle; add mace and allspice. When cold,
add two cloves of raw challots cut small and
half a gill of brandy to each bottle, which
must be corked tight and kept in a cool place."

THOSE TINY, TINY TOMATOES

Have you wondered what the original tomato was like before agriculturists went to work trying to perfect them, make them larger, make them sweeter, and making them juicier? In Europe, the consumer demands fine flavor and high quality, hence breeders are hard at work to meet these standards. Not surprising, many new breeds are coming from the Old World, as well as Asia, and now growers are making them smaller.

Currant Tomatoes: This tomato is actually its own species, related to, but different from every other tomato variety sold. Currant tomatoes are not far removed from their wild forebears, have a delectable half-tart, half-sweet flavor and a remarkable degree of vigor. Currant tomatoes are available both red and yellow.

Green Grape Tomatoes: Not truly grape size, but not a whole lot bigger either, similar to a small prune plum. Green grape tomatoes ripen from a pale apple green to a pleasing golden yellow, lightly suffused with green. The flavor is sweet in a bright, cherry tomato way and is balanced with a nice, slightly acid after taste that makes them a great salad tomato.

Ruby Pearl Tomatoes: From China comes a true grape-sized tomato, about the size of a thumbnail or an olive. Keep a bowl of ruby pearl tomatoes handy; they make perfect snacks to pop in your mouth. – *Shepherd's Garden Seeds*

TOMATO TREE: See TREE TOMATOES

TONGUE: A tough cut of meat from the mouth of a cow, pig, or lamb. Tongue must be cooked slow and long to become tender. Tongues are available at most meat markets, either fresh, corned, pickled, or smoked. Often used in potted meat spreads.

TOPPING: Any food used to create attractive first layer on other food. Toppings add color, crunch and/or eye appeal. Typical toppings include: preserves, sauces, honey, syrups and whipped cream. On hot food toppings might be bread crumbs or melted cheese or toasted onions. .

TORTE: A rich pastry or layer cake made with eggs and a small amount or no flour, baked in layers, filled with rich creams and fruit fillings spread between the layers. The resulting "stacked" cake is then usually iced and decorated. A German word, *torte,* akin to the word *kuchen,* for cake. *Kuchen* was generally less fancy than *torte.*

TORTILLA: (tore-teeya) A flat, round bread made with corn masa or wheat flour. Originally made by our Native Americans, now made in Mexico and Central America. Tortillas are best served hot, either plain or filled with meat, beans, cheese, salsa, and other ingredients. Tortillas are used to make tacos, burritos, and chips. Flour tortillas can be seasoned with sugar and cinnamon, deep fat fried and eaten like a cookie.

TORTILLA TALES

"Tortilla is the name given to the bread made of corn that nourished the ancient inhabitants of the Americas and is used to this day by their descendants, be they poor or well to do . . ." said Nuevo Cocinero Mejicano in 1878. There's much history of the tortilla. One of the most famous events is the arrival of Santa Ana's army at San Antonio's Alamo in 1836. Strange as it may seem, the army had no quartermaster, so it was up to the women camp followers to feed Santa Ana's army. The tortilla got wrapped around any food that was pillaged from farms as they made way north into Texas. The corn tortilla is the basis of Mexican food. It goes back to the Native Americans when they cultivated corn and made their tortillas out of corn masa. The best tortillas come from fresh masa. Masa is corn boiled in lime (to break down some of the indigestible enzymes) and then ground into moist dough. The tortilla can be a meal with chili or beans and rice. Some people use the tortilla as an eating utensil to scoop with. There is no limit to how you can use the tortilla. You can make tacos, either soft or crispy, tortilla soup, enchilades, tostadas, flautas, fajitas, huerfanitos, campesinos, gorditas, quesadillas, chalupas, chimichangas and nachos. It's all up to your imagination. Making a new recipe with tortillas is like a chemistry lesson with ingredients of cheese, chicken, beef, pork, fish, salsa, tomatoes, onions, peppers, and lots of fresh garden vegetables. Some people will not start their meal without a buttered tortilla in one hand and a fork in the other. Today flour tortillas are preferred over corn. Whether made from corn or flour, the tortilla must be served hot - before, during, and after the meal.

Flour tortillas have opened up new recipe ideas from fried bolitas to meat, cheese or fruit filled turnover pies called empanaditas. The tortilla in Mexican cooking is as old as time. In Mexico, in the pueblos, with nothing more than a *molcajete* to grind the chile and tomato and their beans and corn tortillas, the very poor sustain themselves, since that is their daily food. In the United States, the tortilla is a matter of choice. But once you get hooked on the tortilla, you may want one at every meal.

TORTONI: An Italian frozen dessert flavored with wine, rum or other liquor.

TOSS: (verb) Simply it means to mix or combine ingredients. Salad greens are "tossed" with other salad ingredients and dressing.

TOURNEDOS: A very lean filet taken from the tip of the tenderloin. It is usually sautéd in butter or broiled with bacon fat and served on bread with its sauce.

TOURON: (tur-ohn) The name is for a round, layered candy cake (petite four) made from almond paste, royal icing, chopped pistachios and orange zest. See TURRON.

TREACLE: British name for molasses.

TRAIL FOOD:

FOOD ON THE TRAIL

Whether you are going on a day hike, or plan to spend a night or more on the trail, plan carefully. Space and weight are at a premium. Also, many fresh foods just won't make the grade. Dried and dehydrated foods are light weight and take up less space. Some of these foods are on your kitchen shelves, and most can be found at your local supermarket. For some specialty items, visit a nearby camper's store.

Prior to your trip, plan all meals. Keep them simple. Carry only light foods. Pack all foods for that meal in one plastic bag. When cooking, plan one-pot meals. Take a condiment kit with your favorite spices. Always plan for the unexpected, such as bad weather that makes cooking impossible or that might delay your trip home.

BREAKFAST

Your choice of beverage is first on the list. Instant coffee, tea, cocoa, milk, and some juices are available at all supermarkets. There are packaged cereals, instant hot cereals, all providing an easy, nutritious, tasty breakfast. Dried fruit and food leathers are good for breakfast, and also make wonderful snacks.

LUNCH

Instead of taking sliced bread, which doesn't travel well, consider tortillas, pita bread, and prepackaged (not fresh) bagels. For fillings, re-pack peanut butter and jam in small plastic cartons. Jerky, beef sticks, and salami do not need refrigeration. Also there are small cans of tuna, chicken and other meats made into a salad spread which works well with tortilla wraps. Mustard, mayonnaise and ketchup are available in small packages, however, once opened use immediately or discard. Hard cheeses keep well and adds zest to sandwiches.

SNACKS

Make your favorite trail mix with raisins, peanuts, dried fruits, chocolate chips and grains. Granola and "energy" bars also travel well.

DINNER

After hiking, a hot meal is a must. Take along a small camp stove for heating water. Shop for:
- Dried soup mixes and soup-in-a-cup.
- Boil-in-the-bag rice.
- Instant pastas with spaghetti sauce, and other
- Quick cooking dried foods, such as potatoes, vegetables and meats.
- Prepackaged instant sauce mixes available.
- With dehydrated hamburger, taco sauce mix and tortillas, you have a Mexican meal.

Take some jerky, stew sauce mix and when the meat is tender, add some dehydrated potatoes and vegetables for a hardy stew. Some fresh vegetables travel well, such as carrots, zucchini, and cucumbers. Wash them well at home and thoroughly dry them. For dessert consider pound cake, it holds up well. For that sweet tooth, add hot water into flavored gelatin and drink. Meals on the trail won't be like home cooking, but after hiking and fresh air, it's surprising how great they will taste.

TREE TOMATOES:

THE TREE TOMATO
by Pat Smithdorff

 The tree tomato is a Peruvian shrub not related to the tomato family. The tree tomato can be grown in tropical and subtropical countries and produces red or yellow egg-shaped fruit. The fruit is also called *tamarillo*. My doctor friend, Dave Crozier, a former teacher and botanist, tells me the tree tomato is about the size of a kiwi fruit, but with a smooth, rather hard skin, and tapered in shape, not as square as a kiwi. It is more maroon than tomato red. Darker streaks mark the segments like the segments of a tomato. The flavor is tart, the flesh is orangish, with black seeds. Once establish, the plant bears fruit for five to seven months and will continue to produce fruit year after year in a warm climate. In cold climates, the plant must be brought inside or it will die. Tree tomatoes are eaten fresh, stewed, made into a sauce and jam.

TRIFLE: An English dessert made with liquor-soaked sponge cake topped with custard cream. Trifle can also be soaked with fruit juice and topped with whipped cream. A trifle means something of little importance. Its hard to see how anyone could dismiss the traditional English cake and cream dessert as a mere trifle. A trifle is made by arranging layers of dessert in a clear bowl. The result of layering such goodies as sponge cake, pudding, cherries (or blueberries), and nuts is more spectacular than trifling. Maybe it's called a trifle because anyone can do it. Get yourself a big clear bowl. Alternate layers of your favorite sponge cake (in chunks)with slivered almonds or pecans, glazed cherries, peach slices, or blueberries (or all three) and whipped cream.

TRIPE: There are three types of inner lining of the beef stomach: **honeycomb** (the most desirable), **pocket** and **plain**. Tripe is available fresh, canned, and pickled. Fresh tripe is precooked prior to purchase and must be cooked again before eating. Tripe can be eaten as a meat boiled, sautéd, or broiled. In some countries it's used as a bag for sausage stuffings.

TRITICALE: A hybrid of rye and wheat with a superior balance of amino acids and a nearly complete protein. It is milder in flavor than rye, however, stronger than wheat. It is available in some health food stores as whole berries and flour.

TRANS FATTY ACIDS:

At one time, manufacturers of food products thought trans fatty acids were not harmful. Now it is believed they are just as dangerous as saturated fats, because trans fatty acids will raise the bad LDL cholesterol levels in your blood vessels. At the same time, these trans fatty acids will lower the good HDL cholesterol.

Walter Willet from the Harvard School of Public Health says, **"Trans fatty acid is a secret killer."** Food labels state how much saturated fat is in a product, but it is anybody's guess how much trans fat you are eating." So how do you know if a product has trans fatty acids? Read the ingredients on the food label. If it states "partially hydrogenated vegetable oils," then the product has trans fatty acids. A partially hydrogenated oil, is a liquid vegetable oil that has been hydrogenated and has turned the liquid into a soft solid. A good example is shortening. Shortening is basically 100% partially hydrogenated oil. It doesn't make any difference if the oils comes from corn, soybeans or canola, it's still bad for your health.

What products contain trans fat? Most margarines (some exceptions are Feischmann's, Promise and Smart Balance in tubs), most peanut butters, packaged cookies and crackers, bakery cakes and those little cake rolls, refrigerated ready to bake biscuits, doughnuts, pie crust, packaged frosting, microwave popcorn and the list goes on and on. The problem, the label doesn't state how much of these trans fats are in a product, since some foods contain only slightly hydrogenated oils and maybe that little bit is not really enough to harm you.

If the margarine label lists partially hydrogenated oil as one if the first few ingredients, chances are you are eating artificial butter favored shortening. Yuck!

Many food packages are labeled "no cholesterol," but at the same time the product is loaded with trans fats. Today, most fast food restaurants use trans fatty acid oils to deep fry potatoes. A serving of these fried potatoes might contain more harmful trans and saturated fats than the saturated fats from a quarter pound hamburger. Some of the fast food restaurants are converting to 100% liquid vegetable oil or so they say, but how do you know for sure? You don't! Many families have replaced butter with margarine because of the belief that vegetable fats are better for you than animal fats. It has been said that the body doesn't know the difference between these two fats. Let's compare the fats.

One tablespoon of butter:	One tablespoon of margarine:
101 calories	100 calories
11.4g total fat	11.3g total fat
7.1 saturated fat	2g saturated fat
3.3g monounsaturated fat	5.5g monounsaturated fat

.4 polyunsaturated fat	3.4 polyunsaturated fat
Zero trans fatty acids	1g to 3g trans fatty acids
30.7mg cholesteral	Zero cholesteral

A closer look at fats and cholesterol:
- Saturated fats will raise LDL cholesterol levels.
- Monounsaturated fats will lower LDL cholesterol levels.
- Polyunsaturated fats will lower both LDL and HDL cholesterol levels.

In addition, different vegetable oils have varied affects on cholesterol. Oils that are rich in monounsaturated fats, such as olive and canola oils tend to lower LDL without affecting the HDL levels. Oils that are rich in polyunsaturated fats, such as corn and safflower oils, tend to lower both HDL and LDL levels. And once again, trans fatty acid raise the bad LDL cholesterol and lower the good HDL cholesterol. Now that you know some of the facts, it is up to you to read the food labels and decide what is best for you.

TROPICAL ALMOND: From tropical Asia with 2-inch flat fruits, only the oily seeds are eaten raw. The bark and roots are used for tanning.

TROPICAL FOODS: Tropical foods from all over the world are too numerous to include in a general food dictionary but this dictionary contains many tropical foods by their English names. A great many of our most popular foods have originally come from tropical forests before being transplanted for growing around the world. Since the hot, wet conditions of the tropical lands make excellent growing conditions, many fruit and vegetable growers still prefer to farm there year round, whenever possible.

TROPICAL GARDEN YOU CAN GROW
by Billie Jean Hepp

Tropical plants are beautiful, and many can be grown in indoor pots at home. Many can be transplanted in southern California, south Florida, and along the southern Rio Grande River in Texas where prolonged frost doesn't occur. Your will need for each plant:

Paper towels
Garden pots
Potting soil
Seeds

Papaya Tree

At first I didn't think those little black seeds from a papaya would make an interesting plant. When they first sprout, they might look like weeds, but once the secondary leaves come out, you know you have a papaya plant.

To get Papaya seeds:

1. Cut open a papaya you have purchased at the supermarket, and remove the seeds.
2. Pick out the larger seeds, place them on a paper towel for 3 days to allow them to dry a bit.
3. When they look shriveled and almost dry, plant three seeds 1 inch deep in the potting soil.
4. Water well.
5. In about 2 weeks they will sprout. See also GRAPEFRUIT TREE, MANGO TREE, and PINEAPPLE PLANT.

TROUT: A member of the salmon family, most varieties are found in fresh water rivers and lakes. Some varieties such as the rainbow and steeled will enter the ocean, but will return to spawn. Trout is a favorite of sports fishermen because they are great fighters and can be hard to catch. The flesh is lean and delicate. Trout can be fried, baked, and broiled. **Nutrition facts** 3 ounces: 126 calories, 53 calories from fat, 5.7g total fat (9%), 1g saturated fat (5%), 49.4mg cholesterol (17%), 44.3mg sodium (2%), zero carbohydrates and fiber, 17.7g protein (35%), 50 IU vitamin A (1%), zero vitamin C, 37mg calcium (4%), and 1.3mg iron (7%).

TRUFFLE: The truffle is a fungus that grows underground and has an incomparable flavor that is only appreciated by gourmets, since the average person will probably never eat one. They are not found fresh in the United States, but are available canned in some gourmet food stores and are very expensive. Since no part of the fungus is above ground, they are hard to find. Most truffles grow under oak trees. However, there is a variety that is found the deserts. Europeans have trained dogs and pigs to sniff them out. Once found, the animals will dig them out, but you must move quickly once found, as the animals like truffles as much as people do. In Europe, turkeys are stuffed with truffles, chopped and added to a sauce, cut into fancy shapes as decoration on meat platters. Canned truffles are added to salads, diced and mixed with boiled potatoes, and as a dressing for wild game and fowl. Never mix herbs with truffles, as the truffle will lost their flavor. Truffles are low in calories and have almost no nutritional values. Recently a truffle oil has become available.

TRUSS: Prior to cooking poultry, the wings and legs are tied tightly to the body with string. This keeps the bird well balanced during cooking, especially when roasting on a turning rod.

TRY OUT: To heat fat until the fat melts and separates from the solid tissue. This fat is then used in cooking like lard, shortening, and butter.

TUNA: A salt-water fish that is found in almost all of the oceans of Asia, Africa and the America's. Tuna is a member of the mackerel family and there are a number of varieties with albacore the most used for canning. There are also bluefin, bonito, skipjack and yellowfin. Tuna is available fresh, frozen, and canned. Canned tuna is generally packed in water or oil and sometimes seasoned. The Japanese also dehydrate it and add it to their *dashi* soup. Fresh tuna can be fried, broiled, baked, and poached. Most recipe books use canned tuna. However, fresh tuna can be substituted by cooking it first. Fresh tuna is best when soaked in brine for an hour, then poached to be used in canned tuna recipes. **Nutrition facts** 3 ounces, fresh: 123 calories, 40 calories from fat, 4.2g total fat (7%), 1.1g saturated fat (6%), 32.3mg cholesterol (11%), 33.2mg sodium (2%), zero carbohydrates and fiber, 19.9g protein (40%), 1657 IU vitamin A (37%), zero vitamin C, 7mg calcium (1%), and .9mg iron (5%).

TURBOT: This delicate and delicious flatfish is found in European salt waters. A member of the flounder family, it looks like a halibut with an average weight of ten pounds. Turbot is sometimes available frozen in seafood markets. **Nutrition facts** 3 ounces; 81 calories, 24 calories from fat, 2.5g total fat (4%), .7g saturated fat (3%), 40.9mg cholesterol (14%), 127.6mg sodium (6%), zero carbohydrates and fiber, 13.7g protein (28%), zero vitamin A, 2mg vitamin C (3%), 16mg calcium (2%), and .3mg iron (2%).

TURKEY: This wild, native American bird is found from Central America north to Canada. Today, wild turkeys can still be seen close to wooded urban areas. Many states still have hunting season for wild game, including turkey. Our Native Americans domesticated the turkey prior to the European settler's arrival. It is believed that turkey was the main course served by the friendly Native Americans to the Pilgrims when they landed in America. Ben Franklin wanted the turkey to be the national bird, not the eagle. If he had his way, what would we eat for Thanksgiving? Surely it would not be the eagle.

Commercially raised turkeys are available fresh, frozen, smoked, and in parts (legs, wings, breasts). Ground turkey meat can be cooked like hamburger. Young turkey parts can be fried, broiled or baked. Older turkeys are best roasted. The modern commercial turkey is raised to be white, large-breasted, plump but not fat, and ready in the millions for the holiday season from Thanksgiving through Christmas, but still plentiful all year long. Smoked turkey has the taste and aroma of ham but is leaner. **Nutrition facts** 3 ounces, **white meat**: 120 calories, 51 calories from fat, 5.4g total fat (9%), 1.5g saturated fat (8%), 49.8mg cholesterol (17%), 45.2mg sodium (2%), zero carbohydrates and fiber, 16.8g protein (34%), zero vitamins A and C, 40mg calcium (1%), .9mg iron (5%). **Nutrition facts** 3 ounces, **dark meat**: 126 calories, 70 calories from fat, 7.5g total fat (11%), 2.2g saturated fat (11%), 61.3mg cholesterol (3%), 60.4mg sodium (3%), zero carbohydrates and fiber, 16.1g protein (32%), zero vitamins A and C, 15mg calcium (2%), and 1.5mg iron (8%). www.butterball.com

TURKISH DELIGHT: Readers of C.S. Lewis' *The Lion, the Witch, and the Wardrobe* will remember Turkish delight as the special temptation offered to children by the witch. So many children today are not generally familiar with the treat so common in England 100 years ago and no description is given in Lewis's book. Turkish delight comes from the Middle East. It is a jelled, rubbery confection made from sugar and honey, thickened with cornstarch. The flavor comes from almond or pistachio nuts. The usually pink cubes are dusted with powdered sugar. -- *LU*

"I have made turkish delight with gelatin and maple extract. Now Jell-O has a recipe on some boxes for making rubbery Jell-O very similar to turkish delight."–*RSC*

TURMERIC: This tropical herb root is related to ginger and is an important spice in the making of curry, so popular in Indian and Asian cooking. The flavor is a bit bitter. It has a mild aroma and when dried and ground is yellow in color. Turmeric is used for both taste and color in prepared mustard, sauces, relishes and curries. The extract of turmeric is called *curcumin* and used to color certain dairy products. Turmeric can be added to vegetables, eggs, fish, poultry, and rice. Ground turmeric is available is most supermarkets and fresh in herb specialty shops. Turmeric is often used as a saffron substitute in recipes (saffron being the most expensive spice). www.herbco.com

TURNIP: There are several varieties of this European cold weather root vegetable. Both leaves and root are eaten. Turnips have a white flesh, and some have light purple tops. Sometimes called the "purple potato." Turnips are available fresh the year round, with the peak during the winter months. Turnips should feel firm and not spongy when grasped. Generally, smaller turnips are less inclined to be bitter or pithy. Many like turnips raw, with or without dip. Turnips are most often boiled, then seasoned and served with butter or margarine. Turnips are also added to stews and baked in casseroles. **Turnip "sauerkraut"** is made the same way as cabbage sauerkraut. The roots have some vitamin C, while the leaves are an excellent source of vitamins A and C, and a good source for calcium and iron. Both the roots and leaves are low in calories. **Nutrition facts** ½ cup: 18 calories, zero fats, 43.6mg sodium (2%), 4.1g carbohydrates (1%), 1.2g fiber (5%), .6g protein (1%), zero vitamin A, 14mg vitamin C (23%), 20mg calcium (2%), and .2mg iron (1%).

TURNIP GREENS: The turnip leaves that grow above ground on this root vegetable are referred to as "greens." The young, tender leaves are picked fresh for salad.. Avoid dry or wilted leaves. Wash thoroughly and blot dry. Like all mustard and other greens, turnip greens can be cooked in a little water until tender. Boiled greens are a Southern speciality, often cooked with hog jowl (bacon) and served with a touch of vinegar. The nutritious remaining liquid is called "pot likker" and eaten with corn bread or used as a vegetable broth for cooking other dishes. Turnip greens are available canned or frozen. **Nutrition facts** ½ cup: 7 calories, zero fats and sodium, 1.6g protein (1%), 2090 IU vitamin A (42%), 16mg vitamin C (28%), 52mg calcium (5%) and .3mg iron (2%). www.allencanning.com .

TURNOVER: To make, a round pastry crust is filled on one side with plain or spiced meat, poultry, sweetened fruit (pie filling) or a puddling-like cream. The pastry is then folded over, sealed, and baked or deep fat fried. Meat and poultry filled turnovers are served hot, sometimes with a sauce or gravy. Fruit-filled turnovers can be served hot or cold and usually eaten as finger food. Also called "fried pies" or "pasties" in some parts of the country.

TURRÓN: (TOURON) In Catalonia, Spain, Pablo Turróns is given credit for inventing the almond nougat called turrón. Using the only available foodstuffs when the town of Barcelona was under siege around 1700, he made survival rations. War didn't seem so bad when townspeople dined on almond and honey candy. Actually, the Arabs and Jews were making a similar candy long before under the name of *halvo*. Turrón is still a favorite candy in Spain, especially at Christmas.

True turrón is almond and honey whipped with egg white, but modern versions boast of hazelnuts and pine nuts, coconut, candied fruit and even chocolate. It reminds us of Bit O'Honey.

TURTLE: You won't find it in the meat market, but in many parts of American, snapping turtle is still hunted and eaten. A snapper hunter in Pennsylvania recently found one at 65 pounds, which he donated to a wildlife museum. Turtle steak tastes like veal. Turtle eggs are also eaten, mostly boiled. While some turtles may be on the endangered list, snappers are not. You can still find snapper turtle soup on supermarket shelves in some places. *"While living in Jackson, New Jersey we dug a pond and stocked it with fish. When we caught a large turtle, we called a friend who told us how to prepare and cook it. We still have the shell. The stew was delicious."–Kathy Grinley.*

TURTLE BEANS: See BLACK BEANS www.frieda.com

TUTTI-FRUTTI: In Italy it means "all the fruits." Tutti-frutti ice cream contains chopped candied fruits. Tutti-trutti bombe is strawberry ice cream covering a lemon ice cream containing diced fruit.

Uu

UDO: A perennial Japanese plant having leaves and young shoots that are cooked and eaten as a vegetable.

UGLI (UNIQ) FRUIT: In Jamaica, the mandarin orange was crossed with grapefruit and the result was an ugly-looking citrus fruit. Its "ugly" discolored peel, hides tangy, incredibly juicy segments. Ugli fruit is available in most city supermarkets and specialty fruit displays, especially around the winter holidays Ugli is a trademark name. Ugli proves that "ugly is only skin deep" so never judge a fruit by its cover. It's what's inside that counts. In East India, they have a different tree by the same name, which they call *bilva*. It bears medium sized oranges with a leathery skin. They cook these in ashes to make them easier to peel, then they eat them with sugar and make jam. www.frieda.com

UNCOLA: A name used by the 7-Up brand soft drink to distinguish its product from the "cola" drinks such as Coke and Pepsi. The Uncola contains no cola, but is flavored by citrus juices.

UNSALTED: Means foods such as butter, margarine and peanut butter have no added salt.

UNSIFTED: Unsifted flour is packed tightly so you might measure more than the recipe calls for. Recipes will generally be specific about whether to use sifted or un-sifted flour. Sifting makes the flour lighter when measured. Sift a small amount into a bowl and then measure.

UNSWEETENED: On a fruit label, it usually means naturally sweet. Other sweeteners, such as sugar, have not been added. Fruit and juices may be sweet from their own natural sugars. In tea and powdered drink mixes, it generally means "not sweetened at all."

UPSIDE-DOWN CAKE: A cake that is cooked with the topping on the bottom. The cake is turned upside down on a cake plate to be served. Pineapple is the most famous of these cakes, but it can be made with other fruit and berries as well.

UTENSIL: A loose term that applies to pots and pans, cooking spoons and forks, egg beaters, blenders, mixing bowls, colanders, cutting knives, measuring cups and spoons, rolling pin, and other kitchen tools used in preparing and cooking food.

UVALHA: From Brazil and grown in south Florida, this small tree produces medium size, spherical fruit with soft aromatic pulp with one or more large seeds that is used for flavoring drinks. The taste is quite good once you get over the objectionable odor.

Vv

VACHERIN: A dessert cheese similar to Brie, made with whole milk and cream. Vacherin is also the name of a cake made with meringue, usually shaped in a ring and the center filled with fruit and/or ice cream. The name, *vacherin,* comes from both the French and the Swiss.

VACA Y QUESADILLA: (vah-cah kay-sa-dee-ah) Vaca y quesadillas are tortillas filled with cheese and beef. Mexican cooks have many ways of stuffing a tortilla for meals and snacks. Chicken, turkey or ham may be substituted instead of beef. Meatless quesadillas can be made with a tablespoon of cottage cheese or refried beans. *Vaca* means "cow" and *quesadilla* means "cheese cake," and the words have nothing to do with tortilla.

VALENCIA ORANGES are oranges with a thin yellow-orange skin, eaten fresh, and made into juice. Some varieties are hard to peel, and some are seedless or with just a few seeds. Valencias are available from February to November. **Nutrition facts** per orange: 59 calories, 3 calories from fat, .4g total fat (1%), zero saturated fat and sodium, 14.4g carbohydrates (5%), zero fiber, 1.3g protein (3%), 278 IU vitamin A (6%), 59mg vitamin C (98%), 48mg calcium (5%), and .1mg iron (1%),

VANILLA: Believe it or not, the delicate sweetness of vanilla comes from an orchid which has no odor. This tropical plant from Mexico produces a bean pod, and when dried, the pod develops a smell and a taste that almost everyone is familiar with. Most likely it was the Aztecs who first used vanilla. They would grind the vanilla beans with cacao beans to make their chocolate drink. Spanish conquistador, Cortez, discovered its delights and carried it back to Europe. www.spices-and-seasonings.com

Some things are meant to be where they are, or as it is said, "Don't fool with Mother Nature," and the vanilla bean is a case in point. Once the Europeans found the orchid, they transplanted it to other tropical countries. However, the orchid produced no pods. It was found that only Mexican bees can pollinate this plant. Today, these orchids grow in other countries, but the pollination must be done by hand. Mexican vanilla is still the "queen mother" of all.

Vanilla is used in almost every dessert recipe, especially those for baking and ice cream. Pure vanilla is expensive, hence, artificial vanilla is often used. Some flavoring companies combine both the pure and imitation together and it generally can pass for pure vanilla. Some vanilla ice cream makers grind the whole bean in their ice cream. This causes little black specks, and the buyer thinks this is pure vanilla ice cream. The fact is, the natural vanilla does poorly in the cold and is usually reinforced with some of the artificial vanilla. Pure vanilla will lose some of the flavor in baking, whereas artificial vanilla does not. When vanilla is added to fruit, less sugar is required, since vanilla will bring out the sweetness naturally in fruit. Sophisticated chefs even use vanilla in some meat and vegetable dishes.

Activity

It is fun to **make vanilla sugar**. Take a whole bean pod, split it open or break it into little pieces and mix in a cup of powdered sugar. Next day use this sugar to sprinkle on cakes, cookies, breakfast cereal and fruit. Vanilla has the tendency to bring out the natural flavor of foods and beverages. Add a drop or two **in hot tea**. You won't taste the vanilla, but it will bring out the full flavor of the tea. By using a drop or two **in cream or milk** used for your breakfast cereal, you will find that it takes less sugar to make the cereal enjoyable. Add a little vanilla to salad dressing and it will take less dressing for your salad. And yes, by all means, add it to your **hot chocolate** just like Montezuma did centuries ago. Both pure and artificial vanillas are found in supermarkets. Vanilla beans are found in some supermarkets, health food stores, and most specialty food shops.

VANILLIN: The chemical substance that gives vanilla pods their flavor is called vanillin. It can be produced synthetically and is sold widely as a cheaper vanilla. Good cooks always prefer the real thing.

VARIETY MEATS: A broad term referring to the edible organs of animals (heart, liver, kidney, etc.). Also refers to preserved meats, sausages, lunch meats, and meats used in ragout recipes.

VEAL: Often sold as milk-fed beef, veal meat is from young beef under the age of fourteen months that has not been weaned from its mother's milk. Calves that have been weaned, up to the age of one year, are also sold as veal. Veal from the shoulder and the ribs can be roasted or braised, the chops can be panfried, the leg meat is best roasted. Veal "variety meats" include the brains, kidneys, etc.. True veal is generally only available in late winter and early spring. The rest of the year, veal is from older calves. **Nutrition facts**3 ounces: 84 calories, 37 calories from fat, 4g total fat (6%), 1.6g saturated fat (8%), 48.1mg cholesterol (16%), 48.1mg sodium (2%), zero carbohydrates and fiber, 11.4g protein (23%), zero vitamins A and C, 9mg calcium (1%) and .5mg iron (3%).

VEGEMITE: When the Olympics of 2000 were held in Australia, tourists were introduced to a spread Australians are crazy about called Vegemite. It is sold in little jars everywhere in Australia. It's a "yeast extract" (according to Encarta). The taste is said to be salty and bitter.

VEGETABLE: Almost any food coming from a small plant can be called a vegetable. Vegetables can be the roots, the leaves, or the fruit from the blossoms. Some foods are classed as vegetables, such a mushrooms (fungi), beans (legumes), and tomatoes (fruit), because the way they are cooked, and/or the way they are eaten. Vegetables are important to good health, as they contain many vitamins and minerals, and fiber for the digestion system. Vegetables are available fresh during the growing season, canned and frozen the year round. Some vegetables can be dried or dehydrated and others are pickled.

VEGETABLE BRAIN: See AKEE.

VEGETABLE COCKTAIL: A mixture of vegetable juices, such as tomato with carrot and celery juices. An American favorite brand is V-8, a blend of eight vegetable juices. You can make a vegetable cocktail using a blender to liquify your favorite combination of vegetables. In using a blender, you must start with a little water. Best to use a juicer because it separates the pulp from the liquid.

FRESH VEGETABLE COCKTAIL

Take a beet, a couple of carrots, a hand full of spinach and process it through your home juicer, and what do you get? A glass of brown sludge that tastes . . . yuck! What do you do, (a) toss it, (b) hold your nose and gulp it down quick, or (c) look for ways to improve this healthy beverage?

Yes, the correct answer is "C." Many vegetables, especially carrots and spinach, are bitter. Add a natural sweetener, such as an apple and it can improve the over-all flavor. What you need to do is to find the right combination of vegetables and fruits that satisfies you taste buds. Some of the ingredients you should try are sprouts (especially buckwheat and sunflower sprouts), tomatoes, bell peppers, kale, parsley, and cucumbers, to name a few of the more popular vegetables.

Why is it important to drink raw vegetables? There's a belief that when you boil vegetables all the vitamins are cooked out and go into the cooking liquid. Hence, it is far better to drink the cooking liquid and throw out the cooked vegetables. While there might be some truth in that, even cooked vegetables are good for you, especially if they are steamed or baked.

So why the raw vegetables? Raw vegetables not only contain all the vitamins and minerals, but they contain live enzymes, and your body lives on live enzymes. All forms of cooking kills enzymes. Almost all vegetables contain good amounts of vitamins and minerals, especially beets and carrots. Kale is a good source for nutrients, as it is also rich in calcium. Buckwheat sprouts are high in bioflavonoids and sunflower sprouts are a complete protein. Wheat grass is also a popular addition to vegetable drinks, since it is not only high in vitamins and minerals, but has lots of chlorophyll. Chlorophyll provides iron to the body and oxygen to the blood steam. However, wheat grass can not be put through most home juicers, and must be juiced with a meat grinder. If a meat grinder is not available, try a food processor.

It's best to start with one vegetable, then add additional vegetables until you find the right combination of tastes for you. For your first raw vegetable juice cocktail, start with carrots. Even though carrots can be bitter, many are as sweet as sugar. Next add a little spinach, then an apple.

From there, the choice is yours. Your reward will be a healthier you. Try it for breakfast and the high-energy drink will make you feel like running a marathon before school. With that much energy, you can work it off, maybe by mowing the lawn or cleaning your room. But don't forget to add the apple for a sweeter you! Oils can be made from seeds (canola and safflower), vegetables (corn and soy beans), fruit (olives), and nuts (walnut and peanuts). Most are used for sautéing vegetables, blended in salad dressing, and replacing high saturated solid fats in baking.

VEGETABLE OILS: These light, low saturated oils can be made from seeds (canola, sesame, and safflower), vegetables (corn and soy beans), fruit (olives), and nuts (walnut and peanuts). Most are used for sautéing vegetables, blended in salad dressing, and replacing high saturated solid fats in baking.

VEGETABLE SOUP: Although a soup made with one vegetable, such as broccoli soup, could be called a vegetable soup, we generally use "vegetable soup" to mean those made with a variety of vegetables, often including some meat. There are as many recipes for vegetable soups as there are vegetables and cooks.

VEGGIES: Popular short name for vegetables.

VELOUTÉ: a French name for white sauce.

VELVET APPLE: See MABOLO.

VELVET TAMARIND: From southeast Asia, the large tree produces fleshy pods with a black velvety rind and edible sweet pulp. The pulp is eaten fresh.

VENISON: Often called deer meat, venison is also used when referring to moose and elk meat, and all recipes are interchangeable. The flavor of venison depends upon what the animal is eating. The meat is usually on the tough side and should be treated as with other tough cuts of meat by first marinating it, then cooking slowly by roasting with moist heat, such as in a crock pot, dutch oven, or a slow oven. **Nutrition facts** per 3 ounces: 153 calories, 48 calories from fat, 5g total fat (8%), 1.8g saturated fat (9%), 69.8mg cholesterol (23%), 370.9mg sodium (15%), zero carbohydrates and fiber, 25.2g protein (50%), zero vitamins A and C, 11mg alcium (1%) and 5mg iron (28%). See DEER.

VERBENA: This shrub from Argentina is now grown in many mild climates. The leaves have a lemon odor and flavor, and are used as a flavoring for fruit, salads, jellies, some desserts and beverages, and can be used to make tea. Lemon verbena is a great favorite for perfumed oils and soaps too.

VERMICELLI: (ver mi-chelly) Long strings of pasta made thinner than regular spaghetti pasta. Vermicelli can be used in any recipe calling for spaghetti. **Nutrition facts** per ½ cup: 186 calories, zero fats and sodium, 41.1g carbohydrates (14%), zero fiber, 4.6g protein (9%), zero vitamins A and C, 12mg calcium (1%) and 1.1g iron (6%).

VERMOUTH: (ver mooth) A wine fortified with herbs and spices, used for cooking, cocktails, and served plain over ice. There are both sweet and dry varieties.

VICHYSSOISE: (vishy-swas) An elegant chilled soup made with potatoes, leeks, and lots of heavy cream.

VIDALIA ONIONS: One of many varieties of sweet onions, Vidalia onions originated in the sandy soil of Vidalia, Georgia. Most sweet onion varieties are only found locally, while the Vidalia are now distributed nationally. Other sweet varieties includes **Hawaii's Maui Sweets**, Washington's **Walla Walla,** Mexico's **Carzalias,** California's **Italian Reds.** In Texas they are called "**1015**" (because they are planted on October 15).. Sweet onions are mild and easy to digest. **Nutrition facts**½ cup: 15 calories, zero fats, 96.8mg sodium (12%), 3.2g carbohydrates (1%), 1g fiber (4%), .7g protein (1%), zero vitamin A, vitamin C (6%), 36mg calcium (4%), and .1mg iron (1%). www.vidaliaonion.com.

VIENNA SAUSAGE: (Vee-ina) From the city in Austria come small, plain or smoked, pork sausages, available in short, easy to carry tins. The meat is soft enough to spread like liverwurst. Generally eaten as an appetizer or in a sandwich. You'd be very rich if you had a dollar for every tin that went into a fisherman's lunch kit.

VINEGAR: (vin-eh-ger) In French it means sour wine. In the making of wine and cider, a certain bacteria added during fermentation can change the juice of grapes (and other fruit), to a sour acidic liquid. While wine and apple cider vinegars are the most common, vinegar can be made from bananas, berries, dates, honey, molasses, oranges, and rice. Vinegar can be flavored with herbs, garlic and spices. Vinegar needs to be stored in a dark, cool place. If kept too long it will mold and ruin. Vinegar is used for pickling, marinating tough cuts of meat, salad dressings. Cosmetically, it has many uses. When used in shampoo, vinegar will leave your hair soft and silky.

THE WONDER OF VINEGAR

How often do you open up that bottle of vinegar? There are hundreds of other ways to use vinegar.

In the kitchen, use vinegar to kill bacteria and odors from cutting boards and to cut grease from dishes. Just add a tablespoon to hot, soapy water, that's all it takes. Even your hands will smell good. Does your kitchen **drain smell**? Well then, pour about a cup of vinegar down the drain and let it stand for half an hour. Vinegar can be used for **cleaning stains** out of tea pots and to freshen lunch boxes. It cleans and **deodorizes** your refrigerator, microwave and other kitchen appliances. Vinegar is an important ingredient for every cook, as well as gardeners. Check out this list:
1. For **fluffy rice**, add 1 teaspoon of vinegar to boiling water.
2. To **tenderize** meat, soak the meat in vinegar for several hours, even better overnight.

3. Add 2 tablespoons of vinegar to a quart of water when **hard cooking eggs**. This helps to keep the eggs from cracking.

4. If a recipe calls for **buttermilk, substitute** a tablespoon of vinegar in a cup of milk for five minutes.

5. You can **make wine vinegar** by adding 1 teaspoon of dry red wine to 2 tablespoons of vinegar.

6. One teaspoon of vinegar added to a box of gelatin will help to firm up chilled gelatin dessert and **keep gelatin firm** longer out of the refrigerator.

7. **Freshen vegetables** and kill bugs with 1 tablespoon of vinegar in 1 quart of water. This will bring wilted vegetables back to life, in most cases. And bugs will float out of leafy vegetables.

8. When a recipe calls for lemon juice, 1/4 teaspoon of vinegar can **replace** 1 tablespoon of lemon juice.

9. **Fish scales** are removed easier when vinegar is rubbed on the scales about five minutes before scaling.

10. Do you want to **curb your appetite**? You can sprinkle a little vinegar on foods. Some say that will take the edge off your appetite. Also, prior to eating, mix 1 teaspoon of apple cider vinegar with 1 tablespoon of honey in a glass of water, then drink. You will feel good and eat less.

11. Surprise your parents next time you do dishes. **Polish** all the kitchen chrome with a splash of vinegar on a paper towel.

12. In the garden, when used at full strength, vinegar can be used **as a weed killer.** Just be careful not to apply it to good plants. Vinegar can also be used to deter ants and other insects from the garden. **Keep cats out** of your garden by sprinkling vinegar around.

VINAIGRETTE: An easy-to-make salad dressing made of vinegar, vegetable oil, and seasonings, sometimes with herbs.

VITAMINS

WHY YOU NEED VITAMINS

Are you consuming three to five servings of vegetables a day? Two to four servings of fruit? Two to three servings of milk? Two to three servings of meat? And, six to eleven servings from the bread group? If not, you might be vitamin deficient.

Vitamins are important to the growing body. Vitamins do not provide energy (because they have no calories), nor do they construct any part of their body. Vitamins are needed for transforming foods into energy and for maintenance of the body. There are 13 essential vitamins and if any one is missing, disease is possible.

If you consume the average amount of grains, fruit, and vegetables as required by the Food Guide Pyramid, along with recommended milk and meat, you are probably not vitamin deficient. However, if you do not have this balanced diet, it is suggested a vitamin supplement be taken. Vitamins are generally divided into two groups, **oil soluble** and **water soluble**. Oil soluble vitamins are stored in the body for long periods of time, while water soluble vitamins are retained for a very short time.

Vitamin A is an oil soluble type and is stored in the liver. This antioxidant vitamin is necessary for new cell growth, healthy tissues, bone and hair growth, and is essential for vision in dim light (night blindness). Vitamin A deficiency can make you more susceptible to infection, allergies, fatigue, migraines, dry skin, and dry hair. Too much vitamin A can cause pressure inside the skull and mimics symptoms of a brain tumor. Vitamin A is found in milk, butter, fish-liver oils, egg yolks, and vegetables. When vitamin A is found in leafy green and yellow vegetables it is in the form of beta carotene. While vitamin A can be toxic, beta carotene is virtually nontoxic.

The Food and Drug Administration (FDA) of the U.S. Department of Health and Human Services, recommends 5000 IU for kids over four years of age.
If you are taking cod liver oil and a multivitamin, it might raise the levels of vitamin A above safe limits. Vitamin A becomes toxic at 50,000 IU.

Vitamin B1 or Thiamin is water soluble, as are all the vitamins. Thiamin is required for normal digestion, growth, circulation, learning, and normal functioning of nerve tissue. A deficiency can cause beriberi, problems with the nervous system, a loss of appetite, body swelling, nausea, vomiting, muscle contractions, fatigue, depression, irritability, and in some cases heart problems. FDA recommendations for over age four is 1.5mg.

Vitamin B2 or Riboflavin helps you to obtain energy from carbohydrates and protein, growth, and the oxygenation of cells. A deficiency can cause problems with vision, indigestion, baldness, skin disorders, along with lip sores. Riboflavin is found in leafy vegetables, whole grains, cheese, lean meats, milk and eggs. FDA recommends 1.7mg over age four.

Vitamin B6 or Pyridoxine is involved mostly in utilization of the protein and is essential for proper body growth of muscles, skin, nerves, blood cells, and maintaining body functions. Deficiency causes stress, depression, insomnia, irritability, dizziness, nausea, weight loss, and clogging of arteries. Pyridoxine is found in grains, potatoes, red meats, green vegetables and corn. Recommendations over the age of four is 2mg. Pyridoxine may become toxic over 500mg.

Vitamin B12 or Cobalamin is necessary for normal development of red blood cells, the functioning of all cells, especially in the bone marrow, nervous system, and intestines. A deficiency causes anemia, stress, nevousness, fatigue, loss of appetite, and stamina. A prolonged deficiency can cause problems with the spinal cord. Best sources are lean meats, liver, fish, milk, and eggs. This vitamin is not found in plants and it is recommended that vegetarians take supplements. FDA recommends 6mcg over age four.

Vitamin C is the least stable of the vitamins and is necessary in body growth and tissue repair, such as the healing of wounds. This antioxidant aids in the formation of teeth, gum, and bone formation. A deficiency can cause allergies, bruising, scurvy (one of the oldest diseases known to man), and infections. An early sign is bleeding of the gums. Vitamin C is found in green peppers, citrus, tomatoes and other vegetables. The body will receive the minimum daily requirement of vitamin C needed with a daily serving of 4 ounces of the named foods. Recommended is 60mg for over age four.

Vitamin D aids in the absorption of calcium in bone formation. Lack of this vitamin can cause rickets, a softening of the bones which causes bow legs and other skeleton deformation. Insufficient vitamin D can also cause muscle weakness and nervousness. The best sources for vitamin D are found in fish liver oils, fish, egg yolks and milk, along with light from the sun. FDA recommends 400 IU daily for all ages. If you are taking cod liver oil and a multivitamin, it might raise the levels of vitamin D above safe limits. Vitamin D becomes toxic over 1000 IU.

Vitamin K is essential to blood clotting. Natural vitamin K is found in spinach, lettuce, cabbage, cauliflower, and egg yolks. Vitamin K is not usually included in multivitamin supplements. There are no recommendations by the FDA, however, the daily intake should be less than 100mcg. A synthetic vitamin K is available only by prescription.

Vitamin E is an antioxidant or a preservative which helps to prevent oxygen from destroying other substances. Vitamin E aids in circulation, especially to the heart. The E vitamin is found in vegetable oils, wheat germ, milk, beans, eggs, grains, fruit and vegetables, especially lettuce and other leaves. Recommended is 30 IU over age four.

Niacin (B3), Pantothenic Acid (B5), **Folic Acid** and **Biotin** are also essential for the body. Niacin maintains healthy cells, pantothenic acid supports proper growth, and folic acid helps to manufacture red blood cells. Biotin is a member of the B family and is important in the metabolism of carbohydrates, proteins and fats. If you take a vitamin supplement, use common sense. Chewable vitamins can be taken at any time of the day, and should only be taken in doses recommended by the FDA. Vitamin supplements may taste good, but they are not candy. Excess amounts of vitamins is not only a waste, but can be harmful to your health. *–Bernice Erickson*

VODKA: A distilled clear liquor, originally made from potatoes. Today, it is also made from grain mash.

VOL-AU-VENT: A puff pastry shaped like a tower and filled with a sauce or creamed food. The name translates from the French, "flying in the wind."

Ww

WAFER: A very light, crisp cookie. Because of the delicacy, they are usually made commercially. They come plain, rolled, fan-shaped and filled with creme. Some ice cream cones are made from a thin rolled wafer.

WAFFLE: A pancake batter cooked between two hot embossed metal plates (waffle iron) that are hinged for easy waffle removal. The word "waffle" comes from the Germans, meaning "to weave or honeycomb," the impression created by the criss-cross pattern of the waffle iron.

WALDORF SALAD: Named after the famous Waldorf-Astoria Hotel in New York, it is a mix chopped apple, celery, walnuts, and mayonnaise. Raisins or banana sliced may be added. Created by Oscar Tschirky, known as "Oscar of the Waldorf," who began as busboy and rose to become executive in charge of all the dining rooms. He is mistakenly sometimes called a chef but he never was a chef. He was headwaiter for a time in 1893.

WALLA WALLA ONIONS: The seeds for this sweet onion came from the Island of Corsica, off the coast of Italy. The seeds were planted in Walla Walla, Washington by a French soldier, Peter Pieri. The farmers were impressed by the winter hardiness, and soon everyone in Walla Walla were planting these sweet onions. After several generations, this sweet onion has been perfected for its exceptional sweetness, jumbo size and round shape. The name, Walla Walla, is protected under Federal law, and only those onions grown in the Walla Walla region can be labeled as such. www.bmi.net/onion/blue. www.wallawalla.com

WALLEYE: See PIKE or POLLACK

WALNUT: It is believed the walnut originated in Persia, since English walnuts are generally known as Persian walnuts in the Mediterranean region. The name walnut comes from the Welsh word *wealhhnutu* that meant "foreign nut." In America were native black walnuts and these trees became the root stock for the English walnut. Black walnuts are quite rich with oil and are seldom eaten out of hand but used for cakes, candy and ice cream. Walnuts have a hard, brown wrinkled shell, and when cracked open, have two halves. Walnuts are eaten out of hand, used in cooking, especially cakes and cookies, and the Chinese have adopted walnuts in their stir-fry recipes. The United States leads the world in production of English walnuts, which are often called California walnuts, since California leads the nation. **Nutrition facts** per 1/4 cup: 190 calories, 147 calories from fat, 17.7g total fat (27%), 1.1g saturated fat (6%), zero cholesterol and sodium, 3.8g carbohydrates (1%), 1.6g fiber (6%), 7.6g protein (15%), 93 IU, vitamin A (2%), 1mg vitamin C (2%), 18mg calcium (2%), and 1mg iron (5%).

WALNUT TRIVIA

■ Walnuts are one of the oldest tree foods known to man, dating back to 7,000 BC.
■ In ancient Rome, walnuts were considered food for the gods and called *Juglans regia* in honor of Jupiter.
■ There are two major species of walnuts, the English walnut which originated in Persia, and the black walnut, which is native to the United States.
■ The name "English" walnuts refers to the English merchant marines whose ships transported the product for trade around the world.
■ Joseph Sexton planted the first commercial walnut orchard in California in 1867 near Goleta in Santa Barbara County.
■ A walnut tree can bear fruit for as long as 250 years.
■ Black walnuts have a much harder shell and are tart, with a more pungent taste than the mellower English walnuts.

■ California grows 90% of the walnuts produced in the United States, two-thirds of the entire world production. — *The Walnut Marketing Board*

WALRUS: A marine mammal found in the Arctic, north Atlantic and Pacific oceans. It is hunted for its blubber and flesh, as well as the ivory tusks. Walrus meat is not available commercially.

WAMPI: This small tree from south China has round, yellow-green, aromatic fruit that in Asia is eaten fresh, made into juice and jelly.

WASABI: This herbacious plant, a type of horseradish, is cultivated in Japan and Eastern Siberia where the roots, twigs, and petioles are used as a condiment for sushi and fish.

WASSAIL: An English spiced ale popular during the Christmas holidays. The wassail bowl in Medieval England was a huge affair made especially for the high holidays. It needed to hold a lot because the poor went from door to door at Christmastime, singing carols and asking to be rewarded with a drink. Wassailing came to mean caroling. See PUNCH and TOAST.

WATER: If you took two exploding gases and mixed them in the right proportions to form a liquid, would you drink that goop? No! But you do every day. This liquid is made with two parts of hydrogen and one part of oxygen. That chemical formula is H_2O, or what you call water. True, water is not pure hydrogen and oxygen, since water contains many natural minerals (lime, magnesia, etc.) along with man made compounds (chlorine, fluoride, etc.) Heavily mineraled water is known as "hard" water. Many minerals not only improve the taste of water, they are good for your health. Rain water, water from some springs, or distilled water is called "soft" water and generally has a flat flavor. Water is the one most important substance required for life as we know it. As space explorers search for life on other planets, they first look for water. If none is found, they believe there is no life.

WATER:

WATER, WELLS, SPRINGS, AND A CHICKEN

What do you think about water? You turn on the tap, and take a sip. How does it taste? Do you like it? Are you sure the water is safe? Why all the questions, you ask? It's because not many people think about water. They drink it either because they know they need it or because they are thirsty. At one time, you could drink out of any spring or stream, but those days are gone forever. A lot of ground water is now contaminated as a result of chemicals used by farms and factories. Some chemicals seeps into the ground water. Other chemicals are carried by the wind and are deposited in lakes and streams. And some chemicals get dumped into the rivers and oceans.

Sounds bad doesn't it? Thank goodness the public water systems clean your water. True, every once in awhile, the public water gets contaminated. Usually it is just for a day or two, rarely much longer than a week. Then the water is cleaned up and safe to drink. And thank goodness for the news media, who are on top of this and report any problems, and what you should do to use the tap water.

World's Largest Hand Dug Well

You might question where does water come from when you do not live near a lake or a river? Water comes from a variety of sources, and in most cases from deep water wells. Most of these wells are drilled deep in the ground, especially when the water table is not near the ground surface. Some wells are dug by hand where water is just a few feet underground. But this is not always the case, as in Greensburg, Kansas. They claim they have the world's largest well dug by hand. Big Well, as it is called, is 32 feet in diameter, 109 feet deep and contains 15 feet of water. It was begun in 1887 by the Santa Fe Railroad when they needed water for their steam-powered locomotives. Completed the following year, Big Well was used for city water until 1932. Do you have a dollar? If so, the next time you are in Greensburg, you can take a walk down the steps to the bottom of the well. It is open daily year around, except for Thanksgiving and Christmas day, and eight in the morning to eight at night during the summer vacation months.

BIG SPRINGS

Water also comes from free flowing springs and all states have them. In Florida the two most famous are Silver Springs in Ocala and Weeki Wachee in the town of the same name. Silver Springs is reputedly the world's largest formation of all the clear artesian springs. There are more than a dozen water outlets. Boat rides are given. One is the glass bottom cruise where you can view the water bubbling out of the ground. Imagine the rate of 750,000 gallons per day. The water at Weeki Wachee flows at the rate of 170-millon gallons a day. An underwater theater has performances with mermaids. A wilderness river cruise is also available. Texas also boasts many springs, one of special interest is in the town of Big Spring. It was once the only watering place available within a 60-mile radius for those early day pioneers, stagecoach passengers and animals. The spring is now part of a city park where swimming is available.

WATER CAN BE DANGEROUS, EXCEPT FOR CHICKENS
A Strange but True Story

If you do not know how to swim, it's best to stay out of the water until you learn. That's an old joke, but apparently they hadn't heard it in Cairo a few years ago. Some people never learn to swim and have no fear of water, such as the case near Cairo, Egypt. A chicken fell into a large spring. A man jumped in to save the chicken, but the undercurrent pulled him down. One by one five others jumped in to save both the chicken and one another. None knew how to swim, so the men drowned. The chicken, however, is alive and well.

WATER CHESTNUT: A water plant found in Asia produces a crunchy nut-like fruit. It is widely used in Oriental cooking. Added to meat, poultry, fish, shellfish and vegetables recipes water chestnuts add crispness. Canned water chestnuts are available whole or sliced, packed in water and found in most supermarkets. Pickled water chestnuts are available in Oriental markets. **Nutrition**

facts1/4 cup, canned: 18 calories, zero fats and sodium, 4.4g carbohydrates (1%), .9g fiber (4%), .3g protein (1%), zero vitamins A and C, zero calcium and.3mg iron (2%).

WATERCRESS: A member of the mustard family, and sometimes called "peppercress" because of its pungent peppery flavor. Watercress grows wild in cold, shallow, clear water. Americans harvest it in early spring while it is still tender. Watercress adds flavor to mixed green salads, soft cheeses, omelets, potatoes, and soups. Watercress is a popular salad in the American South when dressed by hot crumbled bacon, bacon grease, vinegar and salt. Bunches of watercress can be found in supermarkets. If you aren't fond of the taste, use sprigs for garnish. Watercress is a good source for vitamins A and C, as well as iron, if eaten in large amounts. **Nutrition facts** ½ cup: 2 calories, zero fats and sodium, zero carbohydrates, .4g fiber (2%), .4g protein (1%), 799 IU vitamin A (16%), 7mg vitamin C (12%), 20mg calcium (2%) and zero iron.

WATER LEAF: The edible leaves of this small herb are added to salads. Think twice before planting since the herb will spread quickly like weeds.

WATERMELONS: A native of Africa, the watermelon is a member of the gourd family. Watermelons have been cultivated in Europe, Asia, and Africa since prehistoric times. We know this because holy books in India contain a word for watermelon, and the fruits were depicted by early Egyptian artists drew them in their wall paintings.

The red flesh variety is most common, but there are yellow and white flesh types as well. Watermelons are available whole or cut, and melon balls are found in the frozen food section. The rinds can be stewed like squash or made into sweet spicy pickles. The seeds can be dried and eaten. Most watermelon is eaten fresh, maybe with a touch of salt. Watermelon can be added to gelatin and fruit salads, chilled soups, and made into sherbet. Watermelon is a fair source of vitamin A and vitamin C. **Nutrition facts** ½ cup: 26 calories, 3 calories from fat, .3g total fat (1%), zero saturated fat and sodium, 5.7g carbohydrates (2%), .4g fiber (2%), .5g protein (1%), 293 IU vitamin A (6%), 8mg vitamin C (13%), 6mg calcium (1%) and 1.mg iron (1%). www.watermelon.com/nwa; www.watermelon.org;

WATERMELON, A GIFT FROM HEAVEN

Could the watermelon possibly be any better than nature made it? Most people would say, only if it were chilled or seedless. That's not a problem today. There are smaller seedless varieties which can be chilled without taking up all the room in the refrigerator.

Canteens for the Desert

Watermelons have been around since prehistoric times. Explorer and missionary David Livingston found them growing in deepest Africa in the 1850s. Possibly they originated in the Kalahari Desert region. It may seem strange for such a big juicy fruit to develop in such a dry place. Watermelons need a long, hot growing season in sandy, loamy soil with full sun, well drained earth, and room for the vines to roam. The watermelons provided natural canteens for Africans and other desert travelers. All watermelons are about 95% water.

As American as the Fourth of July

Florida Native Americans seem to have been growing watermelons before 1644, possibly from watermelon seeds brought by the Spanish explorers. Perhaps seeds were dropped while eating a slice of watermelon. American colonists brought seeds with them to Massachusetts in 1629. In his 1774 garden book, Thomas Jefferson noted that on July 31st he "had watermelons from one patch." Not long before World War I, when refrigerated cars made it possible, melons were shipped from California's Imperial Valley to markets across America. And Mark Twain wrote, "One who has tasted watermelon knows what angels eat."

"Men and melons" are hard to know, wrote Ben Franklin. You may see people thumping and shaking melons to know if they are ripe. One of the best ways to tell if they are ready is by the color of the "ground spot," where the melon lies on the ground. When the spot turns from white to a yellowish color, it indicates that the melon is ripe. At one time the grocer would cut a plug from a watermelon for you to taste prior to purchase. Taste plugs are rare today. Melons should be cut and harvested with an inch or two stem left on to retard rot and decay in storage. Uncut watermelons can be stored for about two weeks. Many stores will cut one display melon to show customers the bright red contents and end the guesswork.

July and Independence Day go together, but melons are available all year round now, though they are always tastiest in the summer months. – *LU*

WATERMELON, SWEET WATERMELONS!
A True Story
By Marie Prato

"Watermelons, sweet watermelons," yelled my father from the cab of our large truck. "Come get your sweet watermelons." In the back of the truck, hundreds of watermelons glistened and shimmered with the morning dew. Surrounded on three sides by blue wooden slats, the load shifted and swayed as my father drove slowly up and down the streets of Queens in New York City.

Sitting on the highest watermelon, I watched the load creak and groan with every bump and jolt. Although I was tall for a nine-year-old girl, I was skinny enough to sit on any of the melons or move down the load crab-like without causing any damage.

"We're doing good," commented my dad. "It's not even noon and half the load is already gone."

Getting up at four in the morning and driving to the markets in New Jersey had paid off. We had bought the watermelons for ten to eighteen cents each. That was a nice bit of money in 1955. As we turned onto Northern Boulevard, an elderly woman waved us over.

"Which one do you want?" asked my father as he got out of the truck.

The woman pointed to one of the plump watermelons halfway down the load. I gently dislodged her choice and brought it to the back of the truck.

"Want me to cut you out a plug so you can taste it?" asked my dad with his watermelon knife already in hand.

"No," said the woman shaking her head. "It's not necessary. I've been told your watermelons are good."

By dinnertime our load was almost gone and it was time to head home. It had been a long day but I was wide awake. I knew the best part was just about to begin.

"Watermelons, sweet watermelons," sang my father as we stopped in front of the house where we lived. Jumping down from the truck, I pulled the biggest, juiciest watermelon out - the one I had been sitting on and saving for the end of the day. Before my father finished carving the watermelon up, my friends were standing around the truck waiting to share in my day's reward.

WATERMELON SNOW
by Gretchen J. Huesmann

In the classic Charlie Brown Christmas cartoon, Linus remarks, "It needs sugar," after tasting an early winter snowflake. Perhaps Linus should check out the high mountain peaks where snow that looks and smells like watermelon can be found!

"Watermelon snow," as it is often called, is found on mountains all around the world. The patches and streaks of pinkish snow really do have a fresh watermelon scent. And when you step in the colorful snow, it will tint your shoes and pant cuffs red. What makes the sweet-scented snow? Not sugar, but plants - billions of plants called snow algae. Algae, usually associated with ponds, lakes and oceans, are tiny plants you can't see without a microscope. Snow algae are so small that more than two million of them fit in just one teaspoon of snow!

The tiny plants thrive on leftover winter snow, so they're most often seen in the spring and early summer at altitudes of 10,000 to 12,000 feet, such as in Yosemite National Park in California. However, some species of snow algae have been found at levels as low as 2,000 feet as in the Cascade Mountains in Washington state. "All that is required is continuous snow," say Professor Steve Stefanides of Wenatchee Valley College. He has even found snow algae at sea level in parts of Alaska.

Why does snow algae thrive in freezing temperatures? And how can they survive under the extreme sunlight? These are just a few questions scientists are trying to find out. If they discover the plants' secrets of survival, the scientists hope to use this information to help other plants, such as crops, to live in harsh weather. Scientists believe the red color, or pigment, may work like built-in sun screen protecting the plant against the sun's intense light. Not all snow algae are pink. Many colors, including orange, yellow, green, blue and even purple snow algae have been identified in the western United States alone. Watermelon snow, or *Chlamydomonas nivalis*, is the most common species.

So the next time you're out hiking in the mountains, you may find a winter watermelon patch, a patch of watermelon snow, that is. Can you really eat the snow? Some say "Dig in!" But most experts say it can give you a nasty stomachache. Rather than taking the risk, why not try making your own!

Activity
Watermelon Snow Recipe

All you need is one cereal bowl of clean snow and watermelon-flavored syrup. Watermelon syrup can be found where coffee syrups and snow-cone flavors are sold. Pour about two tablespoons of syrup over the snow and enjoy!

WATERMELON SUMMER

I'm eating
cold watermelon
on a hot afternoon,
a spectacular
Summertime treat.
I'm eating
cold watermelon
in the shade of a tree.
Could anything
taste as sweet?
--Elizabeth Giles

WATER ROSE APPLE: This tree from Southeast Asia produces small, red fruit with crisp sweet, white flesh that is eaten fresh. The fruit is usually seedless; some have one seed.

WAX BEANS: Another name for yellow green beans.

WAX JAMBU: From the East Indies, this large tree bears medium sized, red, sweet, watery fruit that is eaten fresh and made into preserves.

WEDDING CAKE:

THE WEDDING CAKE

A few decades ago, most wedding cakes were plain white home-style with a shortening-based sugar frosting. Today, cakes come in all sizes, shapes, and colors.

British Royal Icing

Some British cakes are coated with an egg white and sugar royal icing. This is the same "royal" icing used to "glue" gingerbread houses. Once this icing harders, it is similar to stucco, some call it "royal armor," because it entombs the cake where not a crumb can get out. It has been seen where the bride would take a hammer and chisel to crack off the first piece of icing in order to get to the cake. Many traditional English wedding cakes are black fruitcakes filled with spirits. English royalty like to go all out with their cakes. One of the largest was when Queen Victoria married Prince Albert in 1840. The cake had a circumference of nine feet and weighed 300 pounds. Wonder what it took to break that royal icing armor?

American Varieties

In America wedding cakes are still made with traditional white batter, but more and more are leaning toward carrot, lemon, orange, mocha, chocolate and spice batters. Another trend is to use different cake batters on each layer. Thus a four tier cake could have as many as twenty different combinations. Celebrities like to show off. When comedian Eddie Murphy married Nicole Mitchell in 1993, their cake was five feet tall and weighted 400 pounds. Each tier was different. Yellow cake filled with strawberries, carrot cake filled with cream cheese, and chocolate cake with mocha filling. Lots of fresh fruits were added, especially bananas and raspberries. On the outside of the cake were hundreds of pastel sugar flowers that cascaded down the sides. On top were a couple hundred hummingbirds made of brown sugar.

A couple of decades ago, a wedding cake cost only a few dollars, in fact $150 was considered an expensive cake. Today some cakes run into the thousands of dollars. Shapes are no longer just round. Many are square, some are oval and heart-shapes are gaining in popularity. Some bakers even combine shapes forming walls, archways and other architectural designs. Not only are flowers and other objects made of sugar used, but many wedding cakes now are adorned with real flowers.

One Cake or Two?

Another trend is when the bride and groom can't decide on what type of cake, two different cakes are made, one for the bride, one for the groom. This trend started in the South, and has now found its way to other parts of the country. What kind of a wedding cake do you want? It's not too early to at least think about it. After all, you will want to keep up with trends. While today the old home-style wedding cake is out, that trend may return when it is time for you to tie the knot.

WEEDS: What is a weed? To most it is an unwanted plant in a garden. Does this mean if there are a dozen or so dandelions in the middle of your lawn, they are weeds? Most would say "yes," but others would pick the dandelions and eat them, roots and all. Of course, people who like to eat dandelions would want to grow them themselves to be sure they were not contaminated with pesticides. What about a rosebush in the middle of a wheat field? Is the rosebush a weed? Yes, as when it is time to harvest, the farmer wouldn't want the rosebush mixed in with the wheat. Hence, in agriculture a weed is an undesirable plant that would damage a desired crop. See CARDOONS, POKE and GIBBONS, EUELL.

WEIGHT: Early day recipes were once weighed instead of using measuring cups and spoons. Today, many chefs and bakers prefer to use scales in measuring their ingredients.

WEINER: (wee ner) Short for the Austrian *Weinerwurst*, a link sausage. The American version is most often called a hot dog.

WEINER SCHNITZEL: A German cutlet recipe made with veal, not to be confused with the fast-food version made with hot dogs. See SCHNITZEL.

WELSH RABBIT: Also known as "rarebit," it is melted cheese made with milk or beer and served over toast. Some like to top the cheese with a poached egg.

WEST INDIAN CHERRY: See ACEROLA

WHALES: For centuries this majestic ocean mammal has been hunted commercially by Europeans, Asians and Americans for its oil, whalebone, meat, sperm and by-products. **Native Americans**, especially the Eskimos still hunt whales for meat with harpoons. During the 1800s civilization depended heavily on whale blubber for lamp oil. Improved whaling methods in the 1900s resulted in several giant species being hunted almost to extinction. International conventions now regulate the hunting of the last survivors. The only commercial whalers today are the **Japanese** and the **Russians**. The Japanese eat it raw and marinated.. **Eskimos** eat it dried In **Iceland**, blubber is preserved in vinegar. **Norwegians** eat grilled whale meat.

NALUKATAQ, A BLANKET TOSSING, FOOD FESTIVAL

Nalukataq (nah-loo'-ka-tahk) is the summer celebration for all the successful whaling crews. During the celebration, the whaling crews will serve, rather than receive, foods to the community residents and visitors. This event is held in the City of Barrow, Alaska, or as some call it, "The Top of the World."

Whaling Holiday

There might be only one, sometimes two *Nalukataq* events, since there are two whaling seasons, the spring and fall. Usually *Nalukataq* is held in June or July. Food is prepared and served by the crew and their wives. The menu includes various kinds of soups, *muktuk* (epidermis and a little blubber from the bowhead whale), whale meat, *mikigaq* (fermented *muktuk* and seal meat), fish, rice with raisins, pudding, Eskimo ice cream (whipped caribou fat with berries, ground caribou meat, sugar, and cooked fish bits), fruit, cake, homemade bread, Eskimo donuts (same as Indian fry bread), coffee, tea and juice. If *Nalukataq* is held in July, the menu will feature native berries: salmon berries, blueberries, black berries and cranberries. While the berries can be quite plentiful, the season can also be shortened by snow.

In between serving the foods, there will be the blanket toss, just one of the Eskimo favorite sporting events you will witness. There's also a candy toss for kids and Eskimo dances. What is a blanket toss? People holding a thick blanket form a kind of trampoline upon which one person is bounced in the air or "tossed." You might be interested to know, that their name, "*Eskimo*," was not chosen by them. This is the name the *Abaki* (an Algonquian tribe) gave to the Eskimo, meaning, "eaters of raw fish." The natives of northern Alaska are properly known as **Inuit** or Yuit, meaning "the people." While in Barrow, a visit to the Iñupiat Heritage Center is a must. For more information and dates on *Nalukataq* call the **North Slope Borough Public Information Office** (907) 852- 0215. Information on other events, accommodations, write Barrow Visitors Bureau, P.O. Box 1060, Barrow, AK 99723 or phone (907) 852-TOUR.

WHEAT: The most used of all the cereal grasses is wheat. It is believed wheat originated in the Euphrates Valley, now part of Iraq. There are both hard and soft varieties of wheat, both ground into flour. Wheat is made up of three parts, bran (the outer covering), endosperm (the inside), and the germ (a tiny part inside the endosperm). When the entire kernel is ground into flour, it is referred to as whole wheat flour. This flour is best for making bread as it contains gluten to make a spongy dough. Some of the starch can be removed from whole wheat flours, producing an even better gluten bread flour. All-purpose flour is flour ground after the bran has been removed. Enriched flour is "enriched" by replacing vitamins and minerals that were lost in the milling process. Wheat kernels are also made into hot and cold breakfast cereals.

WHEAT GERM: A tiny part inside the interior of a wheat kernel. Wheat germ adds a nutty flavor to baked goods, cereals, and casseroles. Wheat germs is high in vitamins B and E, and minerals. **Nutrition facts** 1/4 cup: 90 calories, 20 calories from fat, 2.4g total fat (4%), .4g saturated fat (2%), zero cholesterol and sodium, 13g carbohydrates (4%), 3.3g fiber (13%), 5.8g protein (12%), zero vitamins A and C, 10mg calcium (1%), and 1.6mg iron (9%).

WHEY: It's the liquid left over from making cheese from milk. Whey contains sugar, minerals and proteins. Whey is used to improve texture, color, and other qualities in food products, such as infant formulas, sports beverages, and nutritional supplements. The proteins in whey seem to enhance the immune system. Researchers are hoping to use some of these proteins in the treatment of diseases, such as AIDS. Some people like to drink whey, as did Little Miss Muffet, when she ate her curds (cottage cheese) and whey.

WHIP: Stirring to add air to a liquid such as cream, cake batters, and egg whites to make them puffy.

WHISKEY: An alcoholic beverage made of barley, rye or corn grains.

CALIFORNIA 49ers & THEIR SPIRITUOUS LIBATIONS

When the gold seekers poured into California during the 1849 gold rush, there was generally one thing on their mind, to find a vein of gold and become rich overnight. Others had the foresight to realize there was other wealth to be made. One such man was Bernhardus Berhard. He arrived in Auburn in 1852, first working as a teamster, taking much needed supplies into the mountains. He soon found there was a need for spirits, and began making a variety of whiskeys, brandies, bitters, extracts, and wines. He soon found that different nationalities liked different beverages, hence set forth finding those special ingredients. Many of the ingredients are no longer available, nor are they FDA approved if they were. Also some of those combinations made prospectors sick, some went blind, and a few died. Take a look at the following ingredients and you will understand why you wouldn't want to consume China whiskey.

CHINA WHISKEY

Distilled alcohol
Black tea
Black pepper
Cinnamon
Cloves
Peach Brand tobacco (yuck!)
Strong vinegar

Other ingredients which might sound a bit strange were rock candy, apple ether, acitic acid, fuchel, gunnie keno, Saint John's bread, wacholder berries, calmus, ziefer seed, wormworth, galgaut, entzian and the list goes on and on. In Berhard's whiskey recipes, he used German prunes, not grains as used today. As you noted, rock candy was used in some of the recipes. He would grind the rock candy to a fine powder and dissolve it with rain water to make a syrup. For making tea, he used black tea leaves, dissolved in warm rain water. He let it stand for 24 hours then filtered it through a sponge.

As Berhard's skill advanced, his fine wines (zinfandel, port, sherry and claret) were well received throughout the gold country. His home is now a living museum, restored to its original Victorian splendor. Today, students learn how to make butter, can preserves, and cook on a wood stove with yesterday's kitchen tools. **The Bernard Museum Complex** is open Tuesday through Sunday. Phone (530) 889-6500 for tour hours. For information the Auburn Visitors Bureau, 13411 Lincoln Way, Auburn, CA 95603 or phone (530) 887-2111. www.placer.ca.gov -- RSC

WHITEBAIT: A term used loosely for the small fry of herring, sprat, and smelt, as well as some anchovies. These little fish are used for bait by fishermen, but are also eaten. Best deep fat fried, whitebait can be sautéd and broiled.

WHITE BEANS: A term generally used to refer to great northern, navy, marrow, and white pea beans. Marrow are the largest and pea beans the smallest. Pea beans are the best for making New England Boston baked beans. Navy beans are mostly used for canning with pork and sold as "pork and beans." All white beans are interchangeable in white bean recipes. **Nutrition facts** ½ cup, cooked: 124 calories, zero fats and sodium, 22.5g carbohydrates (7%), 5.6g fiber (23%), 8.7g protein (17%), zero vitamins A and C, 81mg calcium (8%), and 3.3mg iron (18%).

WHITE CHOCOLATE: So-called "white" chocolate is actually cocoa butter. The white chocolate you buy in block form contains sugar, cocoa butter, nonfat milk powder, milk fat, soy lecithin (an emulsifier) and vanilla. We have not been able to find out who first started using white chocolate as a candy and cake icing but it has been relatively recently. Probably it began in the cake decorating industry. Whatever its origin, it is a well established flavor in the candy, cake, and coffee industries now.

WHITE COFFEE is a popular beverage in Damascus. Orange or rose water is stirred into hot water to make it, but it could be made with any spice, herb or aromatic steeped in hot water.

WHITEFISH: A member of the salmon family, fresh water whitefish are fished the year round in the Great Lakes. They are also found in other lakes and rivers in North America. In Alaska, they are found in both fresh and salt water. Whitefish weigh from two to six pounds and can be prepared by any method desired. Whitefish are available smoked whole, frozen whole, and fillets. If a recipe calls for white fish and spelled in two words, this is not the same fish as whitefish. White fish usually refers to cod, sole, and flounder. **Nutrition facts** 3 ounces: 114 calories, 47 calories from fat, 5g total fat (8%), .8g saturated fat (4%), 51mg cholesterol (17%), 43.4mg sodium (2%), zero carbohydrates and fiber, 16.2g protein (32%),102 IU vitamin A (2%), zero vitamin C, 22mg calcium (2%) and .3mg iron (2%).

WHITE MUSHROOMS: See AGARICUS MUSHROOMS.

WHITE PEPPER: See BLACK PEPPER

WHITE SAPOTE: See SAPOTE

WHITE SAUCE: A loose term for a sauce made with milk or cream, flour and butter. Some white sauces are made with veal stock. Some cookbooks refer to white sauce as *béchamel* or *velouté* sauces.

WHITING: Also known as kingfish and silver hake, this salt water fish is found along America's Atlantic coast from New England to the Carolinas. This small fish with a delicate flavor can be fried, broiled, baked, or poached. **Nutrition facts** 3 ounces: 77 calories, 11 calories from fat, 1.1g total fat (2%), .2g saturated fat (1%), 57mg cholesterol (19%), 61.2mg sodium (3%), zero carbohydrates and fiber, 15.6g protein (31%), 84 IU vitamin A (2%), zero vitamin C, 41mg calcium (4%) and .3mg iron (2%).

WHOLE: "Whole" grains, milk, etc., means nothing has been removed. Whole wheat, still contains both the bran and the germ, and whole milk still contains all the cream or fat.

WILD CINNAMON: A tree from South Florida produces leaves and bark as a spice for seasoning. The bark is also used in medicine.

WILD CUCUMBERS: A vine native to south Florida has one-inch fruit that looks like cucumbers. The bright green fruits are eaten fresh and made into pickles. In South Florida it s considered a common weed.

WILD DILLY: Native to south Florida, a small bush bears one-inch, russet skinned fruit, resembling a small sapodilla. The fruit is edible.

WILD FOODS: Foods not cultivated in gardens. "My greatest joy is opening young minds to nature's possibilities," Euell Gibbons said while he researched and rediscovered hundreds of wild plants and food in the American wilderness. As a child in his native Texas, Gibbons invented his first wild recipes - hackberry and hickory nut candy bar. "My lifelong passion," he said, "has been to seek out nature's bounty and subsist on it." Knowing which wild foods are safe to eat, a person would never starve to death in the American wilderness. His first rule remains. "Eat only what you absolutely know is safe." For fascinating reading about the mysteries of wild foods, their history, and recent rediscovery, read Stalking the Wild Asaragus and other books by Euell Gibbons. See GIBBONS, EUELL

WILD LIME: A member of the citrus family, native to Malaysia, it produces 3-inch, round fruit used for food flavoring and hair shampoo.

WILD RICE: This native American grain grows in the western Great Lakes area and the Native Americans have eaten it as a cereal for centuries. Wild rice is quite delicate and should not be over cooked. Wild rice can be cooked and used as regular rice, or blended with either white or brown rice. Wild rice is available at most supermarkets. **Nutrition facts** cup, cooked: 83 calories, zero fats and sodium, 17.5g carbohydrates (6%), 1.5g fiber (6%), 3.3g protein (7%), zero vitamins A and C, zero calcium and .5mg iron (3%).

WILD RICE IN AMERICA
by Linda Huntington

Mahnomen, that's what the Ojibway and Sioux called the stalks of grain sticking out of the water. Today, people call the plant "wild rice," but it is **not rice at all**. Wild rice is actually a grass, some as tall as nine feet, that grows in shallow lakes, rivers and marshy places in Minnesota's and Canada's Lake Superior region. This grass produces purplish black seeds that look like black rice. It has been a great favorite with our Native Americans for centuries.

The Rice Making Moon

Manominikegississ, the rice-making-moon, comes at the end of summer, usually in August, the time for the harvest. Some wild rice is still harvested from the lakes and rivers the way Chippewas did it years ago. Women pole a canoe or wooden boat through the rice bed. Other women bend the tall stems over baskets in the canoe. One whacks the stalks with a stick, making the kernels of wild rice, along with bugs and worms, fall into the baskets. Some of the wild rice seeds fall into the cold water. These will grow the following year when the water warms up in the spring. The green rice is cleaned, the hulls are taken off and some of the moisture is removed. Once the rice is dried, it can be stored for a long period of time without rotting.

Not So Wild Rice

Today some wild rice is not very wild. It is grown on commercial farms where water-flooded fields are known as paddies. The crop is sown by airplanes in leveled fields of shallow water. Prior to harvesting, the fields are drained. Harvesting is done with combines mounted on wide crawler tracks. These commercial operations produce four times as much wild rice, as compared to naturally grown wild rice. However, even with these modern techniques, wild rice still has the roasted-nut flavor that people like. Minnesota leads the world in wild rice production with about 80% of the world's supply; the rest is produced in Canada.

Cooking Wild Rice

To cook wild rice as a side dish, wash 3/4 cup several times in cold water. Add the wild rice slowly to three cups of boiling water, with a teaspoon of salt. Reduce the heat, simmer, covered, for 30 to 45 minutes, stirring occasionally, until the wild rice is tender and all of the water is absorbed. Wild rice is often used as a stuffing for game and poultry, especially a turkey during a Thanksgiving feast. All kinds of foods can be made more nutritious by adding wild rice, such as pancakes, soups, puddings, casseroles, and bread. No wonder people like this high protein tasty grain.

WINE: An alcoholic beverage made from fruit and berries. Most wine is made from fermented grapes. Wines can be sweet or dry (unsweet). Some wines are consumed before a meal, others during a meal, and still others with dessert or after the meal. Wine is also used in cooking, especially with poultry, fish, and beef. A touch of wine puts added zest in salad dressing and some vegetables.

WINESAP APPLES: These small to medium, bright red apples are sometimes splotched with darker red over a distinctly yellow background. The flesh is tinged with yellow and many veins of red. Winesaps are an all-purpose apple with a slightly tart flavor. The firmness makes them nice for both eating raw or cooking, especially in pies.

WINGED BEAN: A vine from southeast Africa sprouts green bean pods with four ridges down the side. The green beans, tubers, dried beans, flowers, and shoots are all eaten. All parts are high in protein.

WINGED YAM: Also known as a water yam. This vine from Southeast Asia produces aerial tubers that are eaten when cooked. These tubers are high in starch.

WINTERGREEN: This member of the heath family is also known as boxberry, checkerberry, partridgeberry, teaberry, and mountain tea. Native Americans drank a tea made from the leaves, as did the American patriots when they boycotted the British tea tax before the American Revolution.

Wintergreen is believed to help rheumatism, relieve headaches and other minor discomforts. Oil of wintergreen is used as a flavoring for cough drops, toothpaste, candy, soft drinks, and chewing gum. The small red berries are also eaten, especially by birds, deer, and other animals.

WINTER SQUASH: These squash are harvested in the late fall months and if stored in a cool, dry place, will keep throughout the winter months. The heavy, course rind ranges from dark green to yellow. Winter squashes include acorn, banana, butternut, and hubbard, as well as the pumpkin. Winter squash is an excellent source of vitamin A, with some vitamin C and iron.

WOK: A round-bottomed pan used for Chinese cooking and stir fry recipes over high heat. Wok frying requires less fat and the cook has constant control over the heat so he/she can judge the perfect timing for tenderness. This allows for crisper vegetables, done to suit the individual. Today there are electric versions. The Chinese wok is made for use over direct flame, such as gas stoves. They don't work as well with electric stove burners, though an adapter can be bought.

WONTON: A Chinese appetizer wherein ingredients such as pork, shrimp, and vegetables are sealed in a thin egg dough and deep fat fried. Wontons are also added to soup. A sweet cookie version is filled with dried fruit and nuts and served with dessert.

WOODCOCK: These game birds are found in both Europe and America and are cooked like other game birds. Frozen woodcocks are sometimes available in specialty food stores.

WOODRUFF: Grown in Europe since the Middle Ages, it is still used to flavor wine (May cups). Put in linen closets to keep away moths. It's fresh hay smell also gives off fragrance. It grows wild throughout the British Isles. Herbalists use woodruff in treating slow-healing wounds, skin ulcers, and rashes.

WONDER BREAD: See BREAD.

WORCESTERSHIRE SAUCE: (wurs-ter-sher) A dark condiment sauce made with malt vinegar, molasses, soy sauce, garlic, anchovies, onion, salt and spices. This sauce originated in Worcester, England. Worcestershire sauce can be added to soups, gravies, meat, and some vegetable juices. The name comes from the town of the man who discovered the sauce in the East Indies. On returning home, Sir Marcus Sanders asked the English grocers Lea and Perrins to make up a sauce as close to the one he loved as they could. they sold the sauce to the public in 1838 and still claim to be the Original and Genuine Worcestershire Sauce.

WORMWOOD: A shrub whose bitter leaves were sometimes used when roasting goose to help cut the grease. As a very old herbal remedy, it appears in tonics for rheumatism, colds, and digestion. Wormwood is also a flavoring used for making absinthe, a green, bitter, licorice-flavored liquid. Wormwood was once used to flavor vermouth. The use of wormwood in alcoholic beverages is now prohibited by law because prolonged used is dangerous.

Xx

XANTHAN GUM: This food thickener is used to maintain a desired consistency similar to what pectin does to jam and jellies. Xanthan gum is added to some baked goods, cake mixes, cheese, ice cream, margarines, puddings and salad dressings. Xanthan gum is derived from a vegetable source, mostly from marigolds and other red plants. Xanthan gum is a potent antioxidant and is sold at health foods stores in capsule form.

XANTHOSOMA: This creeping herb, also known as *yautia*, originated from tropical America where the leaves are cooked like a vegetable. The tubers are of poor quality, but are edible when cooked. In the United States it is grown in green houses and window boxes. In south Florida xanthosoma is grown in very rich, moist soil, and in full sun.

XENIA, OHIO:

THE COLONIAL WILD WEST

Corn was first grown in Xenia by the prehistoric Adena Native Americans. They were followed by the Hopewells, and later the Shawnee tribe. Today, **Old Chillcothe,** just four miles north of downtown Xenia, was the second largest Shawnee settlement in Ohio and the birthplace of the great Chieftain, Tecumseh. After the Revolutionary War, "going West" meant the Ohio frontierland. Xenia was founded by the Europeans in 1803. The name "*Xenia*" means "hospitality" in the Greek language, and is pronounced "Zee-yah." Most of the early Ohio farmers did "all around" farming: tending animals, crops, vegetables and fruit. Now most have specialized, with soy beans being the largest crop followed by corn and wheat. At one time dairy farming was the major industry, with upwards of fifteen dairies at the turn of the century. Milk was processed on the farm, bottled and delivered by the farm family children to those who subscribed to the products from that dairy.

A celebration, called "Blue Jacket," is held each summer with an outdoor epic drama showing the struggle to protect the Shawnee homeland against daring frontiersmen, such as Daniel Boone. The play starts with flaming arrows that light up the night sky, followed by the roar of cannons and the thundering hooves of horses. special events in the Xenia area include the Native American Pow-Wow in late June with lots of food, dancing and singing. A sausage festival is held during Xenia Old Fashioned Days during September. Other food festivals held near Xenia include **April's Sugar Maple Festival** in Bellbrook, **Fairborn Sweetcorn Festival** in August, the **Beavercreek Popcorn Festival** in September, the **Jamestown Bean Festival** also in September, and the **Spring Valley Potato Festival** in October. In nearby Clifton is America's largest operating water powered grist mill where wheat and corn are still stone ground. You can tour the 1802 mill and see how water power runs the incredible mechanical inventiveness of those early millers. For more information, write: **Xenia Area Chamber of Commerce**, 334 West Market Street, Xenia, OH 45385-2843 or phone (937) 372-3591. www.ohio.com

XERISCAPE GARDENING - IS IT FOR YOU?

In dry areas of the United States, gardeners plant xeriscape gardens. Xeriscape comes from the word xeric that means "dry environment," and scape is half of the word from "landscape" which means to improve the appearance of the land. Xeriscape gardens are quite popular in Texas, New Mexico, and Arizona. Two things are needed:

1. Plants that require less water, and
2. The ground around the plants must be covered with mulch.

Most vegetables need an abundance of water. The Native Americans solved this problem by planting corn, beans, and squash together. The saucer-sized squash leaves covered the ground, holding in moisture longer. During the cool months, in areas where the ground doesn't freeze or covered with snow, winter-type vegetables (broccoli, spinach, carrots, cabbage and potatoes) grow well, because moisture is more readily available and irrigation requirements are low. During the hot summer months there are some vegetables and herbs that do well with less water. This includes chili pequin and other small-leaved peppers. Herbs that qualify as low-water-use plants are rosemary, some sages, oregano, and mint marigold. Some varieties of fruits and nuts that will survive with little water are pecans, oriental persimmons, loquats and jujube. To find the best plants for your xeriscape garden, check with your local nursery, agricultural department, the agricultural department of a university, or the U.S. Department of Agriculture. --*Calvin R. Finch*

XIPHOSUPAN: (zif' o sur' on) An anthropod of the order the Alaskan king crabs, horseshoe crabs, and others having extremely long legs. sold for their meat. While any crab meat will do, king crab meat is best for making crab salads. .

XOCHIMILCO'S FLOATING GARDENS

More than 2,000 years ago the Aztecs lived on an island in the middle of a large lake. It was their capital city they called *Tenochtitlán*. Today it is Mexico City. As the Aztecs built their temples, houses, and other buildings, it became impossible to find land for farming. the ingenious Aztecs built rafts called *chinampas* made from reeds, twigs, and tree limbs, then topped the rafts with fertile soil. On the rafts, they built a small hut and planted seven different crops that included corn, tomatoes, chile peppers, squash and a shade tree. These rafts were then floated on the shallow lake and were propelled about the lake with oars. In time, the rafts became rooted, mostly by willow and cypress shade trees. Once the rafts became islands, other *chinampas* were purposely rooted and the Aztecs created a series of canals to reach and to harvest their crops. On these islands they also grew flowers and on many of the islands Aztec nobles made their homes.

Spanish "Breadbaskets"

When the Spanish conquistadors arrived, they tore down the temples, houses, and other buildings, along with the bridges that connected many of the islands and filled the lake with this debris. The Spanish saved the produce-growing islands, because this was their "breadbasket."

Tour the Floating Gardens

Today you can visit these islands on **Lake *Xochimilco*** (soh-chee-MEEL-coh), better known as the "floating gardens." The gardens no longer float, but still grow an abundance of produce and flowers, mostly bound for Mexico City. It also offers you a chance to see how water commerce was like during *Tenochtitlán's* heyday. For a real taste of Mexican merrymaking, you will want to take a gondolas-type, flat bottom boat, which is hand-poled through the canals. As you float through the canals, you will be joined by other families on boats. Boats carrying *mariachi* bands in full costume will play for you for a fee. Canoes filled with hawkers sell hot corn-on-the-cob, tacos and beverages in a carnival atmosphere. Sunday is the most exciting day since you will join Mexican families, as though they are all celebrating a national holiday.

Yy

YAK: In Tibet, the long-haired animal, which looks like a shaggy cow, is eaten like beef. Normally, it's more valuable as a pack animal. Yak milk is used to make cheese and butter.

YAKITORI: A Japanese recipe wherein chicken meat, chicken livers, balls of ground chicken (mixed with scallions, mushrooms, and quail eggs) are marinated (in rice beer, soy sauce, sugar, and ginger), placed on a skewer and grilled.

YAM: The yam and the sweet potato are not the same thing, although they look alike and go by the same name in places. Technically, they are two different plants although no one seems to care except the botanists. According to the plant scientists, both are *rhizomes* (swollen roots) but the yam belongs to the *dioscorea* family and the sweet potato belongs to the *batatas* family. It's not true that African slaves brought yams with them from Africa, since slaves were not allowed to bring anything. What probably happened is that Africans mistook the American sweet potatoes they saw here for African yams back home. According to *The History of Food*, the sweet potato originated in tropical South and Central America long before the slave trade came.

The word "*yam*" does come from Africa, since in some African dialects it means "to eat." Today yams are grown in the West Indies, Africa, and Asia and there are more than 150 species. The most notable difference is in size. Yams can be huge! Some yams grow up to 100 pounds and can be six feet long. That's the size of an alligator! The largest yams are usually cut up for canning. Even though they taste just as great as the smaller ones, the large yams are just too hard to handle uncut.

True yams grow larger, starchier, and drier than the sweet potato, but yams and sweet potatoes can be interchanged in recipes. Yams can be boiled, fried, baked and candied. When boiled, it is best to leave the skins on for better flavor. Yams can be made into soups, casseroles, custards, pies, quick breads and even ice creams. Yams prefer to grow in a hot, moist climate, since they require a long growing season. The yam grows naturally in the clearings of topical forests all over the world. After the yams are harvested, they are cured at a constant temperature of 50 to 70 degrees. This curing helps them stand in storage for up to a year.

The Chinese yam, also called "cinnamon vine," has cinnamon scented flowers and the edible tubers grow deep in the ground. This hard yam can grow further north than most yams. However, in the colder climates they will not always produce edible tubers. In Guinea they are so much a part of the diet that yam flour is a staple in their cooking. Yam flour is made from dried yams, which are beaten to a powder. **Nutrition facts** ½ cup serving of baked or boiled yam without toppings: 89 calories, zero fats and sodium, 20.9 carbohydrates (7%), 3.1g fiber (12%), 1.2g protein (2%), zero vitamin A, 13mg vitamin C (21%), 13mg calcium (1%), .4mg iron (2%), and 612mg potassium. Sweet potatoes have more nutritional values than the yam, but the sweet potato is a good source of vitamin A, where the yam has none.

THE EAST TEXAS YAMBOREE

In Gilmer, Texas, the third weekend of October, the yam is celebrated with parades, yam cooking and decorating contests, arts and crafts shows, livestock exhibits, pageants, carnivals and lots of live music that includes the Old-Time Fiddlers Contest. And what would a yam celebration be without a "Tour de Yam" bicycle ride, and the "Tater Trot" 10-K foot race, and of course the elaborate presentation of Queen Yam and her court. One of the highlights of the Yamboree is the Yam Pie Contest. The contest is for plain yam pies only with little or no spices and no extra ingredients such as nuts or raisins. The pie crust must be homemade. The pie is judged on the taste of the potato, not the flavorings. After the judging, all pies are sold. The basic yam pie recipe has yams, eggs, salt, milk, sugar, butter, and vanilla. It's up to the cook to use more or less to improve the flavor of the yam. Both youth and adult divisions are judged. For more information contact: **Upshur County Chamber of Commerce**, P.O. Box 854, Gilmer, TX 75644 or phone (903) 843- 2413

YAMPAS: Also known as Navaho potatoes. They grow wild in the southern Rocky Mountain states. The tops resemble the wild flower Queen Anne's Lace and the roots are crowded with small tubers that look and taste slightly like carrots. Delicious raw, even better boiled, according to Euell Gibbons. The yampa was so common it once gave its name to the Yampa River and Yampa River Valley in northwestern Colorado.

YANGTAO: See CHINESE GOOSEBERRY, better known as kiwi in the United States.

YARD LONG BEANS: These long, tender, green string beans are quite popular in Asian countries and are sometimes found in American supermarkets.

YASSA: African meat dish.

YAUPON: A low evergreen shrub whose leaves are used to make a bitter, caffeinated tea. In the southern United States, the Native Americans allowed only the women to drink yaupon tea. It gave some relief to feminine "miseries." The rare bushes still grow on the sandy Outer Banks of North Carolina, where the leaves are still sold to make an herbal tea.

YEAST: This tiny organism floats in the air all around you. Yeast is so tiny, a couple thousand packed tightly would take up less than a quarter inch of space. Yet, when mixed with a liquid and sugar or starch, yeast converts to carbon dioxide and alcohol, then begins to ferment. Yeast in bread dough tries to push its way out, thus making the dough to rise. Yeast also turns grapes, fruit, grains into fine wine, beer and liquor such as whiskey. Yeast is also considered fungi, just like mushrooms. They all belong to the same group of living things. **Active dry yeast** is available on supermarket shelves in small packets and by bulk in jars. **Moist compressed yeast** is kept in the refrigerator section. When using yeast to make bread, care must be taken not to get it too hot, because heat will kill it. Liquids should be less than 120° for dried yeast and under 90°F for compressed yeast. Also if the raising place exceeds 145°F, it will kill the yeast. Hence, when the risen bread dough is placed in a preheated oven, the yeast is killed immediately and the bread holds its shape.

YELLOW PEAS: Field peas are yellow, have a hard seed, are dried and usually packaged split. Like green split peas, the yellow variety can be made into soup, especially good with smoked pork. For an Indian flavor, yellow peas are great in curried rice dishes, mixed with cumin and lemon juice, and pureed in a mint and garlic yogurt sauce. **Nutrition facts** ½ cup, cooked: 127 calories, 8 calories from fat, 1g total fat (1%), .3g saturated fat (1%), zero cholesterol and sodium, 22.4g carbohydrates (7%), zero fiber, 8.1g protein (16%), zero vitamin A, 2mg vitamin C (3%), 55mg calcium (5%) and 2.2mg iron (12%).

YELLOW SAPOTE: See CANISTEL.

YIRO: A vertical barbecue spit originally found in Middle Eastern kitchens. Lamb roasts bake on a skewer over the barbeque pit. *Yiro* means "circle." As the meat rotates and cooks, the done meat is sliced off in a thin circle. The slice is generally served in a pita (pocket bread). Lettuce, tomato and a white dressing are often included. In Mexico, beef is the choice of meat and, when sliced, the meat is filled into a hollowed-out soft roll. Chicken and other meats can also be barbecued in this fashion. In the United States, many Greek restaurants have a modern electric version of this ancient cooking equipment.

YLANG-YLANG: In Malaya, a tree produces clusters of half-inch black, tasteless fruit that is eaten fresh. From the flowers comes an oil used in perfume.

YOGURT: When milk is curdled with an acid and with the addition of bacterial cultures, it thickens. Yogurt can be made from whole milk or lower fat milk whether the milk came from a cow, a sheep or a goat. Commercially made yogurt is available plain or combined with fruit and other flavorings such as vanilla and chocolate. Frozen yogurt has all the charm of ice cream but less fat. **Nutrition facts** ½ cup, **whole milk** 70 calories, 33 calories from fat, 3.7g total fat (6%), 2.4g saturated fat (12%), 14.4mg cholesterol (5%), 52.7mg sodium (2%), 5.3g carbohydrates (2%), zero fiber, 3.9g protein (8%), 140 IU vitamin A (3%), 1mg vitamin C (1%), 137mg calcium (14%) and zero iron. **Nutrition facts** ½ cup, **skim milk**: 63 calories, zero calories from fat, 2.1mg cholesterol

(1%), 86.8mg sodium (4%), 8.7g carbohydrates (3%), zero fiber, 6.5g protein (13%), zero vitamin A, 1mg vitamin C (2%), 226mg calcium (23%) and .1mg iron (1%).

YORK IMPERIAL APPLES: These lopsided apples are red striped on a yellow-green, pinkish blush, the flesh is moderately tart and crisp. While only a fair eating apple, Yorks are excellent for baking, especially in pies.

YORKSHIRE PUDDING: It's a British dish, a quick bread batter made with eggs, flour, milk and seasonings, which is added to the drippings from roast beef and baked in a hot oven until puffy, crisp, and golden brown.

YOUNG BERRY: A hybrid bramble fruit, between the southern dewberry and trailing blackberry. The nearly seedless berries taste like raspberries, and are eaten fresh, made into desserts, jam, and juice.

YUCA: Cassava. Not the same as yucca, the cactus. See MANIOC.

YUCCA: Yucca is a family of cactus plants. Parts of the plants are used in various ways. Yucca flowers have long been an important vegetable in Central America and the American Southwest. The clusters are said to be like eating cauliflower. The *Yucca Elephantipes,* better known as Spanish Dagger or izote, can be eaten raw in salads or battered and fried. The *Yucca baccata* has flesh so sweet it can be used as a dessert. Young shoots of yucca resemble asparagus can be peeled, sliced, soaked and fried. Certain kinds of yucca roots contain enough saponin to be used as soap and shampoo, as long used by the Native Americans. .

YULE LOG: During the Christmas holidays, a cake is baked on a sheet pan, removed, spread with a cream filling, rolled up and iced with a chocolate frosting to resemble a wood log.

Zz

ZAATAR: A marjoram-like herb grown and used in the Middle East.

ZABAGLIONE: (zaba-loney) An Italian dessert made with beaten eggs, sugar and wine, which can be served chilled or warm. *Zabaglione* is also served as a sauce with fruit. Same as the French *sabayon.*

ZAKASKI (ZAKUSKI): In Poland this means a first course or appetizers, such as pickled mushrooms and other vegetables, smoked seafood, assorted cheeses, and pumpernickel bread.

ZAMPONE: Stuffed pigs' trotters. An Italian holiday speciality in which the foot and shin are stuffed with ground pork snout and seasonings.

ZANTE CURRANTS: Named after one of the Greek islands, zante currants are tiny, seedless grapes that have been dried. Zante currants have more flavor than raisins and are more tart. **Nutrition facts** ½ cup: 204 calories, zero fats and sodium, 53.3g carbohydrates (18%), 4.9g fiber (20%), 2.9g protein (6%), 53 IU vitamin A (1%), 3mg vitamin C (6%), 62mg calcium (6%), and 2.4mg iron (13%).

ZARTAR: In Lebanon, a blend of herbs, seeds, and olive oil used as a topping on bread.

ZEPPOLE: (ZEP pola or zepoli)) An Italian yeast pastry deep fat fried like doughnuts. Can be filled with cheese (mozzarella or ricotta), cooked vegetables, salted fish (anchovies), if desired. Plain zeppole is coated with sugar and cinnamon or honey and served as a dessert. Filled zeppole is coated with butter and salt and served as an appetizer.

ZEPPOLE
by Pamela Schmidt

It's easy to make sweet little balls of zeppole, all you need is pizza dough and lots of hot oil. Thawed, frozen bread dough works just great if pizza dough is not available. Pinch off inch-sized pieces of dough and roll into a ball. The dough is gently dropped into the hot oil (about 350˚F to 375˚F), and fry until golden. Carefully remove cooked dough with slotted ladle, and drain briefly on paper towel. While still hot, drop in four or five fried balls into a sandwich-sized paper bag, pour about a 1/4 cup of confectioners' sugar into the bag, close bag, shake, and voila! Your have Zeppole! Caution! Just remember not to over-crowd the cooking pieces of dough in the oil. This will drop the temperature and allow the dough to absorb too much oil. *Mangia!*

ZITA: A tubular pasta shape, like macaroni. Use with chunky sauces, salads, stir-fry, and baked dishes.

ZIT-KWA: Also known as "wax gourd," it is about a foot long with a soft rind. The Chinese preserve them. Zit-Kwa grows well on sunny slopes, and can be grown as other melons or cucumbers.

ZIZYPHUS: See JUJUBE

ZUCCOTTO: Layers of sponge cake that are orange glazed.

ZUCCHINI SQUASH: This summer, cucumber-shaped squash was developed in Italy and is also known as vegetable marrow. The skin varies from dark green to a lighter green with yellow strips. There is also a yellow variety. The flesh is a pale-green with a delicate flavor. Zucchini squash found in the supermarkets range from about four to ten inches. In the garden, if not attended, can grow to a couple feet long and three to four inches in diameter. Fresh zucchini is available year round, with the peak season in late spring to mid-summer. Zucchini squash is also available frozen and canned. Zucchini flowers are sold in Mediterranean markets but here you'll only find them in gardens and some farmer's markets. The flowers are eaten stuffed.

Zucchini is eaten raw in salads and with dip, or cooked by boiling in water or baked with a sauce. Small zucchini can be sautéd in butter. Zucchini recipes are endless. It can be made into hot or cold soups, stewed with other vegetables and herbs, cooked with meats, stir-fried or pickled. It can be baked into breads and cakes. Because it has almost no flavor of its own, it picks up the flavors of whatever it is cooked with. You may have or someday eat zucchini pie and never even know it. **Nutrition facts** ½ cup: 9 calories, zero fats and sodium, 1.9g carbohydrates (1%), .8g fiber (3%), .8g protein (2%), 221 IU vitamin A (4%), 6mg vitamin C (10%), 10mg calcium (1%) and .3mg iron (2%).

ZUCCHINI

Come July and August,
it's best to be aware.
Watch out for zucchini,
you'll find it everywhere.

Not just in the garden
but all the food you eat
could have zucchini in it
from normal to offbeat.

Zucchini stuffed with sausage
zucchini in the stew,
zucchini breads and muffins
zucchini cookies too.

Zucchini in the salad
zucchini in the jam
chicken fried zucchini
zucchini with diced ham.

When it's in the garden
and growing everywhere,
watch out in the kitchen,
zucchini will be there.
    —*Eilzabeth Giles*
(previously published in *On The Line*, August 1998)

ZUMO DE COCO Y LIMÓN: (Coconut Lemonade) In Mexico, a coconut lemon beverage is made called *zumo de coco y limón* (zumo-deh-koh-koh-ee-lee-mohn) meaning coconut milk with lemon juice. You can also mix coconut milk with other fruit juices to reduce sugar intake.

1 cup coconut milk, fresh or bottled
½ cup fresh lemon or lime juice
Sugar
Ice, crushed (optional)

1. Combine coconut milk with the lemon juice in a tall
glass.
2. Sweeten to taste with the sugar.
3, Mix thoroughly to dissolve the sugar.
4. Add ice, if desired.
Makes 1 serving.
--Evalyn Neuhaus

ZWIEBACK: Also known as rusk, is a sweet bread, sliced, then toasted dry. It is a German word that means "baked twice." Similar breads are baked twice in French and Italy. A favorite of mothers for their teething babies because it dissolves rather than breaks into crumbs which could choke the baby.

ZWEIBEL KUCHEN: A German onion pie made with bacon, eggs, and sour cream.

BIBLIOGRAPHY

AMERICAN HERITAGE DICTIONARY

AMERICANA MAGAZINE, NY 1981-1987

Berolzheimer, Ruth. *The American Woman's Cookbook,* Consolidated Book

Better Homes and Gardens Cranberry Book, Meredith Publishing In Association with Ocean Spray, Inc., 1971

Better Homes and Gardens Encyclopedia of Cooking, 1973

Better Homes and Gardens Healthy Cooking, CD ROM version, Seattle, Washington: Multicom Publishing.

Bragdon, Allen, D. *The Gingerbread Cook*, NY: Arco, 1984

Bunney, Sarah, Ed. *The Illustrated Book of Herbs, Their Medicinal and Culinary Uses.* NY: Gallary Books, 1984

Coyle, Patrick L. Jr. *the World Encyclopedia of Food*, NY: Facts on File Inc., 1982.,

Davidson, Alan. *The Oxford Companion to Food*, NY: Oxford University Press, Dell, 1966

Eckhardt, Linda. *Great Food Catalog,* NY: Park Lane Press, 1996

Farndon, John. *Children's Encyclopedia*, NY: Carnival, Harper Children's Books, 1992

Feldman, David. *Who Put the Butter in Butterfly and Other Fearless Investigations*, NY: Harper and Row, 1989

Funk and Wagnall's Infopedia, CD ROM version, Israel: Future Vision, Multimedia, 1994.

Haas, Dr. Elson. Staying Healthy with Nutrition. Berkeley, CA: Celestial Arts, 1992

Hale, William. *The Horizon Cookbook and Illustrated History of Food and Drink Through the Ages.*

Hartwig, Daphne. *Make Your Own Groceries*, NY: Bobbs-Merrill Co., 1979

Heinerman, John. *Heinerman's Encyclopedia of Fruits, Vegetables, and Herbs,* Parker, NY 1988

Hooker, Margaret Huntington. *Early American Cookery*, Americana Review, 1981

Kadans, Dr. Joseph M. *Encyclopedia of Fruits, Vegetables , Nuts and Seeds for Healthy Living*, West Nyack, NY: Parker Publishing Inc, 1973

Harvey Long, Jenifer, ed. *Larousse, Gastronomique.* NY: Crown Publishing, Inc. 1984

Miller, John C. *the First Frontier, Called Life in Colonial America*, NY: Dell, 1966

Miller, Joni. *The Collectible Teapot and Tea Calendar for 2000*, Workman Publishing, New York, 1999.

Miller, Amy Bess and Fuller, Persis, Eds. *The Best of Shaker Cooking*, Oxford, England, 1999

Rahaniotis, Angela. *Pizza and Antipasto*, Brimmar, Inc, 1994

Riely, Elizabeth, *a Feast of Fruits*, New York: MacMillan, 1993

Stevens, Patricia Bunning. *Rare Bits: Unusual Origins of Popular Recipes*, Athens, OH: Ohio University Press, 1998.

Swell, Barbara. *Log Cabin Cooking*, Native Ground Music, Inc, 1996

Trager, James: *the Food Chronology, a Food Lover's Compendium of Events and Anecdotes from Prehistory to the Present*, NY: Henry Holt, 1995

Toussaint-Samat, Maguelonne, Tr. By Anthea Bell, HISTORY OF FOOD, Barnes and Noble, Inc with Blackwell, 1992

Wilkinson, Gertrude. *The Attic Cookbook*, Baltimore, MD: Penguin Books, Inc., 1972

Williams, Sallie Y. *The Art of Presenting Food*, NY: Heart Books, 1982

Woman's Day Encyclopedia of Food, Faucett Publications, NY, 1966

ZAK, Victoria. *Twenty Thousand Secrets of Tea*, Dell, NY, 1999

Zimmer, Anne Carter: *The Robert E. Lee Family Cooking and Housekeeping Book*, NC: University of North Carolina Press, 1997

About the Authors

Richard S. Calhoun owns over 400 cookbooks and has cooked food from Alaska to South American. His interest in regional and traditional cooking began as a boy on a visit to Alaska, which later became the basis of his novel, *Cheechako, An Alaskan Adventure*. Excerpts from that novel appear in this book. Richard's career as a writer/editor began as publicity manager for the Alaska Day Festival and eventually led to a career in travel promotion, advertising, and magazine editing. Upon retirement, he began writing for children as a hobby and found himself specializing in articles about history and the world of food. This led to writing *Breakfast Around the World* and eventually to his idea for a food encyclopedia to share his love of food and food history with children who are just becoming old enough to cook by themselves. Richard lives in California with his wife Daisy, learning about his new computer when he isn't creating or researching good food.

As a young teen, **Louise Ulmer** began learning to cook from her Ozark grandmother and her mother, whose cinnamon rolls are still unsurpassed, in the opinion of those who ever had the privilege of eating one. Louise's interest in the vast variety of American foods grew out of living in several states. Her first illustrated quiz on regional food appeared in *Country Living Magazine*. Living in a family in which everyone likes to cook, Louise shared Richard's vision for a book that would make food an education in itself. Her writing began with children's books in the world popular Arch Book Series at Concordia and *The Bible That Wouldn't Burn*. She has been a writing instructor and editor for fifteen years. Recently she has been writing novels for middle grade readers. Her research into life in Shaker villages led to a novel, *Winter Shaker*. Her novel which blends history and science fiction, The *Globster of Glassy Beach*, was chosen as Best E-Book for Kids in 2000. Her romance novel, *Serenade of the South*, can be seen, along with the E-book version of **The ABC's of FOOD,** on the internet at www.ebooksonthe.net.

Peach Blossom Publications

136 Centre Line Avenue - Williamsport, PA 17701 - 570/323-5151

Name _____

Organization _____

Address_____

City_____ State_____ Zip_____

Please send me

The ABC's of FOOD: A Study of Food as History, Story, Tradition & Nutrition

CD-ROM (PDF) ISBN # 0-941367-11-8 @ $20.00 each or 3 for $30 _____
Book ISBN # 0-941367-20-7 @ $45.00 each_____
Subtotal_____

Pennsylvania Residents add 6% Sales Tax_____
US Postage and handling per CD add $1.50_____
US Postage and Handling per book add $3.50 _____
Canadian Postage for book add $9.00_____
Payable with Check or Money Order_____Total_____

THANK YOU for order!   Please allow 3 - 4 weeks for delivery